Political Parties before the Constitution

Jackson Turner Main, professor of history and director of the Institute for Colonial Studies at the State University of New York at Stony Brook, is the author of *The Anti-federalists: Social Structure of Revolutionary America* and *The Upper House in Revolutionary America, 1763–1788.*

PUBLISHED FOR THE
Institute of Early American History and Culture
AT WILLIAMSBURG, VIRGINIA

*Political Parties
before the Constitution*

by Jackson Turner Main

The Norton Library
W·W·NORTON & COMPANY·INC·
NEW YORK

Books That Live
The Norton imprint on a book means that in the publisher's
estimation it is a book not for a single season but for the years.
W. W. Norton & Company, Inc.

Library of Congress Cataloging in Publication Data
Main, Jackson Turner.
    Political parties before the Constitution.
    (The Norton library)
    Reprint of the ed. published by the University of
North Carolina Press. Chapel Hill.
    1. Legislative bodies—United States—States—
History. 2. Political parties—United States—
History. I. Title.
[JK2484.M33 1974]   329'.02   73-20015
ISBN 0-393-00718-9

FOR
JACKSON
AND
EIFIONA
AND
JUDSON

The days this book demanded
You freely lent to me,
I give them back to you, with love
And thanks, paternally.

Contents

Tables and Maps

Tables

Maps

Prepared by Richard J. Stinely

Preface

The American Council of Learned Societies did not know it, but when in 1962 it helped to finance a year's sabbatical leave, it was subsidizing this book. At that time I projected a study of the social structure of the Revolutionary period, part of which would correlate society with politics. The latter part of the plan proved too ambitious. When I returned to the fray, the nature and quantity of the evidence required the use of a computer, and this time the ACLS knowingly came to my aid. Its assistance enabled me to complete my preparations. Mrs. Laura Cummings helped even more. As a research assistant, she took over almost the entire responsibility for preparing the data for computer analysis, did all the programming, and patiently educated me. Even after she had shifted majors, she continued to give unselfishly of her time, and any technical compliments should be directed to her.

Others have also contributed much to this book. The State University of New York supplied money for travel through a research grant. Several graduate students furnished advice and information, notably Louise Allen, Edith Lechleitner, Leonard Sneddon, and Barry Stow. Jacqueline Liebl and Kathy Carne typed carefully and intelligently. My friends Jerome Nadelhaft and Van Beck Hall allowed me to read key portions of their manuscripts on South Carolina and Massachusetts, and the latter criticized chapter 4. My colleague Robert Marcus read the entire manuscript, criticized it brilliantly, saved me from some serious misinterpretations, and suggested ideas that now parade as mine. Ronald Formisano of the University of Rochester performed the same invaluable service. As with other historians, my gratitude goes far beyond any narrow circle to include all those working in the field whose research and ideas I have appropriated. The footnotes will testify to the contribution of the fine state archives and historical society libraries that make the writing of history possible and fun. Finally, I thank my wife, who interrupted her own scholarly career to assist mine.

Introduction

Political parties, as we know them today, developed quite recently. Nowadays they often have national organizations, which may even continue between elections; they write platforms that distinguish them from each other; they attract faithful adherents, so that most voters align themselves with respect to parties; and they campaign vigorously. These attributes appeared gradually during the nineteenth century and scarcely existed before 1800.

During the eighteenth century political divisions remained in many ways amorphous. With a handful of exceptions voting groups even at the local level lacked formal organization, produced no platform, attracted no permanent membership, and electioneered unsystematically if at all. Nevertheless politics were not chaotic. On the contrary, politicians formed into consistent blocs, the precise nature of which varied with time and circumstance but which displayed continuity and cohesion. These blocs took the form of, not national, but legislative parties, which are revealed primarily in the votes of the representatives as well as by their letters, writings, speeches, and occasionally in their campaigns.

Most men of the eighteenth century condemned these political alignments. Ideally all the members of society cooperated with one another, subordinating selfish individual or local interests to the common good. Those in authority acted—or were supposed to act —for the best interests of the whole. Opposition to those in power subverted this harmony, substituted confusion for order, chaos for government. Whig philosophy, of course, did justify resistance to despotism. Ordinarily, however, any challenge to authority was presumed to stem from corrupt men or from demagogues. From their disruptive activities grew the factions or "parties" so characteristic of eighteenth-century politics.

People used both of these terms, *faction* and *party*, loosely and at times interchangeably. Now one critical distinction seems useful. The *faction*, in England and America, referred to a group of men united by a desire for office rather than by any common principle. It usually revolved around one individual or a family. The *party*, on the other hand, possessed some unifying ideology or interest, and its members sought power, not exclusively for its own sake, but to accomplish their aim. One referred to the whig *party* but the Newcastle *faction*, the court or country *party* but the DeLancey *faction*. The faction was ephemeral; the party might endure because it depended upon ideas or interests rather than upon persons. Thus Dr. Samuel Johnson, in his first dictionary (1755), defined a party as "a number of persons confederated by similarity of designs or opinions in opposition to others." This very loose usage of the word, though still preserved in our dictionaries and language, contrasts sharply with its modern connotation. When we encounter it in the seventeenth and eighteenth centuries, therefore, we must divest it of recent accretions.

The precise attributes and the significance of these preparty "parties" in America form the subject of our investigation. With a couple of exceptions, we will not describe organizations, nor must we expect systematic electioneering, though we will discover a little of it. We will find no platforms, though we will devote much space to principles of concert; and we will seldom uncover party or even factional affiliations among the electorate, though we will examine remarkable bloc voting by legislators. We will not find modern parties, but we may explain much about American politics.

Following the Namierist school, the usual interpretation of preparty politics stresses the influence of persons or emphasizes the role of ideology. In recent years historians have minimized disagreements and emphasized consensus in colonial America. Conflicts among social groups, economic interests, and classes have been deemed relatively unimportant. Instead historians have considered religious and factional disputes to be the major determinants of political behavior, together with the century-long contest between the assemblies and the prerogative.

A case can be made for this approach in eighteenth-century England, governed as it was by a ruling elite that agreed on almost every matter of consequence. Factions developed within that elite, but they had little to do with principles. In the colonies, as chapter 1 will show, factions were also the most prevalent form of political division, although not the sole one. Where the reins of authority were slack, "parties" appeared, sometimes directly challenging to the prerogative and occasionally arising out of divisions among the colonists themselves. These "parties" in many ways anticipated the political alignments of the post-Revolutionary era.

After Independence the merchants, lawyers, and great landholders tried to reinstitute the former habits of deference and establish a new consensus. They failed. The Revolutionary experience wrought fundamental changes in attitudes, institutions, and political alignments. The people had been taught to challenge authority in the name of liberty, to doubt the decisions of their governors: the Revolution legitimatized opposition. At the same time ordinary folk had exercised power themselves as never before. They furnished officers for the armies, members for powerful committees, representatives for the legislatures. Political divisions ceased to be simply factional contests; instead they separated men who differed fundamentally.

The very absence of modern parties lends a peculiar interest to the study of post-Revolutionary alignments. The people's representatives in the legislatures could follow their own desires or reflect the wishes of their constituents almost free from external influences. No strong government enforced conformity, no parties required orthodoxy, and (with some exceptions) no entrenched upper class compelled obedience. One might expect that under such circumstances the legislators would vote at random or form into miscellaneous groups, each representing some faction, area, interest, or ideology. Actually, as we will see, they divided into two distinct groups. These appeared sooner or later in every state and everywhere possessed common characteristics. The legislators, then, formed legislative blocs, or *parties*, as Dr. Johnson and others used the word and as we will use it here.

How can we account for this process? Clearly certain general principles, operating throughout the states, await our discovery and analysis. The present investigation grew out of a study of the state senates during the 1780s, which revealed this bloc voting and the existence of similar divisions in the several states. The votes in the senates, while suggestive, proved inconclusive. They were too few, did not involve enough individuals, and above all did not furnish enough different kinds of issues and voters. The senates had been only partly democratized and contained almost no artisans, few plain farmers, and in general few men of the middle rank. Most of the lower houses before the Revolution shared the same characteristics. But after 1776 they changed their nature and became, in many instances, ideal for this analysis. Ordinary farmers, as distinct from large landowners, now formed about a third of the membership, while manufacturers and artisans, together with many lesser professionals, shopkeepers, and the like, furnished a fourth. Indeed, almost every kind of American above the rank of laborer sat in these assemblies. They contained men of small property as well as large, men of little education and college graduates, men of limited experience and cosmopolitan men, men with a variety of church affiliations, of all military ranks, and of all ages. Moreover, the number of representatives in the lower houses increased greatly: this permitted quantitative analysis for our study. In addition, roll-call votes, scarce before 1776, became numerous and involved every important issue. Massachusetts, New York, New Jersey, Pennsylvania, Maryland, Virginia, and South Carolina especially met the requirements for a thorough investigation.

The technique employed for identifying and analyzing the political divisions within the legislatures is described in chapter 2. During the investigation the two major blocs of delegates were denominated party A and party B. These are not memorable names. Instead let us anticipate one aspect of the general conclusion and adopt, as an expedient and without prejudice, the titles *Localist* and *Cosmopolitan*. Chapter 3 discusses the major issues that created these legislative parties. The next eight chapters present the main body of evidence, drawn primarily from the votes but derived also from other sources that explain the pattern. The beginnings of organization and electioneering are noted here. The final two chapters summarize the alignments on major issues and suggest some conclusions concerning the causes, characteristics, and significance of the political divisions.

Part I

Background

Chapter I

Political Parties
before the Revolution

The usual species of political division in colonial America was the faction. In England this became almost the sole form during the eighteenth century. The colonies, however, also produced "parties" based upon broad differences in opinions and objectives. Two primary factors created somewhat different alignments. First, the struggle between the governor and assembly, between the prerogative and local self-government, led to "court," or "proprietary," parties on one side and "country," or "popular," parties on the other.[1] The division resembled that between tory and whig in seventeenth-century England and of course culminated in the debate over independence. While the two groups might differ in principle, they often simply separated the "ins" from the "outs." Second, economic, religious, and political differences created alignments that might or might not correspond with the foregoing groups. These appeared because political arrangements in some of the colonies were less restrictive and more tolerant of variety than in others. A brief summary of politics in the several colonies will indicate the factional or party conflicts during this early period.

No religious or other cultural differences seriously divided the people of New Hampshire,[2] but opposing economic interests contained the elements for potential conflict. One area, centering around Portsmouth, was maritime, while the rest of the colony, much of it isolated, was agricultural. The Wentworth family, how-

1. See particularly Bernard Bailyn, *The Origins of American Politics* (New York, 1968).
2. See Jere R. Daniell, "Politics in New Hampshire under Governor Benning Wentworth, 1741–1767," *William and Mary Quarterly*, 3d Ser., XXIII (1966), 76–105.

ever, transcended sections and encompassed every economic interest. Wielding power through the office of governor and other major posts, they entered into commerce, land speculation, and lumbering (which they monopolized). They succeeded in crushing other family groups that challenged them and, by denying representation to most of the agricultural towns, established an almost monarchical regime that favored entrepreneurial rather than agrarian interests.

In Massachusetts, on the other hand, the governorship changed hands more often, and no one family—not even the Hutchinsons— rivaled the Wentworths' stature in New Hampshire. Moreover every town might elect representatives to the lower house, which had always wielded considerable power. The colony produced various factions, but Massachusetts politics concerned more than just a struggle for power: it reflected religious developments, disputes between the commercial and agricultural towns, and conflicts over economic, especially monetary, policy. One participant, Dr. William Douglass, summarized the alignments as they had existed and as they were in 1749: "The parties in Massachusetts-Bay at present are not the Loyal and Jacobite, the Governor and the Country, Whig and Tory, or any religious sectary denomination, but the Debtors and Creditors."[3] The most spectacular dispute pitted the hard-money merchants of Boston, who backed a bank based on silver that would serve their monetary needs, against the farmers and lesser entrepreneurs of the interior, who preferred a land bank so organized as to loan money with land as security and relieve the general shortage of currency. The victory of the former, made possible by help from England, created bitterness for a generation. A different yet related alignment during the pre-Revolutionary years pitted the "government" party against the "country" party of the eastern agricultural towns, while beginning about 1761 a "popular" party was formed under the leadership of James Otis and Oxenbridge Thacher.[4]

Rhode Island produced the first two-party or, more accurately, two-factional system in America. It resembled the factional type in that it primarily involved a struggle for power rather than a contest between different ideas or interests, but it possessed the

3. Quoted in Carl Bridenbaugh, *Cities in Revolt: Urban Life in America, 1743–1776* (New York, 1955), 12.
4. The fullest account is Leslie M. Thomas, "Partisan Politics in Massachusetts during Governor Bernard's Administration, 1760–1770" (Ph.D. diss., University of Wisconsin, 1960).

stability, continuity, and degree of organization that we associate more with parties than with factions. The Ward group, based in Newport but colony-wide in scope, included merchants as well as farmers and manufacturers; the Hopkins "interest," based in Providence, contained the same elements; and the leading historian of the colony cannot discover any difference in their principles or policies. Both defended Rhode Island's existing form of government, which was unusually democratic, and neither sought change. Their controversy therefore took the form only of "a political dispute between two factions for control of the government."[5] What distinguished Rhode Island's factionalism was the advanced organization built by the leaders of the two groups, who drew up lists of candidates, circulated them, spent large sums of money on campaigns, bribed, published diatribes, and rewarded the faithful with office.[6]

In contrast, Connecticut developed no enduring political blocs. The major officials came primarily from a limited number of families representing the leading business and professional men, including the clergy, together with some large landowners. Drawn from all parts of the colony, they cooperated with one another in most ways and patiently waited their turn along the ladder of preferment until someone died or retired. Their authority, however, was gradually being undermined as the eighteenth century wore on,[7] and the solid phalanx began to crack in the 1760s. At that time disputes over western land policy (the Susquehanna Company), religion, and the Stamp Act created an east-west division and climaxed in the displacement of the governor and several of his supporters. Nevertheless the dispute did not cause any permanent political alignment, and the colony's rulers had repaired most of the breaches by 1776.[8]

New York, like Rhode Island, produced two major political groups that fought for supremacy, but more was involved than just power. True, the DeLanceys and the Livingstons behaved rather like the Wards and Hopkinses, seeking popularity by posing as the colony's friends, defending government while in office and

5. David S. Lovejoy, *Rhode Island Politics and the American Revolution, 1760–1776* (Providence, 1958), 18. Evidently Rhode Islanders used the words "faction," "party," and "interest" indifferently except that the first two, being derogatory, applied to the opposition.

6. *Ibid.*, 21–30; note the method of choosing sheriffs and justices, *ibid.*, 59–62.

7. See Richard L. Bushman, *From Puritan to Yankee: Character and the Social Order in Connecticut, 1690–1765* (Cambridge, Mass., 1967).

8. Oscar Zeichner, *Connecticut's Years of Controversy, 1750–1776* (Chapel Hill, 1949).

attacking while out of it. Both contained merchants, lawyers, and great landowners; both included men of wealth (although the De-Lanceys perhaps attracted a greater number), and both began with, if indeed they did not continue to share, the same political ideology and social values. But New York's parties proved dissimilar in at least three respects. First, the DeLanceys defended the Anglican church and won the support of most Anglicans, while the Livingstons, themselves Presbyterians, attacked the Anglicans and obtained the backing of many dissenters. Second, the DeLanceys' center of strength lay in the south, where they usually carried New York City, Queens, Kings, Richmond, and Westchester, while the Livingstons predominated in the upper Hudson valley and eastern Long Island. The sectional division suggests that the Livingstons, despite their own entrepreneurial nature, may have been more successful than the DeLanceys in attracting agrarian support, but that they enjoyed less success in the trading centers. Finally, during the years immediately before Independence, the Livingstons became whigs, and the DeLanceys, tories. A series of nineteen votes during the period 1768 to 1770, dealing with a variety of issues, helps to identify these two sides. The DeLancey faction consisted of seventeen members who cast 200 out of 263 votes as a bloc (84 percent); of these men nine belonged to the Anglican church and only one was a Presbyterian. The ten Livingstons, who voted just as consistently on the other side, included three Presbyterians, five members of the Dutch Reformed Church, a Quaker, a Lutheran, and no Anglicans. The Livingstons represented the upstate areas and Suffolk County, while most of the De-Lanceys lived near New York City. All of the Livingstons became rebels, but a majority of the DeLanceys remained loyal. Thus, in a very general way, New York's political alignment took the form of an upstate-dissenter-incipiently rebel group versus a downstate-Anglican-tory element, each having some allies in the enemy camp.

The contest between the major "interests" stimulated some lively campaigning. Nominations were made by leaders or even by public meetings. The faithful then circulated tickets and printed broadsides or newspaper articles that announced the issues. Writing in 1907, one historian stated that in certain elections "the voters were as fully informed of the position of the opposing candidate as modern voters are through the party platforms."[9] Although the colony's elite led both factions, they found themselves forced to ap-

9. Carl Lotus Becker, *The History of Political Parties in the Province of New York, 1760–1776* (Madison, 1909). See Patricia U. Bonomi's excellent book, *A Factious People: Politics and Society in Colonial New York* (New York, 1971).

peal to public opinion, especially during the years just preceding Independence. By that time both showed characteristics of the modern parties.[10]

New Jersey's political history had been distinguished, during the early years, by a division between East and West Jersey. The former, settled by the Dutch and by English settlers from New York and New England, maintained economic and cultural relations with New York City; the latter, containing a strong Quaker influence, looked toward Philadelphia. The sectional differences ceased to be politically important by mid-century, though they revived again after Independence. Divisions within each of the sections, including that between proprietors and small landowners, complicated the political situation. Votes in the legislature—if those cast during the 1769/1770 session are typical—followed neither geographical nor religious lines but suggest instead the existence of several groups.

Two such blocs opposed each other fairly evenly on every issue that came to a vote.[11] One consisted primarily of merchants and lawyers who defended their own interests and tended to support the government. In particular they approved subjecting the real estate of nonresidents (absconding debtors) to seizure for debt, defended the dignity of government against abuse, killed a bill to regulate lawyers, granted the governor money in a controversial matter, allowed the chief justice a higher per diem, and approved a resolution condemning Samuel Tucker for taking excessive fees, probably because Tucker was undercutting the lawyers who seem to have started the investigation.[12] Most of these men held offices from the governor, and several belonged to the colony's richest

10. Historians of the subject use the words "party," "faction," and "interest," following the usage of the time. See Roger Champagne, "Family Politics versus Constitutional Principles: The New York Assembly Elections of 1768 and 1769," *WMQ*, 3d Ser., XX (1963), 57–79.

11. "Fairly evenly" means no more than a two-to-one margin for the victors.

12. Richard Stockton Field, *The Provincial Courts of New Jersey, with Sketches of the Bench and Bar*, New Jersey Historical Society, *Collections*, III (New York, 1849), 170. For the votes, see *Votes and Proceedings of the General Assembly of the Province of New Jersey . . .* , especially Nov. 1, 4, 8, Dec. 1, 4, 1769, Oct. 26, Dec. 19, 1770. These records of New Jersey's colonial and state general assemblies are available on microcards in the Early American Imprint Series; see Clifford K. Shipton and James E. Mooney, *National Index of American Imprints through 1800: The Short-Title Evans* [Worcester, Mass., 1969] for directions to this series. The assembly journals of all of the states are also available on microfilm in the Records of the States of the United States of America project; see William Sumner Jenkins, comp., and Lillian A. Hamrick, ed., *A Guide to the Microfilm Collection of the Early State Records* (Washington, D.C., 1950) and the supplement edited by William Sumner Jenkins (Washington, D.C., 1951).

families. The opposite group consisted of men who were engaged in agriculture and who (with one exception) did not hold office or form part of an economic elite. The contrast must not be pushed too far, for only half of the assemblymen divided in this fashion. Thus we deal, not with stable legislative parties, but with a tendency toward bloc voting by different interest groups. Its extent may be judged from these figures: in the sixty votes under consideration, affirmatives formed 55.2 percent of the total; legislators who were not farmers voted pro 80.6 percent of the time, while farmer delegates voted pro 42.1 percent of the time. Clearly parties, even of the colonial species, remained no more than incipient in colonial New Jersey.

A precisely opposite situation existed in Pennsylvania, where parties played so important a role that historians continue to analyze the intricate electioneering. The ingredients, though far from simple, are clear enough in rough outline. The Quakers organized to defend their long-held dominance over the colony. They controlled the assembly, which reflected the Friends' pacifism and tried to protect the Indians. In these objectives they usually obtained the support of like-minded German sects. They posed as a popular party by seeking less interference from the proprietor in local affairs, trying to tax the Penns' land, and attempting to place the colony under royal control. The Penns defended their economic interests and tried to balance what they regarded as the excessive power of the assembly by a stronger executive. They also supported the expansionist desires of the westerners, appealing to anyone who opposed "the eastern, Quaker-dominated, pacifist, Indian-coddling, undemocratic Assembly party."[13]

Politics in Pennsylvania were never dull. At the local level contests for office furnished ample experience in electioneering and even in combat. Much of the furor involved personalities or factions, but colony-wide campaigns, though sometimes undignified, concerned important principles. While it is true that, as one historian has remarked, the parties were "in no way formal organizations, [but] consisted of a loose association of men drawn together by mutual likes and dislikes,"[14] these associations prepared tickets, vigorously attacked each other, stood for well-recognized ideas, got out the vote, and in at least one case established a

13. William S. Hanna, *Benjamin Franklin and Pennsylvania Politics* (Stanford, 1964), 160. See also Theodore Thayer, *Pennsylvania Politics and the Growth of Democracy, 1740–1776* (Harrisburg, 1954), 100.
14. Thayer, *Pennsylvania Politics*, 151.

newspaper as a party organ. One of the most entertaining incidents in American political history occurred when the pacifistic Quakers blocked access to the Philadelphia ballot box and then implored their allies to fend off the sailors that the proprietary party had enlisted to break the blockade. The campaign of 1764 marked the climax of pre-Revolutionary politicking. The proprietary-Presbyterian alliance pushed their "New Ticket," which included Scotch-Irish candidates, ardently supported by their ministers, together with friends of the proprietor, many Germans, and even some Quakers. Both sides spent money and got out the vote. The Quaker party lost in Philadelphia and the westernmost counties, but retained control of the legislature.[15]

After 1765 the Quaker party began to lose ground, and the political alignment slowly shifted. The Friends themselves divided as British measures led some to perceive that life in a royal colony might not be preferable to conditions in a proprietary one. Most Quakers failed to support the resistance movement, so some of their adherents fell away, while the mechanics and shopkeepers of Philadelphia now organized their own "Patriotic Society" in an effort to increase their political influence. Party lines began to blur, as the leaders of both sides tried to preserve the old order. The Presbyterians broke with the Anglicans and the Penns, leading the opposition to British measures, and in 1776 old alignments gave way to the new.

Maryland's legislature contained equally sharp divisions. The party names suggest an alignment like that in Pennsylvania: proprietary versus antiproprietary, court versus country. Maryland, however, lacked the religious differences. Catholics could not vote or hold office and so exercised no political power, and dissenters never became numerous enough to challenge the Anglican majority. The legislative parties did not arise out of local contests, for the proprietor appointed all officials. Therefore, even more than in Pennsylvania, politics revolved around a struggle for power between men who supported the proprietary interest and those who took the more popular side. The division, however, carried over into matters unconnected with the Baltimores. The so-called court and country parties became conspicuous several decades before 1776 and remained central to Maryland's political life.

15. *Ibid.*, 100–103; Hanna, *Franklin and Pa. Politics*, chap. 10. Votes on the attempt to overthrow the proprietary government and on the appointment of Franklin as agent reveal the party lineup. *Pennsylvania Archives*, 8th Ser., VII, 5682–5691. Later votes demonstrate the sectional nature of the division.

The legislative session of 1765/1766 affords a convenient opportunity to examine this alignment. The house, in four meetings, took some fifty roll-call votes on a variety of issues. Among the fifty-eight delegates, eleven cast only a few votes, eleven shifted erratically, and thirty-six divided into two precisely even groups that took opposite sides on almost every issue, casting in fact over 80 percent of their votes in unison.[16] One of their major voting blocs consisted principally of men from the northern part of the Chesapeake and the upper Potomac—from Maryland's more recently settled areas. Almost all lived on the western side of the bay. The other centered in the Eastern Shore, especially the more southerly counties, and the region directly across the bay, south of Annapolis. This area, the oldest part of the colony, contained most of Maryland's slaves but a minority of her electorate. Otherwise economic differences between the opponents seem slight, most of the delegates coming from the planter elite and both containing a few lawyers and businessmen. A crucial factor was the presence in the eastern group of nine holders of proprietary office, whereas the western party contained only one. On the other hand, most of the militia officers (who were unpaid) belonged to the latter. The easterners, therefore, formed the court, or proprietary, party, their opposites the country, or antiproprietary, party.

The character of the two groups appears also in the issues that divided them. Naturally the country party tried to reduce the power of the proprietors—the prerogative. For example, the questions that were debated during the 1765/1766 session included the payment of the clerk of the upper house out of public funds, the control of certain revenues, and the relative strength of the council and the lower house. The country party tended to oppose government expenditures that might fall upon the people, as when the governor suggested that the colony contribute to the victims of a fire in Quebec and when a bill called for a poll tax to maintain roads. The same delegates favored an issue of paper money backed by local resources rather than by Bank of England stock, thus taking a kind of "soft" money position. They vigorously fought plural officeholding, and may deserve the appellation of "popular party" to some degree. Certainly they posed as such.

At the same time, however, circumstances prevented the rise of a genuinely popular party in Maryland. The lively electioneering that would have accompanied such a development was missing.

16. For the votes, see William Hand Browne *et al.*, eds., *Maryland Archives* (Baltimore, 1883–), XIV.

The reason lay primarily in the aristocratic nature of the power structure. The delegates from all counties were large property owners, primarily great planters, so that control of the legislature remained in the possession of an agricultural elite. Probably the representatives divided only because the determined and in some ways extreme position taken by the proprietor and his supporters polarized Maryland's politics.

If that interpretation is correct, then the absence of comparable pressure accounts for the lack of such divisions in Virginia. At first glance one would expect to find in this largest British colony internal disputes that would lead to an advanced stage of party development. Virginia's society had early become so diverse that Bacon's Rebellion seems a natural consequence of social strain, and indeed historians have had difficulty in accepting an interpretation of that event that eliminated sectional and class antagonisms as causes. With their tidewater and piedmont and Shenandoah Valley and mountains, her Northern Neck and Southside; with her extensive trade, rich plantations, and small farms; her merchants, lawyers, pioneers, great landowners, tenants, debtors, and farmers; her cultured elite and remote backwoodsmen; her numerous dissenters, strengthened by the Great Awakening, and her influential churchmen, Virginia seemed destined for a turbulent history. But she experienced no land-bank controversy, no Leisler Rebellion, no Paxton riot, no Regulation, produced no court or country or Quaker or DeLancey party—not even a Ward or Hopkins faction. Instead the colony's politics concentrated on the House of Burgesses's successful struggle for autonomy and the westward advance against French and Indians. Internally Virginia gives the appearance of unity: the Burgesses certainly contained no disruptive elements or basic divisions until a few years before Independence. The reason, as is well known, lay in the unchallenged dominance of the planter elite, who obtained their election even in rather remote areas because the voters were accustomed to choosing such men and either thought them worthy or never questioned their merit. The planter elite itself remained unified by a community of interest and ideas, and the governor never became strong enough to consistently drive a wedge into this solid front. Far from producing parties, Virginia scarcely produced factions.

To some extent this serene uniformity changed after 1760 because of the Two Penny Act and the rise of Henry, the Robinson affair, which called into question the honesty of the elite, and the division of opinion concerning the resistance to England. These events set the stage for the postwar divisions that culminated in the 1790s.

Farther south internal conflicts, far more turbulent than those in Maryland or Pennsylvania, produced violence rather than parties. North Carolina contained several political forces. A number of small trading towns sent delegates to the Commons House. They voted as a bloc and may have exerted considerable influence. The northeast, settled from Virginia, contained many slaves and tobacco plantations and vied for supremacy with the southeast. The latter region may have contained a less stable society and more men who had acquired debts for the purchase of slaves: Governor Martin referred in 1771 to "a Majority from the Southern district in which the people are almost universally necessitous and in debt and whose policy it seems has been to overflow the province with paper money."[17] As a rule the sectional struggle concerned offices rather than issues. The governor's power decreased rapidly with distance from the capital city because primitive transportation and the colony's geography placed most residents beyond his reach. Besides, he had to contend with North Carolina's local officials, whose loyalty lay not with the governor but with the Commons, where indeed many of them sat. Finally, the interior, rapidly expanding in population and area and containing fewer slaves and a more democratic social structure than the east, had its own problems. The legislature failed to cope with western grievances because the eastern majority did not sympathize with them and because the westerners themselves were disunited. The contest took on the appearance of a class war between an arbitrary, powerful group of officials and the majority of the people. As a result westerners did not organize into a legislative pressure group, but engaged in the Regulator Movement.

These elements appeared in the legislature when on rare occasions someone demanded a roll call. Four votes in 1771 show the legislators dividing roughly into two groups: one that included the delegates from the towns plus most easterners and another that consisted primarily of representatives from the interior. The former may have contained the seeds of a court party, but the governor was never able to organize a consistent following. Instead North Carolina's politics remained chaotic.

17. William L. Saunders, Walter Clark, and Stephen B. Weeks, eds., *Colonial and State Records of North Carolina* (Raleigh, Winston, Goldsboro, and Charlotte, 1886–1914), IX, 76. Perhaps Martin meant the western rather than the southern delegates.

In contrast, South Carolina's political system was a little too well organized. It resembled Virginia's in that the planters, together with some native merchants and lawyers, completely controlled the lower house; but whereas Virginia's dominant minority allowed the participation of men from the interior, even from the frontier —from areas characterized by small farms rather than plantations —no such areas chose delegates to South Carolina's House of Commons. Virginia's gentlemen ruled with the assent of the humbler sort, South Carolina's without it. The Commons contained almost no representatives from the interior, and the artisans and shopkeepers of Charleston also lacked a voice except when some radical merchant or lawyer expressed their aspirations. No factions developed among the governing elite. Conflicts took the form simply of clashes between a single harmonious group and outsiders, notably the western Regulators and the British government. The former failed to obtain power, and the latter, though exerting a good deal of influence, never could successfully oppose the united strength of the planters.

A precisely opposite situation existed in Georgia, where we return finally to the New Hampshire style of government. Militarily weak and economically immature, the colony depended on the mother country, and the people dared not oppose their governor. Indeed, Georgia's rulers, unlike the Wentworths, did not need to build a political following in order to govern almost without opposition.[18]

This survey of colonial politics raises the question of what factors or forces existed that might have and occasionally did create factions or the eighteenth-century variety of parties but that normally inhibited their emergence prior to 1776. The answer will clear the way for a discussion of how Independence affected political alignments.

Royal and proprietary governors tried to attract enough support so that they could rule supreme or, if that proved impossible, compete as successfully as the king did at home. They gathered about them a factional following of dependents and sympathizers, and if they received fairly constant support from England, they constructed a court party. The desire for political preferment led colonial leaders to attach themselves to some clique or faction and seek power from the governor or, more rarely, in England.

Local economic interests also affected political alignments. Colo-

18. W. W. Abbot, *The Royal Governors of Georgia, 1754–1775* (Chapel Hill, 1959).

nial merchants, representing the desires of the trading towns, exerted pressure on the legislature. Large landowners always possessed great power. In Massachusetts and perhaps elsewhere creditors determined monetary policy; debtors rarely succeeded. Small farmers could vote and might hold office, but they often identified their interests with that of the large landowners and usually were content to elect someone of superior rank. They emerged, however, as a powerful political force in Massachusetts and Rhode Island and threatened to do so in other colonies. Everywhere their numbers made them potentially strong. On the other hand, artisans, shopkeepers, and other members of the urban middling sort rarely formed a cohesive pressure group, though in Boston, Philadelphia, New York, and some lesser centers politicians competed for their votes. The importance of these economic interests is attested by a petition from Newbury, Massachusetts, requesting a division of the town, "as the inhabitants of one Part of the said Town are mostly Farmers and of the other principally Merchants, Tradesmen, and Sea faring Persons; and as the Interests of said Parties are so different, and in some respects opposite."[19]

Religious differences proved to be the only significant cultural factor. Some had disappeared with time, and several colonies either contained only one major church, or suppressed dissent. However, religious divisions among Anglicans, Presbyterians, Quakers, Old Light and New Light Congregationalists, Baptists, and occasionally some other group affected politics in many areas.

Finally, although most politically important colonists adhered to the whig ideology, American thought ranged all the way from defense of a truly democratic government to toryism. Much political writing took the form of ideological debate that expressed (or in some cases may have concealed) basic differences.

Why did these many influences create divisions in some colonies and none in others? Clearly factions or parties developed only when no single political force became omnipotent. In New Hampshire and Georgia the governors achieved such power that they suppressed dissent. In Virginia and South Carolina members of the colonial elite united sufficiently among themselves and exerted enough weight to prevent the rise either of an effective court party or of an internal opposition.

Elsewhere political power never became so concentrated, and opposition groups appeared. Connecticut stands closest to those colonies dominated by a native elite, but her leaders did divide on particular economic, religious, and political issues. Parties failed to develop in New Jersey, not because any centralized power prevented them, but apparently because no major issue crystallized them, although votes in the legislature do suggest a consistent division along economic lines. Massachusetts produced a fascinating set of factions and interest blocs that coalesced occasionally into major antagonistic groups. In both Pennsylvania and Maryland the proprietors had enough influence to build a court party but not enough to prevent the rise of strong opposition. The proprietary versus antiproprietary dichotomy intersected with or overlapped internal, sectional, religious, and economic divisions. The court, country, Quaker, and Anglican parties became permanent features possessed of continuity, principles, and rhetoric; Pennsylvania added a certain amount of organization and a great deal of campaigning.

Religion and politics also mixed in New York. Here the two major factions, in their struggle for power, appealed to the people through vigorous electioneering. Their constituencies were similar in many respects, yet they drew strength from different areas and religious groups. The DeLancey-Livingston controversy presently coincided with a basic disagreement concerning the resistance to British measures. The term faction clearly seems too limited to describe entities that involved real principles and interests.

Finally, Rhode Island produced her usual unique response to problems in the creation of the Ward and Hopkins factions. The two groups were factional in the sense that they did not differ in their economic, social, or cultural objectives, but they resembled parties in their longevity, their conglomerate membership, and their quite modern techniques. The most democratic colony contained the most uninhibited system of politics.

The events beginning in 1774 profoundly affected political alignments. The earliest, most obvious, and perhaps most important development was the annihilation of the royal and proprietary influences. Their expulsion meant in some cases that internal divisions appeared where none existed before, as in New Hampshire; in others, that a significant force vanished; in still others, that one-half of the power structure disappeared, leaving a huge vacuum. The proprietary parties in Maryland and Pennsylvania and lesser equivalents elsewhere were now destroyed and their like would not be seen for many years. Power in these instances reverted to the legislature or to the locality.

A second factor contributing to a new political situation was the weakening or disappearance of those factions or groups that failed to support the Revolution. These included the Hutchinson family and its adherents, the DeLancey faction, the Anglican party and most of the Quaker party in Pennsylvania, and various less important groups. The positions and influences of these thereupon fell into the possession of different, sometimes new men.

Third, institutional changes also encouraged a different structure of power: (1) several states allowed much greater representation to the backcountry, resulting in a sharp westward shift in the locus of power and at the same time increasing the influence of small landholders, dissenters, and (as will be seen) those espousing certain economic interests and political ideas.[20] This process occurred notably in New Hampshire, Pennsylvania, and South Carolina, and quite possibly the formation of new political units took place more rapidly in Virginia and North Carolina than would have been the case within the empire. (2) The franchise was widened in certain cases (as in Philadelphia), and the right to hold office was extended. The latter reform particularly affected the upper houses, where basic divisions quickly appeared. (3) Access to power widened because more offices became elective or, if appointive, controlled by the legislative rather than the executive branch. This applied even to judges in some states. (4) The political process was gradually democratized in various ways. Secret ballots became less rare. Laws received better publicity, sometimes being printed for consideration before taking effect. In a few states newspapers carried accounts of legislative proceedings. The practice of instructing representatives how to vote increased in frequency. More sessions were opened to the public. (5) Finally, the practice of requiring and publishing roll-call votes, quite limited during the colonial period, gradually became almost universal. Public opinion grew in importance, and politicians could more easily build popular followings.

A fourth circumstance that contributed to a new political era was the greater participation by ordinary folk in public life. They joined various local committees of observation, correspondence, or safety; became officers in the militia or the Continental army; and served in a variety of civil offices, especially during the war. They now sought election to the legislature, and the voters, who had previously selected members of the "better sort" (whatever comprised the local equivalent of a gentry), began to choose men like themselves. This gradual and partial displacement of the elite occurred for several reasons. In many areas they lost the public's confidence because some failed to defend the rebel cause and thus called into question the superior wisdom of any elite. The people turned from Thomas Hutchinson to Samuel Adams, from William Allen to Timothy Matlack, from John Robinson to Patrick Henry, from Cadwallader Colden and James DeLancey to George Clinton, from William Bull to Christopher Gadsden and then to Alexander Gillon—instances that could be multiplied. Simultaneously the people gained confidence in their own ability to judge and to govern. Moreover this change of attitude gained strength ideologically through a greater emphasis upon the democratic element in government. This occurred partly within the whig tradition, as Americans stressed the influence of the popular branch, and partly outside it, as men applauded a government by the people. In either case theorists argued that power originated from the people, and no great leap was required to conclude that the people should govern themselves.[21] That conclusion ultimately justified a popular party.

The implications of these developments appeared unevenly from state to state over several decades. The legislatures gradually opened to admit men or representatives of men previously excluded or possessed of little power: small farmers, debtors, artisans, shopkeepers, those of humble families, little education, limited experience; members of dissenting sects; delegates from small towns, subsistence farm areas, the frontier. These now competed with the merchants and lawyers and planters, the social elite, intelligentsia, cosmopolitans, the Anglicans and Congregationalists, the men from the trading centers and commercial farms. Out of these many elements emerged new political alignments and presently new parties.

21. Gordon S. Wood, *The Creation of the American Republic, 1776–1787* (Chapel Hill, 1969).

Chapter II

The Subject and the Method

The legislative records of the American states during the Revolutionary era offer an embarrassment of riches to the student of political behavior. Whereas before 1776 only a few assemblies recorded any votes for posterity, this practice later became common in all but a few states. The representatives in New York, New Jersey, Pennsylvania, Delaware, and Maryland called for a division on an astonishing array of topics ranging from vital questions of finance to the regulation of dogs. Virginia, North Carolina, Georgia, Massachusetts, New Hampshire, and (beginning in 1787) South Carolina recorded fewer votes, but these generally concerned key issues. Only Rhode Island and Connecticut refrained, and even in the latter state the newspapers have preserved a few exceptions. For various reasons—generally some difficulty in obtaining biographical information on the legislators—the present investigation concentrated on seven states and, for still other reasons, on the postwar years. Even with this narrowed focus, the usable data included some fifteen hundred votes and the same number of individuals. The quantity of facts ultimately required the help of a computer for analysis.

The first step in tackling this data involved analyzing the votes in order to determine whether the legislators divided into significant and consistent groups. In the most commonly used technique the investigator concentrates on a handful of what he considers key votes—the votes on "significant" issues. This procedure enables him to arrange the legislators along some preconceived spectrum, such as radical to conservative, or to scale them with respect to particular questions, such as monetary policy or the slavery controversy. If one is interested solely in a specific subject, the method does sort out the pros, cons, and fence sitters. Our interest, however, extends to all of the issues that divided the legislators of the period, and we should not gratuitously assume the significance of certain questions. The impartial procedure requires a study of the division on every vote without reference to its meaning. If a pattern appears we can investigate the reasons in due course.

One way of discovering voting patterns requires that every voter be compared with every other voter by marking every agreement or disagreement on each vote. The system is exceedingly long and tedious, since a single roll call involving forty men would require 39×39 marks, and an average session might produce twenty such votes. Moreover it proved unnecessary in this study, for simple scanning quickly revealed unmistakable patterns and alignments. Regardless of method, analysis of the roll calls in every state revealed the existence of two major blocs, or legislative parties.

An excellent example of both the analytic method and the alignment it revealed is furnished by the accompanying record of votes in the New York legislature during part of the October–November session of 1784 (see table 2.1). The table is arranged so as to emphasize the pattern. At this preliminary stage the two sides were labeled "A" and "B." During this part of the session, on 14 of the 17 votes (there were 22 more later), the legislators divided into two major blocs. At the extremes Sands, Randall, Vanderbilt, Doughty, Mercereau, and Corsen voted on all 14 exactly opposite to Ford and Sherwood, while the other men fell along a spectrum, 16 casting at least two out of three votes as did the first group, 24 supporting the second bloc two-thirds of the time, and 12 voting independently. The two opposing sides eventually turned out to be, respectively, the anti-Clintonians and the Clintonians.

Although the next session of the legislature contained many new men, the same process again turned up two major blocs, the members of which agreed with one another two-thirds of the time. They contained forty-three of the sixty-five delegates. Thirty-two out of 48 votes showed this pattern. Did the blocs previously discovered continue? We can trace the holdovers as follows: Vanderbilt, Doughty, Youngs, Mercereau, and Townsend cast 91 out of 116 (78.4 percent) of their votes with the new party B. Gilbert, Patterson, Paine, Brinckerhoff, Smith, Cooper, Harper, and Baker voted 216 times out of 252 (85.7 percent) with that session's bloc A. Denning shifted sides, while Goforth, Pell, and Thomas divided their allegiance. Among the neutrals Lockwood stayed put, and James Livingston tended toward side B. Thus fourteen

Table 2.1. *Votes in the New York Assembly, October–November 1784*

	Votes																
	1	2	3	4	5	6	7	8	9	10	11	12	13	14	15	16	17
PATTERN B	+	−	−	+	−	−	+	−		+	−			−	−		−	+
New York City																	
P. V. B. Livingston	+	−	−	+	+	−	+	−	+	+	−	+	−	−	−	−	+
Comfort Sands	+	−	−	+	−	−	+	−	−	+	−	−	−	−	−	−	
Thomas Randall	+	−	−	+	−	−	+	−	+	+	−	+	−	−	+	−	+
Henry Remsen	+	−	−	+		+	+	−	+			+					+
Suffolk																	
David Gelston	+	−	−	+	−	−	+	−	−	+	+	−			−	+	+	−
Jeffrey Smith							+	−	+	+	−	−	−	−	+	+	−
Thomas Youngs	+	−	−	+	−												
John Smith	+	−	−	+	−	−	−	−	−	+	+	−	−	−	−	−	+
Kings																	
John Vanderbilt	+	−	−	+	−	−	+	−	+	+	−	−	−	−	−	−	−
Charles Doughty	+	−	−	+	−	−	+	−	−	+	−	−	−	−			+
Queens																	
James Townsend			−	+	−	−	−	−	+	+	−	−	−				−
Joseph Lawrence	+	−	−	+	−	−		−	+	+	−	+	−	−	+	−	−
John Sands	+	−	−	+	−	−	+			+	+	−	+	−	+	−	−	+
Richmond																	
Joshua Mercereau	+	−	−	+	−	−	+	−	+	+	−	+	−	−	−	−	+
Cornelius Corsen	+	−	−	+	−	−	+	−	−	+	−	+	−	−			−	+
Albany																	
Walter Livingston	−	−	−	+	−	−											
NEUTRALS																	
New York City																	
Daniel Dunscomb		−	−	+	+	−	+	−		−	−	+		+	+	+	−
John Lawrence									+	−	+		+	+	+	−
Aaron Burr						−										−
Westchester																	
Ebenezer Lockwood	+	+							−	+	−	−	−	−	−	+

Table 2.1—Continued

	Votes																
	1	2	3	4	5	6	7	8	9	10	11	12	13	14	15	16	17
Dutchess																	
Cornelius Humphrey	−					+	+	+	+	−	+	−	+	−	−	−	+
Ulster																	
Charles DeWitt	+	+	+	+	+	−	+	−	−		−			+	−	−	+
J. G. Hardenburgh	+	+	−	+	−	+	−	+	−	−	+	+	+	+	−	−	−
Orange																	
John Hathorn	+						−	−	−				+	+	+	+	
Jeremiah Clark	−	+	+	+	−	+			−	−	+	−	+	−	+	+	−
William Sickles	+	+				+	+	−	−	−	−	+	−	+	+	−	+
Montgomery																	
James Livingston	+	−	+			+	+	−	−	+	−	+	+	+	+	+	−
C. P. Yates								+	−	−	+			−	+	+	−
PATTERN A	−	+	+	−	+	+	−	+		−	+		+	+		+	−
New York City																	
William Goforth	+	+	+	−	+	+	+	−	+	−	+	+	+	+	+	+	−
William Denning	+	−	+	−	+	+	+		+	−	−		+	+	+	+	−
Albany																	
Jacob Ford	−	+	+	−	+	+	−	+	+	−	+	+	+	+	+	+	−
Matthew Adgate	−	+	+	−	+	+	−	+	+	+	+	+	+	+	+	−	−
John Younglove	−	+	+	−	+	+	+	+	−	−	+	+	+	+	+	+	−
Abraham Becker		+	+	−	+	+	+	+	+	−	+	−	+	+	−	+	−
Matthew Visscher								−	+	+			+	−	+	+	−
Israel Thompson	−		+	−	+	+	+	+	−	−	+	−	+	+	−	−	
Westchester																	
Philip Pell, Jr.	−	+								−	+	+	+	−	+		−
Abijah Gilbert	−	+	−	−	+	+	−	+	+	−	+	−	−	−	−	−	+
Ebenezer S. Burling	−	+	+	−		+	−	+	+	+	+	+	−	+	+	+	−
Thomas Thomas		+				+	+	+	−	−	+		+	+	+		+
Ebenezer Purdy		+	−			+	−	+	+								

Table 2.1—Continued

	Votes																
	1	2	3	4	5	6	7	8	9	10	11	12	13	14	15	16	17
Dutchess																	
Matthew Patterson	−	+	+	−	+	+	+	+	−	−	+	−	+	−	+	+	−
James Talmadge	−	+	+	−	+			−				−	+	+	−	−	
Brinton Paine	−	+				+		−	−	−		−	+	+	−		
Dirck Brinckerhoff	−	+	+	−	+		+	+	+	−	+	−	+	−	−	−	+
Ulster																	
Nathan Smith	+	+					+	−	−	−	+	−	+	+	+	+	−
Orange																	
Gilbert Cooper	+	+	+	−	+	+	−	+	+	−	+	+	+	+	−	−	+
Montgomery																	
William Harper	−	+	+	−	+	+	−	−	+	+	+	+	+	+	+	+	−
Volkert Veeder		+	+	+	+	−	+	−	−	+	+	+	+	+	+	−	
Washington																	
Albert Baker	−	−	+	−	+	+	−	+	−	−	+	−	+	+	−	−	−
David Hopkins	−	+	+	−	+	+	−	+	−	−	+	−	+	+	−	−	+
Adiel Sherwood	−	+	+	−	+	+	−	+	−	−	+	−	+	+	+	+	−

remained on the same side, one changed completely, and four moved into or out of the neutral group. In subsequent sessions this procedure revealed New York's legislators repeatedly separating themselves into two major, continuous, cohesive groups.

The process also identified a set of votes that served as indicators of bloc affiliation. In the session that was used as an example in table 2.1, votes 9 and 12 obviously failed to do this. On vote 15, bloc B voted con, 4–7, and A voted pro, 14–9, a consistency of about 62 percent. This fell short of the two-thirds established as the norm. All of the others exceeded that standard. In some sessions every vote proved significant. This was usually the case in Massachusetts, where the legislature required votes only on vital matters. In other sessions they might number only half or even less, generally when men were requiring ayes and nays on many minor, personal, or local subjects. Sometimes in sessions such as these the significant votes, from the point of view of party, became apparent only when the affiliation of the legislators had been established from other years. In the end each state furnished a set of critical votes, extending over all of the sessions, which collectively separated the legislators into their two blocs.

This final delineation required the establishment of a dividing line between the bloc members and neutrals. This often presented no problem. Matthew Adgate, whom we saw supporting bloc A on 13 out of 15 votes (table 2.1), scored 60 out of 63 in the four sessions from 1784 to 1788. James Townsend's record, however, was 50 out of 81 in favor of group B's position. The rule eventually adopted required for membership a majority of two votes cast with a bloc for each vote that did not support its position. Townsend was accordingly assigned to the neutrals, having missed bloc B affiliation by about 10 votes.

Several other technical points require explanation. Two kinds of votes did not seem worth recording. First were those with only a small minority on one side. "Small" means fewer than one-third, often only a few individuals. Generally men taking this sort of minority position are reflecting personal, idiosyncratic views rather than the opinions of a bloc. When a nearly unanimous tally seemed to indicate a core group, a separate note took care of it. Another type of "extraneous" ballot resulted from delegates voting to protect the interest of some locality. Thus the allocation of taxes might evoke a series of roll calls in which the representatives of each district tried, for the record, to reduce its burden. The inclusion of these would have tended to distort political sectionalism, a factor that did not need any exaggeration. Lastly, duplicate votes were eliminated, as for example when the advocates of a measure first defeated an attempt to postpone it and then passed it.

In determining bloc affiliation it also seemed desirable to disregard situations in which several consecutive, yet not identical, votes concerned the same issue. For example, three votes might first reject a high salary for an official, then reject a lower one, and finally adopt some compromise. To count these as three might distort the importance of what is really only a single question—whether the salary should be high or low—and they are counted as such. The word "vote" as used here may therefore refer to a set of votes.[1]

1. These sets of votes, condensed for my investigation of blocs, were kept separate when stored into a computer.

The procedure outlined above may not satisfy the student accustomed to the method that indiscriminately casts all of the votes into a matrix. As a check, after the data had been stored in a computer, bloc alignments in New York, New Jersey, and Maryland were determined by comparing the record of every legislator with that of all the others. The result confirmed the conclusions already reached. For example, the computer's matrix for New York's 1784/1785 session showed two major groups of twenty and fourteen men, with a minor bloc of four. The first included eighteen members of party A (Clintonians) and two neutrals; the second contained thirteen members of group B (anti-Clintonians) and one neutral. So precise was the correspondence that, when in another session two men appeared out of place in the computer's analysis, the anomaly induced an investigation that disclosed a key-punching error.

The final result of the voting analysis revealed that each state legislature contained two parties, or blocs, and that the parties in each state shared many characteristics with those of other states—that they divided on the same issues and contained the same sorts of people. These two groups might and often did divide into subgroups, created by factions, sectional similarities, or other circumstances, but these always coalesced into or revolved around the major parties. One proved to be the Constitutionalists in Pennsylvania, the Clintonians in New York, the up-country representatives of South Carolina, the rural legislators of Massachusetts, and so on, while the other included their opposites: Republicans, anti-Clintonians, etc. During the investigation they remained parties A and B, and at the end the titles agrarian-localist and commercial-cosmopolitan seemed most descriptive. We will call them, for short, and without prejudice, the Localists and the Cosmopolitans: evidence will follow. The analysis of voting patterns in the seven states eventually identified 539 Localists, 552 Cosmopolitans, and 412 neutrals.[2]

The next step was to gather biographical data on each legislator. Since the objective of this was to discover the sources of political behavior, research had to comprehend every influence that might affect the political process. Even a wide net does not catch all the fish, and every student of history is uncomfortably aware that he

2. These figures exaggerate the proportion of neutrals, at least after about 1783. They include legislators in several states who served before parties crystallized or when too few roll calls existed to distinguish patterns. Once the legislative parties developed, the proportion of neutrals shrank to an average of 20%.

Table 2.2. *Composition of the State Legislatures*

	No.	%		No.	%
Residence			**Occupation**		
Frontier	157	10.4	Farmer	503	33.5
Noncommercial farm	361	24.0	Large landowner	237	15.8
Commercial farm	433	28.8	Misc. nonfarmer	21	1.4
Commercial farm near city	50	3.3	Artisan	24	1.6
Plantation	226	15.0	Miller	38	2.5
Small town	130	8.6	Iron manufacturer	19	1.3
Second-rank city	24	1.6	Other manufacturer	36	2.4
Major city	114	7.6	Minister	8	0.5
Uncertain	8	0.5	Doctor	62	4.1
			Lawyer	134	8.9
			Other professional	48	3.2
Economic status			Misc. entrepreneur	35	2.3
Poor or moderate	455	30.3	Innkeeper	30	2.0
Substantial	305	30.3	Shopkeeper	40	2.7
Well-to-do	358	23.9	Ship's captain	7	0.5
Wealthy	242	16.1	Merchant or trader	132	8.8
Uncertain	141	9.4	Unknown	128	8.5
Religion			**Age**		
Catholic	3	0.2	Under 40	333	22.5
Espiscopalian	189	12.6	40–49	271	18.0
Methodist	8	0.5	50–59	164	10.9
Quaker	40	2.7	60 and over	67	4.5
Congregational	122	8.1	Unknown	668	44.4
Presbyterian	187	12.4			
Baptist	19	1.3			
Dutch Reformed	63	4.2	**Continental army**		
German Lutheran	22	1.5	Enlisted man	7	0.5
Other	11	0.7	Misc. officer	56	3.8
Unknown	839	55.8	Colonel or general	55	3.6
			Probably served	5	0.3
Political experience					
Local office	303	20.2	**Militia**		
Sheriff, j.p., etc.	227	15.1	Enlisted man	47	3.2
State judge, senator	109	7.3	Misc. officer	322	21.4
Other state office	68	4.5	Colonel or general	208	13.8
Continental Congress	55	3.7	Probably served	13	0.9
Other Continental office	7	0.5	No service known	790	52.5
None	364	24.2			
Uncertain	369	24.6			

Table 2.2—Continued

	No.	%		No.	%
Education			*Intellectual interest*		
None or little	400	26.6	None	1146	76.3
Self-educated	84	5.6	Some	245	16.3
College	133	8.8	Uncertain	112	7.4
Uncertain	886	58.9			
			World view		
			Localist	645	43.0
Father's occupation			Cosmopolitan	297	19.8
			Uncertain	561	37.3
Farmer	346	23.0			
Large landowner	222	14.8			
Artisan	51	3.4	*Father's economic status*		
Manufacturer	30	2.0			
Minister	28	1.9	Poor or moderate	258	17.2
Doctor	21	1.4	Substantial	75	5.0
Lawyer	15	1.0	Well-to-do	190	12.6
Other professional	17	1.1	Wealthy	196	13.0
Misc. entrepreneur	15	11.0	Unknown	783	52.1
Shopkeeper	18	1.2			
Merchant or trader	70	4.7			
Unknown	669	44.5	*National origin*		
			Colonial, English	794	52.8
Social origin			Colonial, Scottish	26	1.7
			Colonial, Scotch-Irish	60	4.0
Humble origin	237	15.8	Colonial, other Irish	2	0.1
Old family	739	49.2	Colonial, German	31	2.1
Above-average family	185	12.3	Colonial, Dutch	96	6.4
Prominent old family	148	9.8	Colonial, New England	26	1.7
Unknown	194	12.9	Colonial, French	28	1.9
			Colonial, misc.	15	1.0
			Immigrant, English	24	1.6
Mobility			Immigrant, Scottish	22	1.5
			Immigrant, North Irish	23	1.5
Mobile	245	16.3	Immigrant, other Irish	6	0.4
Not mobile	1207	80.3	Immigrant, German	13	0.9
Uncertain	51	3.4	Immigrant, other	6	0.4
			Unknown	331	22.0
Slaveholding					
Over 100	45	3.1			
50–99	62	4.2			

Table 2.2—Continued

	No.	%		No.	%
Slaveholding			*Legislative party*		
20–49	168	11.4	Localist	539	35.9
10–19	134	9.1	Neutral	412	27.4
5–9	123	8.4	Cosmopolitan	552	36.7
1–4	181	12.3			
None	603	41.0			
Unknown	156	10.6			

NOTE: This table includes members of the lower houses during the following sessions: Massachusetts, 1784–1788; New York, 1780–1788; New Jersey, 1779–1788; Pennsylvania, 1780–1788; Maryland, 1780–1788; Virginia, 1784–1788; and South Carolina, 1787–1788. It includes about three-fourths of the delegates (nearly 90% of the omissions being in Massachusetts and Virginia) who cast over 96% of all the votes. Those omitted voted on the average four times. For the record, all of the New York delegates received the same investigation—even if they only voted once—but this proved a waste of time.

may not even have conceived of the truly important factor. To guard against such an omission, the search extended to the economic, social, political, and cultural background of the legislators, even when this seemed unlikely to achieve any positive result.

Determining and categorizing the legislator's *residence* proved complicated. Even the simple location of his home was sometimes impossible to discover, for representatives were chosen from counties (except in New England and South Carolina), and where they lived within the county remained, in some cases, a mystery. The major problem, however, was how to characterize the locality. Had politics been simply a matter of generalized sections, such as seacoast versus frontier, it would only have been necessary to determine the rough type of region from which the legislator came. The historian quickly penetrates beyond such simplistic generalizations, but he then puzzles over a substitute formula. What qualities in a delegate's geographical environment are important? How should his constituents be characterized, and what scale should be adopted? An arrangement according to the wealth of the locality was objectionable in this study because the theoretical basis—that degrees of property determine political alignments—was too narrow unless confirmed by other evidence; besides, often the necessary data have not survived.

The final decision, which also suffered from objections but afforded at least a tentative framework, was to arrange the material along a scale from most to least urban, or perhaps more accurately, from most to least commercial.[3] At one pole came the *major cities*: Boston, New York, Philadelphia, Baltimore, Charleston. Next came *towns* of the second rank, such as Salem and Albany, followed by *small towns*. New England "towns," which usually were just agricultural districts with a village, did not qualify as towns at all, unless they contained some trading center such as Springfield. At the other end of the scale, of course, came the *frontier* and the regions just past the frontier stage. In between lay darkness, into which each scholar may peer with a different light. The present system of illumination was as follows: a *plantation* type of community was distinguished, characterized by large-scale commercial farming and most easily identifiable by a concentration of slaves or of tenant farmers. The *commercial farms near cities* formed a category separate from *other commercial farm* areas—regions pretty clearly producing for export, yet not of the "plantation" type. Finally, the rest of the rural countryside by process of elimination belonged to a *noncommercial* variety, presumably characterized by subsistence or semisubsistence farming. In most instances the necessary information for a precise determination was lacking, and decisions involved a good deal of guesswork. All that can be said is that the guesswork was based upon such data as tax lists and local histories and that it presents a picture that seems correct in general though inaccurate in particulars.

The date of the legislator's birth served to distinguish him from other men of the same name and also to test the hypothesis that political attitudes correlate with *age*. This information was lacking in over half of the cases, but sufficed for the purpose.

A representative's *occupation* was clear in most cases. *Farmers* were separated from *large landowners*, or "planters," for two reasons. First, they did in fact differ economically and in other ways. The occupation of a large landowner was distinct from that of the ordinary farmer in that he ran a varied capitalistic enterprise with a labor force (often large), produced a considerable surplus crop for market, often engaged in manufacturing (especially milling and lumbering), and occasionally traded, loaned money, rented farms to tenants, and speculated in land. Although small farmers

3. David Hackett Fischer suggests a division based on stability or instability of population as basic to party distinctions about 1800 (see his *The Revolution of American Conservatism: The Federalist Party in the Era of Jeffersonian Democracy* [New York, 1965]). The difficulty in applying the concept to the 1780s rests in the position taken by delegates from towns, which were socially dynamic. Still, the analytical framework discussed here may prove inferior to some other hypothesis.

also engaged in one or more of these activities, they usually did so for their own subsistence or for a little extra cash. In addition the greater wealth of the large landowner distinguished him socially and often culturally from his less fortunate neighbors. A second reason for the distinction was to test the hypothesis that the two types voted differently (which they did). Assigning the men to the proper category proved difficult in marginal cases. As a rule of thumb, possession of one thousand acres defined one as a large landowner. Exceptions were especially allowed in the North, where land was more valuable.

In other respects the various ways of making a living were separated so as to reflect the actual conditions of the period and to test political behavior. Hypothetically a distinction existed between the large *manufacturer* and the small *artisan*, for the economic activities of a craftsman such as a miller, blacksmith, cooper, or shoemaker differed from those of the large-scale entrepreneur such as an iron manufacturer, distiller, or shipbuilder. *Professional men* included the usual lawyers, doctors, ministers, officials, and miscellaneous persons such as scriveners. Men engaged in trade consisted of several subgroups according to function: *merchants* who specialized in overseas commerce, *traders* who exploited the domestic market, *shopkeepers* with their retail stores, *innkeepers*, and, in a different category, *ships' captains* and mariners. Men who conducted several enterprises were designated by their major vocation or identified as *entrepreneur*.

The occupation of many men remained uncertain. Logic and probability reduced the number labeled *unknown* to fewer than 10 percent. In agricultural communities most inhabitants were farmers. Rural shopkeepers, innkeepers, doctors, lawyers, and owners of manufactories, even millers, were important men at that time and generally conspicuous enough to earn mention in local histories or other records. If a man appeared in none of these sources, the denomination of farmer was a fairly safe choice. Similarly, since few farmers lived in the larger towns, a man of indeterminate occupation could at least be designated a *nonfarmer*. So could representatives from small towns who, according to tax lists or probate records, did not own farm property.

Determining the legislators' *economic status* proved much more difficult. Several categories were adopted: *wealthy* meant the ownership of at least £5,000 worth of property. A southern planter who held a thousand acres of good land and fifty or more slaves would own a total estate of about that size. The larger merchants and most lawyers either possessed that amount in property or earned an equivalent in income. *Well-to-do* meant £2,000 to £5,000. The lower figure did in reality mark a rough dividing line between large property holders, who lived like gentlemen, and small property holders, who could not. Senators in South Carolina and Maryland supposedly held estates of that value. *Substantial* men owned property worth £1,000 to £1,999, typical of prosperous artisans and large farmers with several hundred acres. Most shopkeepers, innkeepers, and doctors had equivalent estates. Men with *moderate* properties were worth £500 to £999.[4]

Precision proved impossible. Generally, if a man had upwards of £5,000, he was conspicuously a man of means and could be identified with some assurance. Otherwise the sources were imperfect. Tax lists proved faulty: often only a few objects were taxed, and personal wealth (such as merchants' stock and money at interest) frequently escaped assessment or was underrated. Invisible wealth, such as income, was ordinarily not taxed, so that a lawyer or official who commanded a large salary might seem poor on the assessment list. Moreover the basis of taxation varied, even from town to town. Probate records afforded only a rough guide, for they omit many men. So do land records. Property, however, could usually be estimated with an error of no more than one point on a scale of ten. For example, James Bonney of Woodbridge, New Jersey (whose family was not mentioned in the local history), owned 135 acres, three horses, and nine cattle in 1784, certainly a small farm. In 1783 he was called a trader—most traders were substantial men—and in 1778 he was taxed for £747 at interest (although this figure may be swollen by wartime inflation). When he died in 1802 he left property worth $3,019 (about £500) in land, cider mills, and distilleries. A designation of barely substantial seemed justified. Another random example is Philip Gardner of Hallam, York County, Pennsylvania, who in 1782 owned 250 acres, four horses, and five cattle. In 1783 his estate was estimated at £722, and the tax lists show his owning two stills and a slave. Because estates were assessed at somewhat less than their full value, he was deemed a substantial man. When specific information was lacking, guesswork was possible up to a point. For instance, in subsistence farm communities almost everyone owned only moderate property, the exceptions being conspicuous. Small errors in

4. These categories correspond quite closely to the realities of the period. See Jackson Turner Main, *The Social Structure of Revolutionary America* (Princeton, 1965), for a description of economic classes.

particular instances presumably canceled each other when scores of cases were involved.

The previous *political experience* of each legislator was also recorded and presently coded in order of descending importance, beginning with *Continental* and then *state offices*, from governor on down, to *local offices* including membership in Revolutionary committees and conventions. Higher ranking officials were easily discovered, but the lesser ones were sometimes very difficult to identify in the absence of local histories or published records. This information did not seem important enough to warrant prolonged search.

Military service also proved difficult to determine. Genealogical interest has led to publications that list officers and soldiers in the *Continental army* and often in the *state militias*, but the latter are not always complete. Where the legislator's name was missing from extensive compilations such as those existing for Massachusetts and Virginia, one could be quite sure that he saw no service, but such certainty was impossible when published records proved unreliable. Apparently only about 8 percent of the representatives served in the Continental army. Two out of five joined the militia, usually as officers.

Whether the representative became a *Federalist* or an *Antifederalist*, and later a *Federalist* or a *Republican*, was interesting for several reasons. It cast light upon his attitudes toward relations with Congress and his political ideology. The conflict over the Constitution became the climactic and most important political event of the decade. It proved fundamentally related to other issues and the history of these early parties. Finally, comparison between the party alignment of the 1780s and that of the 1790s afforded a chance to test the continuity or discontinuity of politics during the early national era. Since these events reach beyond the present study, no systematic effort to achieve completeness seemed necessary, but the final list included about 30 percent of the legislators.

Another subject for investigation was the *religion*, or church affiliation, of the delegates. Ideally the historian needs to know what men believed, but they seldom reveal their convictions to posterity or even to their contemporaries. Instead outward manifestations of their faith have to serve, as recorded in church attendance, burial place, or marriage in a church. Undoubtedly the ratio of success—44 percent—could be greatly increased by the loving attention of a genealogist, but the available information sufficed to test the relation between religion and voting behavior.

Presumably almost all of the legislators could read and write and had acquired a minimal *education.* The sources seldom reveal much about the educational background of the Revolutionary generation, because most men learned at home. The records do identify college men, and in addition they sometimes indicate when one had received a superior education without attending college. These categories, therefore, described the representatives' education, when known: *none or little* (most of them), *college education* (9 percent), and *self-educated* (another 5 percent or so).

Discovering a legislator's intellectual background posed similar problems. The objective here was to identify the "intelligentsia" of the period in order to determine whether such men possessed characteristic voting habits. Evidence of *intellectual interest* was difficult to obtain, and precision proved impossible, but certain facts about a man established a probability: membership in a learned society or library company, sponsorship of a school, known scientific or other scholarly interests, a large or varied private library, the testimony of a contemporary, or the statement of a biographer. If a legislator clearly lacked any such background, he was set down as possessing no intellectual interests, and in doubtful cases he was classified under the heading *uncertain.*

The dichotomy between *cosmopolitan* and *localist* became an important part of this study. The two terms, as applied here, refer to opposing *world views* that are based on the contrasting experience of men. At one pole is the man of broad outlook, usually urban, urbane, and well educated, who has traveled widely and has had extensive contacts with the world because of his occupation, the offices he has held, or his interests. Jefferson and Franklin were cosmopolitan men. At the opposite pole stands the man of narrow horizons—most often rural and sparsely educated—whose experience is limited to his own neighborhood: he is provincial, parochial.

Defining such terms is less difficult than applying them to individuals. Essentially the difference between the two types is subjective, whereas our data are mainly objective. The decision whether a man was cosmopolitan or localist had to be based on indirect evidence that indicated a probability, a presumption about his attitude. If a man had served in Congress or some other federal post; if he had seen military service as an officer that forced him to travel extensively and transcend state boundaries (generally in the Continental army); if he had traveled in the course of business; if he demonstrated intellectual interests or conducted a wide correspondence; or if in general his experiences were such as might cause him to "think continentally" (in Hamilton's phrase), then the term *cosmopolitan* was applied. If none of these facts existed, if he had held only local offices or none, served in the militia or not at all, had apparently never traveled far from home, and possessed no known intellectual interests, then the appellation *localist* seemed appropriate. When information was lacking, the man also probably belonged to this type, because almost by definition the cosmopolitan man was conspicuous. The odds that a delegate would be a localist were especially great in farm or village communities. On the other hand, residence in a large town or city raised such a strong possibility that the man was cosmopolitan in outlook, even if other positive evidence was lacking, that the category of *uncertain* often seemed most appropriate. By such guesswork the proportion of unknowns was limited to 37 percent of the total.

Earlier research into the political attitudes of state senators had suggested that their family background, or *social origin*, was important. Whether a man was raised in wealth or poverty, belonged to a prominent family or fought his way up, seemed to have affected his ideas and behavior. Knowing his family background also helped in assigning the categories of localist and cosmopolitan. Discovering the occupation, wealth, and social rank of the legislators' parents proved so difficult that the problem deserves discussion.

Most of the published biographical research had been written by genealogists. Their books vary in value precisely as do histories: some are unreliable, others are excellent. The student can easily tell the best from the worst; for the rest he should adopt his customary skepticism. As a rule of thumb, detailed histories of particular families are superior to general volumes containing sketches of many families. The good genealogies contain nearly everything knowable about their subjects, for even obscure men are important to the genealogist. The student of a family history will spend days in overgrown cemeteries, in hunting down old Bibles and fugitive letters, or in poring over manuscript court, town, church, and county records to dig up the isolated bits that comprise a biographical sketch. The historian who is dealing with hundreds of cases cannot profitably spend scores of hours on each one. He must therefore rely, whenever possible, upon those who have done so.

Even the best genealogies do not contain all the answers. A model history of the Coit family omits any reference to Isaac Coit of Southwick, Hampshire County, Massachusetts, yet he was an early settler of the town, served as its first physician, and sat in the state legislature. But some fifty miles southeast, in Plainfield, Connecticut, dwelled Deacon Isaac Coit, of the right age to produce Dr. Isaac, twice married but (supposedly) childless. Dr. Isaac never married. The reader can draw his own conclusions.

Second in importance to genealogies as biographical sources are local histories, especially those written before about 1890. The authors, often ministers, were usually well educated and well informed men who knew the locality, studied the records, and worked carefully. They were producing the first substantial accounts and concentrated on the early days, especially the pioneer settlers and their families, carrying the story through the Revolution. Often they included an extensive genealogical appendix. The early doctors, ministers, justices, innkeepers, millers, shopkeepers, and the like appeared, together with public officials and military heroes. Most members of the legislature earned at least a mention.

About the same time the first major county histories appeared, almost entirely for the northern states. These were cooperative enterprises. They opened with a general history that included sketches of prominent men. Then followed an often detailed account of each town, which mentioned practically every inhabitant of consequence down to the Revolution and also contained notices of prominent citizens of the nineteenth century. These histories vary in quality but, discounting local pride, are generally sound.

After 1890 county histories deteriorated rapidly. The second ones to be published contained only a poor historical section, often parroted from the earlier book, and concentrated on the people then alive who might purchase a copy containing accounts of their families but of no others. The genealogical sections were filiopietistic, incomplete, and inaccurate.

These two types of sources—the genealogies and the local histories—identified perhaps three-fourths of the representatives and a third of their fathers in the northern states, but far fewer in the South. Other sources supplied details and missing persons. These included wills and inventories of estates, tax and assessment lists, vital records, land records, miscellaneous data published in local historical magazines or society collections, and manuscript materials in libraries. Eventually these yielded basic data for 90 percent of the legislators and about half of their fathers.

In estimating the social class from which the representatives came, inference filled in many gaps in the data so that the *social origin* of all but 13 percent of the men could be reasonably surmised. The social ranks were defined as follows: the phrase *prominent old family* carries its own meaning. "Old" in Revolutionary America differed from "old" in Europe, for British America was young, and the word signifies merely that one's father had achieved prestige, though sometimes several generations had been prominent. The requirements adopted in the present study for admission into this highest class were stringent. A second major category was *old family* without the "prominent," which was applied to men of the reputable but ordinary middle class—the great mass of farmers, artisans, shopkeepers, or professional men. Next came those of *humble origin*. Most of the legislators whose parents are *unknown* undoubtedly belong here, and were so classified on any slight indication. The ultimate adoption of a more refined scale permitted additional distinctions.

The social *mobility* of the legislators depended on their family background. If a man had risen from a childhood of small property to affluence or had achieved rank considerably above that of his parents, as through high office, he was considered to be mobile; otherwise he was not. John Bacon did not acquire much property, but he graduated from Harvard, became a minister, and finally attained a judicial post and leadership in Berkshire County, Massachusetts, thus rising above the status of his father, John, who apparently was a farmer. About one-sixth of the representatives rose markedly in social class.

Still another possible factor influencing political behavior is the *national origin* of the legislator. Some two-thirds were born in the colony that they later served, of English or Welsh stock. An additional fourth were also born in the same colony but of different stock: Scottish, Scotch-Irish, Irish, German, Dutch, Swiss, French, and miscellaneous others. About one out of ten originally came from another colony and were of various nationalities, usually English. Transplanted New Englanders were especially noted, because some historians have suggested that they voted in a characteristic manner. They formed a significant proportion of the total only in New York and New Jersey. Finally, 7 or 8 percent among those legislators whose birthplace is known had immigrated (the total almost certainly did not exceed one-tenth).

Perhaps the legislators possessed other attributes that affected their votes, but only one more seemed important and easy to discover: whether they owned slaves and how many they possessed. Considered as an economic factor, *slaveholding* already was recorded as part of each man's wealth; however, slavery was more than an economic institution, so that the attitude of slaveowners with respect to noneconomic matters such as the civil rights of Negroes needed testing.

Finally, information on each representative included the years when he served and the quality of the biographical data, ranging from zero up to the reliability of a sketch in the *Dictionary of American Biography*. All together, information concerning 1,503 men in seven states formed the core for analysis. In addition biographical data on the delegates of several other states furnished supporting evidence.[5]

This information, when correlated with the voting records of the representatives, proved conclusively that political behavior did in fact follow certain patterns. A series of hypotheses emerged that called for further testing. The details differed from state to state, and will require extensive discussion, but the general outlines appear in the following example. The forty most consistent legislators in New York during the years 1784 through early 1788 are shown in table 2.3. Table 2.4 (pp. 38–39) indicates the important contrasts between the two groups as well as those factors that seem minor.

Nine or perhaps ten of these criteria indicate lines for further investigation, the exceptions being political experience, military background, age, perhaps the number of slaves, and perhaps national origin, unless the position of New Englanders on one side and Dutch descendants on the other signified something. Two methods seemed plausible: first, to develop some general interpretation that would encompass all of these possible factors; second, to eliminate those differences that proved accidental or that were not independent variables. For example, was a New England origin really significant, or did New Englanders move into geographical areas, engage in economic activities, or possess some other qualities, that were determinative, the place of origin being coincidental? In the case of New York the four New Englanders (Adgate, Hopkins, Ludenton, and Paine) settled in frontier areas, became farmers (in

5. Specifically, research on New Hampshire equaled that on the seven principal states. Research on Delaware and North Carolina was less thorough, and that on the remaining states was negligible.

Table 2.3. *Most Consistent Legislators in New York, 1784–1788*

| | Votes with | | | Votes with | |
Localists	Loc.	Cos.	Cosmopolitans	Loc.	Cos.
Matthew Adgate	60	3	Adrian Bancker	4	22
Albert Baker	69	5	Nicholas Bayard	0	23
Zephaniah Batchelor	28	1	Robert Boyd	2	21
Abraham Becker	51	7	David Brooks	2	33
John Bradner	24	3 .	Cornelius Corsen	0	37
Ebenezer Burling	32	5	John C. Dongan	2	46
Gilbert Cooper	91	10	Charles Doughty	15	82
Lewis Duboys	52	5	Nathanial Gardner	0	23
Jacob Griffin	51	5	Alexander Hamilton	1	26
David Hopkins	43	6	John Laurence	4	22
Ebenezer Husted	23	2	Peter V. B. Livingston	1	37
Henry Ludenton	52	1	Robert C. Livingston	0	28
Joseph McCracken	22	2	William Malcolm	13	63
Brinton Paine	88	3	Joshua Mercereau	4	47
Ichabod Parker	54	3	Thomas Randall	1	33
Nathaniel Satterly	24	3	Comfort Sands	3	36
Johannis Snyder	45	4	John Sands	2	30
Peter Taulman	28	3	Richard Thorne	4	24
Israel Thompson	27	1	John Vanderbilt	2	44
Henry Wisner III	23	2	Peter W. Yates	1	21

one case a miller), never acquired much property, and remained as they began, men of ordinary rank. In the same manner the significance of each fact can be tested, so far as statistics furnish proof, by matching it against every other fact. The process would be tedious, even impracticable, without a computer, but is possible with one. Hopefully, out of the mathematics several valid factors will emerge: these are the independent variables, from among which we must abstract the most probable correlates of the political behavior of our representatives. In this study such "multivariate analysis" permitted a description of political divisions in each state separately and finally of the entire body of biographical data. Subsequent chapters will discuss political alignments state by state.

The student who seeks to explain political behavior in the 1780s must examine not only the characteristics of the legislators and their constituencies but the issues that demanded their roll calls. Some of these topics, while important and interesting, lacked significance for the origin of legislative parties, but others proved

Table 2.4. *Characteristics of Legislative Parties in New York, 1784–1788*

	Number Loc.	Cos.		Number Loc.	Cos.
Residence			**Occupation**		
Frontier	4	0	Farmer	16	2
Noncommercial farm	15	0	Large landowner	0	0
Commercial farm	1	9	Misc. nonfarmer	2	1
Town or city	0	11	Professional	0	7
			Merchant or trader	0	9
			Uncertain	2	1
Economic status					
Moderate	12	2			
Substantial	5	1	**Age**		
Well-to-do	0	3	Born before 1720	0	1
Wealthy	0	10	Born 1720–1729	1	3
Uncertain	3	4	Born 1730–1739	5	5
			Born 1740–1749	4	5
			Born 1750 or later	2	4
Religion			Unknown	8	2
Episcopalian	0	7			
Congregational	2	1			
Presbyterian	5	1	**Military service**		
Dutch Reformed	3	3	Enlisted man	0	1
			Militia officer	9	3
			Continental officer	3	5
Political experience			None or uncertain	8	11
Local office	6	3			
High office	4	6			
None or uncertain	10	11	**Intellectual interest**	0	4
Education			**World view**		
Some education	0	1	Localist	13	3
College	1	5	Cosmopolitan	1	11
None or uncertain	19	14	Uncertain	6	6
Social origin			**National origin**		
Humble origin	6	5	Colonial, English	6	8
Average family	14	6	Colonial, Scottish or Scotch-Irish	1	0
Above-average family	0	2	Colonial, Dutch or German	4	7
Prominent old family	0	7	Colonial, New England	4	0

Table 2.4—Continued

	Number Loc. Cos.			Number Los. Cos.	
Slaveholding			*National origin*		
Over 10 slaves	0	1	Immigrant	0	2
5–9	2	3	Uncertain	5	3
1–4	6	9	*Vote on ratification*		
None	12	5			
Uncertain	0	2	For	1	3
			Against	6	0

fundamental in forming political alignments. The variety of biographical data permitted multiple correlations with many different issues. Thus economic status, occupation, education, religion, place of residence, social origin, world view, and party affiliation could each be considered with respect to approval of the theater, reduced government spending, support of Congress, readmission of the loyalists, procreditor laws, equal rights for Negroes, and higher taxes on land. All told, 1,503 legislators, each possessing nearly a score of characteristics, voted on the average over twenty times on a hundred different kinds of questions.[6] These thousands of facts required the help of modern technology for even rather elementary analysis. Therefore all of the data ended up in a computer and underwent detailed examination (see the following methodological note).

The information derived from the biographical data, when correlated with bloc affiliation, together with the analysis of voting behavior, pointed the way for further research. This subsequent investigation sought evidences of political activities and the contemporary recognition of these alignments, as well as analysis of the arguments used with respect to the major issues creating party divisions. The research now utilized more traditional materials: secondary works, newspaper articles, contemporary pamphlets, legislative debates, petitions, and letters. Each state required separate treatment because the political division in each, while resembling that elsewhere, was in certain respects unique. The results

6. The figure excludes votes on issues on minor consequence or when the reason for the vote was uncertain.

of this research finally combined with the biographical and voting data to produce a general interpretation of political alignments before the Constitution.

METHODOLOGICAL NOTE

The following description may interest the curious and perhaps pacify the skeptical. In preparing the data for computer analysis, the number of votes was first reduced by combining those that pertained to one question and that occurred in succession, as already noted. Votes in which the minority was small were discarded as proving nothing about party divisions (in extreme cases a single dissenting representative might demand a roll call). "Small" means less than one-third, which admitted, for example, a vote of 30–15 but excluded one of 31–14. If the vote nevertheless seemed significant, a note was taken of it, but the fact was not stored in the computer. Some errors crept in, partly no doubt in the process of copying and recopying, but partly because the original records are themselves inaccurate: the totals as recorded by the clerks do not match the total voters, and men are listed as voting on both sides. In two known cases the entire roll of men voting pro was wrongly identified by the clerk as voting con, and vice versa. Since the present objective was to study political alignments, men who voted only a few times were excluded. This step saved several hundred hours of research with no apparent loss. A conscientious research assistant suggested that these men who seldom voted might share peculiar characteristics. To test this and meet other objections, all votes in New York were recorded, and a limited biography of all legislators, however obscure, was compiled. The only results were to expend much time and exaggerate the number of neutrals in New York.

All votes or vote groups, with the exceptions noted, were then coded according to the nature of the issue, and an effort was made to discover the meaning of an affirmative or negative in each of the eleven hundred roll calls. That attempt achieved only partial success. Legislative or other records sometimes do not reveal what the debate was about, as often happens in the case of bills that failed, amendments that lost, and petitions that were never preserved. Every student of politics knows that motions may not be what they seem. The principle followed here was to identify an issue only when its nature was certain, for an error would falsify the meaning of the vote and invalidate conclusions. Did the legislators who

approved a salary of £100 for an official favor high salaries or
low ones? Unless that question could be answered, the vote was
useless. Such votes—and they were numerous—fell into two
categories. Some clearly contributed to political divisions and were
somehow significant for the legislators and therefore for the student of political alignments. These were coded 009. A vote on the
side of the Localists, whether that was aye or nay, was coded 1,
that favoring the Cosmopolitans, 2. Nonparty votes were coded
001, which meant that the issue was unclear or insignificant and
did not separate the protagonists.

Other votes were categorized, numbered, and interpreted. For
example, government expenditures bore the code numbers 010 to
019; governors' salaries were 010. Votes favoring reduced expenditures, whether aye or nay, were given the additional code number
1, and those against, 2. This system enabled the computer, when
instructed, to identify all votes opposing higher salaries for governors, regardless of whether the particular vote had been aye or
nay. Votes concerning taxes were numbered 020 to 039; miscellaneous economic issues, 040 to 049 (such as regulation of prices,
046); debtor-creditor relations and monetary policy, 050 to 059;
local political matters, 060 to 069; relations with Congress, 070 to
079; other political issues, 080 to 089; treatment of loyalists and
social or humanitarian questions, 090 to 099; and cultural affairs,
100 to 109. A given vote entered on a computer card might read
like this:

$$484 \quad 03001 \quad 001 \quad 094 \quad 1 \quad 1$$

The initial number, 484, identifies the session, 03 means New York,
and 001 is Matthew Adgate's number. This is vote number 001,
issue type 094 (readmission of loyalists). The first 1 is a yes vote,
and the second 1 signifies that Adgate lined up against readmission.
This vote was recorded on February 4, 1784, on a petition by
Cadwallader Colden and others praying to be relieved from banish-
ment and admitted as citizens. Jacob Ford's motion for referral to
a committee, which carried, 27–21, postponed immediate consideration. Adgate favored the motion, thereby revealing an antiloyalist position.

A specific example may clarify the process. Votes number 4 and
5 of New York's February 17–18, 1784, session set the price of
unappropriated land at a shilling per acre, a higher price being defeated in vote 4, 12–26, and the lower adopted in vote 5, 26–13.

Those voting affirmatively in vote 4 favored, of course, the higher price, the negatives in vote 5 the lowest possible one, while the other men shifted. The first group, described for computer analysis, consisted in part of those shown in the top section of table 2.5. Ninety-nine is computer language for unknown, the 80 under occupation stands for merchant, 81 for trader, 05 for leisure, 20 for artisan (specific type unknown), 10 for nonfarmer, and 01 for

Table 2.5. Computer Codes for Sample Alignment in New York, 1784

Legislator #	Resi-dence	Occu-pation	Economic Status	Social Origin	World View	Votes with	
						Cos.	Loc.
For higher land prices (*vote 4*)							
03075 [Harpur]	10	20	99	99	9	20	06
03185 [VanZandt]	10	80	08	05	1	15	08
03084 [Hughes]	10	10	04	05	9	17	01
03064 [Gelston]	05	80	06	08	9	30	08
03129 [Platt]	05	80	06	05	9	12	00
03037 [Coe]	06	01	99	05	2	14	06
03068 [Gordon]	09	81	99	02	1	39	17
03207 [Cuyler]	09	80	06	08	9	03	05
03005 [A. Bancker]	05	05	08	09	2	22	04
03126 [Patterson]	04	80	04	02	1	24	107
03035 [J. Clark]	03	01	02	01	2	19	69
03152 [W. Sickles]	05	99	04	01	9	20	28
For lowest prices (*vote 5*)							
03001 [Adgate]	02	01	05	01	2	03	60
03009 [Becker]	02	01	02	05	2	07	51
03056 [Ford]	02	01	02	01	2	13	48
03065 [Gilbert]	02	01	02	05	2	20	70
03131 [Purdy]	05	01	02	03	9	10	54
03020 [Brinckerhoff]	07	70	07	05	2	14	59
03043 [Dennis]	02	01	99	01	9	1	22
03087 [Husted]	02	01	02	03	9	2	23
03142 [Savage]	01	01	02	03	2	19	75
03078 [Hathorn]	03	50	06	07	2	12	18
03074 [Harper]	01	01	02	05	2	22	100
03124 [Paris]	02	81	06	05	9	12	11
03099 [J. Livingston]	05	02	06	10	1	76	27

farmer. Cosmopolitan (as a characteristic, not a party name) is indicated by 1, localist by 2. The reader will observe that the legislators with numbers 037, 126, 035, and 152 differ in their characteristics from the other eight. On the opposite side were the legislators shown in the second half of the table. In the occupation column, 02 signifies a large landowner; 70, a shopkeeper; 50, an entrepreneur. The only important deviant was James Livingston. Isaac Paris was a frontier trader. The number of votes is the total for all sessions, not just this one. This information, with much more, analyzed for each of the coded votes, supplied the basic quantitative data for the study of political behavior.

An important aspect of this study is the statistical analysis of the votes and biographical data. The text will therefore be studded with numbers and percentages that convey a most misleading impression of accuracy. For example, the statement that on a given vote 66.7 percent of the farmers favored a particular position becomes less convincing if one remembers that the identification of a man as a farmer rests often upon a reasonable probability rather than a certainty and, more serious, that the percentage applies to only a handful of persons. When one adds a margin of error in recording and coding, the use of a decimal place becomes absurd and any figure whatever seems dubious. The statistics derive their validity, not from any single vote, which is at best only suggestive, but from the accumulation of a series of percentages. Taken individually they prove nothing; collectively they establish a high probability. Only in the closing chapters, which review the whole body of evidence, are the numbers of cases large enough to bear close scrutiny, and even then the figures are approximate, not precise.

I might add, for the benefit of the students excited by this methodology, that the preparation of data for computer analysis proved exceedingly time-consuming and would have proved impractical without more expert help than anyone has a right to expect. It is a moot question whether the same mathematical processes, performed in the old-fashioned way, might not have been just as efficient. Moreover the data contain so many uncertainties, and doubtless so many errors, that the statistics create an impression of accuracy that is quite false. The computer does offer certain advantages, but one should approach it with caution, preferably accompanied by a statistician.

Chapter III

The Issues

The conflict between the colonies and England cut across factional and party lines. In some instances these lines shifted so as to correspond with the new divisions: thus the Livingston–DeLancey alignment became almost identical with that of rebel-tory. In other cases pre-Revolutionary factions or parties vanished, as in Rhode Island and in Pennsylvania. The struggle over resistance to English measures and then over independence eclipsed all previous questions. After 1776 political divisions developed out of new issues and therefore took new forms.[1]

One of the most important of these new issues was the treatment of the loyalists. At the extremes stood those who hated the tories and those who defended them, those who were radical proponents of independence and those who almost became loyalists themselves. But the alignment was really very complex. Every shade of opinion existed, and the precise situation varied greatly from place to place and from time to time, depending upon the strength of the loyalists and the progress of the war.

In the first place, Americans disagreed over who should be considered loyalists. No one doubted the status of men who joined the British army. Those who fled to enemy territory also condemned themselves, though their crime was less heinous. Not so clear, however, was the standing of those who did not actually flee into British lines but stayed put when British troops came. Some of these took an oath of allegiance to the king that they later retracted; others simply remained passive, sometimes selling goods and services to both sides indifferently. Still another category—

1. The standard history of the Confederation period, which discusses many of these questions, remains Merrill Jensen, *The New Nation: A History of the United States during the Confederation, 1781–1789* (New York, 1950).

perhaps the largest—consisted of those who, although not aiding the British, did not help the Americans either. Who should be punished as enemies? What degree of dissent should patriots tolerate? In certain areas British sympathizers were so few and so quiet that nothing needed to be done. In other sections they were so numerous and so potent that the patriots dared not deal with them. As a rule state governments tried to distinguish friend from foe through a loyalty oath, the precise wording of which proved a subject for debate. As the war waned, many people felt that all but the most outrageous loyalists might be forgiven and restored to full citizenship.

Closely connected with the problem of defining loyalism was the question of punishing the tories, once identified. Mere failure to actively aid the rebellion might be ignored, especially if no means were available to enforce penalties. Often those who refused to serve in the militia or to take a loyalty oath paid a double or quadruple tax but otherwise escaped penalty. More obnoxious tories faced further attacks on their property. Those who fled to British lines but did not aid the enemy might suffer amercement, a fine that involved some considerable portion of their property. Avowed loyalists might expect confiscation of part or all of their possessions, including land, slaves, and debts. The pressure for confiscation became most intense as the states' need for money increased. Extreme measures were opposed by many rebels whose patriotism was unquestioned but who sympathized with the plight of tory families, had tory friends or relatives, or disliked attacks on property. Men who hated the tories, especially those who had suffered from enemy troops, joined those who hoped to gain financially in urging extensive confiscation. Prominent among the latter were men in debt to British citizens or to loyalists, who hoped to reduce payment in some manner. The debate during these years left a legacy of bitterness on both sides.

When the fighting ceased, the nature of the problem changed. All categories of loyalists now sought an end to discrimination, to loyalty oaths, special taxes, and confiscatory laws. The most nearly neutral justified their position as principled, especially if they had acted from religious convictions.[2] Some who had fled now hoped

---

2. An exceptionally able statement of Quaker philosophy is in the Supreme Executive Council, Executive Correspondence, Nov. 22, 1781, Pennsylvania State Archives, Philadelphia. Committee members defended their refusal to celebrate the victory at Yorktown—on the grounds that they opposed shedding of blood and could not rejoice in the advantages so gained—and continued by reviewing their general attitude toward war.

to return and to recover their property. Creditors sued for their debts. These men found allies among the whigs, even some who had previously acquiesced in punitive measures but who now defended their former enemies for various reasons: they looked upon the loyalists as valuable citizens, particularly those who possessed wealth and education; they humanely forgave, especially if through former connections they understood the tory point of view and believed that men might differ honorably; or they hoped to attract political support. Thus the Massachusetts senator and lawyer, Samuel Dexter, felt that the ex-loyalists should be allowed to settle in Massachusetts, where they would enrich the state instead of strengthening the British colonies. He believed that the people demanded the exclusion only of a few *"conspirators."*[3]

On the other side stood men who continued to hate. Usually they either had been injured by loyalist activities, believed that enemies of the Revolution would subvert the new governments, had bought confiscated property or evaded debts, or feared the loss of political power. When patriots had loaned money to the state and could not collect even the interest, why should they suffer enormous loss by paying debts to loyalists?[4] The citizens of Worcester, Massachusetts, declared that readmission of tories "would be not only dangerous, but inconsistent with justice, policy, our past laws, the public faith, and the principles of a free and independent State,"[5] and the townspeople of Londonderry, New Hampshire, similarly combined all refugees into one category and urged the legislature to exclude them.[6] The antiloyalist forces gradually lost ground, but in some states the contest continued throughout the Confederation period.

The controversy swirled around many particular questions. Patriots in the towns, bypassing their legislatures, sought to expel all loyalists and all Britishers by threats.[7] Individual loyalists attempted to regain their position by seeking the unofficial protection of friends, as Henry Van Schaak found a haven through

3. To Robert Treat Paine, Jan. 15, 1785, Robert Treat Paine Papers, Massachusetts Historical Society, Boston.
4. Wensley Hobby to Samuel P. Savage, Dec. 20, 1784, Samuel P. Savage Papers, Box II, Mass. Hist. Soc.
5. *The Pennsylvania Journal, or Weekly Advertiser* (Philadelphia), June 4, 1783.
6. Petition, May 30, 1783, New Hampshire State Library, Concord.
7. For example, a warning letter in a Boston newspaper insisted that the people would not injure persons or property but ordered refugees and their like to leave. *Mass. Centinel* (Boston), Apr. 6, 1785.

Theodore Sedgwick. Others appealed to the legislature, as did William Bull in South Carolina.[8] Sympathizers tried to repeal laws denying equality to the loyalists or neutrals.

The most famous such debate occurred in Pennsylvania, where the Test Oath disfranchised anyone refusing to swear allegiance to the new government. Quakers, among others, could not conscientiously take such an oath. Patriots justified the penalties on the ground "that those who declined to participate in the toils, the sacrifices, and the hazard of the late revolution, should not enjoy all the benefit and advantages arising from that inestimable blessing."[9] The legislature finally repealed the act after long debate and many votes.

Special taxes also gradually disappeared.[10] Loyalists tried to recover such confiscated property as remained unsold, while their enemies hastened the sale of what remained. During the war confiscations had been justified because of financial necessity. Thus when the Maryland Senate rejected a confiscation bill, the House of Delegates asserted that taxes could not be increased, and there remained no other way of raising money for Congress.[11] After 1783 the sale of forfeited estates gradually ceased, though the issue continued important in several states.[12]

Other wartime problems lasted only as long as the British troops remained. Trading with the enemy caused disputes. Few rebels approved of profiteers who enriched themselves by such commerce, but certain necessary articles could be purchased from the British, and if the balance of trade were favorable, gold and silver might help win the war. Therefore between the extremes of no trade and unrestricted trade lay areas of disagreement. Again, while all pa-

8. See South Carolina votes, Mar. 26, 1787, which are available on microfilm (see Jenkins, comp., and Hamrick, ed., *Guide to Early State Records*). Van Schaak chose the winning side during Shays's Rebellion and represented Pittsfield in 1787.

9. *Pa. Jour.* (Philadelphia), Oct. 2, 1784.

10. Thus New York reduced its tax on Quakers who failed to perform militia duty from £15 to £8 in 1782; see vote, Mar. 11. Many New York legislative journals are in microprint in the Early American Imprints Series, but for 1782 see the microfilm listed in Jenkins, comp., and Hamrick, ed., *Guide to Early State Records*.

11. May 5, 1780. For Maryland votes, see *ibid.* for microfilm in the compilation of early state records and Shipton and Mooney, *National Index*, as a guide to the *Votes and Proceedings of the House of Delegates . . .* in microprint.

12. For example, South Carolina votes, Feb. 21, 1787, Feb. 18, 1788; Georgia votes, Jan. 17, 1783, Feb. 18, 25, 1784. Georgia assembly records are largely available on microfilm; see Jenkins, comp., and Hamrick, ed., *Guide to Early State Records*.

triotic Americans supported the war, they differed concerning the vigor with which it should be prosecuted. Each state was tempted when fighting became remote to let others do the job, with the excuse that it had contributed more than its share in the past. Once a state was free of invaders, the legislature might refuse to raise militia or to impose heavy taxes, for such measures were politically unpopular. The representatives might restrict state troops to local action: Maryland voted that no part of her militia should serve out of the state for more than three months.[13] They might also forbid quartermasters to seize supplies, excuse various categories of people from service, or reduce the cost of hiring a substitute. On the other hand, fear of defeat caused legislatures to grant extraordinary powers to the executive branch. In 1780 New Jersey authorized its Council of Safety to suspend writs of habeas corpus; impress provisions, teams, and drivers; remove disaffected persons; and exercise extensive discretionary powers, while the governor might declare martial law.[14] In Maryland, however, at the same time a similar vote went the other way,[15] and Virginia's legislature denied its governor and council the right to enforce martial law.[16] Delegates urged or opposed such actions depending in part upon their enthusiasm for the entire venture or its effect upon their constituents. After the fighting ended, these issues no longer existed.

The subject of wartime price regulation occasioned some interesting arguments. Probably most people upheld the traditional belief that state control over economic activities was justified if the public benefited. But what was an unjust price? As Continental and state currency declined in value and as many goods became scarce, men raised the price of what they sold. The farmer who paid twice as much for salt or shoes as before the war refused to sell pork or wheat or horses to the army or to traders at the old rate. Townspeople complained about the cost of food, while the farmers blamed artisans, storekeepers, and speculators. The wholesale merchants became the principal target, and they probably did in fact start the spiral, because they could anticipate better than anyone else the changing value of money and the state of the mar-

<hr />

13. Jan. 14, 1782.
14. June 5, 16, 17, 1780.
15. Vote, May 3, 1780.
16. Vote, Jan. 11, 1780. See Jenkins, comp., and Hamrick, ed., *Guide to Early State Records,* for direction to Virginia legislative records on microfilm. The Virginia *Journal of the House of Delegates . . . ,* for many years, is also in microprint; see Shipton and Mooney, *National Index.*

ket. Moreover some undoubtedly did engage in monopolistic activities. The attacks on them owed partly to accurate suspicions and partly to a basic antipathy toward city slickers among rural folk and adherents of what one historian has labeled the "puritan ethic."[17] On their side, merchants emphasized the value of their services, the high risk they ran, and the losses from defaulting debtors. They also argued that commerce should be free: traders, if left unrestricted, would benefit the entire people and help win the war. Some appealed to the right of private property. A correspondent of Benjamin Rush's wrote in 1779, "What doth Mr. Roberdeau mean when he says 'that there is no Law to prevent Regulations of prices being made' Is it not part of your Constitution that no man shall be molested in his Person or Property fined or imprisoned not by the Judgment of his Peers and the Law of the Land."[18] To another merchant price-fixing ranked with tender acts, paper money, privateering, and the taxing of nonresident land as a major evil accompanying the Revolution.[19] In the end legislatures divided into economic pressure groups, debated policy, and accomplished little. The whole affair increased the tension between agrarians and businessmen, helping to create an emotional background for the emergence of legislative parties.[20]

The rise in prices, together with monetary difficulties, became central to the problem of financing the war—a problem that remained long after 1783. It involved various issues, each complicated: tax policy, raising money through loans, and the payment of the debt.

From the outset the governments borrowed money in order to conduct the war, as they had in every previous emergency. The most familiar technique, employed everywhere, was the issuance of paper money. The bills of course possessed no intrinsic value, but were essentially "tax anticipation warrants," presumably payable in specie when the state collected taxes. As the years passed, legislatures issued large quantities of paper. Since the governments received little specie, they could not redeem the money, which therefore declined in value. The legislatures passed laws to enforce

17. Edmund S. Morgan, "The Puritan Ethic and the American Revolution," *WMQ*, 3d Ser., XXIV (1967), 3–43.
18. David Smith to Benjamin Rush, June 7, 1779, Rush Papers, Historical Society of Pennsylvania, Philadelphia.
19. Jonathan Jackson, *Thoughts on Government* . . . (Boston, 1788).
20. For a sample vote see New Jersey, Dec. 16–17, 1779. For examples of the antagonism between town and country, see *The Continental Journal and Weekly Advertiser* (Boston), June 12, 1777, Sept. 2, 1779.

a fixed valuation,[21] and other laws made the paper a tender for all purposes including taxes, private debts, and government expenditures. Such laws pleased debtors and taxpayers, but so many people opposed them that they proved impossible to enforce. By 1780 these warrants had depreciated almost to the vanishing point, and legislatures were debating only what fraction of their face value should be established by law for public purposes.[22] During the following year opponents of the legal-tender clauses succeeded in repealing them, often after heated debate.[23]

The states and Congress desperately needed specie. They borrowed some hard money through loan offices, which in return for cash issued loan office certificates bearing interest. These certificates, like the modern government bonds, became primary obligations, and the states made every effort to pay the interest. They could not always do so and sometimes issued certificates for interest called "indents." In consequence the loan office certificates declined in value. As funds ran out, the government paid soldiers in certificates and through "depreciation" certificates compensated men for the decline in value of the money paid to them. Quartermasters and commissaries engaged in supplying the armies also issued IOU's. In the last years of the war the quartermaster and commissary departments seized supplies when necessary, leaving behind a mass of paper notes. The use of these varieties of money, the value assigned to them, and their status as legal tender excited debate during the war.

21. Technically, the legislature would set a "scale of depreciation" establishing the legal value of the money at certain dates. The exchange value of the money usually fell more rapidly than the governments acknowledged.

22. The possessors of paper bills would bring them to the state treasuries and exchange them at a rate of 40:1 for new bills. The states would arrange for the eventual redemption of the new money by taxes. The ratio of 40:1 had been reached the previous fall, but the plan now stabilized the exchange at roughly 60:1, where it remained until 1781. When the legislatures proved unable to collect enough taxes, the old bills began to depreciate fatally. The success of creditors in depriving the money of its legal-tender quality administered the final blow.

23. See votes in Massachusetts, Jan. 11, 16, June 13, 1781; North Carolina, May 16, 1782; Pennsylvania, May 30-31, Dec. 22, 1780, May 16, 1781; New York, June 27, 1780; and New Hampshire, Sept. 1, 1781. Many of the North Carolina House Journals are in the Early American Imprint Series (see Shipton and Mooney, *National Index*), but for 1782 see the microfilm listed in Jenkins, comp., and Hamrick, ed., *Guide to Early State Records*. The Pennsylvania General Assembly records are also largely available in both microprint and microfilm. For New Hampshire votes, the *Journal of the Proceedings of the . . . House of Representatives* is contained in Nathaniel Bouton *et al.*, eds., *New Hampshire Provincial, Town, and State Papers* (Concord and Nashua, N.H., 1867-1943); microprint versions of the journals, after 1784, and microfilm are also available. See Shipton and Mooney, *National Index*, and the *Guide to Early State Records*.

When the war ended, the legislators turned their attention to payment of the public debt, a problem that became one of the chief issues for more than a decade. The question was complicated not only by a growing shortage of specie but by what happened to the debt itself. Originally the certificates were paid to very large numbers of people, including soldiers and officers, farmers, artisans, laborers, officials, and traders. Perhaps their distribution was uneven, but no more so than the distribution of other forms of property. However, like fluid capital generally, the certificates began to flow from the country to the towns and from the poorer citizens to the richer. The process accelerated because during the postwar depression men had to dispose of the certificates, even at considerable loss, to pay taxes and debts or even to buy necessities, while their fluctuating value made them an object for speculation. One Bostonian noted that "the most prudent and sagacious of our wealthy Merchants and Private Gentlemen" were investing in Massachusetts public securities, which brought 12 or 13 percent. People who needed ready money, he declared, were selling 6 percent certificates for half price or less, and the securities were slowly rising in value.[24] In this way many of the widely dispersed soldiers' and quartermasters' certificates, selling at a heavy discount, came into the possession of a comparatively small number of men. Obviously payment of the interest and principal would benefit mostly these large holders, though every public creditor was interested, and anyone to whom they owed money or with whom they did business would benefit indirectly. On the other hand, the majority disliked the heavy taxes required for financing the debt and looked about for some means of minimizing the cost.

One way of reducing the burden was to pay the creditor only what he had given for the certificates. Many people felt that some of the original holders, such as soldiers, deserved face value plus interest but that others did not because they had overcharged the government. Therefore the official responsible for evaluating these debts as they were presented (a process known as "consolidating" or, if new certificates were issued, as "funding")[25] should examine them suspiciously, and the legislature ought to reject most petitions pleading for special treatment. Moreover some regarded those creditors who were not original holders as speculators, reaping a fortune from public distress. Since they had acquired the certifi-

24. Richard Cranch to James Elsworthy, Jan. 1, 1785, Cranch Papers, Mass. Hist. Soc.
25. The term "liquidating" meant fixing the specie value of the debt.

cates for less than their par value, they were entitled only to what they had paid or to the current market value, with interest on the lower figure. By such a reevaluation the state might eliminate most of the burden.[26]

The creditors and their defenders rejected these allegations indignantly. The chief sufferers from a depreciation, they insisted, were widows, orphans, soldiers, and other poor people who depended upon the certificates, together with patriots who saved their country by loans but who now faced financial ruin. Honesty in governments, as well as in the individuals, was ever the soundest policy, and a new, weak nation especially must treasure its reputation. The true policy lay in strict collection of taxes. Besides, once the legislature guaranteed payment, the debt would appreciate to its full value, enriching the country and supplying capital to invigorate the whole economy: foreign investors would loan, specie would reappear, and everyone would benefit from prosperity regained.

One partial solution to the problem was redemption of the debt by selling ungranted land, a technique available to states with extensive territories. Soldiers' certificates and perhaps other securities as well might be accepted in payment for farms or speculative tracts. The town of Groton, Massachusetts, conceded that the state debt ought to be paid off, and justice demanded that public creditors should receive full value. Yet people could not pay taxes. Therefore the state should grant the creditors land for the securities.[27] The adoption of such a policy created a fresh set of disputes. Should the government dispose of its land at a high price or a low one? High prices would benefit the state, especially if the certificates were accepted at a depreciated rate. Thus a hundred-acre tract selling at a dollar per acre would bring in $100 or even $500, and the debt would be reduced accordingly. Speculators and other purchasers might prefer low land prices, but if they could use their certificates at face value, they were perfectly willing that the prices should be high. Ordinary people could not afford to buy, and speculators with the certificates would obtain all of the desirable land. A petition to the Pennsylvania legislature complained that the cost of western land was too high for poor men, who had insufficient hard money and no certificates. The state, the signers

26. E.g., "Public Faith," *The Hampshire Herald; or, the Weekly Advertiser* (Springfield, Mass.), Jan. 31, 1786, reprinted in *Mass. Centinel* (Boston), Feb. 8, 1786.

27. Sept. 1786, Massachusetts Archives, Boston.

added, should pay the certificates in full only to original holders or else the people would be ruined.[28]

Another method of reducing the debt called for the use of securities in payment for confiscated property. Purchasers of loyalist estates especially favored this idea.[29] Still another means of discharging the debt, unpopular with public creditors, was to levy taxes payable in the certificates, after which the certificates would be destroyed. Finally, the state might retire the debt or finance it temporarily without taxes, through issuing more paper money, part of which could be used to pay interest or even the principal. This solution raised problems that intersected with many other issues.[30]

The question of the public debt roughly divided the people into two groups: one possessed no certificates and sought to retire the debt as cheaply as possible, and the other owned certificates or for other reasons joined the public creditors in urging that the state pay its debt in full. From a political point of view, a quick disposal of the debt might return control over monetary policy to the locality, while payment at par with interest thrust financial power upon the state government or Congress.

Paying the debt required the collection of taxes, and taxation was an even hotter issue for the politician. The most common way of raising money during the colonial period was by taxing polls. Its beauty lay in its simplicity—one could not at that time conceal heads, so everyone's contribution was easily determined. We think of a poll tax as regressive, but under primitive economic conditions, when society is relatively undifferentiated, the worth of one's labor does not vary greatly; moreover prosperous citizens had servants or slaves and had to pay the poll tax on them, so that the tax did increase with wealth. As the distribution of property became more unequal, the poll tax ceased to be fair. By the late eighteenth century opposition developed. Poorer communities depended upon it for local revenue but resisted imposition by the state. One critic charged that the poll tax was being imposed by wealthy citizens "to compel the poor labourer to contribute, as to one-third of the public burden, equally with the splendid fa-

28. *The Pennsylvania Packet, and Daily Advertiser* (Philadelphia), Mar. 12, 1785. See vote, Dec. 1, 1786.

29. See votes in New Jersey, Dec. 10, 1783; Maryland, Dec. 4, 1781, Jan. 21, 1782, Dec. 25, 1783.

30. An enlightening contrast is furnished by the separate financial proposals in Pennsylvania by the Constitutionalist party and by Robert Morris. General Assembly Journal, Dec. 22, 1785.

vourites of fortune." Taxes instead should be proportioned to property.[31] In general the larger property holders approved the tax, and poorer men opposed it. A variant of this contest sometimes occurred between men who held slaves and those who did not, the latter trying to tax all slaves, of whatever age or sex, at a high evaluation so as to maximize the tax, the former trying to reduce the number of taxables and the rate per capita.

Land was the next most common source of revenue and the most controversial. Agricultural states such as New Jersey and North Carolina had to rely heavily on land for revenue, and all states collected much of their income that way. The debate over policy involved, first and most simply, landholders versus nonlandholders. Second, owners of cultivated farms tried to shift some of the burden onto uncultivated and unoccupied land. To some extent almost every farmer owned land that he reserved for future use, but the critical question concerned the assessment of large tracts, some granted during colonial days, some obtained during and after the war in exchange for state certificates of debt. Most people felt that some tax should be levied on vacant land, perhaps at a lower rate than that on improved farms. On the other hand, the owners of undeveloped tracts, who often had little ready capital, feared that even a small tax might force them to sell. Another factor to consider was the effect of taxation on land values. If high taxes forced owners to throw their property on the market, land prices generally would fall, benefiting potential buyers but injuring landowners. No tax at all, however, might enable the speculators to keep their property off the market, thus raising land prices. So the settled farmer, who did not want to migrate and who profited by rising land values, might benefit if unoccupied land brought a good price and might favor a low tax on that account, yet would like to shift the tax burden off his property and on to others'. Thus the issue of whether or not to tax unoccupied as well as improved land was complex and controversial.

If the legislature decided to distinguish among different types of land, problems multiplied, for land varied greatly in value. Sometimes the law defined each type of land in terms of its use (meadow, pasture, wood) and fixed the rate. New Hampshire, for example, assessed pasture land at 5d.; arable, tillage, and mowing land at a shilling; and orchard at 1s. 6d. per acre. An acre of orchard land was defined as "so much orchard as will in a common

31. "Leonidas," in *The Weekly Monitor* (Litchfield, Conn.), Sept. 10, 17, 1787. For an example see the interesting vote in New York, Feb. 13, 1781.

season produce ten barrels of cyder."[32] Alternatively the state might require each county or town to contribute a certain sum. The tax collectors could then evaluate each person's real property, levying the same percentage on every holder. The latter method, certainly the fairest if collectors were honest, prevailed in most northern states during the Revolutionary era, but southern planters fought its adoption.

Another conspicuous object for the tax collector was livestock. Cows and horses formed much of the personal wealth in agricultural communities and were usually taxed. Disputes arose over the assessed value of the animal, with farmers naturally trying to obtain the lowest figure. Sheep and hogs, less valuable, were seldom taxed, and other farm animals were never considered, except when total property formed the basis for taxation.[33]

Landowners much preferred to tax nonagricultural property. In the South men without land escaped provincial assessments entirely until the Revolutionary years, except for the tax on polls and certain import taxes. After 1776 the states sought money wherever they could. Thus North Carolina assessed "stock in trade"—the salable goods of merchants, shopkeepers, innkeepers, and artisans—and money, including cash, and debts. The New England states taxed those items, plus ships, wharves, and shops. Men engaged in commerce objected that the risks they ran were so great and their service to the community so important that they ought to be encouraged, not taxed. They also united with creditors in opposing taxes on money at interest.[34] The legislatures found another source of revenue in mills, ironworks, tanneries, and the like. Professional men such as lawyers and doctors, who might own little visible property yet enjoy large incomes, could be compelled to contribute through a tax on "faculties," which required the tax collector to estimate the earning ability of such men, and which farmers approved but everyone else opposed.[35] Maryland's legislators divided upon whether to tax plantation utensils and the working tools of mechanics and manufacturers.[36] New York tried to equalize farm and nonfarm property by evaluating separately all

32. Bouton *et al.*, eds., *N.H. State Papers*, VIII, 685, 849.

33. For example, see New Jersey vote on taxing hogs, June 14, 15, 1781, June 11, 1782.

34. For example, votes in New Jersey, Dec. 8, 1779; Maryland, Dec. 19, 1781; and Pennsylvania, Mar. 10, 1779.

35. See New Jersey vote, May 27, 1783. Maryland rejected a tax on offices of profit, Dec. 21, 1781.

36. Dec. 9, 1782, Dec. 3, 1783.

real and all personal property and debated, but rejected, the imposition of a tax according to each person's ability to pay (November 8, 1781). Delaware actually levied a rudimentary income tax.

Still another kind of tax divided the people roughly along class lines. This was the sumptuary, or luxury, tax, based essentially on moral disapproval of frivolous, evil, or unnecessary consumption. The most frequently taxed items were carriages, silver plate, distilled liquor, and imported wines. Thus Maryland's legislators divided on whether to tax rum and homemade spirits distilled from fruit (April 27, 1780). Taxes of this sort, like Massachusetts's stamp act of 1784, were seldom imposed except in emergencies, for they were unpopular with the politically influential upper class.[37]

Import taxes were also controversial. They were easy to collect and raised a good deal of money. Farmers liked them so long as they did not fall on necessities, especially if land and poll taxes were lightened as a result. They questioned, however, the desirability of a blanket tariff. Artisans who competed with foreign imports approved of a tariff only if it fell on competitive products. Most Americans favored import taxes on such luxury articles as foreign wines and expensive cloth, which they did not buy. Men who opposed slavery or who already owned a sufficient number of bondsmen favored a tax on imported slaves. Merchants disliked any restrictions on trade and preferred taxes on land, polls, or livestock. Commerce, they insisted, must flourish in order for the nation to prosper. They accepted import taxes if they could pass the cost on to consumers, if the tariff was low enough not to disrupt trade, and then only if essential revenue could be obtained in no other way.

A tax on salt, often proposed, divided the legislators along class lines: poor people found it especially burdensome, whereas men of substantial property considered a small tax inconsequential.[38] In Pennsylvania the westerners John Whitehill and William Findley argued that the legislature should help the poor, not increase their burdens. When the wealthy Philadelphian Thomas Fitzsimons insisted that a half crown per year would not distress the poor, and the Pittsburgh lawyer Hugh Henry Brackenridge also supported the tax, Whitehill replied to the former that 2s. 6d. was a great sum to poor people, even though men in easy circumstances might not

37. See the New York vote on taxing wrought plate, Feb. 10, 1781, opposed by most men of means.
38. See Maryland vote, Jan. 12, 1785.

believe it so, and angrily reminded the latter that when elected he was supposed to represent the "popular side."[39]

William C. Houstoun of New Jersey has left us an interesting discussion of the tax question as it appeared to an intelligent man in 1781. He observed that, although the state taxed both necessary and superfluous property so as to raise the maximum amount of money, the latter ought to pay as much as possible, the former only to make up a deficiency. Such a policy, he felt, would make people more willing to pay taxes. He suggested a tax on silver plate, not previously levied in New Jersey, since plate was not only a luxury but harmful in that it withdrew metal needed in trade. A large revenue might accrue from a tax on spirits and such fermented liquor as was not the product of the country. Dogs used for amusement in the chase, race horses "of blood," pleasure carriages, and "adventitious" ornaments of dress were proper objects. Slavery was unnecessary and disgraceful and deserved to be discouraged; so did servants in livery, as distinguished from menial servants, apprentices, and laborers.[40] Despite such good intentions most of the public revenue came from land and poll taxes paid by ordinary citizens, while little came from luxuries owned by the rich.

The state governments often apportioned taxes on real and personal property among the various local political units. Ideally the burden of each locality ought to have corresponded with its ability to pay. A few states tried to estimate such ability by assembling elaborate assessment lists, but the most common method of apportionment was essentially an arbitrary one based on precedent and political power. Inevitably representatives attempted to transfer the burden to someone else's constituents, and the ensuing debates often became heated, notably in New York.

Disputes also arose over the medium in which the tax should be paid.[41] The three major media were specie (gold and silver), specifics (articles such as farm products), and state or federal certificates. The governments tried to obtain as much specie as possible, for its value was certain and everyone wanted it, including the legislators themselves for their own pay. Congress needed it too, above all for interest on the foreign debt. But there was never nearly

39. *Pa. Packet* (Philadelphia), Mar. 3, 1787.
40. May 14, 1781, Etting Collection, Old Congress, II, 36, New-York Historical Society, New York City.
41. See votes in Maryland, Dec. 3, 1783, and Virginia, Nov. 24, 1786.

enough. A certain amount of coin circulated in the port cities, partly imported from areas with which the country had a favorable balance (such as the West Indies), partly left by British and French troops. Small towns and country districts saw little specie and suffered a constant drain of hard money to the urban centers. Therefore resistance to specie taxes centered among farmers, who not only found payment difficult but received little of it in return. Residents of King and Queen County, Virginia, petitioned against such a tax because, they insisted, the people did not possess enough specie. In order to obtain coin they would have to sell their property at a low rate, in effect paying double the tax. Merchants, wrote the petitioners, would enter into combinations to take advantage of the people. Instead they asked to pay part of the tax in commodities.[42]

Payment in commodities, however acceptable to the farmers of King and Queen, was unsatisfactory to the state governments, to the government's creditors, to Congress, and to anyone who wished to support the dignity and authority of the state, for after the war the treasuries could seldom use such products directly but had to sell them, usually at a considerable loss. The legislature might minimize the loss by pegging the value of the specific at the market level, so that, if corn were bringing 2s. per bushel, the taxpayers would be credited with that amount and no more; but the principal point of the medium, as far as the taxpayer was concerned, lay in lightening his burden. He therefore urged that corn or hemp or tobacco be accepted for taxes at a high value.[43] Whether this should be done and what specifics should be accepted became the subjects for long dispute.

In the end the states received a great variety of commodities. New Hampshire, for example, accepted in 1782 rum, cattle, shoes, stockings, cloth, felt hats, blankets, and flour.[44] In general the states during the war welcomed products that the armies needed but afterwards sought to reduce the proportion payable in specifics. Public opinion forced new concessions during the mid-eighties.

A final mode of paying taxes was the use of certificates, less for

42. Nov. 5, 1783, Virginia State Library, Richmond.
43. See, for example, the votes setting the price of tobacco for tax proposed in Maryland, Dec. 20–21, 1780.
44. Bouton *et al.*, eds. *N.H. State Papers*, VIII, 927. Maryland voted in Dec. 1783 to receive specifics for back taxes only. See also Virginia's vote to accept tobacco, Nov. 24, 1786. The legislature kept trying to halt payment in specifics, but every effort drew angry petitions and the delegates would back down.

revenue than to reduce the public debt. Public creditors preferred receiving cash for their securities to paying taxes with them, but most people saw the measure as a relatively painless method of retiring the debt. From western Massachusetts, for example, came a suggestion that the treasury issue new certificates in exchange for the present ones, which would then be receivable for taxes. If the new securities depreciated, that was all to the good, because the debt would be reduced and holders had already received 18 percent on the real value of the money that they had advanced.[45] The suggestion, pushed by rural legislators generally, became a major issue in Massachusetts and occurred elsewhere in various forms.

After all the details had been arranged, the amount of the tax fixed and apportioned, and the incidence determined, someone was likely to move that the bill be postponed until the next session or that collections be delayed for a few months. The motion might result from dislike of some aspect of the measure or from a conviction that people could not then pay the tax.[46] A subspecies of this question concerned unpaid back taxes, which sometimes reached sizable figures, especially in the poorer sections, and legislators whose districts had paid their quota might resent being obliged to carry a new load when much of the money could be raised from delinquents. Few tax laws passed without long debate and frequent roll-call votes.

The legislatures thus debated a variety of questions concerning revenue. But if the number of votes taken by the representatives and the number of articles in newspapers signify anything, even more serious conflicts were fought between debtors and creditors. There were two major types of private debts: obligations growing out of foreign trade and internal debts. Debts originating before 1775, those contracted during the war, and postwar debts also presented different problems, but they all shared certain common features.

The absence of banks and the scarcity of coin forced people to rely upon credit. Over the long run, loans contracted in America were soundly based on the rapid development of natural resources and the expansion of commerce. But at any given time loans were hazardous. Merchants often failed. Fortunes were made or lost on single voyages, despite efforts to spread the risk and to secure ade-

45. *Hampshire Herald* (Springfield, Mass.), Feb. 14, 1786.
46. See, for example, an unsuccessful attempt in Pennsylvania to postpone the collection of taxes for Congress and the prosecution of the war, Dec. 3, 1782, and the passage in Virginia of a bill to postpone collections, Nov. 21, 1785.

quate insurance. Manufacturing was almost as speculative, especially after the war. Farmers suffered from crop failure and defaulted or vanished into the wilderness. Moneylenders therefore charged high interest rates, demanded security for their loans, and anxiously investigated the character of their prospective borrowers. Reputation was essential to the businessman, to any would-be debtor. Reputation—honor—enabled him to attract capital, and the loss of it ruined him. Prompt payment of debts became an article of faith, a rigid formula that he applied to himself, to his debtors in turn, and to public debts as well—especially since much of the public debt belonged to entrepreneurs. "Good" men paid promptly and in the same currency, or its equivalent, as the original debt. To evade a debt by payment in any inferior product, such as depreciated money, was considered a violation of contract, unethical, and in fact might end in bankruptcy through a drying up of future credit.

Foreign debts originated when colonial merchants and consumers bought various necessities, luxury articles, servants, and slaves on credit from Britain. Even before 1774 Americans persistently overestimated their ability to maintain payments, incurring a very large indebtedness amounting to several million pounds. After that date payments almost ceased. Even the most honest American balked at paying interest incurred because of the war, and many not so honest tried to evade payment of the principal as well. One technique for evasion was to obtain a law that forced creditors to accept state or Continental paper at par, under penalty of confiscation by the state or cancellation of the debt by payment of the paper to the state. After 1783 the English and Scottish merchants returned to the fray, strengthened by an article in the peace treaty that required the collection of debts. They were also helped by the reestablishment of adequate courts, some with sympathetic judges, and by the credit needs of Americans who had to acknowledge the old debts in order to resume borrowing.

To these prewar debts the Americans now added a new set. Southern planters who collectively had lost thousands of slaves replenished their stock on credit. Everyone spent wartime profits on coveted consumer goods and then went on spending. An extraordinary flood of imports exhausted purchasing power, and by 1784 shopkeepers could neither sell new goods nor collect old debts. Remittances to Europe almost ceased, and the foreign debt seemed for several years an insurmountable problem.

Domestic debts followed a similar course. Men with fluid capital loaned to traders, manufacturers, and farmers; importing merchants extended credit to retailers, innkeepers, and artisans, who in turn trusted their customers. During the war a great increase in the money supply and the many opportunities for profit caused a further expansion of credit, which the postwar buying spree brought to a peak. The pyramid then collapsed. Most of the specie went to England. Federal and state paper money ceased to exist, while certificates declined in value. The sharp currency deflation was accompanied by lower prices. Other factors made matters worse. Potential foreign markets for domestic exports were closed or restricted by the mercantilistic policies of other nations. (Trade with the British West Indies, for example, was severely limited.) Merchants and farmers producing for export suffered. So did manufacturers: some who had flourished during the war now were ruined by importations, while others (such as shipbuilders) lost their best customers when trade decreased. To make matters worse, farmers suffered several crop failures.

A few illustrations will depict the financial situation in the mid-eighties. The Philadelphia merchant Charles Pettit prophesied trouble ahead early in 1784. During the preceding year, he wrote, importations were not excessive and cash remained plentiful. Country stores still needed large quantities to restock their shelves, and merchants, encouraged by past success, imported heavily. But now little specie remained, and although selling on credit was easy, repayment would be hard. A good many merchants would be ruined, he concluded, and everyone would suffer.[47] A few weeks later another Philadelphian supported Pettit's diagnosis. Country shopkeepers had been at the mercy of European creditors even before Philadelphia merchants advanced goods to them on credit. Now both groups were in a poor position, for specie was scarce and creditors in Europe would soon be pressing. Everyone who valued his reputation and property had become cautious of entering into business.[48] Finally, a country shopkeeper in western Massachusetts lamented that she was selling little: "There was such a Croud of goods got into town before I got home a No. new shops opened with goods credited to large Amount, for eight or ten Months some twelve from Boston, Connecticut, New-York, Albany, Claverick, Kinderhook and most of these People sell on credit for To-Morrow at large—for very little Cash stirring this way—to be pay'd for in old Horses—cows some Boards—cabbages—turnips—

47. Pettit to Joseph Reed, May 27, 1784, Reed Papers, N.-Y. Hist. Soc.
48. William Irvine to his wife, June 12, 1784, Irvine Papers, VIII, Hist. Soc. Pa.

Potatoes etc.— very few of these Capital Articles—To answer well in trade do these people receive for their goods nor are such as grain—butter cheese beef—Mutton etc. now to be had—it would make a Rational Person sick to see the distraction of goods scatter'd in this way—without a Glimpse in Prospect from the Credrs. security and welfare."[49]

Under these circumstances country shopkeepers could not collect their debts and therefore could not pay the wholesalers. Yet many of these importing merchants themselves were being dunned, even threatened with bankruptcy, by foreign firms. In general creditors of whatever variety simply could not collect cash. Their solution was to sue the debtors and require them to sell enough property to pay the obligation. In this way the creditor might realize some specie or might obtain, at a bargain price, property that he could then sell or turn over to his own creditors.[50] Suits in courts and sheriffs' sales began to multiply during the mid-eighties.

The debtors' solution was quite different. Traders in financial straits sought to increase foreign commerce. Manufacturers agitated for a protective tariff. Farmers tried to raise prices in various ways, such as passing a law by which farm products would be received for taxes at a high evaluation. And public creditors petitioned the state for reimbursement. Other debtors who saw no relief in such reforms concentrated on measures that dealt more directly with their problem.

Three methods of aiding debtors became especially popular, all bitterly opposed by creditors. All assumed that abnormal circumstances were placing the debtor at an unfair disadvantage, forcing him to sell his property at a fraction of its true worth and to pay the creditor far more than the debt's original value. A moderate, reasonable article emanating from Medford, Massachusetts, observed that relations between debtors and creditors in commercial states "forms the subject, in three parts in four, of the laws." After an excellent description of the current economic distress, the author concluded that the debtors genuinely needed relief from the legislature. In particular he recommended an appreciation of the currency so that money would return to its previous value.[51]

49. Mrs. Abigail Dwight to Mrs. Morton, Stockbridge, Jan. 10, 1785, Sedgwick Papers, II, Mass. Hist. Soc.

50. On the other hand, specie might be so scarce that property could not be sold at all. In that case the creditor might prefer, even apart from humanitarian considerations, to avoid forced sales and continue simply to dun the debtor.

51. "Rusticus," *The American Herald* (Boston), Feb. 5, 1787.

One solution, the "stay law," called for postponement of payments or payment by installments, so that part or all of the obligation would be delayed until prosperity returned, prices rose, and money became plentiful. Thus New York voted (April 3, 1782) to stop all suits for debt contracted before 1776, and the Pennsylvania legislature passed an installment bill applying to debts before 1777, by which one-third would be paid within a year, one-third in two years, and one-third in three years.[52] An alternative, the "valuation law," required the creditor to accept part of the debtor's property, usually real estate, if offered in settlement, at a value established by some neutral party. For the low price obtained by a sheriff's sale would be substituted an evaluation fixed by sympathetic neighbors, a tax assessor, or a local official. Inhabitants of frontier New Hampshire explained to the legislature in 1785 that the people had contracted a large debt to support the war and, expecting to be paid by the state, had borrowed money subsequently. Creditors, they stated, would be satisfied with nothing but gold and silver, but since none could be obtained, men with ample property were cast into a loathsome gaol and forced to pay high fees and court costs for unnecessary suits. Their solution included the passage of an act providing that "the Estate of Debtors may be a Lawfull tender in Case of Suit to be taken at the appraisal of Indifferent persons under Oath."[53]

The third solution, paper money, was more far-reaching. Paper, said its advocates, could right injustices by returning money to its true value—its value when most debts were contracted. Paper would not only enable private debtors to repay their obligations, thus satisfying creditors, but would permit governments to do the same even to the servicing of public debts. Paper money, if loaned by the state and bearing interest, would reduce taxes, furnish capital for economic growth, prevent the rich from oppressing the poor, and even rescue Congress from its financial problems.

In its most moderate version paper money attracted the support

52. Nov. 30, 1784. See also Maryland's vote, May 15, 1786.
53. Bouton *et al.*, eds., *N.H. State Papers*, VIII, 755–756. They also requested "that the fee Table may be Revised, that Atorneys fees and Entry of actions may be Reduced, and the fees of Jurors, and Evidences be Raised." For a sample vote see Delaware, June 13, 1786 (Shipton and Mooney, *National Index*, lists the available microprints of Delaware's *Votes and Proceedings of the House of Assembly . . .*, and microfilm is listed in Jenkins, comp., and Hamrick, ed., *Guide to Early State Records*). Also see votes in South Carolina, Feb. 21, 26, 1788, the latter of which defeated a bill calling for the valuation of property by a sheriff and two disinterested freeholders and sale at four-fifths of that value.

of public creditors who could see no other way of obtaining payment. The government would issue enough for current expenses and perhaps for business purposes and at the same time levy taxes that would maintain the value of the money equal to gold and silver. This policy would help debtors only indirectly. A different, but still moderate, proposal originated with men who were on the whole financial conservatives but who were also debtors. They proposed that the government issue a limited quantity of paper and loan it on good security, such as land of at least double the money's value, to reliable citizens. The state would require interest and either retire the money gradually by taxes or provide for repayment by the borrower. The value of the paper might then remain on a par with specie. Creditors would be protected by depriving the money of its legal-tender quality.

Such proposals offered nothing to the debtors with small property. More congenial to them was the typical suggestion of "Honestus," who recommended that New York support a state loan office that would loan paper money to farmers. Conceding that paper currency had been issued in excessive quantities during the war, "Honestus" asserted that times were now different. Then the supply of money had exceeded the ability of the country to absorb it; now it fell short of the demand because of adverse trade balances. If the state loaned the paper in small, well-secured sums, the money could easily be redeemed by taxes and the interest paid by improvements. Proposed mercantile banks, he added, served no such useful purpose, for they loaned only to merchants, benefited only a few people, and became too powerful.[54]

The most radical version called for the issuance of large quantities without much backing, which would be legal tender for private debts, public obligations including debts and salaries, taxes, and business transactions of all kinds. Redemption would be postponed until some future date. A classic exposition of this view was expressed by the townspeople of Atkinson, New Hampshire. The town meeting resolved,

> The Citizens of this State now find themselves in a labyrinth of difficulty and distress, like Issachar of old crouching under the weight of complicated burdens, an enormous public debt far beyond their ability immediately to discharge, even if furnished with a medium of trade competent for transacting their other common and ordinary affairs of life.

54. *The New York Packet and the American Advertiser*, Mar. 27, 1786.

Silver and gold hath taken wing and flown to the other side of the Atlantic, without leaving a substitute or even its shadow. . . .

That for want of a suitable medium of trade the Citizens of this State are altogether unable to pay their public taxes, or private debts, or even to support the train of needless and expensive lawsuits, which alone would be an insupportable burden.

They wanted £150,000 in paper bills, with interest of 5 percent, financed by a tax on polls and estates equal to one-tenth of the principal and interest, to be collected first by December 25, 1789, and one-tenth annually thereafter. The tax, they suggested, could be paid in produce. The paper might be used to pay salaries, interest on the state debt, debts due by the state to individuals, private debts, taxes, and court fees.[55]

Creditors and their allies fought every prodebtor proposal. Honor and justice, they insisted, required that debts be inviolable. Laws interfering with private contracts were unconstitutional, immoral, and discreditable to the new nation. The sound-money men condemned advocates of paper as designing demagogues, desperate and corrupt men who sought to rescue themselves from a well-deserved fate by misleading the people. The true solution, they declared, lay in virtue and thrift. The shortage of capital, which everyone acknowledged as a genuine problem, should be alleviated by private, rather than public, bank notes, by the appreciation of public securities through sound financing, and by encouraging business activity, especially foreign trade.

Every legislature contained spokesmen for the procreditor, hard-money view. Delaware's lower house, for example, rejected petitions for a bill that would have prevented for three years the sale of property for debt unless it sold for the appraised value. Experience, the majority asserted, proved such laws to be evil and destructive of faith and credit.[56] William Paterson, the prominent New Jersey judge and legislator, conceded that paper money had

---

55. Bouton *et al.*, eds., *N.H. State Papers*, XI, 122–127. Expressions of the same economic ideas are common if one penetrates below the convictions of the upper class. Town and county petitions are especially useful. A prophetic argument is that of Julius P. Pringle of South Carolina replying to David Ramsay, who had argued that the legislature had no right to interfere with private contracts. Pringle replied that "the ends and purposes of government implicitly give that right in a variety of cases. . . . Whenever the preservation of the majority of the state, and its very important exigencies compel, the right of individuals, though inviolable according to the ordinary language of the law, must in such cases yield." See debates in the South Carolina House of Representatives reported in *The Charleston Morning Post, and Daily Advertiser*, Feb. 19, 1787.

56. Jan. 30, 1788.

been essential during the war, but that by 1786 issuing more would be the height of folly. The proper policy was to support the certificates that already existed. The legislators, he added, seemed quite willing to grant themselves twice as much money as they needed, thus proving that the country's problem was, not a scarcity of money, but luxury.[57] Petitions from distressed debtors were countered by petitions from distressed creditors. Residents of Prince William County, Virginia—many of whom lived in the town of Dumfries—begged the legislature not to pass a stay law or a paper-money bill, "one of the greatest calamities that can possibly fall on their Country."[58] Newspapers made room for numerous articles defending a "sound" monetary policy and attacking schemes for state banks that would loan money to landholders.

Every state legislature spent many hours debating the paper-money issue and called for votes on various aspects of the question. A few examples will illustrate some of the specific issues. The New York legislature voted on whether the interest on a proposed paper currency should be 5 percent instead of 6 percent (which failed) and the time of payment lengthened to fourteen years (which succeeded).[59] Pennsylvania voted that a creditor refusing the state's paper certificates, provided the entire debt was offered, could never recover it, and a majority also supported a heavy fine for anyone who refused to accept the paper in payment for livestock, necessities, manufactured goods, and other articles, or who offered a lower price for payment in gold and silver.[60] The major controversies occurred over the quantity to be issued, the functions of the paper, legal-tender clauses, and terms of repayment.

Private debts and monetary policy aroused important controversies during the Revolutionary era, but the legislators demanded even more legislative votes on questions of government spending. Payments on the public debt formed by far the largest item in every budget and, as previously noted, stimulated much of the argument. Salaries were almost equally important. Americans could not agree whether they should be high or low, permanent or annual. On one side were men who saw only small amounts of cash. Most Americans raised almost all of their own food, provided

57. Article, William Paterson Papers, folder 2, Rutgers University Library, New Brunswick, N.J.
58. May 27, 1782, Va. State Lib. For another example, Amherst County petition, Nov. 6, 1787, *ibid*. The legislature replied by a ringing statement endorsing the hard-money view.
59. Mar. 1, 1786.
60. Apr. 6, 1781. A dissent was printed.

their own housing and some of their own clothes, and traded or bought on credit for the rest. To them £100 was a very large sum, and 4s. or 5s. a day seemed enough for a legislator's pay. One Pennsylvanian complained that, while the citizens were growing poorer, "we daily see our rulers and officers of government growing rich." "It has been calculated," he continued, "that the wages of an Assemblyman amounted annually to more than the profits of an ordinary farm. Hence we find men aspire to seats in the Assembly in order to pay their debts, and purchase land; and hence too they are dependent upon their constituents, that they will not follow the dictates of their own judgements for fear of offending their constituents, and thereby losing their posts of profits."[61] On the other hand, business and professional men handled a good deal of cash and regarded £200 as a rock-bottom salary for respectability; even £500 provided merely a decent living. They argued too that salaries should be high enough to attract the best men and sufficient to remove any temptation toward bribery or profiteering. Low salaries (they told the suspicious farmers) meant that the positions would appeal only to wealthy men, who could live on their own estates, or to low, unscrupulous characters.[62] To this the advocates of economy replied that the rewards of office should not be so great as to encourage luxury in the people's servants, nor should they attract men interested in making a fortune at public expense or seizing power by mere popularity.[63] Public opinion generally feared excessive expenditures by greedy officials. A South Carolinian correctly interpreted the attempt to reduce judicial salaries as a consequence of "that spirit of parsimony not to say envy which too frequently attends democratic government."[64] The dispute involved every level of officialdom, and even popular governors such as John Hancock and George Clinton could not escape salary cuts.[65]

One group of public servants did manage to weather the attack: the legislators themselves. When they considered their own per

61. *The Independent Journal: or, the General Advertiser* (New York), Sept. 20, 1786.
62. *Pa. Packet* (Philadelphia), Mar. 31, 1781.
63. An interesting account of Massachusetts farmers' dislike of high allowances for members of Congress is Henry Van Schaack to Theodore Sedgwick, Pittsfield, July 26, 1789, Sedgwick Papers, Box A, Mass. Hist. Soc.
64. "Diary of Timothy Ford, 1785–86," *South Carolina Historical and Genealogical Magazine*, XIII (1912), 200.
65. See New York votes, Apr. 8–13, 1782, Feb. 21, 1783, and Massachusetts votes, Oct. 19, 1786, Mar. 10, 1787.

diem and travel allowances, the delegates reversed their positions, supporters of high salaries favoring a lower pay, advocates of economy preferring higher rewards. The reason for this reversal grew out of the legislators' situations. Business and professional men, who generally recognized the need for high salaries, often lived or had friends in the capital city and possessed enough specie to support themselves. Their travel costs were minimal because they did not need to travel far and they did not depend upon the per diem for survival. These circumstances enabled them to appear virtuous—always a political advantage—by foregoing pay increases and accusing their opponents of inconsistency. Although they did not say so, they doubtless saw that low allowances would render difficult the attendance of poorer men from the more remote districts.

On the other hand, rural legislators and those from distant parts of the state, who urged economy in general, really needed money. They were obliged to leave their vocations, travel for days, and pay what seemed to them astronomical prices for room and board. Moreover they argued that, unless legislators received a generous reward, ordinary folk could not leave their farms and shops, so that political power would fall by default into the hands of the well-to-do, who alone could afford to serve. Such men might oppress the people.[66] Neither accusations of inconsistency nor fear of the reaction back home prevented them from granting themselves a raise. Votes on this matter were frequent. The New York legislators relieved their own financial problems by a 33 percent raise in 1784, supported by the upstate representatives and opposed by the New York City group, including almost every man of wealth.[67] The same New Jersey legislators who reduced salaries in 1786 raised their own per diem (November 9), while Marylanders who voted themselves a higher allowance were not so generous to the clerk of the council.[68]

Equally important was the question of whether salaries should be granted annually or fixed permanently. The issue really concerned the basic role of public officials, especially judges: should they be independent of public opinion, able to devote themselves

66. *Pa. Packet* (Philadelphia), Mar. 10, 1787.
67. Nov. 23. See also May 1, 1786, Apr. 6–7, 1787.
68. Jan. 9, 11, 1787. For other arguments see *The New-York Daily Advertiser*, Apr. 7, 1787; *The Pennsylvania Evening Herald; and The American Monitor* (Philadelphia), Oct. 29, 1785; *The Independent Gazetteer or, the Chronicle of Freedom* (Philadelphia), Dec. 7, 1786; debate in the Pennsylvania legislature reported *ibid.*, Mar. 12, 1787.

to office without fear of influence and with a sure income, or should they be annually dependent upon the legislature, their actions subject to review, their tenure uncertain because their salaries might be stopped? The debate, familiar to students of early American history, began during the colonial period when Americans tried to free judges from royal control by making their tenure and salaries permanent instead of "at pleasure." Logically everyone should have maintained the same principle after Independence, but relieving officials from royal control was one thing and isolating them from popular influence was quite another. Some state constitutions settled the question of tenure by providing for appointments during good behavior, but even then the issue of permanent versus annual salaries remained debatable. Money varied in value so greatly during the war that the legislatures had to adjust salaries annually; however, by 1783 a fixed arrangement became possible. The controversy then revived and continued throughout the decade.[69]

Other government expenditures also caused dissension. Some legislators favored economy or parsimony. They would reject doubtful claims, reduce others, and insist upon payment in certificates or paper money, often at a depreciated rate rather than in specie. Other legislators favored the state's creditors, supporting their requests and approving payment in specie or specie equivalents.

A variety of economic issues other than those mentioned also created divisions. Debate over the establishment of private banks was limited almost entirely to Pennsylvania, and will be considered in connection with the politics of that state. The controversy, it may here be observed, involved questions of monetary policy and broad issues of social justice. Bills supporting various business enterprises such as manufacturing might encounter opposition, as did a Maryland bill granting £300 for the manufacture of pipe and stoneware and a bill to encourage the manufacture of nails.[70] So also a bare majority in Pennsylvania approved a state loan of £300 for the manufacture of steel.[71] The price of various farm or manufactured products caused dispute, as when lawmakers tried

69. For examples, see votes in New Jersey, Dec. 4, June 1, 1783, and in Massachusetts, Nov. 29, 1780. Maryland established permanent salaries for judges because "the independence and uprightness of judges are essential to the impartial administration of justice." Maryland Session Laws, Nov. 1785, chap. XXVII (Records of States microfilm or Early American Imprints microprint).

70. May 22, 1782, Dec. 15, 1787.

71. Apr. 7, 1786.

to set the value of specifics for tax purposes. Issues involving the rights of tenants and landholders and bills favoring speculators or settlers also divided the legislators.[72] A pathetic petition from Pennsylvania frontiersmen, for example, pled that their land was being bought by others who treated them more cruelly than did the Indians, who at least did not seize their homes.[73] Finally, conservation versus exploitation appeared in the form of a debate over the protection of fish in rivers.

Social and cultural problems arose in every state. The status of black Americans often divided the legislatures. In some instances the question was whether and when slaves should be freed; in others the rights of freedmen were at stake. Arguments for and against slavery anticipated every point in the later nineteenth-century debate and need not be rehearsed here. The specific question usually took the form in the South of whether slaveholders might release their slaves and, if so, under what conditions.[74] An interesting roll-call vote in Virginia (January 1, 1788) defeated a motion that all freed slaves should leave the state within one year after their emancipation, violators being sold into slavery. Efforts to prohibit further importations of slaves created not only moral but economic divisions. Planters who possessed as many slaves as they needed would benefit from the higher prices that would result from the prohibition, but those who had few or no Negroes wanted to buy them at low cost.[75] In the North most people accepted emancipation, but some sought to delay the process. Racial or class prejudices caused efforts to forbid ex-slaves from voting, holding office, or serving on juries, and to restrict miscegenation.[76]

Humanitarians sought other reforms and often encountered opposition. Appeals from debtors in jail, disabled veterans, and other indigents sometimes started a debate, as did bills to establish immigrant-aid societies and other benevolent organizations. The most interesting vote occurred in New York, when the Council of Revision vetoed an act incorporating a German society for encour-

72. See the vote in Pennsylvania to lower the cost of land (Mar. 12, 1788) and votes concerning the interest on debts for land purchased from the state (Apr. 7, Sept. 14, 1783).

73. Feb. 1785, Records of the General Assembly of Pennsylvania, Box 2, Pa. Archives.

74. See Virginia votes, Dec. 14, 24, 1785.

75. Votes in South Carolina, Mar. 17, 23, 1787.

76. See the votes in New York, Mar. 9, 26, 1785, especially on the clause fining a Negro who married a white. For votes on emancipation in Pennsylvania, see Feb. 10, Mar. 1, 1780.

aging immigrants from Germany and relieving distressed immigrants, objecting that the state should not encourage foreigners. The legislature divided on whether to override the veto. Among these humanitarian issues the most important and complex were attempts to aid schools and religious groups.

Appeals for state support of education ordinarily took the form of requests for temporary grants to some private institution. The argument centered primarily around appropriations for colleges. Advocates cited the benefits of education to society as a whole and to the individual recipients. They could rely on the approval of legislators with college degrees or who lived near the college in question. Appeals to patriotism focused on the advantage to a state of training its children at home instead of exposing them to the temptations and expense of a foreign education.[77] Other arguments stressed the need for a universal public system instead of private academies and colleges, which trained only an elite group.[78] On the other hand, opponents of public education asserted that it too would serve the rich without benefiting the poor. "Learning," they argued, "is seldom acquired except by those who enjoy affluent or easy circumstances."[79] Even state colleges seemed designed for an elite; the subjects they taught seemed irrelevant and useless for common people.[80] Why force taxpayers to finance the education of men who could well afford to pay? In spite of these arguments, various states did pass laws establishing a public system. Appropriations, however, did not follow.[81]

Advocates of state support for religion no longer argued that everyone should support some particular denomination but that everyone should support religion in general. Assuming that almost all Americans accepted Christianity and that the encouragement of Christianity was a universal good, if not indeed a supreme duty, legislators introduced bills levying taxes for the payment of ministerial salaries and for other purposes. Critics replied that support

77. *The Maryland Journal and Baltimore Advertiser*, Dec. 7, 1784, Jan. 7, 1785; *The Pittsburgh Gazette*, Mar. 10, 1787; *Thomas's The Massachusetts Spy Or, The Worcester Gazette*, Feb. 13, 1783; *The Carlisle Gazette, and the Western Repository of Knowledge* (Carlisle, Pa.), Aug. 10, 1785; *The Connecticut Courant; and Weekly Intelligencer* (Hartford), Jan. 7, 1788.

78. *Mass. Centinel* (Boston), Mar. 22, 1786; *Pa. Packet* (Philadelphia), Mar. 28, 1787; *Indep. Gazetteer* (Philadelphia), Mar. 28, 1787.

79. *Md. Jour.* (Baltimore), Mar. 29, 1785.

80. *The United States Chronicle: Political, Commercial, and Historical* (Providence), Oct. 19, 1786; *The Maryland Gazette; or the Baltimore General Advertiser*, Feb. 11, Mar. 4, Apr. 1, 1785; *Md. Jour.* (Baltimore), Aug. 19, 1785.

81. The notable votes occurred in Maryland, Dec. 3, 1784, Jan. 14, Dec. 10, 1785.

of religion was a private, not a public, function and elaborated the arguments for separation of church and state and for complete freedom of religion. They pointed out that the largest church group in a community would benefit, whereas members of other churches would be forced to raise money for their own worship while paying tribute to the state-supported minister. Principle and practice therefore combined to arouse opposition among denominations such as Baptists and, in most areas, Presbyterians, together with whatever other church groups expected to pay but not receive. Similarly bills for the support of particular congregations met criticism on grounds of religious principle, prejudice, or economy.[82]

Principle rather than thrift influenced the debate over theatergoing. During the late colonial period the theater flourished in the South and in major northern towns, although many, if not most, people thought it immoral. The Revolution brought a halt to performances, except in those areas occupied by British or French troops. When peace returned so did the theater, quickly and with little comment in the South, gradually and over intense opposition in the North. In northern cities religious prejudices against the theater as godless and immoral united with the conviction of respectable folk that theatergoers were either rich idlers, squandering their money, or inferior riff-raff who ought to learn the virtue of thrift. A Quaker remonstrance lamented the attempt to introduce scenes of "vanity, licentiousness and dissipation, . . . a variety of intemperance, dissoluteness and debauchery," which corrupted the people's manners and was repugnant to good order and subordination in civil society.[83] On the other side, defenders claimed that the theater displayed only the bad effects of sin, improved the mind, polished manners, elevated taste, and provided beneficial relaxation. "The human mind is ever restless," wrote one advocate, "and must have something to keep it in action; if not diverted by laudable and innocent pursuits, it will degenerate into crime and licentiousness." What did Shays's Rebellion proceed from? "From the want of theaters, dances, shows and other public amusements." Not only did plays quiet the common folk, but in

82. Sample votes are: Pennsylvania's rejection of a request for money to print the Bible (Oct. 1, 1781); Maryland's series of divisions on a general tax to support ministers (Dec. 31, 1784, Jan. 8, 1785), which was defeated as unnecessary, impolitic, and injurious to religion (Nov. 19, 1785); and the famous vote in Virginia on a tax to support religion (Nov. 11, 1784).

83. Supreme Executive Council, Executive Correspondence, Nov. 10, 1783, Box 16, Pa. Archives.

Europe the best people attended.[84] Bills legalizing the theater occasioned many newspaper articles, speeches, and votes in the legislature. New York, for instance, narrowly defeated a £10 fine for anyone appearing in a play (April 29, 1786), while a long debate in Pennsylvania involved votes on taxing, regulating, or prohibiting the theater.[85] Other questions involving morality were rare.[86]

Each state faced, in addition to economic, social, and cultural problems, many political issues both local and national in scope. An increasing demand that representatives should be responsive to the people led to at least one vote on permitting citizens to attend sessions.[87] Within several states the formation of new counties became controversial, opposition being local or owing to fears that the change might affect the balance of power. The general arguments in favor of such bills were forcible and in the long run decisive. As a county became more populous, inhabitants of one portion, usually remote from the county seat, wanted their own local governments, their own courts, and their own officials. Especially in the West transportation difficulties caused real hardship for men who had to travel far to reach the center of political life, to sue in a court, or stand trial. Moreover the legislators chosen for a whole county might accurately represent only one part of it. Finally, creation of a new county sometimes meant that additional representatives strengthened the entire section politically. The last consideration caused trouble, for eastern and western delegates disagreed on many issues, and the former might be reluctant to approve more votes for the latter. In Pennsylvania, however, when a new county was formed out of an old one, the seats in the legislature were divided so that no increase occurred, and the voting seldom followed geographical lines.[88] The issue was never exclusively sectional.

Various aspects of the court system caused disagreement. Many people, especially those who were defendants rather than prosecu-

84. *Indep. Gazetteer* (Philadelphia), Jan. 31, 1787. A partial list of citations is given in Main, *Social Structure*, 266–268. The reference for Mar. 5, 1787 should be to the *Pa. Packet*, not the *Chronicle*.

85. Feb. 18, 1784, Nov. 17, 1785, Sept. 21, 1786. See also in Maryland, vote of June 12, 1782.

86. Delaware representatives voted on whether to fine innkeepers who promoted cockfighting, shooting matches, and other idle diversions. June 26, 1786.

87. New Jersey, Mar. 13, 1786.

88. See votes, Apr. 12, Sept. 12, 1782, Mar. 23, Apr. 4, 1784, Mar. 2, 1785, Sept. 19, 1786. The *Pa. Packet* (Philadelphia), Mar. 23, 1787, contains an account of a meeting in Washington County in which advocates and foes of a new county are identified. The same reapportionment took place in New York.

tors, regarded courts as hostile and tried to restrict them. Preferring trials before local magistrates or juries, they sought to limit the number of cases that would be tried in the higher courts and opposed the creation of new courts.[89] They attempted to reduce court costs and especially lawyers' fees. Finally, as previously noted, they endeavored to keep judges subservient to public opinion by frequent elections and annual salaries. On the other hand, men who benefited from the courts preferred to strengthen them and to pay well for the valuable services of judges, other legal officials, and lawyers.

The location of the state capital also provoked controversy. During the years after Independence many capitals were shifted from a coastal town to some interior site, usually after a long dispute. In several states, notably New Hampshire and New York, the legislature voted almost annually on the place for the next meeting. Sessions in the principal town drew support from its residents and from representatives who lived within easy reach, whereas other delegates preferred a meeting in a more convenient, inland community: Augusta to Savannah, Columbia to Charleston, Hillsboro or Halifax to Wilmington or New Bern or Edenton, Richmond to Williamsburg, Harrisburg or Lancaster to Philadelphia, Poughkeepsie or Kingston or Albany to New York, Concord or Exeter to Portsmouth. Delaware was divided between advocates of Wilmington and Dover, Maryland between supporters of Annapolis and Baltimore. The arguments involved more than geography. A large town, some said, contained more rooms for legislators, bigger buildings for the sessions, better transportation facilities, and besides offered social and cultural activities, even economic opportunities, whereas the interior villages had inadequate housing, were isolated, and lacked any advantages whatever. Defenders of small towns, however, considered the cities far too expensive. Worse, they corrupted susceptible legislators, whereas rural communities were cheap, moral, and absorbed the wholesome influence of plain, honest folk.[90]

The powers and limitations of the various state governments were only partially defined by written constitutions. Details remained debatable, and the constitutions themselves continued to be controversial. The extent of the executive authority was never

89. See votes in New York, Mar. 8, 14, 1787, New Jersey, Mar. 7, 1786, and Virginia, Dec. 18, 1787.

90. Sample votes are Pennsylvania, Mar. 27, Apr. 1, 1784, Mar. 21, 1787, and Virginia, Nov. 2, 1787.

entirely settled. During the war the legislatures had entrusted governors with emergency powers, often after much opposition. After the Revolution some favored a continuation and extension of these powers, while others preferred a weak executive. In New York, for example, close divisions occurred on whether the governor and council or the legislature should appoint an auditor and commissioners for Indian affairs.[91] The issue in Pennsylvania lay between the appointive power of the Supreme Executive Council and that of the assembly.[92] The relative power of the lower house and the upper was also controversial. Some men felt that the legislature should contain only one branch that would exercise great power. Others favored two houses of equal authority.

Movements to revise the state constitution occurred in several states for varying reasons. Sometimes the impetus came from men who thought the governments too democratic, the house of representatives too powerful, and the executive lacking in authority (as in Pennsylvania); elsewhere the desire for change originated with men who preferred more democracy than existed, as in South Carolina. The Revolutionary era also saw attempts to restrain the power of public officials. Examples are restrictions on plural office-holding, especially those following the theory that judges should not serve in the legislature (one of Connecticut's few votes concerned this issue), and limitations on the economic activities of legislators, in particular those denying them the right to engage in trade.[93] The first reform made considerable progress, but the latter did not.

A final type of controversy concerned relations between a state and its neighbors, with Congress, and with foreign nations. Interstate affairs sometimes were settled in Congress, sometimes by direct negotiation. The citizens of a state ordinarily united in opposing a neighbor, but exceptions occurred: thus New Yorkers divided over the status of Vermont, while Pennsylvanians disagreed concerning the proper policy toward the settlers who came from Connecticut into the Wyoming Valley.

Congress handled most foreign affairs, but the states sometimes became involved also. Especially controversial was the treaty of peace with England, ratified in 1783. The treaty, though welcomed

91. Feb. 26, 1782, Mar. 20, 1783.
92. Dec. 3, 17, 22, 24, 1784, Apr. 2, 1785. The issue in Pennsylvania seems to have concerned party politics rather than principle.
93. See above, and the vote in New Jersey, Mar. 1, 1780, on whether a legislator could act as tax assessor.

at first, proved unpopular in some of its parts. Clauses requiring Congress to urge that the states repeal all laws injurious to loyalists and any legislation impeding the recovery of British debts raised the specters of a ruinous collection of prewar debts, plus interest, and an invasion of tories demanding the restoration of power and property. The treaty contained no reciprocal provision for the return of slaves carried off by British troops or for payment of damages inflicted on American property. Criticism increased when England refused to abandon western fur-trading posts, reputedly encouraged Indian attacks, and restricted the profitable trade with her islands in the West Indies. This controversy centered in the South, where British debts were especially important. A petition from Northampton, on Virginia's Eastern Shore, stressed the lack of specie and the ruin faced by debtors as the creditors bought land at a fraction of its value. A great proportion of the debt, the signers complained, was due from the warmest friends of independence to those who opposed it and who refused to accept state paper money, while the debtors were patriotically supporting the credit of the government. The citizens could not simultaneously pay the domestic and foreign debts. They suggested a stay law or payment by installments.[94] Bushrod Washington made it clear that the issue concerned more than debts. "As to the British debts," he wrote, "I am afraid that little is to be hoped either from the honesty or wisdom of our assembly in fulfilling this part of a sacred Treaty. Like paper money it has advocates whose interest it is to prevent the payment of them, and there are many honest and even sensible Men who will support such a measure from opinion of principle; they say that Great Britain has first broken the treaty by carrying off our slaves, and farther that if we once give up this advantage, we shall have lost every opportunity of either compelling Great Britain to deliver the western forts or to recompense ourselves if they refuse."[95]

When some representative moved to repeal all acts in conflict with the peace treaty, the Virginia legislature plunged into a debate over foreign policy. Those in favor hoped that if the United States obeyed the treaty, England would do likewise, which meant withdrawal from the West and repayment for lost slaves. Improved relations might lead to commercial concessions as well. They admitted that debtors would have to pay their debts and that the loyalists would be forgiven their sins, but such actions were only

94. June 12, 1784, Va. State Lib.
95. To Dr. Hodgdon, Sept. 15, 1786, Miscellaneous Papers, New York Public Library.

honorable and humane. These arguments failed to convince men who had no interest in trading posts, commerce, or the recovery of slaves, and even less in paying debts, tolerating loyalists, or conciliating the recent enemy.[96]

Relations with Congress involved men, money, and power. During the war Congress appealed for troops and requested funds, stirring up much the same controversy as took place in each state with respect to its own support of the war effort, with the addition that some men accused Congress of excessive demands and self-aggrandizement. On the whole, however, few worried about an abuse of power as long as the very existence of the United States remained doubtful. After Yorktown, support of Congress seemed less vital and its requests increasingly suspect.

One such request concerned payment of the army. At a low point during the war Congress promised half pay for life to officers who would reenlist. After the war ended, Congress asked the states to furnish money for that promise, now modified to a lump sum and called "commutation."[97] Opposition developed because many people feared lest the Continental officers, who had recently formed a secret Society of the Cincinnati, might constitute a threat to the country's liberties. "The power of the sword," men felt, must be carefully watched. The officers' case was weakened by several mutinies in the army and by a suspicion that certain men hoped to use the army to establish a despotism. A Massachusetts colonel complained that the people wanted only to get rid of the army, not to pay it, "for the most part of them look upon an Officer with as Evil an Eye as they did on the British in 74."[98] Other critics saw no reason to treat the officers differently than enlisted men. At the same time Congress asked for a special grant called the "supplementary fund," exclusive of the usual requisition, which would pay interest on the federal debt. Both cost money and created support or opposition depending upon one's attitude toward taxes, spending, and Congress.[99]

The "5 percent impost" symbolized both patriotic support of Congress and fear of an oppressive government. Congress recommended a general 5 percent ad valorem tax on imported articles, to be used for paying the foreign debt, in 1781 and again in 1783.

96. See votes in Maryland, May 10, 1786; Virginia, June 7, 23, 1784, Nov. 12, 1787; North Carolina, May 29, 1784.
97. See discussion and citations in Jackson Turner Main, *The Antifederalists: Critics of the Constitution, 1781–1788* (Chapel Hill, 1961), 86–92.
98. Col. J. Greaton to William Heath, Brookline, Mass., Jan. 13, 1782, Heath Papers, XXIII, 164, Mass. Hist. Soc.
99. See Massachusetts vote, Mar. 16, 1786.

The controversy is too well known to require more than mention of the principal arguments. Some people opposed it because they feared to pay more than their share. Others wished to postpone payment of the debt until the supply of money increased. The major objection was that once Congress could collect taxes without reference to the states, it could act as it chose, and the United States would have a strong national government rather than a confederation. Instead the critics recommended that Congress apportion its debt among the several states, each of which would levy and collect its own taxes and retire the debt in its own way. Congress would then need only a little money and limited power.[100] On the other side, the impost's defenders urged that an apportionment was impracticable, that the tax was fair and would raise the necessary money, and that Congress should collect its own revenue in order to pay its own debts and become respectable in the eyes of the world. Above all Congress must become more powerful if the United States were to survive. The issue then, while partly economic, was primarily constitutional, the essential question being the nature of the Union.[101]

Debates over supporting Congress arose in other connections also. Every year each legislature had to decide how much money to grant, how to raise it, and in what medium to pay it. In general, one set of legislators appropriated money only reluctantly, arguing that Congress had exaggerated its requirements, that other states owed a greater share, and that most taxpayers were overburdened. They recommended that the states pay in certificates rather than in specie. Supporters of Congress urged the justice of its requests and the importance of strengthening the Union. They tried to obtain as much hard money as possible. These "federal" men also supported Congress in other ways—by appointing, for example, an adequate number of delegates and paying them well and by heeding other requests of Congress such as a grant of power over commerce.[102]

100. Thus the town of Dunbarton, N.H., voted in 1787 "that the selectmen proportion the foreign, domestic and State debt to each individual, so that they may have opportunity to pay the same to the State treasurer." Caleb Stark, *History of the Town of Dunbarton, Merrimack County, New-Hampshire* . . . (Concord, N.H., 1860).

101. See votes especially in Massachusetts, May 1, 1782, June 7, 1783, New York, Mar. 27, Apr. 11, 13, 1786.

102. See three close votes in New York on complying with requisitions of Congress, Feb. 7–12, 1783. Votes on the per diem of members of Congress occurred in New Jersey, Nov. 17, Dec. 14, 15, 1783; Maryland, Nov. 27, 1781; and Delaware, Jan. 17, 19, 1785.

All of these issues reached a climax in the most momentous question of the decade: the ratification of the Federal Constitution. Its adoption involved not merely relations between the states and the central government but the many internal disputes that divided the legislatures—paper money, the court system, debts, slavery, taxes, land policy, and ultimately many more. The struggle over ratification therefore became in most states the most bitter of all such contests.[103] The victory of the Federalists began a new political era.

103. See votes in New York, Apr. 15, 1787, Jan. 31, 1788; Pennsylvania, Sept. 27, 1787; and Maryland, Jan. 15, 1788, Nov. 26, 1787.

Part II

Political Parties in the States

Chapter IV

Massachusetts

The issue of resistance to England cut athwart previous political alignments in Massachusetts. A great majority of the people, regardless of rank, favored opposition. By 1776 the loyalists included only a small fraction of the population and proved too weak to assist the British or to cause serious dissension after the war. Despite this harmony the war years witnessed the beginning of disputes that would create, in the mid-eighties, far sharper cleavages than those of colonial times.

The earliest of these controversies proved the least divisive in the long run, though it did contribute to internal differences. The Massachusetts Constitution of 1780 took effect only after the people had rejected two drafts and even then over much opposition. But most of the criticism, such as that directed against property requirements for voting or holding office and the power granted to the governor, subsided after ratification. These faults, if such they were, seemed counteracted by the wide suffrage for the lower house, which granted the vote to almost anyone likely to complain, and by continuation of the traditional system in which every town could send at least one delegate to the General Court. The maritime region of the state, though thickly settled, controlled only a minority of the representatives and could pass no legislation unfavorable to the interior towns, unless these failed to send delegates or unless some inland delegates supported such laws. The sections of the constitution that became controversial—those establishing the court system and a senate—excited less attention. After all, both had always existed and now had been rescued from external influence. The 1780 document seemed moreover to make the senate a trifle more responsive to public opinion than did earlier versions.[1]

If political issues did not excite intense conflict in Revolutionary Massachusetts, economic ones did. During the early 1780s they concerned primarily the payment of the state and federal debts, taxation, private debts, and monetary policy. A brief description of the state's economic background is therefore necessary.

Massachusetts contained several types of society that, while they shared many fundamental characteristics and shaded into one another, differed in crucial ways.[2] Boston epitomized one species, to which belonged lesser urban centers such as Newburyport, Salem, and Marblehead. Economically these towns served as export and import centers. They drew products to their markets from a wide area, in return disseminated consumer goods, and furnished capital to their hinterlands. These towns also contained a good deal of the state's manufacturing, including most of the large enterprises such as shipbuilding and distilling. The social elite either originated here or were eventually attracted by the advantages of an urban center. Culturally the ports constituted the most educated, cultivated, cosmopolitan, urbane atmospheres in a generally isolated and rural country. And politically they served as foci of local power or, in the case of Boston, of the entire commonwealth's power structure. Merchants and professional men, the same people who furnished economic and social leadership, dominated public life. Even after 1776, when a few prosperous artisans attained high office, merchants occupied nearly three-fourths of the seaports' legislative seats.

Associated with the principal trading centers were other ports that relied upon a coastal trade, fishing and whaling, shipbuilding, and a local wholesale-retail business. Examples include a few Maine villages, Lynn, Ipswich, Beverly, Plymouth, and the towns on Cape Cod. These shared many of the same economic interests and in varying degree performed the same cultural and political functions as the larger centers, though their society seems to have been

1. During the colonial period the council was selected by the lower house subject to veto by the governor. The 1778 draft called for election by the people, the number being roughly proportioned to population. However only men with £400 in property could hold office, and the voting requirement was £60 clear of debt. In 1780 the franchise was lowered slightly (no reference being made to "clear of debt"), and senators needed to own only £300.

2. The following description owes much to Van Beck Hall's economic analysis of the Massachusetts towns, *Politics Without Parties: Massachusetts, 1780–1791* (Pittsburgh, 1972).

less aristocratic. Political power belonged to men in trade, professionals, and those following other nonfarm occupations. Similar in some respects were interior trading communities, especially such Connecticut River valley towns as Springfield and Northampton.

Another major kind of Massachusetts community existed in the commercial areas, most of which enjoyed easy access to the coastal towns. They profited from good land and produced a considerable surplus for consumption in the trading centers or for export. Although these towns sometimes contained a few families conspicuous for their property and prestige, and although they always included a large number of laborers and servants, their society was on the whole democratic. Culturally they afforded no great opportunities, but their location near urban centers and their economic prosperity assured them of stimulating connections with the outside world. Eastern Essex, Middlesex, Suffolk, and Plymouth counties contained many towns of this type, such as Dorchester, Medford, Roxbury, Charlestown, Haverhill, Newton, Braintree, Marshfield, and Bridgewater. They chose as representatives a mixture of men in trade, miscellaneous entrepreneurs, manufacturers, professionals, and substantial farmers. At once agrarian and commercial, urban and rural, these communities occupied an intermediate position between the trading towns and the interior farms.

A third type of town, the most numerous, characterized the whole interior of the state. The people produced as much surplus for sale as they could, but they were handicapped by inferior soil, isolation, and lack of capital or of cheap labor. Therefore they earned little cash income, depended on their own resources, and were necessarily more self-sufficient than richer communities. These communities suffered from a chronic money shortage. Since they afforded little opportunity for large profits, they scarcely produced an economic upper class, though a few families often ranked socially above the rest. Physically isolated and lacking surplus wealth, such towns did not develop a culturally sophisticated, cosmopolitan environment, and the people became parochial in their view of the world. They chose as delegates men characteristic of the neighborhood—mostly farmers, or perhaps a local innkeeper or artisan.[3]

Finally, the towns in Maine seem either to have resembled the lesser trading and fishing centers or the semisubsistence towns of

3. Thus the Worcester County representatives who voted several times during the years 1784–1787 included 25 farmers, 4 innkeepers, 3 millers, 2 large landowners, 2 artisans, a shopkeeper, a lawyer, and one whose occupation is unknown.

the interior, yet they possessed distinctive qualities and followed their own erratic political path. Exclusive of York and Falmouth, which were ports of some size, they sent a mixture of farmers (eight) and townspeople of the second rank (thirteen).

Economic developments during the war years caused dissension because some people profited, while others did not. High farm prices, the result of increased demand, of relative scarcity (many farmers served in the army), and of currency inflation, benefited those agricultural communities blessed with good land and located near markets. Commercial farm areas therefore could afford to pay taxes and to purchase needed products even at a high cost. But most interior towns, lacking such advantages, found it increasingly difficult to support the war and buy necessities. Within the trading towns real wages declined, and the fishing industry almost ceased. But men engaged in trade, in certain types of manufacturing, and in other entrepreneurial activity prospered. Most of the money spent by the state or by Congress flowed to the commercial centers and their immediate agricultural hinterland, benefiting the wealthy more than the poor.

Throughout the war the governments needed large sums of money. The people of Massachusetts shared the general reluctance to pay taxes, and at first many feared that taxes might create tories out of rebels. They therefore relied upon deficit financing, borrowing money, and issuing more paper than would have been necessary had heavier taxes been levied. Without adequate backing the paper depreciated more rapidly than was desirable. Laws making it legal tender only postponed the depreciation and defrauded creditors.[4] A general fiscal reform became essential, and creditors of the state, private creditors, and everyone suffering from inflation joined forces to effect a reform. Their efforts produced a conflict within the legislature that foreshadowed the contest of the mid-eighties. Although the present analysis will focus primarily on the later years, a brief discussion of these early issues will shed light on the emerging political alignments.

The program advanced by the reformers called upon the government to rely on loans rather than upon paper. The older paper and certificates would be funded on terms favorable to the holders. Men with money to lend would be encouraged by repealing the

---

4. See for example complaints in *Cont. Jour.* (Boston), Oct. 26, Nov. 9, 1780. For financial policies during the war years, see Oscar and Mary F. Handlin, "Revolutionary Economic Policy in Massachusetts," *WMQ*, 3d Ser., IV (1947), 3–26.

law that made paper a legal tender and by taxes in silver that would pay the interest on the loan. Creditors of the state would be paid with the money thus obtained. Private creditors, of course, need no longer accept the paper money, the value of which was now set by a scale of depreciation. The taxes imposed, part of which must be paid in specie, fell primarily on polls and real property.[5]

This major change in policy aroused widespread opposition. An address from the town of East Sudbury to its representative, Capt. Richard Heard, suggested the objections of the agricultural interior. The residents insisted that the state's paper money had not in fact depreciated until the reformers repealed the tender act. Now, since the state was collecting taxes in silver, the people would be reimbursing the state's creditors for twice what they had loaned. This was money taken from the poor and given to the rich. To make the situation of the poor taxpayer still worse, he could no longer use paper to pay his taxes or debts. If the people were to pay taxes in gold and silver to redeem the bills, they certainly ought to be legal tender. The townspeople detected a conspiracy by men who sought either to spread discord throughout the state or to build fortunes on the ruin of the common people. For the legislature to change the value of these bills was "a piece of arrogance almost intolerable."[6] An angry reply accused the writers of being "men of little property, less honesty, and deeply in debt" who had no right to insult the government. The tender act, the responder insisted, had ruined thousands of respectable creditors.[7]

Perhaps most residents of the commonwealth adopted a middle position, anxious to maintain the state's credit, unwilling to defraud either debtors or creditors, doubtful about the worth of paper money but reluctant to pay the heavy taxes needed to maintain its value. The interests of public creditors, private debtors and creditors, taxpayers, merchants, farmers, the army, and other groups

5. Some articles favoring this program are in *Cont. Jour.* (Boston), Jan. 25, Mar. 22, 1781; *The Independent Chronicle. And the Universal Advertiser* (Boston), July 27, 1780 (very interesting), Aug. 10, 1780, Jan. 4, 15, 1781. The intent of the new law is outlined in *The Boston Gazette, and the Country Journal*, Mar. 26, 1781. For the new policy see Robert A. East, "The Massachusetts Conservatives in the Critical Period," in Richard B. Morris, ed., *The Era of the American Revolution* (New York, 1939), 349–391. The Journals of the House of Representatives contain the details, notably Sept. 26, 1777, Feb. 19, 1778, Jan. 6, May 28, 1779, and June 24, 1780.

6. *Boston Gaz.*, May 14, 1781.

7. *Ibid.*, May 28; see also July 1.

conflicted, and the wisest and fairest policy was by no means clear.[8] These different objectives and views caused dissension in the legislature, too, and led to several close votes.

On January 11, 1781, the Massachusetts House of Representatives agreed to repeal the tender act, 56–47.[9] Support for the measure came primarily from coastal communities and nearby towns, together with a crucially important dozen from the west. The opposition centered in the interior, which also won a few votes from the coastal areas but not enough for victory. Delegates who in the mid-eighties belonged to the eastern, or nonfarm, bloc, presently to be described, favored the bill, 6–2, while their opposites voted nay, 9–4.[10] There followed several almost identical votes in which the legislators agreed to arrange for the prompt settlement of and payments on the state debt, reimbursements to be in specie or money equivalent. The margin averaged about 70 to 50.[11] The alignment on these votes followed precisely that on the legal-tender issue. Those favoring repeal of the tender provision supported the new arrangements without exception, while their opponents demonstrated similar consistency. Delegates who sat in the legislature later in the decade duplicated their voting record with few exceptions, the correlation being 80 percent.

The spring elections altered the personnel of the house and encouraged advocates of a legal-tender act to renew the battle. A motion on June 14 to repeal certain of the offending clauses in the January law carried, 76–47, but later failed in the senate. The shift did not result from individual changes of heart, for most delegates voted consistently. Rather, towns previously unrepresented roused themselves, especially in Hampshire and Berkshire counties. The same east-west division continued. As before, the vote forecast the later alignment: delegates who presently formed part of the western, or Localist, group favoring repeal, 14–2, while their future opponents voted, 7–2, against the attempt.

These new financial arrangements required the imposition of new taxes. Apparently the people of the state recognized the need for revenue, including specie. They tried, however, to minimize the quantity by controlling government expenses, especially payments

8. An example of a middle position is in *Indep. Chron.* (Boston), Oct. 19, 1780.

9. The bill stated that all debts, both public and private, would be paid either in specie or in paper at its actual circulating rate, the precise value to be determined by impartial judges. See also the votes on Nov. 24, 1780, and Jan. 16, 1781.

10. These figures reflect the enormous turnover of personnel in the lower house between the early and later years of the decade.

11. See votes, Jan. 16–18, 24, and Feb. 5.

on the debt, and everyone endeavored to reduce his particular share. The debate focused on two questions: first, What proportion of the tax should fall on polls and real property ("estates") as opposed to personal property or income? and second, Should a tax on imports, called an "impost," be passed?[12]

As for the former, the issue seems clear enough. So much of the state's wealth lay in its land and buildings and the labor of its people that a tax on polls and estates was unavoidable. Yet such taxes fell primarily upon farmers, for men with some nonagricultural occupation, although perhaps owning real estate, derived most of their income from personal property such as money at interest, stock in trade, and ships, or from their special skills, as did artisans and professional men. Rural folk argued that taxes should fall on income or on property such as unimproved land held for speculative gain and on personal estates.[13] On the other hand, men whose wealth lay in personal property applauded a tax on real estate. Owners of unimproved land, of course, sought to exempt their holdings.[14] The critical vote occurred on June 28, 1782, upon a motion to reconsider (and probably therefore to postpone) the tax on polls and estates, which lost, 54–57. Votes against reconsideration came primarily from the eastern towns with important support from the frontier areas, probably because their assessment was low. Most of the other inland towns and those in Maine favored the motion. Three-fourths of the delegates who would presently belong to the two future political groups voted consistently with their subsequent position. The alignment on this vote closely resembled that on previous questions: those who supported the financial changes of 1781 approved the tax, and vice versa.

The debate on the impost proved more complex for two reasons. In the first place, because Congress would collect it for payment of the federal debt, it involved a series of issues relating to external affairs. Second, no one was certain who would pay the tax—the importing merchants, well-to-do consumers, or the people generally. The debate found expression in four votes that show a gradual shift and crystallization of opinion. During the first three votes (May 1 and June 7, 1782) the seacoast towns tended to op-

12. An excise tax seems not to have been controversial. It fell on luxury articles that few people bought and could easily be justified on moral grounds. See Massachusetts Sessions Laws, Sept. 1781, chap. VII (Records of the States microfilm or Early American Imprints microprint).

13. Examples are *Indep. Chron.* (Boston), Nov. 2, 30, 1780, Feb. 8, 1781.

14. See their argument in *Cont. Jour.* (Boston), May 4, 1781, Feb. 6, 1783.

pose the bill because they feared that the burden would fall on commerce and on the larger property holders who would buy foreign products. Interior communities, on the other hand, favored passage by a margin of about two to one.[15] At this point the delegates whom we will later identify as belonging to the Cosmopolitan and Localist blocs split evenly.

Congress reopened the question in 1783, after the earlier request had failed to win unanimous support from the states. The tax became politically more palatable because it was limited in time and because the states would control collections. Proponents argued that Congress needed the money desperately to pay its debts and strengthen the nation, and in fact the central government's finances did require help. Nevertheless opposition rapidly increased in the agricultural towns. Perhaps the farmers changed their minds about the economic effects of the tax, but probably they feared a dangerous concentration of power in Congress. At the same time, many people, especially in the interior, became excited about the special payment, or "commutation," to former Continental officers. During the summer the lower house insisted by a very large margin that the money should not be used in that way, and when the senate disagreed the bill failed (July 8–9).

In the fall (October 16–17) three close votes finally settled the matter: first, the house approved a clause that bound the state for twenty-five years; second, supporters defeated an attempt to prohibit the use of the money for commutation; and finally the bill passed, 72–65. Passage of the bill without restrictions now won the assent of almost all towns on or near the coast, while the interior by a three-to-two margin tried to limit the scope of the act and then defeat it. The correlation on these votes with those in later years was 80 percent.[16]

The debate over the tender act had disclosed the conflict between debtors and creditors that would reach a climax during Shays's Rebellion. The nature of the alignment on that issue appeared also in a roll call of July 2, 1782, which approved a valuation law. Favorable votes came primarily from the interior farming communities, while the procreditor delegates represented the eastern commercial towns. The alignment on this vote resembled very closely (by over 80 percent) that on later roll calls.

The only other major issue that caused the house to divide dur-

15. See Main, *Antifederalists*, 72–102 *passim*.
16. On the final vote future Cosmopolitans cast 9 votes for the impost and 4 against, while Localists opposed it, 8–21.

ing the early 1780s concerned the loyalists. Hostility to tories, until about the middle of the decade, seemed to resemble disapproval of sin. The newspapers contained numerous articles against them, and towns instructed their representatives to prevent the return of the loyalists or the restitution of confiscated property.[17] Although some individuals privately welcomed and protected former friends and although these former miscreants gradually regained the confidence of their neighbors, few if any dared openly to advocate a general amnesty. As a result efforts to modify the punitive laws succeeded only gradually after several years of controversy.

The first recorded vote on the question concerned the petition of Thomas Brattle that he be allowed to return. Brattle belonged to a distinguished family that had chosen the losing side. The senate accepted the report of a joint committee favorable to the petitioner, but the representatives rejected it by a single vote, 52–51.[18] The division on this issue followed, in a general way, that revealed by previous roll calls: eastern representatives usually supported Brattle, and westerners opposed him. Delegates who belonged to the two major groups—soon to be introduced—divided in a way moderately consistent (69 percent) with their later position.

A later vote (June 25) suggests that some men voted to admit Brattle who would not support loyalists in general. The house defeated an amendment to a bill preventing the return of loyalists, which would have enabled a person arrested under the act to obtain his release more easily, and then passed the clause in its harsher form by a huge majority. The next day a motion to reconsider lost by a closer vote, 84–67. This vote revealed a sharp sectional division. Men who presently supported the eastern, nonfarm side favored a reconsideration, 12–3, while those on the other side rejected it, 22–8. Representatives living on the coast had favored Brattle's petition and now advocated the more lenient clause by an even larger margin, with interior towns opposed. The relationship between the voting on the Brattle issue and four other questions is indicated by table 4.1, which traces the votes of individual delegates.

During the next four sessions, extending from November 1784 through March 1788, the legislature called for twenty significant

17. James Sullivan contributed one such article disguised as "Marcus." *Indep. Chron.* (Boston), Apr. 3, 1783. Sullivan to Samuel P. Savage, Apr. 3, 1783, Savage Papers, Box II, Mass. Hist. Soc.
18. Feb. 27, 1783.

Table 4.1. *Interrelationship of Votes on Return of Loyalists and Other Issues*

June 25 Vote on Brattle	Valuation Law	Impost, 1783	Tax on Polls and Estates, 1782	Repeal of Legal Tender, 1781
Proloyalist				
For	4	31	12	9
Against	11	12	11	4
Antiloyalist				
For	24	21	7	6
Against	5	39	20	22
Correlation	80%	68%	64%	76%

roll-call votes. Despite the fact that many towns failed to send representatives or chose different delegates from year to year, and despite frequent absenteeism, a sufficient number of men voted enough times to permit an analysis of the alignment. In all, these 259 men cast roughly four-fifths of the total votes cast.[19] During these years the make-up of the legislature varied somewhat, but its general character is indicated in table 4.2.

Plainly, the subsistence-farm and frontier delegates could block undesirable laws if they stood united, as could the men of moderate wealth, farmers, and those of little education and limited experience. Townspeople, the well-to-do, the educated, the cosmopolitan, those of prominent families and extensive experience, however influential, could accomplish nothing without support.

On every one of these twenty votes the representatives divided into two blocs, the alignment on each strongly resembling that on all the others. One group, basically eastern and nonfarm, included 84 men. Another, primarily made up of farmers from the interior, contained 134, while 41 were neutral. We will call these the Cosmopolitans and the Localists and will trace their position through the votes.

During the session that began in November 1784, the representatives demanded four roll-call votes. The first division again concerned loyalists. The lower house did not consider a general

19. In 1784/1785 the proportion was 73%; in the next year, 78%; during 1786/1787, around 95%; and on the final three votes, about 45%.

Table 4.2. Composition of the Massachusetts Assembly, 1784–1788

	No.	%		No.	%
Residence			*Social origin* (continued)		
Frontier	17	7	Above-average family	16	6
Noncommercial farm	119	46	Prominent old family	9	3
Commercial farm	62	25	Unknown	27	10
Town	43	16			
City	18	5	*Occupation*		
			Farmer	122	47
Economic status			Large landowner	2	1
			Artisan, manufacturer, misc.		
Poor or moderate	148	57	nonfarmer	31	12
Substantial	34	13	Professional	34	13
Well-to-do	31	12	Merchant or trader	51	20
Wealthy	13	5	Unknown	19	7
Unknown	33	13			
			Age in 1783		
Religion			Under 40	50	19
Episcopalian	2		40–49	64	25
Methodist	1		50–59	52	20
Quaker	2		60 and over	21	8
Congregationalist	103		Unknown	72	28
Presbyterian	7				
Baptist	5				
Other	3		*Military service*		
Unknown	136		Enlisted man	14	6
			Misc. officer	79	31
			Colonel or general	24	9
Political experience			Probably served	5	2
Local office	122	47	None or unknown	137	53
Sheriff, j.p., etc.	30	12			
State senate	7	3	*Education*		
State governor or judge	8	3			
Other state office	2	1	None	194	75
Continental office	3	1	Self-educated	16	6
None	5	2	College	27	10
Uncertain	82	32	Uncertain	22	8
Social origin			*Intellectual interest*		
New, native family	12	5	None	175	67
New, immigrant family	7	3	Some	26	10
Average family	188	73	Uncertain	58	23

Table 4.2—Continued

	No.	%		No.	%
World view			*National origin*		
Localist	166	64	Mass. born, English	211	82
Cosmopolitan	32	12	Mass. born, Scottish	2	1
Uncertain	61	24	Mass. born, Scotch-Irish	3	1
			Mass. born, Irish	1	0
			Mass. born, French	1	0
Mobility			Immigrant, English	1	0
Mobile	33	13	Immigrant, Scottish	2	1
Not mobile	224	87	Immigrant, Scotch-Irish	2	1
Uncertain	2	1	Unknown	36	14

pardon, for public opinion still forbade leniency. But some argued that loyalists might bring in a good deal of money and that it was possible to support particular concessions while opposing a general readmission. In this case the representatives, by a vote of 60–59, permitted seven men to remain within the state until the next session. The legislators discussed above—the 259 consistent voters—favored the motion, 43–35. Men in trade and the professions supported the loyalists, 16–4, as did manufacturers, 4–1, but artisans opposed them by the same margin, while farmers furnished most of the negative votes, 32–11. Geographically delegates from the towns cast all but two of their votes for the petitioners; two-thirds of the rural representatives opposed them. The larger property holders voted for the loyalists, 14–2, and the small ones against them, 34–13.[20] Curiously the older men proved more antitory than the younger: perhaps they resisted change. Other significant differences on the issue included the tendency of college men, delegates with intellectual interest, and those of cosmopolitan outlook to support the petitioners, while their opposites voted against the loyalists.[21] Men of relatively prominent families favored readmission; those of ordinary social background opposed it. Finally, the

20. Delegates with intermediate, or substantial, property divided evenly.
21. Voting in favor were: 71% of college men, 41% of those without education, 67% of men with intellectual interest, 36% of those without intellectual interest, 86% of cosmopolitans, and 34% of localists.

Cosmopolitan bloc voted for the resolution, their opponents against it:[22]

	For	Against
Extreme Localists	21%	79%
Moderate Localists	50	50
Neutrals	50	50
Moderate Cosmopolitans	80	20
Extreme Cosmopolitans	86	14

The second vote revealed the delegates' attitude toward the collection of taxes. A senate resolve sharply criticized delinquent collectors and recommended steps forcing them to proceed more vigorously. The lower house refused to concur, 39–55. Although this issue seems to have nothing in common with admitting loyalists, the alignment proved similar, if one can judge from the sixty-three legislators about whom we have sufficient biographical data. In general the offending collectors lived in the poorer parts of the state where, despite a lower tax rate, payment proved difficult. A considerable portion of the taxes paid by the maritime area and by men with substantial incomes took the form of imposts and excises, the collection of which posed no problem, and which the farmers and men with small cash income found agreeable. But land and polls contributed most of the money, created the major problem for collections, and aroused the greatest hostility. Moreover the people understood and resented the fact that their taxes primarily benefited the public creditors. Their distress, as one defender observed, resulted not from imprudence but from a genuine scarcity of money. The war impoverished many; farms, buildings, clothes, and implements fell into disrepair; creditors bore heavily upon them; and crops failed.[23] Such men lived in districts "remote from sea ports and from markets, and destitute of many of those means of procuring wealth and money, which are enjoyed by the mari-

22. "Extreme" refers to those who voted with a bloc at least 80% of the time; "moderates" did so at least two-thirds of the time. The group affiliation of the delegates is based upon all 20 votes. Percentages are approximate.
23. The Handlins identified as suffering from the war men on fixed incomes, wage earners, fishermen, and "farmers in areas only recently settled, where subsistence agriculture still prevailed." "Revolutionary Economic Policy in Massachusetts," *WMQ*, 3d Ser., IV (1947), 18–19.

time towns, and the towns in their vicinity."[24] Farmers could avoid
most of the import taxes simply by frugality and would not feel
small sums incorporated into the cost of salt, rum, sugar, cotton,
or molasses, but they felt oppressed by a demand for cash. On the
other side, towns that had paid most of their taxes and men who
would benefit from strict collection urged justice to those who
loaned money during the war, emphasized the reputation of the
new government, and insisted that delinquents could pay if they
stopped buying superfluities.[25]

The evidence suggests that the farmers had the stronger case.
Most luxuries probably remained in the import centers and appeared inland only in homes of the well-to-do. The crucial factor
undoubtedly was, not the purchase of luxuries, but the absence of
cash in agricultural towns. Young George Richards Minot, who
had just taken his attorney's oath (together with Fisher Ames),
wrote the truth in his journal:

There is always a louder complaint against the payment of taxes in
the Country than in the maritime towns which many have supposed to
have arisen from an equal apportionment of them, but I think there are
other reasons to account for this inconvenience. The taxes are mostly
payable in money, and the whole estates of merchants and traders consist of that article, or of such others as admit of an easy exchange for
it. Whereas the estates of farmers lying in land or such other kind of
property as can be commanded and sold only at certain period of the
year, and is vastly more difficult to be converted into the proper medium for discharging the taxes. The advantages of the one and the disadvantages of the other will upon this consideration appear obvious
whenever the demand of the tax exceeds that is whenever it requires
of the Farmer more than a certain amount, the surplus of his income.[26]

24. *Cont. Jour.* (Boston), Sept. 9, 1784, from Springfield.
25. *Indep. Chron.* (Boston), Apr. 1, 1784, Dec. 1, 1785.
26. "Remarks, etc.," Sedgwick Papers (Minot), Mass. Hist. Soc. Minot continued:

"And this will appear still more striking if we suppose for a moment that the
tax was dischargeable by assigning to Government a certain portion of land in
lieu of paying them money, when the advantages of these orders of men would
certainly be reversed. But the Yeomen of the Country are also more tenacious of
their property than people engaged in commerce for two reasons. First, because
land of which the first are possessed, had always been held of a higher and more
valuable nature than any personal estate. So the Laws have ever required more
solemn ceremonies in the conveyance of it and annexed greater privileges to the
tenure of it than of any other property. A Freehold estate is often necessary for
purposes in civil polity which other estate of much greater value is unequal to.
Hence the possession of it seems to be a greater gratification to the pride and
independence of men. Secondly, people in commerce are more habituated to great

On this issue the interior farming communities formed a nearly solid bloc against the resolution and overwhelmed the urban centers, who united in favor. As might be supposed, farmer-delegates opposed any pressure on the collectors (79 percent), as did the artisans (80 percent), but all of the merchants and most of the lesser tradesmen and professional men favored stronger measures. So did men of large property, college graduates, delegates with intellectual interests, those of cosmopolitan views, and men from prominent families (all these qualities being possessed by a few men). The party division on the resolve was more clear-cut: Localists nixed the proposal, 5–33, neutrals divided, 4–3, and Cosmopolitans favored it, 16–2.

The third vote, on March 10, 1785, introduced an issue closely related to several others. This concerned the grant of a "supplementary fund" to Congress of $224,427 annually. That was a sizable sum, and the lower house rejected it overwhelmingly, 33–96. As with the impost, the supplementary fund involved both support of Congress and money. Much of the resistance to the impost focused on the power that the central government would exercise, opposition to which centered in the rural districts. That objection did not apply to the fund, but the farmers, who had hoped that the impost might fall on the trading towns, knew that they could not avoid paying a substantial portion of the requisition, which would fall on the polls and estates. On the other hand, many merchants who had feared the cost of the impost felt that this grant would not injure them. Therefore even on the first vote when nearly three-fourths of the delegates opposed the proposal, Boston representatives supported the fund unanimously, whereas agricultural areas overwhelmingly rejected it (88 percent). Similarly, while 90 percent of the farmers opposed the bill, only 14 percent of the merchants and 65.5 percent of other nonfarmers did so. The fund appealed to the larger property holders, the better educated, and the more cosmopolitan men. These generalizations, based on the votes of 91 out of 129 delegates, are illustrated by the percentages in table 4.3.

A year later the delegates again considered the fund (March 16,

and sudden losses than those of landed interest who, with common prudence, are almost beyond the reach of the quick reverses of fortune. We all know it is a common case for a Navigator to accumulate vast riches by a single adventure; and as common to loose them again by trifling accident. This gives him an indifference at parting with his property which the husbandman can never attain, and of course makes him yield the more easily to it in whatever way it may happen."

Table 4.3. Percentages of Delegates Opposing the Supplementary Fund

	Against		Against
General vote	74	General vote	74
Economic status		*Military service*	
Moderate	90	Enlisted man	100
Substantial	67	Colonel or general	57
Well-to-do	57	Other officer	96
Wealthy	29	None	67
Political experience		*Intellectual interest*	
Local office	84	Some	40
Sheriff, j.p., etc.	82	None known	84
High office, state or national	20		
		World view	
Education		Localist	91
None or little	79	Cosmopolitan	22
Self-educated	71		
College	33	*Legislative party*	
		Localist	94
Social origin		Neutral	79
Humble origin	60	Cosmopolitan	33
Average family	60		
Above-average family	83		

1786) with a similar result, except that the adverse majority was reduced to 67 percent and the lower house postponed the question instead of rejecting it outright. Again farmers opposed the grant almost unanimously (85 percent), as did all of the six artisans present; however, all six merchants favored it, and other nonfarmers now split evenly. The opposition increased as one left the trading towns (20–4 pro) and moved through the commercial farm areas (18–9 con) into the subsistence farm region (49–4 con) and the frontier (7–1 con). The correlation between the vote and other characteristics of the delegates increased: thus all but 2 of the

65 Localist delegates voted to postpone, whereas 25 of the 29 Cosmopolitan bloc took the other side.[27]

The final vote on the issue came on June 9, 1786, when the legislature approved the fund, 59–45. The sharp reversal resulted partly from a change in public opinion and partly from a power shift within the legislature. The basic nature of the division remained unchanged. Delegates from trading towns voted yea with few exceptions, 27–3, whereas those from subsistence farm towns opposed, though by a reduced margin of 13–30. The shift of representatives of the commercial farm areas, especially those nearest the cities, now proved decisive, as they supported the fund, 15–8.[28]

The final vote of the 1784/1785 session, to which we now return, approved the once-hated stamp tax, 65–46. Twenty years before, resistance to that tax centered in the cities, with merchants and lawyers taking the lead, strongly supported by the printers. These last again protested vigorously, but they were deserted by their former allies, who now either expected the burden to be spread throughout the population or considered the need for money greater than the evil. Every merchant and all but one of the professional men (a doctor) approved the bill, while farmers furnished most of the negative votes, their opposition increasing in proportion to distance from the coast. Every well-to-do or wealthy representative favored passage; substantial men divided equally; but two-thirds of those with less property opposed the tax. Similarly the delegates divided according to various cultural factors, social origin, political experience, and their alignment on other issues. Of the members of the Localist group, 84 percent voted nay, while 89 percent of the Cosmopolitan bloc voted aye.

Thereafter, this very sharp division persisted on other tax bills, the sides shifting according to financial interest. The first vote of the next session proved that townspeople, though supporting taxes generally, drew the line at assessments which fell entirely on them and that the rural prejudice against taxes extended only to those they would pay: men voted their economic interest rather than their principles. Thus men who felt that the government must have money were obliged to accept import and excise taxes in addition

27. Against the measure were 79% of the delegates owning moderate properties, 86% of those with substantial means, 40% of the well-to-do men, and none of the wealthy delegates.

28. See table 4.4. We are dealing here with 96 persons, comprising all but 8 of those voting.

to the tax on polls and estates, else the representatives would balk. Such a bill passed in July 1785 evidently with general approval, but when an amendment included a tax on bonds and bills of lading, the trading interest unsuccessfully objected.[29] Eighty percent of the urban delegates voted against it, but the measure succeeded because rural representatives favored it by a margin of nearly three to one. Similarly delegates who were farmers by occupation overwhelmingly favored this tax, which they would not pay, while professional men and merchants opposed it. Of the Localists, 88 percent approved it, and 80 percent of the Cosmopolitan group voted against it.

The legislature recorded only two more votes on the tax issue. These concerned an assessment of polls and estates that would provide money for the supplementary fund. Support for Congress was not at stake, everyone agreeing that the federal government needed money. The issue rather concerned how the money should be raised and whether the grant should extend for twenty-five years.[30] The first attempt to pass the bill failed, 65–72. An amendment then reduced the proportion that had to be paid in specie, after which the measure succeeded, 73–57. This second vote therefore represented an acceptance both of the grant to Congress and of the consequent tax.

These two votes (June 30, 1786) reveal almost in pure form the political alignment in Massachusetts during this period, combining as they did two important issues. Over 80 percent of the farmers and artisans voted nay on the first vote, while all fourteen merchants and all but one of the other delegates engaged in trade voted aye. A large majority of professional men and a small one of manufacturers also favored the tax. Representatives of subsistence farm communities and of the frontier likewise voted against the supplementary fund, delegates from commercial farms divided about equally, and 90 percent of those from trading towns voted for the bill. All wealthy delegates and three-fourths of those who were well-to-do favored passage, but 72 percent of small property holders objected. Significant differences appeared also between men with and without formal education, intellectual interest, and cosmopolitan outlook; men of above-average social origin unanimously favored the tax, while 63 percent of the rest opposed it. All high-ranking officials voted yes, but holders of local posts voted no by

29. July 1, 1785. The amendment passed, 76–60. See table 4.4.
30. See the full and informative account of the debate in *The Boston Magazine*, III (1785), 142–144, 313–316.

a three-to-one margin. Finally, 95 percent of the adherents of the Localist group opposed, while 94 percent of the Cosmopolitan bloc favored the tax.[31]

On the following vote most of the delegates remained consistent. A handful of neutrals shifted, which had the effect of further solidifying the nonfarm vote, except that artisans maintained their opposition. Localist delegates opposed the tax by 98 percent, Cosmopolitans favored it by 90 percent. These decisions, which finally granted the supplementary fund and levied a heavy assessment on farmers, helped to precipitate Shays's Rebellion.

Before we proceed with the votes of the 1786/1787 session, one more roll call of the previous year should be noted. It pertained to a quite different issue. The two houses, over Governor Bowdoin's veto, set up a joint committee to supervise certain government expenses. The lower house favored legislative control, 111–55. Bowdoin drew some support from all sections, especially from the trading towns (16–6), but he was defeated by an overwhelming majority of the subsistence farm and frontier delegates. The governor's fellow merchants all supported him, as did a majority of lesser tradesmen and professional men, but artisans and above all 85 percent of the farmer delegates voted to override. The same division noted on other issues appeared on this: between large and small property holders, well-educated and uneducated men, and throughout the other categories including that of party. The vote here was 91 percent of the Localists for the resolution, 70 percent of their opponents against, and the neutrals slightly opposed (54 percent).

The legislature that met during the early summer of 1786 failed to take the rather drastic steps that would have been necessary to avert Shays's Rebellion. The lower house continued to appropriate more money and levy additional taxes. When the representatives did adopt a more popular policy, the senate interfered. The most important vote, one of the decade's most significant, concerned the question of how the revenue from imposts and excises should be spent. An unspoken but weighty element in the debate was that these taxes could be collected easily and surely, whereas revenue from polls and estates had proved uncertain. Another aspect of the question was, Who deserved the most favorable treatment: Congress, the state's creditors, or officials and other recipients? At the time the money went entirely to creditors of the state, who col-

31. Data here include 122 of the 137 voters.

lected interest on their securities. Proponents of continuing this policy insisted that creditors deserved support (widows and orphans, as usual, were said to depend on it); the honor of the state was at stake; and the value of the certificates, if properly upheld, would rise, thereby increasing the quantity of money in circulation. Creditors feared that, if they were denied this source of revenue, they might receive only a partial return on their investment or even none at all. On the other hand, a majority of the representatives adhered to a different set of priorities. They believed that the state's creditors consisted of speculators rather than of widows and orphans and preferred that the money go first to Congress and second to the state's civil list. Creditors would presumably rely upon the tax on polls and estates.[32]

The procreditor element in the lower house obtained a favorable verdict from a committee, which in March 1786 recommended continuing the previous policy. The full house, however, rejected the report, 56–51. This division found the frontier and subsistence farm areas, which were about to become the centers of the Shays's revolt, solidly opposed to the report, while the trading towns favored it by a six-to-one margin. The commercial farm communities, which until this time had largely inclined to support their fellow farmers, now divided evenly; they were to continue this shift. Farm delegates voted against the report by a margin of five to one; men in trade voted for it, 17–3; artisans opposed it, professionals favored it, and manufacturers were divided. The other characteristics of the two sides remained unchanged, and the party lines emerged sharply, the correlation exceeding 90 percent.

From this time on the events and issues growing out of Shays's Rebellion became central to all legislative disputes. Documentation for the protestors' grievances and their opponents' reactions is embarrassingly rich, for the newspapers are full of articles and the legislature was flooded with petitions. On the whole, the "rebel" complaints were justified. Nobody on either side denied the prevalence of debts and the existence of numerous suits. Everybody admitted the shortage of money. Clearly debtors were being forced to repay more than they borrowed and to bear excessive court costs. Though a few commentators denied it, taxes did fall severely on farmers and did extract money from them for the benefit of

32. Newspapers contain many articles, but the clearest presentation is in *Boston Mag.*, III (1785), 139–140, 436–437. See also the analysis in Caleb Strong to Theodore Sedgwick, Mar. 14, 1786, Sedgwick Papers, Box A, Mass. Hist. Soc.

public creditors. And clearly the policies might justly have been changed. Contemporary opinion diverged fundamentally in many ways. The Shaysites and their sympathizers discovered a conspiracy of creditors, merchants, moneyed men, and aristocrats who profited from the innocent common people. Critics of the rebellion attributed the whole affair to sin, originating in luxury, profligacy, dishonesty, and now subversion. Solutions similarly conflicted. The first group wanted a change of monetary policy so as to increase the supply of money or (what would have the same effect) the reenactment of a tender law. They advocated tax reform, especially so as to reduce the burden on polls and estates. They wanted expenditures reduced, partly by cutting salaries but primarily by scaling down or postponing payment of the state debt. This would release revenue from the impost and excise, which would go to Congress and take the burden off the farmers. They wanted more lenient treatment for debtors and a cheaper way of trying suits. A few suggested limiting legal fees or even abolishing lawyers (the newspapers printed some entertaining articles on that point). When the senate blocked certain reforms, some recommended that it be abolished too.

The other side clung to existing policies. Restrictions on imports, which it suggested as a means to reduce an outflow of money and stimulate domestic manufacturing, pleased the artisans but attracted only minor attention. Calls for moral reform and the prompt payment of debts, combined with references to suffering widows and orphans, solved no problems. Basically the anti-Shaysites stood pat and demanded that the rebels be suppressed. They succeeded because both the governor and the senate took their side and because even the lower house proved moderate. A major factor favoring the status quo was the reaction of commercial farming areas against radical aspects of the uprising. In addition representatives of non-agricultural occupations opposed the rebels, as did most political neutrals. The totally unfair characterization of the Shaysites as economic levelers and political traitors became widely believed and was ratified by force.

The votes that reveal the division in the legislature concerned three specific issues: the reduction of the governor's salary, which served as a symbol of the desire to limit expenses; the passage of a "stay law" to postpone the collection of debts; and the imposition of penalties on the rebels.

The first issue resulted in three votes. On October 19, 1786, the house decided, 75–47, that it was "consistent with the Constitution to reduce the Governor's salary."[33] On March 6, 1787, it passed, 57–30, a bill to fix his salary permanently at £800 instead of £1,100. Four days later a vote to override the executive veto failed to obtain the necessary two-thirds, 36–29.[34] As might be expected, the alignment remained much the same throughout, and the first may be taken as typical. The division in every way resembled that on previous issues. Sixty-seven percent of the frontier representatives favored a lower salary, as did 89 percent of those from subsistence farm areas. Delegates from commercial farm communities cast a small majority of votes on the same side, but seven-eighths of those from trading towns sided with the governor. Four-fifths of the farmers and three-fourths of the artisans backed the reduction, but almost all of the merchants together with about two-thirds of the professional men and manufacturers preferred the higher salary. The agreement among the latter increased on later votes. Larger property holders supported the governor, as did college graduates, intellectuals, cosmopolitans, men from higher social rank, principal officeholders, and adherents of the Cosmopolitan voting bloc. The proportions remained nearly constant.

The proposed stay law, a major objective of the debtor interest, passed the lower house on October 26, 1786, by a vote of 69–50, but was vetoed by the senate. A year later, it passed again by a 116–74 margin and again failed in the upper house. The issue thus coincided chronologically with Shays's Rebellion and its aftermath, contributing to it and prolonging the resentment. The alignment revealed by the votes indicates both the division between debtor and creditor and that between Shaysites and their opponents and parallels in every respect the alignment on other issues. The stay law won overwhelming support from farmers, artisans, and a bare majority of manufacturers, but was opposed by merchants, other men in trade, and a small majority of professionals. In 1786 three-fourths of the representatives from subsistence farm regions voted for it, as did over five-eighths of delegates from commercial farm areas, but almost all townsmen opposed it. Favoring the stay law were the smaller property owners, men of little education, those holding only local office, and adherents of the Localist group (92

33. See the report of the proceedings in *Boston Mag.*, III (1785), 430–431. A sectional division characterized an earlier vote to fix a permanent salary, Nov. 29, 1780.

34. The figure of £800 was a little low, though Virginia was paying her governor that, while New Jersey appropriated less. On the other hand, New York and Pennsylvania each paid £1,500 and Maryland £1,000.

percent). A year later the lines of division actually sharpened, and the wealthier and nonfarm groups especially solidified against the bil'.

Two votes indicate opinions about the so-called rebels. The first, on November 8, 1786, empowered the state supreme court to try various categories of Shaysites. This passed, 58–52, but an attempt to reconsider lost, 55–56. On June 13, 1787, the lower house accepted a committee report that raised troops and pardoned certain insurgents. An attempt to eliminate a list of exceptions to the pardon having failed, delegates sympathetic with the uprising challenged the report but lost, 100–108. The protest movement had, of course, developed among farmers from the interior and had attracted more support from men who were poor and in debt than from the well-to-do creditors, so the voting naturally resembled that on the stay law. The protagonists geographically were the subsistence farm areas and the towns, with commercial farm delegates at first divided and then opposing the Shaysites. Farmers and many artisans voted for lenient measures, but men in trade wanted repression. The more property one owned, the more one upheld law and order. Cultural attitudes also correlated with voting, in that the cosmopolitan men of education showed little sympathy with the rebels. Finally, only two members of the Cosmopolitan party voted with the insurgents on the two votes, while the Localists lined up, though with decreasing consistency, on the other side.

One last vote deserves mention: in March of 1788 the legislature voted, 52–40, to allow the Phelps-Gorham group of land speculators to pay for their huge grant in £300,000 worth of state securities. The request was backed by the urban, commercial, well-to-do members of the Cosmopolitan bloc and opposed, though by a lesser margin than usual, by the Localists. Meanwhile, outside the legislature in the state ratifying convention, Cosmopolitans were supporting the Constitution, 23–5, while the Localists opposed it, 25–7.

These twenty votes, taken during four sessions and involving a dozen different issues, demonstrate a continuing, consistent alignment in which two major groups of legislators, possessing opposite characteristics, steadfastly confronted each other. The issues, different though they seem, formed a pattern that extended back in time to the preceding legislative sessions, when it embraced votes dealing with questions of monetary policy, the impost, payment of the state debt, taxation, the treatment of loyalists, and commutation. The interrelationship of the issues of the period 1784 to 1788 can be demonstrated by singling out the men who supported the grant of a supplementary fund and tracing their attitudes toward some of the other recorded questions:

	For	Against
Return of loyalists	16	6
Collection of taxes	14	4
Payment of state debt	53	7
Tax on bonds, etc.	8	28
Tax on polls and estates	42	7
Reduction of gov.'s salary	13	29
Stay law	12	37
Prosecution of Shaysites	40	10

The men who, through analysis of these votes, have been identified as forming two legislative parties demonstrated strikingly consistent political behavior. Table 4.4 shows the percentage of cohesiveness of each party on the twenty votes. The top figure records the margin by which the motion won or lost: thus 52 means 52 percent of all delegates favored passage. Below come the proportion of affirmative Localist, neutral, and Cosmopolitan votes. Delegates of the Localist bloc voted together about 85 percent of the time, while the Cosmopolitans were even more consistent (88 percent). With the partial exception of the last vote, the two groups sharply opposed each other on every issue.

Every vote moreover reflected economic, social, political, and cultural factors. The principal ones are shown in table 4.5, which concerns certain votes selected as representative of the various issues. The major generalizations need no comment. The table indicates the intermediate position taken by representatives of commercial farm communities, among whom those near the larger towns tended to vote with the cities and those more remote generally supported the noncommercial farm element.[35] The difference in political behavior of manufacturers and artisans probably lacks statistical validity.

Political alignments in Massachusetts during these years may be

35. Representatives of commercial farms near cities in 1784/1785 cast 33% of their votes with the Cosmopolitans, but in 1785/1786 they agreed by 73% and in 1786/1787 by 78%.

Table 4.4. *Bloc Voting in Massachusetts, 1784–1788*

Percentage of Affirmative Votes on Each Issue

	1	2	3	4	5	6	7	8	9	10	11	12	13	14	15	16	17	18	19	20
All delegates	50	59	26	59	56	67	51	67	52	44	56	48	62	59	46	56	55	52	65	56
Localists	27	13	6	16	88	91	85	97	11	5	10	6	91	92	13	96	93	48	84	53
Neutrals	55	57	21	92	48	46	36	61	59	37	65	37	61	53	67	67	70	10	17	50
Cosmopolitans	84	89	67	89	20	30	10	14	100	94	98	88	15	8	95	8	4	100	4	80

CODE OF VOTES: (also referred to in table 4.5):

1. Readmission of certain loyalists.
2. More stringent collection of taxes.
3. Grant of supplementary fund.
4. Stamp act.
5. Tax on bonds and bills of lading.
6. House supervision of certain accounts.
7. Revenue from impost and excise to Congress.
8. Postponement of supplementary fund.
9. Grant of supplementary fund.
10. Tax on polls and estates.
11. The same.
12. Revenue from impost and excise to state creditors.
13. Reduction of governor's salary.
14. Partial stay law.
15. Punishment of rebels.
16. Permanent reduction of governor's salary.
17. The same.
18. Exclusion of certain rebels from general pardon.
19. Continuation of partial stay law.
20. Phelps-Gorham purchase.

Table 4.5. *Factors Affecting Voting on Selected Issues* (in Percentages)

	Percentage of Affirmative Votes						
	1	5	9	10	13	14	15
Residence							
Frontier	50	63	33	17	67	43	14
Noncommercial farm	33	75	30	20	89	81	31
Commercial farm	30	70	65	44	57	65	58
Trading town	82	24	83	85	20	18	90
City	100	0	100	100	10	0	100
Occupation							
Farmer	26	76	32	19	81	72	35
Artisan	20	50	20	17	75	67	43
Manufacturer	80	50	75	56	57	57	57
Professional	70	27	89	70	39	42	85
Lesser trader	100	42	63	88	33	38	79
Merchant	100	0	100	100	9	9	91
Economic status							
Moderate	28	70	44	38	78	66	43
Substantial	45	56	44	45	60	63	63
Well-to-do	88	30	92	75	18	38	69
Wealthy	80	33	100	100	33	25	100
Education							
None	41	65	44	36	68	58	48
Self-educated	67	63	45	36	77	86	60
College	71	43	100	89	18	27	85
Intellectual interest							
None	36	71	45	32	72	59	46
Some	67	29	92	78	27	31	77
World view							
Localist	34	73	37	27	73	66	42
Cosmopolitan	86	22	100	89	23	25	85

Table 4.5—Continued

	1	5	9	10	13	14	15
Social origin							
Humble origin	40	67	67	29	67	33	67
Average family	42	66	50	38	68	60	51
Above-average family	83	36	92	100	36	46	80
Political experience							
Local office	42	72	38	27	77	66	46
County office	55	36	60	63	47	63	63
State or national office	78	14	100	100	45	13	100

NOTE: See note to table 4.4 for the code identifying the substance of these issues.

summarized from three points of view: the votes taken in the legislature, the characteristics of the representatives, and the expressions
of opinion by the people of the state. The votes reveal a continuous division, which took the same form on every issue throughout the period 1780 to 1788. One set of delegates steadily favored
a monetary policy backing an ample supply of paper money
that would be legal tender in the payment of debts, taxes, and
other financial transactions. A prodebtor attitude, implied by such
a policy, appeared in their support of a stay law. The same men
proved unenthusiastic about payment of the state debt. They
seemed willing to support the federal government as far as contributing to the discharge of the national debt, indeed preferring
federal to state creditors, but they rebelled at payments to army
officers, rejected permanent funds, and opposed the increased
power implied in the impost proposal and explicit in the Federal
Constitution. On the whole, they disliked taxes, especially those
on polls and estates, which seemed especially burdensome to the
poorer people and to farmers; but they favored revenue raised
from nonagricultural sources. They preferred lower government
expenses, at least those that formed the governor's salary. One vote
suggested a lack of sympathy with speculators, and three indicated
hostility toward such loyalists as tried to return. Finally, they
showed sympathy with the Shaysite movement by trying to
weaken punitive measures. With the possible exception of the anti-
loyalism, all of these attitudes reflected a consistent set of objectives concerning economic and political policies.

The characteristics of the delegates who differed on these issues

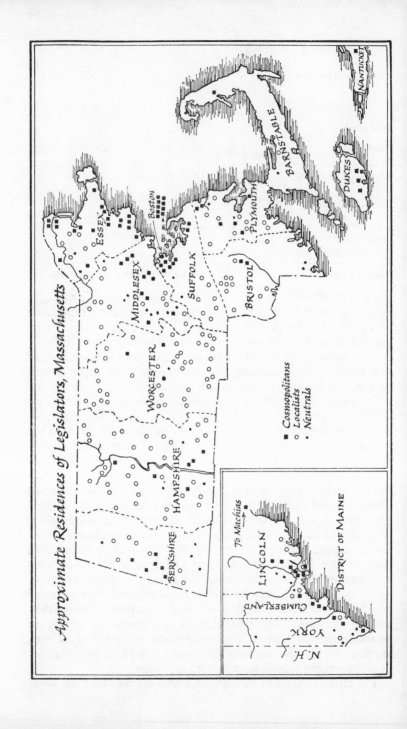

Approximate Residences of Legislators, Massachusetts

■ Cosmopolitans
○ Localists
• Neutrals

are sharply disparate. The geographical contrasts have been sufficiently stressed (see the map, p. 110). The major protagonists
were at one extreme, Boston, which chose thirteen representatives
who voted as a unit, and at the other pole the semisubsistence farm
communities that furnished nearly a hundred opponents of the
Boston bloc, a baker's dozen supporters of it, and eleven neutrals.
The lesser trading towns supported the city thirty-nine to four,
with five neutrals. Two areas divided. The frontier delegates
tended to agree with the subsistence farm groups (nine to three,
with five neutrals), and the commercial farm regions split evenly.
The definition of the last category remains very doubtful, but the
generalization remains valid whatever the definition, for the towns
most clearly commercial in nature—those nearest the coast—voted
decisively with the trading centers, while inland the political record shades gradually in proportion to geographical distance from
the markets.

The correlation between occupation and voting was even
higher, for those delegates who were not farmers tended to agree
even when they represented agricultural communities.[36] Merchants
—importers and exporters—almost never differed; all supported
the Cosmopolitan bloc. Other men engaged in trade generally
voted the same way except in the case of innkeepers. Lawyers and
doctors tended to join the traders, as did ministers, teachers, and
officials. Thus professional men as a group agreed with the commercial interest (23–8, with 4 neutral). Manufacturers divided
evenly, whereas artisans preferred the Localists or remained neutral. Farmers of whatever size furnished the major strength of the
Localist bloc. Eliminating representatives whose occupation is unknown, the parties therefore were composed as is shown in
table 4.6.

The economic contrasts between the two sides extended also to
differences in wealth. Among the thirteen largest property holders,
eleven voted with the Cosmopolitans and two remained neutral;
among thirty-one well-to-do representatives, two-thirds supported
that party. Those with smaller but substantial estates (£1,000 to
£2,000) slightly preferred the Localists, while the lesser property
holders, who comprised over half of the total, voted with the Localists by a margin of three to one. Put differently, the Cosmopolitan group contained the following elements: wealthy, 15 percent;

36. To illustrate: subsistence farm and frontier areas cast 27% of their votes
with the Cosmopolitans or as neutrals, but nonfarm delegates from those areas
cast 46% on that side.

Table 4.6. Composition of Massachusetts Parties by Occupation (in Percentages)

Occupation	Cosmopolitans	Neutrals	Localists
Farmer	16.0	48.0	72.0
Artisan, etc.	1.5	17.0	9.5
Professional	29.0	14.0	6.5
Manufacturer	6.0	7.0	4.0
Trader	47.5	14.0	8.0
Total	100.0	100.0	100.0

well-to-do, 30 percent; substantial, 18 percent; and moderate means, 37 percent. The Localist bloc consisted of: wealthy, none; well-to-do, 7 percent; substantial, 15 percent; and, moderate means, 78 percent.

Social distinctions probably reflected or coincided with the preceding differences in residence, occupation, and property. Men of humble or obscure origin, including immigrants, usually appeared in recently settled areas and preferred the Localists. Representatives from families prominent in the state's history never did so, but voted either with the Cosmopolitan or as neutrals. Those from families of above-average status preferred the Cosmopolitans by a two-to-one margin, whereas delegates of average background supported the Localists by the same majority. Since almost all wealthy and well-to-do men voted with the Cosmopolitans, so necessarily did those representatives who were vertically mobile.

The relationship of cultural factors to political behavior seems difficult to prove, but the evidence suggests some connections. Most of the delegates who attended the Congregational church voted indifferently. Among those of other denominations the two known Episcopalians supported the Cosmopolitans, and the two Quakers divided. The rest, including seven Presbyterians, five Baptists, two Universalists, and a Methodist, almost always voted with the Localists (12–1, with 2 neutrals), but the numbers are too small for significance. Almost all college men and men with known intellectual interests adhered to the Cosmopolitan bloc, which included those with a cosmopolitan world view, whereas four-fifths of those with only local experience supported the Localist group.

Finally, the evidence shows a correlation between the representatives' political and military experience and their attitude toward the major issues. Holders of high political office invariably belonged to the Cosmopolitan group, as did Continental army officers and indeed higher ranking military officers generally. Men who in early 1788 favored the ratification of the Constitution had voted with the Cosmopolitans by a margin of over three to one, while those who opposed it had been Localists by an even larger margin (five to one). Adding all of these characteristics, one can describe a Cosmopolitan party that consisted principally of business and professional men rather than farmers, who usually lived in trading centers and had held an important civil or military office. They owned far more property than most Americans and benefited also from a superior social rank and better education. These advantages contributed to their cosmopolitan outlook. Their opponents, mostly farmers, owned modest estates, came from ordinary families, lacked educational advantages, rarely held high office, and viewed the world from an experience limited to the locality.[37]

Spokesmen for the two opposing viewpoints expounded the series of related ideas typical of their group. Thomas Clarke, a Roxbury tanner who represented his town in the General Court for many years and supported the Cosmopolitans on almost every issue, received instructions in 1783 that probably reflected the opinion of his semiagricultural, semitrading, and manufacturing town. The people urged him to watch for violations of the constitution and malpractices of officials; to reduce expenses but establish permanent salaries for judges; to obey the treaty with England, even though certain parts were obnoxious, but not to repeal confiscation acts or readmit all of the absentees; to support Congress unless it exceeded its power; and to maintain public credit by selling state lands and levying the taxes necessary to pay the interest and principal of the debt.[38] The position taken by this party found emphatic expression in the writing of a Bostonian in November 1787. The people, he asserted, resigned all authority to their representatives and must obey them. Judges and other officials should become entirely independent of the people, for "their election is apt to occasion party-spirit, cabals, bribery and public dis-

37. Neutrals shared at least one characteristic with the Cosmopolitans. Thus 17 out of the 35 lived in commercial farm or trading centers. Of the rest nine followed a nonfarm occupation, two were men of above-average wealth, and one was a Continental army officer. Seven remain, of whom six came from Maine and the last from Berkshire County (he became a Federalist). One of the substantial farmers, incidentally, was the son of a Yale minister.
38. *Indep. Chron.* (Boston), May 29, 1783.

order." The voters might instruct their representatives, but not often, and the instructions should not be binding, since most people lived remote from each other and lacked information. He laid down as basic principles the sanctity of contract for both state and individuals, the injustice and tyranny of tender laws, and the evil tendency of stay laws and paper money.[39] Similarly the judge's charge to the Middlesex County grand jury in October 1786 emphasized that local conventions were treasonable, because everyone must obey the government and might only petition for redress of grievances. He feared attacks on private property, warned against paper money, urged that public credit be maintained, noted that taxes were necessary to that end, pointed out that the evils of the day would be cured only by time, industry, frugality, and the encouragement of manufacturing and commerce, recommended a grant of power to Congress, and closed by emphasizing the duty of the people to support the government.[40]

The opposite view found expression in the numerous petitions drawn up by delegates of the western towns, meeting in conventions. During the early part of the decade these conventions lacked unanimity[41] and called for investigations, greater caution on the part of their representatives, and minor reforms.[42] But opinion had hardened by 1786 and became angry during the following winter, after which the shattering defeat suffered by the insurgents silenced the extremists.[43] The instructions of New Braintree indicate the collection of ideas that characterized the Localist voting bloc. They defended the rebels and asked for an act of indemnity, dismissal of the troops, and repeal of a law that had suspended the writ of habeas corpus. Their sympathy with debtors and distrust of authority led them to request restrictions on lawyers (who would be limited in number and paid by the state), the dismissal of the attorney general, and abolition of the court of common pleas. Local government would be strengthened by empowering constables, selectmen, and town clerks to perform many functions

39. *The American Magazine,* I (1787–1788), 9–11.

40. *Mass. Centinel* (Boston), Nov. 11, 1786.

41. For example, see the split votes in a Hatfield convention, Aug. 9, 1782 (Mass. towns, Force Papers, Vol. II, 205:2:173, Library of Congress).

42. Broadside, Worcester County Convention, . . . *In Convention. Tuesday, April 9, 1782* (Worcester, Mass., 1782).

43. The Shaysites suffered a loss not only physical but moral and intellectual. Their defenders, browbeaten, ceased to write and apparently were silenced for years. See *The Hampshire Gazette* (Northampton, Mass.) and the fate of William Whiting as revealed in the Robert Treat Paine Papers, Mass. Hist. Soc.

such as serving writs, collecting the impost and excise taxes, registering deeds, and taking over the probate court; the court of common pleas and general sessions of the peace would be abolished, and the authority of sheriffs greatly reduced. The people recommended extension of the stay law. Their antiurban bias is suggested by the request that the General Court leave Boston, while their remonstrance against any grant of money to Harvard indicated anti-intellectualism.[44]

The various county petitions covered the same ground. They usually favored an increase in the money supply, control over lawyers, reduction of government expenses and of taxes, reforms in the court system, prodebtor laws, payment of the foreign debt by the impost and excise, postponement of payment of the state debt or an easier method of paying it, and removal of the legislature from Boston.[45] While only a minority of the people approved of violence, undoubtedly a large majority shared the attitudes that these conventions expressed and that, when the legislature failed to act, resulted in the "rebellion."[46]

The increasing acrimony of political disputes led to growing awareness of the differences between the blocs and to "electioneering." The basic divisions within the state never vanished during the Revolution. Eastern spokesmen hoped in vain that the state's constitution would ward off a "levelling spirit" and soon were fearing, during the early years of the decade, that western protests might culminate in "an agrarian law and a revolution."[47] According to one observer the American Revolution encouraged opposition to the elite. "How strangely things alter in a popular government!" wrote Henry Van Schaack, an ex-loyalist, to his protector. "There was once a time when the arrival of Theodore Sedgwick in the Town of Richmont was in every bodies mouth—

44. This petition appeared in several papers as well as in the *Worcester Magazine*, I (1786), 106–107, and the *Pa. Packet* (Philadelphia), June 20, 1787, where it was accompanied by refutations of many points.

45. For example, the Hampshire and Middlesex conventions of Aug. and the Worcester conventions of Aug. and Oct. 1786.

46. "A Freeman" probably expressed the opinion of the townspeople who chose delegates to the conventions. Those who called the meetings unlawful, he remarked, were saying in effect that "when we had other *Rulers*, Committees and Conventions of the people were lawful—they were then necessary; but since I have *myself* become a ruler, they cease to be lawful—the people have no right to examine into my conduct." *Worcester Mag.*, II (1786–1787), 336–338.

47. *The Boston Evening Post: and the General Advertiser*, Dec. 22, 1781; Samuel Allyne Otis to Theodore Sedgwick, Boston, July 8, 1782, Sedgwick Papers, Box A, Mass. Hist. Soc.

The children along the Street announced it as people passed by. But alas it is not so now."[48] Others cast the conflict in economic terms, as a dispute between the landed and commercial interests, featured especially by the farmers' distrust of merchants. One writer took a more inclusive view.[49] The ideas of country people, he observed, were too often "cribbed, narrow and confined," and their minds lacked "the expanding peculiar to the education of the great world." Their reading extended only to *Robinson Crusoe* or *Pilgrim's Progress;* they could talk of nothing but the weather and local scandal. On the other hand, people of populous towns were citizens of the world, who possessed knowledge of men.[50]

During these early years political contests seem to have been restricted to the locality and probably involved persons rather than ideas. Newspapers contain no indication of what transpired, though an occasional private letter testifies to quiet activity.[51] John Hancock's retirement in 1785 caused a conflict between Thomas Cushing and James Bowdoin for the succession, and one newspaper, which plumped for the loser, complained that "perhaps there never was an Election in this state wherein there was more *cunning* and *address* used, than there was in the last election of governor."[52] But the contest seems not to have reached much beyond the gubernatorial race.

Criticisms of government policies increased during the spring of 1786, just preceding the uprising. The right to criticize, which implied a right to formal opposition, found a public defender in "Honestus," the pen name of Benjamin Austin. Austin, a well-to-do ropemaker, cast four votes with the Cosmopolitan party when he sat in the house in 1785, but he now became a leading critic of lawyers and a spokesman of the Boston mechanics, ending as a Jeffersonian. "Honestus" insisted that the people should not acquiesce in authority. It was a grand principle of an "aristocratical party" that a few men knew better than the majority; but the majority ought to instruct their representatives how to act.[53] Appar-

---

48. Jan. 2, 1784, Sedgwick Papers, Box A, Mass. Hist. Soc.

49. *Boston Mag.,* II (1784), 116; *Indep. Chron.* (Boston), Apr. 21, 1785.

50. *Mass. Centinel* (Boston), Mar. 24, 1784.

51. James Warren wrote to Elbridge Gerry, Mar. 2, 1783, concerning a meeting that intended "to fix upon those men who are the most likely to obtain the suffrages." Gerry-Knight Papers, Mass. Hist. Soc.

52. *Mass. Centinel* (Boston), Apr. 16, 1785.

53. *Indep. Chron.* (Boston), May 25, 1786. An attempt to incorporate Boston aroused fears that the "better sort" sought to control the city and oppress the people. *Mass. Centinel* (Boston), Oct. 29, 1785.

ently for the first time, newspapers published lists of approved candidates for the senate, and not for the last time a voter complained at the effort to influence votes: "How happy the Electors of the County of *Suffolk* must esteem themselves," he wrote sarcastically, "seeing *their Masters* have condescended to permit them to choose *one* Senator at the next Election, *provided* they confine themselves, however, either to *Judge* Cranch or General Heath." A slate also appeared in Worcester County, similarly containing the candidates of the Cosmopolitan bloc.[54] During the subsequent election for representatives in May, several Boston caucuses drew up lists that differed, though the reference in them to party distinctions may not refer to the legislative parties presently under consideration.[55]

Not until the following spring, when one Boston paper ran a continuous column called "Electioneering," did political contests begin to develop a form. Evidently the early conventions had concentrated on issues rather than on men; they recommended no candidates. But in February the town of Stoughton, which chose men who almost invariably sided with the Localists and which sympathized with the Shaysite movement, suggested a general conference to select the best candidates for the legislature. The newspaper publishing the resolution accompanied it with an angry editorial terming it effrontery and a result of the spirit of faction. Even so the town of Dorchester approved a county convention to confer, which elicited an almost hysterical editorial condemning conventions. Other towns rejected the proposal.[56] Shortly thereafter the town of Lunenburg in Worcester County called a meeting to discuss the choice of senators. Some towns approved and did in fact choose delegates, but other people defended the government against such implicit criticism and agreed that the proposed method would result in bribery and undue influence. As a result the meeting adjourned without acting.[57] The newspapers published no lists of candidates, and the campaign focused instead on Bowdoin's losing struggle to retain his office. Numerous articles defended his actions upholding law and order and attacked the Shaysites bitterly, though none dared to identify Hancock with

---

54. *Am. Herald* (Boston), Mar. 27, 1786; *Mass. Centinel* (Boston), Mar. 29, 1786; *Worcester Mag.*, II (1786–1787), 52. But voting for the senate that year seems to have followed personal rather than party lines in most counties.
55. *Mass. Centinel* (Boston), May 6, 1786.
56. *Ibid.*, Feb. 14, 1787; *Indep. Chron.* (Boston), Feb. 15, 1787, Mar. 16, 29, 1787.
57. *Worcester Mag.*, II (1786–1787), 638, III (1787), 10–11.

them.[58] Hancock's overwhelming victory, while testifying to his general popularity, clearly represented a victory for the Shaysite sympathizers, for the Localist group, and in general for small property holders. Bowdoin's strength derived entirely from the eastern trading centers and more prosperous farm areas. In Boston the voting seems to have followed class, or at least occupational, lines: newspapers published an apocryphal summary in which physicians, clergymen, lawyers, independent gentlemen, merchants, traders, and printers favored Bowdoin, 391–30, tradesmen preferred him narrowly, 328–299, but laborers and servants chose Hancock, 5–446 (the totals being accurate).

Attention then turned to the contest for the lower house. The Localist party won an overwhelming victory, and even in Boston the dominant merchant-professional group found itself challenged. "Old Rock" called upon the "smaller sort of folks" to attend the election in order to overthrow the "better sort." So bad had the situation become, he noted, that men had been sent to the gallows "for speaking disrespectfully of our Rulers."[59] In the same newspaper "Probus" called for the defeat of the "overgrown rich," especially those owning public securities, and recommended election of patriots who would act in "perfect coincidence" with country members to redress grievances.

Although the eastern group and their allies retained control of the senate and of the coastal area, they lost power in the lower house. The shock reverberated through the state and, taken in conjunction with the "rebellion," caused the leaders of the Cosmopolitan party to undertake a vigorous campaign. Theodore Sedgwick, a Berkshire County lawyer, expressed their alarm: "The natural effects of a pure democracy are already fully produced among us. A very large party in both branches of the legislature filled with a spirit of republican frenzy are now attempting the same objects by legislation, which their more manly brethren last winter would have procured by arms. In both instances it is a war against virtue, talents and property carried on by the dregs and the scum of mankind."[60]

By the end of the year both sides, but Sedgwick's in particular, had become accustomed to vigorous campaigning during the contest over ratification, the politics of which were described by

58. E.g., *The Massachusetts Gazette, or General Advertiser* (Northampton), Mar. 27, 30, 1787.
59. *Mass. Centinel* (Boston), May 5, 1787.
60. To Nathan Dane, Boston, July 5, 1787, Sedgwick Papers, II, Mass. Hist. Soc.

Minot in his journal. And by this time people had become accustomed to speak of Federalists and Antifederalists or Shaysites (the last as an epithet). The contest during the spring election of 1788 focused on the senate, and newspapers published lists of candidates. Where once this had been considered indecent, now the "newly adopted" system was applauded as useful to the people.[61] The climax came when the *Massachusetts Centinel* printed, and the *Hampshire Chronicle* republished, senatorial candidates for every county, reportedly drawn up "at a meeting of influential citizens from divers part of the Commonwealth," who if elected would guarantee a "good and stable government." It consisted of Federalists, most of whom had been associated with the Cosmopolitans, though it included also three members of the Localist bloc who had crossed lines on ratification. The campaign succeeded: Henry Jackson wrote that the senate would be "Federal to a fault," and "a very great check to an *Anti* and insurgent lower house."[62]

The period therefore ended with two clearly identifiable sides that usually lacked definition or organization but that did conduct ad hoc campaigns. These contests now were bitterly fought, and upon their outcome hinged the principal questions of the time.[63]

61. *Mass. Gaz.* (Northampton), Apr. 4, 1788.
62. To Henry Knox, Boston, Apr. 20, 1788, Knox Papers, XXII, 19, Mass. Hist. Soc.
63. See letters during 1789 in Theodore Sedgwick Papers, Box A, Mass. Hist. Soc.

Chapter V

New York

If Massachusetts, with her narrow littoral, her hilly interior divided by the Connecticut valley, and her detached counties in Maine, Nantucket, and Martha's Vineyard, developed almost inevitably a political sectionalism, so also did New York with its one great seaport, its Hudson valley, its mountains, its several frontiers, and its islands. Moreover New York lacked the general cultural uniformity possessed by Massachusetts. There most of the population was descended from old English, Congregational stock; New York, however, contained a mixture of established Dutch and British families as well as recent immigrants of various national origins, including German, and these attended a variety of churches. Finally, whereas the Revolutionary movement and the war united most people of the Bay Colony, New Yorkers divided violently in their sentiments, and the long British occupation further cut off New York City and its environs from the rest of the state. Any analysis of political alignments must therefore begin with a summary of New York's complex regions.

The commercial center of the state was of course New York City, with a population of about twenty thousand in 1776. Surrounding the city were counties containing many fertile farms that furnished food for the townspeople and for export. These were Kings (now Brooklyn) and Queens on Long Island, Richmond (Staten Island), and on the north a section of the mainland that formed part of New York County (the Bronx). The Dutch predominated in Richmond and Kings counties, shared influence with the British in New York City, and gave way to an English majority in Queens County on the east.[1]

Further east, Suffolk County extended nearly a hundred miles into the Atlantic. Settled primarily from Connecticut, its people imported their theology and town form of government from New England, but their land system was a mixture of large grants ("manors") and small holdings. Its population in 1776 equaled that of Kings and Queens and included about a thousand Negroes. Most of the people were farmers, but they also fished, whaled, built ships, and traded.

During the colonial period New York stretched not east and west, as it does now, but north and south in a narrow ribbon of settlement along the Hudson, much as French Canada reached up the Saint Lawrence. At the northern end the people had begun to fan out, penetrating even before 1776 about seventy miles to the west, though the pioneers clung to the Mohawk and a few subsidiary streams.

The people of this area, some 150 miles long by less than 40 miles wide, settled under very different conditions and developed diverse attitudes. Everywhere, but primarily along the east bank of the Hudson, certain Dutch and British families had acquired huge landed estates, many of which survived the war. They contained a mixture of freeholders and tenants who apparently voted for the magnates before 1776 but became less reliable thereafter. The eastern parts of these counties (Westchester, Dutchess, and Columbia) were being invaded by New Englanders, whose influence controlled Washington County (called Charlotte until 1785) on the far north opposite Vermont. They brought with them, among the institutions and attitudes of their homeland, a leveling influence (as detractors then called it) that caused them to question extreme economic and social inequalities and lean toward democratic political ideas. During the war years this influx of yeoman farmers joined a stream of refugees from the occupied south. As a result this northeastern section grew in population very rapidly.

Orange and Ulster counties, on the western side of the river, primarily contained small farms. Property was much more equally distributed than on the east bank: some Orange County tax lists indicate that the 10 percent of the people who were assessed for

1. Queens then included Nassau County and as a result contained more small farms and a smaller population that one would expect. Politically, it resembled Suffolk rather than Kings.

the highest tax owned about a third of the taxable property, whereas across the Hudson the same proportion held, on the average, 45 percent. No doubt the western area produced a surplus of farm products, but the presence of fewer towns than existed on the left bank suggests a smaller volume and more subsistence farming.[2] Certainly the profits were more equally distributed.

Albany County, when the war began, sprawled over almost the whole state north of Ulster and Dutchess and contained more people than any other county in 1771—one-fourth of the whole number. By the mid-eighties Washington and presently Columbia were set off, as noted above, between the Hudson and New England, and Montgomery (called Tryon until 1785) included the western frontier settlements. Even after these divisions the county contained a great variety of peoples: the three thousand inhabitants of Albany, an important commercial town; the tenants and owners of some large landed estates; and a great many independent farmers, some with highly developed holdings, others with new, untouched plots. As a result the county's political scene constantly changed. Thus the most commercial parts of the state included New York City, the nearby farming area, and a narrow but rich ribbon north to Albany along the Hudson, especially on the east bank. The least commercial sections lay on either side of this ribbon.

In 1777 a special convention drew up a constitution for the state. Representation in both houses of the bicameral legislature was based roughly upon population. Since British troops controlled the five southern counties, the constitution provided that their current delegates would serve until elections could be held. As matters turned out, the incumbents remained until January 1784, when all but four lost their offices. As a result nearly one-third of the legislators did not truly represent their constituencies. These southern delegates belonged to the more "radical" element and agreed with the upstate delegates on many vital issues, especially upon vigorous prosecution of the war. Although many of the votes recorded during this early period anticipated the later political alignment, the abnormal situation distorted and delayed the development of parties. We will concentrate upon the later, normal period when the southern representatives again presumably reflected the desires of their electorate.

In 1784 the lower house contained nine delegates from New

2. Kingston was the only town of consequence on the west bank, whereas Fishkill, Poughkeepsie, and Hudson developed on the eastern side.

York County and two each from adjacent Kings and Richmond. Queens and Suffolk on Long Island chose four and five respectively. On the left bank of the Hudson, Westchester sent six, Dutchess seven, and in the north Washington four. Orange and Ulster across the river elected ten between them. Albany's ten became seven when Columbia separated, and the frontier county of Tryon-Montgomery chose six. The property qualification permitted about 60 percent of the adult white men to vote for the lower house and to hold office in it.[3] Since balloting now became secret, the assembly was reasonably representative of public opinion except, of course, for those with little or no property.

During the 1780s the lower house contained members of all New York's economic, social, and cultural groups except for those of less than average wealth and status (see table 5.1). Geographically about one out of seven lived on the frontier, specifically near the Massachusetts and Vermont border and along the Mohawk. One-fourth came from agricultural communities that produced relatively little surplus, and over one-third from commercial farming areas. The remaining fourth lived in New York City (one-sixth), Albany, or the lesser Hudson valley trading centers. Farmers, mostly of substantial property, held nearly two-fifths of the seats, and would almost have formed a majority had the large landowners voted with them—which they did not. Artisans and manufacturers contributed only about one out of twelve delegates, and were outnumbered by the professional men, primarily lawyers, with one-sixth of the total. Men in trade, consisting of assorted innkeepers, shopkeepers, entrepreneurs, and above all merchants, held more seats than any occupational group except for the farmers— about one-fifth. Thus despite the agricultural character of the state and despite the fact that three-fourths of the legislators lived in rural areas, one-half of them were not farmers.

Similarly the legislature contained a mixture of large and middling property holders. The former had furnished nearly 90 percent of the prewar assembly. This proportion now dropped to half that figure, but since not over one out of ten Yorkers owned large estates, wealth remained greatly overrepresented.[4] About one-fifth of the delegates owned substantial properties and presumably

3. Alfred F. Young, *The Democratic Republicans of New York: The Origins, 1763–1797* (Chapel Hill, 1967), contains the best discussion.
4. As explained earlier, "large" property as used here means an estate worth £2,000. The lack of data prevents any exact estimate of how many heads of families held that amount, but it certainly could not have exceeded 1 in 10.

Table 5.1. Composition of the New York Assembly, 1780–1787

	No.	%		No.	%
Residence			**Occupation**		
Frontier	33	14.2	Farmer	86	37.1
Noncommercial farm	59	25.4	Large landowner	19	8.2
Commercial farm	80	34.5	Artisan, manufacturer, misc.		
Town	21	9.1	nonfarmer	23	9.9
City	39	16.8	Professional	42	18.1
			Merchant or trader	45	19.4
			Unknown	17	7.3
Economic status					
Poor or moderate	60	25.9			
Substantial	40	17.2	**Age in 1783**		
Well-to-do	56	24.1	Under 40	57	24.6
Wealthy	32	13.8	40–49	54	23.3
Unknown	44	19.0	50–59	28	12.1
			60 and over	16	6.9
			Unknown	77	33.2
Religion					
Episcopalian	22	9.5			
Quaker	1	0.4	**Military service**		
Congregationalist	10	4.3			
Presbyterian	44	19.0	Enlisted man	8	3.4
Dutch Reformed	48	20.7	Misc. officer	63	27.1
Lutheran	3	1.3	Colonel or general	46	19.8
Unknown	104	44.8	Probably served	6	2.6
			None or unknown	109	47.0
Political experience			**Intellectual interest**		
Local office	62	26.7	None or uncertain	185	80.1
Sheriff, j.p., etc.	10	4.3	Some	46	19.9
State judge	10	4.3			
Other state office	33	14.3			
Continental office	14	6.0	**National origin**		
None	40	17.2			
Uncertain	63	27.2	N.Y. born, English	67	28.9
			N.Y. born, Scotch-Irish	2	0.9
			N.Y. born, German	4	1.7
Social origin			N.Y. born, Dutch	69	29.7
			New England	24	10.3
New, immigrant	17	7.3	Immigrant, French	6	2.6
New, native family	26	11.2	Other immigrant	14	6.0
Average family	122	52.6	Miscellaneous	6	2.6
Above-average family	32	13.8	Unknown	40	17.2
Prominent old family	24	10.3			
Unknown	11	4.7			

earned incomes well above the average, and the rest, comprising nearly one-third of the total, held moderate property.[5]

Socially the legislature reflected the state's diverse origins. One out of ten representatives came from families long prominent in the state's history, and a somewhat larger number ranked just below them in status. More than half belonged to average families— to the great middle class of small property owners. Finally, one-fifth had risen from humble origins, beginning either as immigrants or children of poor parents, or from obscure backgrounds. The occupation of the fathers, as far as this is known (60 percent) emphasizes the same situation: one-fifth had been traders or professional men, about the same proportion were large landowners, 10 percent were artisans and the like, and half were ordinary farmers.[6] As might be supposed some of the legislators had surpassed their fathers in status, though the proportion—15 percent—suggests stability, rather than major change, and emphasizes the large number who never attained high rank.

New York's legislature reflected not only the social but the cultural diversity of the state. However, men of English ancestry contributed a disproportionate number of representatives, nearly half of those whose background is known. Most of these were native Yorkers, though an important two dozen migrated from New England. The Dutch furnished about one out of three delegates, and the rest were a mixture of colonial-born Germans, Scotch-Irish, and French, together with miscellaneous immigrants. Similarly the religious affiliation of the representatives indicates both the supremacy of Britishers and the effect of a more varied society than that of Massachusetts. Among the known church members, over 40 percent were Presbyterians or Congregationalists, nearly as many belonged to the Dutch Reformed Church, and one-sixth were Episcopalians. Few Yorkers received much formal education, nor did their legislators. Less than one in ten attended college, though an additional 6 percent or more educated themselves. One in five had shown intellectual interest. Perhaps a fourth came from a cosmopolitan background, and 35 percent clearly did not.

The military and political experience of the representatives testifies to the opportunities created by the Revolution. While only twenty-seven had served in the Continental army (all as officers),

5. The figures in the text exclude those whose economic status is unknown (19%).

6. Again the figures eliminate those not known. The middle class backgrounds of the politicians would become even clearer were the unknown fathers considered as yeomen or laborers.

another eighty-five to ninety had fought as militia, so that half of the total had proved their patriotism in the field. An even higher proportion had occupied a civilian post, usually minor but sometimes important. Thus the assembly contained men who shared the complex background of their constituents and reflected their different opinions.

The New York Senate also contained a variety of men, for anyone with a freehold might serve, and every part of the state chose its share. More large property holders held that office, and a larger proportion of the urban elite, yet farmers other than large landowners made up two-fifths, and men of relatively small estates one-third. Only a minority represented the elite families.[7]

The events of the war left several legacies to postwar politics. First, antiloyalist feeling continued with unusual animosity. It flourished particularly in that part of the state that had not been occupied and was directed toward the areas under British control, especially New York City, because the people who remained there were suspected of loyalism. Men who had left the city during the war and now returned to it attempted to expel and replace the British adherents. Second, people in the unoccupied counties felt that they had borne the major financial, as well as the military, burden for seven years and that taxes should now be imposed on the southern district. Residents of the latter protested their patriotism and complained of their own sufferings. They wished to participate equally in the blessings of independence, not be deprived of its fruits. These circumstances magnified the sectional division already evident in the state's politics. Third, Gov. George Clinton emerged as a popular hero almost above party and unchallengeable for some years. His popularity remained strongest in those areas and among those people who clung to wartime emotions, neither modifying nor advancing much beyond them: they constituted a sort of GOP of New York State. Others, including many of the state's elite, never had been enthusiastic about Clinton. The northernmost counties had begun by preferring Schuyler, the southernmost backed John Morin Scott or John Jay, and opposition continued.[8] Until long after the war it remained private, each side always heading their tickets with the governor's name, and Clinton himself may have felt above party; but in fact he strongly attracted

7. Jackson Turner Main, *The Upper House in Revolutionary America, 1763–1788* (Madison, 1967), 134–135.

8. Henry P. Johnston, ed., *Correspondence and Public Papers of John Jay* (New York, 1890–1893), I, 141–147, III, 151–152.

only certain New Yorkers.[9] Accordingly there gradually emerged a group or coalition that supported the policies associated with Clinton and another that opposed both the policies and eventually the man. Finally, rural and upstate New Yorkers, perhaps more than most Americans, inherited an antagonism for speculators and entrepreneurs generally. This feeling increased after 1776 when people blamed such men for trading with the enemy, raising prices, profiteering, and thus prolonging the war. This hostility helped to shape the state's postwar politics.

The attitude of such men is suggested by an interesting series of articles appearing in the Poughkeepsie newspaper during 1779.[10] The writer, calling himself "the real Farmer," blamed monopolists, engrossers, and traders for the depreciation of currency and rise of prices. The entire commerce of the United States, he claimed, was "a shameful system of monopoly and distortion"; not a single trader had "contented himself with an old fashioned profit, from twelve and a half to twenty-five percent." He urged strict laws regulating prices and business activities, including the supply of the army. The state itself should import foreign goods, sell them at moderate prices, and use the profit to reduce the public debt. Moreover the tax system needed reform in order to relieve farmers. The yeomanry, he insisted, ought especially to be favored, for they loved liberty and were neither rich nor poor, yet bore a heavy pecuniary burden because their property was visible. The mercantile and mechanical classes, on the other hand, were the most dangerous part of the community, yet they escaped taxation. "The security of American liberty," the farmer observed, "requires a more equal distribution of property than at present." This point of view pitted the agrarians against the townsmen, paralleling and reinforcing the prejudices left by the war years.[11]

The outcome of these internal divisions was the emergence of two legislative parties, one of which—the Localists—consisted of men who supported Clinton and the policies associated with him, while the other—the Cosmopolitans—opposed them. A number of votes during the sessions prior to 1784 anticipated this political alignment, but continuous patterns really began in the spring of

9. Linda Grant DePauw, *The Eleventh Pillar: New York State and the Federal Constitution* (Ithaca, 1966), strongly urges that Clinton stood above party. This argument, however, is based on the assumption that the legislature contained no blocs.

10. *The New-York Journal, and the General Advertiser* (Poughkeepsie), Jan. 18, 25, Feb. 1, 8, 15, 1779.

11. See also *ibid.*, Nov. 30, Dec. 21, 1778.

that year. During the next five sessions the legislators recorded nearly two hundred votes or vote groups, 70 percent of which proved significant as indicators of party. Among the 157 legislators who cast enough votes so that their positions can be ascertained, 65 belonged to the Cosmopolitans, 52 to the Localists, and 40 remained neutral.[12]

Roughly the same alignment developed in the senate. All told, some twenty senators consistently opposed the twenty-one Clintonites, and half a dozen remained neutral.[13]

The definition and treatment of loyalists remained an important issue in New York. During the British occupation, while refugees were representing the southern counties, the legislators generally agreed in their hostility to loyalists and differed only on details. This agreement is shown in the votes, during the session beginning in October 1781, that concerned loyalist property, debts owed by or to persons who remained within the enemy lines,[14] and a motion to tax doubly those who sought protection with the enemy.[15] These show no consistent sectional pattern, nor are party lines apparent. Since they concerned payment of debts as well as the treatment of loyalists or neutrals, the issue was complex. In these war years the senate recorded several votes that reveal the beginning of party divisions. Thus the basic confiscation act won the support of all but one of the men who presently would become Clintonians, while on the other side stood most of their future opponents.[16]

After the British withdrawal an antitory campaign began. These attacks emanated both from inhabitants of New York City, especially those who had fled and now returned, and from the upstate counties. Meetings held in the Saratoga district, Cambridge, and King's districts in Albany County, Amenia in Dutchess, Westchester, and of course the city opposed any concessions.[17] On the

12. Beginning in 1780, 232 legislators served. These divided as follows: anti-Clintonians, 30.6%; neutrals, 47.4%; Clintonians, 22%. Intensive biographical research was limited to the legislators sitting in 1784 and thereafter.

13. The remaining four cast only a handful of votes. Every senator who served during the years 1777–1788 is accounted for in these figures.

14. Nov. 8, 1781, Mar. 23, 25, 1782.

15. July 18, 1782. Several earlier votes concerning the sale of confiscated estates show an alignment anticipating that of the mid-eighties. See note at end of chapter.

16. N.Y. Senate Journal, Mar. 9, 1779. Richard Morris, Isaac Roosevelt, and Isaac Stoughtenburg, all anti-Clintonians, signed a protest.

17. *The New-York Gazetteer, or, Northern Intelligencer* (Albany), May 26, June 9, 30, July 2, 1783; *The New-York Packet, and the American Advertiser*

other hand, loyalist sympathizers abounded in the southern district, although they did not advertise themselves in the press or by open meetings. Thus Alexander McDougall, sheltered behind a pen name, advocated the strict payment of debts to those who remained within enemy lines,[18] while the Trinity Church in New York City chose an outspoken loyalist as its rector.[19] Whatever the artisans and mechanics thought, the loyalists and neutrals had powerful defenders on Manhattan, among the staid farmers of Long Island, and elsewhere. By 1787 their right to vote was openly defended in the legislature by Alexander Hamilton, John Tayler of Albany, and William Malcolm.[20]

Several roll-call votes show the alignment on the issue. These included the famous case of *Rutgers* v. *Waddington*, in which the Clintonians strongly condemned a court decision favoring Waddington, a loyalist merchant defended by Hamilton, over a widow, Mrs. Rutgers, who sued Waddington for damages to her property during the war.[21] A New York law supported her; the British treaty favored him. The case therefore involved one's opinion whether a court and a treaty were superior to the state. The critics of the decision thus expressed a localist or states' rights point of view as well as an antiloyalist bias. The Clintonians also opposed the return of such prominent men as Cadwallader Colden and Henry Van Schaack;[22] tried to force neutralist and loyalist creditors to accept the state's securities and bills of credit (February 20, 1784); attempted to exclude from citizenship members of the Anglican vestry of New York City during the occupation and to proscribe others as well (April 5, 1784); supported a measure that would have required certain lawyers to obtain certificates attesting to their patriotism before they could practice (March 21–23, 1785); tried to limit the number of names in a bill restoring citizens to their rights (April 26, 1786) and later to disqualify any loyalist from sitting in the legislature (January 27, 1787); and attempted to hamper the recovery of debts due to persons who had remained

---

(Fishkill), Apr. 17, July 10, 1783; *N.-Y. Jour.*, continuously during Dec. 1783 (when it was called *The Independent New-York Gazette*) and Jan. 1784, and Apr. 8, 29, 1784, Dec. 29, 1785.

18. McDougall Papers, Box 6, N.-Y. Hist. Soc.; *N.Y. Packet* (New York), Feb. 19, 1784.

19. Robert R. Livingston Papers, Jan. 1784, N.-Y. Hist. Soc. He was forced out.

20. A good general discussion of the issue is contained in E. Wilder Spaulding, *New York in the Critical Period, 1785–1789* (New York, 1932), 120–131.

21. Oct. 29, Nov. 2, 1784.

22. Feb. 4, Nov. 12, 1784, Mar. 1, 26, Apr. 2, 1787.

within the enemy lines (April 4, 1786, April 12, 1787). Similarly in the senate they were opposing a plea by John Watts that he be allowed to buy land from the forfeited estate of his father and trying to deny former loyalists the right to vote.[23] In these cases the New York City delegates started by adopting a cautious anti-loyalist position but moved gradually to the other side. The final alignment can be illustrated by a study of the assembly votes concerning the Rutgers-Waddington case, the restriction on lawyers, the seating in the legislature, restoration of other civil rights, and the effort of Miles Sherwood to recover his position.[24] Delegates from the frontier and noncommercial farm areas consistently voted against the loyalists, while those from commercial farms and towns usually supported the ex-tories or neutrals. The division along occupational lines primarily pitted the farmers against merchants and lawyers. Loyalists found defenders among larger property holders but not small ones, Episcopalians but not Presbyterians, cosmopolitans but not localists (only a tendency), members of prominent old families more than those of humble origin, civilians more than military men, and the anti-Clintonians rather than their opponents.

The tax issue in New York involved, more than anything else, an attempt by delegates from unoccupied areas to shift the burden on to the southern counties after the British evacuation. In 1784 the legislature imposed a special assessment of £100,000 on the southern district. Thereafter each county contributed a quota, New York City alone paying over a fourth and its neighbors (Suffolk, Queens, Kings, and Richmond) a like proportion. The Clintonians, delighted with the situation, voted to raise £200,000, while the anti-Clintonians tried to halve the tax. The compromise of £150,000 carried primarily by the votes of the former (March 18 and 27, 1784). Despite the lighter burden on the Clintonian strongholds, they fell behind and pressed for a delay in collection. Representatives from the south opposed a postponement almost unanimously, and when the Council of Revision vetoed it they successfully upheld the veto.

Under the time-honored system, taxes rested both on real and personal property. The assessors estimated the taxable value of each person's property, varying the valuation within each county depending upon its quota. Several interesting votes deal with the

23. Apr. 20, 1784, Feb. 3, 1787. See also votes of Apr. 29, 1784, Apr. 8, 1785, and Apr. 4, 1787.
24. Nov. 2, 1784, Mar. 23, 1785, Apr. 26, 1786, and Jan. 27, Mar. 26, Apr. 2, 1787.

details of the assessment. On February 10, 1780, a motion to levy a tax on wrought plate carried, 19–18. The affirmative votes came particularly from the frontier, where few indeed would own such a luxury, from farmers, men of moderate or substantial property, localists, those of humble origin, and future Clintonians. Merchants, lawyers, large property owners, cosmopolitans, men of prominent family, high-ranking civil officials, and the anti-Clintonian group opposed the tax.[25] Another interesting vote exempted ministers from certain taxes. Two-thirds of the legislators approved this, but no correlation exists with any of the criteria being used here: the vote serves as a good example of a question that divided the delegates according to abstract opinion rather than according to some interest.[26]

The tax laws throughout the decade allowed payment in a mixture of media. Only one clear-cut vote exists on this matter. On February 26, 1785, a motion to bring in a bill enabling tax collectors to receive public securities of the state for arrears of taxes lost, 17–26. Theoretically one might expect support to come from the larger property owners and delegates from New York City, who held most of the securities. But upstate, rural counties, especially Dutchess, Ulster, and Orange, owed most of the taxes,[27] and the supervisors of Albany had petitioned the legislature for this relief. As a result the voting followed no set pattern.

The assembly failed to furnish votes on import taxes with one exception: a duty on molasses, cocoa, and sugar imported by foreigners on foreign vessels carried, 21–18. The variety of special interests involved in this assured a split vote by almost any criterion, and the only clear facts are that merchants and representatives from the towns liked the tax.[28]

The major debate on taxation came during the session of Feb-

25. A vote on a poll tax followed similar lines, but the division was less sharply drawn.

26. Over 80% of the known church members voted for the exemption, while less than half of the legislators did so (Feb. 6, 1783). A motion to reduce the tax on Quakers who refused to serve in the militia involved both attitudes toward loyalists and perhaps religion (Mar. 21, 1782). The alignment took a curious form in that the anti-Clintonians voted for the higher tax. The Quakers found friends among the farmers rather than the townspeople (except for the artisans), the smaller property owners, and localists.

27. See *N.-Y. Daily Adv.*, Jan. 22, 1788.

28. Apr. 21, 1785. The senate recorded an interesting vote on whether to raise the tax on goods sold at auction, the anti-Clintonians favoring this six to one, Clintonians opposing it one to nine. The issue at stake probably concerned not taxation but auctions, which merchants disliked because goods sold cheaply. The tax would raise the cost.

ruary-March 1787. Alexander Hamilton led the delegates from the New York City area in a general attack on the existing system. It was, he declared, arbitrary because the tax depended upon the assessors, who might discriminate against individuals (Robert R. Livingston, for one, was complaining bitterly).[29] The tax bill as drawn up to replace the quota system levied a land tax of a shilling per hundred acres on woodlots and 2d. per acre (16s. 8d. per hundred) on meadow, pasture, and arable land. Unimproved land, except that being used for wood, no longer would form part of the basis for assessment, whereas it had done so previously. A tax on houses began at 2s. per room for log houses, rose to 6s. for larger houses and even to 20s. if the ceiling was stucco. Other taxes would fall on storehouses, mills, carriages, taverns, male servants, marriage licenses, and plays. Ebenezer Purdy,[30] speaking for the rural legislators, objected to the tax on houses and land because it would tax country people more than city folk, and land thirty or forty miles from a river or market was taxed as heavily as more accessible property. He noted that, although a tax was imposed on mills, none fell on merchants' goods or ships. Hamilton defended the proposal, pointing to the tax on carriages, servants, and special rooms, and observing that merchants paid a duty on their ships.[31] The lower house took three roll-call votes. The first, on February 28, agreed to adopt the tax on buildings, 36–20, opposition coming from the central and northern counties. The decisive votes came on March 9, when a motion to defeat the clause taxing houses and lands lost, 24–27, but then the bill as a whole was defeated, 23–29, owing to a shift of two Dutchess County delegates, one from Queens, and one from Ulster, who had just voted to tax real estate. Three of these were among Clinton's most consistent supporters and may have deliberately voted for a clause that would defeat the bill. The old system of taxation by quota on counties therefore continued, and the delegates engaged in a free-for-all on March 22 that ended with the outnumbered southern counties suffering defeat.

On the last two votes the legislative party lines appear clearly.

29. Assembly Journal, Feb. 21, 1787; Livingston to Hamilton, Mar. 3, 1787, Harold C. Syrett and Jacob E. Cooke, eds., *The Papers of Alexander Hamilton* (New York, 1961–), IV, 103–104.

30. Purdy, a Westchester farmer of moderate property, served as major in the militia, voted consistently with the Clintonians (54–10), and became a Republican. His father, Abraham, seems to have been a small farmer. Josephine C. Frost, *The Strang Genealogy* (Brooklyn, N.Y., 1915), 40–41.

31. *N.-Y. Jour.*, Mar. 22, 1787; *N.-Y. Daily Adv.*, Mar. 9, 15, 1787.

The anti-Clintonians voted with few exceptions for the controversial clause and supported the bill as a whole, while the Clintonians suffered a few defections on the first vote but closed ranks on the second (81 percent). Farmers, especially those from more nearly subsistence areas, small property owners, and localists opposed the proposed change in the tax system while townspeople, merchants, lawyers, large property owners, and cosmopolitans favored the new plan. The most impressive correlation was along lines of wealth. In the end no change in the incidence of taxation took place.

Monetary policy and the relations between debtors and creditors became exceptionally important during the mid-eighties. The only votes on a stay law came earlier (April 3, 1782), when the legislature defeated a clause that would have stopped suits for prewar debts until an indefinite time after the war and also turned down a clause that would have made a delay effective even for suits already in the court. These found the delegates divided erratically. Beginning in 1784, however, the lower house debated a series of paper-money proposals resulting in over a dozen votes. The series started with a decision on April 3, 1784, to issue £150,000 in bills of credit, and another vote three days later that the money should be legal tender for debt when a court case was involved. The senate vetoed this measure. In the fall (October 28) a majority of the delegates agreed to bring in a bill to emit paper on loan, but the senate vetoed that too. The spring session brought votes to introduce a paper-money bill, to make it legal tender in all payments, even retroactively, public and private, to issue £100,000 rather than a lesser or greater sum, and to pass the bill.[32] The senate again refused its assent. Finally in February and March 1786, the paper-money advocates introduced a new bill that again required a series of votes concerning a legal-tender provision, the quantity, the interest rate and period for repayment, and various senate amendments reducing the amount and requiring other changes. Meanwhile the upper house recorded roll calls on the same question, the most important being the rejection of the 1785 act (April 19) and a series the following year on such questions as the legal-tender clause, the amount to be issued, and the interest rate.[33]

These votes show certain legislators, sharing particular characteristics, voting consistently for larger sums of paper that would be legal tender, loaned at a low interest rate and payable over a long

32. Mar. 7–8, 17–18, Apr. 8, 12, 1785.
33. Mar. 29–Apr. 1, 1786.

period. In both houses members of the Clintonian group favored every propaper motion almost unanimously (well over 90 percent), while the anti-Clintonians took the negative side by a nearly equal majority. A state loan of paper won the overwhelming support of the men from subsistence farm areas (over 90 percent), of farmers (about three-fourths), of artisans, manufacturers, and the like (four-fifths), of small property owners, militia officers, localists, and men of humble origin. On the other side were representatives from the cities and commercial farm areas, merchants, lawyers, and large landowners, wealthy and well-to-do delegates, Episcopalians, Continental army officers, and cosmopolitans. The alignment resembled in certain respects that depicted by "A Citizen of Dutchess County" who listed as antipaper the "importers, stockholders, speculators in cash, monied men and creditors," and as the propaper advocates "the shopkeepers in town, merchants in the country, manufacturers, and debtors of every denomination." The facts certainly substantiate his generalization that "interest is, and ever has been the predominant bias of man's actions," but one could add various categories to both sides of his list, not all of them economic.[34]

A few other votes also concerned the relations between debtors and creditors. The Clintonian group almost unanimously agreed to increase the number of cases concerning small debts that would be tried before a justice of the peace instead of a higher court.[35] This principle won the support of men from all sections except the towns, and while some delegates of every sort approved it the most nearly unanimous were small property owners, farmers, Presbyterians, and localists. An interesting vote approved (23–16) a clause that any prisoner for debt who could not support himself could apply for maintenance by the creditor and, if the creditor refused, then be released.[36] These debtors owed their freedom to most interior and frontier delegates, farmers, men of moderate property, Presbyterians, localists, and men of humble origin; Clintonians were nearly unanimous.[37]

34. *The Country Journal, and the Poughkeepsie Advertiser*, Feb. 23, 1786, reprinted in *N.Y. Packet*, Mar. 6, 1786, and *Am. Herald* (Boston), Mar. 20, 1786.

35. Mar. 14, 28, 1787.

36. Apr. 26, 1786.

37. The situation of distressed debtors awakened the humanitarian sympathies of some legislators the next year when, after adjournment, John Lansing read a list of prisoners confined for debt, 10 of whom had debts totaling £24. All of the members contributed a day's pay, which released the prisoners. *N.-Y. Daily Adv.*, Mar. 26, 1787.

New York's lower house recorded only a few votes concerning the spending of money. The governor's salary constituted a special case because of Clinton's popularity. Thus a reduction in 1782 from £2,000 to £1,500, insisted upon by the senate, succeeded because every attending member of the presently emerging anti-Clinton bloc voted for the lower figure, while the governor's supporters could not remain entirely united. A year later the assembly voted a further cut to £1,200, again due primarily to Clinton's political critics.[38]

The per diem that the legislators granted to themselves also was a special case. This question arose during several sessions beginning in 1780, when they established the rate of 12s.[39] Four years later the delegates treated themselves to a 4s. raise.[40] In 1786, however, they first returned the rate to 12s., then presently compromised at 14s., and when the senate tried to reduce the per diem the assembly voted to retain its own figure.[41] Finally a year later a new effort to raise the per diem to 16s. failed and 14s. again succeeded.[42] Meanwhile the senate also recorded several votes on the question.[43] The alignment on all of these votes followed a consistent pattern. The anti-Clintonians steadily favored the lower rate by a majority ranging from two to one to ten to one, while the Clintonians almost as determinedly supported the higher pay. Farmers and men such as artisans and innkeepers were most apt to vote for a raise, lawyers the least. The great majority of delegates from subsistence farm and frontier areas wanted more money, as did the smaller property owners. The more educated men, those from commercial farm and urban areas, and delegates with more wealth, accepted less reward for their time. The evidence suggests that the legislators responded both to their own interests and attitudes and to the presumed desires of their constituents.

The alignment on the other expenditures was entirely different. Higher salaries for judges received the assent of the anti-Clintonians, almost all townsmen, delegates from commercial farm

38. Apr. 8–13, 1782, Feb. 21, 1783. This time the senate came to the governor's aid.

39. Oct. 6. The vote was 20–15. There is no direct evidence whether the advocates favored the figure because it was high or because it was low, but since all known members of the anti-Clinton group voted con, while 5 of 8 known Clintonians pro, the per diem was probably high. See also a vote on Oct. 28, 1779, on which the alignment is clear.

40. Nov. 23, 1784.

41. Mar. 30, Apr. 17, May 1, 1786.

42. Apr. 6–7, 1787.

43. May 6, 1784, Apr. 17, 1787, Mar. 20, 1788.

areas, merchants, lawyers, large landowners, wealthy and well-to-do representatives, those with education, and cosmopolitans. The rest of the legislators opposed such rewards to the judiciary, though with less cohesiveness.[44] The judges' earnings in New York had been quite low, perhaps because of the state's financial problems, but probably also because the dominant group in the assembly preferred it that way. Egbert Benson, an eminent lawyer and attorney general, felt that the judicial salaries were "incompetent." Writing before the war ended, he hoped that when the southern counties were regained, "wealth and a liberal spirit" would produce more adequate allowances.[45] The division did in fact follow sectional lines, correlating also with wealth and probably with Benson's "liberal spirit."

The legislators voted similarly on salaries of other government employees. These included the per diem for the auditor's clerk, the auditor's own salary, a payment to the attorney general for his services, the salary of the collector of New York port and his aides, the chancellor's salary, the auditor's travel expenses, and the grant of two large tracts for services rendered during the war.[46] Payments to the attorney general and the port officials do not conform to the general alignment, which varied with the issue. Especially interesting because it involved the general principle of government costs was the vote to reduce all salaries by one-sixth, which failed, 19–29.[47] The original, higher rate attracted the support of all the delegates from towns, from lawyers, merchants, large landowners, wealthy and well-to-do delegates, cosmopolitans, and anti-Clintonians. Rural legislators, smaller property owners, and the Clinton bloc favored the reduction.

A somewhat different question involved the establishment of permanent salaries for judges, which the legislature rejected.[48] This divided the legislators more sharply than did most preceding votes, the alignment taking the same form as that just described, the rural-urban and party divisions being particularly clear.

---

44. Feb. 21, 1783, Apr. 9, 1787. See senate votes, Mar. 10, 1779, Mar. 24–25, 1783, Apr. 17, 1787.

45. To John Jay, Oct. 27, 1781, Johnston, ed., *Papers of Jay*, II, 139. Morris thought his enemies in the legislature were trying to drive him off the bench. Judges, he felt, should earn enough to guarantee their independence and integrity. To. R. R. Livingston, Apr. 8, 1788, R. R. Livingston Papers, Box 4, N.-Y. Hist. Soc.

46. Nov. 1, 1781, Mar. 1, 1782, May 7, 1784, Nov. 16, 23–24, 1784, Apr. 6, 1787, and Mar. 13–15, 21, 1788.

47. Feb. 29, 1788.

48. Mar. 7, 1788.

Various other economic issues required votes. An import duty on butter obtained the support of country legislators, especially those who owned farms and small estates; townspeople opposed it.[49] A higher price for the state's land appealed to men most distant from it and best able to afford the cost if they wished to buy; the anti-Clintonians favored it but the Clinton group opposed.[50] Another vote, which lost, 14–22, concerned the question of whether to allow certain rights to squatters on land that had been sold but not cultivated (March 28, 1785). The division pitted the anti-Clintonians against the Clintonians, the townsmen against the most rural delegates, and the largest against the smallest property owners, but cultural factors seem not to have affected the voting except that Episcopalians opposed the squatters' rights while Presbyterians defended them.

Several votes suggest a pro- or antibusiness bias among the legislators. One dealt with a clause that required a particularly heavy bond and other restrictions on reexported goods when the import duty was deducted.[51] Another denied a petition for the remission of duties on the cargo of a foreign vessel.[52] In 1787 the legislature refused to exclude owners of privateers or vessels of war from the legislature, and later in the session it denied a plea from New York merchants that they receive some relief for their prewar debts.[53] On all of these the representatives from towns and from commercial farm districts, with nonfarm occupations, large property, and cosmopolitan tastes, together with members of prominent old families, composed the probusiness bloc, the two groups voting with a consistency of over 80 percent. Somewhat different was a bill to encourage the manufacture of pantile, which the legislature narrowly approved.[54] The lines here were in many respects blurred, though the anti-Clintonians favored the act while the Clintonians disapproved it, and a wide gap appeared between cosmopolitans who voted pro and localists who voted con. A pro- or antiurban bias seems evident in a senate vote in which the anti-Clinton bloc defeated a clause placing the burden of proof on anyone accused of trading with the enemy, the two sides voting almost unanimously (June 21, 1780).

49. Feb. 25, 1784.
50. Feb. 17–18, 1784.
51. Nov. 5, 1784.
52. Nov. 12, 1784.
53. Feb. 6, Apr. 5, 1787. See *N.-Y. Jour.*, Apr. 19, 1787, for a brief account of this. A senate vote of Apr. 19, 1785, seems related.
54. Apr. 16, 1787. Pantile is a type of roofing tile.

The handling of the public debt never became an issue in New York as it did in Massachusetts, except in relation to the federal debt. During the war years the state was concerned with spending rather than saving, and from 1780 on, at least, the legislature recorded no important votes on the question. Perhaps an exception was an attempt to defeat a clause that provided that certain tax money, if not needed to meet Congress's requisition, should be paid for interest on state loan office certificates and liquidated debts owed by Congress to citizens of the state. The future Clintonians opposed this proposal almost unanimously, while their political opponents stood just as firmly on the other side. Probably the Clinton group preferred to use the money for payments on the state debt.[55]

After the British evacuated New York, a profitable, noncontroversial tariff raised a good deal of money, and as we saw earlier, the Clintonians happily imposed half of the property tax on the southern counties. This money, together with the sale of some confiscated estates, put the state's finances into reasonably good condition—or would have done so had the central and northern counties paid their quotas. No votes cast further light on this question. One on whether tax collectors should receive state securities for taxes divided the legislators irregularly.[56] Another vote defeated a motion to accept various federal certificates for payment of money owed for confiscated estates.[57] Clintonians opposed this unanimously, but of course it concerned the federal rather than the state debt.

Although the Clintonians showed no reluctance to pay the state's creditors, once they adjusted the tax system to their satisfaction, payment of the federal debt created a different attitude. Immediately following the vote just mentioned, the lower house rejected a senate amendment to a tax bill that would have raised £100,000 for interest on Continental securities.[58] This question separated the legislature into its opposing blocs with only a couple of exceptions and confronted townsmen with rural legislators, large property owners with small. This repeated an alignment of three years before (February 7, 1783), when a motion to comply with Congress's requisition had passed, but the division had been less sharp then.

55. Feb. 13, 1783. Thomas C. Cochran, *New York in the Confederation: An Economic Study* (Philadelphia, 1932), contains a good account of financial affairs.
56. Feb. 26, 1785. Continental army officers were more enthusiastic than any other group.
57. Apr. 10, 1786. See also senate vote of Apr. 20, 1784.
58. Apr. 27, 1786.

In the meantime the 5 percent impost had developed as the crucial issue.

When Congress first proposed the impost, the outcome of the war remained doubtful, and the British occupied New York City. The state therefore acceded promptly. By 1783 the situation had changed in every respect, and New York was preparing her own financial arrangements based partly upon import taxes. Thereafter she had every selfish economic reason to reject the grant to Congress; the wonder is that so many legislators approved it. But the issue, as previously noted, involved not simply the payment of the debt, but who should collect and disburse the money: it concerned power as well as cash. And the New York legislature contained men who would willingly grant power, while others strongly opposed this. As a result the impost dispute emerged as an important political contest, well documented in the press.[59]

A series of votes in the assembly during 1786 and 1787 reveals the nature of the alignment. The votes concerned whether the collectors should be appointed by Congress and the money paid to that body and the general question of whether the power should be granted at all.[60] On all of them the ballot followed nearly straight party lines. Delegates from towns almost unanimously supported the grant, and opposition increased in proportion to distance from the urban centers. Merchants favored the impost but farmers did not; large property owners, cosmopolitans, and Continental officers voted for it while localists, small property owners, and militia officers voted against.

A similar shift by the Clintonian supporters from full cooperation with Congress to independence of it can be followed in other instances. When in 1784 Congress failed to provide for garrisoning the state's western posts, the anti-Clinton bloc voted to proceed without further delay, whereas the Clintonians did not want to act independently of Congress.[61] But already the latter were becoming suspicious of Congress's authority. Earlier in the year Abraham Yates, a Clintonian, had introduced into the senate a motion to abolish the office of the Continental receiver of taxes in New York, vesting its functions in state officials. Philip Schuyler then moved that Congress's collector receive a permanent salary; this carried on February 24, with the vote following party lines.

59. Main, *Antifederalists*, 97–99; Spaulding, *New York*, 174–180; Cochran, *New York in the Confederation*, 167–176.
60. Apr. 13, 15, 1786, Feb. 15, 1787.
61. Apr. 2, 1784.

When Congress decided that Vermont should be granted her in-dependence, New York agreed because the anti-Clintonians almost unanimously accepted the decision whereas the Clinton group strongly opposed it.[62]

The issue of federal-state relations reached its climax with the struggle over ratification. Beginning with the senate vote on a resolution instructing New York's delegates in Congress to recom-mend a convention for revising the Articles (February 20, 1787), the two blocs opposed each other almost unanimously in both houses. The Clintonians sent two future Antifederalists (for the moment neutrals on the political scale) to join Hamilton at the Federal Convention and defeated Hamilton's resolution to send additional delegates.[63] The following winter William Floyd, a neu-tral, replaced Hamilton in Congress.[64] Votes on these questions pitted the two parties decisively against each other, dividing urban from rural legislators; merchants, lawyers, and large landowners from the lesser nonfarm and farm delegates; and the educated, cul-tured cosmopolitans from the provincials. In January 1788 the legislature, in an identical alignment, defeated an Antifederalist attempt to preface the call for a ratifying convention with a clause critical of the proposed constitution. Finally, the Clintonians fur-nished 18 votes against ratification and 4 in favor (of which 2 originally were Antifederal), while their opponents supported rati-fication by 13 to 4.[65]

A few other votes that revealed the differences between the two parties deserve mention. The location of the capital naturally split the legislature sectionally, with the southern delegates favoring New York City, and the others preferring Kingston or Pough-keepsie.[66] The delegates also divided according to wealth (though not by occupation). The anti-Clinton group agreed to a petition of a citizen to sell goods deposited by him under the act prohibit-ing illicit trade with the enemy, while their opposites rejected it.[67] The Clintonians refused to grant land to certain prewar claimants (March 16, 1785). An effort to expel the Clintonian Ephraim Paine

62. The vote also pitted townspeople against the rural delegates, wealthy and well-to-do men against men with less property, educated and cosmopolitan rep-resentatives against their opposites. Mar. 28, Apr. 11, 1787.

63. Apr. 16, 1787.

64. Jan. 22, 1788.

65. Later 7 Clintonians became Republicans, one a Federalist, while 20 members of the anti-Clinton group became Federalists and 12 were Republicans.

66. See Apr. 27, 1785, Apr. 21, 1787.

67. Feb. 13, 1783.

because he was a minister failed because his party supported him (March 5, 1784). For some reason most Clintonians did not want Samuel Loudon to become the state printer, but their political opponents got him the job by a solid vote (February 11, 1785). Payment of legislators by the state treasury instead of by each county won only the Clintonians' assent; both groups voted almost unanimously (March 30, 1786). No doubt the advocates felt their pay would be much more secure. The Clintonians naturally defended the governor's refusal to call the legislature into special session after Congress had received news of the impost's rejection and had requested reconsideration (January 9, 1787). Finally, the Clinton bloc voted to reject a bill for repairing the highways of Kings County (March 6, 1788).

Several interesting cultural questions forced the legislature to record its opinions.[68] A clause encouraging the use of the state land for founding colleges was rejected, 23–19, because the Clintonians strongly opposed it. Support came from towns and commercial farms, lawyers and large landowners (but not merchants), large property owners, Episcopalians, and cosmopolitans. Against it were notably men from noncommercial farm areas and the frontier, farmers, men in trade, smaller property owners, localists, and men of humble origin.[69] On another occasion the Council of Revision vetoed an act incorporating a society for encouraging and assisting German immigrants, on the ground that the state should not encourage foreigners, and the assembly failed to override the veto in a tie vote.[70] The two parties divided evenly, and no significant correlation exists between the vote and most characteristics of the legislators. Merchants, however, wanted to override the veto, lawyers to uphold it. Men of Dutch descent generally and all known members of the Dutch Reformed Church favored the immigrants, while the English divided equally, except those from New England, who took the anti-German side. A quite different issue also found the legislators dividing erratically. The house voted, 24–22, to retain the death penalty for stealing from a church.[71] The most sympathetic toward criminals were farmers, men of moderate property, and Presbyterians; least forgiving were merchants and lawyers, wealthy men, and Episcopalians.

68. A clause fining anyone £10 for performing in a play seems to have presented no clear-cut issue, for men voted erratically (Apr. 29, 1786).
69. Mar. 31, 1787.
70. Apr. 20–22, 1785.
71. Jan. 29, 1788.

Finally, the legislature recorded an extremely interesting series of votes on the rights of Negroes. The specific questions concerned the rapidity with which emancipation should proceed, whether Negroes could testify in court against whites, and whether they could vote, hold office, and marry a white without being fined. The delegates voted twice on the general bill, once when the Council of Revision vetoed the measure.[72] Unfortunately all of these votes occurred in the same session so that fewer than fifty men are on record. The alignment remained much the same throughout, and the series can be treated as a unit (see table 5.2).

Table 5.2. Correlation of Slaveholding and Votes on Negro Rights

No. Slaves Owned	For Negro Rights	Against Negro Rights
Over 10	0	3
4–9	3	5
1–3	10	10
None	12	2

The delegates most unfriendly to the Negroes were large slaveowners, while those most favorable held none. With some exceptions, the wealthiest men proved least sympathetic, and the poorest, most so. Geographically, those favorable to civil rights came from the frontier and to a lesser extent from noncommercial farm areas, those unfavorable from commercial farms, while townspeople divided. None of the religious groups distinguished themselves, the Dutch Reformed Church being most anti-Negro, as were the Dutch generally, while former New Englanders always took the side of the blacks. Educated men opposed Negro rights more than those without learning, and on every vote the localists outshone the cosmopolitans. Social origin evidently meant little, as did military and political experience. Finally, although this was not a "party" issue, the Clintonians sided with the Negroes by a ratio, on the average, of 62 percent, while their opponents scored 41 percent.[73]

72. Feb. 26, Mar. 1–3, 9, 26, 1785. The council vetoed it ostensibly because it deprived the Negroes of civil rights, but the legislators who upheld the veto had shown themselves to be anti-Negro on previous votes.

73. Since neutrals voted for the Negroes only 37% of the time, these party figures probably lack significance. Too few men voted for certainty, and more-

Although the legislators of New York agreed with one another on many vital issues of the period, especially during the war, they divided into two major groups that opposed each other on a variety of important questions. During the sessions between the spring of 1784 and the spring of 1788, one set of legislators cast, on two-thirds of the roll calls recorded, over 80 percent of their votes as a bloc, while another set adhered to the opposite side with equal consistency. Only about a fourth of the delegates remained neutral in their voting. Each of these groups contained a score of men who opposed one another on almost every vote (see appendix). One became associated with the policies of, or implemented under, Governor Clinton. These people, mostly farmers or representatives of agricultural districts in the middle and northern counties, became antiloyalists, obtained and kept a tax system favorable to themselves, supported the interest of debtors and strove for legal-tender paper money, usually voted for lower salaries except if a reduction threatened their own per diem or the governor's income, opposed permanent salaries for judges, preferred a low price for vacant land, tended to demonstrate an antibusiness or antiurban bias, opposed an increase of federal power beginning about 1785, and favored a northern location for the capital. Their political opponents took the opposite position on these, as well as on minor matters (see table 5.3).

The two legislative parties, Clintonians and anti-Clintonians, varied in their attitudes toward important issues because they contained different sorts of people, dissimilar economically, socially, and culturally as well as politically. Sectionally, the contrast between the southern counties on one side and the central and northern on the other, is striking, but the division by the residence of the delegates went beyond mere north and south: Albany and other towns lay well upstream from New York City, yet their representatives voted on the same side (see map, p. 146). The towns formed the core of the anti-Clinton bloc. Among New York City delegates, twenty-eight (71.8 percent) voted with that group, eleven were neutral, and none allied with the Clintonians, while those from Albany and the lesser towns also either voted with the anti-Clintonians (one-third) or were neutral (all the rest). Legislators who lived on farms near these trading centers joined them (38.9 percent) or remained neutral (55.6 percent), with a single

---

over on an earlier occasion the pro-Clinton delegates had opposed a bill freeing Indians and Negroes who enlisted in the Continental army (Feb. 25, 1780).

Table 5.3. Illustrative Votes, New York (in Percentages)

						Votes								
	1	2	3	4	5	6	7	8	9	10	11	12	13	14
All delegates	52	65	57	33	38	42	45	40	59	51	44	51	46	60
Legislative party														
Clintonian	20	42	18	8	0	4	0	6	39	6	18	5	22	37
Neutral	47	69	75	31	33	50	80	13	74	68	29	67	50	55
Anti-Clintonian	71	80	100	70	77	96	100	89	81	75	82	79	80	89
Residence														
Frontier	0	50	50	0	0	0	0	0	17	0	25	0	33	100
Noncommercial farm	50	56	29	22	0	14	7	0	35	37	36	28	20	60
Commercial farm	56	50	67	31	79	67	71	65	81	45	25	65	63	38
Town	56	83	100	71	44	89	100	78	75	100	100	83	63	100
Occupation														
Farmer	23	56	43	15	22	19	23	27	41	32	20	30	28	52
Large landowner	50	50	100	0	0	—	100	0	67	80	60	100	100	67
Misc. nonfarmer	50	100	25	38	33	0	0	0	40	40	22	44	57	17
Lawyer	100	67	67	—	100	100	100	50	100	55	63	67	80	100
Merchant or trader	75	60	83	67	58	70	80	82	78	75	78	60	33	71

Economic status

	1	2	3	4	5	6	7	8	9	10	11	12	13	14
Moderate	30	45	30	9	0	6	13	0	17	37	24	22	36	57
Substantial	0	40	25	50	33	0	40	25	60	14	17	50	0	38
Wealthy or well-to-do	75	90	88	36	56	78	71	82	88	82	65	71	69	61

World view

	1	2	3	4	5	6	7	8	9	10	11	12	13	14
Localist	29	67	39	18	29	22	16	32	49	39	16	33	31	45
Cosmopolitan	80	57	86	63	47	75	80	53	63	78	55	57	63	72

NOTE: The position taken by members of the anti-Clinton bloc establishes the norm. All figures are rounded percentages.

CODE OF VOTES:

1. Against tax on wrought plate, Feb. 10, 1780.
2. For lower governor's salary, Feb. 21, 1783.
3. For higher judges' salaries, Feb. 21, 1783.
4. For higher price on vacant land, Feb. 17, 1784.
5. Pro-Waddington, case of *Rutgers* v. *Waddington*, Nov. 2, 1784.
6. Against paper-money bill, Mar. 7, 1785.
7. Against legal-tender provision, Mar. 17, 1785.
8. For repeal of act requiring lawyers to produce a certificate of loyalty, Mar. 23, 1785.
9. For lower delegates' per diem, Mar. 30, 1786.
10. For 5% impost, Feb. 15, 1787.
11. For reform tax bill, Mar. 9, 1787.
12. Against trial of small debts before justice of the peace, Mar. 28, 1787.
13. For college land grants, Mar. 31, 1787.
14. Against general reduction of salaries, Feb. 29, 1788.

Approximate Residences of Legislators, New York

To Washington

MONTGOMERY

VERMONT

ALBANY

ALBANY

MASSACHUSETTS

COLUMBIA

ULSTER

Hudson River

DUTCHESS

CONNECTICUT

ORANGE

NEW JERSEY

WESTCHESTER

New York City

SUFFOLK

KINGS

QUEENS

RICHMOND

■ Anti-Clintonians
○ Clintonians
• Neutrals

exception. Commercial farmers farther away from the city voted similarly, but the margin narrowed (36.1 to 19.7 percent with 44.3 percent neutral), while delegates probably living in a semisubsistence farming area cast nearly half of their votes with the Clintonians, most of the rest being neutral. One out of three frontier representatives sided with the Clinton bloc, and the rest were unaligned. Put differently, the Clintonian group consisted of the following elements: from towns, none; from commercial farms, 25.5 percent; from subsistence farms, 52.9 percent; and from the frontier, 21.6 percent. Among anti-Clintonians, 49.3 percent lived in towns, 40.9 percent in commercial farm areas, and 9.9 percent in subsistence farm regions.

The division by occupation reinforces and adds detail to the analysis by residence. Farmers supplied about three-fifths of the Clintonians' members, the rest being almost entirely artisans and lesser tradesmen. Although 90 percent of the farmers either favored that party or were neutral, all large landowners belonged to the neutrals or to the anti-Clinton bloc. All of the lawyers and all but one of the merchants voted with the anti-Clintonians or were neutral. Doctors behaved the same way. The rest of the delegates who were not farmers—artisans, manufacturers, innkeepers, storekeepers, and the like—divided almost equally, with a slight preference for the Clintonians. The anti-Clintonians consisted primarily of men other than farmers, notably men in trade (over one-third) and professionals (another third). A few large landowners and a handful of farmers made up a minor agrarian wing comprising about 30 percent of the total.

Since there is a close relationship between where a man resided and his occupation, the question arises of whether these factors are independent variables or whether they are aspects of the same factor: that is, did men with a nonfarm occupation prefer the anti-Clintonians regardless of where they lived? This can be tested by examining the alignment in the farm areas. In these the anti-Clinton group attracted 26 percent of the vote, and their opponents, 45 percent. Of the nonfarm delegates, however, 50 percent supported the anti-Clintonians against 27 percent for the Clintonians. Thus occupation seems to be a variable independent of residence.

Another clear difference between the two parties was their relative wealth. Wealthy men either voted with the anti-Clintonians (65.6 percent) or were neutral (31.3 percent), only one person excepted out of thirty-two. Well-to-do legislators voted similarly but less unanimously: for the anti-Clintonians, 35.7 percent; neutral, 53.6 percent; and Clintonians, 10.7 percent, six persons out of fifty-six. On the other hand, delegates of substantial property favored the latter, 25 to 10 percent, while the rest were neutral. Those with less wealth voted even more decisively, 47 percent for the Clintonians, 12 percent on the other side, and the rest neutral. Expressed differently, the Clintonian group contained these elements, excluding those whose economic status remains unknown: wealthy, 2.2 percent; well-to-do, 13.3 percent; substantial, 22.2 percent; and moderate, 62.2 percent. The anti-Clintonian bloc consisted of: wealthy, 40.4 percent; well-to-do, 38.5 percent; substantial, 7.7 percent; and moderate, 13.5 percent. Analysis reveals that wealth was a variable independent of residence, for men of large property voted more frequently with the anti-Clintonians than did other delegates from their own counties, while men of moderate means supported the Clintonians more often than one would anticipate (see table 5.4).

Table 5.4. Party Preference in New York: Economic Status in Relation to Residence (in Percentages)

Party Divisions in Two Residential Groups	Economic Status		
	General	Well-to-do or Wealthy	Moderate
Noncommercial farm			
Clintonian	45.8	16.0	54.6
Neutral	42.4	44.0	36.4
Anti-Clintonian	11.9	40.0	9.1
Commercial farm			
Clintonian	19.7	11.1	50.0
Neutral	44.3	40.7	37.5
Anti-Clintonian	36.1	48.2	12.5

These economic contrasts go far toward illuminating the characteristics of the two parties. They also differed in religious composition, in that almost all of the Episcopalians favored the anti-Clinton group. However, members of other religious groups showed no preference. The national origin of the legislators does not seem important. The Clintonian bloc contained the following: English, 27.3 percent; Dutch, 21.6 percent; New England immigrants, 19.6 percent; other non-English, 7.8 percent; and unknown, 23.5 percent. The other group consisted of English, 40.9 percent;

Dutch, 28.2 percent; New England immigrants, 1.4 percent; other non-English, 7.0 percent; and unknown, 22.7 percent. Those born in New England settled along the frontier, which probably accounts for their political behavior. As the following percentages show, age seems to have made little difference:

	Under 40	40–49	50 and Over	Total
Clintonians	37.5	43.8	18.7	100.0
Anti-Clintonians	41.4	32.8	25.8	100.0

Men of education almost never belonged to the Clintonians. It is true that the legislature contained only a few such delegates, but their unanimity probably had some influence. Delegates known to demonstrate some intellectual interests preferred the anti-Clintonians almost as decisively, but they too were few in number. The division between cosmopolitans and localists was significant: the former supported the anti-Clintonians by a ratio of six to one, while the latter took the other side by a margin of five to two. The cultural attitude that these words connote is closely connected with residence, and the New York data do not indicate whether they are identical.

Military experience probably played a minor role except on particular issues. Continental army officers appeared on both sides, but favored the anti-Clintonians. On the other hand, half of the Clintonians had served as militia officers, while only one-eighth of their opponents had done so. Civil officials belonged to the anti-Clintonian bloc if they had held some Continental post or a high state office, but lesser officials took the other side.

The parties differed considerably in their social orgin. All of the legislators who came from prominent families either voted with the anti-Clintonian or the neutral group. The same held true for those of above-average status, but those of lower rank—especially the immigrants—preferred the Clintonians. So did the sons of farmers and of small property owners, but delegates whose fathers had not been farmers favored the anti-Clintonians by a margin of over three to one.

These characteristics create a composite description of the two sides. The anti-Clintonians drew their support from New York City, Albany, the other towns, and commercial farm areas, especially in the south. They usually engaged in trade or the professions, owned property worth £2,000 or more, came from families of above-average social rank, often held a high civil or military post, and tended to have a cosmopolitan outlook. Their opponents lived in semisubsistence farm areas in central or northern New York, were farmers themselves, owned small estates, came from ordinary or humble homes, seldom held high office, rarely obtained an education, and were parochial in their view of the world.[74]

The contest within the legislature reverberated outside. Although the modern political party lay in the future, its seeds can easily be seen in the acrimonious disputes of the eighties. New Yorkers had long been accustomed to parties of the factional species and to active electioneering. The struggle between loyalists and rebels educated them further, and the divisions during the 1780s added a new excitement. Even before the war ended, newspapers had published "tickets" and citizens worked for their favorites; John Lansing wrote humorously that "the Air becomes infected when a

74. The senate's parties shared identical features, as this table shows:

Composition of Legislative Parties in New York Senate

	Clintonians	Neutrals	Anti-Clintonians
Occupation			
Farmer	11	3	1
Large landowner	2	2	4
Misc. nonfarmer	4	0	1
Lawyer	3	0	7
Merchant	1	1	7
Economic status			
Poor or moderate	10	2	0
Well-to-do	7	1	9
Wealthy	4	3	11
World view			
Localist	10	3	1
Cosmopolitan	7	1	15
Uncertain	4	2	4
Social origin			
Humble origin	13	2	3
Average family	7	3	7
Prominent old family	1	1	10
Vote on ratification			
Antifederalist	14	0	3
Federalist	0	2	10

number of politicians assemble."[75] When the British evacuated New York, elections could be held in the city for the first time since the occupation. A committee of artisans published a slate that included the wartime popular heroes (such as Lamb, Willett, Sears, and Malcolm) and that contained a mixture of artisans and self-made merchants. A meeting of "Whig Inhabitants" presented a list that overlapped but incorporated three merchants, of whom two represented the prewar elite. Robert R. Livingston described the state's "parties" (as he called them) as consisting, on the one side, of violent whigs who wanted to expel all tories in hope of retaining power and, on the other, of men who wished to avoid violence, soften the laws against loyalists and not banish them, yet who did not want to shock people's feelings by destroying at once all distinctions between them and the "royalists."[76]

The following spring New York City's voters again had a choice. A group of "real whigs" nominated a slate similar to that put forward by the mechanics in December, including Sears, Stagg, Malcolm, and Dr. Isaac Ledyard, to which the Sons of Liberty agreed. A list recommended by "respectable inhabitants" contained no duplicates, but a mixture of wealthy merchants and lawyers. This ticket succeeded; as R. R. Livingston put it, the outcome was what one would expect "when one of the parties were so jealous of power as to endeavour to exclude property and abilities from the weight that they must and will have in every society." Apparently the other counties held quiet elections at this period.[77]

The upstate calm broke during the 1785 elections. Both Hamilton and Schuyler expressed alarm at the legislature's activities. Schuyler blamed it all on Clinton (an old antagonist) who, he asserted, sought popularity at the expense of good government. Hamilton feared for the *"security of property"* and urged the choice of men whose principles were "not of the *levelling kind*." He attributed the situation to a "junto" headed by Ford and

75. To Richard Varick, Poughkeepsie, Sept. 5, 1780, Richard Varick Papers, N.-Y. Hist. Soc.; *N.-Y. Packet* (Fishkill), Apr. 19, 1781, Apr. 4, 1782; Gouverneur Morris to R. R. Livingston, Philadelphia, Sept. 22, 1788, and Livingston to G. Morris, June 20, 1781, R. R. Livingston Papers, Box 6, N.-Y. Hist. Soc.

76. R. R. Livingston to John Jay, Jan. 25, 1784, Johnston, ed., *Papers of Jay*, III, 108; *Indep. Jour.* (New York), Dec. 22, 29, 1783, Jan. 1, 3, 7, 1784. Some upstate politicking appears in the R. R. Livingston Papers; also see Peter W. Yates to Richard Varick, June 21, 1783, Richard Varick Papers, N.-Y. Hist. Soc.

77. *N.-Y. Jour.*, Apr. 22, 29, 1784; *Indep. Jour.*, May 1, 1784; Livingston to Charles DeWitt, May 9, 1784, R. R. Livingston Papers, Box 13, N.-Y. Hist. Soc.

Adgate (both prominent leaders of the Clintonians, the latter especially voting with remarkable consistency), which was trying "to
subvert the constitution and destroy the rights of private property."[78] From the north Henry Livingston reported that his county
"never had such a hard tryal since the Revolution between Demo-
[cracy] and Aristo[cracy], as it will have this Election all parties
are alive, Letters and Lists contending [*illegible*] and every Sub-
terfuge invented by both Parties."[79] Determined efforts by the
Livingstons, Van Rensselaers, Schuylers, and "other Gentm. of
property" resulted in a major victory in Albany County, where
both Adgate and Ford lost, giving way to John Livingston, John
Tayler, an Albany merchant and friend of the Livingstons', and
other Albany businessmen.[80] New York City experienced another
hot election in which (after the newspapers had confused the issue
by publishing various tickets) the mechanics produced one slate,
and the "respectable Whig citizens" another. The two overlapped,
but the former succeeded in the conflicting cases.[81]

In 1786 New York City voters again chose between tickets offered by some "respectable inhabitants" and by mechanics. The
latter incorporated a few nominees of the former, but left out the
lawyers Richard Varick, Hamilton, and the wealthy merchant
Nicholas Bayard (all of whom won).[82] The outcome perhaps was
influenced by newspaper articles that warned against choosing mechanics, who themselves could not frame good laws and could not
be relied upon to elect "gentlemen of education and abilities."[83]
Meanwhile in Dutchess County, evidently for the first time, the
local newspaper printed a Clintonian ticket including many of the
party's most extreme members (such as Brinton Paine, Henry
Ludenton, and Lewis Duboys). This succeeded despite a criticism
that the practice was "contrary to all rules of modesty, of sound

78. Schuyler to Jay, May 30, 1785, Johnston, ed., *Papers of Jay*, III, 151; Hamilton to Robert Livingston, Apr. 25, 1785, and to William Duer, May 14, 1785,
Syrett and Cooke, eds., *Hamilton Papers*, III, 609, 611.

79. To Walter Livingston, Apr. 24, 1785, R. R. Livingston Papers, Box 14,
N.-Y. Hist. Soc.

80. Robert Livingston to Hamilton, June 13, 1785, Syrett and Cooke, eds.,
Hamilton Papers, III, 615. For the politicking, John Livingston to John Tayler,
Apr. 24, 1785, John Tayler Papers, N.-Y. Hist. Soc.

81. *N.Y. Packet*, Mar 31, Apr. 4, 7, 14, 18, 21, 25, 1785; *The New-York
Gazetteer, and the Country Journal*, Apr. 22, 26, 1785.

82. *N.Y. Packet*, Apr. 3, 17, 22, 24, 1786; *N.-Y. Daily Adv.*, Apr. 15, 1786;
Indep. Jour. (New York), Apr. 22, 26, 1786; *Country Jour.* (New York), Apr. 25,
1786.

83. *N.-Y. Daily Adv.*, Apr. 1, 15, 1786.

policy, and of wisdom."[84] In the north the Lansing and Yates families took the lead in publicizing nominations and getting out the Clintonian vote, appealing, as one put it, to "the far better part of our Society, the Yeomanry of the County." They held their own in Montgomery, but lost in Albany.[85]

Electioneering continued in the spring of 1787. In New York City the mercantile paper published a merchant-lawyer slate, presently countered by a somewhat similar one drawn up at a joint meeting of committees chosen by mechanics and "respectable inhabitants," clearly a mechanic's ticket.[86] In Kings County an unsuccessful effort was made to dislodge Cornelius Wyckoff because he lacked "property or connections of any consequence" and had voted to abolish slavery.[87] In Columbia County delegates from almost every district met at Claverack and recommended one slate that the Livingstons did not approve. A subsequent meeting put forward a somewhat different group, which won (with a Livingston substituted for one candidate).[88] Robert R. Livingston himself intervened in the Dutchess County campaign and accurately predicted that five of the incumbents—all strong Clintonians—would be beaten by the efforts of "most of the leading people at this end" of the county.[89] Competing tickets also appeared in Albany and Montgomery counties.[90]

Perhaps most New Yorkers felt obliged to agree with the observation that "party is the madness of many, for the gain of a few."[91] Certainly parties in any formal sense had not yet become

84. *Country Jour.* (New York), Apr. 20, 27, 1786. An article later defended the method because the electoral district was so large that candidates could not make themselves known otherwise. *Ibid.*, May 11.

85. Abraham G. Lansing to Hendrick Gardinier, Albany, Apr. 19, 1786, Abraham Yates, Jr., Papers, #177, N.Y. Pub. Lib.; announcement of Apr. 11, 1786, in Peter W. Yates Misc. Papers, N.-Y. Hist. Soc.; R. R. Livingston to Robert Livingston, Oct. 3, 1786, R. R. Livingston Papers, Box 15, N.-Y. Hist. Soc.; John Tayler to Leonard Gansevoort, Mar. 29, 1786, L. Gansevoort Papers, Rutgers Univ. Lib.; John Myers to James Duane, Duanesburgh, May 1, 1786, Duane Papers, N.-Y. Hist. Soc.; "A Freeholder," *To the Public. I was Sorry to Observe. . . . April 21, 1786* (Albany, 1786).

86. *N.-Y. Daily Adv.,* Apr. 20, 23, 1787; *N.Y. Packet,* Apr. 24, 1787; *Indep. Jour.* (New York), Apr. 11, 1787.

87. *N.Y. Packet,* Mar. 30, 1787.

88. Livingston Papers; *The Hudson Weekly Gazette* (Hudson, N.Y.), Mar. 29, 1787.

89. To Hamilton, Mar. 3, 1787, Syrett and Cooke, eds., *Hamilton Papers,* IV, 104.

90. *The Albany Gazette,* Apr. 12, 19, 1787; Abraham Yates to ?, June 2, 1787, A. Yates, Jr., Papers, #185, N.Y. Pub. Lib.

91. *N.Y. Packet,* Jan. 13, 1785.

part of the political scene. Neither the letters nor the newspapers of the period reveal any statewide organization. Even the contest over the Constitution failed to inspire united action until, late in the game, the Federal Republican Committee tried to coordinate an opposition. Yet an increasing number of men engaged in political contests, still local in character, but with obvious implications for the makeup of the legislature. The issues at stake were emerging clearly in the newspapers and in meetings. As early as 1781 three hundred inhabitants of the manor of Livingston had convened and drawn up a list of ten grievances.[92] Five years later the freeholders of Amenia, in Dutchess County, approved a series of resolves including a criticism of loyalists, a request for paper money, lower court costs, and trials in the locality, a sort of embryonic platform for the Clintonians.[93] The elements for statewide parties clearly existed and one could readily anticipate much about the form they would take, but they remained potential before the Constitution.[94]

NOTE TO CHAPTER V

During the final revision of this manuscript, I looked at the supplementary items to Charles Evans's *American Bibliography*. These included the journals of two meetings of the New York Assembly's third session (1779/1780) previously presumed missing. Although New York's political alignment took form several years later, a test of the hypotheses presented in this chapter seemed worthwhile. The hypotheses passed with flying colors. The most interesting meeting was the second (January–March 1780), but all furnished significant votes. Briefly, the delegates divided into the customary two groups, in this case consisting of twenty-three

92. Walter Livingston to R. R. Livingston, Jan. 7, 1781, Walter Livingston Letterbook, R. R. Livingston Papers, Box 10, N.-Y. Hist. Soc.

93. *Country Jour.* (New York), Dec. 22, 1785.

94. The student of New York politics who wishes to examine the evidence in greater detail will find the effort rewarding. Many votes other than those mentioned reveal the alignments. For example in selecting the Council of Appointment on Oct. 19, 1784, the Clintonians voted down the line for Ward, the anti-Clintonians for Roosevelt. A parenthetical warning: on Feb. 4 the assembly failed to pass, over the Council of Revisions's veto, a bill that would have enabled Yorkers to discharge in state securities and state money debts owing to persons who remained in British line. The vote to override was 31–17, short of the necessary two-thirds. The clerk recorded the 31 as voting nay, probably because he thought of them as being on the losing side, an error that cast the Clintonians in the unaccustomed role of procreditors.

and twenty-five legislators, with seven neutrals. One contained all of the New York City delegates, most of the delegates other than farmers, about three-fourths of the large property owners, and probably most of the cosmopolitans (no effort was made to gather fresh biographical data). The bloc just described contained all of those known to have become anti-Clintonians. The "parties" appeared on two-thirds of the votes. The potentially anti-Clintonian party adopted the following positions: for delay in the sale of confiscated estates and exclusion of unimproved land from sale (September 14, 16, 1779, and February 4, 15, 22, June 13, 1780); for higher taxes (September 23, October 6, 21, February 9, 15, 16, 1780); for lower pay to the legislators (October 25, 1779); against a general consideration of ability to pay taxes, in assessments (January 30, 1780); for concessions to refugees from occupied areas (February 8, March 1, 1780); to earmark funds for the exclusive use of Congress (February 28, 1780); and to accept a senate proposal that the state try to borrow money before selling confiscated land (March 10, 1780).

Chapter VI

New Jersey

On October 29, 1779, New Jersey's assembly rejected, 11–17, a council resolution to prosecute the author of a newspaper article critical of the government. A modern observer might congratulate the majority for protecting freedom of the press, but the war was going badly, and the eleven who sided with the council doubtless thought of themselves as fighting sedition. Whatever the correct interpretation, the vote revealed the existence of two distinct political groups in the legislature. All but one of the eleven who favored suppression lived in the northeastern half of the state; the majority included four men from the east and thirteen from the southwest. All of the wealthy and most well-to-do delegates protected the author, while the smaller property holders sided with the government. Localists favored prosecution, cosmopolitans opposed. Quakers unanimously defended the critic, whereas Presbyterians and members of the Dutch Reformed Church divided. This division exemplifies the character of political alignments during the decade.[1]

That vote on freedom of the press (or on suppressing sedition), the first of the session, was followed by some three hundred others during the next nine years. Among these votes, 70 percent demonstrate a pattern formed by two opposing groups of legislators, one including fifty-six persons, the other fifty-two, the members of which agreed with each other about 85 percent of the time. Each contained a dozen or so men who adhered almost unanimously to the "party line." Another forty-five assemblymen conformed to

1. All members of the Cosmopolitan, or West Jersey, party, as later defined, voted against, while 80% of the Localist, or East Jersey, bloc were for it. The council vote was 5–3, Localists voting 4–0, Cosmopolitans, 1–3.

neither pattern but remained neutral. The Legislative Council during the same years contained identical blocs, one side with twenty-eight men, the other with twenty-four, and four neutrals.[2]

The most obvious difference between the two legislative parties was sectional. One predominated in East Jersey, including Essex, Morris, Bergen, Middlesex, Somerset, and Monmouth counties. Three-fourths of the other group lived in West Jersey, comprising the counties of Burlington, Gloucester, Salem, Cumberland, and Cape May. The remaining two counties, Sussex and Hunterdon, often held the balance of power and contributed men to both sides. During the war years Sussex, which contained many loyalists, tended to support neutralist West Jersey, but it shifted subsequently when the legislature concentrated on economic issues. Hunterdon always inclined toward East Jersey, especially after 1783.

The reasons for this geographical division seem to have included both economic and cultural factors originating in the colonial past.[3] East Jersey had been settled by a mixture of Dutch and English Calvinists, the latter being strongly influenced by migration from New England. Presbyterians provided much of the leadership, especially during the Revolutionary movement. The Anglicans, also numerous, proved lukewarm toward independence, as they did in New York, and indeed produced some prominent loyalists. Loyalists and neutralists appeared also among the Dutch settlers in Bergen and Somerset. During the war East Jersey became the scene of heavy fighting, extensive damage, and great bitterness. The whigs, who retained control, punished their enemy by confiscations, and

2. This conclusion resulted from a careful examination as described in chap. 2, which involved the elimination of those votes that did not contribute to party divisions and the assignment of bloc affiliation on the basis of all the sessions. In order to check the reliability of that procedure, all of the votes taken by the lower house, regardless of their importance, were key-punched. Through analysis performed by a computer, a matrix for each session identified the delegates who voted as blocs. The result corresponded closely to what inspection already revealed. In 1779, for example, the matrix separated one group of 13 men, another of 16, and 8 in a third. The first consisted of 11 members of the West Jersey group and two neutrals; the second contained 12 members of the East Jersey bloc and one neutral, while the third included two neutrals, four members of the East Jersey party, and two members of the West Jersey group. All told, analysis revealed the two major groups and one minor one, consisting respectively of 60, 53, and 20 persons, which corresponded almost precisely with the parties described in the text.

3. The authority on New Jersey during the Confederation period is Richard P. McCormick, *Experiment in Independence: New Jersey in the Critical Period, 1781–1789* (New Brunswick, N.J., 1950). Chap. 1 contains a general description of the state during the Revolutionary years.

almost all of the property that the state seized lay in the north. The East Jersey whigs supported the war financially too, so that the people there owned most of the state and federal debt. Although East Jersey contained some large estates and two lesser commercial centers (Perth Amboy and Elizabeth), it consisted primarily of small farms. Most of the farmers lived above the subsistence level, but were far from well-to-do.

West Jersey, on the other hand, contained a very strong Quaker influence, which led that section to be less enthusiastic than the east about armed resistance. The Quakers and their allies opposed the use of taxes, loans, or soldiers to support the rebel cause. West Jersey, in short, sat out the war, experiencing few invasions and few losses. The small commercial towns such as Burlington were surrounded by fertile agricultural land where the farms were larger and (judging from tax records) the people more prosperous than those of the northeast, perhaps because they suffered less during the war.

The legislature contained an equal number of representatives from both sections and included men of various economic interests, cultural and social backgrounds, and political experience. During the years from 1779 to 1788 over 150 men attended. Each county chose four annually. Property qualifications allowed men of small property to vote and hold office, so that fully one-third of the assemblymen held but moderate estates. About the same number owned large properties. Farmers contributed half of the members, the rest consisting of mixed manufacturers, professionals, and traders. The people chose few men of education or intellectual interest and few cosmopolitans, a fact that probably reflects the rural character of the state. West Jersey sent a mixed group of Quakers, Episcopalians, and Presbyterians, almost all of English ancestry, while from East Jersey came both Dutch and English delegates, with Presbyterians especially prominent. The composition of the legislature remained almost unchanged during the decade (see table 6.1).

The 1779 attempt to muzzle the press of course reflected the determination of East Jersey legislators to prosecute the war vigorously. Many other votes during that session and the three that followed also testify to that determination. These included the passage of an act to prevent forestalling, engrossing, and other nefarious activities; the grant of extraordinary powers to the executive; rigorous restrictions on trading with the enemy; measures for military defense; generous payment for those assisting the war ef-

Table 6.1. Composition of the New Jersey Legislature

	No.	%		No.	%
Residence			*Occupation*		
Noncommercial farm	36	23.5	Farmer	70	45.8
Commercial farm	77	50.3	Large landowner	9	5.9
Town	32	21.0	Misc. nonfarmer	21	13.7
Unknown	8	5.2	Professional	23	15.0
			Trader	22	14.3
			Unknown	8	5.2
Economic status					
Moderate	50	32.9	*Military service*		
Substantial	35	23.0			
Well-to-do	43	28.3	Enlisted man	6	4.0
Wealthy	10	6.6	Misc. officer	28	18.3
Unknown	14	9.2	Colonel or general	23	15.0
			Probably served	2	1.3
			None or uncertain	94	61.4
Religion					
Episcopalian	5	3.3	*National origin*		
Quaker	17	11.1			
Presbyterian	45	29.4	New Jersey, English	89	58.2
Baptist	8	5.2	New Jersey, Scotch-Irish	2	1.3
Dutch Reformed	14	9.2	New Jersey, Dutch	26	17.0
Unknown	64	41.8	New Jersey, other	3	2.0
			Immigrant, English	6	3.9
			Immigrant, Scottish	3	2.0
Social origin			Immigrant, Scotch-Irish	1	0.7
			Unknown	23	15.0
Humble immigrant origin	8	5.2			
Old family	91	59.5			
Above-average family	29	19.0	*Legislative party*		
Prominent old family	4	2.6			
Uncertain	21	13.7	Localist (East Jersey)	52	34.0
			Neutrals	45	29.4
			Cosmopolitan (West Jersey)	56	36.6

fort; levying sizable taxes; and acts to maintain the value of state money. The same group cracked down on loyalists, as they so often did in other states, and favored higher salaries, which elsewhere they usually opposed. During these years they also supported Congress, including the grant of the 5 percent impost and the supplementary fund.[4] At the same time in the Legislative Council the East Jersey representatives adopted identical policies. They too backed Congress,[5] voted for higher taxes and more troops, approved the confiscation act, pushed the sale of loyalist property, opposed leniency to men who could not take the oath of allegiance, and favored the prosecution of delinquent tax collectors.[6]

The nature of the alignment on this assortment of issues appears in table 6.2. The representatives from East Jersey in each case are

Table 6.2. Illustrative Votes, New Jersey, 1779–1783 (in Percentages)

	Delegates Voting with East Jersey Bloc on Seven Issues						
	1	2	3	4	5	6	7
All delegates	68	57	43	38	62	62	35
Section							
East Jersey	80	100	67	69	80	83	62
West Jersey	50	28	36	0	33	42	0
Sussex	33	0	100	0	0	25	33
Hunterdon	100	0	50	50	100	67	0
Residence							
Noncommercial farm	89	67	83	25	71	71	56
Commercial farm	47	44	47	39	52	53	43
Town	100	80	50	67	80	71	33
Occupation							
Farmer	67	62	58	43	53	65	44
Large landowner			0			0	33
Misc. nonfarmer	67	36	57	50	64	71	60
Merchant	100	100	0	0	100	67	—

4. These votes occurred as follows: prevention of forestalling, etc., Nov. 26–27, Dec. 6, 1779; powers granted to the executive, June 5, 16, 17, 1780; restrictions on trading with the enemy, Oct. 5, 1781, June 15, Dec. 9, 1782; measures for defense, Nov. 25, Dec. 9, 1780, June 7, 1781; payment for assisting the war effort, Dec. 22, 1779, Mar. 8, 17, 1780; levying taxes, Nov. 20, 1779, June 14, Dec. 4, 1781, June 10, 1782; maintaining value of state money, Mar. 17, 1780; antiloyalist measures, Nov. 28, 1782; raising salaries, Nov. 27, Dec. 13, 1782; grant of the 5% impost and supplementary fund, May 31, 1781, June 11, Dec. 16, 1783.

5. For example, they defeated an attack on Congress for its declaration of martial law (Apr. 2, 1778).

6. See votes, Dec. 8, 1777, Dec. 1, 1778, May 15, 1779, Mar. 1, 13, 1780, Dec. 4, 16, 1783.

Table 6.2—Continued

	1	2	3	4	5	6	7
Economic status							
Moderate	77	69	69	63	77	69	75
Substantial	80	50	38	33	71	43	25
Well-to-do	55	40	50	14	37	67	44
Wealthy	50	100	0	—	50	0	50
Religion							
Quaker	33	50	0	0	0	67	67
Presbyterian	100	57	44	55	63	43	33
World view							
Localist	100	—	—	—	—	57	50
Cosmopolitan	100	—	—	—	—	100	100
Legislative party							
East Jersey party	87	92	75	73	80	92	88
Neutral	71	43	57	0	38	67	44
West Jersey party	33	13	45	18	50	11	11

CODE OF VOTES:

1. Act to prevent forestalling, etc., Dec. 6, 1779.
2. Grant of exceptional powers to Council of Safety, June 5, 1780.
3. To establish forfeiture of estate for second offense of trading with the enemy, June 15, 1782.
4. Tax bill, Dec. 4, 1781.
5. Act for redeeming U.S. bills of credit, May 31, 1780.
6. Grant of 5% impost to Congress, June 11, 1783.
7. To establish higher salaries, Nov. 17, 1783.

considered as voting pro. Too few men sat in the legislature to furnish accurate statistics, but the table makes clear, first, that significant sectional differences existed; second, that these corresponded with party divisions; and third, that no other factors seem important except perhaps a persistent tendency among men of moderate property to support the East Jersey group. The Quaker vote tended toward the West Jersey side on issues directly related to the war, but on other questions the Friends supported the government.[7]

7. Only a few Quakers held seats, and these probably were not typical of their sect.

The session of 1783/1784 saw the beginning of a political re-alignment, anticipated earlier, that developed as the legislators turned their attention to internal problems. The major subject for debate in New Jersey, as in other states, grew out of the economic situation, so that the representatives now lined up, not according to issues relating to the war, but according to their own or their constituents' economic objectives. This reorientation involved some individual shifts of position, but the two blocs continued and retained certain of their characteristics, notably their sectionalism.[8] The denominations East and West Jersey remain appropriate, though each group drew some support from the other's stronghold.

The first circumstance that created the new alignment was the concentration of most of the state and federal debt in the eastern counties. Their representatives accordingly favored the payment of interest. At the same time losses due to the war deprived that section of enough hard money to pay taxes. The obvious solution was to collect as much specie as possible from the western counties and pay the rest of the tax in state money and certificates, keeping these equal to specie for tax purposes. What the easterners lost in taxes they would soon gain through the payment of interest on the debt. The West Jersey delegates, now that the war had ended, became more willing to support Congress's demand for a specie tax, but resisted the rest of the easterners' financial program.

A second circumstance was the depression of the mid-eighties. The easterners took up the cause of the debtors, demanding among other reforms an issue of paper money. Obviously this increase in the money supply would enable people to pay taxes more easily and thus enable the government in turn to pay its creditors. West Jersey delegates opposed relief for debtors. Therefore by 1786 the character of the political divisions within the state began to resemble those in Massachusetts and New York. This major realignment can be traced through most of the significant questions, including government spending, taxation, relations between debtors and creditors, monetary policy, and the public debt.

During the earlier years the East Jersey delegates had proved more willing than their opponents to grant higher salaries. William Livingston, an exceptionally vigorous and able leader, won general

8. The cohesiveness of the East Jersey delegates diminished somewhat during this later period from roughly 70% to about 60%. On other hand, West Jersey delegates voted as a bloc more often (from about 60% to nearly 75%). On many votes no sectional pattern existed. When it did appear, the delegates voted with their neighbors about 70% of the time.

support, and the other principal officials evidently shared his popularity. This attitude continued through 1783, but by 1786 the easterners opposed an increase for Chief Justice David Brearly and
voted almost unanimously that the entire civil list be cut from
£10,000 to £4,000.[9] None of these votes reveals any consistent
urban-rural division, nor did men's occupations affect their voting.
Relative wealth also seems unimportant—indeed Governor Livingston received a good salary because the poorer legislators desired
it.[10] Cosmopolitan men, however, favored higher salaries and localists opposed them. But the delegates reversed their stand when their
own pay was at stake. On the same day that the easterners reduced
the civil list they raised their own per diem. The division on this
issue depended somewhat on the delegates' financial need, for
while only 40 percent of the wealthy and well-to-do men voted for
a higher per diem, 60 percent of the substantial delegates and 85
percent of those with moderate property granted themselves a
raise.

Ideas about other types of government spending also changed
over time. During the war years delegates of East Jersey approved
most appropriations, but their attitude shifted as early as December 1782, and from this point forward they tended to oppose spending money.[11] The largest expenditure, in New Jersey as in other
states, went to payments on the state debt. As previously noted,
the easterners, who owned most of it, would gladly receive the
money, but because they lacked specie they could not furnish hard
money for the purpose. The westerners could better afford to pay
specie taxes, and once the war ended they became more willing
than their opponents to support the government—except for payments on the certificates. At first the result was an impasse. In
January 1783 the legislators defeated the tax bill. A Bergen County
correspondent explained,

> The case was thus, from the different Situation of East and West
> Jersey the Members from each were differently influenced—West
> Jersey has few publick Certificates and less State Money. We have very
> considerable of both. The Eastern Members were for exceeding the
> requisitions of Congress and to receive a certain proportion in State
> Money and Certificates that by it the Credit of the One and the other

9. Nov. 9, 1786.
10. Votes of Nov. 27, Dec. 13, 1782. When Livingston requested a special fund
to be spent without strings, a motion to raise the amount from £60 to £75 was
supported by most legislators of moderate properties but by none of the wealthy
ones (Dec. 19, 1782). New Jerseyites were indeed peculiar.
11. E.g., May 29, June 12, Nov. 25, 1783, Feb. 28, 1786.

might be preserved as much as possible which the Western Members would not accede to and by a Majority got a Bill thro the House for hard Money only which was rejected by Council. . . . (N.B. The Eastern Members were for Raising 130,000 £ hard and 225,000 £ State money and Certificates)—The Expence of our Civil List is considerably lowered.[12]

For several years the East Jersey group was reluctant to raise taxes and once voted to postpone collections.[13] In November 1785, however, they obtained control of the assembly and presently introduced their own financial system. Not only did the easterners recover by interest on their certificates what they lost in taxes, but an issue of paper money made taxes easier to pay.[14]

Votes on other aspects of taxation also suggest the change from an entire lack of pattern to a more complex one. During the earlier period a motion to tax stock in trade (December 8, 1779) found men from both sections and of various occupations, levels of wealth, and cultural attributes voting indifferently on either side. A tax on hogs (June 15, 1781) divided the East Jersey men voting pro from the West Jersey delegates opposed, but representatives from noncommercial farm areas actually cast more votes for the measure than did those from towns, and relative wealth made no difference. Similarly a faculty tax won more support from urban than from rural delegates, but both merchants and farmers opposed it in equal proportions (May 27, 1783). The incidence of taxation ceased to be an issue after 1783, with one major exception: the excise of 1787, which the eastern group pushed through and defended. The vote on this matter followed both party and economic class lines, as the division of May 30, 1787, indicates:

	For	Against
Moderate and substantial property	16	7
Well-to-do and wealthy	2	9
East Jersey group	14	1
Neutral	6	3
West Jersey group	3	13

The circumstance that primarily caused the postwar realignment and fresh crystallization of the state's politics seems to have

12. Dirck Romeyn to Richard Varick, Hackensack, N.J., Jan. 16, 1783, Richard Varick Papers, N.-Y. Hist. Soc.
13. Oct. 31, 1786.
14. See votes, Nov. 13, 21, 1786, May 25, 1787.

been the financial crisis of the mid-eighties. As in other states, the postwar contraction, combined with commercial difficulties, left debtors vulnerable and crying for relief. In December 1785 "Willing to Learn" drew a gloomy picture of the economy.[15] The laws, he said, that enabled debtors to pay their just debts for less than a fourth of their real value, combined with a stay law, had halted the circulation of hard money so that honest men with good security could not borrow.[16] Some debtors had been forced to sell their estates for much less than their true worth, thus increasing poverty and promoting that inequality of property that was dangerous in a republican government. He urged that the government issue £200,000 in legal-tender notes and loan them on good security at 6 percent interest. Debtors would be relieved, creditors would receive their money quickly without court suits, and the additional money would permit payment of taxes that in turn would enable the state to pay interest on the public securities. These would rise in value. Meanwhile the treasury would be receiving £12,000 in interest annually. This argument drew forth some angry replies, and the ensuing debate followed the course familiar everywhere.[17]

In the legislature the contest required a number of votes dealing with the relations between debtors and creditors and with monetary policy. The sectional divergence continued, East Jersey invariably supporting the debtor, soft-money view. But now the alignment revealed other conflicts. Delegates from the towns backed the creditors, those from noncommercial farm areas the debtors. Men in trade and large landowners opposed paper money and relief for debtors, farmers favored them. Most larger property owners voted with the creditors, men owning smaller estates with the debtors. Creditors also usually received the support of Quakers and cosmopolitans, debtors of Presbyterians and localists. The alignment can be illustrated by the series of votes shown in table 6.3. In each case the prodebtor vote is given first.

During the same years the Legislative Council recorded a series of votes that revealed an identical alignment. Indeed as early as

15. *The Political Intelligencer. And New-Jersey Advertiser* (Elizabethtown), Dec. 14, 21, 1785.

16. The law actually referred only to debts owed to loyalists and to prewar obligations. New Jersey Session Laws, 8th session, chap. 59, Sept. 2, 1784, and 9th session, chap. 65, Dec. 8, 1784 (see Records of States microfilm or Early American Imprints microprint).

17. *Political Intelligencer* (New Brunswick, then Elizabethtown, N.J.), Dec. 28, 1785, Jan. 4, 25, Feb. 1, 8, 1786; *New-Jersey Gazette* (Trenton), Feb. 6, 1786. A South Carolina newspaper commented on the volume of articles in New Jersey papers. *The Columbian Herald, or The Independent Courier of North-America* (Charleston), Jan. 30, 1786.

Table 6.3. *Illustrative Votes, New Jersey, 1785–1787 (in Percentages)*

	Delegates Taking Procreditor Position on Six Votes					
	1	2	3	4	5	6
Section						
East Jersey	24	53	39	24	15	25
West Jersey	87	86	77	87	62	87
Sussex	33	0	0	0	0	0
Hunterdon	0	20	0	0	0	0
Residence						
Noncommercial farm	18	33	9	9	9	9
Commercial farm	62	53	60	56	50	60
Town	44	100	78	67	67	67
Occupation						
Farmer	45	33	35	36	29	41
Merchant	67	100	67	83	50	83
Economic status						
Moderate	36	40	25	36	25	36
Substantial	38	29	45	23	18	25
Well-to-do or wealthy	73	92	70	91	60	91
Religion						
Presbyterian	20	50	22	10	0	0
Quaker	83	75	83	100	67	100
World view						
Localist	38	33	33	33	13	25
Cosmopolitan	33	67	75	89	50	67
Legislative party						
East Jersey party	13	23	31	7	0	6
Neutral	44	67	25	57	38	57
West Jersey party	92	80	90	100	70	100

CODE OF VOTES:

1. Stay law, Mar. 23, 1786.
2. Act for relief of insolvent debtors, Nov. 1, 1787.
3. Division on paper-money bill, Nov. 25, 1785.
4. The same, Mar. 9, 1785.
5. Motion to reduce quantity of paper, Nov. 25, 1785.
6. Legal-tender provision, Mar. 1, 1786.

1780 the West Jersey bloc was protecting creditors against paper money.[18] Now it succeeded in delaying the paper-money bill, defeated a stay law, and opposed acts relieving men imprisoned for debt.[19]

The new elements in this realignment extended to other economic questions. As previously noted, the East Jersey group reflected the problems of farmers by delaying the collection of taxes (October 31, 1786), cutting government costs by reducing the amount appropriated for the civil list, and at first voting against payments on the state debt (December 4, 20, 1784; March 18, 1786). Meanwhile the same group ceased to support Congress by blocking consideration of the federal requisition, opposing the supplementary fund (March 21, May 30, 1786), and denying Congress the money for payments on its debts, which the state now assumed (November 13, 21, 1786). A few years earlier they had willingly granted, while the West Jersey group had opposed, the 5 percent impost (June 11, 1783). The vote of March 21, 1786, clearly shows the new alignment: in this ballot Congress received support from all of the West Jersey party members, large landowners, and Quakers; 91 percent of large property holders; 60 percent of town dwellers; and 67 percent of cosmopolitans. On the other hand, only 7 percent of the East Jersey group, 9 percent of delegates from noncommercial farm areas, 33 percent of farmers, 20 percent of small property owners, 10 percent of Presbyterians, and 25 percent of localists backed Congress with their votes.

A variety of other issues also caused divisions within the legislature. The treatment of loyalists during the war aroused little debate because, whatever public opinion may have been, most of the representatives were committed to the war effort. Confiscation of loyalist property was nonpartisan (except for some council votes), and a 1780 vote on the temporary suspension of sales revealed no pattern except that the more property a delegate owned, the more he defended the loyalists' estates. Once the war ended, men might protect neutrals and moderate tories with less risk of ostracism. In 1781 the legislature suspended the sale of confiscated estates, a delay that continued for several years without causing a division. An act for the sale of an estate in Bergen County (December 10, 1784) created support or opposition because of individual opinions. Nor did the parties disagree when sales were resumed in 1786, unless the change reflected the East Jersey group's majority. A roll

18. Sept. 29, Oct. 3; see also June 1, 1781.
19. Nov. 25, 1785, Mar. 14–15, 23, May 26, 1786, June 1, 1787.

call granting nonjurors the right to vote, on the other hand, clearly divided the two parties. Supporters of the nonjurors included the western bloc, all of the large property holders, every Quaker, and almost every cosmopolitan, together with merchants, lawyers, and large landowners (May 23, 1786).[20] On the whole, however, loyalism seems not to have created a serious conflict within the assembly.

Various other questions need only brief notice. The easterners favored, while westerners opposed, a motion to impose a limit of £70 per hundred acres at which land could be valued for tax purposes (December 11, 1781). West Jerseyites backed a motion to tax only improved land (December 10, 1779), which would relieve speculators and owners of large estates. This divided the legislators primarily by economic class (three-fourths of the large property holders pro, four-fifths of the lesser ones con).[21] The establishment of courts for the trial of small causes (March 7, 1786) lost because almost every member of the East Jersey party, almost every delegate from a semisubsistence farm area, most men of moderate property, practically all Presbyterians, and three-fourths of the localists opposed it. Probably they preferred the settlement by justices and juries, who would favor debtors. A bill establishing permanent salaries for the judges of the supreme court passed (June 1, 1786) when it received unanimous or almost unanimous support from West Jerseyites, townsmen, lawyers, well-to-do delegates, Quakers, intellectuals, cosmopolitans, and high civil officials.[22] As noted at the beginning of this chapter, the issue of freedom of the press divided the legislature in much the same way.

Several social and cultural issues, while interesting, did not affect political alignments. East Jersey delegates twice voted for measures leading to the abolition of slavery[23] and twice supported the chartering of Presbyterian churches,[24] but an attempt to authorize the Supreme Court to grant divorces was disapproved by almost every sort of people outside of the educated townspeople. A special tax on strong liquor found men from both sections on either side (May 21, 1787). The vote followed both economic class and

20. May 23, 1786.
21. Wealthy and well-to-do, 75%; substantial, 29%; moderate, 15%; West Jersey party, 64%; East Jersey party, 7%; cosmopolitan, 50%; localists, none.
22. An earlier bill lost (Dec. 4, 1784) when it failed to attract such solid backing, though the vote followed the same general lines.
23. Nov. 7, 1780, Feb. 21, 1786. In the council a vote seems nonpartisan (Feb. 28, 1786).
24. Dec. 19, 1782, Dec. 20, 1784.

religious lines, the richer delegates and Quakers voting for, while farmers, small property holders, Presbyterians, and localists opposed such a tax.[25]

A broad view of New Jersey's history during the years after 1776, whether in peace or in war, discloses the existence of two basic political groups. One drew its principal strength from West Jersey (see the map, p. 170). During the war, its members were less anxious to pursue vigorous measures. On various occasions they opposed calling out the militia and providing for their pay in times of emergency, fought the grant of extraordinary power to the executive, voted against tax increases and various government expenditures, opposed heavy penalties for trading with the enemy, negatived antimonopoly bills and price controls, defended newspaper criticism of the government, seemed a little more sympathetic with loyalists, and were much less anxious to support Congress than were their political opposites. With peace they began to shift ground and adapt to new circumstances. They now became eager to uphold the government and concentrate power in Congress, they approved government expenses, the collection of taxes, and permanent salaries, they defended the rights of large landowners and of creditors, and fought paper money. On all of these issues an equally determined group of delegates, primarily from East Jersey, supported opposite policies.

Compared with the sectional character of the two protagonists, other aspects of the alignment seem relatively unimportant until the closing years of the decade. Delegates who lived in towns appeared on both sides, though those from the largest trading centers did tend to favor the West Jersey group in later sessions. Representatives from noncommercial farming areas showed a mild preference for the East Jersey bloc. Farmers voted indifferently, but large landowners supported the westerners by a two-to-one margin. Artisans, manufacturers, professional men, and lesser tradesmen divided evenly, while merchants tended toward the West Jersey side, again only in the later years. The parties differed clearly in wealth, as table 6.4 shows. The difference reflects the

25. The division is interesting. The tax lost, 12–23. The minority in favor included notably Quakers (4–1), large property holders (8–2), men of above-average social origin (6–4), and the West Jersey bloc (7–5). Those opposed were men from noncommercial farm areas (1–10), farmers (3–15), Presbyterians (1–8), and Baptists (0–4), small property owners (8–19), localists (0–7), and the East Jersey bloc (1–13).

Approximate Residences of Legislators, New Jersey

■ West Jersey Party
○ East Jersey Party
• Neutrals

economic characteristics of East and West Jersey and is obviously related to the positions taken by the parties on debtor-creditor relations and monetary policy.[26]

Table 6.4.   Party Preference in New Jersey by Economic Status (in Percentages)

	East Jersey Party	Neutral	West Jersey Party	Total
Economic status				
Moderate	46	30	24	100
Substantial	40	23	37	100
Well-to-do	21	33	47	101
Wealthy	20	10	70	100

These last issues seem primarily responsible for the transformation of the later eighties. Prior to 1784 the two groups contained identical components economically; both attracted equal support from men of various occupations and levels of wealth. Beginning in that year, however, the men who made their first appearance in the legislature divided in a new manner. Now practically all of the business and professional men combined with the large landowners to form the West Jersey party, while the East Jersey bloc attracted farmers and some of the artisans, shopkeepers, and their like. Fourteen out of the nineteen well-to-do and wealthy delegates among these new legislators voted with the westerners, and

26. The figures below show the strength, in percentages, of each party in the various sections and the economic status of the delegates there. Men of small property (moderate plus substantial) voted with the East Jersey group slightly more often than did other representatives from the same area, while men with large property (well-to-do plus wealthy) consistently tended toward the opposite side. Taken by itself the table lacks significance, but it must be considered as part of a general pattern.

	East Jersey			West Jersey			Sussex and Hunterdon		
	E.J. Party	Neutral	W.J. Party	E.J. Party	Neutral	W.J. Party	E.J. Party	Neutral	W.J. Party
All delegates	63%	33%	4%	7%	25%	69%	18%	36%	46%
Moderate, substantial	71	25	5	8	24	68	29	29	43
Well-to-do, wealthy	47	42	10	7	13	80	0	40	60

three remained neutral, while most of those with small properties belonged to the East Jersey group. The same change occurred in the voting preference of delegates who lived in the towns.

Also interesting was the difference in the religious affiliation of the delegates. Almost all of the Quakers supported West Jersey, while the Presbyterians and Dutch Calvinists preferred East Jersey by about a three-to-one margin. In the latter cases this voting record is somewhat misleading; among the legislators generally three-fourths of the Presbyterians lived in East Jersey, but a smaller proportion belonged to that side. Probably, therefore, that a delegate was a Presbyterian did not affect his political behavior except insofar as religion formed part of the general cultural environment of East Jersey. Even the Quakers, all of whom lived in the western counties, voted less uniformly than their geographical distribution would lead one to suppose. Religion, then, formed a part of the composite description of each section and of each party, but did not operate independently of other influences.

Military experience predisposed the delegates toward the East Jersey side, presumably because of wartime policies; on the other hand, men who did not serve in any capacity preferred the West Jersey group by about two to one.

Political background had almost no effect. Since New Jersey's ratifying convention accepted the Constitution without dissent, the delegates' subsequent political careers cannot shed much light on the ideology of the 1780s. Still it is probably significant that the one known Antifederalist (Abraham Clark) belonged to the East Jersey party, and that, of the eleven known Federalists, six voted with the westerners, two with the easterners, and three remained neutral. During the next decade East Jersey produced six Jeffersonian Republicans and three Federalists, while their opponents furnished three to the latter and two to the former.

Other factors did not affect the political alignment. Age seems to have played no role at all; most social and cultural characteristics were also insignificant. Neither education nor intellectual interest influenced the voting, and the cosmopolitan-localist dichotomy appeared only on certain votes. Social origin and national origin seem unimportant. While clues to political behavior may be found in various circumstances, the key components appear to be, first, sectionalism; second, economic status; and third, religion.

This interpretation of the alignment gains force from an analysis of the voting in the Legislative Council. There one bloc was also a predominantly West Jersey group. In addition it included most of the wealthy councillors and consisted primarily of men other than farmers; it attracted members of various religions and generally those from prominent families (but no more than its share of cosmopolitans). On the other side were men from East Jersey and such relatively small property holders as reached so high an office. Practically all were Presbyterians, and nearly half were farmers or artisans. In the upper house as well as in the lower a realignment occurred after about 1784.

These political divisions apparently existed only within the legislatures. They do not appear as parties among the primary sources of the period. There is evidence of active campaigning, and in at least one county interested men nominated candidates, but the practice seems not to have become general, nor did the voters furnish these candidates with particular instructions.[27] Newspapers and legislative records reveal certain contested elections,[28] but the combatants seem to have been individuals rather than organized groups. New Jersey contained the seeds for political parties, but they remained latent and almost unrecognized.

27. Cornelius Ten Broeck Papers, Box 1, Rutgers Univ. Lib. McCormick discusses this point in *Experiment in Independence*, 91–93, where he notes contested elections in Burlington County.

28. *N.-J. Gaz.* (Trenton), Oct. 23, 1782; Dec. 25, 1784; Oct. 31, Dec. 12, 1785.

Chapter VII

Pennsylvania

Parties in Revolutionary Pennsylvania began with the Constitution of 1776, the debate concerning the treatment of loyalists and neutrals, and a struggle for political power. They were strengthened and sharpened by subsequent economic and political issues and reached a climax with the conflict over constitutional reform during the period 1787 to 1790. These controversies were so intense that the two sides assumed names, nominated candidates, fought election campaigns, adhered to clearly understood though unwritten platforms, and voted in the legislature with soldierly precision.

Most states adopted constitutions without starting such a furor. Ordinarily compromises resulted in governments that were controversial only in detail. A few states established governments too undemocratic for the populace, but the people did not exercise sufficient power under them to challenge the outcome effectively. In Pennsylvania, however, the constitution was so democratic that it antagonized powerful elements in society. These groups immediately organized against the new order, fought it for over a dozen years, and finally overthrew it in 1790. The Pennsylvania Constitution of 1776 brought about the first party system.

The legislature that served as the political arena contained a single house, to which all taxpayers elected representatives. The city of Philadelphia sent five, and the counties chose delegates roughly in proportion to their population. By the mid-eighties the older counties nearest the city (Philadelphia and Chester) sent seventeen, and the politically allied two immediately to the west (Lancaster and York) chose nineteen. These forty-one furnished the core of one party. Three other counties east of the mountains (Berks, Bucks, and Northampton) selected sixteen, while the area

Table 7.1. Composition of the Pennsylvania Assembly, 1780–1788

	No.	%		No.	%
Residence			**Occupation**		
Frontier	39	15.1	Farmer	95	36.7
Noncommercial farm	48	18.5	Large landowner	6	2.3
Commercial farm	100	38.6	Artisan, etc.	9	3.5
Commercial farm, near city	16	6.2	Miller	17	6.6
Small town	27	10.4	Iron manufacturer	14	5.4
Second-rank city	4	1.5	Other manufacturer	16	6.2
Major city	25	9.7	Doctor	7	2.7
			Lawyer	14	5.4
			Other professional	18	6.9
Economic status			Misc. entrepreneur	7	2.7
Poor or moderate	98	37.8	Innkeeper	12	4.6
Substantial	95	36.7	Shopkeeper	16	6.2
Well-to-do	34	13.1	Merchant or trader	17	6.6
Wealthy	24	9.3	Unknown	11	4.2
Unknown	8	3.1			
			Age		
Religion			Under 40	38	14.6
Catholic	1	0.4	40–49	60	23.2
Episcopalian	16	6.2	50–59	30	11.6
Quaker	16	6.2	60 and over	9	3.5
Presbyterian	61	23.6	Unknown	122	47.1
Baptist	3	1.2			
German Lutheran	14	5.4	**Military service**		
Other German	7	2.7			
Miscellaneous	5	1.9	Enlisted man	19	7.4
Unknown	136	52.5	Misc. officer	50	19.4
			Colonel or general	67	26.0
			Probably served	2	0.8
Political experience			None	120	46.5
Local office	49	18.9			
Sheriff, j.p., etc.	56	21.6	**Intellectual interest**		
State judge, council	23	8.8			
Other state office	14	5.4	None known	215	83.0
Continental Congress	10	3.9	Some	44	17.0
None	55	21.2			
Unknown	52	20.1			
			World view		
			Localist	123	47.5
			Cosmopolitan	49	18.9
			Unknown	87	33.6

Table 7.1—Continued

	No.	%		No.	%
Education			*Father's economic status*		
Little or none	8	3.1	Moderate	43	16.6
Self-educated	28	10.8	Substantial	13	5.0
College	9	3.5	Well-to-do	19	7.3
Unknown	214	82.6	Wealthy	15	5.8
			Unknown	169	65.3
Father's occupation			*National origin*		
Farmer	64	2.7	Colonial, English or Welsh	49	18.6
Large landowner	5	1.9	Colonial, Scottish	4	1.5
Artisan	9	3.5	Colonial, Scotch-Irish	47	18.1
Manufacturer	13	5.0	Colonial, German	26	10.0
Minister	4	1.5	Colonial, misc.	9	3.5
Lawyer	2	0.8	Colonial, unknown	15	5.8
Other professional	1	0.4	Immigrant, English	5	1.9
Innkeeper	2	0.8	Immigrant, Scottish	4	1.5
Shopkeeper	6	2.3	Immigrant, Scotch-Irish	12	4.6
Merchant	8	3.1	Immigrant, other Irish	3	1.2
Unknown	145	56.0	Immigrant, German	8	3.1
			Immigrant, other	1	0.4
Social origin			Unknown	76	29.3
Humble origin	49	19.0			
Old family	114	44.0			
Above-average family	26	10.0			
Prominent old family	9	3.5			
Unknown	61	23.6			
Mobility					
Mobile	49	18.9			
Not mobile	190	73.4			
Uncertain	20	7.7			
Slaveholding					
10–19 slaves	2	0.8			
5–9 slaves	1	0.4			
1–4 slaves	35	13.5			
None	174	67.2			
Uncertain	47	18.1			

west of the first ranges chose seventeen in 1783. These northern and western counties became the center of the other party. According to the scale used here to identify different types of residence, the frontier furnished 15 percent of the delegates; noncommercial farm areas, 19 percent; commercial farms, 44 percent; towns of various sizes, 12 percent; and the city, a little less than 10 percent.

Almost half of the representatives were primarily farmers, and the agricultural interest exercised considerable weight in Pennsylvania. Artisans, manufacturers, shopkeepers, and other lesser entrepreneurs contributed over 30 percent, and the rest of the assembly consisted of merchants and professional men. Delegates of relatively small property held most of the seats, fewer than one-tenth being rich and not many more well-to-do. The assembly contained men from a variety of religious backgrounds, but the Presbyterians were more numerous than they ought to have been (half of those known), the German groups much less. Half had seen military service. Probably a fifth of the delegates were cosmopolitan men. Men from old families were rare, being in fact outnumbered by immigrants. The legislature must have had quite an international flavor, being about equal parts English, Scotch-Irish, and non-British (mostly Germans). In general the assembly came as close to reflecting the state's society as did any in the country. Very likely its diversity contributed to political discord.

Hostilities among Pennsylvanians did not cease with Independence. Within a few months critics began to attack the constitution. First they condemned a recommended oath of allegiance, presently embodied into law, that disenfranchised Quakers and all those whose religious convictions forbade them to swear oaths. Most Quakers refused to give in and fought the law. Why should we suddenly change, they asked, when "we are still under the same God, we ever was?"[1] Next critics charged that a one-house legislature, though traditional in Pennsylvania, had proven faulty. "A *single* legislature is big with tyranny," observed Benjamin Rush.[2] "The friends and enemies of the new frame of government agree in the necessity of a *check* for the single legislature," wrote "Andrew Marvell."[3] The opponents of the constitution, he con-

1. James Burd to Edward Shippen, Nov. 6, 1776, Shippen Papers, XII, Hist. Soc. Pa.

2. To Anthony Wayne, May 19, 1777, Lyman H. Butterfield, ed., *Letters of Benjamin Rush* (Princeton, 1951), I, 148.

3. *Pa. Packet* (Philadelphia), Nov. 26, 1776. All of the Pennsylvania newspapers cited in this chapter (except the *Carlisle Gaz.*) were located in Philadelphia. Thus their location will not be mentioned in this chapter after the first citation.

tinued, want to add an upper house, while its supporters locate the check in the hands of the people. "The latter supposes all men to possess *equal* understanding, knowledge and leisure. It requires that the husbandmen should neglect his farm, that the merchant should forsake his compting-house, and the tradesman shut up his shop to examine the acts of every session of Assembly." Such a check simply meant bad government. The only solution was a senate.

Third, the power of the legislature to appoint, pay, and impeach most executive and judicial offices also seemed an error. Since judges served for only seven years and since most of these men owed their existence to the assembly, that body could rule despotically, possessing "the most *unbounded* liberty, and yet no kind of barrier to prevent its degenerating into licentiousness."[4] Finally, no true executive branch existed, for instead of a governor the state had only a presiding officer and a "Supreme Executive Council" without power.[5]

Writers of newspaper articles and private letters elaborated these criticisms. Most influential was the statement of a mass meeting held in Philadelphia that adopted a series of objections, demanded that the constitution be submitted to the people, and instructed the city's representatives to obtain a reform.[6] From that meeting stemmed the "Republican Society" and presently the Republican, or anticonstitutional, party. Their attack on the constitution was both theoretical and practical: theoretical in that they truly preferred a bicameral legislature, a separate executive branch, and independent judges; practical in that the constitution symbolized and to some extent institutionalized a shift of power. The new government was associated in the minds of many people with a dangerous revolutionary movement, directed through a provincial convention instead of the legal assembly by "violent wrongheaded people of the inferior class."[7] In the process prominent citizens were brought low. "I don't wonder," wrote the Quaker doctor William Shippen, "to see some of our Friends offended and full of resentment upon the change—who have heretofore been at the head of

4. "K" in *ibid.*, Sept. 24, 1776; "Addison" in *ibid.*, June 3, 1777.

5. The Republicans in the Council of Censors advocated the abolition of rotation in office except for members of Congress, a longer residence requirement for voting and officeholding, elimination of an assemblyman's right to enter dissents in the minutes, and an end to the publication of bills for consideration by the public. These proposals illustrate the antidemocratic bias of the party.

6. See *Pa. Packet*, Oct. 8, 22, 29, 1776; *At a Meeting of a Number of the Citizens of Philadelphia in the Philosophical Society-Hall, the 8th of November, 1776* [Philadelphia, 1776].

7. Joseph Shippen to Edward Shippen, Philadelphia, Feb. 29, 1776, Shippen Papers, XII, Hist. Soc. Pa.

affairs and in short have in many instances behaved as though they thought they had a sort of Fee simple in them, and might dispose of all places of Honor and Profit to such as pleased them best. Now to be ousted or at least brought down to a level with their fellow Citizens."[8] To such men, and even to many who did support the Revolution, the constitution was excessively democratic. "It supposes perfect equality, and an equal distribution of property, wisdom, and virtue, among the inhabitants of this state."[9] From the very beginning of Pennsylvania's history as a state, therefore, "the Sensible and Virtuous part" of the residents were "indavouring to set the Villanous Constitution aside."[10] They naturally denied that they formed a party or that they sought power: "That the present opposition to government is only a faction, and that we are contending, only for power and office; is mere declamation without proof."[11] Instead those who upheld the government were guilty of factionalism. Despite the denial, parties in Revolutionary Pennsylvania clearly began in 1776.

Attacks on the constitution continued during the years that followed.[12] The Republican Society kept up the criticism based on political theory, emphasizing the evils of a one-house legislature and demanding a new convention to amend or replace the new form, while other opponents lamented the shift of power. At the provincial convention, wrote "Agricola," "an absurd and foolish doctrine was too successfully propagated among the unthinking *many*—that men of property, however much they might have at stake, men of experience and knowledge, however well they might have acquitted themselves in former trusts; were to be carefully avoided on that occasion."[13] From this point of view the government should be reconstituted so that the best men would hold office. The virtual elimination of Quakers, who had provided much of the experience and ability in former years, cast power into the hands of men with little experience or ability.[14] What could be done?

8. To Edward Shippen, July 27, 1776, *ibid.*

9. "Ludlow," *Pa. Jour.* (Philadelphia), May 21, 1777.

10. William Thompson to James Wilson, Apr. 14, 1777, Gratz Collection, Generals of the Revolution, Hist. Soc. Pa.

11. "An Associator," *Pa. Jour.*, May 21, 1777.

12. *Pa. Packet*, Mar. 25, 1779; *Pa. Jour.*, May 21, 1777. See the account in Robert L. Brunhouse, *The Counter-Revolution in Pennsylvania, 1776–1790* (Harrisburg, 1942), 30–32. The assembly journal for Feb. 27, 1779, contains a full statement by critics of the constitution.

13. *Pa. Packet*, Feb. 6, 1779.

14. Charles W. Peale to David Ramsey, Philadelphia, 1779 (?), Peale Letterbook, American Philosophical Society, Philadelphia.

In 1778 they obtained from the legislature a resolution to discover whether the people wanted a convention. Such replies as
have survived suggest that the people did not.[15] Indeed these early
attacks may have damaged the Republican cause, for criticisms of
the constitution could easily be interpreted as treasonable when the
fate of the nation was at stake. That Quakers and some who were
really unfriendly to the Revolution joined in the complaint seemed
further evidence that the Republicans lacked patriotism. A correspondent of Benjamin Rush's warned the doctor that he had made
a mistake. The nonjurors and neutrals with whom Rush had allied, being more numerous and determined than in other states,
could more effectively oppose the government and would indeed
have done so whatever the constitution's nature. He warned Rush
that friends of the Revolution must unite and support the constitution, suppressing neutralists and tories until the war was won.
Once that had been accomplished, people could be reasoned with,
and constitutional reform obtained.[16] Failing in these early efforts,
the Republicans abandoned their futile attempts and waited im-
patiently for the day when the Council of Censors would meet to
examine the need for changes. Meanwhile they worked within the
existing system. "The great struggle at present," wrote one, "is
for men, that the measures wished for by one party and detested
by the other, may be favored or counteracted."[17]

As the day approached for the election of the censors, both parties again focused on the form of government. The Constitutionalists defended their handiwork, calling themselves patriots and
democrats. The Republicans renewed their propaganda, smearing
Constitutionalist leaders and urging radical change.[18] They won a
majority of the Council of Censors, who reported that the constitution was defective. Pennsylvania should add a second house chosen
for three years, judges with fixed salaries serving during good
behavior, and a governor with a veto power. The principle of rotation, they felt, had been carried to such an extreme that it deprived

15. Cumberland County remonstrance, Jan. 1, 1779, and York County remonstrance, 1780, Supreme Executive Council, Executive Correspondence, Pa. Archives; York County remonstrance, Jan. 15, 1779, Records of the General Assembly, Box 1, Pa. Archives; undated petition, Box 2, *ibid.* The assembly journals
note petitions from almost every county, totaling over 15,000 by 1779. Thereupon
the assembly rejected a revision, 47–7. June 11, 17, 1777, Feb. 16–Mar. 13, 1779.
See Brunhouse, *Counter-Revolution*, 53–60.
16. David Smith to Rush, June 7, 1779, Rush Papers, Hist. Soc. Pa.
17. "W. C.," *Indep. Gazetteer* (Philadelphia), Oct. 19, 1782.
18. *Ibid.*, Oct. 11, 1783.

the state of able men.[19] A minority of the censors published a rebuttal that defended every article in the constitution. "The grand objection," they asserted, was "that it retains too much power in the hands of the people, who do not know how to use it, so well as gentlemen of fortune, . . . and that it gives no advantage to the rich over the poor."[20] Since the Republicans comprised fewer than the two-thirds needed to call a convention and in the censors' second session lost control entirely, they accomplished nothing, and the constitution survived for six more years.

The nature of the division on this fundamental question cannot be studied through votes in the assembly, for none exist. The general characteristics of the two parties reveal it, as do several other bits of evidence.[21] Several votes by the Council of Censors indicate that the demand for change came from the city of Philadelphia and the southeast, whereas men from more western areas defended the constitution. The former group consisted primarily of merchants, lawyers, and others with a nonfarm occupation—men with considerable property, often high-ranking officers, who became Federalists in 1788; while opposed to them were mostly farmers of moderate property and future Antifederalists.[22]

Another suggestive list of names includes the signers of a petition calling for a convention to amend the constitution. They included the prominent Philadelphia merchants Robert Morris, George and Daniel Clymer, Sharp Delany, Thomas and Richard Peters, William Gray, Thomas Barclay, and J. M. Nesbitt, together with the iron manufacturer Mark Bird, the lawyer James Wilson, and the socially elite John and Lambert Cadwalader. Benjamin Rush's name led all the rest.[23]

Probably neither party gained politically from this dispute. The

19. *Pa. Packet,* Jan. 24, 1784.

20. *Pa. Jour.,* Jan. 31, 1784. The newspapers contain many articles. For other defenses of the constitution see *Pa. Packet,* Feb. 12, 1784, and a reply in *The Pennsylvania Gazette* (Philadelphia), Apr. 3, 1784; *The Freeman's Journal: or, the North-American Intelligencer* (Philadelphia), Feb. 18, 23, Mar. 3, 1784.

21. *Pa. Gaz.,* Jan. 7, 21, 28, 1784.

22. A quick survey of obvious sources shows the following men among the censors: Constitutionalists—farmers (large and small), 7; lawyers, 2; millers, 1; unknown, 1. Republicans—merchants, 4; lawyers, 3; doctors, 1; millers, 3; unknown, 1.

23. A visitor from Maine remarked that Rush was "the tool of a party, whilst his vanity leads him to imagine himself the principal, who are labouring to destroy the present constitution of Pennsylvania, and to introduce in its room one which is in a great measure aristocratical, and in my opinion, very inimical to liberty." William Hazlitt to Richard Price, Nov. 15, 1785, Massachusetts Historical Society, *Proceedings,* 2d Ser., XVII (1903), 335.

Republicans alienated moderates by their intemperate attacks. Although some privately conceded that the constitution was not altogether bad (John Dickinson among them),[24] publicly they viciously assaulted it and their opponents, meanwhile revealing an antidemocratic bias not calculated for popularity. A writer in the *Pennsylvania Journal*, for example, advocated higher property qualifications for voting, favored a longer period for naturalization on the ground that foreigners did not make good republicans, and warned the constitution's defenders that they faced defeat because the influence of wealth in elections was great and "a great proportion of the wealth of the state, you know, is in the hands of men who are opposed to your views and principles in government."[25] The Constitutionalists for their part obstinately refused to acknowledge any flaws in the government and launched vitriolic attacks on their opponents. They themselves were the whigs, theirs the government of the people, while their opponents were friends of the loyalists and traitors who proposed "a System of aristocratick or monarchical Despotism."[26] That their attack gained some temporary advantage is suggested by the victory of George Bryan over Samuel Miles when the latter resigned as censor and by their subsequent gains in the next election. But as Gen. John Armstrong observed, both sides were guilty of extremism and appeals to emotion.[27]

While the state's constitution divided the people most sharply, other issues contributed to the formation of parties. The Constitutionalists controlled the government during the years preceding 1781, when Philadelphia was taken, Charleston occupied, and Gates overwhelmed at Camden. Inevitably they were blamed for the military defeats and for the financial collapse of 1779–1780. The petition just discussed pleaded that a new convention to revise the constitution was essential to a restoration of confidence and unity. The signers complained of inadequate provision for resistance, the lack of regular administration of justice, high prices, and a failure to support public credit. On the other side, the

24. To Joseph Reed, Jan. 4, 1783, Logan Papers, VIII, Hist. Soc. Pa.

25. Mar. 20, 1784. See attacks on Bryan and others, for example, *Indep. Gazetteer*, Oct. 14, 1783.

26. Circular letter sent by the Constitutionalists of Philadelphia, Aug. 2, 1783, broadside, Hist. Soc. Pa.

27. Armstrong was especially disappointed in the obstinacy of the Constitutionalists, who included, he felt, some excellent men. They ought to have accepted certain reforms, especially an upper house. He feared that their refusal would be blamed on "the Presbyterian body." To John Harris, Carlisle, Pa., Mar. 25, 1784, Lamberton Scotch-Irish Collection, II, Hist. Soc. Pa.

Constitutionalists accused their critics of raising prices through war profiteering, monopolies, and speculation. When the British troops entered Philadelphia and many citizens remained in the city, the antiurban and anti-Quaker prejudices of many Pennsylvanians were intensified. The extreme measures thereafter taken, together with the apparent failure of the war effort, led to a Republican resurgence in 1781.

The treatment of loyalists or neutrals became, next to constitutional reform, the most significant issue in Pennsylvania politics. Attention centered on the Test Oath, which required an oath of allegiance to the new state and its constitution and in certain cases extended to belief in one God and the divine origin of the Bible. Nonjurors could neither vote nor hold office, were regarded as enemies to the country, and became subject to other punitive legislation.[28] During the war years the refusal of most Quakers to support the cause exposed them to punishment. A vote recorded by the assembly early in 1781 indicated the alignment. A clause in the tax bill of that year required payment entirely in gold and silver, except for those who had taken the oath or served in the militia, plus a few others. These might pay half the tax in paper. This section was approved, 28–23 (June 11, 1781). Adherents of the Constitutionalists favored the requirement almost unanimously (20–1), while the Republicans opposed it by an equally large margin (19–1). The division in various other ways introduces the differences between the two sides that continued throughout. Sectionally the Constitutionalists dominated the interior counties, while the Republicans controlled or were strong in Philadelphia, Chester, Lancaster, and York. Because of the Test Oath, only two Quakers sat in the legislature at this point, and they divided their votes. Presbyterians voted pro, Episcopalians con. On the side of the neutralists were merchants, property owners, and cosmopolitan men; opposed were most notably farmers, men of moderate property, and localists.

After the war hostility to the nonjurors was prolonged by antitory sentiment, fanned by newspaper articles and public meetings. These expressed particular resentment against ex-loyalists who tried to return. A meeting in Philadelphia's "Liberties" ward called for the expulsion of anyone who aided the enemy and resolved that their estates should not be restored. The citizens advised their

---

28. For measures taken against the nonjurors, see Brunhouse, *Counter-Revolution*, 40–44.

representatives to pass the necessary laws, "in the exercise of that unquestionable right of the freemen of the state of Pennsylvania to instruct their representatives on matters of political importance."[29] Meetings at Newtown in Bucks County, Germantown, Philadelphia, and East Caln (Chester County) also requested the exclusion of loyalists and warned against repealing the oath.[30] The men associated with these activities were obscure, often militia officers, with rarely someone of wider reputation such as Blair McClenahan, a merchant; Samuel Miles, a prominent Philadelphian; Elias Boys, a shopkeeper; and Col. Robert Smith, a well-to-do farmer and engineer.[31]

Attention turned to the legislature in 1784 and 1785, when the Republicans tried to repeal the Test Oath. They argued the justice of granting civil rights to respectable citizens who differed from the rest out of religious conviction, had been inoffensive, and would now strengthen the state. Constitutionalist spokesmen bitterly criticized those who failed to aid the country in its hour of distress and attacked prominent Republican leaders for inactivity during the war. These included Richard Willing, of a prominent merchant family; James Morris, son of a wealthy brewer; Samuel Ashmead, a wealthy merchant of eminent family; the iron manufacturer Thomas Bull; and Isaac Gray, a member of the Quaker elite.[32] According to one correspondent, thousands of Pennsylvanians denied that Quakers were Christians and believed that nonresistance was always wrong, the true policy being to injure or oppress no one.[33] The controversy had political significance, for the Republicans expected that the nonjurors would support them; as Rush was informed, the agitation for relief would fix their children to his interest.[34] The Constitutionalists naturally wished to prevent this.

In March 1784 the legislature began to receive petitions for the repeal of the test laws. After two roll-call votes these were tabled. When the assembly reconvened in the late summer, the Constitutionalists found themselves in the minority and finally prevented a third and final reading of the bill only by absenting themselves and preventing a quorum. Five votes were taken at this time. The

29. *Pa. Packet,* May 31, June 7, 12, July 8, 1783.
30. *Ibid.,* June 17, 19, 26, 1783; *Indep. Gazetteer,* June 21, 1783.
31. See newspaper articles such as the *Pa. Packet,* Jan. 8, 1784; *Pa. Jour.,* Sept. 17, 1783; and *Indep. Gazetteer,* Aug. 14, 1784.
32. *Pa. Packet,* Oct. 6, 1784.
33. John Black to Benjamin Rush, Jan. 26, 1785, Rush Papers, Hist. Soc. Pa.
34. George Lux to Rush, Feb. 18, 1785, *ibid.*

first two did not reflect a party division, the issue evidently not being clear-cut. Some delegates who wished to repeal the Test Oath voted against postponement, hoping for immediate action, while others thought a delay advisable. On the opposite side those who opposed repeal could not agree whether to reject the petition outright or put off consideration.

In September the lines solidified. Members of the Republican party supported the bill almost unanimously, while only one Constitutionalist deserted his party. The cause of nonjurors won support from most delegates living in towns and nearby farming areas, from men in trade and the professions, delegates with larger property, education, and cosmopolitan qualities. All of the known Quakers and Episcopalian representatives voted for repeal. On the other side were the delegates from subsistence farming areas and the frontier, most farmers, a majority of small property holders, localists, and the Presbyterians.

The next session (1784/1785) found the Constitutionalists firmly in control of the legislature, and they easily squelched an attempt to introduce a new bill. The Republicans won the fall 1785 election, however, and succeeded in passing a law that restored to citizenship all nonjurors except outright loyalists. This time the Republicans supported the bill unanimously, whereas the Constitutionalist minority could not hold together, six members breaking completely and others occasionally. The nature of the division appears in two typical votes on December 13, 1785, and March 1, 1786. The majority (which consisted of nearly two-thirds) included almost all of the Philadelphia delegates together with those from other towns and commercial farming regions; merchants, lawyers, and other men with nonfarm occupations (except artisans, who divided); larger property holders, Episcopalians and Quakers, men of education, and cosmopolitans. The minority consisted of representatives from less commercial areas, farmers and to some extent manufacturers, smaller property holders, Presbyterians, and localists—though some of all these groups shifted sides. This repeal of the Test Oath proved final.

A third major issue that separated Republicans from Constitutionalists concerned the Bank of North America. The bank was created by a number of merchants, notably Robert Morris and his associates, partly as a means of financing the debts left by the war, partly as a service to the business community, and partly for private profit. The usefulness of the bank at first delayed any essential criticism of it, and opposition focused only on certain features. Two votes in the Pennsylvania legislature during its spring session of 1782 indicated the character of the division at this point. These were cast first on whether the bank could own land (approved, 35–21) and on a motion that the assembly might alter, amend, or repeal the charter in 1789 or thereafter (defeated, 27–24). The Republicans approved the bank's ownership of land and blocked revision of the charter almost unanimously, losing only two votes to the Constitutionalists. The latter were scarcely less consistent, losing out of their 48 votes on the two roll calls only 7, of which 3 were cast by frequent defectors. The alignment in many ways resembled that on the loyalist issue. The bank drew its support from townsmen other than artisans and manufacturers, who divided their votes. All of the wealthy and most of the well-to-do members favored the Bank of North America, as did intellectuals and cosmopolitans. The attackers consisted primarily of farmers, especially from the more distant counties, smaller property owners, and localists.

By the mid-eighties attacks on the bank reached a climax with the repeal of the charter. No votes were recorded on that step, though the arguments on both sides were fully recorded in the press. From the start the opposition was partly political, for as one writer observed, the Constitutionalists "do not wish any thing to prosper which has originated and is supported by their opponents the republicans, however useful and beneficial it may be."[35] But the critics concentrated on economic and social evils. They emphasized that the bank served the businessman but injured farmers, who could not borrow, that it concentrated capital in the hands of a few men, which enabled them to dominate the state's economy, and that it created an aristocracy, dangerous alike to social equality and to republicanism. The solution to the monetary problem, they declared, was a public, not a private, bank that would create and loan money with land as security, at low interest. On their side the bank's defenders stressed the usefulness of the bank to merchants, to the government, and through them to everyone. Bank notes, they claimed, furnished a more stable medium of exchange than any other currency.[36]

35. John Wilson to Joseph Pemberton, Apr. 1, 1782, Pemberton Papers, XXXVI, Hist. Soc. Pa.

36. Some attacks: "A Mechanic," *Indep. Gazetteer*, Mar. 13, 1784; "A Friend to Liberty," *Pa. Packet*, Oct. 9, 1784; "Colbert," *ibid.*, Mar. 31, Apr. 1, 1785; "A Citizen," *The Pennsylvania Mercury and Universal Advertiser* (Philadelphia), Dec. 10, 1784; and "Philadelphiensis," *Freeman's Journal*, Mar. 2, 1785. An undated petition in the Records of the General Assembly, Box 2, Pa. Archives,

The bank suffered from the selfish policy of its directors, who alienated influential Philadelphians by restricting the number of shares. This monopolistic practice surely contributed to the Republican defeat in fall 1784. Crucial was the Constitutionalist victory in Philadelphia city and county, where a mixture of manufacturers and merchants, disillusioned with the narrow policy of the Morris group, brought a total reversal. The legislature then repealed the charter without ceremony or roll calls.[37]

A year later the Republicans, encouraged by political gains in Philadelphia city and county, attempted to reverse the repeal but failed, 36–28 (April 7, 1786). They now introduced some new and interesting arguments, featuring the doctrine that to deprive stockholders of property was "most dangerous and most tyrannical." The assembly, they felt, had no right to revoke the charter.[38] The antibank speakers repeated their objections, again pronouncing in favor of state control over the money supply. The Constitutionalist leader John Smilie asserted that "the question is not whether we shall have paper money—but who shall emit it—the bank or the state? . . . If the state is obliged to borrow, she must necessarily pay 6 per cent.—whereas, if she emits on loan, she gains 6 per cent."[39] As before the vote followed party lines with scarcely an exception, Constitutionalists being unanimous, the Republicans losing only Isaac Gray, a marginal adherent from

---

declared, "That your petitioners are mutch alarmed at the fatal Effects upon the Community which flow from the bank Established in Philadelphia. That whilst monied men are enabled by Means of the bank, to receive near three times common Interest, and at the same time to receive their money at a very short warning when Ever they have occasion for it, it will ever be impossible for the husband man, or mechanick, to borrow on the former terms of Legal Interest and distant payments of the principle."

37. See *Pa. Packet*, Mar. 25, 29, 1785; *Pa. Evening Herald* (Philadelphia), Sept. 8, 1785.

38. *Pa. Evening Herald*, Apr. 15, 1786; *Pa. Packet*, Mar. 28, 1786.

39. *Pa. Evening Herald*, Apr. 5, 1786. See also Whitehill in *ibid.*, Apr. 15, 1786. The *Packet* and *Freeman's Journal* contain numerous articles. The antibusiness, antiurban bias of the bank's opponents appear often. "A Fellow Citizen" wrote in the *Indep. Gazetteer*, Feb. 28, 1787, "The contest appears to me to be in short this—whether the Bank or the state shall issue paper bills of credit in lieu of hard money, to give that aid to agriculture so often mentioned in the debates? No system can be devised equal to a Loan-office, established on a permanent footing; the benefits arising from a Loan-office goes into our Treasury, to be applied by the legislature in lieu of taxes; the profits arising from the Bank goes into the pockets of the stockholders. . . . The Bank appears to me to be the favorite of a few overgrown fortunes in our capital, who, in a little time, from their unlimited credit with the Bank when once established, will be able to govern the trade of Philadelphia."

the city of Philadelphia, and one other. The small neutral group opposed the renewal.

The bank became a major issue again in the fall election of 1786. "The late returns," wrote a newspaper correspondent, "fully evinces that the Bank of North America has recovered its popularity, and that paper money has lost its credit throughout the state. On those two points the late general election *turned* in every county. In Bucks County, it is confidently asserted that the friends to the prevailing ticket, openly declared they voted only for men who would *restore* the honor and credit of the state, by *reviving* the Bank."[40] The division even more than before seemed to separate those interested in commerce from the farmers. One writer observed that the effects of the bank were evident to Philadelphians and in all parts of the state that had trade communications by land or water with the city. The fact was proven, he noted, by the defeat of eastern representatives who had voted against the charter. But the rest of the state remained antibank, influenced in some instances by narrow motives of party spirit, in other cases by trade with Baltimore or because the western counties produced few articles of exportation.[41] Another writer, attacking the bank, wrote simply that "the commercial interest is already too powerful, and an overbalance for the landed interest."[42]

A final series of votes ended with the bank's recharter in 1787. These adopted a report calling for its revival (December 13, 1786), defeated postponement, rejected a clause that would have restricted stockholders in their voting for directors to one vote each, defeated an attempt to rotate directors, adopted a clause punishing embezzlers of the bank by death, and called for the bill to be printed (all on December 28). The Republicans then fought off further efforts to delay and rejected an amendment that would have enabled stockholders to withdraw easily. Both sides voted with extraordinary consistency as though some powerful, conforming voice forced every aye and nay. Only George Logan, usually a Republican, broke party lines on that side, and Isaac Gray, often a neutral, voted for some of the restrictive clauses but finally favored recharter. By this time the Bank of North America had come to prove, rather than cause, party divisions.

40. *Indep. Gazetteer*, Nov. 27, 1786.
41. *Ibid.*, Dec. 2, 1786.
42. *Freeman's Journal*, Feb. 7, 1787. The writer preferred a loan office as better for farmers. Interesting articles that emphasized the antidemocratic nature of the bank are in *ibid.*, Jan. 3, Aug. 22, 1787.

These roll calls, like the earlier series, indicate the kinds of people who supported and opposed the bank. The antagonists continued to be from the commercial areas and the counties more remote from Philadelphia; the traders and lawyers versus the farmers; the large against the small property holders; the Episcopalians and Quakers versus the Presbyterians. Party distinctions, however, overshadow these other contrasts.[43]

The Republicans and Constitutionalists clashed on many other issues. One such was the debate over the College of Philadelphia. In 1776 the college was controlled by Anglicans, some of whom were tories and others neutrals.[44] The Constitutionalists therefore revoked its charter in 1779 and reestablished the college under a new board with new teachers who were ardent rebels.[45] After the war the former president, the distinguished Anglican minister William Smith, petitioned for the repeal of the 1779 act and reinstatement of the trustees.[46] The assembly recorded seven votes before it approved the requested bill, after which the Constitutionalists blocked final passage by preventing a quorum. The Republicans supported Smith with only three exceptions: Isaac Gray, who as just noted defected on the bank and other issues, Jonas Hartzell, whose record was erratic, and John Steinmetz, who also broke ranks on the Test Oath. The question evidently did not involve what kind of college would furnish the better education, for college graduates upheld the former trustees, and men without formal learning divided evenly. Instead the significant division pitted the commercial areas and nonfarm occupations against the agrarians, Episcopalians and Quakers against Presbyterians, and most of all party against party.

Disputed election results provided another source of party conflict. The assembly considered several contested vote counts, in cases of dubious merit that were mainly argued according to which side would benefit. In November 1781 the Philadelphia County election was challenged. Although the Republicans had carried seven of the nine seats, they attacked the election result in order

43. In this case educated and cosmopolitan men differed little from their opposites.

44. The Constitutionalist members of the Council of Censors stated, in 1784, that among the 21 trustees in 1778, 11 were nonjurors, three others had been attainted of treason, and another trio had remained in the city during the British occupation, leaving only four above suspicion. *Pa. Packet*, Sept. 7, 1784.

45. Brunhouse, *Counter-Revolution*, 77–79. The dissent is in the assembly journals, Oct. 2, 1779.

46. Assembly journals, Sept. 4, 7, 8, 21, 22, 1784.

to embarrass their opponents, who evidently had tried to steal it. The Constitutionalists defended the election with complete unanimity, while the Republicans were almost as solid.[47] Two years later the Constitutionalists challenged the election of William Maclay, William Cook, and James M'Clenaghan for Northumberland. The issue probably concerned Maclay, for M'Clenaghan died and Cook, a political neutral the previous session, never attended. Although Maclay won fame in later years as a backwoods democrat, he appeared in a different guise at this period. He was well educated, married into a good family (the founder of Harrisburg was his father-in-law), and became a lawyer and large landowner. By 1781 he owned 3,100 acres, a gristmill, and a sawmill, paying by far the largest tax in his area. In 1781/1782 he usually supported the Republicans, notably on the bank question. The next year he was absent much of the time, but otherwise voted with the Republicans, especially on financial issues. This record doubtless explains why the Constitutionalists challenged his seat. The Republicans, however, voted in a solid phalanx and gained the support of most neutrals as well as two renegade Constitutionalists.[48]

Maclay was also involved in a contested election in 1785. One slate of delegates, Frederick Antes, Samuel Dale, and Daniel Montgomery, consisted of leading Constitutionalists. They apparently carried every district except the first, which returned Maclay and two others. The question revolved around illegal voters, the Republicans trying to substitute Maclay for Montgomery. In this they succeeded, after two very close votes in which party lines were unanimous except for one Constitutionalist, Thomas Newharter, whose shift assured Maclay's victory. The vote revealed a very sharp sectional division between the two sides, and differences in the wealth and occupations of the delegates are also impressive. Maclay never took his seat, but the Republicans had succeeded in ousting Montgomery.

The parties also divided over the 1786 Bedford election, from which a large number of voters were reportedly excluded. The Republicans, who were happy to settle for one occasional supporter in that county, blocked an investigation, and both sides voted a strict line.[49]

47. Brunhouse, *Counter-Revolution*, 106–107.
48. Maclay cast a few votes, all with the Republicans, the most important of which was in favor of issuing £50,000 in paper instead of £100,000.
49. The contestants were John Canon, who voted with the Republicans two-thirds of the time, and John Piper, who supported the Constitutionalists on 58 votes out of 60.

Certain other votes also concerned politics rather than principle. Such was probably the roll call on a resolution in April 1782, which replied to Pres. William Moore's message by denying any attempt to reduce the power of the executive and terming his charges improper. Moore, a wealthy Philadelphia merchant, was a moderate Constitutionalist who during a subsequent term in the assembly voted with that party more often than not. His affiliation probably explains why the Constitutionalists cast an almost unanimous vote against the resolution. Political theory seems to have had little to do with a series of votes in the 1784/1785 session that defined the appointive power of the Supreme Executive Council. The question was whether the council should elect certain officers or whether these should be chosen by the assembly. Theoretically the Constitutionalists ought to have lodged all power in the assembly, and they did so in the case of some officials, but in most cases they agreed to the council's authority, probably because at this time they controlled the council and could rely on it to appoint their own men. In a series of nine votes[50] the two parties faced each other in military array, members following the party line with scarcely an exception. In the same year they voted almost unanimously on whether to retain a clause in a message to President Dickinson that was highly critical of him (February 17, 1785).

Various other political issues required votes during the 1780s. Efforts to organize new counties out of old ones resulted in the creation of Franklin, Fayette, Montgomery, and Dauphin. Despite an eastern reluctance to increase the number of western counties, the division did not follow sectional lines.[51] In Pennsylvania a new county received its share of the representatives out of those chosen by the old county, the number of men in the legislature remaining constant, so that westerners did not gain politically. The argument therefore focused on the justice of the measure together with the politicians' estimate of whether different men might be chosen. In 1782 the Constitutionalists supported almost without dissent a bill that eventually created Franklin County out of Cumberland. Since they controlled this region solidly, they anticipated no political danger and experienced none. Republicans however opposed the bill with few exceptions.

The separation of Dauphin from Lancaster, on the other hand, found the parties divided. The initiative came from John Harris and his son-in-law, William Maclay, whose town of Harrisburg would become the county seat and much later the capital. In

50. Dec. 3, 1784, Mar. 3, 18, Apr. 2, 1785.
51. *Indep. Gazetteer*, Mar. 20, 1787.

general legislators from counties west of Berks voted for the division, while the easterners voted against it; yet the Lancastrians opposed it, and some of the Philadelphians favored passage. The next session the act finally passed (March 2, 1785) with the Constitutionalists now casting most of their votes against, even though they gained ultimately when they lost the older county but carried the new one. Moreover they presently opposed the creation of Huntingdon from Bedford and blocked the formation of a county in the far west (September 14, 19, 1787).

The location of the state capital created a sectional rather than a strictly party division. The first two votes, on March 21 and April 1, 1784, found only one easterner breaking ranks on the first roll call and three on the second. Of these, two were Constitutionalists and two were neutrals. The western representatives formed a less solid bloc. York County delegates opposed the proposal because the capital would be located in Lancaster. Otherwise six westerners opposed the shift on one or both votes, of whom two were Constitutionalists, two Republicans, and two neutral. A second pair of votes on March 3 and March 21, 1787, resulted in delaying the removal. This time the potential capital was Harrisburg. Again some delegates from York County hoped for a closer site and voted in the negative. So did those from Lancaster now, because Harrisburg lay in newly created Dauphin County. Otherwise the voting was almost entirely sectional. One exception, the westerner Hugh Henry Brackenridge, had already won unpopularity by breaking ranks.

The two parties usually agreed in supporting Congress, dividing only on financial aid. The first important vote occurred on December 3, 1782, when the Constitutionalists tried to postpone half of the tax intended for Congress. They favored delay by a margin of 17–4, while the Republicans supported an immediate collection, 17–5, two of the five being marginal members. The latter succeeded when Speaker Muhlenberg broke a tie. Again, on March 8, 1785, the Republicans moved to postpone for one year the state's contribution to Congress. This lost, 46–23. The issue was complex, for the Constitutionalists proposed to pay the requisition in paper money, whereas the Republicans felt this was unjust, preferring to raise money by the sale of back lands. In that way (asserted the minority in a dissenting report) taxes could be lowered. The voting followed strict party lines.

A variety of economic questions divided the two parties. Probably most important were monetary policy and the closely related dispute between debtors and creditors. The debate over the Bank of North America, as already noted, was connected with the question of paper money. In 1784 the Constitutionalists tried to resolve the state's financial problems in part by printing paper money and establishing a loan office. The attempt resulted in a series of votes that, for example, increased the amount to £100,000, restricted loans to a maximum of £100, and limited the legal-tender quality of the money. The Constitutionalists favored the paper generally, supported a larger quantity, wanted it to be legal tender, and deferred the loan office bill until the next session rather than see it defeated.[52] The following year they pushed through the bill as part of their general financial program.

The need for additional currency won popular support in the mid-eighties. Petitions and newspaper articles testify to the demand for more money, especially in rural areas and among artisans and farmers who could not borrow from the bank.[53] Even some moderate Republicans favored paper, usually the artisan and western elements in the party, while Constitutionalists almost solidly supported the plan. Votes on March 31 and August 24, 1784, reveal the nature of the division on this question. In both instances the anti-paper-money forces drew primarily from the merchants, lawyers, other professional men of the towns, and the wealthy and well-to-do delegates. Episcopalians and Quakers also backed a hard-money policy. Legal-tender bills received their most enthusiastic support from the noncommercial agricultural areas, from delegates of small property, farmers, and localists. Artisans and representatives from commercial farms divided. That only a handful of Republicans borrowed from the loan office, while many Constitutionalists did so, made its purpose obvious.

Several votes on debtor-creditor relations also reveal the attitudes of the two sides. The debate over whether Continental currency should remain legal tender required several votes during the spring of 1780 (March 21, 23, May 25–31), in which the Constitutionalists defended the tender law while the Republicans tried to protect the creditors. A year later (April 6, June 16), the Constitutionalists favored and Republicans opposed a clause that anyone refusing a bill of credit, provided the entire debt or demand was offered, could never recover it. The same alignment continued on a clause heavily fining anyone who refused to accept bills of credit equal

52. Mar. 31, Aug. 24, Sept. 27, 1784.
53. E.g., petition from Westmoreland County, Aug. 1784, Records of the General Assembly, Box 1, Pa. Archives.

to gold and silver in payment for various products. Finally, the Constitutionalists succeeded in striking out a clause that would have protected creditors against loss on debts prior to 1777. The Constitutionalists were almost unanimous on these measures, while the Republicans lost half a dozen possible votes. The lines of division followed that on paper money, the extremes being city versus frontier, wealth versus moderate property, and cosmopolitan versus localist. Several years later the legislature passed a stay law for certain debts contracted before 1777 (September 2, 1784). Payment was postponed until the end of the session following June 21, 1785. The two parties split internally on this bill. In the fall (November 30, December 23), on the other hand, Constitutionalists overwhelmingly favored an installment bill applying to the same debts, which provided that, after a decision against the debtor, he needed to pay only one-third after a year, one-third after two years, and the rest after three years. The Republicans, who were outnumbered that session, closed ranks in opposition with a few exceptions.

That same year the Constitutionalists put through their general financial program. They proposed to fund (settle all accounts and issue uniform certificates for) both the state and federal debt, paying the interest by levying taxes.[54] The necessary currency supply would come from new state paper, issued on loan through a state bank. Although the proposal did not discriminate between original holders and subsequent purchasers of the debt and would require additional taxes, the taxpayers would not suffer greatly for several reasons: the principal would be paid only gradually, little money need be sent to Congress because the state would be handling the internal debt, part of the certificates would be received for western lands, and both the paper money and the appreciated securities would furnish more money for taxes.[55]

The Republicans urged that the debt ought to be paid to original holders as well as to speculators, and that the price of

54. See Brackenridge's description of the state debt, *Pa. Packet*, Mar. 27, 1787. Certain types of certificates, especially the quartermaster, commissary, and soldiers' certificates, were quite widely held. See Cumberland County petition, Records of the General Assembly, Box 2, Pa. Archives.

55. The assembly journal, Dec. 22, 1785, contains the majority's proposals and a detailed financial statement. Preliminary arguments appear *ibid.*, Dec. 4, 24, 1784, Feb. 3, 17, 1785. Newspapers published various favorable accounts, e.g., *Freeman's Journal*, Feb. 2, 1785, and *Pa. Packet*, Mar. 18, 1785. "A Constitutional Mechanic," broadside, Sept. 23, 1787, N.-Y. Hist. Soc., is interesting; see also William Findley to Gen. Irvine, Mar. 22, 1788, Irvine Papers, X, Hist. Soc. Pa.

western land ought to be raised so as to realize as much money as possible. Moreover they considered the plan "antifederal" in that it eliminated Congress from the whole affair.[56] Meetings of merchants pronounced against paper money and the funding plan.[57] Their substitute proposal, presented by Robert Morris, rejected paper money and relied instead upon the state's borrowing £2,000,000 in loan office certificates at 6 percent, the state paying the interest and ultimately the principal by taxes.[58] The money supply would be based on these certificates, but primarily would consist of the Bank of North America's notes. Morris's proposal was defeated, 39–23, probably because it would not help the small debtors, because it depended upon the bank and upon profitable loans from private individuals, because it would have left the payment of the federal debt in the hands of Congress, and because it involved heavier taxes. Two days later the Constitutionalists rejected a motion that the state borrow money to pay the debt and levy taxes to repay the loan. The Republicans cast an almost solid vote on these two questions, supporting Morris, 23–4, and taxes, 23–2, while Constitutionalists opposed both, 29–0 and 26–3.

Table 7.2 shows the principal characteristics of the opposing sides on the two crucial votes, age being included to indicate, by contrast, a factor that did not affect the voting.

The price of western lands was connected with the funding program because the Constitutionalists hoped to pay off part of the debt and so reduce taxes by receiving certificates for the land. At the same time they did not want to raise land prices beyond the ability of settlers to purchase farms, and the use of certificates would enable settlers to pay easily. The debate extended not only to future purchases but to past claims that had never been patented. Many of these lands also were occupied by poor settlers.[59] Although Pennsylvania lacked the great semimanorial estates characteristic of her neighbors in New York and Maryland, some large tracts had been purchased, and speculators hoped to obtain more. Such men would willingly pay in certificates. From the Constitutionalist point of view, that would help retire the debt, but if the speculators engrossed all the land the settlers would have to buy or rent from them. The Constitutionalists therefore opposed

56. *Indep. Gazetteer*, Feb. 5, 12, Mar. 5, 1785; *Pa. Packet*, Mar. 2, 1785.
57. *Pa. Packet*, Feb. 24, Mar. 12, 1785.
58. Assembly journal, Dec. 22, 1785.
59. See petition from Lancaster County, Nov. 20, 1785, Supreme Executive Council Correspondence, Box 20, Pa. Archives.

Table 7.2. Two Illustrative Votes, Pennsylvania

	Morris's Motion			Tax Proposal		
	No. Pro	No. Con	% Pro	No. Pro	No. Con	% Pro
All delegates	23	39	37	27	33	45
Residence						
Frontier	0	10	0	1	9	10
Noncommercial farm	0	12	0	2	9	18
Commercial farm	18	13	58	18	11	62
Small town	1	3	25	1	3	25
Major city	4	1	80	5	1	83
Occupation						
Farmer	8	18	30	9	19	32
Misc. nonfarmer	3	8	27	4	2	67
Artisan or manufacturer	4	8	33	7	3	70
Lawyer	3	0	100	1	0	100
Trader	4	2	67	4	2	67
Economic status						
Moderate	4	21	16	5	21	19
Substantial	11	13	46	14	8	64
Well-to-do	5	1	83	4	1	80
Wealthy	3	1	75	3	1	75
Religion						
Presbyterian	2	16	22	3	14	18
Quaker	5	0	100	4	1	80
Episcopalian	5	0	100	2	0	100
Age						
Over 50	5	4	56	4	5	44
40–49	6	14	30	8	10	44
Less than 40	6	4	60	5	4	56
World view						
Localist	8	22	27	10	21	32
Cosmopolitan	7	7	50	7	5	58
Legislative party						
Constitutionalists	0	29	0	3	26	10
Neutrals	0	6	0	1	5	16
Republicans	23	4	87	23	2	92

the speculators. Republicans argued that speculators served a useful purpose because they advanced credit, and urged the merits of higher land prices because the state would profit.[60]

Several votes indicate the attitudes of the two parties. The price of land required two roll calls. On December 29, 1786, a committee report opposed the Supreme Executive Council's recommendation that the price of land in the last Indian purchase be reduced. The committee felt that to do so would mean that the best locations would sell, but the rest would decline in value and the state treasury would suffer. The Constitutionalist leader Robert White-hill then moved that the price be lowered, but this lost, 28–30. Republicans opposed the motion almost unanimously (Bracken-ridge for once voting with the westerners), while the Constitutionalists all backed Whitehill. On March 12, 1788, a committee report lowering the price of state-owned land passed, 35–32; Republicans opposed it with only one exception, while Constitutionalists favored the reduction unanimously. The sectional nature of the division appeared very sharply in these votes, occupation being much less significant. Striking too is the correlation between property and attitude toward land prices, for no wealthy and only one well-to-do delegate favored a reduction, whereas over two-thirds of the men with small properties preferred the lower price.

A related series of votes concerned the collection of payments for land purchased before Independence. An amendment to a bill introduced in 1785 canceled interest after 1775 owed by all actual settlers west of the Alleghenies. This at first carried (April 7), 28–26, Constitutionalists supporting it by 19–7, Republicans opposing it by 11–3. The following September the decision was reversed, such support as the amendment received coming primarily from westerners regardless of party. A motion then carried (September 14) canceling interest only for those who had been driven out by the Indians. The Constitutionalists supported this suggestion, 25–5, while Republicans opposed it by 11–5; the exceptions were westerners.

The final issue involving western lands was whether certificates could be used in payment for arrearages. In December 1786 the Constitutionalists tried to introduce a law permitting certificates to be used in payment due for land purchased before the Revolution,

60. Various opinions are J. Okely to Benjamin Rush, Dec. 25, 1784, Rush Papers, Hist. Soc. Pa.; John King to Rush, Jan. 24, 1786, *ibid.*; *Indep. Gazetteer*, Feb. 12, 1785, Dec. 6, 1786; *Pa. Jour.*, Feb. 19, 1783; *Pa. Packet*, Mar. 12, 1785.

but the Republicans defeated the measure, both parties voting unanimously. The following March a bill was introduced to help redeem the state's debts by collecting arrearages. At first only Pennsylvania money of 1781 and soldiers' certificates could be received. The Constitutionalists voted to give this form of the bill its third reading, while the Republicans opposed it, both by a very large majority. The latter then tried to postpone it until the next session, attempted to amend it so as to accept in payment certificates for supplies furnished, money lent, and services rendered to the state or to Congress, and finally opposed enactment, all unsuccessfully. The Constitutionalists voted in a solid block, while the Republicans lost because on each vote several members from the central and western counties defected.[61]

The only important debate concerning tax policy occurred in 1779, when the Philadelphians tried to reduce their share of the burden, but failed on a party vote (March 14). Thereupon the residents of the city and county refused to pay taxes until a general reassessment followed a new census of taxpayers. In the same year an interesting debate arose over whether ready money should be taxed (March 10, 1779). The Republicans voted against, 2–14, the Constitutionalists for, 17–9. A petition favoring the tax led to a reversal in the fall (September 10, 14). Two other votes deserve mention. On September 23, 1786, the Constitutionalists opposed unanimously a bill relieving owners of nonresident land in Wyoming from taxation. A motion to tax imported salt was favored only by the most extreme Republicans, all from Philadelphia city and county, Bucks, Chester, and Lancaster (November 22, 1787).

An interesting debate between Robert Morris and the Constitutionalist spokesman John Smilie enlivened the assembly in 1786. Morris suggested an export tax instead of a land tax, to fall on commercial farmers especially in good years, relieve subsistence farmers, and collect from residents of New Jersey and Delaware. He would also impose a one-dollar poll tax and an excise, which would be "farmed out" (collected by some person or persons who would guarantee the state a fixed sum). This plan would raise money for all purposes, and he remarked that Philadelphians might refuse to pay their proportion unless the rest of the state

61. The arguments can be followed by the debates as reported in *Pa. Packet,* Mar. 27–Apr. 4, 1787. See especially the exchange between Whitehill and Brackenridge, who deserted his fellow westerners on this issue also. It seems likely that soldiers' certificates and perhaps the state money were widely held, whereas the certificates suggested by the Republicans belonged to merchants and monied men, who had supplied the army and loaned money to the governments.

collected back taxes. This disgraceful delinquency, he felt, resulted from disinclination, not inability. Smilie replied that most
of the specie lay in and near Philadelphia. More remote areas could
not pay the taxes, which had been much too heavy. No increase
should be imposed now. He objected that a poll tax had always
been unfair, that a tax on exports was impolitic and might dis-
courage agriculture, and that Morris's plan would exempt from
taxation all property in cities and towns. In reply Morris insisted
that attacks on the poll tax by "the country members" were merely
"unfounded clamour," for anyone who worked for half a crown
a day could pay it; but he had to give way, and indeed his proposal
never came to a vote.[62]

Salaries and other payments divided the assembly on numerous
occasions. The Constitutionalists ordinarily preferred lower expenditures. Party politics confused the issue, for on several occasions the Republicans attempted to force Constitutionalist judges
and other officials to resign by impoverishing them. Thus while
the Constitutionalists voted to reduce the chief justice's salary in
1781, they took the reverse position on several occasions.[63] Despite
newspaper criticisms, the Constitutionalists tried to hold the legislators' per diem at 15s. when other salaries were being reduced.[64]
Other votes concerning salaries included a division presenting state
officials with an increase retroactive for six months (December 19,
1781), opposed by the Constitutionalists as requiring too much
money; raising the salary of the secretary to the Supreme Executive
Council by £250 (September 16, 1785), also opposed by the
Constitutionalists; and a further increase for the same person,
which the Constitutionalists defeated (April 5, 1786). The same
party rejected a report that the state maintain certain roads (February 27, 1787) and reduced certain other grants of money,[65] but
the two sides seldom differed on these minor expenditures.

Government aid to business involved both money and principle.
A few votes suggest that the parties differed on this as on other

62. *Pa. Evening Herald*, Jan. 4, 7, 1786.
63. Dec. 17, 1781. The Constitutionalists voted against £900, 13–8. Brunhouse,
Counter-Revolution, 103, 117–118.
64. See, specifically, *Indep. Gazetteer*, Dec. 7, 1786; in general, *Pa. Packet*,
Sept. 3, 1785; David Jones to Anthony Wayne, Feb. 7, 1782, Wayne Papers, XV,
Hist. Soc. Pa.; William Irvine to Wayne, Apr. 28, 1784, XIX, *ibid.* A writer in
the *Pa. Evening Herald*, Oct. 29, 1785, argued that $2 per diem was profitable.
The vote was Constitutionalists, 16–10 for a higher rate, Republicans, 21–8 for a
lower one.
65. E.g., Mar. 4, 1788.

policies. A loan of £300 for the manufacture of steel won a narrow victory, perhaps because both parties contained manufacturers (April 4, 1786)—though these men themselves divided. The Constitutionalists opposed the loan, 18–12, while Republicans favored it, 17–9. Constitutionalists defeated a bill that would have authorized the Supreme Executive Council to loan cannon to a ship sailing to the East Indies (December 3, 1785), explaining that the cannon might be needed for defense, that the property of the state might be squandered, thus wasting the taxpayers' money, and that such a principle was liable to be abused. All but one of the Republicans defended the bill. The Constitutionalists also protected the taxpayers' interests by opposing a resolution that relinquished the state's share of a forfeited ship in favor of its owners and a bill giving the Supreme Executive Council blanket power to restore such forfeitures (November 9, 1787). These two votes followed party lines except for one individual. A division between the commercial and noncommercial interests appears clearly on these votes, for representatives from commercial farm areas supported the businessmen almost as enthusiastically as did Philadelphians, while delegates from the distant areas strongly opposed them. Affirmative votes came from the larger property owners rather than small, and Episcopalians and Quakers rather than Presbyterians, but other cultural factors seem unimportant.

A few miscellaneous votes on economic matters are noteworthy. Although Republicans opposed aid to most kinds of debtors, they favored almost unanimously a stay law for suits against debtors to the state (November 25, 1782). They also were willing to enable Mark Bird and James Wilson, both members of their party, to collect tolls forever for using a bridge across the Delaware (November 27, 1783), while Constitutionalists tried to limit the duration. Finally, the Republicans unsuccessfully tried to give Pennsylvania officers and soldiers who had served in the Continental army preference over all other state creditors (December 23, 1785), an effort blocked by a solid Constitutionalist vote. That three-fourths of the legislators who had served in the Continental army were Republicans no doubt influenced this division.

Most social, cultural, and humanitarian issues were nonpartisan. The treatment of Quakers was political rather than religious, though some antagonism on the part of Presbyterians may have affected the Constitutionalists' attitude. Only a few votes pertained to religion. A petition for money to publish the Bible received the support of most Constitutionalists despite their reluctance to spend money (October 1, 1781).[66] Another vote pertained to a bill freeing the Scots Presbyterian Church of Philadelphia from its subjection to the Edinburgh Synod. An amendment that would have limited the application of the law to temporal concerns barely lost when almost every Constitutionalist opposed it.[67] A bill to incorporate a society for the relief of distressed Germans (September 19, 1781) probably was not a party issue. The city delegates favored it, as did the wealthier members, cosmopolitans, and of course the Germans, but the Scotch-Irish did not.

A series of votes concerning slavery proves that the conflict over emancipation was a cultural and social rather than a political or party issue. The basic bill passed early in 1780. A vote on March 1 shows the legislators dividing without respect to party, opposition centering in Lancaster, Berks, Northampton, and Westmoreland. Subsequent votes concerned details. One forced Negroes to continue to serve if their masters, through ignorance, had neglected to register them under the act for gradual abolition. Another vote amended a bill that permitted citizens of other states forced to take refuge in Pennsylvania during the war to keep their slaves, changing it in such a way as to protect Negroes who were being freed from such continued service. On March 4, 1782, further relief to neglectful masters was denied, but later (April 13, 1782) slaveholders in the frontier counties were granted the right to register slaves and servants who were less than thirty-one years of age and to hold them in servitude. Finally, the house voted on whether a committee should bring in a bill to levy a fine for engaging in the slave trade (January 29, 1784). All these questions found the delegates divided with little respect to party.

Another group of votes suggests some cultural difference between the two sides, although the issue was not really partisan.[68] These determined whether and under what conditions the theater would be allowed. One such vote, concerning a report taxing and regulating the theater, was overwhelmingly defeated, perhaps

66. The division is quite interesting. City delegates cast all their votes against publication, while men from the frontier favored the appropriation unanimously. Men of small property and localists approved, their opposites did not. Publication found friends among Presbyterians but not Episcopalians.

67. Sept. 5, 1786. See the discussion in *Pa. Packet*, July 6, *et seq.* Brunhouse states that the real issue was whether the legislatures could modify charters and that the Republicans defended, not religious liberty, but the sanctity of contracts, while the Constitutionalists did not hesitate to attack private property. Brunhouse, *Counter-Revolution*, 183.

68. See the discussion in Brunhouse, *Counter-Revolution*, 112–113.

because it allowed the theater to exist (February 18, 1784). On another occasion the assembly narrowly rejected a motion to bring in a bill authorizing the construction of a theater "under such regulations and restrictions as may be necessary to confine the management thereof within the bounds of utility and decency" (March 30, 1785). Foes of the theater tried to prohibit it entirely as part of an act for suppressing vice but failed (November 17, 1785). Later they did succeed in attaching a clause forbidding anyone to build a theater or put on a play (September 21, 1786). On another occasion the opponents of the drama tabled an act licensing the theater (November 21, 1785). Not until 1788 did a theatrical company receive the assembly's approval. On these votes the Constitutionalists opposed the theater by a margin of nearly three to one, while the Republicans supported one by a majority of about five to three.[69] The Constitutionalists' position suggests both moralism and anti-intellectualism, which may be confirmed by their opposition to a request by the American Philosophical Society that it be granted a lot. On the second of two votes (March 26, 1785, March 15, 1786), the Constitutionalists opposed, 27–7, whereas Republicans voted for the society, 27–5.[70]

The final issue that requires notice was the ratification of the Federal Constitution. Before the selection of delegates to the convention that drew up the new plan, leaders of both parties conceded the need for reform.[71] But the state's delegation was (except for Franklin) exclusively Republican, including some of the party's most trusted (or mistrusted) leaders.[72] Constitutionalists were therefore prepared to dislike the proposed changes—their opposition was predicted as early as August—and immediately at-

69. The significant differences in Pennsylvania on this issue appear to have been as follows: for the theater, townspeople, large property owners, Episcopalians, and those of English descent; against it, the delegates farthest from Philadelphia, most farmers, smaller property owners, Quakers, and especially Scotch-Irish Presbyterians. Curiously, education and similar factors seem unimportant. Newspapers contain many articles, some of which are listed in Main, *Social Structure*, 267–268. See also a protheater petition from Philadelphia, Records of the General Assembly, Box 2, misc. folder undated, Pa. Archives; discussion in Brunhouse, *Counter-Revolution*, 147, 184, 219.

70. The legislature recorded no votes on education. A difference in party attitudes may be inferred from Whitehill's objection to establishing a German college as expensive and unnecessary. Fitzsimons in reply urged that the state should help the Germans educate their children. The question, of course, may have depended upon national prejudices. *Pa. Evening Herald*, Mar. 7, 1787.

71. See especially George Bryan's reminiscence, undated, in Bryan Papers, Hist. Soc. Pa.

72. *Indep. Gazetteer*, Aug. 16, 1787.

tacked the document. The Republicans introduced and supported unanimously a resolution calling for prompt elections and an early meeting of the ratifying convention (September 26, 1787). The Constitutionalists opposed this, 19–6. In the election campaign that followed, the two parties attacked each other bitterly, and the alignment both in and out of the convention showed that party lines were steadily maintained. No Constitutionalist legislator is known to have favored ratification, and not a single Republican assemblyman is known to have opposed it.[73] The same division affected politics for the next decade or more, every known Constitutionalist becoming a Jeffersonian Republican, and almost every Republican becoming a Federalist.

During these years of intensive political conflict, the two parties coalesced, adopted names, associated themselves with certain policies, put forward candidates, and campaigned for election. The degree of cohesion is shown by the votes themselves. Pennsylvanians seem to have formed parties reluctantly, impelled by circumstances rather than by approval of such a system. They recognized that parties existed and that they were important, but they lamented the fact and sometimes urged an end to party warfare.[74] Benjamin Rush, who helped to create parties when he took the lead in opposing the state constitution, referred to his party as a "society" and deplored the division; at one point he thought that the differences had ceased except those between Presbyterians and other religious groups.[75] Most observers knew better, and the papers are full of onslaughts and counterattacks in which the term "party" is used casually. For example, on October 10, 1783, the *Freeman's Journal* published a hilarious and scurrilous series of sketches of Philadelphia Republicans, in which one was termed "the bell-weather of his party," another a "staunch party-man," a third a "hot party man," and a fourth a "devoted tool of party."[76]

73. John King wrote to Rush, "Every thing among our people, must be reasoned with party, but it is astonishing to think that this great national question should have gotten so intirely involved in it, as it is in this state." Nov. 5, 1787, Rush Papers, Hist. Soc. Pa.

74. E.g., to Col. Bayard, July 2, 1783; Rush Papers, Hist. Soc. Pa.

75. To Gen. Armstrong, July 30, 1783, *ibid.*

76. Two other examples: "A Citizen" lamented "the baleful influence of party" and called upon legislators to "loose sight of private interest, either as merchants, mechanics, or farmers." *Carlisle Gaz.* (Carlisle, Pa.), Mar. 29, 1786. Another lengthy attack asserted that "the man of party is a man of violence, and sees every thing through a medium tinged with prejudice." *Pa. Evening Herald,* Feb. 4, 1786.

Both parties worked hard at election time. Apparently candidates were put forward and their names circulated, and men exerted themselves for the common good.[77] The 1784 election in Lancaster involved twenty-one candidates for eleven positions, for which the eleven leaders (in five of the six districts) all were Constitutionalists or neutrals, polling 1,627 to 2,660 votes; the other ten candidates were Republicans who drew 103 to 1,079 votes. The next year, after Dauphin County had been separated from Lancaster, Republicans swept the election. Not a single Constitutionalist succeeded, while Republicans who the previous year had scarcely received a hundred votes were now chosen.[78]

The election of October 1785 was fought with particular vigor, at least in southeastern Pennsylvania. The artisans had supported the Constitutionalists the previous year because the Republicans had paid no attention to their requests for a protective tariff. Unfortunately neither did the Constitutionalists, whose attitude may be indicated by an article explaining that protection for American manufacturers was impossible, which was too bad but unavoidable, so the mechanics ought to become farmers—a suggestion indignantly rejected.[79] Nevertheless the mechanics (according to newspaper accounts) supported the Constitutionalist ticket, consisting of the incumbents, perhaps because that party hastily passed a tariff of sorts two weeks before the election. The Republicans made certain concessions in the city of Philadelphia's ticket, for while Thomas Fitzsimons, Robert Morris, and George Clymer represented the extreme wing of the party, William Will was a moderate who appeared on the Constitutionalist ticket also, and James Irvine, a military hero, had served on the Supreme Executive Council as a Constitutionalist.[80] "The ensuing election," wrote Matthew Carey in his *Herald*, "bids fair to produce a most violent contest. No exertions are spared on either side. All the arts of electioneering are put in force." Carey later wrote an angry editorial in which he described the "undue steps" taken by the campaigners who went from door to door begging for votes. He also published an entertaining and revealing imaginary talk of

77. Thus Thomas Hartley wrote to Thomas Fitzsimons, Oct. 7, 1784, that "exertions are not wanting at York and we are not idle at Lancaster." Gratz Coll., Provincial Delegates, IV, Hist. Soc. Pa.

78. *Pa. Gaz.* Nov. 17, 1784.

79. *Indep. Gazetteer*, Jan. 8, 15, 22, 1785. Examples of requests for protection are in *Pa. Packet*, July 22, 1783; *Indep. Gazetteer*, May 22, 1784; *Freeman's Journal*, Sept. 14, 1785.

80. Irvine voted more times with Constitutionalists than with Republicans and was replaced in 1786 by the reliable Jacob Hiltzheimer, who voted the straight party line. Will changed parties at this time.

election day: "Well, Tom, going to vote? My dear fellow, here's the staunch supporters of the constitution—your approved friends —men who have taken care of the mechanic's interest—huzza!— they are for the paper-money—Damn the bank—down with the bank for ever!—We'll have no nabobs—no great men—no *aristocrats*—huzza boys! Success to the constitution for ever!"[81] According to some accounts many mechanics were prevented from voting because the polls closed too early in the evening.[82] However some probably preferred the Republican ticket because they hoped for better treatment. The Republicans won an exceedingly close victory, obtaining only 52.4 percent of the votes cast.

The "wide spreading flame" of party continued during the elections that followed. Each side recognized that control over the legislature was essential. A fellow Republican warned Benjamin Rush that their party must unite if they were to win. The Constitutionalists, he observed, were neither so numerous, wealthy, nor talented, but their "strict concert" gave them strength. He recommended that all leaders of subdivisions within the party should be assembled and consulted and that compromises should be arranged. He advocated generals throughout the state with captains in each district.[83] During 1786 the two parties were equal in strength, and local leaders exerted themselves. From Chester County, Gen. Anthony Wayne described the situation as follows:

I arrived from Philadelphia last evening. Our friends Morris, Clymer, Fitzsimons etc. are exceedingly anxious about the Chester Election and requested me to write you on the subject—*Frazer* is the person who will be run by the Constitutionalists to a man—we must have no division in our ticket. Your People must make sacrifice of private prejudice to public utility—for rest assured you will not have one man to spare on the third reading of the Law for modifying the test—I fear that the person who will be returned for *Montgomery*—will be of a different Complexion to *Reece*—Proctor is a weather cock ready to turn with any wind that blows—*Brown* of Northampton has already told us he goes no farther than the publication with us—thus Circumstanced I am Confidant that you will exert every influence and argument in your power to returning Willing—I shall be in Chester where I will endeavor to keep things right.[84]

81. Oct. 5, 12, 1785.
82. *Indep. Gazetteer*, Oct. 8, 1785; *Pa. Evening Herald*, Oct. 12, 1785; petition, Records of the General Assembly, Box 2, Pa. Archives.
83. George Lux to Rush, Feb. 18, 1785, Rush Papers, Hist. Soc. Pa.
84. To John Hannum, Waynesborough, Pa., Jan. 9, 1786, Wayne Papers, XIX, Hist. Soc. Pa. Frazer (actually a neutral) lost. Reese, Brown, and Willing won; Proctor lost.

Accompanying this energetic campaigning were accusations of unfair practices, diatribes in the newspapers, disputed elections, and punishment of those who failed to support their party.[85] Thus when Brackenridge violated the clear wishes of his constituents, they replaced him promptly.[86] By 1786, at least, every member of the legislature had to openly reveal his party affiliation because the delegates seated themselves in two opposing groups.[87]

The outcome of an election resulted not simply in the victory of one set of politicians or one "faction" or another, but major changes in policies. When the Constitutionalists conquered in 1784, they not only rewarded the faithful with office and punished the enemy in various ways[88] but forced through a totally different financial program, repealed the Bank of North America's charter, issued paper money, and passed a protective tariff to help the artisans. The later Republican success similarly led to basic reversals.

The character of the parties developed from their fundamentally different points of view on several crucially important issues. Thomas McKean defined the two opposing groups as "the few and the many . . . aristocraticks and democraticks." The Republicans preferred a less democratic constitution than that of 1776. On the whole they had been moderates in the contest over imperial affairs, and defended the Quakers against punitive measures. Centering in Philadelphia, led by business and professional men, they advanced policies useful to trade and beneficial to creditors, especially the establishment of the bank. They paid taxes promptly, advocated the payment of public and private debts, and favored a strong central government.[89] They were, wrote one observer, "whigs of a more moderate and deliberate cast, of more property and more respectable capacities—Many of them old hands in the

85. The newspapers contain many articles. For an example of a disputed election see petitions to the Supreme Executive Council, Executive Correspondence, Box 21, Pa. Archives. Evidently the judges deliberately reduced the votes of one candidate in Bedford so that another, with whom they agreed politically, could be chosen. Various groups of people instructed their representatives how to vote, and the delegates usually obeyed.

86. Richard Butler to William Irvine, Jan. 8, 1787, Irvine Papers, IX, Hist. Soc. Pa.

87. According to Dr. Logan, "It was notorious to every body the state was divided into two parties. Every one that comes into our gallery sees we arrange ourselves on opposite sides in this house; and it cannot be, nor is not concealed from the world." *Pa. Packet*, Sept. 19, 1786.

88. Brunhouse, *Counter-Revolution*, 166–167.

89. See the proceedings of a Philadelphia town meeting, reported in *Pa. Evening Herald*, June 22, 1785, and other papers.

legislature—Many Quaker Whigs."[90] On the other side stood defenders of the 1776 constitution—who were or posed as democrats —critics of the bank, the former College of Philadelphia, Quakers, creditors, and the Federal Constitution, and defenders of paper money, low land prices, and the interests of inland farmers. They were, wrote one, "country members, who are yet uninformed, jealous of and opposing the cities and people in trade."[91]

The Constitutionalists and Republicans—our Localists and Cosmopolitans—differed radically in their composition. Among the twenty-five Philadelphia representatives who held office between 1779 and 1788, only one voted with the Constitutionalists, and half a dozen remained neutral. Republicans also obtained a majority of delegates from other towns and from commercial farm areas, but those from subsistence farms and the frontier preferred the Constitutionalists by a large margin (see map, p. 208, and table 7.3). Farmers divided depending upon where they lived, but pre-

Table 7.3. Party Preference in Pennsylvania by Residence (in Percentages)

	Constitutionalist	Neutral	Republican	Total
Frontier	67	18	15	100
Noncommercial farm	64	15	21	100
Commercial farm	31	19	50	100
Town	29	13	58	100
Philadelphia	4	24	72	100

ferred the Constitutionalists by a margin of about five to two. Merchants and lawyers, who furnished the intellectual leadership for the Republicans, favored them six to one.[92] The rest of the delegates, including artisans, manufacturers, professionals, and lesser tradesmen, divided more equally, since they found neither party really sympathetic, but being townsmen they inclined toward the Republicans (see table 7.4). A final economic characteristic also clearly divided the two opponents. Wealthy men almost al-

90. Barnabus Benney to Nicholas Brown, Mar. 17, 1781, Brown Papers, misc. letters, John Carter Brown Library, Providence.

91. Samuel Vaughan to Richard Price, Nov. 4, 1786, Mass. Hist. Soc., *Proc.*, 2d Ser., XVII (1903), 356.

92. Joseph Reed observed that "our lawyers here, of any considerable abilities, are all, as I may say, in one interest, and not the popular one." To Jared Ingersoll, Dec. 15, 1778, William B. Reed, *Life and Correspondence of Joseph Reed* (Philadelphia, 1847), II, 39-40.

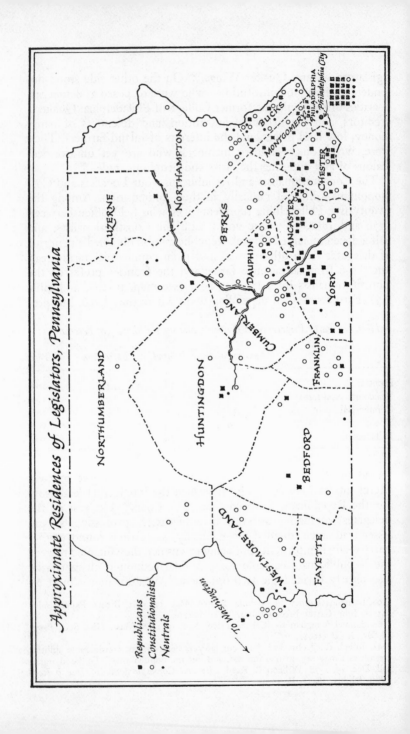

Approximate Residences of Legislators, Pennsylvania

■ Republicans
○ Constitutionalists
• Neutrals

Table 7.4. Party Preference in Pennsylvania by Occupation (in Percentages)

	Constitutionalist	Neutral	Republican	Total
Farmer	59	17	24	100
Large landowner	33	17	50	100
Artisan	26	26	48	100
Manufacturer	40	23	37	100
Lawyer	21	0	79	100
Other professional	24	20	56	100
Lesser tradesmen	34	23	43	100
Merchant	6	18	76	100

ways sided with the Republicans, and well-to-do delegates did likewise by a three-to-one margin, whereas men with substantial properties preferred that party only slightly and those with still less wealth voted overwhelmingly for the Constitutionalists. This factor acted independently of residence. Thus, while the Constitutionalists won 67 percent of the frontier delegates, 76 percent of the frontier delegates with small properties favored that side (see table 7.5). The same trend existed elsewhere: men of small prop-

Table 7.5. Party Preference in Pennsylvania: Economic Status in Relation to Residence (in Percentages)

Party Divisions in Economic Groups	Residence				
	Frontier	Noncommercial Farm	Commercial Farm	Town	City
Constitutionalist					
General (see table 7.3)	67	64	31	29	4
Moderate	76	65	52	50	0
Substantial	49	74	17	15	0
Well-to-do	0	50	17	13	13
Wealthy		0	25	0	0
Republican					
General (see table 7.3)	15	21	50	58	72
Moderate	10	13	24	11	67
Substantial	20	16	66	62	100
Well-to-do	50	50	69	50	63
Wealthy		100	63	100	80

erty belonged to the Constitutionalists, and those with large property to the Republicans, no matter where they lived.

Religion also played a role in forming Pennsylvania's parties. Notably, the Quakers had been alienated by the Constitutionalists from the outset, and the controversy over the Test Oath confirmed their Republicanism. Twelve out of fourteen voted with that party at least 80 percent of the time. Episcopalians were almost as strongly Republican, a position perhaps due as much to geographical location as to their peculiar history. Presbyterians voted for the Constitutionalists about two to one, but such prominent Republicans as Benjamin Rush and James Wilson belonged to that denomination, and on the whole their preference seems to grow out of their location in the more western counties. Lutherans inclined toward the Republicans, and all three Baptists as well as the single Catholic supported that party.

Table 7.6. *Pennsylvania Constitutionalists: Presbyterianism in Relation to Residence (in Percentages)*

Preference for Constitutionalists	Residence				
	Frontier	Noncommercial Farm	Commercial Farm	Town	City
General (see table 7.3)	67	64	31	29	4
Presbyterians	71	50	48	63	0

The Constitutionalists, strongest in the interior, naturally attracted the Scotch-Irish, who furnished much of their leadership. Yet many joined the Republicans (among them Brackenridge, William Maclay, and Anthony Wayne), and all told 49 percent became Constitutionalists; 32 percent, Republicans; and 19 percent remained neutral. Germans divided evenly, but men of English descent, reflecting their more eastern homes, decidedly preferred the Republicans (59 percent as against 13 percent Constitutionalists and 28 percent neutrals). There was little difference in age:

	Republicans	Constitutionalists
Under 40	34%	24%
40–49	40	46
50 and over	26	30
Total	100	100

Continental army officers voted with the Republicans three to one, but militia officers supported both indifferently.[93] Previous political experience did not affect party. All of the men from prominent families cast almost every vote with the Republicans, but those of obscure origin are found equally on either side.

Very few of the legislators had gone to college, and almost all of them preferred the Republicans. However those who had obtained a good education without much formal training expressed no preference. Intellectually inclined men generally adhered to the Republicans. Cosmopolitans almost always did so, whereas localists voted with the Constitutionalists. This factor seems to be independent of residence, though a relationship of course exists. At almost every point the cosmopolitans voted less often and localists more often with the Constitutionalists than the general average for a section (see table 7.7).

Table 7.7. Pennsylvania Constitutionalists: World View in Relation to Residence (in Percentages)

| Preference for Constitutionalists | Residence | | | | |
	Frontier	Noncommercial Farm	Commercial Farm	Town	City
General (see table 7.3)	67	64	31	29	4
Localists	83	75	40	50	0
Cosmopolitans	67	50	6	11	6

Parties in Pennsylvania resulted from various factors: the antagonism between urban and rural, commercial and agrarian, cosmopolitan and localist, eastern and western, large and small property holders, and among religious groups. These divergences took form because to such usual issues as taxation, expenditures, monetary policy, debtor-creditor relations, and the form of government were added traditional hostilities, the struggle over the state constitution, the debate over the bank, and the treatment of neutralists. The outcome was the formation of party organizations far in advance of those elsewhere and prophetic of the future.

93. Brunhouse states that "the militia furnished the rank and file of the Radical party." *Counter-Revolution*, 94. It probably is true that the Constitutionalists favored the militia over Continental army troops, but whether the ordinary militiaman (as opposed to the officers) preferred that party to the Republicans remains to be demonstrated.

Chapter VIII

Maryland

The Revolutionary leader Samuel Chase wrote from experience when he declared, "There is no government in which parties do not sometimes arise, and party as naturally creates factions, as summer produces heat, or winter cold."[1] Words change their significance, and Chase probably meant, by parties, various interests and, by factions, loose coalitions of like-minded individuals. Certainly that is what developed in Maryland.[2]

Once the war started, the distinction between country and court parties vanished permanently. Overt loyalism appeared on the Eastern Shore, stronghold of the old court party, but the rebels crushed it quickly.[3] The tories in Maryland were connected with the unpopular Calverts (rather than with the respected Hutchinsons, DeLanceys, or Bulls), and punishments such as confiscations remained a minor issue in state politics. The various questions that had created the long conflict between the council and the assembly also, for the most part, followed the royal prerogative into oblivion. On the other hand, a new series of issues pitted the senate against the assembly. In Maryland political alignments took the form of a contest between the upper house allied with a part of the lower against the rest of the delegates.

The composition of both houses produced this division. Maryland's constitution, created by the state's elite, provided for the

1. *The Maryland Gazette* (Annapolis), June 7, 1781.
2. This chapter was published in a slightly altered form as "Political Parties in Revolutionary Maryland," *The Maryland Historical Magazine*, LXII (1967), 1–27. The article contains details not included here.
3. The unrest, which continued into 1777, can be followed in the legislative journals. See also Purdie's *Virginia Gazette* (Williamsburg), Apr. 4, 1776.

protection of the status quo despite the Revolutionary upheaval.[4]
Primarily the rights of the planter class were protected by the
senate, which consisted of large property owners (£1,000 current
money in real and personal property) serving for five years. A
method of indirect election assured senatorial conservatism: the
people chose electors, who then selected the upper house. Moreover the senators, once in office, filled vacancies as they developed,
so that they themselves replaced about a third of the empty seats.
Since the electors usually returned incumbents, the senate consisted of a small ingroup. Far from representing the people as a
whole, it reflected the views of merchants, lawyers, and great
planters, the educated, cultured, wealthy, influential elite.[5]

The lower house also could not be termed a democratic body,
but it certainly was more so than during the colonial period (see
table 8.1). Every county sent four representatives, while Baltimore
and Annapolis chose two apiece. About a tenth of the delegates
lived in these and other towns such as Georgetown, Port Tobacco,
or Fredericktown. Over half resided in areas dominated by
plantation-type agriculture, containing many slaves and large estates. About one-fourth came from commercial farming settlements that featured smaller farms and fewer slaves but that
nevertheless produced for export. Those counties generally returned as their representatives men of the middling sort. They drew
support from a small semisubsistence farm area, and the two combined contributed the purely agrarian element in the lower house.
Delegates from the frontier cannot be distinguished unless the four
from Washington County are so denominated, but these men were
not themselves pioneers. Much of the state's frontier lay in the
western and northern parts of Harford, Baltimore, Anne Arundel,
Montgomery, and Frederick counties, where its influence cannot
be clearly distinguished from the sections of those counties that
bordered the Chesapeake and Potomac. We can only infer that its
effect may have partly accounted for the political behavior of the
representatives who came from these counties but who themselves
lived in the more settled districts.

By comparison with the northern states, Maryland's lower house
contained a relatively small proportion of men other than farmers.
Aside from those whose occupation is unknown (5 percent of the
total), 35 percent followed some nonfarm vocation, many of whom

4. Beverley W. Bond, Jr., *State Government in Maryland, 1777–1781,* Johns
Hopkins University Studies in Historical and Political Science (Baltimore, 1905).
5. See Main, *Upper House,* 101–114.

of course held considerable land. Scarcely 10 percent engaged in trade, so that the purely commercial interest had to depend upon the senate for protection. Lawyers and other professional men comprised about 20 percent and included many of the most prominent leaders. Only five delegates at most were artisans or manu-

Table 8.1. *Composition of the Maryland Assembly, 1780–1788*

	No.	%		No.	%
Residence			*Occupation*		
Noncommercial farm	15	7.2	Farmer	64	30.6
Commercial farm	53	25.4	Planter	65	31.1
Plantation	118	56.5	Artisan	1	0.5
Town	16	7.7	Manufacturer	1	0.5
City	7	3.3	Misc. nonfarmer	9	4.3
			Doctor	12	5.7
			Lawyer	23	11.0
Economic status			Other professional	7	3.3
			Merchant or trader	17	8.2
Moderate	31	14.8	Unknown	10	4.8
Substantial	44	21.1			
Well-to-do	75	35.9			
Wealthy	47	22.5	*Age*		
Unknown	12	5.7			
			Under 40	53	25.4
			40–49	29	13.9
Religion			50–59	18	8.6
			60 and over	5	2.4
Catholic	2	1.0	Unknown	104	49.8
Episcopalian	62	29.7			
Quaker	3	1.4			
Presbyterian	8	3.8	*Military service*		
Misc.	3	1.4			
Unknown	131	62.7	Enlisted man	7	3.3
			Misc. officer	59	28.2
			Colonel	23	11.0
Political experience			Probably served	1	0.5
			None known	119	57.0
Local office	27	12.9			
Sheriff, j.p., etc.	39	18.7			
State judge, senator	12	5.7	*Intellectual interest*		
Other state office	5	2.4			
Continental Congress	8	3.8	None known	173	82.8
None	41	19.6	Some	22	10.5
Unknown	77	36.8	Uncertain	14	6.7

Table 8.1—Continued

	No.	%		No.	%
Education			*World view*		
Little or none	4	1.9	Localist	76	36.4
Self-educated	13	6.2	Cosmopolitan	36	17.2
College	9	4.3	Uncertain	97	46.4
Uncertain	183	87.6			
Father's economic status			*Father's occupation*		
Poor, moderate	32	15.3	Farmer	37	17.7
Substantial	12	5.7	Planter	64	30.6
Well-to-do	50	23.9	Artisan	6	2.9
Wealthy	42	20.1	Minister	6	2.9
Unknown	73	34.9	Doctor	11	5.3
			Lawyer	3	1.4
			Other professional	1	0.5
Social origin			Merchant or trader	13	6.2
			Unknown	68	32.5
Humble origin	38	18.2			
Old family	99	47.4			
Above-average family	25	12.0			
Prominent old family	35	16.7	*National origin*		
Unknown	12	5.7			
			Colonial, English	151	72.2
			Colonial, Scottish	8	3.8
Mobility			Colonial, Scotch-Irish	1	0.5
			Colonial, French	6	2.9
Mobile	27	12.9	Colonial, other	2	1.0
Not mobile	177	84.7	Immigrant	8	3.8
Uncertain	5	2.4	Unknown	33	15.8
Number of slaves					
Over 100	6	2.9			
50–99	14	6.7			
20–49	67	32.0			
10–19	45	21.5			
5–9	30	14.4			
1–4	17	8.2			
None	3	1.5			
Unknown	27	12.9			

NOTE: This table includes 88% of the delegates, 1780–1788. They cast over 98% of the votes.

facturers, though a few others invested in such enterprises. There-fore the great majority engaged primarily in agriculture. Some 30 percent owned large enough estates to be denominated planters, and about the same proportion were farmers. As they usually owned several hundred acres and a few slaves, these last, to be sure, were not impoverished, but they brought to the lower house a kind of person seldom seen there in colonial days. In addition many other delegates had been brought up in the same environment. Thus the desires of ordinary Marylanders might be reflected by men such as these and by other representatives who took the same side. The farmer-delegates by themselves could accomplish noth-ing, but by joining with the planters they could and did protect the state's agriculture.

Large property owners held almost every senate seat and they also formed a majority in the house. Nearly one-fourth were wealthy, and three-eighths were well-to-do. About a fifth owned substantial properties, while the remaining 15 percent had less wealth. This last group generally voted together, but the others divided irregularly.

Culturally the delegates seem comparatively uniform. Most of them were Anglicans, for few of the state's many Catholics served in public offices, and the other denominations also lacked political influence. A large majority of the representatives were between thirty and fifty years of age, which had nothing to do with their voting. Few Marylanders enjoyed a formal education, and indeed the senate contained more college men than did the much larger lower house. Some delegates acquired an excellent education without attending school, but the great majority must have pos-sessed limited knowledge of the world. Only one in ten showed intellectual interest. As in other states, the data essential to defining the localist or cosmopolitan rarely exist, but probably the localists outnumbered the cosmopolitans by at least two to one.

Most of the delegates came from rural backgrounds. Although their fathers held more than an average property, only one in five could be called wealthy and one in four, well-to-do. Between one-sixth and one-fourth belonged to Maryland's prominent families, and at the opposite end of the social scale perhaps a fifth were of humble origin. Neither of these opposites voted as a bloc except on particular issues. At least three-fourths had been born in Maryland of English stock. Only one in eight was a self-made man.

The representatives brought to their offices less military and political experience than one might expect. Only a handful—8 percent—had served in the Continental army, and 35 percent in the militia, almost always as officers. Twelve percent had occupied a high political post. Considerably more were sheriffs, justices of the peace, and the equivalent, who voted quite differently from the men of higher rank. In addition some delegates served on local committees, but well over half seem never to have held office of any kind.

The common background of a very large majority of the delegates—living in the country, earning their living by farming, and sharing a common culture—meant that most of them agreed on fundamentals. As a consequence the lower house seldom or never divided on certain issues important elsewhere, such as the handling of the state debt. On a number of occasions the delegates united solidly in opposition to the senators, for only a minority of the lower house shared the opinions of the upper. At the same time only a minority went to the opposite extreme. The localist bloc, which in many state legislatures equaled or exceeded its opponents in strength, included in Maryland fewer than 30 percent of the delegates. The house contained a majority of moderates who opposed both the senate and its extreme adversaries, so that the legislature followed a middle course. Still, its sessions were enlivened by contests with the upper house and by various internal disputes.

During the eight sessions beginning in November 1780 the legislature recorded some 350 votes. On five-eighths of these the delegates divided into two clear-cut groups. Whereas in Pennsylvania the two sides bore names and took on many attributes of modern parties, in Maryland the division existed only as legislative blocs, unnamed and apparently unorganized. We will call them, as in Massachusetts, Cosmopolitans and Localists. A variety of economic, political, social, and cultural questions polarized the delegates. Most important and most numerous were economic issues, especially concerning taxation, expenditures, and relations between debtors and creditors.

In every session the delegates argued about the salaries of public officials. With minor exceptions each vote produced the same alignment: the delegates from cities and towns could be counted on to favor the higher salary. Men from areas that contained many large plantations did so more often than not (about 60 percent of the time). On the other hand those from smaller commercial and noncommercial farming regions usually tried to keep salaries low. Practically every lawyer and most merchants supported the higher figure, planters divided evenly, and farmers took the other side by a two-to-one margin. A majority of large property owners favored higher salaries, whereas three-fourths of the delegates owning moderate properties backed lower ones. In the cultural categories men of education and intellectual interest agreed that officials needed good incomes. Cosmopolitans were twice as apt as localists to vote for high salaries. Men who had held a state or federal office themselves naturally saw the desirability of good pay, whereas sheriffs and justices of the peace (who depended upon fees) did not, but the lack of an office did not influence one's opinion. Sectionally, men from the Eastern Shore and the two towns favored higher pay by a five-to-one margin, the opposition coming from the three northernmost counties together with Washington and Montgomery in the west, which voted twelve to one for lower figures. Finally, the sharpest difference separated the delegates of the Cosmopolitan and Localist blocs, which cast 85 and 11 percent for high salaries respectively (neutrals divided fifty-fifty).[6]

An example, in most respects exaggerated, is furnished by a vote on the whole civil list (January 22, 1782), which approved salaries for all of the public officials, 24–15. Voting in the minority were at least three-fourths of farmers, men of little property, delegates from small commercial or subsistence farms, and members of the Localist group. The majority included the same proportion of the high state and federal officials, educated and cosmopolitan men, wealthy and well-to-do delegates, merchants, lawyers, town dwellers, planters, and all thirteen members of the Cosmopolitan bloc.[7]

The alignment changed entirely when the delegates considered their own per diems. Four votes show the members with the least amount of property trying to obtain the most pay, while the most affluent favored the lowest. Similarly the highest per diem appealed to farmers and localists, and the lowest to merchants, lawyers, planters, cosmopolitans, and high-ranking officials. The senate also

6. Technically these figures are the medians of percentages on 20 roll calls selected to include votes on various sorts of officials, from the governor and members of Congress to clerks of the house, as well as one concerning permanent salaries and one on the civil list generally, discussed below. These occurred on Dec. 19, 1780; Jan. 29, 1781; Jan. 22, 1782; Jan. 5, Nov. 21, Dec. 23, 1783; Dec. 2, 1784; Jan. 6–7, Nov. 28, Dec. 9, 1785; Jan. 9, May 23, 26, Nov. 28, Dec. 5, 1787. Interesting earlier votes were recorded on Dec. 22, 1777, Dec. 4, 11, 1778.

7. The sectional vote was as follows: Eastern Shore, 9–0; cities, 4–0; southern (St. Marys, Calvert, Charles, Prince Georges), 8–13; northern (Anne Arundel, Baltimore, Cecil, Harford), 1–8; western, 2–4.

debated this question, the Cosmopolitan group there voting for a low salary, Localists for a higher one (December 24, 1779). The most significant factor affecting opinions on this issue seems to have been neither party nor the delegates' constituencies but their wealth.[8]

On other expenditures the lineup closely resembled that on salaries. Typical financial votes included those reimbursing the citizenry for losses caused by enemy action during the war,[9] compensating the governor for his moving expense (November 27, 1783), and paying individuals for services rendered—a doctor for his wartime work (January 15, 1785), a lawyer for codifying the state's laws (December 31, 1785), and a printer for publishing the legislative proceedings (December 31, 1787). Another ballot concerned improvements on a road from Baltimore to the Susquehanna (January 18, 1785). On all of these issues the delegates from Baltimore and Annapolis almost invariably favored paying the maximum amount, and those from the more remote areas, especially from noncommercial farm regions, just as uniformly preferred to pay as little as possible. Merchants, planters, and especially lawyers defended the petitioners; farmers opposed. In the same way the larger property holders, more educated and cosmopolitan delegates, and those who held high office voted affirmatively, their opposites negatively. Finally, delegates of the Cosmopolitan bloc strongly approved these expenditures, their vote averaging about 85 percent pro, while the Localist group generally cast at least 90 percent of their votes against such appropriations.[10]

Taxes in Maryland fell primarily on land and slaves, though the state tapped other sources as well. The delegates' attitudes clearly reflected their own economic interests and the interests of their constituents, but throughout runs an element of principle dividing those who approved of taxation from those who resisted it. One set of roll calls concerned the number of shillings per £100 worth of real and personal property that the people would pay, the rate

8. These votes were: Jan. 17, 1782 (for 22s. 6d.), Jan. 8, 1783 (for 21s.), Jan. 11, 1787 (for 14s.), and May 3, 1787 (for 17s. 6d.). These are the votes on which the issue was most clearly drawn. On all except the next-to-last, the affirmative favored a relatively high per diem.

9. May 8, 1783. A bill to pay for tobacco burnt created a somewhat different division, following above all relative wealth—the wealthiest favoring payment—but not of party.

10. Not every money bill resulted in such a division. A motion to pay members of the lower house who were absent without leave, for instance, found the sides reversed in some respects and in others without any pattern whatever (June 7, 1782). Appropriations for education will be discussed below.

gradually declining over the years from about 30s. to less than 10s. In these votes one set of delegates consistently supported a higher tax rate, the other a lower, until March 1786 when the two reversed for no apparent reason. Cultural and social factors seem unimportant throughout, though a small difference did persist. Until the last vote delegates owning little property favored a lower tax rate than did wealthier representatives, though the difference was seldom great.[11] Merchants and lawyers almost always supported high taxes of this type (which fell principally on land), farmers opposed them by a margin of about two to one, and planters divided. No significant sectional divisions appeared except on a few votes, but the two parties took opposite sides, the Localists of course trying to reduce the ratio.

The alignment on other taxes varied. A duty on salt was vigorously favored by townspeople, cosmopolitans, larger property owners, merchants, lawyers, planters, educated men, holders of high office, and members of the Cosmopolitan group, but opposed by others. One's position undoubtedly depended upon whether one had to buy considerable amounts (as farmers did) and whether one could afford a higher price.[12] The sides reversed when the question concerned a tax on faculties, lawyers, or offices of profit (April 15, 1778; December 17, 1781). Planters, wealthy delegates, and most affiliates of the Cosmopolitan bloc tried to place a low estimate on the value of slaves for tax purposes. Taxes on land won approval from townspeople and men with nonfarm occupations generally, but representatives from rural areas, especially more remote sections, were unenthusiastic.[13]

Import and export taxes received the assent of townsmen, representatives from plantation farm districts, and representatives from the economic and social upper class. Other delegates usually disagreed, but the lineup depended on the particular question. The attitudes of the two parties and of other interest groups appear in table 8.2.

The most exciting political contests in Maryland as in other states concerned private debts. The battle lines took a peculiar form in Maryland for two reasons. First, many well-to-do planters were in debt, so that at times both large and small property holders supported debtor relief. Second, the state's senate, procreditor in

11. See particularly Dec. 20, 1781, Nov. 21, 1782, Jan. 6, 1785, Mar. 1, 1786. Early votes (Apr. 13, Dec. 12, 1778) indicate a sharp division along party lines.
12. See Jan. 12, 1785, May 26, 1787.
13. Jan. 5, 1785, Jan. 25, 1786. Party lines correlated about 70%.

Table 8.2. Illustrative Tax Votes, Maryland (in Percentages)

	Delegates Favoring Five Tax Proposals				
	1	2	3	4	5
Occupation					
Farmer	40	32	35	42	44
Large landowner	56	62	69	62	50
Misc. nonfarmer	100	50	100	50	83
Lawyer	100	100	100	100	100
Merchant	67	50	33	67	0
Economic status					
Moderate	28	20	10	20	44
Substantial	55	50	50	50	50
Well-to-do	64	64	73	71	60
Wealthy	80	80	80	80	42
Intellectual interest					
None	52	47	48	50	53
Some	75	100	75	100	80
World view					
Localist	29	38	35	45	63
Cosmopolitan	82.5	83	100	87.5	53
Legislative party					
Localist	0	0	18	12.5	78.5
Neutral	70	40	50	60	62.5
Cosmopolitan	95	95	94	94	70

CODE OF VOTES:

1. For tax on imports, Jan. 13, 1785.
2. For tax on exports, Jan. 22, 1785.
3. For agricultural impost, Jan. 13, 1785.
4. For tax on agricultural exports, Jan. 13, 1785.
5. For tax on imported bar iron, Jan. 8, 1787.

composition, consistently and successfully blocked or moderated action. The dispute between the two houses touched off an animated controversy in the press that broadened to include the basic issue of whether the senate should be bound by public opinion.

Essentially, however, the question concerned economic policy. Both houses contained spokesmen of creditors and debtors who frequently demanded roll calls.

The earliest of these concerned payment of interest on private debts contracted before the war. Probably so many Marylanders owed money that an aversion to interest, at least until the war ended, was hardly controversial. The legislature recorded two votes on particular aspects of the general question. The first, an amendment to a money bill, allowed the debtor to deduct one-sixth of his interest during the year. An attempt to eliminate the clause failed, 14–24.[14] The second concerned a motion to bring in a bill abolishing all interest on prewar debts (November 14, 1783), an extreme proposal that also failed, 13–27. On these votes the creditors received their support from the Cosmopolitan party, the towns and the plantations, the large property owners, and the cosmopolitans, while delegates of the Localist bloc favored the debtors, as did the farmers, men of moderate property, and localists.[15] The correlations, however, are not very impressive and suggest that Marylanders of all types divided on the question.

Much more important and informative about political alignments was the series of votes on the issuing of paper money recorded during 1785 and 1786, which ended with a major dispute. In December 1785 the lower house passed a paper-money bill, 38–22, after a motion to postpone it had failed, 34–25 (December 13, 22). But the senate rejected it unanimously. In the view of most Marylanders, according to one report, the upper house considered the bill "incompatible with the interest of the extreme rich, and opulent class of our citizens, some of whom were members of that branch of our Legislature."[16]

During the summer of 1786 the usual shortage of specie and increasing prosecutions for debt, both internal and that owed

14. The explanation for this clause is given in Maryland Session Laws, 1st session, chap. 22 (see Records of States microfilm or Early American Imprints microprint). The debtor deducted, from his payment to the creditor, that portion of the interest that the creditor otherwise would pay in taxes.

15. The divisions in the text appear much more sharply on the second vote than on the first. In the senate the Localists backed, and the Cosmopolitan bloc unanimously opposed, a compromise proposal to deduct half of the interest (Dec. 19, 1783). Earlier an act had suspended suits for prewar debts (session laws, Apr. 1782, chap. 55). An interesting vote on Apr. 12, 1777, rejected overwhelmingly a motion allowing British citizens to sue for debt. Cosmopolitans furnished the small minority.

16. William Kilty, *History of a Session of the General Assembly . . . of Maryland* (Annapolis, 1786), 23. Kilty then proceeded to attack paper and defend the senate.

to British merchants, created growing distress. The *Maryland Journal* reported that in Charles County the court had been "compelled to adjourn all *civil* causes by a tumultuary assemblage of the people, and it is to be apprehended, that other counties are disposed to follow the baneful precedent." In Harford County, the article continued, no one was permitted to bid at auctions for property seized for debt.[17] The same paper presently announced a second riot in Charles County, this time directed against the recovery of British debts (July 21), and other instances of mob action occurred in Calvert County, adjacent to Charles on the western shore, and Cecil County at the head of the Chesapeake Bay.[18] These accounts may be exaggerated, for they appear in a pro-paper-currency journal, but they undoubtedly reflect a popular protest. During the summer of 1786 the newspapers published several articles insisting that more currency was essential for taxes, as well as for public and private debts, and attacking the "LORDS or MIZERS of the State."[19]

In the fall paper-money advocates promptly introduced another act providing for three issues of paper on loans totaling £150,000. The lower house defeated an amendment, 30–31, that would have permitted the loans only if the currency remained at par with specie and then passed the bill, 37–25.[20] Once again the senate vetoed the measure, supported, one critic declared, by "importing merchants, traders, retailers, Money lenders, rich men and lawyers, and their connections, friends, and dependants."[21] Both sides appealed to the people, paper-money advocates arguing that a majority favored the emission and that the senators should bow to the will of the people. The senators, however, defended their right to independent judgment.[22] As an alternative to paper money, they proposed that the government solve its financial problems by levying taxes payable in specie; a people whose income was £800,000, they argued, should willingly support the government.

17. June 27, 1786.
18. The basic account of Maryland during the Confederation remains Philip A. Crowl, *Maryland during and after the Revolution* (Baltimore, 1943). For these debts, see 89–95.
19. *Md. Jour.* (Baltimore), June 6, July 11, 14; *Md. Gaz.* (Annapolis), Aug. 31, 1786. The last is ironic.
20. Dec. 12, 15, 1786.
21. *The Maryland Chronicle, or the Universal Advertiser* (Fredericktown), Feb. 21, 1787.
22. For examples, *ibid.,* Jan. 31, Feb. 14, 1787. The major defense of the senate, written by Thomas Stone, appeared in *Md. Gaz.* (Annapolis), Apr. 5, 1787. See Maryland House Journals, Jan. 5, 1787.

The evidence does not make clear where the majority lay. On the one hand, a few articles in the newspapers, including some reports of grand juries, reported antipaper opinion in Washington, Frederick, Montgomery, Queen Annes, St. Marys, and Talbot counties.[23] On the other, two accounts from Anne Arundel County testified that over 90 percent of the people in the rural areas wanted debtor relief including an emission of paper. A communication from Fredericktown bragged that the principal gentlemen there supported the senate, but admitted that a great many people in the country wanted paper. In Baltimore County a delegate felt that a majority of his constituents hoped for paper although "a very respectable Body of them, who could support or affect the Credit of the Paper Money, much more than the Advocates, were against it." The senate continued its opposition, and the state could issue no money.[24]

The foregoing statements suggest that the division, besides pitting debtor against creditor, also involved the country versus the towns and the less respectable people versus the principal gentlemen, a distinction presumably both cultural and economic. The four votes taken in the legislature confirm such an analysis, but only as a very rough tendency. Samuel Chase, a considerable debtor, and other men of property and status who usually voted with their kind changed sides on this question, thus blurring party and other lines. Delegates of the Cosmopolitan party did oppose paper money but with less than their usual cohesiveness, averaging 68 percent on the four votes, while their antagonists sided with the debtors more decisively (85 percent). Most townspeople voted against paper, while representatives from small farm areas and men who were farmers themselves strongly favored it. Delegates from regions containing many large plantations divided evenly, as did those who were planters. The second vote on passage showed no difference between men of small and large properties, but the other three votes did do so. Cosmopolitan men, like planters, divided evenly, while three out of four localists wanted paper. Sectionally, the Baltimore town and Annapolis representatives—except Chase—opposed paper. Country delegates divided and the bills received their strongest support from the western and northern counties.

The same alignment continued when in the spring of 1787 the delegates passed an installment bill. No such act could pass the

23. *Md. Jour.* (Baltimore), Feb. 20, Mar. 30; *Md. Gaz.* (Annapolis), Mar. 22, 29, Apr. 26.
24. *Md. Jour.* (Baltimore), Dec. 19, 1786, Feb. 16, Mar. 8, 13, 1787.

lower house, to say nothing of the senate, unless well-to-do debtors as well as small ones found relief. Therefore the delegates began by granting those indebted for large sums the right to appeal for relief. An attempt to apply that principle to debts of £500 or more lost, but the debtors succeeded with a lower sum of £300. The procreditor group then tried to restrict installments to debts of more than £20, which failed, after which the figure of £10 carried. Other significant votes included the approval of a clause stating that all debts of more than £80 would be installed for five years, and the final passage.[25]

These votes indicate a division primarily economic, as the nature of the issue suggests. The urban delegates, those with nonfarm occupations, and the planters took the creditors' side except on the vote concerning those indebted for more than £500, whose cause they advocated (though lawyers divided on that). Larger property owners voted the same way, but education, intellectual interest, cosmopolitan taste, and political background had little influence. The localists, however, and men occupying county posts, did favor the installment of small debts, as did three-fourths of the farmers, men of moderate property, and representatives from small commercial or (notably) subsistence farm areas. Delegates belonging to the Cosmopolitan group voted with the creditors two to one, while the Localist bloc favored the debtors four to one. The same alignment occurred in the senate. Geographically, the creditor stronghold lay in several counties of the lower Chesapeake, while northern and to a lesser degree western counties generally voted for the bill.

Three other votes cast light on the question of domestic debts. One concerned a bill to prevent frivolous appeals, which, by fining debtors who appealed adverse decisions but lost, would have assisted the creditors in recovering their debts. The bill originated in the senate, but was rejected by the lower house.[26] In this vote cultural factors played no role, but delegates divided according to their occupation and wealth (see table 8.3). Again the Cosmopolitan group sided with the creditors (77 percent), Localists with the debtors (94 percent).

Quite different was the vote on an insolvency act, designed to comfort bankrupt entrepreneurs (May 19, 1787). This won the

25. Apr. 30, May 15, 16–22, 1787. The senate, for a wonder, assented, 6–4 (Maryland Senate Journals, May 12, 1787).

26. Feb. 20, 1786. See James Lloyd to Gen. John Cadwalader, Annapolis, Jan. 21, 1786, Cadwalader Collection, Hist. Soc. Pa.

almost unanimous approval of the Cosmopolitan party, city and town dwellers, merchants, and lawyers, and the support by at least two to one of men from plantation-type areas, planters, well-to-do delegates, educated, intellectual, and cosmopolitan men, and those

Table 8.3. *Prodebtor Support in February 20, 1786, Vote (in Percentages)*

	Prodebtor		Prodebtor
All delegates	41	All delegates	41
Occupation		*Economic status*	
Farmer	82	Moderate	100
Large landowner	66	Substantial	56
Misc. nonfarmer	60	Well-to-do	43
Lawyer	20	Wealthy	62.5
Merchant	0		

holding high office. Opposition came from the Localist bloc (85 percent), representatives of small farm communities (67 percent), and men with moderate property (60 percent). Finally, the same kinds of people who thus protected one group of hopeless debtors tried to assist creditors who were not citizens of the state, with the same groups in opposition (December 14, 1787). In all of these votes cultural and social factors seem minor on matters concerning debtors and creditors. The most significant elements in the voting alignment were, first, the delegates' wealth, for while larger property holders took the debtors' side about half the time, men of moderate means almost always did so, and second, the type of constituency, for men from towns and plantation-dominated areas favored the creditors, while those from regions of small farms supported the debtors. Finally, delegates of the Cosmopolitan party cast over 70 percent of their votes against paper money, installment bills and the like, whereas over 80 percent of the Localist bloc supported the debtor cause.

A few other economic issues deserve brief mention. The legislature recorded several votes concerning the treatment of men who owed money to the state, mainly for the purchase of confiscated loyalist property.[27] Many Marylanders were concerned with this, for although much of the property passed into the hands of well-to-do speculators, lands in certain areas—notably Harford and Cecil counties—apparently were taken over by former tenants

27. Dec. 4, 1781, Dec. 25, 1783, Mar. 2, 1786, May 24, 1787.

who thereupon became owners of the land. As a result voting became confused and resembled previously discussed patterns only roughly: in particular, delegates of the Cosmopolitan group consistently favored this species of debtor, as did townsmen. A wartime decision allowing retailers the relatively high markup of 30 percent (June 26, 1777) passed because the Cosmopolitan bloc favored passage, 22–3, while the Localists opposed it, 3–15. An interesting roll call concerned the question of whether the valuation of real property in Annapolis should be reduced for tax purposes.[28] This especially pitted the wealthier, cosmopolitan delegates against the poorer localists; representatives from small farming communities almost unanimously voted for the higher figure. Party lines appeared on this and also on a bill to regulate auctions (January 20, 1781), the alignment on the two being very similar. Block voting failed to develop on votes concerning agricultural prices, which correlated with wealth and geography. Finally, two roll calls dealt with the price of vacant land (January 7, 1782). On these the lower price (first 2s. 6d., then 3s. 6d. per acre) was supported by representatives of small farming communities, by farmers, less well-to-do delegates, and members of the Localist group, while higher prices appealed to city folk, planters, men of large property, and the Cosmopolitan bloc.

Certain political issues require attention for their importance or because they help further to illustrate political alignments. An interesting vote removed the restriction that prohibited the state's delegates to Congress from engaging in trade (January 14, 1781). The original law related to the moral attitudes of certain delegates. One is not surprised to find the merchants, most of the lawyers, and townspeople generally approving the change, for trade to them must have seemed legitimate, and four-fifths of the Cosmopolitan bloc agreed. But so did one-third of the Localist party and over half of the farmers. Education, previous political or military experience, and family background seem unimportant. Religion may have played a role, but unfortunately too few known dissenters sat in the lower house at the time to prove anything; Anglicans favored the change three to one. Curiously the younger men (less than forty) voted to remove the restriction, while only a third of the older delegates (fifty or more) did so. For some reason Eastern Shore representatives supported the townspeople unanimously, perhaps because they usually did vote together.

28. Jan. 7, 1781.

Relations with Congress never became divisive in the lower house. The impost of 1781 required only two votes. One of these defeated an amendment that would have authorized Congress, instead of the state, to collect the revenue, a procedure much desired by nationalists. The voting took no clear form, however, and men of all kinds voted on both sides indifferently (June 4, 1782). Unlike the alignment in most states, the Cosmopolitan party gave the proposal only feeble support, while the Localists were less united than usual in opposition to it (69 percent). On the other hand, a motion to approve Congress's request for altering Article VIII of the Articles of Confederation (which set land as the basis for determining the state's financial contributions) won the strong support of representatives from towns and plantation farm areas, of merchants, lawyers, planters, men of large property, college men, cosmopolitans, holders of high office, and members of the Cosmopolitan bloc (91 percent), with the other delegates either opposed or divided.

A curious affair with parallels then and later developed when, after most of the fighting had ended, a motion was introduced that no part of the militia should be kept out of the state longer than three months (January 14, 1782). This lost, whereupon a two-month limit passed. Those who voted in the affirmative thus were voting, not to prohibit out-of-state service, but to permit the militia's absence for a three-month period rather than for only two months; the negative votes expressed a narrower, not a broader, view. The minority favoring the longer time consisted of cosmopolitans, merchants, lawyers, the larger property holders, educated men, representatives from the towns and plantation areas, and the Cosmopolitan group. Three out of four Continental officers voted on that side, but militia officers opposed, 4–8. Particularly interesting is the vote of the localists, who opposed this longer service ten to one, a margin nearly equaled by farmers, small property holders, and the Localist bloc. Thus most people preferred to keep the militia at home, and they also defended military duty for everyone regardless of rank, voting against exempting the governor and other high state officials from service other than active duty (January 8, 1783).

Questions regarding the treatment of loyalists seldom arose in Maryland, and opinion seems to have depended primarily on individual attitudes and the particular issue. A motion to expel certain categories of loyalists, who sought permission to remain, lost (December 28, 1780), the division following no clear lines. The basic confiscation act, designed to favor large purchasers and limited in scope, passed over the opposition of men from the small farm districts, who usually favored such laws. Delegates from Cecil, Harford, and Baltimore counties, where most of the property lay, opposed the bill unanimously, as did most of the Cosmopolitan group.[29] Later in the decade the upper house unexpectedly rejected a bill to remove political disabilities of nonjurors because they felt that those persons continued to threaten the state. The delegates protested that such men as Quakers and Methodists were inoffensive, indeed useful, and advocated liberality. The position of the senate was defended by the Localists, farmers, and small property holders, who opposed concessions to the loyalists or neutralists, while the wealthy members, cosmopolitans, lawyers, and planters found themselves in the curious position of attacking the senate.

A final important political issue concerned the "intendant," appointed in 1782 to supervise finances and reappointed regularly thereafter. This step encountered considerable criticism in which the two parties consistently opposed each other in both houses. Probably the Localist group saw no need for still another powerful official, whereas the Cosmopolitans recognized the importance of efficient control.[30] The newspapers printed many articles on the subject.

The distinction between political, economic, and cultural matters, while definable in theory, is often blurred in politics, and in Maryland the line was seldom sharp. A clearly humanitarian issue involved whether some of a murderer's property should go to his widow or all to the state. The widow's cause won sympathy from the poor members, not the rich, who voted unanimously against her, from farmers rather than merchants or lawyers, from localists rather than cosmopolitans, and from men of humble origin, not delegates of prominent families (January 5, 1782). The only clear vote concerning slavery (December 7, 1785) found the representatives divided erratically with respect to most criteria except that of section. A motion to reject petitions favoring emancipation received its principal support from commercial farming areas, especially the western shore of the Chesapeake, while men from the towns and subsistence farm areas approved the petitions.

29. Jan. 28, 1781. Two senate votes also illustrate the party division. The Cosmopolitan bloc there defeated a loyalty oath in 1777, and in 1779 rejected a confiscation act, both unanimously, while the Localist group favored passage of both.
30. Votes Jan. 17, Nov. 30, 1782, Jan. 13, 1783, Jan. 14, 1786, May 26, 1787.

One roll call that reveals something about attitudes toward morality took place on an act granting the theater in Annapolis to the American Company of Comedians.[31] As in the two preceding questions, the alignment did not follow party divisions. Religion may have exerted a considerable influence, for 92 percent of the Anglicans present voted affirmatively; the two known dissenters (a Quaker and a Presbyterian) voted negatively. Geographical and occupational differences were minor, except that all of the merchants and most of the lawyers and planters favored the grant, while two-thirds of the farmers opposed it. The amount of property owned seems to have been more significant, as the following percentages of favorable votes indicate: wealthy, 83 percent; well-to-do, 70 percent; substantial, 20 percent; moderate, 33 percent. All of the cosmopolitans but only three-eighths of the localists voted for the theater.[32]

The same kind of person who liked the theater favored the establishment of colleges. Certain additional factors sharpened the cleavage in the lower house. In 1784 the legislature appropriated a permanent fund for salaries in Washington College, on the Eastern Shore.[33] One vote approved a grant not to exceed £1,200 current annually, another passed that bill, and a third chartered the college. The next year the delegates granted leave to bring in a bill establishing a college on the western shore and then passed it. Later an unsuccessful attempt was made to reverse the decision by repealing both of these acts and substituting one that would have created the University of Maryland.[34]

According to one observer, the opposition came from Presbyterians who supported education but feared Episcopal control of the colleges.[35] While it is true that such Presbyterians as became delegates took that stand, they were too few to affect the outcome; moreover Anglicans themselves split on the issue. Nor did the vote reflect simply the desire of the two "shores" to have their own colleges. More important were the questions of who would pay and who would benefit. Articles in the newspapers as well as the voting in the legislature indicate that many people regarded higher education as benefiting the rich at the expense of the poor. Of what use were colleges, inquired one writer, to the poor man who "is

31. This passed, 22–18, on June 12, 1782.
32. The senate also divided on the theater (Nov. 30, 1778).
33. Nov. 30, Dec. 3, 30, 1784.
34. Votes Nov. 18, 22, Dec. 10–19, 1785.
35. George Lux to Benjamin Rush, Feb. 28, 1785, Rush Papers, Hist. Soc. Pa.

scarcely able to feed and cloath his family, pay his public just and necessary demands, and teach his children to read the bible and write their names; what are colleges to these? why should they support them?"[36] Whatever the real effect of the colleges (and the critics were correct in thinking that only certain kinds of people would benefit), the division of opinion formed along not only cultural but economic lines.

Those who voted for the establishment and financial support of these two colleges included, above all, the merchants, lawyers, and planters from the towns and plantation farm areas, educated delegates with intellectual tastes and cosmopolitan outlook, and members of the Cosmopolitan party. These voted at least three to one and usually nine or ten to one for the colleges. Well-to-do men did also, but wealthy delegates split fifty-fifty, perhaps because they had alternative ways of educating their children. At the other extreme almost no one from a subsistence farm area ever favored these plans. Also strongly in the negative were localists, farmers, men of moderate property, those of humble background, and members of the Localist bloc, who were 80 percent opposed. Unfortunately no votes exist on the question of common schools, for the legislature took no action.

The final important issue arose concurrently with the debate over public funds for education, and the two became related. This concerned public support for religion. That subject produced two crucial votes, one of which approved the need for a general law to support Christianity, and the other declared that to levy a tax for the benefit of ministers was constitutional.[37] Although one observer felt that the Anglicans and Presbyterians opposed one another,[38] the votes give no evidence of it, and on the whole the dispute does not seem to have followed doctrinal lines. One side argued the moral advantages of a strong church and the need for general support, regardless of denomination, while the other felt that the money could better be spent on economic reforms, given the state's financial problems. Moreover the critics attacked the proposed method of financing by a poll tax. One suggested sarcastically that the people might be persuaded to combine all taxes into

36. *Md. Jour.* (Baltimore), Aug. 19, 1785; see also *Md. Gaz.* (Annapolis), Feb. 11, Mar. 4, Apr. 1, 1785.

37. Both votes occurred on Jan. 8, 1785.

38. George Lux to Benjamin Rush, Baltimore, Feb. 18, 28, 1785, Rush Papers, Hist. Soc. Pa. In these letters Lux either was telling Rush what he wanted to hear or reflecting the writer's own prejudices. They illustrate the danger of taking letters at their face value.

one poll tax so that the burden would lie where it ought, "on the sturdy shoulders of the rabble, on the lower class, or commonalty." The common sort could also then be made very pious, which "will comfort them under oppression—and make them submissive to the yoke—and look out for a *better world;*—whilst we, taking as much Religion as suits *us*, will govern *this* to our own interest." A few Marylanders at least had a remarkable grasp of realities![39]

The alignment in the lower house strikingly resembled that on the college issue. Favoring support of religion by a majority of at least two to one, and in some instances unanimously, were merchants, lawyers, planters, delegates from the two principal cities and the plantation farm districts, wealthy and well-to-do men, educated delegates, those with intellectual interests, cosmopolitans, descendants of prominent old families, and holders of high offices. Particularly opposed were representatives of the smaller towns and subsistence farm areas, farmers, delegates with moderate property and of humble origin, and (in less degree) localists. The Cosmopolitan bloc supported the proposal about seven to one, the Localist group opposed it four to one. Anglicans divided evenly. Obviously the issue was not primarily religious but financial.

The votes on these various issues reveal different alignments. Yet resemblances exist, forming persistent patterns that continued throughout the period. The way in which these patterns appear is illustrated in table 8.4 by the votes taken during the 1784/1785 session. In the table absent delegates are omitted, as are votes in which the minority constituted less than one-third. In addition a few roll calls are left out because they dealt with details and merely duplicated the vote on the main question. The issues concerned, most importantly, the college (1, 3, 8), salaries (2, 13, 16–18), the religious question (19–20, 28), alteration of Article VIII of the Articles of Confederation (6), import taxes (22–26, 33–35), taxes in general (11, 14, 15), the depreciation pay of an army doctor (29), the civil rights of nonjurors (30, 32), the road from Baltimore to the Susquehanna (31), and adjournment (36). A plus means affirmative, minus a negative. The order of votes has been arranged so as to present, in order, those of the lower western shore, the Eastern Shore, the two towns, the northern counties, and the upper Potomac, thus bringing into proximity the men who agreed with one another. The reader will easily perceive that one group of legislators voted as a bloc on almost every vote, typified

39. *Md. Jour.* (Baltimore), Feb. 25, 1787. See also *ibid.*, Mar. 1, 1785, and "Planter," Worcester County broadside, Feb. 1, 1785, Hist. Soc. Pa.

Table 8-4. *Alignments on Maryland Votes, 1784/1785 Session*

County	Delegate	Votes																																			
		1	2	3	4	5	6	7	8	9	10	11	12	13	14	15	16	17	18	19	20	21	22	23	24	25	26	27	28	29	30	31	32	33	34	35	36
Lower western shore																																					
St. Marys	Key	+	+	+	+	+				−		+		−	−	+	−	+	+	+	+	+	−	+	−	+	+	+	+	+	+	+	+	+	+	−	+
	DeButts	+	+	+	+	+				−		+		−	−	+	−	+	+	+	+	+	−	+	−	+	+	+	+	+	+	+	+	+	+	−	+
	Plowden	−	−	−						−				−	−																						
Calvert	Grahame	+	+	+	+	+	+	+	+	−	+	+	+	+		+	+	+	+	+	+	+	+	+	−	+	+	+	+	+	+	+	+	+	+	+	+
	Taney	−		+	−	−		−	+	−	+	+	−			−	+	+	+	+	−	+	+		−	+		−	−		−	+	−	+	+	+	+
	Frazier	−	−	+	−			−	+	−	+	+	−	+	−	+	+	+	+	+	−	+	−	+	−		+	−	+	+	−	+	+	+	+	+	+
Charles	Ware	+	−	+	−	+	+	+	+	−	+	−	+		+	+	+	+	+	+	+	+	+	+		+	+			+	+	+	+	+	+	+	+
	Hanson	−	−	−	−	+		−	+			−	−	−	+	+	−	−	+	+	+	−	+	+		+	+		+	−	+	+	+	+	+	+	−
	Dent	−	−	−																																	
Prince Georges	Gantt	+	+	+	+	+				−		+	−		+	+	+	+		+	+	+		+		+	+	+	−		+	+	+	+	+	+	+
	Digges	+	−	+	+	+	+	+	+	−	+	+	+	−	−	+	−	+	+	+	+	+	−	+	−	+	+	−	+	−	+	+	+	+	+	+	+
	Johnson			+	+		+	+	+	+	+	+	+	−	−	+	+	+	+	+	+	+	+	+	−	+	+	−	+	+	+	+	+	+	+	+	+
	Bowie				+	−	+	+	+		+	+	+	−	−	+	+	+	+	+	+	+	−	+	−	+	−		+	+	+	+	+	+	+	+	+
Eastern Shore																																					
Kent	Scott	+	+	+	+	+	+	+	+	+	−	−	+	+	−	−	−	−	+	+	−	−	+	−	+	−	+	+	−	+		+	+	+	+	+	−
	Letherbury	+	+	+	+	+	+	+	+		−	−	−	−	+	+	−	+	+	+	+	+	+	+	+	−	−	+	+	−	−			+	+	+	+
	Graves			−		+	+	+	+			−	−	−	+		−	+	+	+	+	+		+	+		+	−	+	+	+	+	+	+	+	+	+
	Cadwalader	+			+	+	+	+	+	−	−	−	−	−	+	+	−	+	+	+	+	+	−	+	+	−	+	−	+	+	+	+	+	+	+	+	+
Talbot	Harris			−	+	+	+	+	+	+		+				+		+	+	+	+	+	+	+	+	+	+	−	+	+	+	+	+	+	+	+	+
	Gibson			+	+	+	+	+	+																							+					
	Hindman	+	+	+	+	+	+	−	+	+			+		+	+		+	+	+	+	+	+	+	+	+	+	+	+	+	−		+				
	Roberts			+	+	+	+		−	+		−		+	+		−	+	+	+	+	+	−	+	−	−	+	+	+	+	+	−	−	−	+	+	+
Somerset	Dashiell	+	+	+	+				+		−	−		+	+	−	−	+		+	+		+	+	+	+	+		+	+	+	+		+	+	+	+
	Waters	+	+	+					+	+	−	−	+	+	−	−	−	+	+	+	+	−	−	+	−	+	+	+	+	+	+		−	+	+	+	+
	Elzey	+	+	+	+	+	+	+	+	+				−	+	−		−	+	+	+	+		+	+	−	+	−	+	+	+		+	+	+	+	+
	Gale	+	+	+	+	+	+	+	+	+				+	+	+		+	+	+	+	+		+	+	−	+	+	+	+	+	+		+	+	+	+
Dorchester	Shaw			+			+	+		+	+													+					+							−	
Queen Annes	Scott	+	+	+	+	+	+	+	+	+		+	+	+	+	+	+	+	+	+	+	+	+	+	+	+	+	+	+	+	−	+	+	+	+	+	+
	Steel	+	+	+	+	+	+	+		+		−																+		+							
	Seney	+	+	+	+	+	+		+	+	−	+	+	+	−	+	−	+	+	+	+	+	+	+	+	+	+	+	+	+				+	+	+	+
	Wright	+	+	+	+	+	+		+	+	−		+	+	−	+	−	+	+	+	+	+	+	+	−	+	+	+	+	+				+	+	+	+
	Coursey	+	+	+					+	+		+		−	+		+						+					+								+	+
	Sewall			+					−	+	−		−	+	+	+	+	+	+	+	+	+	+	+	−	+	+	+	+	+	−	+	+	+	+	+	+
Worcester	Townsend	+	+	+	+	+	+	+	+	+	−	−	+	−	+	+	−	−	−	−	+	+	+	−	−	+	+	+	+	+	+	+	+	+	+	+	+
	Chaille		+	+	+	+	+	−	+	−	−	+	+	+	+	+	−	+	+	+	+	+	+	+	−	+	+	−	+	+	+	+	+	+	+	−	−
	Dashiell		+	+	+	+	+	−	+	−	−	−	−	+	+	+	−	+	+	+	+	+	+	+	−	−	+	−	+	+	+	+	+	+	+	−	−

Table 8.4—Continued

County	Delegate																				Votes																
		1	2	3	4	5	6	7	8	9	10	11	12	13	14	15	16	17	18	19	20	21	22	23	24	25	26	27	28	29	30	31	32	33	34	35	36
Caroline	Hardcastle	+	+	+	−	+	+	−	+	+	−	−	−		−	+	−	+	+	+	+	−	−	+	−	+	+	−	−	−	+	+	+	+	+	−	−
	Hughlet	−		−	−	+	+	−	+	+	−	−			+	+	−	+	+	+	+	−	−	+	−	+	+	−	−	+	+	+	+	+	+	−	−
	Downes																													+	+	−	+	+	+	−	+
Towns																																					
Annapolis	Chase	+	+	+	+	+	+	−	+	+	−	−	−	+	+	+	−	+	+	+	+	−	−	+	−	+	+	−	−	+	+	+	+	+	+	+	+
Baltimore	Quynn	+	+	+	+	+	+	−	+	+	−	−	−	+	+	+	−	+	+	+	+	−	−	+	−	+	+	−	−	+	+	+	+	+	+	+	+
	McMechen			+	+	+	+	−	+	+	+	−	−	+	+	+	−	+	+	+	+	−	−	+	+	+	+	−	−	+	+	+	−	+	+	−	+
	Steret	−		−	−	−	−	−	+	+	+	−	−	+	+	+	−	+	+	−	−	−	−	+	+	+	+	+	−	−	+	+	−	+	+	−	+
Northern counties																																					
Cecil	Job	−	−	−	+	−	−	−	+	+	+	+	+	+	+	+	+	−	−	−	+	−	+	+	+	+	+	−	−	−	+	−	+	−	−	+	+
	Miller	−	−	−	−	+	−	−	+	+	−	+	+	+	+	+	+	−	−	−	−	+	+	+	+	+	−	−	−	−	−	−	−	−	−	+	+
	Brevard	−	−	−	+	+	+	−	+	+	−	+	+	+	+	+	+	−	−	−	−	+	+	+	+	−	−	−	−	−	−	−	−	−	−	+	+
	Oglevee			−	+	−	−	−	+	+	+	+	+	+	+	+	+	−	−	−	−	+	+	+	+	−	−	+	−	−	−	−	−	−	−	+	+
Harford	Norris	−	−	−	−	−	−	−	+	+	+	+	+	+	+	+	+	−	−	−	−	+	+	+	+	−	−	+	−	−	−	−	−	−	−	+	+
	Love			−	+	−	+	+	−	−	+	+	+	−	−	−	−	+	+	−	−	+	+	+	+	−	−	+	−	+	−	−	−	−	−	−	−
	Wheeler			−	+	−	−	+	−	−	+	+	+	−	−	−	−	−	−	−	−	+	+	−	−	−	−	+	−	−	−	−	−	−	−	+	−
	Bond			−	−	−	−	+	−	−	+	+	+	−	+	+	+	−	+	−	−	+	+	−	+	−	+	+	−	+	−	−	−	−	−	+	+
Baltimore	Ridgely			−	+	−	+	+	−	−	+	+	+	+	+	+	+	−	−	−	−	−	−	−	−	−	−	+	−	+	−	−	−	+	+	+	+
	Ridgely of William	−	−	−	−	+	+	+	−	−	+	+	−	+	+	−	+	−	+	+	+	−	+	−	+	+	+	−	+	−	−	+	−	−	+	−	+
	Stevenson			−		−	−	+	−	−	−	+	−	−	−	−	+	−	−	−	−	+	+	−	−	−	+	−	+	+	−	−	−	−	+	+	+
	Deye			−	+	+	−	+	−	+	+	+	−	−	−	+	+	−	−	+	+	−	−	+	+	+	+	+	+	+	+	+	+	+	+	+	−
Anne Arundel	N. Worthington	−	−	−			−	+	−	−	+	+	+	+	−	+	+	−	+	+	+	−	−	+	+	−	+	+	+	+	−	+	+	+	−	+	−
	Hall	−	−	−	+	+	+	+	−	−	+	−	−	−	+	+	+	+	−	+	+	−	+	+	−	−	+	+	+	+	+	+	+	−	−	−	−
	Carroll			+	+	+		+	+	−	−	+	−	−	+	+	+	−	−	+	−	+			+	+	+	+	+	+	+	+	+	+	+	+	−	+
	B. T. B. Worthington			−	−	−	+	+	+	+	−	−	−	+	+	+	+	+	+	+	+	+	−	−	−	−	+	+	−	+	−	−	+	+	+	−	−
Upper Potomac																																					
Frederick	Beatty	−	−	−	+	−	+	+	−	+	+	−	−	+	+	+	−	+	+	−	−	−	−	−	+	−	+	−	−	+	−	+	−	−	−	+	+
	Gantt	+	+	+	+	+	−	+	−	+	−	−	−	−	−	−	−	+	+	+	−	−	+	+	+	+	+	+	−	−	+	−	−	−	−	+	+
	Carey	+	+	−	+	−	−	+	−	+	−	−	−	−	−	−	−	+	+	+	+	−	+	+	+	+	+	+	−	−	+	−	−	−	−	+	+
	Shriver	−	−	+	+	+	−	+	−	+	−	−	−	−	−	−	−	+	+	+	−	−	−	−	−	−	−	−	+	−	−	−	−	−	−	−	−
Washington	Stull	−	−	−	−	−	−	+	−	−	+	+	+	−	+	−	−	+	+	+	+	−	+	−	+	+	−	+	+	−	+	−	−	−	−	+	+
	Cellars	−	−	−	+	−	−	+	−	−	+	+	+	−	+	−	−	+	+	+	+	−	+	−	+	+	−	+	+	−	−	−	−	−	−	+	+
	Swingle			−	+	−	−	+	−	−	+	+	+	−	+	−	−	+	+	+	+	−	+	−	+	+	−	+	+	−	−	−	−	−	−	+	+
Montgomery	Oneale	−	−	−	−	−	−	+	+	−	+	+	+	+	+	+	+	+	+	+	−	−	+	−	+	−	−	+	+	−	+	+	+	−	−	+	+
	Cramphin			−	+	−	−	+	+	−	−	−	−	+	+	+	+	+	+	+	+	−	+	+	+	−	−	+	+	−	+	+	−	−	−	+	−
	Edwards			−	+	−	−	+	+	−	+	+	+	+	+	+	+	+	+	+	+	−	+	+	+	−	−	+	+	−	−	+	+	−	−	+	+
	Wooton			−	−	−	−	+	+	−	−	+	+	+	+	+	+	+	+	+	+	−	+	−	+	−	−	+	−	−	−	+	−	−	−	+	+

especially by the legislators in table 8.5, which traces the alignment only halfway. Other legislators such as Key, DeButts, Digges,
Johnson, Scott, Steel, and Townsend clearly belong to the same
group. This is our Cosmopolitan bloc. On the opposite side are,
most decisively, Seney, Job, Miller, Brevard, Oglevee, Norris, Love,
Bond, Wheeler, Stevenson, Hall, Shriver, Stull, Cellars, Swingle,

Table 8.5. Bloc Voting in Maryland

	Votes																	
	1	2	3	4	5	6	7	8	9	10	11	12	13	14	15	16	17	18
Type	+	+	+	+	−	+	−	+	?	−	−	−	−	+	+	−	+	+
Frazier	+	+	+	+	−	+	−	+		−	−	−		+	+	−	+	+
Gantt		+	+	+			+	+		+	+	−				−	+	+
Gibson	+	+	+	+	+	+	−	+		−	−	−	−	+		−	+	+
Hindman	+	+	+	+	−	+	−	+	−	−	−	−	−	+	+	−	+	+
Dashiell	+	+	+	+	−	+	−	+	−	−	−	−	+	+	+	−	+	+
Waters	+		+	+	−		−	+	+	−	−	−	−	+		−	+	+
Elzey	+	+	+	+	−	+	−	+		−	−	−	+	+	−	−	+	+
Chaille		+	+	−	+	−	+	+	−	−	+	−	+	+	−	+	+	+
Dashiell	+	+	+	+	−	+	−	+	+	−	−	−	+	+	+	−	+	+
Hardcastle	+	+	+	−	+	+	−	+	+	−	−	−		−	+	−	+	+
Chase	+		+	+	−	+	−	+	−	−	−	−	−	+	+	−	+	+
Quynn	+	+	+	+	−	+	−	+	−	−	−	−	−	+	+	−	+	+
M'Mechen		+	−	+	−	+	+	+	−	−				+	+	−	+	+
Carroll		+	−	+		+				−	−	−	+	+	−	+	+	+

Oneale, and Edwards. These two sets of delegates polarized on
nearly every issue during the whole session. This is an extreme example, but during the eight years under consideration the two
groups of men cast 80 percent of their votes as a unit on significant
issues that included three-fifths of the votes cast.[40]

40. "Significant votes" include about two-thirds of the whole number and
means those votes that distinguished the parties. In order to check the accuracy
of this analysis, each delegate's votes were compared with those of all other delegates by use of a computer, each session being taken separately. The result always
corresponded closely with that described in the text. All told, the machine analysis
separated two major groups. One contained 62 persons, including 46 Localists,
3 Cosmopolitans, and 13 neutrals. The second included 61 Cosmopolitans, 1 Localist, and 19 neutrals. A collection of misfits was made up of 3 Localists, 1 Cosmopolitan, and 15 neutrals. Thus the two blocs accounted for roughly seven-eighths
of the delegates.

The two major parties differed from one another in many ways. Geographically, the Cosmopolitans drew nearly half of their support from the Eastern Shore, primarily the five southernmost counties, and one-third from the four southern counties of the western shore between the Potomac River and the Chesapeake Bay (see map, p. 237). Together with the delegates from the two towns, these men account for over 90 percent of the bloc's membership. The Localists, on the other hand, lived principally in the counties along the northern part of the bay, especially on the western shore, or in the state's western area along the upper Potomac. All but one of their leaders, in terms of voting consistency, represented those sections. Table 8.6 shows the voting patterns of these districts.

Table 8.6. Party Preference in Maryland Sections (in Percentages)

Section	Cosmopolitans	Neutrals	Localists	Total
Eastern Shore	47	38	15	100
Southern Chesapeake/Potomac	51	30	19	100
Annapolis and Baltimore	89	11	0	100
Northern Chesapeake	11.5	27	61.5	100
Western	10	37	53	100

Any attempt to describe the economic characteristics of the homes of these men founders on the absence of detailed studies. Obviously some lived in towns, some in areas containing a heavy concentration of slaves and large estates, a few probably resided in areas sufficiently remote to be termed semisubsistence, and the rest came from communities that concentrated on cash crops but contained relatively few real plantations. While so much imprecision makes any conclusions tentative, certain generalizations seem valid. Over half of the delegates from towns of all sizes voted with the Cosmopolitan bloc, and most of the rest were neutrals. Representatives from what seem to be plantation-type areas divided in a similar fashion, 47 percent with the Cosmopolitans, 33 percent for the neutrals, and 20 percent with the Localists. Those from smaller commercial farms preferred the latter by a small margin, while delegates probably living in partly subsistence, partly commercial farming settlements voted with the Localists, four to one.

The occupations of the delegates may have exerted more influ-

Approximate Residences
of Legislators, Maryland

■ Cosmopolitans
○ Localists
· Neutrals

ence on voting than did geographical location (see table 8.7).
Lawyers, doctors, and merchants provided a fundamental core of
strength for the Cosmopolitan party, furnishing over 40 percent of
the membership and half of the leaders. On the other hand, the
Localist group drew only 7 percent of its delegates from trade and
the professions. Planters divided quite evenly, while ordinary
farmers much preferred the Localists. Thus the Cosmopolitan bloc
consisted primarily of business and professional men and of plant-

Table 8.7. Occupation and Party Preference in Maryland (in Percentages)

Party Choice of Occupational Groups					Occupational Composition of Parties			
	Loc.	Neu.	Cos.	Total		Loc.	Neu.	Cos.
Farmers	45.3	29.7	25.0	100.0	Farmer	49.2	27.9	19.5
Planters	30.7	32.3	36.9	99.9	Planter	33.9	30.9	29.3
Lawyers	8.7	21.7	69.6	100.0	Lawyer or			
Doctors	0.0	33.3	66.7	100.0	doctor	3.4	13.1	29.3
Traders	11.8	17.6	70.6	100.0	Trader	3.4	4.4	14.6
Other non-					Other non-			
farmers	22.2	61.1	16.7	100.0	farmer	6.7	16.2	3.7
					Unknown	3.4	7.4	3.7
					Total	100.0	99.9	100.1

ers, the Localists of farmers and planters. Even in those areas dominated by the Localists, which as we have seen were rural and
comparatively small farming districts, the nonfarmers tended to
vote on the other side. Thus in the seven counties where the Localists had a majority, 58 percent of the delegates supported them,
31 percent were neutral, and 11 percent favored the Cosmopolitans, but nonfarm representatives seldom followed the Localist
voting pattern: they either preferred the Cosmopolitans (32 percent) or more often remained neutral (50 percent). Occupation,
then, defines the Localist bloc as primarily agrarian, the Cosmopolitan group as urban (49 percent) and commercial farm (27
percent).

The factor of wealth seems comparatively minor except on particular votes. Most of the small property owners among the delegates either sided with the Localist party or remained neutral, but
the larger property owners showed only a slight preference for
the Cosmopolitans. The latter might appropriately be called a

party of well-to-do Marylanders (72 percent), but half of the
Localists consisted of the same species. That wealth was an independent variable is indicated by again examining those counties in
which the alignment was Localist, 58 percent; neutral, 31 percent;
and Cosmopolitan, 11 percent. Well-to-do or wealthy delegates
voted as follows: Localist, 46 percent; neutral, 32 percent; and
Cosmopolitan, 22 percent. However property was less important
than other factors.

Among cultural characteristics neither age nor religion made
much difference. Educated men and those with intellectual interests inclined toward the Cosmopolitan party, but their numbers
were too small to exert much political pressure. The distinction
between cosmopolitan and localist world views was less politically
significant in Maryland than in most other states, and if we were
studying Maryland alone, the party names would not seem apro-
pos. The cosmopolitan men supported "their" party by a considerable majority (56 to 22 percent), while localists voted by a lesser
margin with the party of that name (46 to 26 percent), much depending on the issue.

Family background seems to have lacked significance, delegates
from humble backgrounds being found equally on both sides,
though men of good family usually voted with the Cosmopolitans.
Military service and political experience were unimportant except
on certain questions and except for a tendency for high-ranking
officials to support the Cosmopolitan group and for local officials
(sheriffs, justices of the peace, and the like) to prefer the Localists.
In the division over ratification, the Antifederalists drew almost
all of their support from the Localist party (Samuel Chase being
an exception), while the Federalists consisted principally of men
belonging to the Cosmopolitan bloc (14) or neutrals (11), whose
position on this question probably exerted much weight.

The characteristics of the two groups appear with particular
clarity in those delegates who voted most consistently. The "leaders" of the Cosmopolitans came from the southern counties of both
shores, the longest settled centers of plantation agriculture, and
from the two major towns, while the leaders of the Localists represented the more rural, small farm, recently settled areas to the
north and west. The most consistent Cosmopolitans made their
money through trade (3) or the law (10), large-scale commercial
farming being of secondary importance (4), but the Localists'
steadfast supporters were relatively small farmers (14 of 20). The
archetypal delegate of the Cosmopolitans owned large property,

including at least twenty slaves, and was a man of cosmopolitan taste. His equivalent on the other side, while far from poor, held moderate or substantial property including ten or a dozen slaves and was a localist in his interests. Briefly, then, the Cosmopolitan party represented the business, professional, and planter interests, whose outlook tended to transcend their locality, while the Localist group reflected the parochial views of the more purely agrarian Marylanders.

The position taken by the two blocs on major issues, when they disagreed, confirms the implications of this description. To summarize, the Cosmopolitans supported, and the Localists opposed: higher salaries for state officials except in the case of the delegates themselves; payment of government costs generally; higher taxes except on certain objects such as offices of profit, slaves, and Annapolis property, but including import and export taxes; the interests of speculators, particularly with regard to confiscated property; higher prices for land; a hard-money, procreditor policy except for insolvent businessmen and debtors of large property; state support both for colleges and for religion; and a stronger central government. These attitudes constitute a unified point of view toward the problems of the time (see table 8.8 for the divisions on these issues).

The existence and continuity of these two sides is clear enough now, but only rarely does the literature of the period reflect them. Apparently the people of Maryland continued to vote as they always had voted, for the man rather than for the principle. Hints of change appear first in 1786, when the senate so vigorously upheld the creditor cause as to provoke attack upon it, and at that time accusations reached the press of a combination, motivated primarily by the paper-money question, that hoped to change the political balance of power.[41] An increased activity in electioneering led one Marylander to assert that competition "subjects the voters to an influence destructive of free Elections" and to recommend the use of ballots.[42] At least one segment of the voting public, the traders and artisans of Baltimore, came out publicly for a particular candidate;[43] and in the fall of 1787 for the first time a newspaper

41. In particular, *Md. Gaz.* (Annapolis), Aug. 31, 1786; *Md. Jour.* (Baltimore), Mar. 6, 1787.
42. *Md. Gaz.* (Annapolis), Oct. 3, 1786.
43. James McHenry, running for elector: *Md. Jour.* (Baltimore), Sept. 1, 1786.

Table 8.8. *Illustrative Votes, Maryland (in Percentages of Pro-Cosmopolitan Votes)*

	Votes																
	1	2	3	4	5	6	7	8	9	10	11	12	13	14	15	16	17
All delegates with Cosmopolitan position	55	48	37.5	52	62	52	65	48	57	59	47	49	42	37	39	54	57
Legislative party																	
Localist	27	6	40	21	13	5	41	19	13	43	11	21	18	25	12.5	24	6
Neutral	37.5	55	31	22	82	63	67	55	70	69	40	70	50	32	36	65	70
Cosmopolitan	79	93	42	89	100	95	100	71	84	70	65	67	67	59	82	88	95
Residence																	
Noncommercial farm	0	0	0	0	(2)50	17	(2)50	25	40	(1)0	(2)0	33	0	12.5	(1)0	0	50
Commercial farm	22	30	18	25	12.5	40	20	50	46	37.5	14	21	35	35	0	47	33
Plantation	83	61	61	68	71	58	83	48	60	80	66	60	50	44	55	65	52
Town	50	75	43	75	87.5	100	75	100	83	37.5	56	67	71	40	43	80	100
Occupation																	
Farmer	33	33	14	25	18	29	33	50	30	27	44	27	11	25	10	26	33
Planter	55	44	46	68	56	50	64	44	73	89	33	65	55	40	30	68	56
Misc. nonfarmer	0	100	(1)0	33	(2)50	67	33	(1)0	—	50	(1)0	83	0	0	0	0	40
Professional	90	71	50	40	100	82	100	86	100	80	70	17	78	44	73	78	78
Trader	60	75	75	100	80	67	100	67	67	40	50	67	60	67	60	100	100

Table 8.8—Continued

								Votes									
	1	2	3	4	5	6	7	8	9	10	11	12	13	14	15	16	17
Economic status																	
Moderate	25	30	17	14	25	36	50	40	36	25	0	25	27	31	0	25	25
Substantial	60	33	20	33	50	55	55	62.5	30	37.5	50	45	18	33	25	42	62.5
Well-to-do	59	70	37.5	59	67	58	73	75	67	58	50	60	50	39	43	70	67
Wealthy	67	75	75	80	72	55	75	40	100	87	64	55	61	60	58	64	50
Education																	
None	45	too few	33	too few	51	51	37	too few	54	59	38	too few	too few	37	33	47	52
Some	100	too few	75	too few	80	56	80	too few	75	60	100	too few	too few	67	80	100	71
World view																	
Localist	25	37	22	39	31	29	40	50	32	36	20	40	8	19	9	32	45
Cosmopolitan	90	100	62.5	75	90	77	91	55	78	70	78	40	56	39	78	100	82
Social origin																	
Humble origin	55	60	22	62.5	50	44	62.5	62	47	33	22	40	33	40	25	33	70
Prominent old family	80	62.5	64	60	75	56	71	40	86	88	75	64	60	60	59	76	54

CODE OF VOTES:

1. For higher salary for governor, Dec. 19, 1780.
2. For higher salary for judges, Dec. 23, 1783.
3. For lower per diem for delegates, Jan. 8, 1783.
4. For permanent salaries, May 23, 1787.
5. For payment of civil list, Jan. 22, 1782.
6. For payment for digest of laws, Dec. 31, 1785.
7. For higher tax rate, Dec. 20, 1781.
8. For higher tax on land, Jan. 5, 1785.
9. For import tax on salt, Jan. 12, 1785.
10. For higher price for western land, Jan. 7, 1782.
11. For lower tax on Annapolis land, Jan. 7, 1781.
12. Against stay law, May 22, 1787.
13. For postponing paper-money bill, Dec. 13, 1785.
14. Against paper-money bill, Dec. 22, 1785.
15. For longer out-of-state militia service, Jan. 14, 1782.
16. For money for college, Nov. 22, 1785.
17. For position of intendant, May 26, 1787.

published the votes of the winning and losing candidates for the house, which apparently represented distinguishable sides.[44] The materials for formal parties clearly existed, but political alignments had not progressed beyond legislative blocs.

44. *Md. Jour.* (Baltimore), Oct. 5, 1787. In Baltimore County the victors included Edward Cockey, Charles Ridgely, and T. C. Deye, all among the most consistent leaders of the Localists, while both of the losers were neutrals. In Baltimore City, Chase and M'Mechen, both prominent Cosmopolitans, emerged victorious over McHenry, the artisans' candidate, and another man.

Chapter IX

Virginia

Stability, continuity, consensus: these terms more nearly apply to Virginia than to any other state during the Confederation. She contained relatively few loyalists, and her people agreed on most matters during the war. She experienced no storm over a constitution, no bitter division over economic matters. After the war, when the legislature received petitions concerning paper money, the delegates condemned the proposal, 85–17. When disagreements arose, the legislature divided, not into two almost unanimous parties, as in Pennsylvania, but into several groups, the members of which voted with a consistency of two or three to one rather than four or five or even ten to one, and more delegates acted independently. Legislative blocs did form, but whereas in other states a mere glance at the assembly is enough to reveal them, in Virginia they require some hard looking. Moreover two of the most conspicuous controversies—those concerning religious freedom and manumission of slaves—created quite different alignments.

The reasons for this comparative uniformity lie in Virginia's history. Although we will focus on sectional conflicts, harmonious elements are also impressive. The immigrants were mostly English and Anglican. Almost all became farmers. As everyone knows, Virginia developed no city, few towns, and no urban society. This economic and social homogeneity continued as the colony expanded, for Virginia's west was settled primarily by Virginians. Of course some diversity arose out of the Scotch-Irish settlements, the southward movement of Pennsylvanians, and the Great Awakening, but these factors, important as they were, modified but did not fundamentally alter the colony's civilization. The farmers lived and worked much alike, regardless of where they resided.

Sharing the same culture and similar economic circumstances, the Virginians also agreed politically in many ways and therefore chose as their delegates men of a uniform type. During the colonial period at least four-fifths of the men in the House of Burgesses owned large estates. About 70 percent were primarily farmers, and two-thirds of the rest also owned plantations. Most (conceivably all) held slaves, and close to half belonged to the famous First Families—relatively few can be termed self-made. Almost all were Anglicans, and in general they seem much of a piece culturally; the exceptions exerted little political influence. Most historians agree that Virginia's internal political controversies are best described as factional, which is to say superficial, the eruption of Bacon and the intrusion of Patrick Henry forming dubious exceptions.

Independence brought many changes (to our profit, the legislature now recorded roll-call votes) but no fundamental alteration in the power structure. More delegates came from the frontier or from semisubsistence farm areas, but most of them represented commercial farm communities (see table 9.1). The towns of Williamsburg and Norfolk had only one vote apiece, though some of the counties occasionally did send delegates from towns such as Richmond, Alexandria, or Fredericksburg. As in colonial times a majority of the delegates owned farms or plantations. Men who engaged in trade, even including innkeepers, held only 8 percent of the seats, artisans but one out of forty. Professional men, notably lawyers, did exert considerable weight, with over a fifth of the seats and more of the prestige. Dissenters clearly gained in strength, but still comprised a minority of perhaps one-third. Men of non-English stock were few. The overwhelming number had been born in Virginia of good family, grew up on farms, owned slaves, and received their education at home. The major changes were that relatively more delegates held no office before election, that they owned less property, probably included fewer men of ability (at least of training), and that the center of political gravity had shifted westward and downward.

The political gains scored by the interior areas contributed to, and perhaps primarily accounted for, the divisions within the legislature and the emergence of a consistent political alignment. The major protagonists were the counties of the Northern Neck and the Southside, especially the southwestern piedmont. The geo-

Table 9.1. *Composition of Virginia's House of Delegates, 1784–1788*

	No.	%		No.	%
Residence			**Occupation**		
Frontier	24	11.9	Farmer	40	19.9
Noncommercial farm	54	26.9	Planter	73	36.3
Commercial farm	62	30.8	Artisan or manufacturer	6	3.0
Plantation	55	27.4	Minister	3	1.5
Town	6	3.0	Doctor	6	3.0
			Lawyer	32	15.9
			Other professional	2	1.0
Economic status			Misc. entrepreneur	3	1.5
			Innkeeper	3	1.5
Poor or moderate	30	14.9	Merchant or trader, etc.	13	6.5
Substantial	34	16.9	Unknown	20	10.0
Well-to-do	69	34.3			
Wealthy	50	24.9			
Unknown	18	9.0	**Age**		
			Under 40	55	27.3
Religion			40–49	24	11.9
			50–59	17	8.5
Episcopalian	46	22.9	60 and over	7	3.5
Methodist	3	1.5	Unknown	98	48.8
Presbyterian	8	4.0			
Other	5	2.5			
Unknown	139	69.2	**Military service**		
			Enlisted man	4	2.0
Political experience			Misc. officer	57	28.4
			Colonel or general	56	27.9
Local office	24	11.9	Probably served	2	1.0
Sheriff, j.p., etc.	37	18.4	None or uncertain	82	40.8
State judge, senator	9	4.5			
Other state office	5	2.5			
Continental Congress	9	4.5	**Intellectual interest**		
None known	106	52.7			
Uncertain	11	5.5	None	131	65.2
			Some	46	22.9
			Uncertain	24	11.9
Education					
Little or none	161	80.1	**World view**		
Self-educated	7	3.5			
College	33	16.4	Localist	89	44.3
			Cosmopolitan	63	31.3
			Unknown	49	24.4

Table 9.1—Continued

	No.	%		No.	%
Father's occupation			*Father's economic status*		
Farmer	28	13.9	Poor or moderate	25	12.4
Planter	53	26.4	Substantial	6	3.0
Artisan	1	0.5	Well-to-do	25	12.4
Minister	4	2.0	Wealthy	47	23.4
Doctor	3	1.5	Unknown	98	48.8
Lawyer	5	2.5			
Other professional	4	2.0			
Innkeeper	2	1.0	*National origin*		
Merchant	8	4.0			
Unknown	93	46.3	Colonial, English	159	79.1
			Colonial, Scotch-Irish	3	1.5
			Colonial, misc.	5	2.5
Social origin			Immigrant, English	2	1.0
			Immigrant, Scottish	4	2.0
Humble origin	32	15.9	Immigrant, Scotch-Irish	1	0.5
Old family	80	39.8	Unknown	27	13.4
Above-average family	40	19.9			
Prominent family	34	16.9			
Unknown	15	7.5			
Mobility					
Mobile	35	17.4			
Not mobile	156	77.6			
Uncertain	10	5.0			
Slaveholding					
Over 100	15	7.7			
50–99	23	11.8			
20–49	58	29.7			
10–19	44	22.6			
5–9	21	10.8			
1–4	13	6.7			
None	7	3.6			
Unknown	14	7.2			

NOTE: This table includes less than 60% of the delegates, but they cast over 80% of the votes.

graphical division is so striking, and so exceeds other characteristics in statistical significance, that the explanation of Virginia's politics at this time clearly requires an understanding of these regions. Several points of contrast seem indisputable.[1]

First, the conditions under which the people obtained their land differed, for the Northern Neck (between the Potomac and the Rappahannock rivers, extending across the Blue Ridge) was granted to the Fairfax family and by them sold in large tracts. By the 1780s plenty of small farmers had moved in, but the region always contained an unusual number of great plantations, as well as an exceptional population of tenants and slaves. Society was in short aristocratic. On the other hand, settlers moved into the Southside (the area south of the James River) more normally; some obtained sizable grants, but most bought small farms. Slaves had become plentiful by the 1780s, comprising indeed from a third to a half of the population, but they were more widely held, as was property in general. Society was in short more democratic.

Second, the Northern Neck enjoyed unusual transportation and communication facilities, since every farm (except those near the mountains) lay near either the Potomac or the Rappahannock. Economically, geography encouraged large-scale commercial agriculture. Culturally, it may have contributed to a cosmopolitan environment, urbane despite the lack of cities. Socially and politically, the great planters moved easily upstream, becoming dominant even in the northern end of the Shenandoah Valley—Washington first sat in the House of Burgesses for Frederick County. On the other hand, the southern part of the state, except for the area around the James River valley, was less well supplied with waterways. The Roanoke, which flows through the southwestern piedmont, enters North Carolina and, after encountering rapids, ends in Albemarle Sound, where it finds no major port and no easy egress.

This section remained frontier until not long before the war and continued somewhat isolated, looking perhaps less westward or eastward than inward. Politically, the difference between the two regions showed partly in the kind of representatives that they chose, for the Southside elected far more men of small property than did any other area, and partly because their representatives voted differently.

1. This chapter supersedes my article "Sections and Politics in Virginia, 1781–1787," *WMQ*, 3d Ser., XII (1955), 96–112, which however contains many citations not repeated here.

The Northern Neck interests drew most of their support from eastern counties that shared some of the Neck's characteristics, especially in containing many large plantations and in lying along the major river valleys (particularly the James) with their economic and cultural advantages. Similarly the Southside found allies in several eastern counties and those of the northern piedmont, exclusive of the Northern Neck. East of the mountains, the two were evenly matched.

The rest of Virginia lay beyond the Blue Ridge. The Shenandoah, or Great, Valley, settled by a mixture of English, German, and Scotch-Irish immigrants from Pennsylvania and eastern Virginia, had a history of its own and followed its own course politically, except that the two northernmost counties had been part of the Fairfax grant and accordingly became a frontier of the Northern Neck.[2] Kentucky contained a mixture of Virginia-oriented land speculators and independent-minded pioneers. The former chose most of the delegates, who tended toward the Northern Neck view on most matters. On the other hand, the area now West Virginia, while containing similar basic elements, leaned the other way.

Politically, the House of Delegates during these years contained the usual two basic voting blocs. The consistency of voting behavior, however, was relatively low, applying only to a little over half of the votes, and one-third of the delegates aligned with neither group. Of the two principal legislative parties one centered in the Northern Neck, but won support elsewhere; the other also consisted of delegates from all over the state, but was concentrated in the Southside counties. For the sake of consistency, we will continue to call them, respectively, Cosmopolitans and Localists, although the terms are not descriptive of Virginia's alignment.

During the war years the legislature united in support of the struggle for independence, and few controversies disturbed its harmony. Since loyalists presented little problem, except briefly near Norfolk, restrictions on the tories never became politically important. Only one vote indicated a difference in attitude, when in 1779 a bill was introduced to repeal the treble tax that the state had collected from all those refusing to take an oath of allegiance. This carried by a narrow margin (December 3). The division showed no distinct sectional pattern, or any other except perhaps

2. The authoritative study of the valley during these years remains Freeman H. Hart, *The Valley of Virginia in the American Revolution, 1763–1789* (Chapel Hill, 1942).

that men who were not farmers voted to reduce the tax and that the Southside delegates showed least enthusiasm for the change. Men who, judging from the more numerous votes in later years, sided with the Northern Neck group favored passage, whereas their future opponents opposed it, but only a few delegates were involved.

In the same session some delegates tried to delay the removal of the capital from Williamsburg to Richmond, but failed, 40–45. Perhaps the pro-Richmond group justified their stand by the more exposed position of Williamsburg, but the vote was basically sectional in nature. Other correlations, such as the division along occupational lines, probably reflect the characteristics of east and west. The question did not recur and the capital, of course, soon moved.

Payment of the state and federal debt, often the most important and sometimes the crucial problem in the states, rarely divided Virginians. The only votes required occurred in 1780 when the legislature agreed to retire the state's share of the federal debt by taxes over a period of fifteen years and resolved generally to follow the new procedure recommended by Congress, which, as already discussed, attempted to introduce a sound-money policy pleasing to creditors and holders of public securities.[3] This policy received the support of the Northern Neck delegates (excepting those of the Shenandoah Valley) by a large majority and of their usual allies, while opposition centered in the piedmont. Merchants and professional men were enthusiastic, planters divided, and farmers opposed. Noneconomic factors seem to have exercised no influence. Adherents of the Localist party voted against this measure by a large majority, with the Cosmopolitan bloc on the other side (but only twenty-nine men were involved). Debates over policy continued, but Virginia's ability to retire part of her own debt in land and a general agreement that the federal debt ought to be paid restricted the dispute to a question of means rather than of ends.[4]

Even the dispute over means remained relatively minor. Virginia's wealth lay in land and slaves, and taxes on these raised most of the money. The planters and farmers naturally assessed other types of wealth, but they realized that they themselves had no

3. Votes of June 6, 22, 1780.
4. See petitions in the Va. State Lib., notably Charles City, Nov. 8, 1780; Surry, June 8, 1782; Amelia, May 16, 1783; Prince Edward, June 1, 1784; Pittsylvania, Nov. 5, 1787.

choice but to pay and did so with less wrangling than one would expect. Petitions complaining about taxes often admitted their necessity, and the legislature actually received one urging higher taxes to support the war and to maintain economic health.[5] The legislature made a real effort to follow Edmund Pendleton's principle that "a proportion of every man's clear income, if it could be come at, would be the just mode of taxation,"[6] and the dictum of Orange County petitioners that taxes should fall "on all visible property, in proportion to its value."[7] The delegates evolved a fair method for evaluating land and assessed in addition slaves, livestock, faculties, trade,[8] and other sources of revenue.

In 1786 the legislature levied an additional tax on carriage wheels and also assessed lawyers, doctors, and retail merchants. Several petitions opposed this,[9] and one from Fredericksburg[10] produced a bill modifying it, which the legislature eventually rejected. The single vote, which lost, 40–53, came on a motion to postpone the issue until the next year (December 27, 1787). Postponement would of course have had the effect of continuing for another year the taxes in question. The effort to postpone came from the Southside and West Virginia; it was defeated by the Northern Neck group and its supporters, who voted against the motion by a three-to-one margin. As might be expected, farmers disliked the bill and sought to postpone it by a margin of three to one, but two-thirds of the planters and almost all traders and professional men approved. Men of larger property hoped to modify the tax; delegates of moderate wealth wanted no change. This vote shows clearly that on the tax question men tended to defend their economic interests.

The delegates tried to obtain as much specie as possible, but always recognized that they must accept specifics and various money equivalents. When in 1783 they tried to collect only gold and silver, they received some outraged remonstrances and backed

5. Culpeper County petition, May 18, 1779, Va. State Lib.
6. To Madison, Dec. 19, 1786, Mays, ed., *Letters of Pendleton*, II, 491. A Cumberland County petition urged that every man should contribute in proportion to his wealth, for "Equality, we conceive to be the Very Soul of our Government; destroy it, and there is an end to democracy." Nov. 3, 1788, Va. State Lib.
7. Two petitions, Orange County, Nov. 3, 1777, Va. State Lib.
8. An interesting group of petitions complaining of this are Alexandria, May 27, 1780; Winchester, May 17, 1780; Norfolk County, Norfolk Borough, and Portsmouth, June 1, 1780; and misc. petitions, May 15, 1780, all in Va. State Lib.
9. Williamsburg, Nov. 3, 1787, Cumberland, Nov. 3, 1788, Harrison, Oct. 22, 1787, Va. State Lib.
10. Dec. 10, 1787, Va. State Lib.

down.[11] As a rule the people demanded and received permission to pay in hemp, deerskins, tobacco, flour, paper money, and various certificates.[12] The only vote resulting from this question came after the legislature decided not to accept tobacco. At the time various delegates were urging paper money, a general reduction of taxes, postponement of collections, and other remedies, so that the legislature had to make at least one concession. As Madison explained it, payment in tobacco had to be granted to avoid something worse, and Pendleton believed that otherwise collectors could not have obtained the money.[13] These considerations may explain why merchants and lawyers proved more enthusiastic than farmers or planters.[14]

More controversial was the issue of collecting taxes once imposed. Beginning in 1781, collectors encountered resistance, and the legislature received petitions from sheriffs praying for more time and from the people asking postponement. Every part of the state experienced financial problems. In the spring of 1781 Governor Jefferson learned of an insurrection against the tax collector in far-off Hampshire County, beyond the Great Valley, and of trouble on the Eastern Shore.[15] Two years later tax records were destroyed in Lunenburg County in the Southside,[16] and the people of Rockingham County in the Valley announced that they could not pay taxes.[17] By the middle of the decade every section of the state had clamored for postponement, and such prominent men as George Mason and Benjamin Harrison admitted the need for concessions.[18] In response the legislature almost annually allowed sheriffs a few extra months before they must take legal action and twice postponed collections for a longer period.[19]

11. King and Queen, Nov. 5, 1783, Essex, Nov. 5, 1783, and Culpeper, Oct. 5, 1783; Virginia Session Laws, May 1783, chap. 182, and Oct. 1783, chap. 188 (see Records of States microfilm or Early American Imprints microprint).

12. The people requested other methods of payment: thus westerners asked that they work out their taxes on a road. Harrison, Dec. 5, 1786 and Greenbrier, Dec. 9, 1785, Va. State Lib.

13. Letter of Dec. 4, 1786, Madison Papers, VII, Lib. of Congress; Pendleton to Madison, Dec. 19, 1786, Mays, ed., *Letters of Pendleton,* II, 491.

14. Vote of Dec. 18, 1786.

15. William P. Palmer, ed., *Calendar of Virginia State Papers* (Richmond, 1873–1893), II, 28–29, 97–99.

16. Randolph to Madison, Apr. 26, 1783, Madison Papers, IV, Lib. of Congress.

17. Petition, June 18, 1783, Va. State Lib.

18. Mason to Patrick Henry, May 6, 1783, Robert A. Rutland, ed., *The Papers of George Mason, 1725–1792* (Chapel Hill, 1970), II, 769–774; Harrison to Monroe, Nov. 20, 1783, Monroe Papers, I, Lib. of Congress.

19. William Waller Hening, ed., *The Statutes at Large; Being a Collection of All the Laws of Virginia . . .* (Richmond, 1809–1823), XI, 194, 368, 540, XII,

Debates on this question led to three votes. The first occurred on an amendment that would begin the period of "distress" for taxes, which is to say of compelling collection, in October rather than November. The legislature defeated the earlier date, 48–62 (May 26, 1783). Support for it came from the Northern Neck (15–4) and its allies (11–6). Western delegates divided, and the rest of the representatives opposed the bill, the Southside and its supporters rejecting it by a four-to-one margin. The minority consisted mainly of planters, lawyers, and merchants, while farmers overwhelmingly opposed enforcing collection.

The second vote concerned tax collections, and the third defeated another postponement.[20] The latter provides the clearest test. Again the Northern Neck and its allies, with the Kentucky delegates, favored prompt payment, the margin being more than two to one, while the Southside opposed by over three to one, joined by all the West Virginians. Farmers tried to postpone, but nonfarm delegates, with the help of about half of the planters, defeated the attempt. Men of small property and men of wealth took opposite sides, but cultural factors seem unimportant except that cosmopolitans and localists divided sharply, the latter voting for delay. Finally, Localists favored postponement almost unanimously (24–2), while the Cosmopolitan bloc opposed with equal determination (20–2).

The same economic circumstances that made it hard to pay taxes affected the payment of private debts. As usual the depression hurt everybody: debtors faced bankruptcy, creditors might be ruined unless they received their money, and merchants suffered along with farmers and planters.[21] Complaints by debtors mounted during the decade. As with the protest against heavy taxes, the petitioners lived in all parts of the state. In October 1786 some four hundred residents of Brunswick County deplored a lack of specie that they "Conseive proceeds from the political views of the british Merchants and traders of this Commonwealth. . . . The Merchants well new at the Close of the late war that a Set of men deprived of all the Comforts and nessesaries of life as we then were

---

93–96, 368–369, 540–543. For accounts of this matter see Archibald Henderson to Washington, Nov. 21, 1783, Washington Papers, CCXXXIV, #48, Lib. of Congress; Madison to Jefferson, Jan. 22, 1786, Madison Papers, IV, Lib. of Congress.

20. These came on Nov. 19 and 21, 1785, on a bill further to extend the delay of one-half of the taxes; it lost, 48–50.

21. For some merchant and trader complaints see petitions from Winchester, May 17, 1780; Alexandria, Nov. 14, 1786; Fredericksburg, Dec. 2, 1784, Nov. 14, 1785; Portsmouth, Nov. 5, 1785; Norfolk, Nov. 4, 1785; all in Va. State Lib.; also citations in Main, "Sections and Politics," *WMQ*, 3d Ser., XII (1955), 100.

would be Eagerly greedy to obtain those nessessaries on Credit which was the only method we then had to obtain them." But as soon as the people's hands were tied, the merchants only accepted specie. The supplicants noted that before the war paper had filled the need for money, and they suggested that it might do so again. Other petitioners recommended installment or stay laws or payment of debts in produce so that "the landlord and Tenant, the Creditor and Debtor, the Gentleman and the Peasant" would share alike the inevitable evils.[22] In response the legislature did pass an installment act and a moderate valuation law.[23]

These arguments were countered by petitions on the other side that pleaded the cause of creditors, protested the installment act (a "violation of the Social Compact itself"), and recommended economy instead.[24] While Virginia made enough concessions to the debtors so that she experienced only scattered uprisings, she did reject inflation, and on the whole creditors fared rather well.

Only a few votes indicate the delegates' opinions concerning debts, and only one pertained exclusively to domestic private obligations. This came on an amendment to a bill that regulated the recovery of debts. A clause gave the debtor three months of grace after his property had been seized, if he signed a bond to pay the full debt, costs, and interest. The amendment provided that, if the property brought less than three-fourths of its appraised value at sale, the debtor might sign a bond for payment in twelve months, upon which his property would be restored.[25] The amendment lost, 44–55. It received some support everywhere except, curiously, in West Virginia. The vote indicated only a slight sectional division, with Northern Neck delegates opposing the amendment by a two-to-one margin and Southside representatives favoring it, 12–5. A small majority of farmers voted aye, while merchants and

22. Prince William, Nov. 2, 1776, Va. State Lib. See Spotsylvania, Nov. 10, 1787, Northampton, June 12, 1784, New Kent, Dec. 5, 1785, Louisa, Nov. 20, 1786, Campbell, Oct. 30, 1786, Albermarle, Nov. 3, 1787, and Amherst, Dec. 5, 1783, all in Va. State Lib.

23. Paper money won the support of only 17 delegates from the southwestern Piedmont and the west. Among these seven belonged to the Localist group (two being among the leaders), one to the Cosmopolitan bloc, and one was a neutral.

24. Botetourt, Oct. 17, 1787 (oversize), Va. State Lib. See also Amherst, Nov. 6, 1787, Chesterfield, May 22, 1782, Cumberland, Nov. 19, 1787, Henrico, June 12, 1784, misc. petitions, Nov. 22, 1787, Va. State Lib. and *Virginia Gazette and Alexandria Advertiser*, Sept. 21, 1786. The Henrico petition explained that one act (Oct. 15, 1784) tended "to take away that confidence between man and man so essential and necessary between merchants and traders."

25. Dec. 15, 1787.

planters voted nay. A clear correlation appears with relative wealth, small property holders being prodebtor. Delegates belonging to the Localist group favored the amendment by a very large margin (85 percent), while three-fourths of the Cosmopolitan bloc opposed it.

Another vote concerning debtor-creditor relations came three years later (January 5, 1788) on a bill to enable Virginians who were partners of British subjects to recover their share of any debts due to them. This failed of passage by a single vote, 50–51.[26] Creditors obtained support from the Northern Neck group (three to one) and Kentucky, but lost primarily because the Southside delegates opposed them by a four-to-one margin. Not a single member of the Localist group took the creditor side, while 86 percent of the Cosmopolitan bloc did so. Farmers voted with the debtors, merchants and professionals with creditors, and planters divided. The larger property owners among the delegates favored the creditors, smaller ones the debtors. The educated, cosmopolitan men also voted for passage. These votes suggest a consistent division on the issue of debts.

Two votes on June 23, 1784, may have affected debts owed to the British, but probably pertained rather to the losses suffered by Virginians during the war. The first, which took place during a debate over the British treaty, called upon the governor to gather and send to Congress all claims for damages. Most of these would have resulted from the carrying off of slaves, but British troops had destroyed much other property. The delegates defeated this, 33–55. A second clause proposed that the state retain enough of the debts owed by Virginians to British subjects as would satisfy the claims. Probably the adoption of this procedure would have meant, in practice, payment of the debts at less than their nominal value, though the outcome remains uncertain. This proposal also lost, 33–50. The alignment was primarily sectional. On both votes the Northern Neck representatives and their allies along the coast, where the damage centered, strongly favored the motions, whereas the Southside opposed almost unanimously. Cosmopolitans supported the claimants by a margin of six to one, with Localists almost as decisively on the other side. Other correlations probably relate to sectionalism.

26. The clerk, by error, listed the majority as voting in the affirmative, when they actually opposed, as a count of the voters and comparison with the motion to postpone will show.

The question of British debts and wartime losses were among several problems arising out of the treaty with Great Britain. The treaty remained important in Virginia politics throughout the Confederation period. As previously explained, an adherence to the terms by both sides would require, on the part of England, abandonment of fur-trading posts in the Northwest Territory, as well as reimbursement for damages caused by the war, while Virginians would have to pay their debts and repeal all antiloyalist laws. Therefore, if one wished to enforce the treaty in every particular and repeal all laws conflicting with it—the form in which the issue usually appeared—one would be proloyalist, procreditor, interested in recovering damages, and anxious to expand westward, an unusual though not incredible combination. Perhaps also a vote for enforcement registered a willingness to regard treaties as superior in authority to state laws and a diminished hostility to England.

Five votes, extending from 1783 to 1787, disclose the alignment.[27] In these the Northern Neck delegates and their allies, with increasing consistency, voted to obey the treaty. The arguments in favor of enforcement stressed the principle that debts should be paid, the possibility of reprisals especially against shipping, and the importance of the western posts.[28] The Southside group opposed enforcement by a margin averaging about three and a half to one. The evidence indicates that the latter were motivated partly by dislike of the loyalists and a reluctance to pay debts to former enemies. Presumably they had little interest in western lands or in obtaining commercial concessions. The people of the Shenandoah, Kentucky, and West Virginia held the balance of power. At first they showed no interest in enforcing the treaty, probably because they had no reason to forgive loyalists, pay creditors, or worry about reprisals, and apparently they were not yet concerned about the posts. However in 1787 they cast a unanimous vote for enforcement, providing the margin of victory.[29]

The alignment followed not only sectional but party lines, with Localist delegates voting against enforcement of the treaty by a margin varying from 83 to 100 percent, increasing over time.

27. Dec. 17, 1783, June 7, 1784, Nov. 1787.
28. Citations in Main, "Sections and Politics," *WMQ*, 3d Ser., XII (1955), 103; Essex County petition, May 19, 1784, Va. State Lib.; Pendleton to Madison, Mar. 31, 1783, Mays, ed., *Letters of Pendleton*, II, 440–441.
29. See petitions of Augusta, Oct. 26, 1786, and Botetourt, Oct. 17, 1787, Va. State Lib.

Similarly the Cosmopolitans voted for adherence by an equal margin of 80 to 98 percent, also increasing during the period.[30]

Other aspects of Virginia's external relations furnish only two votes, neither very useful. Aside from payment of the federal debt, already discussed, early relations with Congress centered upon the impost, which though controversial did not produce a roll call. In 1782 the lower house postponed, 46–28, an attempt to reduce the number of delegates representing the state in Congress. Probably the question had more to do with saving money than supporting Congress. The Northern Neck group opposed the reduction by voting for its postponement, 17–3, while the Southside delegates favored it by a small margin. Farmers and small property owners voted for fewer congressmen, those not farmers and large property owners preferred more. The absence of any division along cultural lines suggests that the issue was primarily economic.

The second vote concerned granting Congress power over commerce. By 1785 many merchants and commercial farmers, in Virginia as elsewhere, had concluded that only Congress could take effective measures against foreign restrictions and foreign control over American trade. On the other hand, even those who recognized the need for centralized authority feared its political implications, and resistance extended throughout the state. As formulated the resolution limited the grant to thirteen years. This the supporters of congressional power tried to remove, but they won scarcely more than a fourth of the votes. Thereupon eight delegates, as Madison put it, "chose rather, to do nothing than to adopt it in that form," voting against the resolution and helping to defeat it.[31] In order to analyze the alignment correctly, therefore, one must consider these eight as voting with the advocates. The Northern Neck group divided equally, furnishing about half of the positive votes. The Southside delegates opposed the grant by a margin of slightly more than two to one and accounted for its defeat. The Cosmopolitan bloc (including as affirmative voters Madison and his mavericks) supported commercial powers four to one, while the Localists opposed it five to one. Economic status, age, military career, education, social origin, and other factors did not correlate with voting, but farmers decisively and planters nar-

30. These divisions seem more meaningful than any others. Farmers opposed enforcement, while planters, professional men, and merchants favored it, but other factors lacked significance.

31. To Jefferson, Jan. 22, 1786, Gaillard Hunt, ed., *The Writings of James Madison* . . . (New York, 1900–1910), II, 218.

rowly negatived the proposal, and professional men and traders agreed to it. These two votes suggest, though they do not prove, that the Cosmopolitan bloc favored a stronger central government and that the Localists opposed centralized authority.

On a few other votes the delegates divided in a similar way. The Cosmopolitan group, Northern Neck delegates, and representatives other than farmers all enthusiastically approved the establishment of district courts and probably courts of assize. The two parties also divided in the same way on the power of the admiralty court. They also opposed each other on various minor issues that lack statistical or historical significance. Unusually divisive was the case of Anthony New, an exceptionally consistent adherent of the Localist bloc from Caroline County. With Parke Goodall, Garland Anderson of Hanover, and Joseph Jones of Dinwiddie—all equally consistent Localists—New formed a private committee to expel from the state certain persons whom they thought undesirable. Probably their targets were British or Scottish merchants and factors. New, as chairman, called upon one Mr. M'Aulay and gave him four hours to get out of town. M'Aulay thought that New acted as a member of the legislature and complained to that body, arguing that he was a citizen. The delegates decided that New had not pretended to act under the authority of the legislature and had not lessened its dignity. The vote came on a clause that condemned M'Aulay's complaint as "vexatious, frivolous and groundless." New's supporters wanted to retain this, but the delegates struck it out, 60–49.[32] Probably the question involved more than just New's behavior, but the records do not supply details. In any event, the alignment closely followed party lines, four-fifths of the Localist group backing New, while 27 out of 29 members of the Cosmopolitan bloc voted to omit the clause. The Northern Neck delegates and the Southside clearly opposed each other, but other factors lack significance.[33]

Two other issues, of quite a different type than those previously discussed, were important throughout the period. The manumission of slaves divided the delegates in a way similar to that on most

32. Oct. 27, 1787.

33. A minor vote upon which the parties differed concerned the salary of the delegates' clerk. The Localists favored a lower figure, Cosmopolitans a higher one, but the correlation is barely 67%, while the sectional vote was still closer. The major factors, statistically, seem to have been occupation—farmers voted for a lower salary and nonfarm delegates for a higher one—and wealth, the small property holders being strongly opposed to spending. Jan. 11, 1787.

other questions, while conflicts arising out of the relations between church and state cut across "party" lines.

Several votes reveal the alignment on manumission. In 1785, after the legislature had passed an act authorizing the freeing of slaves, a flood of petitions arrived demanding its repeal. These anticipated the proslavery argument of later decades, basing the case on the Bible, property rights, and social evils. Most of them came from the Southside. Other petitions had developed an attack on slavery, usually taking a high moral stance. The Frederick County petition of November 8, 1785, insisted that Negroes were equal to whites and that arguments drawn from physical differences were "beneath the Man of Sense, much more the Christian." Liberty, the Valley residents argued, was "the Birthright of Mankind, the right of every rational Creature without exception"; that right had been taken from the Negroes and ought to be restored. The legislature voted, 52–51, that one of these proslavery petitions was reasonable (December 14, 1785), but later defeated a bill to repeal the act in question, 35–52 (December 24). During the next session the delegates agreed to carry out the will of Joseph Mayo freeing his slaves.[34] On all of these votes the Southside opposed emancipation by a large margin, while the Northern Neck group favored it slightly. The most solid support for freeing the slaves came from the west, where the margin was six to one. Roughly, and with a good many exceptions, delegates from the most economically advanced and commercialized areas and those from counties containing few slaves supported manumission. Lawyers and merchants were most willing to free the Negroes, farmers least so, while planters split evenly. Wealth did not matter, nor did education, intellectual interest, the cosmopolitan-localist factor, age, one's military career, social background, or offices held. On the other hand, limited biographical data suggest that dissenters were more favorable to manumission than Anglicans. Finally, the Localist group very strongly opposed it (about five to one), whereas the Cosmopolitan bloc voted just as strongly for freeing the Negroes.

The exceedingly important issue of church-state relations may be dismissed briefly because it did not at this time affect party alignments. The legislators recorded various votes concerning taxation for religious purposes, the incorporation of the Episcopal Church, and financial support for the teaching of Christianity. Members of the Localist bloc tended to oppose these measures, the

34. Two votes, Nov. 4, Dec. 18, 1786.

Cosmopolitans to support them, and a clear sectional division existed in which the extremes were the westerners, voting against state support, and delegates from the eastern plantation area, voting in favor. No difference appeared in the attitude of different occupational groups, but a very sharp division occurred between the delegates of small property, who opposed any state support for religious purposes, and wealthy delegates, who favored this; the question of course involved taxation as it did in Maryland. Educated men were more inclined to approve close state-church relations than those without education. As one would expect, Episcopalians felt that their church should be encouraged, while dissenters disagreed, though on the question of state aid to religious education differences seem slight.

These votes, together with a few others, furnish the evidence for a description of a consistent political alignment in Virginia. One set of delegates favored the special interests of the Southside and attracted the support of an equal number who lived elsewhere. These men preferred debtors to creditors, and low taxes except when the burden fell on others; probably were antiloyalist and anti-British; and opposed the grant of power to the governor, Congress, and the courts.[35] Their opponents came almost entirely from counties and towns in the Northern Neck or the eastern James River area.[36] They defended creditors, the British treaty, loyalists, the collection of taxes except on nonfarm groups, and authority in government. Both sides secured help from western representatives, depending on the issue, Kentuckians usually inclining toward the Northern Neck, or Cosmopolitan, bloc, West Virginians toward the Localists, while the Shenandoah Valley counties split evenly (see map, p. 261).

Table 9.2 presents the alignment as shown by votes on most of the major issues, selected to illustrate the general pattern. In each case the position taken by the Cosmopolitan group is treated as the norm against which every factor is measured. Except in a few instances, age had no influence. Occupation, on the other hand, seems important in almost all of these roll calls, farmers forming one extreme, merchants and lawyers the other, with planters and men with other occupations usually divided equally. Relative degrees of wealth proved to be significant in about half of the issues.

35. See the note at the end of this chapter for a petition incorporating some of these attitudes.
36. Specifically Charles City, Elizabeth City, James City, New Kent, Powhatan, Surry, York, Princess Anne, and Norfolk Borough.

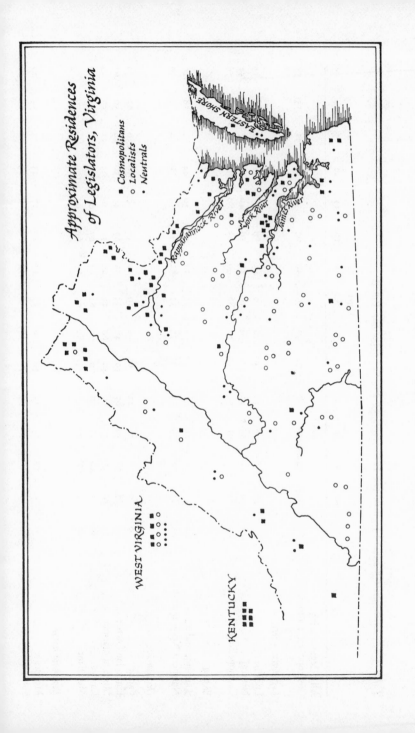

Approximate Residences
of Legislators, Virginia

■ Cosmopolitans
○ Localists
• Neutrals

EASTERN SHORE

Rappahannock River

York River

James River

WEST VIRGINIA

KENTUCKY

Table 9.2. Illustrative Votes, Virginia (in Percentages of Pro-Cosmopolitan Votes)

								Votes							
	1	2	3	4	5	6	7	8	9	10	11	12	13	14	15
All delegates with															
Cosmopolitan position	60	62	44	48	57	37	40	49	39	63	36	60	52	55	55
Legislative party															
Localist	25	23	0	8	32	19	16	0	13	0	17	22	32	21	15
Neutral	22	50	42	55	48	50	50	38	27	59	46	79	57	52	52
Cosmopolitan	83	82	72	91	79	83	87	86	90	95	80	93	63	93	76
Section															
Southside and allies	46	41	20	28	52	3	3	21	10	27	30	44	44	18	26
Northern Neck and allies	63	85	72	75	74	80	75	75	82	63	53	70	64	89	59
Occupation															
Farmer	0	0	0	22	25	0	0	19	10	38	29	50	30	63	50
Large landowner	46	67	33	54	67	50	48	55	54	67	43	50	48	50	62
Misc. nonfarmer	33	50	33	50	60	40	60	22	40	71	50	63	71	57	50
Lawyer	80	75	40	71	78	70	70	82	64	67	67	91	60	80	50
Merchant	100	50	(1)	75	100	75	80	100	67	60	67	100	(1)	50	50
Economic status															
Moderate	0	0	17	15	23	40	0	17	17	50	17	45	13	33	25
Substantial	60	17	40	38	55	50	50	50	33	78	46	100	36	80	59

	1	2	3	4	5	6	7	8	9	10	11	12	13	14	15
Well-to-do	33	60	43	56	62	41	54	52	41	50	65	53	57	65	67
Wealthy	67	78	40	71	75	68	61	60	65	65	35	56	67	47	50
Age															
Under 40	67	44	44	66	68	73	80	60	59	68	52	68	71	63	76
50 and over	67	80	50	38	55	43	29	50	43	69	50	0	25	55	55
Education															
None known	48	48	38	47	52	42	46	42	36	60	39	64	51	55	52
Some	50	67	33	59	77	69	60	83	71	73	44	53	50	75	70
World view															
Localist	33	45	25	29	46	41	38	41	29	61	32	64	39	67	51
Cosmopolitan	57	79	27	65	72	58	55	67	67	68	55	57	69	76	52
Social origin															
Humble origin	33	75	17	11	22	25	20	33	20	78	38	71	60	67	47
Prominent old family	83	60	33	64	69	88	80	100	79	88	29	42	67	78	65

CODE OF VOTES:

1. For paying of federal debt, June 22, 1780.
2. Against reducing number of congressional delegates, Dec. 14, 1782.
3. For enforcing tax collections, May 26, 1783.
4. Against postponing of tax collections, Nov. 21, 1785.
5. For removing taxes on nonfarmers, Dec. 27, 1787.
6. For pressing claims for wartime damages, June 23, 1784.
7. For withholding debts due to British creditors, June 23, 1784.
8. For paying debts due to Virginia creditors, Jan. 5, 1788.
9. For enforcing British treaty, June 7, 1784.
10. The same, Nov. 1787.
11. For granting power to Congress, Dec. 1, 1785.
12. For manumitting slaves, Dec. 24, 1785.
13. For raising salary of clerk, Jan. 11, 1787.
14. Against Anthony New, Oct. 27, 1787.
15. Procreditor, Dec. 15, 1787.

Education made only a slight difference; the cosmopolitan-localist factor was minor; and social origin was somewhat more important in a few cases.

The nature of the alignment appears from the characteristics of the legislators who composed the two parties. The most striking difference between the two sides remains the sectional distribution. A line drawn northwestward from Norfolk city at an angle of about ninety degrees, passing through the town of Orange and across the Blue Ridge, would separate four-fifths of the Cosmopolitan group, including all but one of its leaders, from almost all of the Localists. The latter intruded into Caroline and Essex counties, while the former added support from the upper James and the area beyond the Blue Ridge. The secret of Virginia's politics during this period lies, therefore, in contrasting characteristics of these two major areas. Their similarities, such as their essentially rural nature and the predominance of agriculture based on slave labor, account for the state's relative harmony; their differences created conflicts.

The western counties of the state followed their own interests. The representatives of the southern Shenandoah Valley and from what is now West Virginia began by supporting, on most issues, the Localists, but shifted during 1785. Kentuckians normally, though not invariably, voted with the Cosmopolitans.

Since all sections of the state east of the Blue Ridge contained commercial farms and produced at least a few wealthy planters, traders, and professional men, and since Virginians continued to prefer such men as they traditionally had done, the delegates belonging to these two sides resembled one another more than one might expect, given the clear sectional pattern and voting behavior. The Cosmopolitan group contained slightly more wealthy men and slightly fewer men of small properties than did the Localists. More significant was the division by occupation that appeared on a considerable number of issues. Merchants and lawyers supported the Cosmopolitans by a margin of more than four to one, while on the other side farmers preferred the Localists almost as decisively. The remaining delegates with a nonfarm occupation and the planters divided equally. The Cosmopolitan bloc thus contained these elements; merchants and lawyers, 37 percent; other nonfarmers, 14 percent; planters (a thousand acres or forty slaves), 41 percent; farmers, 8 percent. The nonagrarian or commercial orientation of this party is evident. The Localist group in contrast included merchants and lawyers, 9 percent; other nonfarmers, 18 percent; planters, 39 percent; farmers, 34 percent.

Cultural factors seem unimportant in forming Virginia's political alignment insofar as voting analysis furnishes evidence. Men of high social status favored the Cosmopolitans, but the correlation is unimpressive. Religion, education, and intellectual interest made little difference, though men of education showed a mild preference for the Cosmopolitans. Men who had attended Congress almost always voted with that party, and Continental officers did so more often than not. About half of the cosmopolitan men belonged to the bloc of the same name, one-fourth to the Localist group, and one-fourth remained neutral. Given the nature of the opposing sections, this factor may very well have been highly significant in separating the two constituencies, but only traces of it appear among the delegates. Finally, delegates who favored ratification in 1788 supported the Cosmopolitans almost unanimously (32–3, with 14 neutral), while Antifederalists came overwhelmingly from the Localist group (29–6, with 10 neutral). Still later the Cosmopolitans usually remained Federalists (26–10), and the Localists always became Republicans (20–0).

A glance at the delegates who had the most consistent record highlights the differences between the two voting blocs (see the Appendix). Northern Neck counties contained over half of the Cosmopolitans' seventeen, and the rest, with only one exception, came from contiguous counties of the James River area. Most of the Localist leaders lived south of the James. All but three of the latter engaged primarily in agriculture, whereas the Cosmopolitan bloc's leading members might be either lawyers or planters and were all large property owners. The leaders of the Cosmopolitans were more apt to be educated, intellectual, cosmopolitan, and of higher social origin. All of these interrelated factors created the two sides.

The emergence of these two groups seems to have affected Virginia's election campaigns little or not at all before 1788. Indeed as late as the spring of 1787 a resident described the candidates separately soliciting votes at the "pole," "stooping into the dirt that they may ride the poor people."[37] Other descriptions clearly identify the electoral process as based on personalities or factionalism without organization. If it was true that competition had in-

37. David Thomas to Griffith Evans, Mar. 3, 1787, Mass. Hist. Soc., *Proc.*, XLVI (1912–1913), 370–371.

creased since 1776, and men testified that it had,[38] parties nevertheless had not yet emerged. A few indications other than voting
behavior suggest that they might soon appear. Edmund Randolph
observed to Jefferson as early as 1784 that parties were beginning
to form, and by 1787 two writers urged that the old system of in-
dividualistic anarchy no longer worked well because desperate and
corrupt men bought votes for selfish reasons. The solution, they
insisted, was for men of influence to organize meetings that would
nominate men "of clear and independent property."[39] These observers did not refer to the alignment in the House of Delegates,
but one of its members surely drew on his experience when, a few
months later, he wrote in a passage too familiar to quote at length,
"the most common and durable source of factions has been the
various and unequal distribution of property."

NOTE TO CHAPTER IX

Petition from Washington County, November 3, 1787

This petition contains an exceptionally clear statement of the monetary policy
popular among Localists. Washington was then a frontier county in southwestern
Virginia. (Virginia State Library, Richmond.)

That from a serious and deliberate consideration of our affairs
we consider our selves in a critical and dangerous situation: we
have considered the load of taxes we have to pay, the annual interest arising on the several kinds of Certificates, the great scarcity
of Gold and Silver in circulation amoungst us to answer both our
public and private demands which has impelled us to apply to you
our Representatives that some expedient may immediately be
adopted that will afford us some prospect of relief.

We have taken into our view the gallant Officers and Soldiers
that served us during the war, the virtuous Citizens that parted with
their property to carry on that war, and our generous Allies that
lent us money to assist us in time of need, and to do justice to all
is our greatest wish. We have considered the necessity of answer-
ing the Requisitions of Congress to support the feoderal Union
without which we could not be a respectable Nation and the neces-

38. Archibald Stuart to Jefferson, Oct. 17, 1785, Boyd, ed., *Jefferson Papers*,
VIII, 645; Pendleton to R. H. Lee, Mar. 14, 1785, Mays, ed., *Letters of Pendleton*,
II, 477.
39. "Aristides" and "Observator," *The Virginia Independent Chronicle* (Richmond), Mar. 21, 28, 1787.

sity there is to revive and support Public credit, to obtain these desirable ends and to releive us we know is an arduous task, but if we remain inactive political ruin must soon follow. No mode occurred to us so proper as an emition of paper Money and that proper funds might be provided for its redemption, we have therefore thought that if a sum was emitted equal to the sum we pay an annual interest for at six percent; and that all the Certificates of whatever kind or description be called in and the owners and holders be paid off and that part of the revenue that was applied to paying the interest on those Certificates be applied as a sinking fund we humbly conceive might in some measure releive us. We also conceive it would be sound policy and Justice that the paper Money thus emitted should have all the credit the Legislature could give it and that it should be made a tender equal with Gold and Silver. We doubt not but it will be objected against us that paper Money will answer us no purpose out of the State and that it will depreciate and that we cannot with paper money answer the requisitions of Congress or pay our foreign debt. In answer to such objections we would observe that the credit of the paper money will much depend on proper funds being provided for its redemption: the faith of Government and the virtue of its Citizens and that if the credit of it is maintained it will purchase our flower, our hemp and tobacco which by sending to proper markets will answer the Requisitions of Congress and pay our foreign debt.

Chapter X

South Carolina

South Carolina's legislature recorded no roll-call votes until the 1787 session. By that time many of the major controversies had already exploded and settled, and must be analyzed through sources other than the legislative record. As in other states these issues developed out of the history of the colony and the more immediate experience. Fundamental was the well-known sectional division between the coastal parishes and the up-country.

For some decades almost all of South Carolina's people lived within a few miles of the coast. Beginning about the middle of the century, however, the demography began to change. Population statistics scarcely exist, but apparently in 1770 the colony contained upwards of 150,000 persons of whom probably 50,000 were whites. At that time some 6,000 men reportedly lived along the frontier, which, if true, indicates a white population there of at least 30,000, more than half of the total. By 1790 four-fifths of the whites resided in the backcountry. Charleston contained 8,000, the other coastal parishes 10,000, a contiguous area (including Prince Frederick, Prince George Winyaw, Prince William's, and part of St. Peter's) about 8,000, and the interior perhaps 120,000. But the Negroes were concentrated near the coast: in Charleston they equaled the white population; to the north and south they outnumbered the whites five to one; and just inland they were twice as numerous as the free men. Further west, however, they formed only one-fifth of the people. If representation had been proportioned to voters, therefore, the up-country ought to have held power. If it were determined by wealth, then the low country, with three times the number of slaves and probably more property generally, might merit a majority of the seats. Actually the coastal area chose at least two-thirds. This dominance of the low country predetermined the outcome of most questions: if the planters united, they succeeded.[1]

One controversy that had ended before 1787 concerned control of Charleston. During the war a popular party, consisting mainly of artisans, challenged the rule of the upper class, but by the mid-eighties the latter conquered. The artisans thereafter either supported or ceased effectively to oppose the merchants, and the few artisans who sat in the legislature voted consistently with the other Charleston delegates.

Questions concerning the relations between the state and Congress also arose earlier in the decade. After some delay South Carolina first passed, then repealed, and finally reenacted the 5 percent impost law. The arguments evidently duplicated those elsewhere, but the alignment on this issue remains doubtful. Evidently the opposition centered in the agricultural areas rather than in the city. On the other hand, a grant of commercial power encountered some objections from merchants. By 1786 it too had succeeded.[2]

The various issues arising out of the need for revenue also had been settled, for the time being, before 1787, and did not come to a vote. Until 1784 the state's money came primarily from a tariff together with taxes on land and slaves, most of which serviced the state debt.[3] Land was assessed at a flat rate of one dollar per hundred acres, regardless of value. In that year pressure from the interior aided by some eastern support obtained a general reform. A tax of 1 percent was levied on the value of the land, and the valuation varied from £6 down to as little as a shilling, so that most of the burden fell on the wealthier people.[4]

1. The best political study of South Carolina during the Confederation is the unpublished manuscript by Jerome Nadelhaft, and I have profited greatly from it.

2. The only one known to have opposed it in the legislature was Patrick Calhoun of Ninety-Six district. *Charleston Morning Post*, Feb. 9, 1786. According to one account, British merchants and loyalists caused the delay. Thomas Farr to Caleb Davis, Feb. 20, 1786, Caleb Davis Papers, XIIIa, Mass. Hist. Soc. However they could not possibly have exerted decisive influence.

3. Of the revenue, 88% was reserved for interest on the domestic and foreign debt. *Columbian Herald* (Charleston), July 15, 1785. The state also assessed bonds, stock, and the income from faculties and professions. Acts of Jan. 16, 1777, Mar. 28, 1778, and Mar. 12, 17, 1783.

4. Thomas Cooper, ed., *The Statutes at Large of South Carolina* (Columbia, 1836–1841), IV, 627–637. The popular spokesman William Hornby, writing under the pseudonym "Democratic Gentle-Touch," asserted that the act passed because "the back country members are more numerous, and NOW more clearsighted than formerly; and that they are, in future, determined to oppose all attempts to filch the money out of their pockets, to ease the *rich Rice* and Indigo planters." *The Gazette of the State of South-Carolina* (Charleston), July 29, 1784.

Another important issue that also divided the legislature without resulting in a recorded vote concerned the removal of the capital from Charleston. The alignment undoubtedly was sectional, for people living in or within easy reach of the city naturally preferred that site, which offered more comforts and diversions, whereas those more remote saw the advantages of a less expensive, cooler, and to westerners, a closer location. Perhaps also the aristocratic society of Charleston influenced the votes of country folk and led their spokesmen to seek a more democratic environment. However the up-country lacked the votes to force a change and must have drawn support from certain coastal parishes, probably those farthest from Charleston. This supposition is strengthened by a vote recorded on whether the legislature should meet at Camden rather than Charleston while the building proceeded at Columbia. The proposal, which failed, 63–69, naturally pitted the west against the east, but joining the former were over half of the delegates from the intermediate area.[5] Similarly a senate vote on appropriating money for new state capital buildings (which carried, 12–9) found westerners approving, 9–0, and easterners opposed, 2–9.[6]

During the sessions beginning early in 1787 and in January 1788, the representatives voted some thirty times on seven subjects, and the senators recorded another dozen. The outcome of these debates depended to a large extent upon the composition of the legislature at that time (see table 10.1). In the lower house Charleston delegates cast almost one-fifth of the total votes. From the nearby coastal parishes, the stronghold of the great rice planters, came nearly one-fourth. A little farther away lay parishes of an intermediate type, not quite so rich, often raising crops other than rice (such as indigo), but still containing commercial farms; these chose about one-sixth of the delegates.[7] The remaining parishes, beyond the pine barrens, contained few slaves and few large plantations. They ranged from districts settled a generation earlier and economically advanced, such as St. Matthew's and Orange, to frontier areas. These sent 40 percent of the representatives. There-

5. South Carolina House Journal, Feb. 25, 1788 (see Records of States microfilm or Early American Imprints microprint).
6. Senate Journal, Mar. 28, 1787. A delegate from the intermediate region voted pro.
7. These included Prince William's, St. Bartholomew, St. Helena and St. Peter's in the southwest, All Saints and Prince George Winyaw near the North Carolina line, and two other lowland but not coastal parishes, Prince Frederick and St. Stephen's.

fore Charleston, together with the nearby coastal parishes, controlled only a few more seats than the interior, and the balance of power lay with eight lowland parishes lying some distance from the capital and extending farther toward the up-country. In the senate, however, the easterners enjoyed a clear majority.

At least half, and perhaps as many as two-thirds, of the representatives engaged in agriculture as their primary occupation. Most of these may be denominated planters, judging from their wealth and place of residence. Another 15 percent were professional men, principally lawyers and doctors, many of whom also owned plantations. Merchants and a few other traders held one-eighth of the seats, while a blacksmith, a mason, a couple of other artisans, and a few more townspeople cast not over 6 percent of the votes. The proportion of representatives with a nonfarm occupation considerably exceeded the ratio for the people as a whole, and since these men gained some support from the planters, they exercised a considerable, though not always a decisive, influence in the legislature.

Most of the delegates held sizable estates. Indeed, more than a third were wealthy and fully one-fourth were well-to-do, these two groups probably controlling five out of eight seats. About 22 percent had only moderate property. Undoubtedly a majority were Episcopalians, though we know the affiliation of only a fraction of the representatives. The legislature also contained Methodists, Congregationalists, a Baptist, a Lutheran, and (the second most numerous) more than a dozen Presbyterians. The body was young, averaging less than forty years of age. Only seven had served in the Continental army, but 30 percent belonged to the state militia, all except one as officers. One in twenty of the delegates had attended Congress, and one in ten had held an important state office. In addition, a tenth had served as sheriff, justice, or the like, but fully half had never occupied a political post before their election.

In their social origins the representatives included every sort of person. The pre-Revolutionary elite survived with enough influence to hold one-sixth of the seats—far less than before, but they did control the senate. Another tenth belonged to families of above-average status, 30 percent came from an average background, and all the rest were of humble origin, usually outside of the state in some colony to the northward or in Europe. Almost certainly at least 40 percent of the legislators were socially new men—the

Table 10.1. *Composition of the South Carolina Legislature, 1787–1788*

	No.	%		No.	%
Residence			**Occupation**		
Frontier	44	23.4	Farmer	26	13.8
Noncommercial farm	30	16.0	Planter	61	32.4
Commercial farm	32	17.0	Artisan	6	3.2
Plantation	52	27.7	Doctor	13	6.9
Major city	30	16.0	Lawyer	13	6.9
			Other professional	2	1.1
			Misc. entrepreneur	3	1.6
Economic status			Merchant or trader	22	11.7
Poor or moderate	37	19.7	Unknown	42	22.3
Substantial	23	12.2			
Well-to-do	50	26.6			
Wealthy	66	35.1	**Age**		
Unknown	12	6.4	Under 30	22	11.7
			30–39	30	16.0
			40–49	19	10.1
Religion			50 and over	9	4.8
Episcopalian	36	19.1	Unknown	108	57.4
Methodist	2	1.1			
Congregational	4	2.1			
Presbyterian	14	7.4	**Military service**		
Other	3	1.6	Enlisted man	1	0.5
Unknown	129	68.6	Misc. officer	40	21.3
			Colonel or general	24	12.8
			None known	123	65.4
Political experience					
Local office	5	2.7	**Intellectual interest**		
Sheriff, j.p., etc.	13	6.9			
State judge, senator	14	7.4	None	134	71.3
Other state office	5	2.7	Some	41	21.8
Continental Congress	11	5.9	Uncertain	13	6.9
None	96	51.1			
Uncertain	44	23.4			
			World view		
			Localist	90	47.9
Education			Cosmopolitan	42	22.3
None or little	11	5.9	Unknown	56	29.8
Self-educated	4	2.1			
College	25	13.3			
Uncertain	148	78.7			

Table 10.1—Continued

	No.	%		No.	%
Father's economic status			*Father's occupation*		
Poor or moderate	12	6.4	Farmer	18	9.6
Substantial	10	5.3	Planter	48	25.5
Well-to-do	14	7.4	Artisan, etc	3	1.6
Wealthy	47	25.0	Doctor	2	1.1
Unknown	105	55.9	Lawyer	1	0.5
			Other professional	1	0.5
			Merchant, etc.	15	8.0
			Unknown	100	53.2
Social origin			*National origin*		
Humble origin	48	25.6	Colonial, English	66	35.1
Old family	43	22.9	Colonial, Scottish	7	3.7
Above-average family	17	9.0	Colonial, Scotch-Irish	2	1.1
Prominent old family	33	17.6	Colonial, French	13	6.9
Unknown	47	25.0	Colonial, other	13	6.9
			Immigrant, English	3	1.6
			Immigrant, West Indian	3	1.6
Mobility			Immigrant, Scottish	2	1.1
			Immigrant, Scotch-Irish	5	2.7
Mobile	40	21.3	Immigrant, other	4	2.1
Not mobile	142	75.5	Unknown	69	36.7
Uncertain	6	3.2			
Slaveholding					
Over 100	24	12.8			
50–99	25	13.3			
20–49	43	22.9			
10–19	31	16.5			
5–9	21	11.2			
1–4	5	2.7			
None	11	5.9			
Unknown	28	14.8			

highest proportion of any state.[8] The precise occupation and economic status of most fathers is unknown, but apparently a majority

8. Only 26% surely began in humble homes. The origin of 25% remains unknown. Of these, however, two-thirds lived in the backcountry, where the great majority, perhaps three-fourths of the people and 73% of the delegates, had immigrated. Several of the low-country men whose parents remain unidentified probably came from overseas.

were farmers. While most of the representatives descended from English stock, men of Scottish, Scotch-Irish, Irish, French, Dutch, and German ancestry also served.[9]

The legislature thus reflected many of the state's varied interests, the clash of which occasioned the roll calls of 1787 and 1788. The most numerous votes concerned loyalists, and indeed loyalism had seriously divided the state for many years. During the war a considerable number of Carolinians in all sections favored the English side. In the interior they received little British support and were crushed, though only after a savage guerrilla warfare that left the backcountry rebels bitterly antitory. Along the coast the planters tolerated the loyalist minority. Charleston was much divided. When British armies occupied the city in 1780, only the most patriotic or the most conspicuous rebels departed. Others remained to take an oath of allegiance. As British rule spread along the coast, some planters fled, a few became open tories, and a good many sat out the war. In 1782 the legislature, meeting at Jacksonborough, passed a strict—some thought harsh—law that confiscated the property of the greatest offenders, levied heavy fines (the "amercement") on others, and deprived a large number of the right to vote or hold office.[10] The confiscated estates could be bought on credit by those giving adequate security.[11]

With the signing of the peace treaty and the evacuation of Charleston, opinions gradually changed. Some British subjects remained in the city, and others arrived. While they were bitterly attacked in the press and even in the streets, they found defenders among prominent residents who finally (as previously noted) succeeded in dominating city politics. A movement gained strength to forgive all but the most notorious tories, to remit the fines, restore unsold property, and allow civil rights especially to such people as had taken the oath of allegiance during the occupation but who had otherwise remained inactive. On the other hand, men

9. During the sessions of 1787 and 1788 the senate contained a majority of great landowners, and wealthy men held nearly two thirds of the seats. However those from prominent old families just equaled the humbly born.

10. [Aedanus Burke], *An Address to the Freemen of the State of South-Carolina* (Philadelphia, 1783).

11. Only men of means could give such security, so the law did not radically redistribute property. One critic objected that the poor people would therefore remain poor while "the Wealthy are thus invited to a dangerous Accumulation of Riches." He remarked further, "It is notorious that the unequal Division of Property in Carolina is a real Grievance." George Turner to ?, Oct. 13, 1782, Miscellaneous Manuscripts, South Caroliniana Library, University of South Carolina, Columbia.

who had risked their lives and lost property fought concessions. Petitions for relief from confiscation and amercement flooded the legislature, which in one session modified the penalty on eighty-nine individuals.[12]

Seven votes reveal the alignment on this question. The first released an estate from amercement, 67–62 (February 8, 1787). This step was supported by two-thirds of the Charleston delegates and by practically all of the representatives from neighboring parishes, but was opposed by three-fourths of the westerners. A more significant vote occurred later in the session on the more general motion to repeal the entire confiscation and amercement act. This lost, 61–97 (February 21). Support again centered in the city and its environs, but 90 percent of the western delegates and nearly 70 percent of the easterners who lived some distance from Charleston opposed the change.

These two roll calls indicate other aspects of the division. Farmers voted almost unanimously against the loyalists. A majority of planters forgave the individual, but would not yield on the principle of confiscation. Professional men and other delegates with a nonfarm occupation voted the same way, but were less antiloyalist. Merchants, however, supported repeal of the act by a four-to-one margin. The more property a delegate owned, the more favorably disposed he was to leniency. Also willing to remove restrictions were the more educated, the more intellectually inclined, and the more cosmopolitan.[13] Loyalists found more defenders among representatives of prominent families than among those of humble origin, and among Episcopalians rather than among dissenters.

Near the end of the session a bill was introduced restoring to an ex-governor, William Bull, the rights of citizenship. Bull, though a loyalist, had been a popular governor, and some members of his family took the patriot side (including his cousin Gen. Stephen Bull, a representative who discreetly remained silent on this question). His petition therefore succeeded and presently became law.[14]

12. Spring session, 1784. For a sample debate, see *The Charleston Evening Gazette*, Feb. 16, 1786. The legislature, by a narrow margin, allowed British merchants to remain in Charleston (Feb. 26, Mar. 1, 3, 1783). Unfortunately, the clerk did not record pros and cons. See also Mar. 5, 1783, and Mar. 4, 1785.

13. Surprisingly, military service made no difference, nor did civil career, at least on the second vote. In the long run the moderates succeeded in relieving the lesser offenders. For an example of their views, see Gov. Guerard's message in the legislative journals, Feb. 2, 1784.

14. Mar. 26, 1787. The vote considered here stood 61–49. The bill presently passed, 75–40, and the senate approved it, 18–6.

The overwhelming majority of easterners voted in favor of this bill, only one Charlestonian opposing it. On the other hand, 85 percent of the westerners voted in the negative. Similarly among occupational groups only the small farmers still resented Bull's loyalism, as did small property owners and men of little education or limited experience. The highest correlation occurred along sectional lines. Probably Bull was favorably known in the east, where most men were natives of the state and admired the family, but he was either unknown or disliked among the westerners, who, if immigrants, might detest Bull as they would any tory governor or, if natives, might inherit prewar antagonisms.

The 1788 session also produced several votes concerning the loyalists. On January 26 a motion to receive no further petitions from men seeking relief from amercements lost, 37–50. The proposal met defeat because almost everyone in or near Charleston sympathized with the ex-loyalists and voted against it. Three subsequent votes concerned the restoration of a particular confiscated estate.[15] On all these votes Charleston's representatives and those from nearby parishes overwhelmingly favored the restoration. Other eastern delegates fluctuated: at first a majority joined their low-country neighbors, but presently some changed sides, though the margin remained small. On the other hand, four out of five backcountry delegates tried to defeat the restoration. A few farmers voted in the affirmative on the first roll call, but they unanimously opposed the bill thereafter. A considerable majority of planters supported the measure at first, but later the proportion fell to 58 percent. Artisans, professional men, and merchants overwhelmingly voted for the bill.[16] Men of moderate property opposed restoration three to one, but wealthy delegates favored it six to one. Age and military service made no difference. College men, those with intellectual interests, and cosmopolitan delegates almost always voted yea, their opposites generally nay. Men of prominent family sympathized with the loyalist petitioners, but those of humble origin usually did not. Finally, Episcopalians voted yes, dissenters no—the division on the second vote being particularly marked.

The senate also contributed several votes on the same question. One agreed to receive no further memorials from anyone who

15. Feb. 8, 81–53; Feb. 18, 64–56; Feb. 22, 58–55; and in a final vote (not analyzed), 51–48 for passage.
16. Delegates with a nonfarm occupation voted 78% pro on the first vote, 81% pro on the second.

had been banished, and two approved Bull's readmission and the restoration of his property. These also reveal a sharp sectional division, the antiloyalist votes coming almost entirely from the west.

All of these facts conform to a general pattern of opinion growing out of the state's history and the nature of loyalism. The legislature was debating, not loyalism in general and decidedly not the species that had flourished in the west, but eastern loyalism, specifically the loyalism of the larger property holders who possessed estates worth confiscating or taxing or trying to defend. These loyalists now were being protected by men of their own section, class, and social, cultural, and economic interests, some of whom perhaps might have been tories themselves, who had loyalist friends or relatives, and who acted from a mixture of magnanimity, sympathy, and confluence of interest. On the other side, the back-country delegates shared none of these feelings, but instead remembered their traditional antagonisms to the eastern merchants and planters as well as to loyalists; and they may have read and believed the newspaper articles that warned that to forgive the loyalists was to strengthen aristocracy. Fundamentally the division reflected economic and social class antagonisms.

Issues arising out of government expenditures created no major conflict in South Carolina. Once the legislature had apportioned taxes in a manner satisfactory to both farmers and planters and provided for payment of the state debt in a way that offended few (at least among the articulate), only details remained. The question of government spending occasioned several votes early in the 1787 session. These concerned the salaries of the governor, the commandant of Fort Johnson (who was Gen. Francis Marion), and the collector of customs at Charleston. Related yet quite different was the question of the legislators' own per diem.

The first roll call of 1787 challenged a salary of £1,300 for the governor, which the delegates rejected, 54–63, as too high. Representatives from Charleston agreed to that figure by a large majority. Two-thirds of the other low-country men also felt it reasonable, but almost all delegates from the interior thought it excessive. Farmers, with few exceptions, preferred a lower salary, while planters divided evenly, but merchants and professional men, who perhaps received that much cash annually, considered the salary fair. As might be supposed, men of moderate or even substantial properties voted overwhelmingly in the negative, while a slight majority of well-to-do delegates and three-fourths of the wealthy ones favored the motion. Army officers divided about as everyone else. Higher-ranking civil officials naturally preferred the better salary, lesser ones did not. Men of education, of intellectual taste, and of cosmopolitan outlook sided with the governor, as did delegates from prominent families, but those of more humble origin tried to reduce the expense.

A few days later the legislature debated the commandant's salary, first defeating £500 (52–63), then £400 (51–60), and finally accepting £200 (61–46), the first and third votes being recorded. In all probability the post was a sinecure, and in fact the legislature soon reduced the force there to a commander, a sergeant, and six men. Perhaps because the post guarded Charleston, city delegates and those from nearby parishes supported the highest income, while those more remote proved even more parsimonious than in the case of the governor. The former voted ten to one in favor of £500 and against £200. Westerners cast 98 percent of their votes against £500 and unanimously favored £200. In between, the low-country representatives who lived some distance from Charleston divided evenly. Similarly the collector of the port of Charleston failed to gain the top figure and ended with £400, winning support from his neighbors but losing allies in proportion to distance and ending with only one friend on the frontier.[17] The division along occupational lines proved just as decisive. No farmer agreed to the higher salary of either official, and every one voted for the low income granted the commandant, whereas a very large majority of delegates other than farmers favored the higher figure. Planters divided equally on the commandant's salary, but most of them found the collector's £500 too high. Small property holders seldom agreed to the larger income, well-to-do representatives split, but wealthy men (as in the case of the governor) proved willing to support the officials in style. In other respects the division also closely paralleled that on the governor's salary.

The legislature voted on one other question involving revenue: a motion that all taxes should be paid to the collector of the county where the property lay. This lost, 55–67 (February 16, 1788). No direct evidence explains the issue. Clearly, however, most of the money collected all over the state flowed to and remained in Charleston or nearby parishes. Payments on the debt took much of the money, and what remained furnished salaries to officials. Since easterners certainly held most of the debt and probably a majority of offices, the outcome was a steady drain of specie from

17. Feb. 5, 1787. The vote on £500 was 48–57.

the interior eastward, even though taxes were lower in the west. The sectional nature of the division substantiates this analysis. No Charleston representative and only two from the nearby parishes voted for the proposal. On the other hand, some men from more distant eastern parishes favored it, as did almost all of the westerners. In other respects also the alignment on this vote resembled that on revenue issues generally. Farmers favored the plan, but everyone else rejected it. Almost all wealthy men opposed it, while smaller property holders voted for it. Perhaps curiously, military and civil officeholders divided equally. Men with good education and those with none, men of intellectual interest and those without, cosmopolitans and localists, all opposed each other decisively, but social origin probably meant nothing.

After combining these few votes with other evidence, the conclusion seems clear that questions of taxation and expenditure divided Carolinians along lines primarily of economic interest, though ideas of what was good or bad for the state doubtless influenced the delegates too. Men from the west, those with relatively small properties, and those of limited education and experience hoped to limit taxes by reducing salaries, tried to shift the burden onto others, and hoped to keep the revenue in their own district for local use. Opposed to them, Charlestonians and other low-country delegates, men with large property, representatives who were not farmers, and well-educated or cosmopolitan men saw the desirability of higher salaries and accepted the tax burden more willingly because most of the money remained in their hands.

One vote that seemingly concerned government expenditures actually involved a different question. This rejected, 47–75, a per diem payment of 7s. to members of the legislature in addition to the usual allowance for traveling. The disagreement concerned, not the specific figure (which was relatively low), but whether the delegates should receive anything at all. They had previously served without pay, and (as debates elsewhere reveal) some men defended that policy. The reformers could cite the financial sacrifice of a long trip, the expense of staying in the city, and the beneficial effects of enabling the best men, regardless of wealth, to serve the people.

The division followed sectional, cultural, and economic class lines. The farther a delegate lived from Charleston and the less property he owned, the more he favored the change. Almost all farmers liked the plan (they saw little cash), planters divided equally (they too often lacked specie), but professional men and merchants voted against it. Military service did not effect voting, and neither, probably, did one's political career. Educated, cosmopolitan men of high social rank agreed to serve without pay, but their opposites would not. As a result delegates received no per diem until a constitution provided for it several years later.

The most heated debate, save that over the loyalists, and certainly the most complex, involved the relations between debtors and creditors. After the war Carolinians increased their already considerable burden by enormous purchases of slaves and imported goods. British merchants both in England and Charleston, together with native traders, advanced liberal credit. Unfortunately exports failed to keep pace. The people bought excessively, crop failures and a decline in the foreign market hurt the farmers, and the loss of a British bounty on indigo added to their difficulties. Although people in the backcountry, like most residents of a newly developed agricultural region, owed money, the loudest outcry came from eastern planters. Blaming the British merchants—convenient scapegoats—they demanded aid and got it, after some riots had frightened waverers. In March 1784 a combined stay and installment law delayed payments on debts contracted before and during the war.[18] In October a valuation law (the "pine barren" act) enabled the debtors to offer some of his poorer land as payment at a price set by sympathetic neighbors rather than at auction.[19] As a result suits for debt ceased. During the same session the legislators debated paper money, expounding the usual arguments, but defeated it, 48–38.[20]

When the legislature reassembled early the next year, it agreed to issue paper on loan under conditions that assured that only men of large property could borrow it. The bill clearly favored the planters, but they must have attracted some backcountry support to pass the act. On the other side, the creditors vigorously opposed measures that they considered both unwise and unfair. Fortunately the quantity of paper money did not exceed the ability of the state to maintain its value, and both merchants and planters supported it. A law that fined anyone who refused to accept paper in exchange for goods seems to have been unnecessary, for merchants presently were bragging about their currency supply and

18. Cooper, ed., *Statutes of S.C.*, IV, 640–641.

19. Technically, after an evaluation the sheriff would conduct an auction, and if the property was not bid for up to two-thirds of the set value, the creditor might either accept the property at the established valuation or refuse and receive nothing. See the debate in *Charleston Evening Gaz.*, Sept. 29, 1785.

20. *Ibid.*, Sept.–Oct. 1785 for the debate, Sept. 30 for the vote.

happily accepting payments on their debts.[21] Indeed the City Council of Charleston issued nearly £3,000 worth of paper in small denominations.[22]

At the same time the creditors urged that the valuation law ought to be repealed; debtors now could pay, they claimed, and lacked further excuse for cheating. How, they asked, could honest American merchants discharge their own debts? The only effect of the law was to encourage licentiousness and dishonesty.[23] When the legislature met early in 1787, creditors renewed their appeal, calling for honesty and economy.[24] David Ramsay, speaking on their behalf, denied the right of the legislature to interfere with private contracts. Instead it should maintain justice between debtors and creditors. The recent laws, he felt, had been unconstitutional. But spokesmen for the backcountry together with a segment of the planting interest (specifically, an indigo-growing district) demanded a valuation law and defended the "pine barren" act as essential to save the poor planter from prison.[25]

The debtors had their way. Two votes during that session suggest the alignment on this question, though they deal only with particular aspects of it. The first struck out of an installment bill a clause exempting from installment all contracts that had been made upon the condition that the borrower would not take advantage of any law.[26] The vote clearly pitted those who appreciated the creditors' position with those who did not. Sectionally, the antagonists were the westerners, 86 percent of whom voted to remove the restriction, and Charlestonians, who opposed the amendment by nearly the same margin. In between, however, the low-country parishes divided equally, those near Charleston barely supporting the creditors, those more remote backing the debtors by a very small majority.

Almost an identical alignment occurred on an amendment, this time initiated by the creditors, that would exempt from the bill all debts under £10. These could be recovered beginning July 1. This lost, 57–64. Charleston representatives sided with the creditors

21. John Cripps & Co. to Caleb Davis, Jan. 6, 1787, Caleb Davis Papers, XIVa, Mass. Hist. Soc.; Samuel Wilcox to Jeremiah Wadsworth, Dec. 8, 1786, Wadsworth Papers, Box 137, Conn. Hist. Soc.
22. *Charleston Evening Gaz.*, July 5, 1786.
23. "Rusticus," in *Columbian Herald* (Charleston), May 8, 1786, and especially his fine article in *ibid.*, Nov. 13, 16, 20, 1786.
24. *Charleston Morning Post*, Feb. 15–16, 1787.
25. *Ibid.*, Feb. 13, 16, 1787.
26. Mar. 22, 1787. The margin was 70–57.

by an even larger majority than before, only two out of twenty-two excepted. Again the westerners voted for the debtors, though by a reduced margin, and the eastern parishes again divided.

Other factors than residence may have affected the result. Farmers were prodebtor, men who were not farmers favored the creditors (though only by a two-to-one majority), and planters divided evenly. A correlation with wealth exists, but seems less significant than residence; clearly the question concerned, not how much property a man owned, but his debts or those of his constituents. Military service made no difference, nor did one's civil office, and the correlation with social origin is unimpressive. Cultural factors may have exercised some influence, but men with good education and cosmopolitan outlook divided more evenly than usual. The evidence strongly indicates that the impetus for a prodebtor law, at this time and of this nature, drew its support from western farmers, who found half of the planter delegates also favorable to the plan.

Debtors triumphed over creditors on another vote during the same session.[27] The former tried to repeal a clause in a 1783 ordinance that had established a depreciation table for state money by estimating the value of that money in rice, indigo, Negroes, and specie for several years while the money gradually depreciated. The clause required that the table must be used in settling private contracts, and since the paper's value had been set at a low rate, debtors could not profit from the depreciation. Only one Charlestonian (future Antifederalist Aedanus Burke) voted for the bill on its second reading, whereas three-fourths of the westerners did so. Rural, low-country delegates separated sharply. Of those near the city, 91 percent joined the Charleston bloc, but those more remote divided about equally. Again, whereas at least two-thirds and probably three-fourths of the farmers favored the bill, planters opposed it more than two to one, and representatives who were not farmers voted against it, four to one. The alignment on this issue correlated significantly with wealth. Nearly three-fourths of men with moderate properties voted yea, and those with substantial holdings favored it five to three. Well-to-do delegates, however, opposed it by a small margin, and wealthy men disapproved overwhelmingly (36–5). Evident also was a division by education and other cultural characteristics and by social origin.

Four votes early in 1788 also pertained to debts. The first oc-

27. The controversial bill originated with the senate, Mar. 9, 1787.

curred upon a motion offered by Alexander Gillon, onetime Charleston radical now representing Saxe Gotha, a western district. Gillon, a wealthy merchant and large landowner, did not invariably support up-country views, but he consistently voted for the debtors. He now moved that a committee "Report a plan which may avert the ruin which threatens both Creditors and Debtors." This lost, 48–97.[28] Every Charlestonian except one voted against it. A third of those delegates living near the city favored it, as did nearly half of the other low-country representatives. Only the west furnished a slight majority for the motion. Some days later the legislature divided on a more specific question: "Is it expedient to pass a Valuation Bill?" Answer: no, 53–92.[29] Again only one Charleston delegate voted for the motion, and again the proportion of favorable votes increased with distance from the city, though this time not quite half of the westerners supported the proposal.

The division of opinion thus followed sectional lines to some extent, but the agricultural districts, far from uniting, disagreed. Men who were planters by occupation rejected Gillon's proposal and the later motion two to one. Men not farmers voted much the same way, for although Charleston representatives disapproved almost unanimously, those elsewhere favored both motions. Farmers found themselves much divided. Counting only those positively identified as such, they voted against by the same margin as did planters. Including delegates whose occupation is unknown but who lived in rural areas and seem to have owned small properties, farmers split equally on the first motion and opposed the second by a margin of two to one. Economic status made little difference, and the correlation between votes and other characteristics of the legislators is unimpressive, with one exception to be noted presently.

Later in the session one group of debtors tried again. This time they limited the scope of the proposal to a "bill to fix the time for sales under execution." An effort to tack on a valuation clause failed. The lower house then passed, 63–57, what evidently was the critical section, limiting sales for execution to the period between January 15 and April 15. The timing almost certainly favored the rice planters, whose crop, harvested in the fall, would be sold or ready for sale by the end of the year and whose financial condition would be most favorable then. On the other hand, the interior

28. Feb. 8, 1788.
29. Feb. 21, 1788. The motion included an explanation that the bill would alter the method for the appraisement of property seized under execution.

farmers would not be helped at all. Charlestonians would be unaffected except as creditors. The bill, however, never took effect, for the legislature refused passage, 54–56 (February 26).

On these two votes men divided in almost random fashion. Property made no difference. Wealthy delegates voted yea both times (by a small margin), as did men of intellectual interest and education. The key to the bill's nature lies in one circumstance: planters supported the amendment by a two-to-one margin and favored passage by a majority of five to three, while other occupational groups including farmers divided evenly or opposed the bill. This question, then, did not involve the major issue of relations between debtors and creditors, but only whether certain planters would receive more favorable treatment before the law. Their position emphasizes the generalization that, on the general question of debts, the planters divided depending upon particular circumstances. Normally western farmers furnished most of the impetus for pro-debtor policies, while Charlestonians steadily opposed them.

Several votes in the senate support these generalizations. They concerned a bill setting up a depreciation table that fixed the value of paper currency at various times, a bill relative to the collection of debts, and an installment bill. The upper house contained too few men for reliable statistical analysis, but the sectional division appears very clearly on all of these roll calls, with westerners casting over 80 percent of their votes for the debtors (39–8), and easterners nearly as solid on the creditor side (40–11). The three senators who were farmers and localists with moderate properties contributed just one vote out of twelve to the creditors. Men who were not engaged in agriculture divided depending on their residence, and so did the large landowners. The evidence strongly suggests that the desires of one's constituency predominated over other influences.

Closely connected with the planters' debts was the question of whether to restrict the importation of slaves. At first sight one might suppose that the Charleston merchants, who profited from the trade, and planters, who profited from slave labor, would resist any restriction, whereas interior farmers, mostly slaveless and engaged in a diversified agriculture, would willingly limit importation; or that the controversy would follow religious or other ideological lines. The second assumption probably has merit, for delegates known to be church members did in fact favor a limitation by a margin of nearly two to one, whereas other delegates divided evenly. But the first assumption is quite wrong, and the religious factor is statistically much less significant than are other influences. The initiative in fact came from merchants and creditors. A majority of planters concurred, but the proposal lost when the westerners rejected it.

As soon as the war ended, planters hastened to replace the Negroes who had died or fled with the British troops. In 1784 they spent almost a quarter of a million pounds sterling on slaves. By 1785, as already discussed, they had exhausted their credit. The merchants now perceived that they must make money, not by further sales of goods and extensions of credit, but by collecting their debts. And only if the planters refrained from buying slaves could they pay those debts. Few men argued that importations should cease because slavery was wrong; the appeal was entirely pragmatic. The planters must have recognized that the plan made sense, yet many wished to continue buying. The major opposition, however, came not from them but from western farmers who hoped soon to become slave owners. They defeated the measure.

The economic nature of the issue appeared immediately upon its introduction into the legislature. In September 1785 the lower house in a special session debated what to do about debts and bad crops, and along with proposals to stop suits for debt and issue paper came the bill to forbid the importation of slaves for three years, which lost, 51–47. This vote was not recorded, but two taken in 1787 reveal the nature of the alignment.

On March 17, 1787, in conjunction with the installment bill discussed above, the lower house approved a clause prohibiting the importation of slaves for three years, 57–54. A week later an attempt to eliminate the amendment failed, 56–73. Delegates from Charleston cast only four votes against the restriction, two of which came from great planters (Thomas Heyward, Jr., and Charles Cotesworth Pinckney), and one from a blacksmith. Merchants favored this restraint on trade, 22–2. Also voting to retain the clause were the delegates from parishes near Charleston, by a margin of better than two to one, but a slight majority of those easterners living farther away took the other side. The low-country majority for a restriction did not come from the planters, only half of whom agreed to deprive themselves of more Negroes, but from business and professional men: thus two-thirds of the latter accepted the amendment. In contrast, western representatives voted by a two-to-one majority to continue importations, the frontier areas in fact being the most anxious of any section to obtain more slaves. Most farmers wanted to buy their first or an additional

Negro. So did the men with moderate property, whereas almost three-fourths of the wealthy delegates favored a temporary embargo. Educated men, intellectually inclined delegates, and cosmopolitan representatives also supported the proposal by a large majority, whereas their opposites opposed it. These factors may have exercised some influence, but the connection of this issue with that of planter debts demonstrates that economic considerations were paramount.

One other issue required two roll-call votes, recorded on March 14–15, 1787. This concerned a convention to amend the state's constitution. Pressure for a revision developed primarily in the west, which lacked adequate representation, but some easterners also advocated a change, either because they believed that the government should be more responsible to the people or for quite different reasons, such as a desire to strengthen the executive branch. The debate began in 1784, when the lower house backed, but the senate rejected, a convention. The following year the representatives, stimulated by petitions from the backcountry (January 27, February 22, 1785), renewed their efforts, but the senate again blocked action. Two years later the delegates once more attempted a revision. The crucial vote came on a motion to postpone reading the report on proposed amendments, which lost, 52–93. The two geographical extremes continued to be the city, which favored postponement by a margin of over three to one, and the interior, which opposed delay nine to one. In between, the lowcountry parishes near Charleston sided with the city (62 percent), while those more distant divided almost evenly. An overwhelming majority of farmers wanted to consider the report. They were joined by a small majority of planters, but other delegates tended toward postponement, the margin being about three to two. Military and civil officials divided, as did the other voters. Revision won support from men of little education, no known intellectual interest, and limited experience, all by very wide margins, whereas their opposites fought revision by about two to one. Almost all delegates of small property voted for a change, as did, indeed, two-thirds of those who owned substantial estates or were well-to-do, but the wealthy voted to delay. Meanwhile the senate also recorded a vote, specifically on a clause stating that the constitution needed revision. The westerners approved this almost unanimously, while the easterners opposed it, 10–3. Again the three ordinary farmers, all westerners, voted with their section, as did men of other occupations, and the evidence points decisively to a sectional explanation of the alignment in the upper house.[30]

Judging from this analysis, the existing arrangements satisfied most of the eastern, urban, economic, and cultural upper class. The most nearly unanimous element in the legislature consisted of western farmers with moderate property and little education, who desired reform. In the end the senate prevented a change, which ultimately came only after the ratification of the Federal Constitution.

Throughout these sessions of the legislature, on almost every vote the representatives divided consistently into two major blocs. One, which may be as usual designated the Cosmopolitans, favored higher salaries and leniency for the loyalists. They opposed constitutional reform and prodebtor legislation, voted against paying the legislators per diem expenses, favored a moratorium on the importing of slaves, and opposed turning over taxes to county collectors. Their votes, taken collectively, establish the now familiar "party line" against which can be measured the consistency of each delegate. A few of these own a perfect record of conformity; forty-eight men cast at least 80 percent of their votes with this group, and another thirty adhered to that party two-thirds of the time. On the other side, forty-nine men opposed the Cosmopolitans by at least four to one (eighteen unanimously), and twenty-two by at least two to one. These two groups cast nearly a thousand individual votes, of which 85 percent conformed to the voting pattern typical of the party. In the center, thirty-nine representatives held the balance of power as neutrals.

This method of examining the political alignment seems even more revealing than that based upon other criteria, such as occupation or residence. The consistency with which the delegates voted according to "party" on the principal issues is illustrated by table 10.2. In each case the basis is conformity to the Cosmopolitan position.

The geographical division within the legislature is strikingly supported by this analysis of individual voting behavior (see the map, p. 289). All of Charleston's representatives voted with the Cosmopolitans, and the city furnished ten of the group's most consistent adherents. Delegates from nearby parishes supplied eleven of the leaders and almost half of the Cosmopolitan bloc's

30. In the Little River district, 192 inhabitants complained "that in the present representation property is consulted and Represented more than the Number of free Men." House Journal, Mar. 25, 1785. See also *ibid.*, Feb. 22, 1786.

Table 10.2. Bloc Voting on Representative Issues, South Carolina (in Percentages of Pro-Cosmopolitan Votes)

	Votes							
	1	2	3	4	5	6	7	8
Localists	9	4	3	18	15	16	14	40
Neutrals	52	35	33	64	59	64	44	51
Cosmopolitans	78	64	75	84	77	97	80	86

CODE OF VOTES:

1. For raising governor's salary.
2. For ending amercement on a loyalist estate.
3. Against revising the constitution.
4. For prohibiting the importation of slaves.
5. For excepting small debts from the installment bill.
6. For restoring Gov. Bull's citizenship.
7. Against paying taxes to counties.
8. Against a valuation bill.

membership, producing only two delegates who took the opposite side and two neutrals. Representatives from the other low-country parishes, in contrast, scattered along the entire political spectrum. One, Robert Heriot of All Saints, on the northern coast, cast all of his votes with the Cosmopolitans, and another, William Ferguson of St. Bartholomew, was one of the Localists' most consistent members. Eleven others cast two-thirds of their votes with the Cosmopolitans, eleven joined the other side, and seventeen remained neutral. In the up-country districts, one delegate joined the Cosmopolitans and sixteen were neutral, while nearly sixty favored the Localists. The four westernmost districts contained two-thirds of the latter's leaders.[31]

Other characteristics of these two opposing groups help to indicate the nature of the alignment. No ordinary farmer voted with the Cosmopolitans, and probably a dozen were neutrals, so that at least two-thirds and perhaps as many as three-fourths of the farmers belonged to the Localist group.[32] Planters, exclusive of

31. Using the criteria of scale for residence established for other states, the alignment is as follows:

	Frontier	Noncomm. farm	Comm. farm	Plantation	City
Localist	80%	73%	28%	10%	0%
Neutral	21	17	34	27	0
Cosmopolitans	0	10	38	64	100

32. Out of 26 known, 17. The occupations of over one-fifth of the delegates are unknown, of whom 70% were Localists. Probably about half of these were farmers, nearly all of whom voted with the Localist bloc.

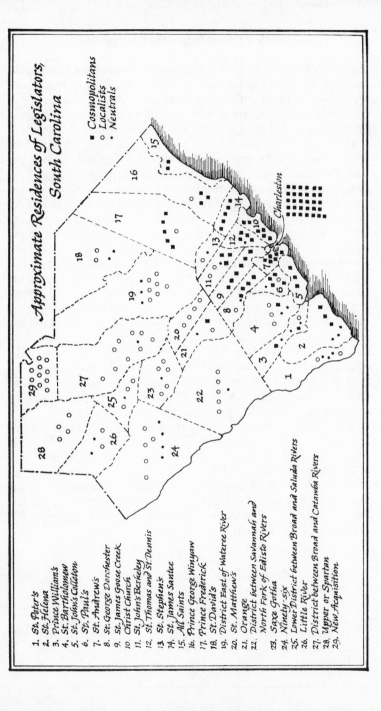

Approximate Residences of Legislators, South Carolina

■ Cosmopolitans
○ Localists
· Neutrals

1. St. Peter's
2. St. Helena
3. Prince Williams
4. St. Bartholomew
5. St. John's Colleton
6. St. Paul's
7. St. Andrew's
8. St. George Dorchester
9. St. James Goose Creek
10. Christ Church
11. St. John's Berkeley
12. St. Thomas and St. Dennis
13. St. Stephen's
14. St. James Santee
15. All Saints
16. Prince George Winyaw
17. Prince Frederick
18. St. David's
19. District East of Wateree River
20. St. Matthew's
21. Orange
22. District between Savannah and
    North Fork of Edisto Rivers
23. Saxe Gotha
24. Ninety-six
25. Lower District between Broad and Saluda Rivers
26. Little River
27. District between Broad and Catawba Rivers
28. Upper or Spartan
29. New Acquisition

those following an additional occupation, favored the Cosmopolitan side but by no great margin. Eight were among the party's leaders as compared with only two at the opposite extreme, but of the whole number nearly half voted with Cosmopolitans, about 30 percent supported the Localists, and the rest remained neutral.

Delegates other than farmers preferred the Cosmopolitan bloc overwhelmingly. Among its leaders were three artisans, six lawyers, three merchants, and a doctor, together constituting thirteen of the twenty-two. Only one merchant (Alexander Gillon) supported the Localists, whereas eighteen voted with the Cosmopolitans. All but one of the thirteen lawyers did likewise. In general, among those with a nonfarm occupation (who formed one-third of the legislature), almost three-fourths voted with the Cosmopolitans, about one-sixth with the Localists, and a tenth were neutral. The alignment, then, was as follows: the Cosmopolitan group consisted of 43 percent planters, 22 percent merchants, 16 percent lawyers, 1 percent farmers, and 18 percent others; the Localists included probably about 30 percent planters, one merchant, no lawyers, about 46 percent farmers, 10 percent whose occupation cannot be surmised, and 14 percent others. The Localists obviously were the agrarians, while the Cosmopolitan group, though it attracted support among the large landowners, primarily consisted of business and professional men. Analysis proves that occupation was an independent variable transcending place of residence.

The two sides also differed in their composition along lines of economic class. Men of moderate property supported the Localists with few exceptions, as did those with slightly larger holdings. Well-to-do delegates divided evenly, but wealthy men almost always voted with the Cosmopolitans. Thus, as table 10.3 shows, the Localist bloc consisted principally of the smaller property holders (64 percent of those known), the Cosmopolitans of the larger (91 percent of those known).

Table 10.3. *Party Preference in Economic Groups, South Carolina (in Percentages)*

	Cosmopolitan	Neutral	Localist
Moderate	8	19	73
Substantial	8	23	59
Well-to-do	35	30	35
Wealthy	81	12	7

Economic status was independent of residence, though obviously closely connected with it.[33]

Socially, too, the composition of the parties reveals contrasting characteristics. Among the nearly three dozen delegates who descended from the prominent old families, only two supported the Localists and three were neutral. Among other above-average families also, a considerable majority voted with the Cosmopolitans. Men of average background divided evenly, but those of humble origin, mostly immigrants, preferred the Localist group by a margin of two to one. Put differently, 55 percent of the Cosmopolitan bloc's members came from families of social stature; 30 percent, from average backgrounds; and 15 percent, from humble environments. Among the Localists 12 percent were of above-average social origin; 32 percent, of average background; and 56 percent, from humble homes. On the other hand, nationality did not matter because most of the delegates were English.[34]

Various cultural factors also seem significant. Most Episcopalians, as far as is known, favored the Cosmopolitans, probably because most of them lived in the low country. The backcountry's religious diversity is reflected in the preference of non-Episcopal denominations for the Localists, an affinity somewhat greater than that of the district generally. The correlation of education and intellectual interest with voting record is so high as to suggest a causal relationship. Among college men, nineteen supported the Cosmopolitans against three neutrals and three who sided with the Localists. Forty-one representatives left evidence of intellectual interest, among whom only two favored the Localists.

Men of presumably cosmopolitan outlook overwhelmingly supported the positions taken by the group of the same name, the proportion being 85 percent, whereas of the localists 65 percent favored the objectives of their bloc and only 11 percent supported the Cosmopolitans. As table 10.4 shows, the correlation far exceeds that which one would expect from the residence of the men. The cosmopolitan-localist factor thus existed independently of residence and also of occupation: whereas nonfarmer delegates (to take an example) supported the Localist bloc only 16 percent of the time, the localists among them did so 56 percent of the time, and cosmopolitans, but 7 percent.

33. Thus in frontier and noncommercial farm areas, where neutrals drew 19% of the votes and the Cosmopolitans 5%, the well-to-do and wealthy delegates lined up 35% and 9% respectively.

34. However, men of Scottish and French descent preferred the Cosmopolitans, whereas the Scotch-Irish voted with the Localists.

The political experience of the delegates seems to have had little effect on their voting except that the higher-ranking officials tended to support the Cosmopolitan bloc. Political ideology, however, probably did influence party alignments. Among the Localists whose attitude concerning the Constitution is known, 88 percent opposed ratification, whereas all but one out of forty-nine delegates voting with the Cosmopolitans supported the new government—a combined correlation of 95 percent. The ideological or party affiliation continued into the nineties, when the Cosmopolitan bloc produced twenty-two Federalists against two Republicans, and on the other side, the Localists yielded three Federalists and eight Republicans.[35]

Table 10.4. Party Preference in South Carolina: World View in Relation to Residence (in Percentages)

Party Divisions in Residential Groups	All Delegates	World View	
		Localists	Cosmopolitans
Frontier–noncomm. farm			
Localist	77	82	50
Neutral	19	15	25
Cosmopolitan	5	3	25
Comm. farm–plantation			
Localist	16	33	10
Neutral	30	48	10
Cosmopolitan	54	19	81

The senate contained a similar alignment. The Localist bloc there consisted almost entirely of westerners, while the Cosmopolitan group was made up of men living near the coast. Two-thirds of the wealthy senators favored the latter, all of those with moderate property (there were only three), the former. The cosmopolitan-localist division appeared, though less prominently than the sectionalism, and the only other striking contrast occurred between the men of humble origin and those of prominent family. Also the Localists in the senate opposed ratification, 5–4, and Cosmopolitans favored it, 6–0.

These facts create a composite picture of a Cosmopolitan dele-

35. The age profile indicates that the Cosmopolitans were somewhat younger than the Localists, but this seems to be related to residence and is a tendency only.

gate. He lived in or not far from Charleston, followed a business or professional career or owned a large plantation, was wealthy, belonged to a good family, exhibited a cosmopolitan outlook, often acquired an education and sometimes intellectual tastes, and probably became a Federalist. His opposite, the typical Localist representative, lived in the interior a hundred miles from the city, engaged in farming, owned a comparatively small property, started his career with few advantages, often as a newcomer to the state, received little education, inclined toward provincialism, and became an Antifederalist.

Politics in South Carolina were a product of this dichotomy. The outlook of the Charleston-centered group needs no elaboration. Although they sometimes referred to their society as democratic, since most white men owned property and could vote, it was of course profoundly aristocratic, resting upon slave labor, and the ruling planter-professional-merchant elite enjoyed a high standard of living. They became well informed less through formal education than through their visits to the city and their economic, cultural, and political relations with the Atlantic world. These advantages fitted them for leadership in the legislature. As the traveler Johann Schoepf observed, "The members from the city are for the most part attorneys, considerable merchants, and others, intelligent and well-informed; hence they are fluent, enterprising, and easily get the upper hand of the representatives from the country, when it is a matter of address and a little intrigue."[36] Four out of five members of the Cosmopolitan bloc lived within a day's journey from the city.

The other low-country politicians, politically neutral, differed from the foregoing in what clearly were crucial aspects. They lived upwards of fifty miles from the city, which they must have visited rarely, and in which many had no relatives or social connections. Probably they marketed their crops through Georgetown on the north or through Beaufort and Savannah in the south. Several of these parishes specialized in indigo, which meant depressed conditions during the 1780s. Tax lists for St. Bartholomew and Prince George Winyaw parishes reveal a more democratic society in that they contained many small farmers and, in the latter, far fewer slaves than in the Charleston district. While large planters certainly dominated these parishes, they seem to have remained more isolated and more purely agrarian at least at this time. Few

36. Johann David Schoepf, *Travels in the Confederation*, trans. and ed. Alfred J. Morrison (Philadelphia, 1911), II, 198–199.

actually sided with the opposition—and these few lived along the
western edge—but they adopted an intermediate position.

The interior contained much variety. The districts of Orange,
St. Matthew's, and Saxe Gotha, along the Broad, Saluda, Catawba,
and Santee rivers, in the center of the state, had been occupied
earliest, contained a sizable number of slaves together with some
large plantations, and possessed good transportation. Otherwise
the western two-thirds of the state remained in, or had just passed,
the frontier stage. The people shared few attributes or interests
with the low-country men, being, to quote Schoepf again, "a
little obstinate, or even a little suspicious." They sought a more
democratic, responsive, and conveniently located government,
economy, relief for debtors, paper money, and local autonomy.[37]

Despite what must have been some bitter battles in the legislature, the sources contain few traces of election contests and few
comments on the political alignments other than that within the
city. There are indications of an extensive struggle in 1784. At
that point Ralph Izard had to send out an overseer "to engage as
many votes as he could for another party," with the object of defeating Thomas Tudor Tucker. More than just personal power
was at stake here, for Tucker, though a doctor of reputation,
voted with the Localists and presently became an Antifederalist
and a Jeffersonian, whereas Izard took the opposite side.[38] The
same year John Lloyd, a Charleston creditor and merchant, wrote
to his nephew that "the Malecontented party having by several
publications endeavoured to influence the Electors throughout the
State to make choice of Men to represent them in the General
Assembly, from the lower class; the gentlemen of property to preserve their necessary consequence in the community and in order
to prevent anarchy and confusion, have almost unanimously exerted
themselves in opposition to them, and it is with particular pleasure
I inform you that they have pretty generally carried their point,
especially in this City, so that I expect we shall have an exceeding
good representation, and by that means support the honor and
credit of the Country."[39]

The emergence of "factions" in South Carolina was, as Edward
Rutledge observed, manifest.[40] Whether it was good depended

37. Petition from Ninety-six district, 1785, in Nadelhaft, chap. 7; petition from
Camden, Senate Journal, Oct. 5, 1785.
38. George C. Rogers, Jr., *Evolution of a Federalist: William Loughton Smith
of Charleston, 1758–1812* (Columbia, 1962), 128.
39. Dec. 7, 1784, Charleston Library Society.
40. To John Jay, Nov. 12, 1786, Johnston, ed., *Papers of Jay*, III, 217.

upon one's point of view. The merchant-planter elite, accustomed to governing without challenge, at least from other Carolinians, resented the emergence of opposition first in Charleston, then in the west. To the westerners parties meant that they might at last hold power: parties and a more representative government went together. Popular elections, wrote "Rusticus," were favorable to liberty. Nay, he continued, "even the spirit of party and opposition which generally reigns there, when kept within certain bounds, may be not only exceedingly useful, but necessary in a commonwealth."[41] Whether useful or distressing, the spirit of party had become a fixed element in Carolina's political system.

41. *Columbian Herald* (Charleston), Nov. 20, 1786.

Chapter XI

The Other States

The seven states considered thus far all furnish adequate information concerning political alignments. They supply enough votes, cast by legislators of many different characteristics, about whom sufficient data are available, to permit satisfactory generalizations. The remaining six are, for one reason or another, less satisfactory. Yet most of these also present points of interest and further our understanding of political contests before the Federal Constitution.

NEW HAMPSHIRE

New Hampshire's House of Representatives recorded over thirty votes between 1781 and 1789, sufficient for analysis, yet considerable study discloses only the outlines of a pattern. The state almost entirely lacked those distinct sectional divisions that constituted so important a factor in political alignments elsewhere. A prolonged and complicated examination of voting by towns revealed, not two or three, but eight sets of towns that voted as blocs, and even these groupings omitted a substantial number that fitted no pattern whatever. Worst of all, these eight did not fall into any neat geographical pattern, but instead occurred in a miscellaneous fashion throughout the state: two in the southeast, two in the south-central, two in the southwest, and two in the north. Thus, although Portsmouth, the principal commercial center, and a few neighbors constituted one bloc, allies occurred not so much among the other eastern trading centers as scattered irregularly about the state. If the state's politics possessed some subtle order, then, it must be sought apart from sectional considerations, although the attitudes of the Portsmouth group certainly must be included.

Why did the usual sectional divisions play a relatively small role? Evidently because they did not exist on the same scale as in most other states. During the 1780s New Hampshire might be said to contain only two sections: Portsmouth and a few other trading towns near the coast and the rest of the state. The former exported the lumber products and a small agricultural surplus drawn from the limited drainage system to the north and a commercial farm area confined to a radius of at most two dozen miles. Newburyport, lying less than a score of miles to the south, competed for the trade not only of the towns in between but of the Merrimac valley, from which Portsmouth is separated by hills. In fact Portsmouth proved to be at a disadvantage, for her communications with the interior remained unsatisfactory during these years. The villages along the Merrimac and those of the Connecticut valley possessed the potential for wealth, especially in manufacturing, but during the 1780s they remained mostly underdeveloped with some small-scale shops and good farms but little wealth. Indeed much of the state either was still frontier or had scarcely passed the stage of subsistence farming. Most towns contained a handful of artisans, a shopkeeper or two, a minister, a justice or country lawyer, a doctor, perhaps a few substantial landowners, and a great majority of small farmers. Probably these agricultural villages were politically, socially, and economically democratic and therefore essentially agreed on most matters. Internal division might lead to a victory first of one group, then of another, but the towns would show no consistent sectional differences because none existed.

Despite this general similarity, voting in the legislature did not occur entirely at random, for when the examination turns from the votes of towns to those of individuals, a pattern emerges. This pattern applies to two out of three votes and to 40 or 50 percent of those delegates who voted more than a few times. The number involved is small, for a roll call rarely found more than seventy delegates present and the personnel changed considerably from year to year, but some sixty persons composed two blocs, casting among them nearly five hundred votes with a consistency of about 86 percent, or seven to one. The protagonists voting most consistently included, on one side, George Gains, a Portsmouth artisan, John Pickering, a lawyer of Portsmouth and Newington, John Sparhawk, a Portsmouth merchant, and Ephraim Robinson, a merchant from Exeter; on the other, Moses Leavitt, a Northampton innkeeper, Jonathan Dow, a Quaker farmer-preacher from Weare, Jonathan Gaskett, a Richmond farmer, and Stephen Powers, a Newport farmer.

The issues that divided the legislators resembled those in neighboring Massachusetts. The treatment of loyalists, however, was much less important. A segment of the well-to-do Portsmouth elite, notably the Wentworth faction, joined the foe and lost their property. These found defenders in Portsmouth but apparently not elsewhere.[1] Interior loyalism developed among ordinary citizens, some Anglican, some not. The only votes concerning this issue related to a doctor from an inland town who had been not only a loyalist but reputedly a counterfeiter. The question was therefore not clear-cut, and the legislators voted erratically.[2]

Economic developments in New Hampshire also paralleled those in the Bay State, except that New Hampshire possessed less wealth and the debtor, paper-money influence was stronger. In September 1781, however, the creditor influence succeeded in depriving paper currency of its legal-tender quality and making gold and silver tender for debts.[3] Most of the affirmative votes came from the small coastal area. Indeed a majority of the forty-three representatives present came from Rockingham, the easternmost county, so that the commercial region had almost enough strength to pass the bill without help. In addition half a dozen delegates from the interior replaced the same number from the southeast who took the soft-money position. The alignment therefore stood:

	Southeast	Interior
For gold and silver	15	7
For paper	7	14

The bloc alignment—insofar as one can be traced at this date—was as follows: Cosmopolitan group (Portsmouth, etc.), 6–1 in favor; Localists, with only one member present, opposed.[4]

1. See "Journal of the House of Representatives," Mar. 25, June 21, 1782, Bouton *et al.*, eds., *N.H. State Papers*, VIII, 938, 944.
2. "House Journal," Feb. 24, 1786, and Jan. 4–5, 1787, *ibid.*, XX, 519–520, 772–774. The doctor proved innocent of counterfeiting.
3. *Ibid.*, VIII, 913.
4. Since most votes occurred during the 1786 and 1787 sessions, parties must be determined by these, and only a few delegates who served then sat at this earlier period.

This decision aroused little interest at first, but by the fall of 1783 the onset of the postwar deflation created a demand for more money and measures favorable to debtors. The town of Chester instructed its representatives that "it is with Concern of Mind we consider the uncomfortable Circumstances we are in by reason of high Taxes, the scarcity of Cash, and the surprising number of Law-Suits, which have an evident Tendency to distress the good People of this state; you are therefore to endeavor that something be done either by cutting down the Table of Fees, by making States Security, or Produce a tender for executions; or making a Small Bank of Money, which may enable the People to pay their Taxes; and therefore prevent the growing Evil. . . ."[5] Agitation reached a climax in 1786 when county conventions, petitions, and newspaper articles urged relief. Arguments familiar elsewhere stressed the difficulties of the debtors, especially the shortage of money and low prices for property sold at auction, and criticized creditors. "I do not hesitate to declare," wrote "Impartiality," "that the debtor's motives for wanting a paper medium, appear to me to be, not only just, reasonable and honest, but patriotic; And the creditor's, on the contrary, to be, not only unjust and cruel, but anti-republican."[6] Towns all over the state joined in the chorus, but interior communities expressed the greatest unrest.

Procreditor, antipaper feeling centered in Portsmouth. A town meeting rejected paper money, 79–6. The residents backed this opinion by an able statement that insisted the present money supply would be adequate if the legislature maintained its value by upholding public credit and called for the collection of taxes, payment of public debt, frugality, economy, and industry.[7] One writer recommended, as the proper solution, reducing imports and increasing exports by lowering both wages and prices. He opposed paper money unless backed by silver and strongly criticized making it legal tender, which he considered arbitrary and unwise: men, he insisted, need not be compelled to accept good money.[8]

---

5. Sept. 30, 1783, Bouton *et al.*, eds., *N.H. State Papers*, XI, 318.

6. *The New-Hampshire Mercury, and General Advertiser* (Portsmouth), Sept. 6, 1786, continued on Sept. 13. Newspapers of the period contain many articles. One of the most revealing is by "A. Z.," *The New-Hampshire Spy* (Portsmouth), Dec. 8, 1786. One of the best statements in the town records is that of Barrington, Nov. 18, 1786, N.H. State Lib.

7. *N.-H. Mercury* (Portsmouth), Nov. 1, 1786. See also "Amicus Reipublicae" [Benjamin Thurston], *An Address to the Public Containing some Remarks on the Present Political State* [Exeter, N.H., 1786].

8. *N.-H. Mercury* (Portsmouth), Sept. 13, 1786.

Although the legislature never recorded a roll-call vote on the money question, the general outline of the division within the state seems clear from the numerous resolutions passed by town meetings and by two votes that concerned debtor-creditor relations. The first came on a senate amendment to an act forcing creditors to accept real or personal estate, when offered, which would have excepted certain debts based upon specie. The Cosmopolitan bloc took the creditor side, though narrowly, while Localists backed the debtors almost unanimously.[9] The second, in June 1787, occurred on a bill to repeal a previous law that had helped the creditors recover small debts. This failed, 32–18, with the Cosmopolitans going against repeal, 3–13, and the Localists voting for it, 10–3.

The tax issue stimulated less excitement, but occasioned more votes. The earliest defeated a motion to change the method of apportioning real estate taxes, but its nature remains unknown. An interesting series concerned the collection of back taxes, which the Cosmopolitan bloc favored nearly unanimously and the Localists opposed with equal solidarity.[10] Import taxes won the support of the Cosmopolitans, who also attempted to include glass, steel, and iron among taxed articles[11] and to place particular restrictions upon the British carrying trade.[12] On the other hand, the Localist group preferred an excise tax by which, as one writer affirmed, "the rich will pay their proportion with the poor—it being observed that the rich are entirely exempt, according to the present plan."[13] The Cosmopolitans voted against the excise by a large margin.[14] A poll tax of 8s. proved satisfactory to the Localists, but the Cosmopolitans succeeded in rejecting this and then obtaining a higher rate.[15] Finally, the Localist bloc voted that public securities be receivable for taxes, whereas the Cosmopolitans preferred payment in specie.[16]

Several other issues also divided the representatives. An attack on the courts apparently grew out of the feeling that they favored

9. "Journal of the Senate," Nov. 8, 1785, *ibid.*, XX, 406; "House Journal," Nov. 3, Nov. 8, 1785, *ibid.*, 434–435, 446.

10. "House Journal," Dec. 26, 1786, *ibid.*, XX, 760–761, and June 20, Sept. 19, 1787, *ibid.*, XXI, 59–117.

11. "House Journal," Feb. 23, 1786, *ibid.*, XX, 516; Feb. 17, 1786, *ibid.*, 502–504.

12. See also the vote on June 27, 1787, and the protest in *ibid.*, XXI, 75.

13. *N.-H. Spy* (Portsmouth), June 26, 1787.

14. "House Journal," June 28–29, 1787, Bouton *et al.*, eds., *N.H. State Papers*, XXI, 84, 87.

15. "House Journal," Dec. 30, 1788, *ibid.*, 420.

16. "House Journal," June 22, 1786, *ibid.*, XX, 656.

creditors, cost too much money, and benefited the judges and lawyers rather than the people. From this it followed that suits should be conducted by local justices.[17] Criticism centered on the Rockingham County judges, who were exonerated of wrongdoing by two votes.[18] The Cosmopolitan bloc backed the judges almost unanimously, 12–0 and 13–1, while the Localist group united against them, 0–13 and 3–9. The Cosmopolitans also supported, 12–2, payment of Congress's requisition of 1785, which the Localists opposed, 0–9.[19] An act to comply with the British treaty first failed, 32–34, then succeeded, 44–34.[20] Cosmopolitans voted in the affirmative unanimously, Localists in the negative, 2–10. Finally, the two groups also divided on miscellaneous issues.[21]

These votes indicate the presence in New Hampshire of the same two legislative parties that existed elsewhere, though one must look hard to discover them. They stood for many of the same ideas. On one side were men, associated with the trading centers and nearby towns, who sympathized with creditors, backed a hard-money policy, tried to collect taxes, approved an import tax and a poll tax but not an excise, and supported the courts, Congress, and the treaty. They tended to become Federalists politically (7–1). Opposed to them were representatives of different opinion on these matters; reflecting the desires of noncommercial communities, they generally became Antifederalists (8–2).

The characteristics of the men who composed the two groups also conform to the alignment in other states, again with the qualification that roughly three-fifths of the delegates are omitted (though most of these voted only a few times). The Cosmopolitan bloc included eight merchants, six professional men, and eight others who were not farmers, totaling two-thirds of the whole and 73 percent of those whose occupations are known. Among the eight farmers, four had large estates. The Localist group contained no merchants, one lawyer, a preacher-farmer, eight others with a nonfarm occupation, and twelve farmers among whom none owned large properties. Of those whose occupations are known,

17. *The New-Hampshire Gazette, and General Advertiser* (Portsmouth), June 1, 1786; *N.-H. Spy* (Portsmouth), June 30, 1787. On the other side, *N.-H. Mercury* (Portsmouth), Sept. 6, 1786.

18. "House Journal," June 26–27, 1787, Bouton *et al.*, eds., *N.H. State Papers,* XXI, 73, 79.

19. "House Journal," June 27, 1786, *ibid.*, XX, 666.

20. "House Journal," Sept. 14–15, 1786, *ibid.*, 697–699.

21. Such as votes of Feb. 7 and Nov. 12, 1788. "House Journal," *ibid.*, XXI, 212–216, 357–360.

55 percent were farmers. The division by economic status was as follows:

	Cosmopolitans	Localists
Wealthy	1	0
Well-to-do	15	1
Substantial	4	2
Moderate	3	17
Unknown	10	7

Religious affiliation seems unimportant. Few on either side received much education, the advantage resting with the Cosmopolitans. Perhaps more important, men probably cosmopolitan in their outlook voted with the bloc of that name, 9–2, while on the other side was a slight majority of the localists. The point of view of the latter is suggested by the instructions of Richmond, in the southwest hill country, to its representatives "to motion to the general Cort at the Next Seting first to not grant the Requsition of Congress at present second to Receive final settlements at six shillings and Eight pence on the pound untill the fifteenth Day of December next for all outstanding taxes third to Call in all publick securitys Drawing Interest that was Isued by this state and Cut them into Certifycates and said Certifycats to pay all state County and town taxes and to pay all Executions or to make paper money to Redeem said securitys and to answer the purposes above said."[22]

These generalizations represent only a tendency in New Hampshire's politics. Although a statewide contest for governor took place annually, senators were chosen by counties and representatives by towns. Until after the Constitution no organized campaigning occurred and even the potential for party divisions seems to have attracted little attention. When observers perceived it, they deplored its appearance. "A Consistent Republican" warned the voters to divest themselves of "prejudice, party spirit, and every other sordid motive that may tend to injure the public good," and advocated for president, not the candidate who had been inactive at the beginning of the Revolution and only participated when victory was in sight (Theodore Atkinson?), but a true patriot, who also had a fortune and extensive acquaintance abroad (John Langdon?).[23] Basically New Hampshire's politics remained fragmented.

22. Sept. 4, 1786, *ibid.*, XIII, 317.
23. *N.-H. Mercury* (Portsmouth), Feb. 1, 1785; see also *ibid.*, Mar. 15, 1784.

RHODE ISLAND

Rhode Island's traditional two-party system revived after the war. It now took the form, however, not of merely factional division, but one that by the mid-eighties reflected economic interests. "It has long been the Practice," wrote a critic, "of the leading Men in this State, at the February Session of Assembly, at each Year to make what they call a Prox, containing a Nomination of the General Offices of Government for the Year."[24] He interpreted the procedure as the conspiracy of "a few Gentlemen" to dictate politics, but as we have seen, before the war the gentlemen had divided, not united, in their objectives. Now however the merchants and other entrepreneurs combined to control the government. They could count on support from such trading centers as Providence, Newport, Portsmouth, and Warwick, and in addition their extensive business activities won allies in other towns.[25] Until 1784 they seem to have ruled unchallenged, aided by a rural upper class of large landowners. They pursued a conservative economic policy and opposed the 5 percent impost because they feared any burden on the state's commerce.

After the mid-eighties an opposition developed reflecting agrarian discontent with economic depression and the government's policies. Theoretically the farmers could have seized power at any time, since they had the vote and the numbers, and country towns chose a majority in both houses. In practice they had been accepting the nominations of the central caucus. Now the agrarians challenged the established order, constructing a new two-party system based, not on factionalism, but on issues.

Several factors led to the political revolution. The depression of course lay at the heart of the unrest. It seems to have hit Rhode Island with particular severity and caused merchants to exert unusual pressure against their debtors. The businessmen and their allies, who held much of the state debt, had imposed high taxes. By the mid-eighties they had changed their minds about the federal impost and began to adopt a nationalistic attitude, replacing their former particularism. In 1785 they therefore agreed to that grant. Meanwhile they refused to alleviate the monetary crisis,

24. *U.S. Chronicle* (Providence), Feb. 16, 1786.
25. The first thorough study of Rhode Island's politics is Irwin H. Polishook, *Rhode Island and the Union, 1774–1795* (Evanston, Ill., 1969). See his description of parties in chap. 2.

trying to remain on a specie basis. The agricultural towns began to agitate for prodebtor measures, tax relief, paper money, and protection against speculators in the state debt. At one time or another almost every town expressed a desire for paper money, opposition being limited to a few trading centers such as Newport and Providence.[26]

The farmers accomplished their objective after some exciting campaigns in 1786 and 1787. Their "Country Prox," ably led by a mixture of merchants, artisans, landowners, and politicians, got out the vote and won a majority in the legislature.[27] The merchants managed to retain control of the commercial towns and a few other communities, mostly along the Narragansett. In Newport, wrote "A Whig" in 1787, the merchants carried the election because they exerted themselves, obtained proxies and "signed them for such as they knew dare not do otherwise than they requested."[28] Their candidate, Gov. William Bradford (who had run on a hard-money platform), carried the election over John Collins, 211–83.[29] In the state generally, however, the men who were "in the Country Prox" won almost every contest by margins of over two to one. Thus the advocates of paper money, Peleg Arnold, Jonathan J. Hazard, and Daniel Manton, were chosen to Congress over James M. Varnum, George Champlin, and Nathan Miller.[30] The victors then filled all the other offices with their own supporters— a time-honored practice in Rhode Island—including even local justices of the peace.[31] The agrarians pushed through an inflationary monetary policy by issuing legal-tender paper money on loan, refused to pass laws for enforcing the British treaty, ordered holders of state securities to receive interest in paper money under penalty of forfeit, insisted upon a relatively light tax that could be paid in state notes, and as is well known, refused to send delegates to the Federal Convention and rejected the document that it produced.[32] The representatives from commercial centers fought all this with little success. Even in the absence of recorded

26. See *ibid.,* 120.
27. For an account of enthusiastic politicking in 1786, see Samuel Ward to Welcome Arnold, Apr. 7, 1786, Peck Collection, Box VIII, #5, R.I. Hist. Soc.
28. *The Newport Mercury,* May 14, 1787.
29. *The Newport Herald,* Apr. 19, 1787.
30. *U.S. Chronicle* (Providence), May 10, 1787.
31. See Polishook, *Rhode Island,* 40–41.
32. *Newport Herald,* Nov. 8, 1787; *Worcester Mag.,* III (July 1787), Journals of the House, especially June 15–16, Sept. 14, 1787 (Rhode Island legislative records are available on microfilm; see Jenkins, comp., and Hamrick, ed., *Guide to Early State Records*).

votes, it is obvious that Rhode Island's political alignments closely resembled that of other states.

CONNECTICUT

Whereas the farmers in Rhode Island succeeded in gaining power and implementing their economic and political program, their equivalents in Connecticut failed to do either. Did they lack the desire? Had they different objectives? Or were they prevented, and if so, by whom and by what means? The answer to these questions, which lies deep in the history of the two states, is far beyond the scope of the present inquiry; and the almost entire lack of votes deprives us of that useful type of evidence. A few observations must suffice.

Connecticut's form of government seems almost identical to Rhode Island's, but it operated very differently. No "factions" made nominations for the legislature. Each town chose its representatives without reference to any general contest. Nominations for the upper house came from a statewide vote in September, and in the absence of any prox or candidates, the people voted for the most familiar names. The twenty victors therefore enjoyed a wide reputation. These twenty nominees then stood for election in the spring, the freemen in each town voting in succession for each candidate beginning with whoever had polled the most votes in the fall. The process almost ensured the election of incumbents. Moreover throughout the election the leading men, especially the ministers, exerted great influence. The lawyer David Daggett described Connecticut's government before 1776 as "a most perfect aristocracy" in that "the minister, with two or three principal characters were supreme in each town. Hence the body of the clergy, with a few families of distinction, between whom there was ever a most intimate connection, in effect, ruled the whole state." Daggett went on to lament the declining influence of the ministers, but the system that he described survived the Revolution with only minor changes.[33] Connecticut's "aristocracy" continued to dominate the upper house and to exert a strong, though not an exclusive, influence in the lower.

As a consequence Connecticut's equivalent of the Cosmopolitan party won every contest. The loyalists returned to the state with relatively little opposition and presently voted and held office,

33. *An Oration*, . . . *July 4, 1787* (New Haven, 1787).

perhaps because they came from all ranks of people.[34] The legislature did not invariably pass a tax law, but imposed enough burdens to arouse complaints (an excise on rum proved especially profitable and controversial). A major debate developed over commutation and the impost. Judging from town resolutions, a convention at Middletown, and one of the representatives' rare votes, the opposition centered in the towns some distance from the coast, probably those least commercial, while support came notably from the merchants, the members of the upper house, and the principal trading towns.[35] Finally, the usual controversy over paper money divided the state much as it did people elsewhere, the propaper stronghold being in the areas most remote from the transportation network.

These contests stimulated some active political campaigning. In 1783, for the first time, two lists of nominations for councillors were circulated. According to one defender of commutation, the impost, and the political status quo, the people were trying "to drop every man of ability, of liberal and independent sentiments and in their room, to choose men of intrigue, who are artfully working upon the passions of the multitude to answer their own selfish purposes."[36] In 1784 the anti-impost forces held a convention that drew up a slate of candidates for the upper house. Eight out of the fourteen succeeded, and one of the losers was chosen to Congress.[37] This activity, like the county conventions a few years later, aroused much criticism and counter campaigning by those who, as one of them observed, favored the payment of debts, granting money to Congress, and "appointing Men of Worth and Property to rule us."[38]

By 1786 Connecticut clearly contained two opposing political groups. One included the localists. "There are," wrote one observer in 1786, "two parties in the state—jealous of each other; *federal and anti-federal.*" The latter included men of "indifferent" education, who thought "on the small scale" and lived "remote

34. *The Connecticut Gazette and the Universal Intelligencer* (New London), Apr. 4, May 16, 1783; *Conn. Courant* (Hartford), Apr. 6, 1784; Franklin Bowditch Dexter, ed., *The Literary Diary of Ezra Stiles* (New York, 1901), III, 111–112.

35. E.g. *Conn. Courant* (Hartford), Mar. 2, 1784. Main, *Antifederalists*, 90–92.

36. *Conn. Courant* (Hartford), Sept. 2, 9, 1783, reprinted in *Mass. Gaz.* (Boston), Sept. 23, 1783.

37. *The Norwich Packet; or, the Chronicle of Freedom*, Apr. 8, 1784.

38. Peter Colt to Jeremiah Wadsworth, Feb. 28, Mar. 28, 1784, Wadsworth Papers, Box 135, Conn. Hist. Soc.

from the best opportunities of information." They were not rogues but were ignorant. The state would be poorly governed, he feared, "till our old influential characters acquire confidence and authority."[39] At the same time William Williams lamented the progress of "Factions," especially one that sought to demolish lawyers like himself; these men had actually succeeded in replacing all of the Lebanon selectmen, "a thing never done before since the Town existed."[40] What that faction wanted was spelled out by "An Old Whig." He called for the election of men neither too poor nor too rich, not judges or lawyers, and for high duties on luxury articles, popularly elected sheriffs, restrictions on attorneys, no imprisonment for debt if it could be discharged in land, an act declaring certain articles legal tender for debts at a value set by freeholders, and a general reduction of officials' fees—an excellent summation of the position characteristic of the Localist party.[41] Similarly a list of grievances, supposedly from Windham, included the following items: yeas and nays in both houses to be recorded and published, a valuation law as recommended by "An Old Whig," voting by all taxpayers, and an easier method of paying the state and federal debt.[42] This cluster of objectives clearly related Connecticut's politics to that of other states.

DELAWARE

Delaware's legislature began to record votes at once and preserved for posterity a substantial number of political contests. It is instructive that the legislators separated into two well-defined blocs on four-fifths of the votes, that these blocs included four-fifths of the delegates, and that the members of the two groups voted in unison 85 percent of the time. The usefulness of these roll calls is limited, however, by two circumstances. First, only twenty-one men sat in the lower house, of whom several were always absent, and the Legislative Council contained but nine at full strength.[43] Second, a shortage of genealogies and local histories severely limits the biographical data. Therefore analysis of the state's politics must depend more on description than on statistical methods.

39. *The New Haven Gazette, and the Connecticut Magazine*, Nov. 30, 1786.
40. To Benjamin Huntington, Jan. 4, 1787, photostatic copy, Mass. Hist. Soc.
41. *Conn. Gaz.* (New London), Apr. 20, 1787.
42. *Ibid.*, Mar. 23, 1787.
43. For an account of the council see Main, *Upper House*, 149–154.

If the number of votes on an issue indicates its relative importance, we can assume that the relations between debtors and
creditors caused the greatest conflict. This took three forms.
First, a stay law, halting all suits for debt, passed on February 1,
1785, lost a year later, January 25, 1786, and passed again in the
fall of 1786 (October 26, 28), after which the council vetoed it.
Second, the assembly defeated a loan of paper money (June 4,
1785), but then passed the bill (January 28, June 13, 1786). The
council rejected this too, advancing the usual antipaper arguments
and adding that debts resulted from "men's living beyond their
income, or speculating indiscreetly upon their neighbor's property,
and but very rarely from inevitable misfortune."[44] Third, valuation
bills required four votes. The first rejected a motion (January 25,
1786) that a committee be appointed to bring in a bill postponing
suits for debt, unless property was evaluated. The next two passed
a bill compelling creditors to accept property at its appraised value
(June 22, 1786). Finally, the legislature accepted, on January 30,
1788, a report condemning another evaluation bill. On all of these
votes the legislators lined up consistently, one group—the Localists
—always taking the debtors' side, and the other—the Cosmopolitans—invariably protecting the creditors.

In contrast, taxes caused almost no debate. Delaware's system
assessed each man proportionately to his economic status, supposedly a sort of income tax. Although far from perfect, it probably was as progressive as any system then in effect, and the
legislators stood pat. On one occasion the Localist bloc voted
against raising the sum of £21,000, probably preferring a lower
amount.[45] The Cosmopolitans favored a method for the more
efficient collection of taxes (February 2, 1788).[46] The Localists
successfully reduced the salaries of justices of the orphans' court
(February 1, 1786), but failed to prevent the delegates to Congress
from receiving more money (January 17, 19, 1785).

Although—or because—Delaware contained numerous loyalists,
only a few votes concerned restrictions on them. During the war
the council modified punitive laws. On June 5, 1783, the lower
house refused to bring in a bill that would have prevented nonjurors from voting, holding office, or serving on juries for seven

44. Journals of the Legislative Council, June 16, 1786.
45. Jan. 26, 1786. An earlier council vote found the Cosmopolitans supporting
higher taxes, 4–0, while the Localists' only member present opposed the increase
(Feb. 4, 1783).
46. See also vote of June 21, 1783.

years. The Localist group was responsible for the defeat of this motion, which was in fact sectional; the Kent County delegation was solidly opposed. In 1786 the legislature passed an act providing for a loyalty oath. Four men, two from each side, voted against any oath of allegiance at all. On three other roll calls the Localists took the opposite side from those four, 19–8, while the Cosmopolitans supported them by a very slight margin, 10–8. On the whole, therefore, this issue did not divide the representatives along party lines.

A few other questions did so divide them. A bill "to prevent vexatious suits against citizens of the state who acted in defence of the country, though not strictly according to law," carried by the votes of the Localist bloc (June 17, 1783). That party preferred Dover to Wilmington as a site for the capital (November 5, 1785; January 25, 1786). Finally, the Localists unanimously supported a resolution extending the time for collecting money for Congress, while the Cosmopolitans first tried to delay until Congress assented to this procedure and then voted, 5–3, against the resolve (January 31, 1787).[47] On almost all of these votes the attitudes of the two groups of representatives agreed with those in other states.

The composition of the two blocs also conforms to the situation elsewhere. For example, sectional differences separated the groups. Twelve of the nineteen Cosmopolitan delegates came primarily from New Castle County in the north. This county contained the town of New Castle, at that time Delaware's most important trading center, and Wilmington, so that most of the state's commerce and manufacturing was located there. The Localist bloc attracted only one New Castle legislator, who favored that side by a bare two-to-one margin. Otherwise it obtained all of its support from the middle county of Kent (10–4) and Sussex County in the south. (9–3). Both of these counties were rural and agricultural. The only two towns of note (Dover in Kent and Llewes in Sussex) provided support for both sides, while elsewhere the southern counties favored the Localists by a margin of fifteen to three.[48]

The rural-urban division indicated by this sectionalism is confirmed by an analysis of the delegates' occupations. An unfortunately large proportion remain unknown, for Delaware historians and genealogists have been less active or less successful than those

47. A number of other votes seem minor, e.g., June 10, 1788.
48. Therefore the towns voted for the Cosmopolitans, 8–4, the country for the Localists, 16–9.

of other states, but the general alignment is suggested by the following:

	Cosmopolitans	Localists
Traders	1	0
Professionals	5	3
Other nonfarmers	2	2
Farmers	3	3
Unknown	8	12

Information on economic status does not permit generalization, nor does that on family background.[49] Eight members of the Cosmopolitan group and only three of the Localist held high civil or military posts; and eight or possibly nine delegates voting with the Cosmopolitan party can be labeled cosmopolitans (42 to 47 percent), as compared with four of the Localist party (20 percent). Among the latter the only well-known figures were Dr. Charles Ridgely and Thomas Rodney, while the Cosmopolitans produced Gunning Bedford, Jacob Broom, Dr. Henry Latimer, Thomas McKean (the Pennsylvanian), and John Vining. This body of biographical data, sketchy though it is, when taken in conjunction with the sectional and especially the town-country character of the party alignment and with the votes, indicates that Delaware's political alignment closely resembled that in other states.

GEORGIA

A few observations about Georgia's politics must suffice. The two old, coastal counties, Chatham (seat of Savannah) and

49. In the council the following alignment appears:

	Loc.	Cos.		Loc.	Cos.
Occupation			*Social origin*		
Farmer	5	1	Humble, unknown	4	0
Large landowner	2	2	Average family	5	4
Nonfarmer	3	4	Prominent old family	1	3
Economic status			*World view*		
Moderate, unknown	7	1	Localist, uncertain	6	1
Well-to-do	6	1	Cosmopolitan	4	6
Wealthy	1	5			

Liberty, contained most of the wealth and generally sent about two-fifths of the delegates in attendance. Wilkes and Richmond were the frontier counties, represented as a rule by a slightly smaller number. Effingham and Burke, lying in between, together with Glynn and Camden on the south coast held the balance of power. A survey of the legislature's votes during the two years from 1783 to 1785 reveals the usual two blocs, appearing on the usual two-thirds of the votes, and involving as expected about 70 percent of the delegates. One group consisted primarily of the Chatham and Liberty men, with scattered support in Richmond, Burke, and Effingham. To it belonged almost all of the important representatives, the well-known men such as James Jackson, William Gibbons, John and William Houstoun, three Habershams, Jonathan Bryan, and Joseph Clay. This certainly was the Cosmopolitan party of Georgia. The opposing or presumably Localist bloc consisted of men from Richmond and Wilkes plus a handful from Burke, Effingham, and Camden. The only prominent leader was William Few. It seems very likely that a biographical analysis of these legislators would disclose further parallels to alignments in other states.[50] After 1785 these blocs became more fluid, except that the Chatham delegates, like those of Portsmouth, formed a consistent core.

NORTH CAROLINA

Biographical information on North Carolina's legislators also leaves a good deal to be desired and is too incomplete for accurate statistical analysis, yet it does permit a general discussion. Both houses published votes on various issues and both contained the ubiquitous two parties.

During the 1780s the state's House of Commons consisted of four representatives from each county and one from each of half a dozen towns. At full strength it would have included some two hundred members, but usually half and even two-thirds were absent. The North Carolina Senate contained a fourth as many men, who attended more faithfully. The state was composed of several sections ranging from the counties of what is now Tennessee, eastward to the semifrontier piedmont, now beginning to fill up with small farmers, and to the older tidewater counties with their

---

50. See particularly William W. Abbot, "The Structure of Politics in Georgia: 1782–1789," *WMQ*, XIV (1957), 47–65.

planters and slaves. No single town served as the center for activities; instead Wilmington, New Bern, and Edenton divided the
import-export trade and performed the other urban functions together with the interior communities of Halifax, Salisbury (in the
hills near Winston-Salem) and Hillsboro (near Durham). The
historical contest between the Albemarle region and the Cape Fear
district now had become minor.

The lower house contained a great variety of persons—indeed
more different types than the senate, perhaps because towns sent
no representatives to the latter. Among the nearly one hundred
men who voted several times during the sessions from 1783 to
1787 were six merchants, seven lawyers, six following some other
nonfarm occupation, twenty-seven large landowners, and twenty-
five farmers, the remaining twenty-eight being unknown. Wealthy
men comprised about 15 percent of the total; well-to-do delegates,
32 percent; and those with less wealth, 30 percent. Between one-
fourth and one-third were probably cosmopolitan men. In the
senate farmers and planters together controlled 80 or 90 percent
of the seats, large property holders about half, cosmopolitan men
perhaps a third. Thus the two houses resembled one another in
most respects.

Both houses divided into two blocs of nearly equal strength,
each containing about a third of the voting delegates, the rest
being neutral. During the four sessions under consideration, party
lines applied to two-thirds of the votes, and the members of the
two groups voted with their fellows over 80 percent of the time.
Economic issues here as elsewhere created the most dissension, but
the same alignment appeared on a variety of other questions.

Taxes in North Carolina fell primarily on land and polls, including slaves. The rural legislators attempted to keep their rate
as low as possible and to transfer part of the burden to nonfarm
property such as stock in trade. In 1785 (December 24) a motion
to increase the general tax rate found the Localists opposed by a
four-to-one margin, while the Cosmopolitan bloc favored it almost
unanimously.[51] The Localists also opposed levying a tax on goods
imported by land equal to that by water. Goods needed by the
inland farmers often, perhaps usually, traveled by road from
Virginia or to a lesser extent from South Carolina, and the tax
would fall upon these people, whereas a tax on seaborne commerce

---

51. Saunders, Clark, and Weeks, eds., *State Records of N.C.*, XVII, 394–395. See
also the vote on Feb. 8, 1779, upon which a sharp east-west division is clear.

affected men in or near the coastal trading towns.[52] The land tax occasioned two roll-call votes. The first defeated a proposal to tax land according to its value, which would have relieved the poorer farmers, and substituted a tax by quantity. This carried when the Cosmopolitans voted unanimously for it, 31–0, even though the Localists united almost as solidly against.[53] The same day the decision was to some extent reversed by setting the tax at only 2s. 6d. per hundred acres. The Localist bloc favored this rate unanimously, 24–0, while the Cosmopolitans united in opposition.[54] A bill to ascertain what property was taxable and to determine the method for assessing and collecting the tax carried because the Cosmopolitans favored it, 19–1, the Localists voting in the negative by about three to one.[55] Finally, the Cosmopolitan bloc succeeded in limiting the proportion of the tax payable in certificates, probably because they wished to obtain as much hard money as possible. Members of the Localist bloc presumably knew that certificates were commoner and cheaper than coin.[56]

The few votes concerning the spending of money are inconclusive. In 1779 higher salaries for both governor and council carried, and in 1785 the clerk of the house suffered a pay cut, both with bipartisan support.[57] On the other hand, the Localists declined to pay a business firm £1,000 for losses during the war and refused to allow a French army officer £68 8s. 4d.[58] A grant of funds to establish an academy at Hillsboro and for other academies passed because the Cosmopolitans voted in the affirmative while Localists divided.[59] This probably involved both economic and cultural considerations.

An interesting senate vote concerned a clause permitting naval officers to import for their own use goods less than £200 sterling in value annually. Probably the motion to eliminate this, which failed, expressed a determination to prevent a conflict of interest

52. Nov. 22, 1784, *ibid.*, XIX, 816. See also senate vote, Nov. 19, 1784, on which both sides were unanimous.

53. In the senate also the Localists favored and Cosmopolitans opposed classifying the land so as to levy higher taxes on more valuable farms. Dec. 27, 1786, Dec. 13, 1787.

54. Dec. 19, 1786, *ibid.*, XVIII, 344–345.

55. May 29, June 1, 1784, *ibid.*, XIX, 676–677, 688.

56. Apr. 24, 1783, *ibid.*, XIX, 262–263. The question pertained to certificates issued for clothing furnished to the militia. The treasurer was authorized to receive these, but the vote confined their use to only three-fourths of the tax.

57. *Ibid.*, XVII, 424–425.

58. Dec. 23, 1785, *ibid.*, 387; Nov. 27, 1786, *ibid.*, XVIII, 257–258.

59. Dec. 9, 1786, *ibid.*, XVIII, 297–298.

and an agrarian distrust of entrepreneurial activity. The Localist bloc voted to strike out the clause, 12–3, while the Cosmopolitans approved it, 11–0.[60]

Policy regarding western land included three questions. First, should North Carolina cede her western lands to Congress? In 1784 the Cosmopolitan bloc obtained such a law, voting almost unanimously, while the Localists voted against just as unanimously. Later in the same session, however, the act was suspended, once more by a strict party vote.[61] A related question was whether Richard Henderson should receive compensation for the loss of his huge grant, which the legislature refused, the Cosmopolitans supporting Henderson and the Localists voting against him.[62] Finally, the latter bloc obtained a price of £10 instead of £20 per hundred acres for land sold to redeem state certificates and soldiers' pay.[63]

The relations between creditors and debtors helped to create party alignments in North Carolina, as they did generally. The Localist delegates tried but failed to obtain a valuation bill in 1783.[64] They voted for an emission of paper money, passed an act to prevent the sale of goods in hard money only, and later attempted unsuccessfully to pass a bill restraining the fraudulent depreciation of paper currency.[65] In the senate, where the same political alignment appeared, the Localists twice voted to issue a larger quantity of paper (December 22, 27, 1785).

The confiscation of loyalist estates, carried out during the war, continued as an issue only because a small, influential minority tried to moderate the policy. A protest on November 10, 1779, against the confiscation was signed by fifteen legislators from the coastal counties.[66] Again in 1784 a small group of eighteen legislators objected, almost all of whom belonged to the Cosmopolitan bloc.

60. Dec. 17, 1787, *ibid*. See also a vote concerning lawyers, Dec. 30, 1786, *ibid*.
61. May 18, 20, 24, Nov. 9, 13, 18, 1784, *ibid*., XIX, 613, 622, 643, 773, 794, 804–805. See senate votes, Nov. 18, 1784, and Dec. 7, 1787, showing the same alignments.
62. May 18, 1784, *ibid*., 613–614.
63. Dec. 12, 1786, *ibid*., XVIII, 312. Another vote dividing the two parties came on May 31, 1784. This concerned a clause that levied a fee on anyone not completing his purchase of land. *Ibid*., XIX, 681. An amendment to except land west of the Appalachian Mountains carried, 36–20, because the Cosmopolitan group voted for it. Probably this exempted speculators.
64. May 8, 1783, *ibid*., XIX, 324–325.
65. Dec. 19, 1785, *ibid*., XVII, 364–365; Dec. 22, 1786, *ibid*., XVIII, 362; Dec. 1, 1787, *ibid*., XX, 179–180.
66. See also May 29, 1784, *ibid*., XIX, 617.

Two senate votes show the same party alignment (May 3, 1783; December 17, 1785). Finally, the Localists favored and Cosmopolitans opposed an act to secure the purchasers of forfeited estates, thus preventing recovery by former owners.[67]

Three political issues further illustrate the division. The Localists favored removing the capital to an interior site.[68] A bill to repeal acts inconsistent with the British treaty passed when every Cosmopolitan but one voted for it and every Localist but one voted against it.[69] Lastly, when the state considered the Federal Constitution, delegates belonging to the Cosmopolitan bloc favored ratification, 14–2, while Localists opposed it, 18–0.[70]

The most obvious feature of North Carolina's political alignment was its sectionalism. A line drawn from just west of the town of Halifax in the north to Wilmington on the southern coast would enclose an area containing one-third of the total members of both parties but not a single member of the Localist group; and another, starting at the same point in the north and running southwest to where the border makes an angle, would form the eastern boundary of a region containing an even greater number of delegates, of whom only three belonged to the Cosmopolitans. The most consistent voters of the Cosmopolitan bloc clustered in the Albemarle region, where seventeen out of nineteen lived within seventy miles of Edenton. In contrast, all but one of the Localist party leaders lived west of the second line described above. This interior, as previously noted, contained few slaves, few rich planters, few towns, but many small farmers who probably raised for sale a much smaller part of their crop than did the easterners; certainly they were economically and culturally more isolated.

Another distinction between the two groups lies in the different occupations of their adherents. In the lower house no merchant, no lawyer, and only one person with an occupation other than farmer belonged to the Localist bloc, whereas the Cosmopolitans included six merchants and the same number of lawyers. All told, 46 percent of that party and 57 percent of those whose occupation is known earned their living by some nonagricultural activity. Large landowners voted indifferently with either side, a considerable number being neutral, while of the farmers only three (12 per-

67. Dec. 29, 1786, *ibid.*, XVIII, 399. See also senate votes, May 3, 1783, and Dec. 17, 1785.
68. Dec. 16, 1785, *ibid.*, XVII, 354–355.
69. May 29, 1784, *ibid.*, XIX, 674–675.
70. Neutrals divided evenly, 8–8. In the senate Cosmopolitans voted to ratify, 12–9, one of the opponents shifting in 1789, while Localists opposed, 14–3.

cent) supported the Cosmopolitans, 48 percent voted with the Localists, and the rest remained neutral. If those of unknown occupation engaged in agriculture, and if we classify as planters those probably well-to-do, then the resulting occupational makeup of the parties is roughly that described in table 11.1. The division

Table 11.1. Composition of North Carolina Parties by Occupation (in Percentages)

	Cosmopolitans	Neutrals	Localists
Farmer	34	62	73
Planter	12	32	24
Misc. nonfarmer	34	3	3
Merchant or lawyer	20	3	0
Total	100	100	100

by wealth is almost as striking. Almost all of the wealthy legislators and a considerable majority of those who were well-to-do composed virtually the entire membership of the Cosmopolitan bloc, while the smaller property owners with few exceptions supported the Localists or were neutral. The economic composition of the two groups is shown in table 11.2. Naturally the larger slave

Table 11.2. Composition of North Carolina Parties by Economic Status (in Percentages)

	Cosmopolitans	Neutrals	Localists
Wealthy	26	10	6
Well-to-do	48	26	15
Substantial	3	13	18
Moderate	6	19	27
Unknown	17	32	33
Total	100	100	99

owners, with twenty or more, strongly preferred the Cosmopolitans, those with a dozen or so divided equally, while men with a few or no slaves almost always voted with the Localists.

Politically, those few legislators who had served outside the state as Continental officers or in civil posts were Cosmopolitans; those of only local or militia experience favored the Localists. Men of above-average social origin, most of whom naturally lived near the coast in the older regions, confronted men of humble origin, usually westerners. The Cosmopolitan bloc attracted a majority of delegates with good educations or intellectual interest (there were only fifteen of the latter). Culturally, the most significant distinction contrasts the cosmopolitan men, who voted for that group with few exceptions, and the localists on the other side. The nature of the evidence on this point, in North Carolina as in other states, makes the data quite inaccurate, but the figures in table 11.3, if not taken literally, are suggestive. As in other states,

Table 11.3. Composition of North Carolina Parties by World View (in Percentages)

World View	Cosmopolitans	Neutrals	Localists
Cosmopolitans	57	10	12
Localists	23	58	76
Doubtful	20	32	12
Total	100	100	100

the contrasts between the two blocs appear in an exaggerated form if the leaders of both sides are compared, emphasizing the sectional, occupational, economical, and the cosmopolitan-localist characteristics. Thus, North Carolina conforms in almost every particular to the political situation by now so familiar.[71]

71. The alignment in the senate roughly resembles that in the lower house:

	Loc.	Neu.	Cos.		Loc.	Neu.	Cos.
Occupation				*Social origin*			
Farmer	7	3	8	Humble origin	11	1	2
Large landowner	13	5	17	Prominent family	0	1	3
Nonfarmer	3	1	1	*World view*			
Unknown	7	1	4				
				Localist	18	7	14
Economic status				Cosmopolitan	7	2	9
Poor, moderate,				Uncertain	5	1	7
or substantial	13	7	8				
Well-to-do	8	2	16				
Wealthy	2	1	6				
Unknown	7	0	0				

SUMMARY

The analysis of the politics of the foregoing states has been relatively superficial. Nevertheless the conclusion emerges unmistakably that the same factors that created political divisions in the seven states examined in detail shaped political alignments in New Hampshire, Rhode Island, Connecticut, Delaware, Georgia, and North Carolina. Moreover the similarity of issues and the similar components of the two groups strengthen our confidence in proceeding to a more general analysis of the voting patterns and the composition of the legislative parties.

Part III

Conclusion

Chapter XII

Conclusion: The Issues

An impressive variety characterized the political history of the thirteen states during the 1780s. Each experienced a separate development, from the relative calm in Virginia to the turbulence of Pennsylvania, from the sharp sectional antagonisms in South Carolina to the geographical uniformity of New Hampshire, from the bitter economic conflicts of Massachusetts to the occasional mild contests in Delaware. Yet these states faced many of the same problems, and these problems stimulated a similar response, notably the emergence in each state of two major, opposing political blocs. The questions that created these parties were primarily economic, but they were also social, political, and to a lesser extent cultural as well.

Just as most men devoted their major attention to getting and spending money, so expenditures and taxation occupied much of the legislatures' time, and matters so vital caused friction in every state. Broadly speaking, one segment of society, probably the larger, wanted to minimize government costs and revenues, while other men proved more willing to spend and to tax. The precise alignment, however, varied with the particular issue.

The question of governors' salaries presents a somewhat special case because the bills often concerned a particular person and in consequence involved political considerations. New York's George Clinton, New Jersey's William Livingston, and Massachusetts's John Hancock, for example, all enjoyed great popularity. Probably as a consequence, the Cosmopolitan, or anti-Clintonian, party in New York advocated a lower income for Clinton. In New Jersey and North Carolina the issue was nonpartisan. More often the Cosmopolitans supported a higher figure, as they did in Massachusetts, Maryland, and South Carolina. This question therefore cannot be properly understood without considering the particular circumstances of each vote. Nevertheless an analysis of the alignment in five states reveals the general trend (see column 1 of table 12.1, pp. 323–325).[1] A lower salary received very strong support in the noncommercial farm areas and from the frontier. The small commercial farms agreed by a slight margin, but those of the plantation type voted five to one for a higher pay, as did the townsmen, by about two to one. Men with certain occupations voted in a distinctive way, notably farmers, who favored a low salary, and on the other side doctors, lawyers, and traders. Among various other correlations the most significant contrasts the localist with the cosmopolitan, and the lowest-ranking officials with the highest, the former in each case voting for the lower salary.

Another special case is the legislators' own pay (column 2 of table 12.1). In every state on record, the Localist bloc tried to obtain the highest possible salary, the Cosmopolitans the lowest, thus reversing their stand on other expenditures. The reversal can only be accounted for by the selfish pecuniary interest of the Localist representatives combined with the argument that even poor men should be encouraged to act as the people's representatives. The Cosmopolitans, on the other hand, either took advantage of their own economic position and place of residence to contend that legislators should serve for little reward or urged that only men of property should hold office. The political advantages of the latter's position were considerable, for they could damn the Localists as selfish. The evidence indicates that both interest and ideology affected the voting on this issue. The delegates from least urban areas and those with the least property and the most limited view of the world wanted the highest per diem, while the men living in or near towns and in plantation farm areas, owning the largest estates, and sharing a cosmopolitan attitude agreed to serve for less. In most respects the alignment was the opposite of that on other government expenses.

Judges generally received good salaries, but the legislators disagreed on exactly what the judiciary merited. As usual much depended upon the local situation. In North Carolina judges obtained their appointments from the legislature and, being therefore relatively "popular," they encountered no trouble over their pay. In Pennsylvania the Constitutionalists supported them for political

1. Massachusetts, Oct. 19, 1786, Mar. 10, 1787; New York, Feb. 21, 1783; New Jersey, Nov. 27, 1782; Maryland, Dec. 19, 1780; South Carolina, Feb. 2, 1787.

reasons. Voting followed no distinct pattern in New Jersey, but elsewhere (New York, Maryland, Delaware) the Cosmopolitans defended higher salaries, Localists lower ones. Examination of these votes (column 3, table 12.1) indicates that the judges usually could count on the delegates from towns and commercial farm areas, from professional men and traders, men who had served in the Continental army or in Congress, college graduates, and cosmopolitans, while delegates possessing other characteristics tended to oppose higher salaries or to divide irregularly.

The question of judicial income had been and continued to be closely related to the issue of whether the salaries would be fixed or subject to annual review. If the judges could rely upon a certain and ample pay, they could arrive at decisions with relative independence from public opinion or legislative pressure (assuming long-term appointments), so the same sort of men advocated permanent salaries as urged ample rewards. In Massachusetts, New York, New Jersey, and Maryland, the Cosmopolitan group pressed for fixed salaries, and the Localists opposed this step. The urban delegates, professional men, and men of the broadest experience approved of judicial independence (column 4, table 12.1).

Table 12.1. Votes on Government Expenditures (in Percentages)

	Votes						
	1	2	3	4	5	6	7
All delegates	58	49	47	50	51	52	56
Residence							
Frontier	75	19	40	100	85	85	80
Noncommercial farm	86	37	68	71	66	61	78
Commercial farm, noncity	55	49	53	45	58	58	56
Commercial farm, near city	63	63	33	67	77	33	50
Plantation	17	62	45	54	27	41	50
Small town	36	64	29	13	28	33	40
Second-rank city	20	80	25	0	29	0	50
Major city	38	71	13	10	4	29	25
Occupation							
Farmer	73	34	62	68	71	67	68
Large landowner	57	55	48	40	49	40	46
Misc. nonfarmer[a]	55	64	53	55	43	53	57
Artisan	70	50	17	75	50	50	100
Manufacturer	63	100	—	—	43	75	—
Doctor	25	46	30	0	50	44	33

Table 12.1—Continued

	1	2	3	4	5	6	7
Occupation							
Lawyer	36	87	25	13	16	13	50
Merchant or trader	21	76	29	35	21	26	36
Economic status							
Moderate	67	27	53	62	75	73	71
Substantial	58	34	58	54	60	57	67
Well-to-do	44	58	40	41	40	36	35
Wealthy	42	70	42	33	22	30	47
Age							
Under 40	51	59	40	54	40	38	46
40 to 49	57	63	49	48	48	60	63
50 and over	52	57	33	57	49	50	58
Religion							
Episcopalian	45	60	39	42	21	44	41
Quaker	50	80	56	0	67	50	—
Congregationalist	66	86	—	—	29	—	—
Presbyterian	67	51	46	82	61	64	75
Dutch Reformed	83	65	54	33	40	43	46
Other	75	36		33	50	62	
Unknown	52	41	48	46	57	51	63
Military service							
Militia officer	70	52	53	63	55	51	67
Continental officer	25	60	13	40	27	24	33
None known	51	47	49	42	51	54	58
Political experience							
Local office	71	44	49	58	44	63	54
Sheriff, etc.	56	26	67	65	52	67	70
High state office	46	59	47	45	44	42	71
Continental office	14	93	14	0	11	20	40
Education							
None known	67	45	50	52	53	53	—
Self-educated	50	67	40	20	42	46	—
College	20	79	19	40	26	25	—
Intellectual interest							
None known	66	44	52	57	57	56	—
Some	22	74	22	21	28	35	—

Table 12.1—Continued

	1	2	3	4	5	6	7
World view							
Localist	73	34	57	66	71	66	70
Cosmopolitan	24	74	19	36	24	31	30
Father's occupation							
Farmer	70	41	57	58	66	70	—
Large landowner	47	61	45	42	27	41	—
Misc. nonfarmer[a]	36	48	32	57	44	52	—
Lawyer or trader	44	86	34	38	9	27	—
Social origin							
Humble	65	38	51	55	54	56	52
Average	61	51	48	53	58	57	63
Above-average	50	63	45	27	36	33	38
Prominent	27	68	29	54	18	30	50
Legislative party							
Localist	83	30	70	60	55	87	81
Neutral	66	41	47	65	43	46	57
Cosmopolitan	24	60	26	14	43	25	29
Vote on ratification							
Antifederalist	78	32	52	73	71	86	75
Federalist	35	63	48	25	18	39	25

NOTE: [a] Includes innkeepers, shopkeepers, entrepreneurs, and men who could be identified only as nonfarmers.

CODE OF VOTES:
1. For lower salary for governor (212 votes).
2. For lower per diem for legislators (304 votes).
3. For lower salary for judges (224 votes).
4. For salaries not permanent (128 votes).
5. For lower salaries, general (436 votes).
6. Against general costs (237 votes).
7. To accept certificates for taxes (91 votes).

The same kinds of people sought to grant members of Congress the highest possible per diem. Except in New Jersey the Cosmopolitan bloc, professional men, college graduates, and those who themselves held high political posts, usually voted for the maximum rate, while the representatives from subsistence farm areas, farmers, small property owners, localists, and men of little political experience sought to reduce the expense.

Roll calls concerning the salaries of other officials occurred in almost every state legislature, often frequently, and these, taken collectively, furnish a large body of evidence concerning the legislators' attitudes toward government expenses (column 5, table 12.1).[2] Except in New Jersey and perhaps Virginia, the Cosmopolitan group favored high salaries on almost all of the several dozen votes. Most urban delegates agreed, as did those from plantation-type farms, but other rural legislators either divided or opposed. Farmers voted against, traders and lawyers for. The more wealth a representative owned, the more apt he was to support good incomes for officials, as were former Continental army or civilian officeholders, college men, cosmopolitans, and men of high social rank, while the poorer delegates and localists were especially likely to oppose such government costs.

An even longer list of votes dealt with the payment of other debts owed by the state, varying from the obligations in the form of certificates to individual bills for services rendered, from elaborate funding plans to a simple aye or nay on a petition for a few pounds. The alignment always depended in some degree on the particular circumstances. Thus during the war years the Localist group might be most anxious to pay expenses arising from the war, and where that party originated some general plan, as they did in Pennsylvania and in New Jersey, they would vote in favor of payments arising out of their scheme. Other things being equal, however, the Localists tried to restrict or reduce payment of these public debts. The reasons lay in the factors that led the Localists to oppose most such expenditures: the benefits flowed to men and to areas connected with the Cosmopolitans, while the money had to be raised by everyone. Moreover the party's general attitude reflected a suspicion that the bills were too high or unnecessary (A. C. Hanson's charge for digesting the laws of Maryland is a case in point). The characteristics of the men who most often accepted or rejected such expenditures reveal much about their motives (column 6, table 12.1). As in the case of salaries, the opposition increased with distance from an urban center. Farmers usually disapproved, for they seldom received such money, but large landowners, men in trade, and especially lawyers agreed more often than not. The more property a delegate owned, the more likely he was to favor the grant. Continental officers both

2. This is based upon computer analysis of 8 votes in 6 states involving 436 persons. They include some key votes such as 3 on a general reduction of the entire civil list and accurately represent the alignment.

civil and military, educated men, and cosmopolitans also usually voted for payment. Other types of delegates either opposed, as did localists, or divided irregularly.

A review of these data concerning the votes on government costs suggests that certain factors affected the delegates' attitudes. These include their place of residence, their occupation, economic status, and world view. Other characteristics seem less significant and appear to have operated only in certain types of cases or to have involved so few people that their influence cannot have been very extensive. (For example, relatively few Continental army officers, college men, and members of Congress sat in the legislature, and they are probably comprehended in the category "cosmopolitan.") The four seemingly primary influences may, however, be aspects of the same general factor, operating as a single force rather than as independent variables, so that one or more may be merely coincidental. To determine whether each was real or only apparent, the maximum number of cases is desirable. The best issues for this purpose involve general salaries (column 5, table 12.1), covering 436 individual votes in six states, and general expenses (column 6), including 237 votes in three states. Although the evidence permits a very extensive analysis, brevity recommends only a few examples.

Did men's occupations affect their voting independently of their residence, or did, for instance, farmers behave in a certain way, not because they were farmers, but because they came from a rural environment? Men from noncommercial farm areas favored low salaries by 58–30, or 65.9 percent, but representatives who were farmers so voted, 27–10, or 73 percent. Delegates from commercial farm regions (including plantations) cast 98 votes for the lower figure, 106 for the higher (48 percent), while farmers from the same districts preferred the lesser sum, 44–23 (65.7 percent). Thus, regardless of where they lived, farmers tended to favor lower salaries. On the other hand, nonfarm delegates voted for a high salary far more often than did delegates generally:

For Higher Salaries (%):	Frontier	Noncomm. Farm	All Comm. Farm
All Delegates	15	34	52
Nonfarmers	25	50	67

The same conclusion emerges from an examination of the votes on general government expenditures:

For Lower Costs (%):	Frontier	Noncomm. Farm	All Comm. Farm
All delegates	85	61	50
Farmers	93	64	62
Nonfarmers	40	54	40

Indeed, in all of these votes on government costs, occupation seems to have exercised an effect apart from residence.

Similarly the economic status of the delegates and their world view can be examined in conjunction with their residence in order to discover whether they are independent or coincidental. As table 12.2 shows, men of small property usually opposed, and larger

Table 12.2. Multivariate Analysis: Votes on Salaries (1) and Government Expenses (2), (in Percentages)

	Delegates for Higher Expenditures, by Residence							
	Frontier		Noncomm. Farm		All Comm. Farm		Town–City	
	1	2	1	2	1	2	1	2
All delegates	15	15	34	39	52	50	86	73
Economic status								
Moderate	6	7	24	30	29	30	77	50
Substantial	21	33	35	40	39	43	69	57
Well-to-do	29	—	41	67	58	63	92	67
Wealthy	33	—	60	67	78	67	88	78
World view								
Localist	7	100	28	31	33	39	82	75
Cosmopolitan	25	100	60	50	78	74	88	75

NOTE: Votes in column 1 were on salaries; votes in column 2 were on other expenditures.

property holders accepted, government costs regardless of where they lived. Also cosmopolitan men voted for high salaries and expenses, while localists voted against them more often than did the general representation from their area. The same test indicates that, regardless of their occupation, men with more property supported higher expenses. In one example only—the case of higher salaries—table 12.3 illustrates the generalization.

Table 12.3.   Occupation with Economic Status: Votes on Higher Salaries (in Percentages)

| | *Delegates for Higher Salaries, by Occupation* | | |
	Farmer	*Large Landowner*	*Trader or Professional*
All delegates	29	51	73
Economic status			
Moderate	20		56
Substantial	38	22	58
Well-to-do	44	49	82
Wealthy		67	88

To summarize: higher salaries of most types and most species of government expenditures primarily won the support of representatives of towns and commercial farming areas, delegates of large property, men who were lawyers or traders, other non-farmers, and cosmopolitans.[3]

During these years the men who favored government expenditures either saw the need for them or expected to benefit directly from them. As a rule they recognized an obligation to pay taxes. However, much depended upon the type of tax and, as has been sufficiently discussed, the particular situation. Taxation as an issue included several specific questions, notably the general quantity to be raised, whether collections should be compelled or delayed, the incidence of taxation, and whether taxes or other obligations owed to the state should be paid in specie, certificates, or kind.

Seldom did the Cosmopolitan bloc fail to support an increase in taxes. The principal exceptions were in New York, where the anti-Clintonians felt that the tax basis discriminated against the

3. Education, however, was not independent of economic status. For example, on salaries:

For Lower Salaries (%):	*Moderate*	*Substantial*	*Well-to-do*	*Wealthy*
All delegates	75	60	40	22
College education	50	75	44	0
No education known	77	58	40	29

Instead, men of little property voted against high salaries even when they had gone to college.

southern counties, and in New Jersey, where the West Jersey delegates at first took a position hostile to high taxes; but in both states a change occurred later in the decade. Meanwhile, in Massachusetts, Maryland, North Carolina, Delaware, and Rhode Island, Cosmopolitan delegates consistently favored larger amounts. Several factors evidently influenced their view: the need for an effective government that could keep order, enforce the laws, and encourage economic progress (especially trade); the need to raise money for various purposes, notably the state and federal debt and payment of the civil list; and the happy circumstance that non-Cosmopolitans paid much of the total. In contrast, the Localists might have felt the disadvantages rather than the benefits of a strong government, would have profited little from expenditures, and often found taxes difficult or impossible to pay.

The inclusion of votes from New Jersey and New York in the total tends to obscure the sharpness of the contrasts between the opponents on this issue, as they appeared for example in Massachusetts; but since complexities are common in politics, the alignment reflects the general situation with some accuracy. Column 1 of table 12.6 (pp. 336–338) totals 349 individual votes from four states (the three just mentioned plus Maryland). A smaller tax burden won the support of men most remote from the towns, whereas representatives from urban centers regardless of size, from their nearby farm areas, and from regions characterized by plantation agriculture favored heavier taxes. Occupation seems to have exercised less influence, though farmers and men in trade clearly opposed each other. Wealth affected the voting only at opposite ends of the scale. Among other factors the cosmopolitan-localist dimension alone seems significant, though other types of delegates did show a characteristic attitude and tendencies can be discerned throughout that would become obvious in particular instances.

The legislators' point of view towards taxes appears even more clearly in the votes on whether to postpone collections (column 2, table 12.6). These were recorded in Massachusetts, New Jersey, Virginia, Delaware, and New Hampshire. They occurred during the depression period and reflected a general inability to produce money on demand and a reluctance to force sheriff's sales. Usually the motion asked postponement only for a few months, in which form it won the support of many, such as planters, who expected to obtain money after a short time. The issue therefore did not starkly pit those who favored taxes against those who opposed them, but indicates only a tendency. The characteristics of the alignment nearly duplicate and therefore reinforce that on the amount of tax money to be raised, with the Cosmopolitans and Localists decisively opposed to each other.

Analysis of three sample votes in Massachusetts and Virginia involving 161 persons (column 2, table 12.6) reveals several distinct features of the alignment. The most significant factor statistically was the kind of constituency that the legislator represented, thus indicating that he reflected the economic conditions and point of view of his locality. The seven delegates from towns of the first and second rank all favored prompt collections. Representatives of commercial farming areas divided evenly, but those from noncommercial areas cast a heavy vote for postponement. Farmers and artisans sought to delay payment, while men of other occupations divided irregularly. The legislators with least property, localist experience, and humble origins usually tried to defer collections. Other factors seem minor or doubtful for lack of evidence.

Probably most people acknowledged that they should pay taxes, but sought to reduce their own proportion. As a tax on land was universal, only the degree could be debated. The Cosmopolitan delegates supported a relatively high rate whenever the question arose, as it did in New York, New Jersey, Maryland, and North Carolina. However they favored either excluding or imposing a low tax on unimproved land (New Jersey and Pennsylvania). The effect of this policy was to raise much of the money from the improved land that formed a large proportion of the small farmers' property; this explains much of the Localists' opposition to the tax on polls and estates in Massachusetts. The votes on this question all demonstrate the especial significance of the sectional factor. The percentages favoring low land taxes and taxes on unoccupied land in four legislatures (137 persons) were as follows:

Delegates for Low Taxes, by Residence (%)

All delegates	57
Frontier	87
Noncommercial farm	74
Comm. farm, noncity	59
Comm. farm, near city	50
Small town	56
City (18 men)	0

Interesting correlations exist also with the delegates' occupation, economic status (78 percent for men with moderate property, o percent for wealthy men), and the cosmopolitan-localist dichotomy.

Both import and excise taxes found the delegates much divided, because their effect seemed doubtful. In some instances the importers and their followers at first feared that import taxes would penalize trade, and many continued skeptical, but on the whole town dwellers came to favor this method of raising money, and rural legislators opposed it. The Cosmopolitan party voted for it in Massachusetts, New York, Maryland, and New Hampshire (except that in the first state the sides reversed on taxing bills of lading, bonds, and the like). A clear division appeared according to wealth, but the correlation reflected a continuing doubt over the

N.Y. and Md. Delegates for Low Import Taxes,
by Economic Status (%)

All delegates	53
Moderate	74
Substantial	44
Well-to-do	46
Wealthy	31

effect of such a tax. Much depended upon the specific content of the bill. Import duties on agricultural products received the approval of farmers and planters from both parties but the opposition of townspeople, while tariffs on manufactured goods brought a mixed result. The general excise tax was not controversial in Massachusetts, where, indeed, the Cosmopolitan bloc secured a stamp act, but in New Jersey and New Hampshire that side opposed it, as it did a luxury tax in New York. The same party approved a tax on hard liquor in New Jersey. A tax on faculties usually found the Cosmopolitan group, representatives of towns, men with non-farm occupations, larger property owners, and cosmopolitans voting against, as one would expect. Detailed analysis indicates that each of these influences affected the result. Scattered votes show the Cosmopolitans providing the support for a tax on salt (Maryland and Pennsylvania), on polls (New Hampshire and Massachusetts), and exports (Maryland).

Few votes exist concerning the media in which taxes should be paid, although petitions are common. Objections to demands for specie usually came from the Localist strongholds or were coupled with complaints characteristic of that party. The only vote on the subject, in New Jersey, found West Jersey supporting payments in gold and silver. Several votes related to whether the state should accept certificates of various types for obligations owed to the government (see column 7, table 12.1, pp. 323–325). Much depended on what public securities and what debts were involved. As a rule the certificates were held by men of means living in towns and commercial farm areas, and the debts had been incurred by the same sort of people, most often for the purchase of confiscated loyalist estates or of large tracts of land. These people accordingly favored payment, not of taxes, but of such obligations in certificates, as did the Cosmopolitan bloc in New York, New Jersey, Pennsylvania, and Maryland. The same sort of people also favored a sort of stay law for debts due to the state both in Pennsylvania and in Maryland. On the other hand, they inclined to oppose payment of taxes in certificates, preferring hard money (North Carolina and New Hampshire, but the reverse in Maryland and a split vote in New York).

Sufficient data for detailed analysis of opinions regarding taxes exist only in the cases of votes on the quantity, though the similarity of the division concerning postponement increases one's confidence in the conclusions. The most important influences, as with the issue of government expenditures, include residence, occupation, wealth, and world view (political ideology will be considered later). Testing occupation, economic status, and the cosmopolitan-localist factor against residence shows that each seems in some degree independent, especially the cosmopolitan characteristic (see table 12.4), and economic status and occupation also seem separate (table 12.5). These investigations confirm the conclusions reached by a study of the division on government expenditures.

Next only to questions of taxation and government expenditures, debtor-creditor relations and the intimately related issue of monetary policy required the greatest number of votes in the state legislatures; and if we can judge by the number of articles in the press, together with the volume and emotional intensity of petitions and letters on the subject, these matters surpassed all others in their impact on political alignments before the Constitution. They include the passage of stay laws and installment bills, evaluation laws,

Table 12.4. Multivariate Analysis: Votes on Lower Taxes and Postponement (in Percentages)

	General		Noncomm. Farm		Comm. Farm		Town-City	
	1	2	1	2	1	2	1	2
All delegates	54	58	75	80	50	47	31	17
Occupation								
Farmer	68	79	87	94	55	63	60	—
Large landowner	44	53	25	63	35	46	—	—
Lawyer or trader	30	43	33	55	36	40	25	75
Economic status								
Moderate	68	79	87	95	54	60	43	25
Substantial	53	58	71	75	48	50	38	33
Well-to-do	47	44	50	62	54	42	25	0
Wealthy	25	39	0	33	30	45	21	0
World view								
Localist	64	74	80	84	53	65	36	—
Cosmopolitan	26	42	20	50	26	46	25	—

The column group header reads: *Delegates for Low Taxes (1) and Postponement (2), by Residence*

Table 12.5. Occupation with Economic Status: Votes on Lower Taxes (in Percentages)

Delegates for Low Taxes, by Occupation

	General	Farmer	Large Landowner	Lawyer or Trader
All delegates	54	68	44	30
Economic status				
Moderate property	68	72	—	67
Substantial property	53	64	—	57
Well-to-do	47	60	55	30
Wealthy	25	0	31	22

various other aspects of relations between debtors and creditors, paper-money bills, the quantity of money, whether it should be legal tender, and other questions involving the currency.

Almost every legislature considered bills to delay the recovery of debts, and many passed them. Their popularity arose from several circumstances: prewar debts owed by numerous rebels, some of whom had considerable property, to loyalists or Britishers; the postwar buying spree that also involved men of wealth; and the severe deflation of the mid-eighties. A very large proportion of the people must have owed money. A general act to delay suits, or to provide for payment by installments, would therefore find some friends everywhere. Nevertheless the issue polarized the representatives in Massachusetts, New York, New Jersey, Pennsylvania, Maryland, and Delaware.

Ordinarily stay laws won the wholehearted approval of the Localist bloc and the opposition of the Cosmopolitans. In Massachusetts the vote was 92 percent and 8 percent respectively; in New Jersey, 92 percent and 13 percent; in Pennsylvania (on the second vote), 88 percent and 0 percent; in Maryland, 80 percent and 33 percent; and in Delaware, on several votes, about 85 percent and 10 percent. Less decisive votes usually concerned some particular type of debt that aroused less enthusiasm and hostility.

Analysis of several of these votes shows patterns other than the party division. The demand for postponement came primarily from delegates representing the areas most distant from the marketplace, notably from subsistence farm regions and secondarily from commercial farms, if these were neither close to towns nor of the plantation type. Resistance centered in the towns, nearby farms, and plantations. Occupation seems less influential, except that farmers generally approved and men in trade opposed. Probably more important was property, for the more wealth a man possessed the more apt he was to vote against these bills; however the correlation did not exceed two to one. The strong support given by Presbyterians and the opposition of Quakers may reflect their geographical location rather than religious convictions. One might expect young men to contract more debts than the old, but age did not affect voting on this issue. Military and civil career made little difference, nor did most social and cultural factors, though localists favored stay laws more than did cosmopolitans.

Valuation laws also caused controversy. Although few votes exist, the legislators evidently divided in much the same way as they did over stay laws. The issue was similar: whether the advantage should be granted to the debtor, or whether he should be forced to sell his property for what it would bring at auction in order to satisfy a claim. If such a law passed, the creditor must accept, in discharge of the debt, property that would at the moment be worth considerably less than he felt he merited. In the four states where the issue came to a vote (Massachusetts, Delaware, and the Carolinas) the Cosmopolitan bloc always opposed such bills, and the alignment followed sectional lines.

A considerable number of other votes also concerned relations between debtors and creditors. They dealt, for example, with the method of prosecuting for debts, the kind and value of money or other property in which the debt would be paid, whether interest should be charged during the war years, and whether particular categories of debtors or creditors should receive special treatment. On almost every vote the Cosmopolitan party took the creditor side and Localists the debtor, usually by wide margins. An interesting and revealing exception occurred in Maryland, when Cosmopolitans approved a bankruptcy act that relieved businessmen. Somewhat comparable was the action of South Carolina rice planters in trying to extricate themselves from their obligations.

Table 12.6. Economic Issues I (in Percentages)

	Delegates Favoring Seven Types of Economic Proposals						
	1	2	3	4	5	6	7
All delegates	54	58	56	58	59	57	58
Residence							
Frontier	67	75	38	62	100	92	69
Noncommercial farm	75	80	85	82	94	80	78
Commercial farm, noncity	62	51	62	60	56	51	60
Commercial farm, near city	33	40	20	20	20	58	33
Plantation	26	43	38	57	55	—	—
Small town	36	27	25	24	46	41	50
Second-rank city	25	0	38	0	0	0	33
Major city	22	0	0	8	30	9	9
Occupation							
Farmer	68	79	70	69	74	76	68
Large landowner	44	53	37	61	57	50	50
Misc. nonfarmer	55	60	39	48	62	40	67
Artisan	53	83	67	38	80	56	67
Manufacturer	54	50	56	60	50	46	63

Table 12.6—Continued

	1	2	3	4	5	6	7
Occupation							
Doctor	42	20	75	46	40	—	—
Lawyer	42	44	73	47	32	36	27
Merchant or trader	23	20	22	37	28	20	29
Economic status							
Moderate	68	79	67	71	82	79	67
Substantial	53	58	60	53	71	63	71
Well-to-do	47	44	36	56	49	37	41
Wealthy	25	39	33	50	31	6	10
Religion							
Episcopalian	33	44	50	55	53	27	21
Quaker	42	—	22	57	13	22	30
Congregationalist	46	61	51	—	—	50	—
Presbyterian	56	100	80	53	61	77	76
Dutch Reformed	69	—	67	40	55	67	55
Other	75	50	67	71	72	53	50
Unknown	57	59	57	60	63	57	65
Age							
Under 40	42	40	46	50	54	42	43
40 to 49	47	64	54	64	53	68	41
50 and over	58	60	53	49	54	55	64
Military service							
Militia officer	63	54	68	62	75	62	66
Continental officer	31	28	50	56	50	0	17
None known	50	54	48	54	48	53	56
Political experience							
Local office	65	62	67	59	76	62	74
Sheriff, etc.	57	68	68	59	78	53	64
High state office	49	33	24	55	52	61	55
Continental office	39	25	67	35	36	50	20
Education							
None known	57	60	61	68	—	58	60
Self-educated	61	67	67	40	—	71	50
College	25	40	37	49	—	0	0
Intellectual interest							
None known	57	61	58	59	62	61	62
Some	43	41	44	46	45	36	37

Table 12.6—Continued

	1	2	3	4	5	6	7
World view							
Localist	64	74	67	69	78	77	74
Cosmopolitan	26	42	41	54	42	28	25
Father's occupation							
Farmer	60	80	54	60	64	72	70
Large landowner	38	45	35	50	49	31	47
Misc. nonfarmer	35	46	57	41	55	55	62
Lawyer or trader	37	40	40	47	28	0	17
Social origin							
Humble	57	82	56	56	72	63	55
Average	59	61	59	58	62	68	68
Above-average	35	41	29	57	39	37	35
Prominent	22	45	41	52	39	0	0
Legislative party							
Localist	77	90	90	76	95	97	90
Neutral	60	52	48	52	60	46	53
Cosmopolitan	24	14	14	44	19	15	27
Vote on ratification							
Antifederalist	69	68	77	75	88	91	93
Federalist	33	32	38	46	58	22	18

CODE OF VOTES:

1. For lower taxes (349 votes).
2. To postpone collections (161 votes).
3. For stay law (220 votes).
4. Prodebtor, general (376 votes).

5. Pro-paper money (187 votes).
6. For paper as tender (169 votes).
7. For more paper (136 votes).

In examining the detailed statistics on eight of these votes in four states (including 376 individuals; see column 4, table 12.6, pp. 336–338), one is struck primarily by the sectional division. The figures are a little misleading, because three of the four states are in the South, where the planters tended to favor the debtors' position more often than did most men of equivalent economic status, social position, and cultural characteristics. Votes in northern states on stay laws, tender laws, and the like prove a correlation along lines of wealth and, in other respects, greater than the data in table 12.6 indicate. Nevertheless the table clearly shows certain tendencies. The delegates from the most rural areas supported prodebtor legislation. Those from plantation districts and commercial farms in general voted for relief more than half the time. On the other hand, urban representatives seldom did so.

Occupation seems less important than the delegates' constituency. Few townspeople favored these bills, yet roughly 40 percent of the men with some nonfarm occupation voted for them. This means that country artisans, traders, and professionals voted as did their farmer neighbors, and indeed an examination of residence against occupation indicates that the latter had almost no effect at all:

For Debtor Laws (%):	Noncomm. Farm	All Comm. Farm
All delegates	82	58
Farmer	77	61
Large landowner	88	58
Misc. nonfarmer	83	60
Lawyer or merchant	79	53

Economic status affected the voting somewhat more than table 12.6 actually indicates, since on other issues involving debtor-creditor relations most wealthy people adopted a procreditor position. Still, that half of the large property owners favored the debtors tells a good deal about the period. The table below makes it apparent that regardless of their wealth men voted with their section on these questions, although the men with moderate property were more prodebtor than the wealthier delegates:

For Debtor Laws (%):	Noncomm. Farm	All Comm. Farm	Town-City
All delegates	82	58	13
Moderate	84	69	14
Substantial	69	47	17
Well-to-do	87	57	15
Wealthy	78	54	11

Table 12.6 shows no close relationship between these votes on economic issues and religion, age, military record, political expe-

rience, education, intellectual interest, or social origin. Rather surprisingly, cosmopolitans favored debtor laws of this type almost as much as did localists. It should again be emphasized, however, that an abnormal proportion of the votes included in this table reflect the peculiar situation of southern planters.

The issue of paper money arose in every state, and almost every legislature recorded a vote of some sort. The roll calls analyzed (see columns 5–7, table 12.6, pp. 336–338) may somewhat exaggerate the propaper sentiment among the delegates, since Virginia's almost unanimous rejection is excluded, as are the decisions of New Hampshire, Connecticut, and Massachusetts not to issue such currency. On the other hand, the data fail to reflect the opposite actions of Rhode Island, North Carolina, and Delaware. Moreover the support for paper money among the people at large unquestionably exceeded that within the legislature.[4] All things considered, the general figure in column 5 of almost 60 percent voting for paper minimizes the popular majority.

The complexities of this question need not be reemphasized here, but the data cannot be interpreted without remembering that paper money under certain circumstances might win approval from every kind of person. If a severe currency contraction developed, as it did in the mid-eighties, and if the value of the paper could be properly secured, "sound"-money advocates might favor such bills. But if the quantity were excessive, if it were legal tender regardless of circumstances, and if no adequate provision were made for redemption, then opinions divided sharply. Votes on these issues were crucial, and much more divisive, than the simple question of whether some kind of paper should be issued.

In every state the Localist bloc approved the passage of paper-money legislation. Votes in New York, New Jersey, Maryland, North Carolina, and Delaware show that side voting from two to one on up to twenty to one for paper, and they clearly took the same position in other states such as Rhode Island and South Carolina. The Cosmopolitans' opposition was less solid, for though it might reach unanimity in the northern states (and in North Carolina Cosmopolitans favored postponement five to one), the margin in Maryland and probably in South Carolina dropped to two to one. On the whole, however, the conflict over this issue was so intense that it served to solidify party lines.

The most notable feature of the alignment other than the party division was the sectional split. Almost all of the pressure for paper

4. Thus New Hampshire's legislature refused to issue paper, but the votes of the towns clearly demonstrate a popular majority for it.

money came from the agricultural interior, notably from such small farming areas as the southern "piedmont," western Pennsylvania, upstate New York, rural Delaware and Rhode Island, and the hilly interior of Connecticut, Massachusetts, and New Hampshire. Column 5 of table 12.6 shows the frontier and noncommercial farm areas casting almost every vote (40 of 43) for passage. Other farming regions divided about evenly except those close to urban centers. Small towns also cast almost as many votes for as against paper, but the larger trading cities opposed it (22 percent). Occupation seems less significant, for the major propaper advocates were ordinary farmers, artisans, and lesser nonfarm groups. Lawyers and merchants took the other side about two to one. Analysis indicates that occupation exercised relatively little influence.

On the other hand, the delegates' economic status mattered a good deal. While fewer than a third of the wealthy delegates favored paper money, four-fifths of those with moderate property voted for it. Property seems a variable independent of residence:

For Paper Money (%):	Noncomm. Farm	All Comm. Farm	Town-City
All delegates	94	54	32
Moderate	90	67	100
Substantial	100	65	50
Well-to-do	75	50	33
Wealthy	33	42	0

Since most of these paper-money laws were primarily intended to relieve farmers by loaning the currency with land as security, the data confirm the commonsense conclusion that the major pressure came from less well-to-do farmers plus, no doubt, men in debt generally. Economic status was a factor independent of occupation:

For Paper Money (%):	Farmer	Large Landowner	Lawyer or Trader	Misc. Nonfarmer
All delegates	74	57	28	63
Moderate	80	—	—	100
Substantial	79	—	50	46
Well-to-do	50	61	23	25
Wealthy	—	46	0	—

The only religious sect to deviate from the norm was the Society of Friends, who opposed paper more solidly than the average and whose position cannot be accounted for by residence. Militia officers, enlisted men, and local officials voted for passage as did the localists, while cosmopolitans tended to adopt a hard-money position.[5]

Other aspects of the paper-money question were even more important than passage of an act, for they determined who would benefit and who would suffer. The quantity to be issued and its character as legal tender, together with such related matters as the interest rate, security for loans, and the number of years before redemption, involved the whole broad issue of monetary policy. Votes on these problems occurred in many states, notably New York, New Jersey, Pennsylvania, Georgia, North Carolina, and Maryland, while both New Hampshire and Massachusetts witnessed exciting debates over the legal-tender quality of Revolutionary certificates. In every case the Cosmopolitan bloc fought for a lower quantity, against any legal-tender provision, and in favor of other restrictions favoring the creditor, the alignment closely resembling that on passage of the bill.

Examination of these roll calls (see columns 6 and 7, table 12.6) once more demonstrates a sectional alignment, with the opposites as usual being the frontier and noncommercial farm areas on the debtor side and the cities on the creditor, and with small towns and commercial farming areas in the middle.

Property ownership and occupation affected a man's reaction to these clauses. Farmers supported the debtors, as did artisans and half of the large landowners, while about two-thirds of the lawyers and men in trade defended the creditors. Much more important was the effect of property, for very few wealthy men approved of large amounts of paper or legal-tender provisions, while two-thirds of the small property holders did so. The evidence suggests that wealth plus residence together account for the alignment (among economic factors), occupation lacking significance except in the case of farmers (see table 12.7).[6]

Both Episcopalians and Quakers opposed these provisions more often than chance would dictate, but Presbyterians, on the other

5. Note that, as 59% of the votes here analyzed favor paper, the figure of 42% for cosmopolitans in column 5, table 12.6, is well below the norm.

6. The small number of cases deprives the figures in table 12.7 of statistical reliability, but data concerning the quantity of money confirm them, so that the general conclusions seem accurate.

Table 12.7. Multivariate Analysis: Votes on Legal Tender (in Percentages)

	Delegates for Legal Tender, by Residence		
	Noncommercial Farm	Commercial Farm	Town-City
All delegates	80	52	27
Occupation			
Farmer	96	60	—
Misc. nonfarmer	46	44	27
Lawyer or trader	100	22	24
Economic status			
Moderate	81	78	40
Substantial	85	46	43
Well-to-do	50	30	17
Wealthy	50	0	0

side, probably acted as representatives of particular constituencies rather than from religious conviction. Continental army officers and civil officials strongly supported the creditors; militia officers, enlisted men, and local officials, the debtors. College graduates, cosmopolitans, and men from prominent families also disapproved of these provisions, while localists favored them. The cosmopolitan-localist factor was independent of residence.

All of this evidence demonstrates the importance of issues concerning debts and money in forming political alignments. The data also indicate that the legislators reflected primarily the circumstances of their constituencies and secondarily their own economic status and their point of view as cosmopolitans or localists. Other factors influenced individuals, among them occupation, religion (in a few cases), military service (notably in the case of enlisted men who seem to have suffered from the war), and education. The impressive difference between the votes of Federalists and Antifederalists will be noticed later.

Other economic issues afford no such series of votes as the money question, but taken collectively they reveal as much about the political alignment. The price of vacant land sold by the state interested everyone. Most people remote from the land hoped to raise money by the sale, and the Cosmopolitan bloc's consistent stand for high prices probably resulted from geographical location plus their objective of obtaining funds for the state. The Localists voted for a low price wherever the question came to a vote—in New York, Pennsylvania, Maryland, and North Carolina. The division, as column 1 of table 12.8 (pp. 345–347) shows, followed sectional lines, with areas near the vacant land (including some small towns) providing most of the affirmative votes. Occupation was less important: where the delegates lived, rather than what they did for a living, controlled their votes. Small property holders favored low prices, more wealthy ones voted for a high price, but this factor was also related primarily to the section. The same holds for the cosmopolitan-localist dichotomy and probably for other apparent influences, except that of party.

Several votes show a consistent preference by the Localist delegates for the western settlers and tenants over land speculators. These occurred in Massachusetts, New York, Pennsylvania, New Jersey, and North Carolina. Column 2 of table 12.8 shows the alignment in the first three states. The most important influence again was the representatives' constituency, those from rural areas supporting the settlers, those from towns, the speculator or large-landowner interest. The divisions by wealth and occupation are less significant, though the delegate's family background may very well have affected his point of view on this matter.

Other roll calls also show a consistent division on economic issues. Notable ones were: New York votes to exclude owners of privateers from the legislature (column 3, table 12.8) and to relieve certain New York merchants from their prewar debts; a Maryland vote on lowering taxes in Annapolis; one in New York to require special bonds (and other annoyances) on reexported goods (column 4); the long series of Pennsylvania votes on the Bank of North America, represented by two in column 5; several votes involving aid to business, of which three are combined in column 6; a New York refusal to remit duties on a ship from Dominica; Pennsylvania's rejection of a request that cannon be furnished for a ship; and in the same state a grant of £300 for making steel. In each of these the Cosmopolitan bloc took a pro-urban, probank, probusiness position. Taken singly, they do not furnish a sufficient number or variety of votes, but viewed as a whole, these three-hundred-odd individual votes become significant.

The most striking sections of table 12.8 (other than the vote on ratification) are those dealing with residence and economic status. Representatives from the frontier and semisubsistence farm areas

Table 12.8. Economic Issues II (in Percentages)

	Delegates Favoring Six Types of Economic Proposals					
	1	2	3	4	5	6
All delegates	52	50	40	44	52	62
Residence						
Frontier	95	80	100	80	87	89
Noncommercial farm	79	59	53	85	95	96
Comm. farm, noncity	39	46	33	8	34	48
Comm. farm, near city	40	63	25	33	57	50
Plantation	24	—	—	—	—	—
Small town	60	18	0	—	33	44
Second-rank city	50	25	0	—	—	—
Major city	28	33	13	13	17	18
Occupation						
Farmer	66	59	68	67	65	81
Large landowner	27	—	0	—	75	—
Misc. nonfarmer	55	62	17	40	44	70
Artisan	43	60	100	—	44	38
Manufacturer	75	50	—	—	63	67
Doctor	17	—	0	—	—	0
Lawyer	33	14	29	0	20	18
Merchant or trader	31	36	13	18	13	20
Economic status						
Moderate	72	67	65	78	76	80
Substantial	52	39	57	60	41	63
Well-to-do	40	52	12	27	31	47
Wealthy	19	21	0	17	9	20
Religion						
Episcopalian	25	40	17	—	13	20
Quaker	13	—	—	—	0	29
Congregationalist	50	59	—	—	—	60
Presbyterian	75	59	55	—	74	84
Dutch Reformed	64	40	33	—	—	67
Other	27	25	—	—	42	63
Unknown	54	47	40	—	55	63
Age						
Under 40	49	32	47	40	46	64
40–49	66	68	39	56	61	67
50 and over	39	38	38	36	38	38

Table 12.8—Continued

	1	2	3	4	5	6
Military service						
Militia officer	61	52	60	56	55	78
Continental officer	50	50	57	—	56	36
None	44	48	24	38	46	52
Political experience						
Local office	55	50	13	44	48	64
Sheriff, etc.	63	35	—	—	45	56
High state office	63	63	38	75	67	67
Continental office	46	—	0	—	25	17
Education						
None known	50	44	—	50	50	65
Self-educated	75	42	—	0	—	39
College	50	27	—	0	—	41
Intellectual interest						
None known	54	53	46	50	54	63
Some	50	50	11	22	41	57
World view						
Localist	63	54	55	59	64	76
Cosmopolitan	44	48	31	25	35	45
Father's occupation						
Farmer	61	72	56	57	77	76
Large landowner	29	20	0	25	0	57
Misc. nonfarmer	50	37	0	33	31	30
Lawyer or trader	31	17	0	0	0	25
Social origin						
Humble	56	71	50	67	56	68
Average	59	50	50	52	62	69
Above-average	36	56	0	17	25	36
Prominent	31	0	0	10	0	25
Legislative party						
Localist	94	68	94	86	98	98
Neutral	61	52	22	17	67	59
Cosmopolitan	16	24	0	0	2	27

Table 12.8—Continued

	1	2	3	4	5	6
Vote on ratification						
Antifederalist	94	66	33	75	94	91
Federalist	18	11	—	—	0	0

CODE OF VOTES:
  1. For low land prices (158 votes).
  2. Favorable to settlers in West (124 votes).
  3. Antiurban (53 votes).
  4. For regulation of business (41 votes).
  5. Anti-Bank of North America (110 votes).
  6. Against to business (115 votes).

voted overwhelmingly against the urban and business interests, while the townsmen obtained support from the commercial farming regions. Delegates owning moderate property sharply opposed those with large estates—the contrast being indeed more impressive than that of residence. Were these two characteristics independent or aspects of the same influence? Combining all four furnishes the needed data on 309 votes (see table 12.9). Clearly the

Table 12.9. Residence with Economic Status: Pro-Localist Votes (in Percentages)

	Pro-Localist Delegates, by Residence				
	General	Frontier	Noncomm. Farm	Comm. Farm	Town-City
All delegates	51	88	83	33	26
Economic status					
Moderate	76	91	87	67	43
Substantial	52	71	100	32	0
Well-to-do	33	—	40	29	42
Wealthy	18	—	67	33	0

delegates' attitudes toward these economic issues stemmed both from their own economic interests and from the kind of constituency that they represented.

As one would expect, farmers consistently adopted an antiurban, antibusiness position, as far as these votes provide evidence, while lawyers and traders defended their own interests. Episcopalians and Quakers voted for the urban-business position more often than their geographical distribution would lead one to expect, but Presbyterians acted like other similarly situated delegates, as did both cosmopolitans and localists. Apparently the occupation and social rank of the parents exercised some influence on the delegates' attitudes. The major factors, however, remain residence and economic status.

Compared with these economic questions, social, cultural, and even most political issues played a minor role in forming legislative alignments, however important they might have been otherwise. The treatment of loyalists, which occasioned many votes, was controversial because it often involved economic and political issues. Oaths of allegiance, generally required during the war years, disappeared gradually afterwards, causing debate in certain states. Delaware's loyalists concentrated in the southern counties so that party positions became blurred. In Maryland the Cosmopolitan bloc opposed modification of the oath in one vote, but only religious minorities were involved. Elsewhere that group attempted to remove the oaths, ostensibly on idealistic grounds, but probably because the restriction disenfranchised potential allies: this is certainly true in Pennsylvania, where the major debate took place; in New York, where loyalists concentrated in the southern counties; and in New Jersey, where they were most numerous in the west, especially among Quakers. In reality the people discriminated against had seldom become outright loyalists (whom everyone opposed), but were neutrals or principled nonjurors.

In these last-mentioned states the alignment seems to involve almost every possible factor (see column 1, table 12.10, pp. 348–

Table 12.10. *Social and Political Issues (in Percentages)*

	Delegates Favoring Six Types of Social-Political Issues					
	1	2	3	4	5	6
All delegates	40	52	44	51	55	40
Residence						
Frontier	85	88	82	96	82	27
Noncommercial farm	70	54	59	70	73	68
Comm. farm, noncity	31	53	34	38	56	38
Comm. farm, near city	20	20	56	10	31	—

Table 12.10—Continued

	1	2	3	4	5	6
Residence						
Plantation	—	36	11	—	—	27
Small town	31	78	14	33	24	25
Second-rank city	0	50	25	75	0	—
Major city	7	26	10	20	13	—
Occupation						
Farmer	47	67	65	65	70	65
Large landowner	50	46	21	20	64	38
Misc. nonfarmer	50	27	39	39	59	43
Artisan	50	40	64	60	61	—
Manufacturer	50	75	20	67	47	—
Doctor	0	44	23	0	9	—
Lawyer	0	0	10	35	42	36
Merchant or trader	7	29	11	37	12	29
Economic status						
Moderate	49	81	66	67	66	64
Substantial	47	66	47	52	54	38
Well-to-do	15	49	36	39	40	44
Wealthy	8	21	10	16	21	36
Religion						
Episcopalian	0	22	12	18	17	46
Quaker	0	—	—	25	31	—
Congregationalist	—	—	53	80	55	—
Presbyterian	63	60	57	73	60	57
Dutch Reformed	—	58	25	46	52	—
Other	47	100	67	42	42	—
Unknown	44	56	45	51	57	36
Age						
Under 40	38	39	33	50	41	34
40 to 49	42	61	33	56	59	38
50 and over	13	60	50	21	60	43
Military service						
Militia officer	46	57	48	56	63	48
Continental officer	14	33	33	50	35	26
None	36	48	40	46	51	39
Political experience						
Local office	30	50	48	50	66	50
Sheriff, etc.	47	65	46	63	53	54

Table 12.10—Continued

	1	2	3	4	5	6
Political experience						
High state office	42	45	33	46	48	40
Continental office	0	25	11	0	25	29
Education						
None known	—	56	55	51	60	43
Self-educated	—	75	20	73	50	—
College	—	19	14	20	16	36
Intellectual interest						
None known	43	59	51	53	62	41
Some	27	32	11	42	42	31
World view						
Localist	59	75	61	62	71	43
Cosmopolitan	13	33	16	39	24	33
Father's occupation						
Farmer	60	59	51	53	71	32
Large landowner	8	36	18	18	57	33
Misc. nonfarmer	29	45	36	50	39	38
Lawyer or trader	0	20	19	22	25	25
Social origin						
Humble	50	64	47	55	71	32
Average	51	54	47	55	62	52
Above-average	20	35	5	38	44	54
Prominent	0	17	13	15	6	11
Legislative party						
Localist	78	75	75	84	80	84
Neutral	44	60	67	41	57	50
Cosmopolitan	5	24	5	25	14	4
Vote on ratification						
Antifederalist	93	75	55	90	80	77
Federalist	9	31	19	30	18	17

CODE OF VOTES:
1. For loyalty oaths (137 votes).
2. For confiscation (190 votes).
3. Against readmittance (266 votes).
4. For capital in West (190 votes).
5. Against financial support of Congress (381 votes).
6. Against enforcement of British treaty (136 votes).

350). A great majority of delegates from the frontier and non-commercial farm districts opposed repealing the oath, while most other delegates favored removing this restriction. The nonjurors found allies among merchants and professional men, the large property owners, Episcopalians and Quakers, older men (apparently), Continental army officers and officerholders, men of intellectual taste, cosmopolitans, and men of prominent economic and social background. Other sorts of people divided equally, though Presbyterians distinguished themselves for opposition to repeal. Clearly social, cultural, and economic considerations combined with the political. The same influences applied also to the removal of other restrictions, the precise alignment again varying from state to state.[7]

The confiscation of loyalist property, initiated as a wartime measure, slowed after 1783. Critics attacked it as an extreme and unfair punishment, which penalized honest men who held a different opinion or were victims of circumstance. Those defending confiscation sometimes had acquired a personal stake, but they usually argued that the loyalists were enemies of their country and had forfeited their rights. The only post-1780 vote in New York showed the two parties divided irregularly, but previous roll calls there, as well as votes in New Jersey and in both Carolinas, prove that the Cosmopolitans normally defended the loyalists. As a rule the Localists favored confiscation, as did delegates from the interior parts of the state, farmers and men with lesser nonfarm occupations, those with small property, Presbyterians, localists, and men of humble background (see column 2, table 12.10). Defenders of the loyalists included, notably, residents of major cities and the most commercialized farm areas, lawyers, traders (though some of these, being purchasers, took the other side), wealthy delegates, Episcopalians, Continental officials, college graduates, cosmopolitans (with exceptions), and men of prominent family.

The payment of debts owed to loyalists also involved certain complexities. In a few cases, notably in New York, men normally voting with the Cosmopolitans opposed payments because some merchants faced ruin by the recovery of these obligations. As a

7. The Localists rather than the Cosmopolitans favored removing the special tax on Quakers (New York, Maryland), perhaps because of their generally low-tax position. One suspects, however, that the Localists sympathized with the loyalists where these came from the same background as members of that party. Most of the punitive legislation was directed against men of property whose estates were worth confiscating—against influential men who might be dangerous. The Cosmopolitans defended such men as these.

rule, however, the Cosmopolitan bloc backed payment both because of a general procreditor conviction and for the same reason that led them to defend loyalist rights in other ways. The principal features of the alignment included residence, occupation, economic status, education, world view, and socioeconomic origin, resembling in every way the division on the confiscation of loyalist property.

A final major controversy of this type concerned the readmission of loyalists, usually of certain individuals or in some cases generally. Analysis of votes in Massachusetts, New York, and South Carolina (column 3, table 12.10) confirms the generalization that Cosmopolitans generally favored loyalists, while Localists opposed them. Frontier areas in particular objected to the return of these men, most of whom were once-wealthy city dwellers. Also unfriendly were farmers, artisans, men of moderate property, and localists. Those favoring readmission most often included townsmen and men from plantation areas, lawyers, traders, large landowners, and wealthy delegates. Episcopalians, Continental officials, college graduates, intellectuals, cosmopolitans, and men of above-average economic and social backgrounds also defended the former enemies.

The nature of the division on the treatment of loyalists is not surprising, since most of the men in question were men of property who would naturally tend toward the Cosmopolitan side. An examination of the votes on confiscation of property and readmission

Table *12.11. Multivariate Analysis: Votes for Confiscating Estates (1) and against Readmitting Loyalists (2), (in Percentages)*

	I. By Residence									
	General		Frontier		Noncomm. Farm		Comm. Farm[a]		Town-City	
	1	2	1	2	1	2	1	2	1	2
All delegates	52	44	88	82	54	59	43	29	40	12
Occupation										
Farmer	67	65	92	81	62	67	50	52	67	—
Large landowner[b]		21		—		43		16		—
Misc. nonfarmer[c]	40	46	100	100	33	63	25	40	38	23
Lawyer or trader	17	12	—	0	0	33	13	8	22	14

Table 12.11—Continued

	1	2	1	2	1	2	1	2	1	2
Economic status										
Moderate	81	66	89	85	67	41	100	65	67	9
Substantial	66	47	100	100	63	36	46	33	33	40
Well-to-do	49	36	67	100	55	36	38	35	60	17
Wealthy	21	10	—	0	0	50	24	8	14	6
World view										
Localist	75	61	88	91	65	60	76	51	0	10
Cosmopolitan	33	16	—	67	0	33	35	6	32	16
Religion[d]										
Episcopalian		12		—		—		8		10
Presbyterian		57		76		62		33		0

II. By Occupation

	General		Farmer		Large Land-owner[b]		Misc. Non-farmer[c]		Lawyer or Trader	
	1	2	1	2	1	2	1	2	1	2
All delegates	52	44	67	65	46	21	40	45	20	6
Economic status										
Moderate	81	66	86	71	—	—	50	53	—	0
Substantial	66	47	46	50	100	0	33	40	30	33
Well-to-do	49	36	57	40	57	33	33	37	20	20
Wealthy	21	10	—	—	28	15	—	—	17	7

NOTES:

[a] Includes plantations.

[b] Data for this category are not included for votes on confiscation of estates, column 1.

[c] Includes artisans, manufacturers, innkeepers, shopkeepers, and unidentified nonfarm occupations but not professional men.

[d] Same as note *b*, above.

of loyalists in table 12.11, above, indicates that residence, occupation, economic status, world view, and religion (except for Presbyterianism) all affected the voting patterns. The conclusion follows that a combination of economic, cultural, and political factors determined the legislators' attitudes toward this species of loyalism.

Other social issues require little discussion because, however interesting, they did not contribute to the legislative bloc voting. Attitudes toward the emancipation of slaves and civil rights for Negroes differed with the locality. In New York the anti-Clintonians opposed equality consistently, but in Virginia, Northern Neck delegates inclined to the other side, while no bloc pattern whatever developed in Pennsylvania and Maryland. The issue of importation in South Carolina was economic, not social. In a general view, the particular situation of a state or a section seems to have been the most important element, except that Quakers, Baptists, and Congregationalists favored civil rights for the slaves. Enthusiasm for humanitarian reform depended upon the reform in question, and the data will not support any general interpretation.[8]

Cultural questions usually cut across "party" lines. Support of religion seems primarily to have been a moral matter. In North Carolina, Maryland, and (in a close vote) Virginia, the Cosmopolitan bloc supported state aid, but in Pennsylvania the Republicans refused to appropriate money for publishing the Bible. Smaller property holders tended to oppose state support, notably in Maryland, because they feared economic loss, but the slight correlation suggests that noneconomic factors were more important. Attitudes toward the theater did not involve our legislative parties. The division was partly moral, with Episcopalians for and Quakers, Presbyterians, and the Dutch against. Large property holders approved of the theater by a margin of more than two to one, but delegates with less wealth divided irregularly.

On the other hand, state support of schools separated the two parties wherever it came to a vote (New York, Maryland, and North Carolina). Representatives from the towns and most highly commercialized farm areas favored state aid, those from noncommercial farm regions opposed. Planters and lawyers were for, farmers against. Small property owners strongly disapproved, for they expected to share the cost without obtaining any benefit. Well-to-do delegates voted just as solidly on the other side, but wealthy men did not: presumably they could educate their children privately and saw no need for a public system that might require taxes from them, whereas men who were only well-to-do

8. Aid to immigrants was approved by city dwellers, Dutch, Germans, and wealthy men; aid to paupers was favored by the delegates with the least property from outlying areas. Divisions on other reforms show no pattern except that Quakers approved. Lawyers generally disliked all of them. Conceivably a careful study might reveal some correlations.

earned too little for private education and realized the advantages of a public system. Most college graduates, intellectuals, and cosmopolitans voted for state aid, their opposites against. If Pennsylvania's alignment on support of the American Philosophical Society can be regarded as evidence, a similar division formed with respect to educational institutions in general.

Political issues naturally divided the two parties. Many of the questions already discussed involved political considerations, and others arose in every state. Highly important was the nature of the state constitution. The absence of roll-call votes precludes quantitative analysis, but the general nature of the division seems clear. Wherever a controversy continued into the eighties, the alignment coincided with bloc lines. Pennsylvania supplies the most obvious evidence, but the debate both in South Carolina and in Massachusetts was sectional. The architects of Maryland's conservative constitution became Cosmopolitans, and the difference of opinion within New York's constitutional convention also anticipates the later party division. The evidence from North Carolina and New Hampshire, such as it is, points in the same direction.

A few constitutional questions continued to concern the legislators. The power of the executive—soon to be increased by new constitutions in Georgia and Pennsylvania—received support from the Cosmopolitan party both in New York and in Massachusetts. The same men defended the independence of judges, as already discussed above. The establishment of new courts also won their approval (New Jersey and Virginia), and they preferred that suits be tried in these rather than before local magistrates or juries. Whether new counties should be formed divided the delegates irregularly depending upon circumstances, parties becoming involved only when some political advantage seemed likely.

The location of state capitals was almost exclusively a sectional issue. The Localist delegates, representing primarily the agricultural interior, tried everywhere to move the governments to some inland site: the Shaysites petitioned unsuccessfully in Massachusetts, and votes were recorded in New York, Pennsylvania, Virginia, and both Carolinas (column 4, table 12.10, pp. 348–350). Economic status also affected the alignment, and the smaller property holders favored removal wherever they lived. Older men tended to prefer the traditional location, perhaps because they were willing to pay for the comfort. Other factors seemed related to geography or economic status.

Adherence to the British treaty created a division that differed in certain respects from other political questions (column 6, table 12.10). One circumstance that remained constant was the attitude of the two parties, the Cosmopolitan bloc favoring and the Localists opposing such obedience in every state on record—Virginia, North Carolina, Maryland, New Hampshire, and Rhode Island. Since abiding by the treaty required the repeal of antiloyalist legislation and payment of British debts, the positions taken by the parties coincided with their other objectives. As a result the alignment resembled that on loyalism and debtor-creditor relations, but with certain exceptions: western Virginia eventually supported obedience because of the western posts. Economic status seemed less important than on other questions, while religion, education, and the cosmopolitan-localist factors mattered little (at least in Virginia).

Relations between the states and Congress became controversial in several areas, notably with respect to commutation (New England), the supplementary fund (primarily in Massachusetts), the impost, and general support, especially financial. With very few exceptions the Cosmopolitans supported Congress's requests and authority. In New Hampshire its members agreed to grant money as asked; they voted for troops in Pennsylvania; for the supplementary fund in Massachusetts and Connecticut; for general support in New York and New Jersey; for the commerce power in Virginia; for the land cession in North Carolina; for the impost in Massachusetts, Rhode Island (eventually), Connecticut, and New York;[9] and they favored paying the federal debt in New York, New Jersey, Pennsylvania, and Delaware. Most of these questions involved money, so that the two blocs acted in accordance with their economic ideas. Most also involved power, which introduces a new element into the analysis of party objectives.

The alignment on paying the federal debt, including the supplementary fund, followed the usual division (see column 5, table 12.10). Differences in residence appear in the four states analyzed (New Jersey, Massachusetts, Pennsylvania, and New York). The extremes consisted of the frontier and subsistence farm areas on the one side and the towns and contiguous farming districts on the other. Most farmers voted against financial aid to Congress, while traders and professional men approved. Larger property holders tended to support Congress, as did the Continental officials, college

9. In New Jersey the two groups reversed, while in Maryland the impost cut across bloc lines.

graduates, cosmopolitans, and men of prominent family, but localists opposed. Other differences seem minor or coincidental. In
general the sectional contrast and that between cosmopolitans and
localists appear most sharply.

One final category of issues might be termed miscellaneous or
"party" conflicts. These arose in particular states where, if important, they might have helped to shape legislative blocs and otherwise serve as indicators of political divisions. They included, in
Massachusetts, the decisions during 1786 on how money arising
from the tax on polls and estates should be appropriated and on
the policy that the legislature should adopt concerning the rebellion. The votes on seating Paine in New York and censuring Anthony New in Virginia are a similar type. Examples from Pennsylvania include the series of roll calls on the College of Philadelphia,
the arguments over the 1781 Philadelphia County election and
over the seating of William Maclay in 1783 and 1785, and the debates over the Supreme Executive Council's power of appointment
and over a clause critical of the assembly president, John Dickinson. Delaware's legislature also divided along party lines over an
election (Sussex County, January 1788), while Maryland's became
involved in a protracted debate concerning the office of intendant.
Sometimes these issues reveal little about the principles and composition of the parties, but all testify to the existence and intensity
of political disputes. They suggest that "party" spirit was itself
becoming a motive for political behavior.

The climactic issue of the period was, of course, that over the
ratification of the Constitution. While a detailed treatment of that
subject lies outside the scope of this investigation, a few observations cast further light upon political alignments during these years.

As the tables 12.1, 12.6, 12.8, and 12.10 have shown, future
Antifederalists and Federalists consistently opposed each other on
these roll calls. Indeed the correlation between this factor and the
various issues sometimes exceeded any other except that of legislative party itself. At least four out of five among the 20 percent
who were known Antifederalists took the following positions: for
a general reduction of salaries, for low land prices, for paper
money, for paper to be tender and issued in large quantities,
against banks, against aid to business, for loyalty oaths, and for the
removal of state capitals. The proportion fell only a little short of
four to one in support of reducing the governor's salary, cutting
expenses, passing a stay law, and confiscating loyalist property,
and in opposition to payments to Congress and enforcement of

the British treaty. The 259 identified Federalists stood united in favor of permanent salaries, high land prices, less paper money without the quality of tender, banks, aid to business, measures unfriendly to settlers, repeal of loyalty oaths, readmittance of loyalists, payments to Congress, and enforcement of the treaty. The list could be considerably lengthened by noting particular issues. The division over ratification, in brief, was organically related to that over other questions of the time.

The Antifederalists may have disagreed with one another, and the Federalists may have had various motives for their position, but one central conviction united each group: the Antifederalists defended local autonomy, while the Federalists sought centralization. This basic ideological difference obviously resembles, if it does not in fact result from, the localist-cosmopolitan dichotomy. A correlation, therefore, between our bloc alignment and the vote on the Constitution seems inevitable. The alignment in the seven states analyzed in detail was as follows:

Legislative Party	All Delegates	Anti-federalists		Shifting		Federalists	
Localist	158	132	84%	2	1%	24	15%
Neutral	89	30	34%	4	4%	55	62%
Cosmopolitan	178	24	14%	2	1%	152	85%

In addition, party lines in Rhode Island held fast on the Constitution, a clear relationship existed in Connecticut, while in New Hampshire, Delaware, and North Carolina the following may be added to the above:

	Antifederalists	Federalists
Localists	17	1
Cosmopolitans	4	27

All together, then, data on 474 individuals show that the members of the two blocs voted, on the issue of ratification, with a consistency of about 86 percent.[10]

10. The Localist group furnished 149 Antifederalists and 27 Federalists including the two who shifted; Cosmopolitans voted the other way, 28 to 181 including as Federalists the two who shifted. The positions taken by these men

A review of this survey shows that the two legislative parties habitually confronted each other on most of the major issues of the Confederation period. Moreover the positions that they adopted display an internal consistency, form a unified whole, rather more than do the platforms of many modern political parties. Furthermore the factors that seem to have created this persistent alignment also apply to most issues and form the same logical pattern.

The legislators of the Localist bloc almost always tried to minimize government costs, whether these be salaries paid to officials, other payments to persons, the principal or interest of the state debt, or miscellaneous expenses. The major exception concerned their own salaries, for precisely because they lacked wealth and came from poorer districts, they at once tried to reduce the burden of government and to relieve themselves. They could and did argue too that, if men like themselves were to hold office, they must at least meet expenses; at the same time they denied that judges and other officials should profit unduly. They violated their principles occasionally, when the stake concerned some favorite person (such as Clinton) or some payment clearly beneficial to themselves (as during the war).[11]

At the same time they tried to reduce the tax burden in several ways. Primarily they attempted to lower the rate on property held by themselves or their constituents, particularly land, while raising that on property owned by others, especially nonfarm property and luxury goods. They also tried to reduce the level (unless they had succeeded in shifting the burden), to postpone collections, and to pay in articles other than specie. Low taxes and reduced expenditures formed critical aspects of their creed.

The Localist delegates also favored the cause of debtors over creditors—indeed they approached nearer to unanimity on this than on any other type of issue. They backed stay laws, installment bills, valuation laws, and other relief measures. They also supported an inflationary monetary policy that would ease the lot of debtors, relieve taxpayers, provide money for the government,

were determined not only by votes in the conventions but from other sources (but no systematic search was undertaken). These figures coincide with those gathered in a study of the senates. A word of caution: these men, as relatively public figures, had often openly committed themselves to a political position and probably found it hard to break ranks. The correlation between ratification and "party" alignments is probably much lower in the case of ordinary citizens.

11. They violated it too in many cases that do not concern the present study, for when the two groups agreed the question never came to a vote. The present study tends to exaggerate the differences between blocs.

furnish loans to farmers and others at low interest, solve the currency shortage, and, one might say, act as a general economic panacea. They wanted a plentiful money supply that would be legal tender for debts, taxes, and all other purposes.

Other laws that would help men such as small farmers also attracted the Localists' particular approval. These included low prices for vacant land and any provision that aided western settlers and renters. They opposed acts beneficial to townspeople or to business (symbolized by the Bank of North America). Public support for colleges and the like they fought, because they saw the cost but not the benefits of education. Disliking loyalists, especially propertied ones, they generally defended loyalty oaths and other restrictions, advocated the confiscation of loyalist property, and tried to prevent both the readmission of loyalists and payment of debts owed to them.

Politically, these men opposed permanent salaries for judges, voted against the establishment of new courts, and preferred trials by local magistrates. They sought to remove state capitals to interior towns. They disapproved of the British treaty. They granted funds to Congress with great reluctance, preferring to keep both money and power in their own hands. Finally, they voted against ratifying the Federal Constitution without amendments. These various positions agreed with a general attitude characteristic of farmers, of men from noncommercial areas, of small property holders with a limited, parochial view of the world.

What factors influenced the political behavior we have been examining? Age rarely affected voting. Occasional correlations seem due to the small number of cases or to a coincidence with other circumstances, notably residence. More will be said on this and on other biographical matters in the next chapter. Religion exercised only a limited influence. The Presbyterian tendency to follow the Localist "party line" probably resulted from the geographical distribution of that denomination, not from theology. The same holds true of the Quakers except in certain instances. Episcopalians showed an appreciation of the Cosmopolitan's point of view that also seems related to their residence in the towns and the plantation areas of the south. Military service in the Continental army clearly disposed the officers toward the Cosmopolitan bloc on certain issues. These included, especially, the salaries of judges and some other expenditures, collection of taxes, inflation (though not the mere issuing of paper), loyalty oaths, and support of Congress. One can trace through these attitudes various aspects of their experience and special interest, and probably also the environment from which they originally came. An opposite tendency among militia officers almost certainly tells more about the recruitment of that class of men than their careers. In both cases a comparison of their votes with the data on economic status suggests that military service by itself was not a basic factor in creating political blocs.

The same is true of the delegates' political careers. The only significant contrast, that between local and Continental officials, corresponds with the correlation by residence and by wealth. Continental officials clearly reflect their experience in many ways, but seldom were they present in sufficient numbers to exert a decisive effect. Educated men also voted with the Cosmopolitan group, and on many issues the difference between their attitude and that of men without any known education indicates that the college men did share a particular point of view. Yet education does not seem separable as a variable from residence, occupation, or wealth. It sometimes did not operate at all, and too few men were affected for it to have exerted more than a peripheral influence. The same can be said of intellectual background, and indeed the "intelligentsia" behaved with much less consistency than one might expect. The occupations of the delegates' fathers and their social origins were minor factors insofar as they counted for anything, correlating less than other influences, except that men of prominent family voted against inflation, were strongly prourban and probusiness, proloyalist, and favored authority in government. The national origin of the legislators made no difference whatever.

Four major variables, other than party itself, remain. Sectional influences played an extremely significant, probably the primary, role in every state except perhaps in New Hampshire. The crucial poles were occupied by the least and the most commercial areas: seacoast New England versus the upstate counties, Philadelphia—city and county—versus the western mountains, Charleston and the nearest parishes versus the backcountry. Second in importance was the opposition between two kinds of agricultural communities: that of large, prosperous commercial farms such as those of the Northern Neck and its allies, the east bank of the Hudson, parts of West Jersey, and eastern North Carolina, against the smaller, less prosperous farm regions typified by the Virginia Southside and the Carolina "piedmont." Delegates from the frontier and from "subsistence" or "noncommercial farms" took the Localist position on almost every vote, ranging from virtual unanimity (propaper, antibank, and antibusiness) to an average agreement of nearly 75 percent. Arrayed against them, in addition to the commercial farm areas, were the representatives of major cities, who favored most types of government expenditures except to pay legislators, supported high taxes (sometimes even on themselves), defended the rights of creditors, fought paper-money and tender laws, aided their own cities and business but not the westerners or farmers, opposed loyalty oaths and confiscations, voted for the readmission of loyalists, urged adherence to the treaty, led the drive for a stronger Congress, and finally obtained the Constitution. In all this they cast over four-fifths of their votes as a bloc.

Only in a few states could these city delegates exert much influence. With them, however, usually voted the men of the smaller towns, who broke ranks only when some interior representatives supported their own section, as in the case of land prices and the confiscation of the loyalist property. In addition, delegates living just outside the cities often supported the townspeople. Although they tried to keep down government expenditures, they tended to agree with the urban representatives on such questions as taxes, debts and monetary policy, loyalty oaths, and federal affairs. The position taken by delegates from the "plantation" areas varied considerably, but they stood as a rule closer to the towns than to the subsistence farms, while the representatives of small commercial farms some distance from the cities divided equally on almost every type of vote.

The delegates' occupations also influenced their politics, though the cohesiveness of their voting fell short of that based on residence. Especially evident was the agreement among farmers (as opposed to large landowners), two-thirds of whom could generally be found on the same side of an issue. They shared all the attitudes of the Localists, being most enthusiastic about postponing taxes, issuing paper as legal tender, opposing special favors to business, and blocking excessive grants of power and money to Congress. If they came from noncommercial farming areas or had little property, their vote became almost a certainty. Large landowners, on the average, divided just about in half and only rarely united: although they were farmers, they also shared many characteristics with men in nonagricultural walks of life. Moreover they owned considerable property. At the opposite pole from the farmers stood the professionals and men in trade. Yet their consistency seldom exceeded two to one, for factors other than occupation affected their attitudes. Lawyers united especially in support of loyalists, high and permanent salaries, and aid to business and to urban interests, while the traders, following a similar course, added a dislike of taxes and a desire to support Congress and the British treaty. Doctors generally agreed with the lawyers. Artisans, manufacturers, and other men with a nonfarm occupation behaved irregularly. The first two voted with farmers more often than not, particularly on government expenses and certain debtor laws, while the latter tended the other way.

A third influential factor was the delegates' economic status. While this had something to do with both residence and occupation, it acted independently. Men with moderate property voted together about 70 percent of the time—a better record than farmers—while wealthy delegates even exceeded that solidarity. The latter failed of virtual unanimity only on the subjects of government spending, postponement of tax collections, and certain aspects of debtor relief; they united concerning the price of land, legal tender, the quantity of money, urban and business policies, loyalism, the capital, and support of Congress. Men with "substantial" property slightly but steadily supported those with less (especially on debtor relief), while well-to-do delegates joined the wealthy ones more often than not, but unreliably. The factor of wealth became significant only at the extreme ends of the scale, but there it was usually important.

Finally, cosmopolitans and localists opposed each other on many of the votes. The cosmopolitans, by definition, included practically all Continental army officers and civil officeholders, college graduates, and most of the prominent men from the cities and plantation areas, thus combining in one cultural species men who inclined for related reasons toward a certain set of objectives. At the same time they did not invariably follow the Cosmopolitan "party line," deviating on the issue of land prices, the postponement of taxes, debtor relief, laws favoring settlers, and bills aiding business. Lacking (by definition) any uniform economic interest, they acted independently on economic matters without forming a solid bloc on other issues. The localists also combined several characteristics. They too voted with a cohesion of about 67 percent and united on certain types of issues, in their case primarily on questions of government spending, taxes, debts, loyalist property, and the Constitution.

Thus far in our analysis we have discovered two parties that differed on a long series of issues. The opposing points of view reflected two consistent attitudes. A study of what kinds of delegates voted together on these questions reveals several factors that help to account for the alignment. These are: first, the sectional division in each state; second, the occupations of the delegates; third, the legislators' economic status; and fourth, the cultural outlook of these men as expressed by the terms "cosmopolitan" and "localist." Certain additional influences affected a few individuals or the alignment on particular questions. These included religion, military service, education, and social status. The opposing viewpoints of the two legislative parties also took the form of divergent political ideologies that came to a focus in the struggle over the ratification of the Federal Constitution.

Three problems remain for consideration. First, the composition of these voting blocs requires more detailed analysis. Second, we must inquire whether contemporary opinion recognized and expressed these related sets of attitudes. Finally, we ask what general principles or hypotheses about the origin of parties and the factors affecting political behavior emerge from this investigation.

Chapter XIII

Conclusion: The Parties

Our investigation has disclosed the existence, in every state, of two legislative blocs or parties similarly composed and expressing, in their votes, resolutions, petitions, instructions, pamphlets, and letters, the same attitudes toward major issues of the period. The "Cosmopolitans" and "Localists" of Massachusetts, Maryland, and the Carolinas appear almost identical with the anti-Clintonians and Clintonians of New York, the Republicans and Constitutionalists in Pennsylvania, and the Northern Neck and Southside blocs of Virginia. Even the West-East division in New Jersey about 1785 took a similar form, and we can trace the same political alignments in New Hampshire, Connecticut, Rhode Island, Georgia, and Delaware.

We are now ready for an explanation of why these alignments developed and why they assumed everywhere the same characteristics. In seven state legislatures, some 1,500 persons placed themselves on record through their votes, which form the core of our analysis. Supplementing this data is information concerning over two hundred men in three additional legislatures, which reinforces our conclusions. A study of these representatives will go far toward revealing the reasons for their political behavior and will prepare the way for an attempt, through more detailed analysis, to distinguish the truly significant from the irrelevant. This investigation will finally produce a general explanation of political alignments before the Constitution.

Perhaps the most important influence on the legislators' votes lay in the kind of constituency that they represented (see the map, p. 367). The Cosmopolitan party drew almost all of its support from a narrow strip of land along the Atlantic, occasionally broken, and with extensions inland along several streams. The Localist stronghold lay in a much broader band extending from the western edge of settlement to within twenty or thirty miles of the coast, which it reached at a few points.[1] Neither region presented a united front, for each had allies within the other's boundaries and each contained men who remained neutral, yet in both a majority adopted clearly articulated, opposing opinions regarding most important issues of the time.

Each of these major areas possessed certain crucial characteristics. The Cosmopolitans lived in communities that were either urban or well populated—the long-established counties and towns. Socially, these communities included practically the entire upper class, both the colonial "better sort" who had become whigs in 1776, retaining their rank and influence, and the nouveaux riches. Most of the slaves and white servants lived there too, making the society aristocratic rather than democratic. Economically, all of the overseas trade, much of the internal commerce, the large-scale manufacturing, and the production of staple crops concentrated in this region, as did most of the fluid capital. It was the business, financial, commercial part of the country. The same districts contributed most of the nation's culture. Almost all of the newspapers and books were published there, and there too were located the educational institutions, theaters, societies, and men of taste and learning. Politically, the centers of power, with very few exceptions, coincided with the Cosmopolitans' strongholds.

The region was discontinuous, consisting of a series of sections, each containing as a core some important town or the commercial nexus of a major river. The major cores included Portsmouth, Boston, other coastal towns of Massachusetts and New Hampshire together with nearby farming communities, the Narragansett Bay region, southern Connecticut, New York City and the other southernmost counties of the state, Philadelphia and its environs in New Jersey and Delaware as well as in Pennsylvania, the southern Chesapeake and both banks of the Potomac, especially on the Virginia side, the lower James River valley, Albemarle Sound, and the Carolina plantation country dependent upon Charleston. The principal extensions reached up the Connecticut into Massachusetts, the east bank of the Hudson as far as Albany, the farmlands of southern Pennsylvania westward across the Susquehanna, and the

1. These few places are: Sussex and Kent counties in Delaware (see chap. 11), coastal East Jersey, if the term Localist is appropriate, a few towns in Rhode Island, and some Maine villages.

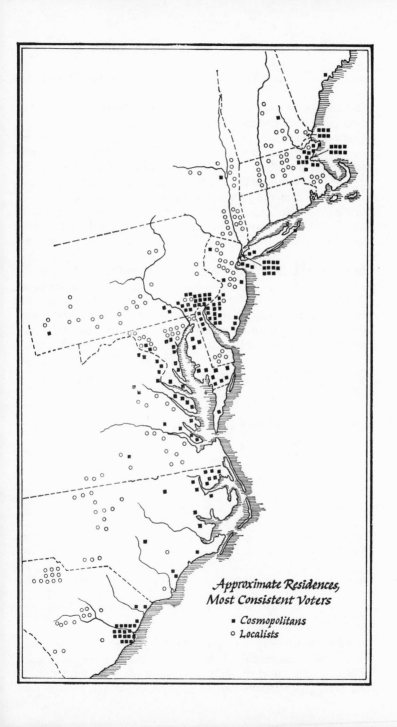

Approximate Residences,
Most Consistent Voters

■ Cosmopolitans
○ Localists

upper Potomac including the northern part of the Shenandoah Valley.

The delegates who comprised the Localist party lived primarily inland from their opponents. They represented the upland villages in New England and easternmost New York, the farm country west of the Hudson extending up to the Mohawk and down into East Jersey, the interior of Pennsylvania beginning with the first range of hills, southern Delaware, northern and western Maryland, Virginia south of the James, and thence south through the piedmont of the Carolinas. The region was not contiguous, but all parts shared one fundamental feature: they lacked short, cheap access to markets. In addition, the Localist strongholds had been more recently settled, and the population continued to be somewhat scattered. Socially, few important families lived there, the people coming from average homes or humble circumstances. They held few servants or slaves, so that the social structure was relatively democratic. Economically, they depended upon agriculture with few business enterprises of any size. Lacking major cultural centers and without surplus wealth or leisure, the people tended to be culturally backward. Finally, they had previously enjoyed little political influence and only now were gaining substantial power.

Table 13.1. Residential Scale I (in Percentages)

	% Votes with Cosmopolitans	Frontier	Noncomm. Farm	Comm. Farm, Noncity	Comm. Farm, Near City	Plantation	Small Town	Second-Rank City	Major City	Other	Total
Localist	0–20	17.8	44.5	27.1	1.8	4.7	3.4	0.0	0.3	0.5	100.1
↑	20–33	12.3	35.5	28.4	2.6	13.5	7.1	0.0	0.0	0.6	100.0
	34–66	11.9	20.4	29.6	3.6	17.2	10.2	1.9	4.4	0.7	99.9
↓	67–79	3.7	16.0	31.9	5.5	24.5	4.9	2.5	11.0	0.0	100.0
Cosmo-politan	80–100	3.9	6.4	28.5	3.9	19.5	14.4	3.1	19.8	0.5	100.0

Any terms defining these geographical entities bear connotations that prejudice the result. The most obvious series, adopted in previous chapters, ranks the delegates' residence from most rural to least rural and attempts also to incorporate, in the case of rural areas, distinctions among the types of agricultural societies. The scale has its faults, but pragmatically it has proven useful, as table 13.1 demonstrates. For greater precision the members of each legislative party are separated into groups in this table: those who voted with a bloc at least 80 percent of the time and those who conformed less often. The percentages show how often the representatives voted with the Cosmopolitans, so that those who did so least often (the top row) formed the extreme wing of the Localist party. The middle group (34–66 percent) consists of the neutrals. As presented in this table and in more simplified form in figure 13.1, the Localist bloc consisted primarily of delegates from semi-subsistence (noncommercial) farm areas, with a secondary element of men from commercial farming regions; the Cosmopolitan group contained principally members from the commercial farms and secondarily from the towns.

Table 13.2. Residential Scale II (in Percentages)

	Frontier	Noncomm. Farm	Comm. Farm, Noncity	Comm. Farm, Near City	Plantation	Small Town	Second-Rank City	Major City
Localist	55.4	62.6	34.2	22.0	17.2	18.5	0.0	0.9
Neutral	31.2	23.3	28.2	30.0	31.4	32.3	33.3	15.8
Cosmopolitan	13.4	14.1	37.6	48.0	51.3	49.3	66.7	83.3
Total	100.0	100.0	100.0	100.0	99.9	100.1	100.0	100.0

A more exact breakdown of the party division in these several types of communities is given in table 13.2, which shows that the Cosmopolitans' strength diminished proportionately with the distance from a major city, where one existed, and also decreased from the most highly commercial and most favorably situated farm country—that nearest the cities and that charactertized by plantations—to the least commercial. The controlling factor was not simply distance, however, for the frontier supported the Localists no more strongly than did the subsistence farm areas: the general nature of the environment, broadly defined, rather than just geographical location, affected the voting.

What the delegates did for a living also influenced the political

Figure 13.1. Residential Composition of Parties

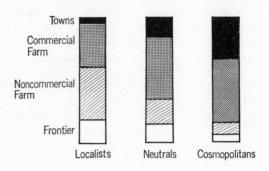

Figure 13.2. Occupational Composition of Parties

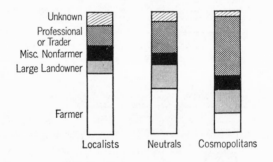

alignments. Among farmers, over half voted with the Localists and only one-sixth with the Cosmopolitans; large landowners slightly preferred the latter; professional men supported the Cosmopolitans as decisively as farmers opposed them; traders did so by an even greater majority, while other men such as artisans, manufacturers, and innkeepers divided evenly. Table 13.3 reveals the details: the Localist party was made up of farmers, 50.3 percent; large landowners, 11.7 percent; miscellaneous nonfarmers, 14.5 percent; professionals, 7.6 percent; traders, 5.2 percent; and men of unknown occupation, 10.8 percent. Most of these were probably farmers or artisans. The Cosmopolitans consisted of farmers, 15.6 percent; large landowners, 17.2 percent; miscellaneous nonfarmers, 14.9 percent; professionals, 26.5 percent; traders, 20.5 percent; and men of unknown occupation, 5.4 percent (see also figure 13.2).

The figures in table 13.3 demonstrate unmistakably the agrarian nature of the Localists, for fully two-thirds of them lived primarily by farming. In contrast, not more than a third of the Cosmopolitan bloc's adherents did so, and of these the great majority lived near cities or on plantations. The rural artisans, manufacturers, innkeepers, and shopkeepers, whom the farmers sometimes chose to represent them, did in fact favor the Localists, but by no great margin; evidently they could easily be persuaded to join the townsmen. The distinction earlier postulated between artisans and manufacturers does not come off very well, for they voted much alike. These people, together with the lesser tradesmen, clearly found themselves torn between the two political pressure groups, able to support neither the farmers nor the professional-merchant group with any enthusiasm. The latter voted with striking uniformity, merchants in particular adhering to their "party line" with few exceptions. The evidence amply demonstrates the difference between farmers and large landowners. The large landowners apparently included an agrarian element and a large entrepreneurial segment: the former varied from one-fifth in the northern states to one-half in parts of the South but was in general a minority, while the latter group, the entrepreneurs, acted as a business wing and preferred the Cosmopolitans. Finally, the difference between the occupational composition of the parties at the two extremes of the political spectrum is especially striking:

% With Cosmo-politans	Farmers	Large Land-owners	Profes-sionals	Trad-ers	All Other Non-farmers	Un-known	Total
0–20	54.4	8.3	6.0	4.4	15.4	11.5	100.0
80–100	15.2	14.4	28.5	21.1	16.4	4.4	100.0

Table 13.3. Occupational Scale (in Percentages)

	% Votes with Cosmopolitans				
	0–20%	21–33%	34–66%	67–79%	80–100%
Farmers	42	12	29	5	12
Large Landowners	14	13	33	17	24
Misc. Nonfarmers	10	10	29	10	43
Artisans, Unspecified*	25	0	13	13	50
Millers	37	16	13	8	26
Blacksmiths*	29	14	43	—	14
Carpenters*	50	—	33	—	17
All Artisans	36	11	21	7	26
Iron Manufacturers	37	5	16	11	32
Tanners	29	12	18	0	41
All Manufacturers	31	6	20	9	35
Entrepreneurs	18	12	30	9	30
Innkeepers	37	10	13	13	27
Shopkeepers	28	15	15	15	28
Traders	20	20	20	20	20
Merchants	3	2	24	19	53
All in Trade	10	6	21	17	46
Ministers	0	13	13	13	63
Doctors	20	2	27	18	34
Lawyers	5	8	24	13	51
Judges*	0	0	44	11	44
Officials	17	10	27	13	33
All Professionals	10	7	23	15	46

NOTE: * Indicates categories in which the cases are too few to be meaningful.

The leadership of the Cosmopolitans, judged by consistency of voting, thus came from the large landowners, professionals, and traders, who contributed nearly two-thirds, while farmers and the lesser nonfarm occupations furnished the Localist bloc with an even greater proportion of their most reliable supporters.

The difference in voting between farmers and large landowners, and between men such as artisans and innkeepers on the one side and lawyers and merchants on the other, suggests a contrast in wealth as well as in occupation. The division along lines of property was great, especially among the most consistent voters and at the extreme ends of the economic scale—between men of wealth and those with moderate property. Three-fourths of the Localists' voting strength came from men of moderate or substantial property, while about five-eighths of the Cosmopolitan bloc were well-to-do or wealthy (see the top section of table 13.4). The bottom part of table 13.4 shows the party differences in the poles of economic status more clearly. (Note again that the percentages voting as neutrals here are exaggerated.) Among men of moderate holdings, 60 percent favored the Localists; an even higher proportion of wealthy delegates supported the Cosmopolitans.

So far three factors, two primarily and one partially economic,

Table 13.4.   Economic Status and Party Preference (in Percentages)

	Economic Status					
	Moderate	*Substantial*	*Well-to-do*	*Wealthy*	*Unknown*	*Total*
% *Votes with* *Cosmopolitans*						
0–20	54.6	20.9	12.3	4.4	8.0	100.2
21–33	36.1	20.6	25.2	12.3	5.8	100.0
34–66	27.9	21.6	26.9	13.1	10.4	99.9
67–79	11.7	21.0	32.7	20.4	14.2	100.0
80–100	14.4	18.0	27.8	30.6	9.3	100.1
Legislative party						
Localist	58	37	24	15		
Neutral	25	29	31	22		
Cosmopolitan	17	34	45	63		
Total	100	100	100	100		

seem to have affected the political alignments. All bear an obvious
relationship to one another: did they affect behavior independently,
or are they merely different manifestations of the same factor? If
farming, for example, instead of being an independent variable,
coincided with residence—if men voted as they did because they
lived in a rural environment rather than because they farmed—
then the proportion of pro-Localist farmers ought to be the same
as the proportion of all pro-Localist voters in the locality. Instead
we find that farmers did favor the Localists by a slight, but consistently greater, percentage margin than did their neighbors generally:

	Frontier	Non-comm. Farm	Comm. Farm, Noncity	Plantation
All pro-Localists	55	63	34	17
Pro-Localist farmers	58	75	46	21

The same technique, applied to various groups, provided the
evidence in table 13.5. Here, by reading across, we can see that
large landowners, lawyers, and traders voted with the Cosmopolitans regardless of where they lived, but that the political preference of artisans depended upon their residence, not their occupation. Men of moderate property invariably joined the Localists
more often than did their neighbors, while wealthy and well-to-do
delegates preferred the Cosmopolitans regardless of residence. The
evidence also shows that residence itself was a factor independent
of both occupation and property.

Table 13.6 tests economic status as an effective variable by comparing it with occupation and residence. The figures indicate that
men of moderate property preferred the Localists, whatever their
occupation, while those with the largest estates chose the Cosmopolitans. The table also suggests that, regardless of occupation,
men voted pro-Localist if they lived on the frontier or in noncommercial farm areas and that, if they lived in and represented plantations, other commercial farm regions, or cities, they sided with the
Cosmopolitans. Therefore the tables indicate that all three factors
affected political behavior.

Most social and cultural characteristics influenced the delegates'
voting only occasionally. Young men demonstrated a slightly higher

Table 13.5. *Residence and Party Preference (in Percentages)*

	Frontier			Noncomm. Farm			Comm. Farm, Noncity			Plantation			Small Town			Major City		
	Loc.	Neu.	Cos.	Loc.	Neu.	Cos.	Loc.	Neu.	Cos.	Loc.	Neu.	Cos.	Loc.	Neu.	Cos.	Loc.	Neu.	Cos.
All delegates	55	31	13	63	23	14	34	28	38	17	31	51	19	32	49	1	16	83
Occupation																		
Farmer	58	37	5	75	21	5	46	26	28	21	45	33	20	53	27	—	—	—
Large landowner	18	46	36	55	29	15	28	41	31	20	27	53	—	—	—	—	—	—
Artisan	71	29	0	67	17	17	32	14	55	—	—	—	57	43	0	0	16	83
Lawyer	33	33	33	33	39	28	4	21	75	11	26	63	16	24	60	0	5	95
Trader	40	27	33	51	27	22	26	17	57	16	18	67	19	24	57	2	21	77
All nonfarmers	47	29	24	48	26	26	24	21	56	9	27	64						
Economic status																		
Moderate	64	27	8	72	21	7	54	24	22	23	46	31	39	37	34	0	27	73
Substantial	54	36	10	67	18	15	27	29	44	7	28	44	26	23	52	0	20	80
Well-to-do	36	36	29	44	37	19	24	32	44	24	29	47	13	34	53	3	18	79
Wealthy	17	67	17	43	30	26	30	25	46	13	25	62	0	20	80	0	13	87

Table 13.6. Occupation and Party Preference (in Percentages)

	Farmer			Large Landowner			Artisan			Doctor			Lawyer			Merchant		
	Loc.	Neu.	Cos.	Loc.	Neu.	Cos.	Loc.	Neu.	Cos.	Loc.	Neu.	Cos.	Loc.	Neu.	Cos.	Loc.	Neu.	Cos.
All delegates	54	29	17	27	33	41	47	21	33	22	27	52	13	24	64	5	24	72
Economic status																		
Moderate	65	25	10	—	—	—	58	31	13	25	42	33	17	33	50	—	—	—
Substantial	39	36	25	20	40	40	40	10	50	20	20	60	22	22	56	25	50	25
Well-to-do	32	38	30	29	39	33	38	13	50	25	19	56	14	18	68	5	30	66
Wealthy	—	—	—	24	25	51	—	—	—	10	20	70	7	24	69	3	18	77
Residence																		
Frontier	58	37	5	18	46	36	71	29	0									
Noncomm. farm	75	21	5	55	29	15	67	17	17	25	50	25	33	39	28	40	40	20
Comm. farm, noncity	46	26	28	29	41	31	32	14	55	32	24	44	4	21	75	0	14	86
Plantation	21	45	33	20	27	53	—	—	—	7	14	79	11	26	63	6	25	69
Small Town	—	—	—	—	—	—	57	43	0	—	—	—	16	24	60	11	33	56
City	—	—	—	—	—	—	0	16	83	0	0	100	0	5	95	2	19	79

percentage for the Cosmopolitans, though men over forty divided evenly:

Party	Under 30	30–39	40–49	50–59	Over 60
Localist	26	27	38	37	36
Neutral	25	25	24	26	33
Cosmopolitan	49	48	39	37	32

The explanation lies to some extent in the habit among rural constituencies of choosing older men than did town dwellers; however, this tendency existed apart from residence:

	Delegates under 40, by Residence (%)				
Party	Frontier	Noncomm. Farm	Plantation	Small Town	City
All delegates	13	14	51	49	84
Cosmopolitans	20	17	61	46	94

The composition of the two parties, in percentages, was:

Party	Under 40	40–49	Over 50	Total
Localist	32	37	31	100
Cosmopolitan	47	30	33	100

The median age for the Localist bloc was about forty-four; for the Cosmopolitans, about forty-two. This difference cannot be traced in the voting patterns except on a few issues, and, on the whole, age seems to have exercised only a minor influence.

The church affiliation of the delegates, determined for nearly half of the whole number,[2] indicates several clear tendencies. The Episcopalians preferred the Cosmopolitan bloc by a margin of five to two, and among the party's most steadfast adherents they outnumbered the next three religious groups combined. Also voting with the Cosmopolitans were 70 percent of the Quakers, almost all of whom lived in New Jersey and Pennsylvania. Methodists and

2. 664 out of 1,503, or 44%.

Baptists favored the Localists, while Lutherans and members of the Dutch Reformed Church divided about equally. The Presbyterians and Congregationalists both cast the majority of their votes with the Localists. In the latter case, the figures probably do not mean much, the differences being so slight as to indicate a trend only, subject to statistical error. The Presbyterians, on the other hand, had a long history of conflict with the Quakers and Anglicans in New York, New Jersey, and Pennsylvania. The controversy had theological roots, acquired political importance, was affected by differences in the pattern of settlement, and took on new life during the Revolution, when most Quakers and many Anglicans in these states remained loyal or neutral while the Presbyterians became active in the rebellion.

The preference of Presbyterians for the Localists, therefore, seems reasonable. Yet their voting can be explained almost entirely as a result of where they lived; they might very well have voted as they did had they belonged to some other denomination.[3] By contrast, Episcopalians and Quakers voted more often with the Cosmopolitans than did other delegates from the same areas (see table 13.7).

The data for those whose church affiliation is unknown correspond quite closely with the general percentage and increase one's confidence in the reliability of the table; still, the figures cannot be taken literally, but are suggestive only. They show that the Congregationalists preferred the Localist bloc more than one would expect in certain areas but not in others, so no general trend appears. Presbyterians voted as everyone else did except in the small towns, so that for them also religion by itself lacks statistical significance. Both Quakers and Episcopalians, however, supported the Cosmopolitan group more and the Localists less at almost every point, which suggests (though it does not prove) a causal relationship. Religion can be considered as a factor that operated in certain circumstances, primarily for these two denominations, and on particular issues.[4]

3. It could be argued that the areas of Localist strength might not have voted as they did without the Presbyterians to affect political attitudes. We can, however, trace Localism in areas quite devoid of Presbyterians. Perhaps we may concede Presbyterianism local importance while denying it any fundamental, pervasive significance. Whether localism as a world view was necessarily connected with a particular religious orientation remains to be proven.

4. The reader must remember that the data being analyzed derive from roll calls on economic, social, and political issues and that the alignment on cultural questions rarely conforms to the patterns under consideration. Such issues as slavery and the relation between church and state probably did involve religious convictions.

Table 13.7. Religion with Residence: Party Preference (in Percentages)

	Residence									
	Frontier		Noncomm. Farm		Comm. Farm, Noncity		Small Town		Major City	
	Loc.	Cos.	Loc.	Cos.	Loc.	Cos.	Loc.	Cos.	Loc.	Cos.
All delegates	55	13	63	14	34	38	19	49	1	83
Religion										
Episcopalian	0	40	60	20	36	42	0	75	0	89
Congregationalist	25	0	87	8	46	24	8	83	0	100
Presbyterian	57	14	57	14	31	35	48	22	0	71
Quaker	—	—	—	—	16	69	0	100	0	83
Unknown	60	14	64	13	35	37	13	53	2	83

The legislators' national origins exerted no discernible influence on the political alignment (see table 13.8). Two possible exceptions are the French preference for the Cosmopolitans (50 to 14 percent), which seems due to their concentration in the South Carolina low country, and that of former New Englanders for the Localists (42 to 4 percent), which occurred primarily because they settled on the New York frontier and in East Jersey. Otherwise the principal groups divided in random fashion. Slight variations from the norm can easily be explained by statistical inadequacies and patterns of settlement.

Table 13.8. National Origin and Party Preference (in Percentages)

	Colonial, English	Colonial, Scottish	Colonial, Scotch-Irish	Colonial, German	Colonial, Dutch	Immigrant, English	Immigrant, Scottish	Immigrant, North Irish
Localist	34	39	48	42	23	29	32	43
Neutral	26	19	17	19	53	29	23	22
Cosmopolitan	41	42	35	39	24	42	46	35

The social and economic family background of the delegates proved much less influential than expected. Men who grew up on farms did prefer the Localist bloc by a margin of two to one (47 to 24 percent, with 29 percent neutral), but men who themselves farmed supported the same group by a much greater majority. Table 13.9 compares the votes of the delegates generally with those whose fathers can be identified. It indicates that the sons of large landowners, artisans, manufacturers, and shopkeepers, like the sons of farmers, tended to vote a little less often with the Localists than one would anticipate, while the sons of ministers, doctors, lawyers, and merchants voted more often with the Localists than might be expected. For example, 13 percent of the lawyers voted with the Localists, but 27 percent of the sons of lawyers did so. Environment seems therefore to have exerted a reverse effect, if it had any at all. The bottom half of table 13.9, which compares the legislators' (sons') economic status with that of their fathers, reinforces the conclusion that what the delegates themselves did and became influenced them more than what their fathers had been.

The social status of the delegates' families may have affected their lives in many ways, but its political significance seems minor.

Table 13.9. Family Background and Party Preference (in Percentages)

	Localist		Neutral		Cosmopolitan	
	All Delegates	Sons Only	All Delegates	Sons Only	All Delegates	Sons Only
Occupation						
Large landowner	27	20	33	29	41	51
Artisan	47	38	21	30	33	32
Manufacturer	37	17	20	30	44	53
Minister	13	25	13	39	76	36
Doctor	22	33	27	19	52	48
Lawyer	13	27	24	33	64	41
Shopkeeper	43	25	15	25	43	50
Merchant	5	11	24	22	72	67
Unknown	45	40	31	25	24	35
Economic status[a]						
Moderate	58	46	25	31	17	23
Substantial	37	32	29	43	34	25
Well-to-do	24	26	31	33	45	42
Wealthy	15	15	22	27	63	58
Unknown	28	41	31	24	42	36

NOTE: [a] Based on half of the representatives.

Social rank, as defined here, incorporates the data concerning the father's economic background with other factors, such as the mother's family, the prestige of the parents, and whether the representative began as an immigrant. The basic information derived for over 90 percent of the men, but involving a good deal of guesswork, is presented in part I of table 13.10.

Table 13.10. Social Origin and Party Preference (in Percentages)

I. Social Origin, All Delegates

	Humble Origin					
	Colonial	Immi-grant	Average Family	Above-Avg. Family	Prominent Old Family	Unknown
Localist	43	40	41	19	15	41
Neutral	30	21	28	37	20	24
Cosmopolitan	27	39	31	44	65	35

II. Social Origin, Steadfast Party Voters

	Humble Origin	Average Family	Above-Avg. Family	Prominent Old Family	Unknown	Total
Localist	19	60	5	2	14	100
Cosmopolitan	14	41	13	20	12	100

The slight preference of the man of lowly birth for the Localist bloc, shown in this table, becomes insignificant when compared with the much greater allegiance of men who owned moderate properties or farmed. Also, the voting behavior of men coming from prominent families corresponds precisely with that of wealthy delegates. The influence of social origin is less visible near the center of the political spectrum than at its extremes. The most steadfast voters of the two parties and their social origin are shown in the second part of table 13.10; on the whole, the difference between them seems unimpressive. The effect of high social rank can be traced in the alignment on certain issues, but it forms only a small part of the total pattern.

About one out of six delegates had risen above his parents' social and economic rank. Some of these became important leaders of the Localist bloc, but even more often they joined the men of wealth and prestige on the other side:

	Mobile	Not Mobile	Unknown
Localist	27%	38%	28%
Neutral	24	29	18
Cosmopolitan	49	33	55

The influence of education appears in certain votes and is especially traceable among college graduates. The areas that chose Localist delegates contained few men of education, who clustered instead in towns and on large landed estates. Residence alone would therefore incline the college man toward the Cosmopolitans. In addition, most men of learning probably owned large properties to start with or quickly acquired them and became professional men, thus naturally tending toward the same side. The question becomes, then, did they vote as Cosmopolitans even more frequently than men of the same economic status and occupation? The figures in table 13.11 support the conclusion that a college education predisposed men to support the Cosmopolitan bloc independently of occupation or wealth, while the lack of any known formal schooling influenced them, though in a less degree, toward the Localists. Since fewer than 10 percent of the representatives obtained a college education or its equivalent, the factor had a limited effect, but entered as a minor element in the total equation.

The same generalization applies to the characteristic of intellectual interest. Although men who exhibited no intellectuality favored the Localists, they did so to a degree too small for significance—even less than men with no education. Those who can be considered intellectuals voted as did college men, though less uniformly, but they made up only one-sixth of the delegates and affected the voting only occasionally.

Intellectual Interest	Localist	Neutral	Cosmopolitan
Some	17%	26%	57%
None	41	28	31

On the other hand, the distinction between world views, cosmopolitan versus localist, gains strength upon examination. Those

Table 13.11. Education and Party Preference (in Percentages)

	Loc.	Neu.	Cos.	Total	Loc.	Neu.	Cos.	Total	Loc.	Neu.	Cos.	Total
	Farmers				Large Landowners				Lawyers			
All delegates	54	29	17	100	27	33	41	101	13	24	64	101
No education known	66	23	11	100	30	34	35	99	25	25	50	100
College	75	—	25	100	32	23	44	99	8	23	70	100
	Merchants				Moderate Property				Substantial Property			
All delegates	5	24	72	101	58	25	17	100	37	29	34	101
No education known	0	25	75	100	67	21	12	100	49	30	22	101
College	0	28	72	100	18	27	55	100	7	20	73	100
	Well-to-do				Wealthy				All delegates			
All delegates	24	31	45	100	15	22	63	100	36	27	37	100
No education known	27	33	40	100	27	17	56	100	47	25	28	100
College	24	26	50	100	5	22	73	100	14	23	63	100

with the former outlook supported the Cosmopolitan party nearly four to one, while delegates with the latter world view voted with the Localists by a margin of not far from three to one. As table 13.12 shows, the contrast becomes sharpest among the most consistent voters. The top part of the table outlines the political spectrum, gauged by the percentage of votes cast with the Cosmopolitans. (Thus the column headed by "0–20 percent" represents the most loyal Localists.) The bottom section expresses in a different way the world views that predominated in the parties' various elements. Although only one out of five delegates was a man of cosmopolitan view, they made up nearly a third of the Cosmopolitan bloc. If one out of three adherents of that bloc whose world view is unknown were a cosmopolitan (a fair guess), then nearly half of the party and 60 percent of the most consistent voters were cosmopolitan men.

Table 13.12.   World View and Party Preference I (in Percentages)

I. % Votes with Cosmopolitans

World View	Localist ◄———— 0–20%	21–33%	34–66%	67–79%	————► Cosmopolitan 80–100%	Total
Localist	40.8	14.1	25.0	7.0	13.2	100.1
Cosmopolitan	8.4	8.1	23.9	10.8	48.8	100.0
Uncertain	17.2	7.2	31.8	15.4	28.4	100.0

II. Political Spectrum

World View	Extreme Localist	Moderate Localist	Neutral	Moderate Cosmopolitan	Extreme Cosmopolitan
Localist	68.5	58.7	39.3	27.6	21.9
Cosmopolitan	6.5	15.5	17.3	19.6	37.3
Uncertain	25.0	25.8	43.4	52.8	40.9
Total	100.0	100.0	100.0	100.0	100.1

The dichotomy between world views bears a close relationship to the delegates' residence and probably also to their occupation and economic status, so its influence must be tested in comparison with these. As the first segment of table 13.13 indicates, the cultural point of view sharply distinguishes the two parties in every locality except the last, "major city." However, the table also demonstrates that the delegates' residence influenced their voting regardless of whether they were localists or cosmopolitans.[5]

The cosmopolitan man usually enjoyed a larger income than his cultural opposite because as a rule only wealth's advantages enabled one to become a cosmopolitan (note the figures in the "number" columns of 13.13). Which factor, then, wealth or world view, really affected voting—or did both? The data in 13.13 show that regardless of economic status the cosmopolitan man always preferred the Cosmopolitan bloc and the localists, vice versa. Nevertheless property also influenced political behavior independently of world view, for the more wealth a delegate owned, the greater his preference for the Cosmopolitan group (see the table). The two factors reinforced each other.

The same question of independence or interdependence arises with respect to occupation and world view, for the farmer seldom, and professionals usually, became cosmopolitan men. The facts confirm this obvious relationship (again note those under the "number" headings in table 13.13), but at the same time, regardless of occupation, cosmopolitan men voted with the Cosmopolitan bloc (farmers excepted), and localists voted with the Localist party (merchants excepted). Conversely, the independent influence of occupation upon voting is very clear in table 13.13, especially in the case of farmers and merchants at the two extremes of the political spectrum. We conclude, then, that the cosmopolitan-localist factor contributed substantially to the political alignment, but was not by itself determinative.

On the other hand, the military and political experience of the legislators influenced their conduct only in limited ways. Service as an officer (not an enlisted man) in the Continental army had the same effect as, and probably formed part of, the cosmopolitan attitude. Colonels and generals in particular heavily favored the Cosmopolitan bloc, but lower-ranking officers shared the same preference. High-ranking militia officers, by contrast, divided evenly, and the rest more often supported the Localists. Enlisted men usually did so, while those who saw no service voted indifferently.

5. Thus among localists voting with the Localist bloc the proportions varied with residence as follows: major city, 1%; town, 32%; commercial farm, 48%; noncommercial farm, 73%; and frontier, 65% (characteristic decline); among cosmopolitans voting with the Cosmopolitan party the percentages varied with residence as follows: noncommercial farm, 27%; commercial farm, 50%; small town, 59%; city, 83%.

Table 13.13. World View and Party Preference II

	General			Localist World View						Cosmopolitan World View					
	Loc.	Neu.	Cos.	Loc.		Neu.		Cos.		Loc.		Neu.		Cos.	
				No.	%	No.	%	No.	%	No.	%	No.	%	No.	%
All delegates					55		25		20		17		24		60
Residence[a]															
Frontier	55	31	13		65		27		8		50		14		36
Noncommercial farm	63	23	14		73		19		8		47		27		27
Comm. farm, noncity	34	28	38		48		26		26		20		30		50
Plantation	17	31	51		21		38		41		16		25		59
Small town	19	32	49		32		29		39		9		32		59
Major city	1	16	83		1		15		83		0		17		83
Economic status															
Moderate	58	25	17	(212)	65	(74)	23	(38)	12	(6)	29	(6)	29	(9)	43
Substantial	37	29	34	(77)	51	(35)	23	(40)	26	(9)	26	(11)	31	(15)	43
Well-to-do	24	31	45	(42)	44	(33)	34	(21)	22	(14)	15	(24)	26	(55)	59
Wealthy	15	22	63	(8)	28	(10)	35	(11)	38	(17)	13	(25)	19	(87)	67
Occupation															
Farmer	54	29	17	(223)	62	(87)	24	(49)	14	(7)	47	(4)	27	(4)	27
Artisan-manufacturer	42	21	38	(23)	46	(12)	24	(15)	30	(3)	23	(5)	39	(5)	39
Large landowner	27	33	41	(26)	34	(30)	39	(21)	27	(12)	24	(14)	27	(25)	49
All professional	17	23	61	(9)	41	(5)	24	(8)	36	(15)	12	(29)	24	(80)	65
Merchant	5	24	72	(1)	13	(2)	25	(5)	63	(4)	6	(15)	22	(48)	72

NOTE: [a] Numbers of delegates are not included in this section of the table.

	Continental Officer (%)			Militia Officer (%)		
	Loc.	Neu.	Cos.	Loc.	Neu.	Cos.
Lt.—Capt.—Major	20	41	39	47	27	26
Lt. Col.—Col.—Gen.	15	25	60	39	28	34

The following percentages show that political experience also did not affect the alignment except for the holders of Continental posts, who usually belonged to the Cosmopolitan bloc.

	None	Local	Sher-iff, etc.	Misc. State	Sena-tor	Judge	Conti-nental
Localist	34	44	40	25	40	23	19
Neutral	26	28	32	24	23	23	23
Cosmopolitan	40	29	28	41	36	54	58

Finally, political ideology probably influenced the delegates, as their vote on ratification suggests. Their subsequent party affiliation confirms that influence and suggests further implications. Among 84 members of the Localist bloc, 71 (85 percent) became Jeffersonian Republicans, while 102 out of 143 Cosmopolitan delegates became Federalists (71 percent). The correlation was even higher among the most consistent voters, reaching 80 percent (130 out of 162).

This extensive examination has revealed several factors that, taken together, seem to account for political alignments during the 1780s. The most important single influence was the delegates' residence, which included their own environment and the kind of constituency that they represented. Although the situation varied from state to state, and New Jersey seems an exception, the differences based upon residence may be described by three sets of adjectives: first, urban versus rural, in that the core members of one party lived in or near towns and reflected urban interests in their voting, while their opposites centered in the regions more remote from the towns and expressed rural objectives; second, commercial versus agrarian, since one bloc attracted support from the most highly commercial farms as well as from the towns, whereas the other dominated the least commercial agricultural regions; third, cosmopolitan versus localist, for the delegates who lived in cosmopolitan areas—or who themselves had viewed the world extensively —opposed those who dwelled in areas isolated from the world and who themselves had limited experience. The last contrast also appeared in the voting with respect to affairs that were external to or transcendent of the community—this applies to most important issues. Environment, then, includes facets usually termed economic but in reality involves the culture of the people.

Other factors reinforced or modified the sectional influence. The representatives' occupation was of course related to their residence, for most men in subsistence farm areas were farmers and sent farmers to the legislature about half of the time, just as plantation counties chose planters half the time and towns sent men who were not farmers almost all of the time. But occupation itself affected the alignment. Wherever they lived, delegates who were farmers (again as opposed to large landowners) voted with the Localists more often than did other representatives from the same area, while professional men and men in trade opposed them by margins that reached four or five or even a hundred to one in plantation counties and towns. Farmers as here defined generally lived a restricted existence, well described as parochial or narrow. Circumstances forced them to concentrate on farming, to think of little but farming: to become agrarian in their view of life. Large landowners, doctors, lawyers, judges, and most traders generally had a much broader view—continental, cosmopolitan, urbane. Thus residence plus occupation equals most aspects of the two parties. These might most accurately be called *agrarian-localist* and *commercial-cosmopolitan*, designations that express the unity, the cluster of influences, making up the two political cultures.

The economic status of the delegates also affected their political position. Men of "substantial" property showed little preference. But men owning less, which is to say possessing only slightly above the average, supported the Localists more often than did delegates from similar districts, the same occupation, or with any other quality in common. Therefore the Localist group was not just an agrarian-localist party, but the party of the small property holder (three-fourths of the total). In contrast, over half, and probably over 60 percent, of the Cosmopolitans owned large properties (64 percent of those whose economic status is known), and such men favored that side regardless of their other characteristics. The bitter controversies over debtor relief and monetary policy, together with some other issues, become explicable only if this difference in wealth is added to the equation. In every section conflicts appeared between economic classes and interests.

Finally, several minor influences affected the alignment. They are minor because they applied only to a small proportion of the delegates, concerned few issues, or were components of other factors. These influences included a tendency on the part of the younger delegates to side with the Cosmopolitans; a Quaker and Episcopalian preference for the same group; a division between college graduates and intellectuals, who voted with the Cosmopolitans, and men lacking education, who opposed them; very strong support for that bloc by men with experience in Continental military and civil offices, which service formed part of the cosmopolitan attitude; an equally emphatic preference by men of upper-class origin, related also to cosmopolitanism and probably to economic status; and a nationalistic, strong-government ideology, leading many of the Cosmopolitan members to Federalism, versus a particularistic, weak-government political attitude influencing Localist delegates toward Antifederalism and Jeffersonian Republicanism—a factor that intersects with and reinforces the foregoing dichotomies. All of these forces created the persistent political alignments of the 1780s. Collectively they make possible a profile of each party as it had developed by 1787.

Both major groups resulted from a combination of four major factors: residence (or the nature of a delegates' constituency), occupation, wealth, and world view. The proportions of these factors varied from state to state and party to party. In all four of the northern states studied in detail, the most significant influences in forming the Localist bloc were wealth and world view. Of the Localist delegates in those legislatures, 95 percent were either small property owners or localists or both, while the northern Cosmopolitans represented above all the towns and commercial farming areas; most were engaged in occupations other than farming. These two factors of residence plus occupation accounted for 92 percent of the members of that bloc. In the South different components seem more important. The localist world view again was a major ingredient in forming the Localist bloc, this time in conjunction with residence, so that 96 percent of the Localists lived in areas characterized by small farms and a parochial world view. The southern Cosmopolitans, like the northern, were primarily men other than farmers, plus large property owners, the two combined accounting for 93 percent of the bloc. To summarize:

northern Localists = small property owners + localists
southern Localists = farming areas other than plantations + localists
northern Cosmopolitans = commercial areas + men not farmers
southern Cosmopolitans= large property owners + men not farmers

Of the four factors, place of residence exercised the most influence statistically, accounting for at least 96 percent of the bloc members either as a primary or a secondary factor. Next most important was world view, affecting 90 percent. Third in significance came occupation, 84 percent, and finally economic status, 79 percent.[6]

The agrarian-localist bloc, or Localists, drew over four-fifths of its supporters from a hundred counties, almost all of which lay inland from the coast. These counties were rural, containing mostly small farms with only scattered large estates and a few towns. While the counties did produce a surplus, primarily of agricultural products, it was insufficient for wealth, and the people themselves had to provide most of what they needed. Few could acquire large property or purchase slaves and servants. The typical representative was himself a farmer. He owned property worth

6. The following figures show what proportion of the delegates in a given bloc can be accounted for by each major factor. The most significant percentages are in italics. The table understates the importance of residence throughout. For example, the division in New Jersey was basically sectional, but this does not appear in the table, which records most to least commercial.

	Northern Localists					Northern Cosmopolitans				
	General	Mass.	N.Y.	N.J.	Pa.	Gen.	Mass.	N.Y.	N.J.	Pa.
World view	88	*99*	87	58	87	57	49	70	56	55
Residence	71	76	76	26	55	*85*	*81*	93	*81*	84
Occupation	64	71	70	48	60	78	85	87	60	76
Economic status	89	93	*84*	77	*91*	49	45	75	52	39

	Southern Localists					Southern Cosmopolitans				
	General	Md.	Va.	N.C.	S.C.	Gen.	Md.	Va.	N.C.	S.C.
World view	88	*81*	63	88	94	62	49	60	69	73
Residence	*81*	54	87	91	92	70	*81*	50	56	83
Occupation	45	53	37	57	41	90	79	93	89	*100*
Economic status	53	39	65	68	65	*81*	73	76	90	*91*

about £1,000, well above the average and sufficient for a decent living, though not for luxuries. Even in the South he probably lacked a slave. It seems likely that a good many of these legislators owed money: certainly their constituents did. Most of them, if they attended church at all, belonged to the Congregational or Presbyterian churches or, in the South, to the Episcopal Church. About half saw military service, almost always as militia officers, so that they served briefly and seldom far from home. If they held any civil office before their election, it required only local duties. Their fathers probably had been farmers of small property.[7] They lacked formal education or intellectual interest and, since their experience was so restricted, they did not envision a world much greater than that of the locality. These delegates primarily sought to help their own people—their fellow farmers and small property holders. The appellation "agrarian-localist" applies to 90 percent of the party's more consistent members.

The party also contained two major subspecies. First, about one in nine was a large landowner, and perhaps an equal number were prosperous commercial farmers, living fairly near markets or along major transportation routes. Such men often voted with the Cosmopolitans, but a fourth or a third of them supported the Localists. The obvious reason is that they regarded themselves primarily as agrarians, and no doubt some, despite their advantages, shared a localist viewpoint. The southern planters, as everyone knows, produced many such men.

Second, about one-fourth of the lesser nonfarm delegates also belonged to the Localist party. These artisans and mechanics, shopkeepers, innkeepers, millers, and the like often lived in the same noncommercial farm areas as did the majority of the bloc, where they were chosen to represent the agrarian-localist interest and did so.[8] Moreover they generally owned small properties (over two-thirds) and shared that characteristic together with the various other qualities that distinguished the Localists.

The party did of course attract a few merchants and professional men, but not very many (about fifty, or less than 10 percent of the total), and as a rule these had relatively small properties (58 percent of those known) or represented the farm communities.

7. Three out of five fathers were farmers. Among those whose economic status is known, half had moderate properties and a ninth possessed substantial wealth.
8. Among 92 such men, 52 (57%) lived in noncommercial farm areas or on the frontier, and 22 (35%) lived in commercial farm communities that were not of the plantation type.

Only a fraction failed to conform in some characteristic to the agrarian-localist type.

The commercial-cosmopolitan delegates, or Cosmopolitans as we will continue to call them, concentrated in a different hundred-odd counties[9] that also held over 80 percent of the bloc. Almost all of these districts lay on the coast or along a navigable river. The typical delegate lived in a town or a highly commercialized farming area within easy reach of a trading center. He himself engaged in trade, a profession, or large-scale commercial agriculture, occupations that necessarily placed him in touch with the world and enabled him to participate in the social and cultural life of the towns. He was well-to-do or wealthy, owning at least £2,000 worth of property, which enabled him to purchase luxury goods, live in comfort, educate his children, and acquire a little "culture" himself, if he wished. He usually had several slaves or servants. He might owe money, but his assets probably exceeded his debts. He attended the Episcopal or Congregational or (in the middle states) the Quaker church. He was much more apt than his political opponent to have served as a Continental army officer or in a high civil post, he perhaps obtained some formal education, and he probably had an extensive view of the world. Most of these men started with social advantages, occasionally coming from prominent families. Although some owned farms, they were fundamentally businessmen rather than farmers, and while some lived in the country, they were more urban than rural.

The Cosmopolitans also attracted two secondary elements. Most important numerically were the farmers, who contributed one out of six members. Almost all of these (87 percent) lived in commercial farming areas, and they were apt to have substantial or even fairly large properties. A group almost equal in number consisted of artisans, lesser tradesmen, and the like. Of these, half owned large property, and many lived in towns, so that they shared at least one characteristic with the commercial-cosmopolitan group.

Once the composition of the two legislative parties is clearly understood, their attitudes toward the issues of the day are seen to form a logical, consistent whole, and the patterns made by their voting becames natural, if not indeed inevitable (see table 13.14). The agrarian-localists, or Localists, tried to reduce government costs because they received very little benefit from such expenditures once the war ended: they and their constituents held few

9. Among the 288 most consistent members of the two parties, only 28 lived in areas controlled by their opponents.

Table 13.14. Bloc Votes on Major Issues

Type of Vote	No. of Votes	No. of States	Number of Voters Loc.	Neu.	Cos.	Total	Percentages Loc.	Neu.	Cos.	Total	Loc. Less Cos. (%)
For lower salary, governor	7	4	164– 30	55– 45	39–118	258–193	85	55	25	57	+60
For lower salary, judges	12	4	113– 71	63– 63	67–108	243–242	61	50	38	50	+23
For lower salary, Congress	7	3	63– 31	32– 40	28– 50	251–247	67	44	35	51	+32
For lower salary, assembly	8	4	36–138	61– 60	115– 56	212–254	21	51	67	45	–46
For lower salary, misc.	19	7	310– 74	122–117	89–300	522–490	81	51	23	51	+58
Against paying state debts	9	6	128– 49	56– 90	43–124	227–263	72	39	26	46	+46
Against state expenses	19	4	225– 88	106–130	73–234	404–452	72	45	24	47	+48
Against permanent salaries	3	3	38– 10	23– 13	8– 40	69– 63	79	64	17	52	+62
Against taxes, general	8	6	111– 48	48– 75	42–103	201–226	70	39	29	47	+41
Against collection of taxes	8	7	109– 44	43– 53	28– 82	180–172	71	45	25	51	+46
Against land taxes	6	3	85– 31	43– 44	27– 80	155–155	73	49	31	50	+42
For nonfarm taxes	5	4	90– 29	33– 45	27– 61	150–135	76	42	31	53	+45
For low land prices	5	4	89– 15	30– 30	14– 95	133–140	85	50	14	49	+71
Favoring settlers, tenants	8	5	117– 33	37– 35	31– 91	182–159	78	51	25	53	+53
Antiurban	5	3	59– 9	17– 27	11– 66	87– 92	87	40	14	48	+73
Antibusiness, banks	5	1	98– 14	11– 18	20–121	129–153	88	38	14	46	+74
Against aid to business	4	3	67– 23	16– 14	15– 65	98–102	74	53	19	49	+55
For stay, installment laws	12	6	221– 59	75– 63	51–198	347–320	79	54	20	52	+59
Favoring debtors	15	5	231– 92	101–120	105–263	437–475	71	46	28	48	+43
For passage of paper money	11	5	153– 22	75– 37	25–116	253–175	87	67	18	59	+69
For more paper money	6	3	88– 15	32– 30	18– 77	138–122	85	52	19	53	+66
For paper as legal tender	8	3	147– 8	32– 44	21–102	200–154	95	42	17	57	+78

Table 13.14—Continued

Type of Vote	No. of Votes	No. of States	Number of Voters				Percentages				Loc. Less Cos. (%)
			Loc.	Neu.	Cos.	Total	Loc.	Neu.	Cos.	Total	
For paper money, misc.	7	5	117– 10	51– 44	30– 99	198–153	92	54	23	56	+69
Against Congress's requisitions	4	2	47– 45	19– 23	26– 44	92–112	51	45	37	45	+14
Against other grants	9	5	218– 31	73– 51	27–149	318–241	88	59	15	57	+73
Against impost	4	3	49– 17	25– 33	21– 40	99– 90	74	43	33	52	+41
For loyalty oaths	7	3	126– 26	31– 35	8–145	165–206	83	47	5	44	+78
Antiloyalist, misc.	4	2	57– 8	15– 20	12– 62	84– 90	88	43	16	48	+72
For confisc. loyalists' property	7	4	174– 34	67– 65	53–178	294–277	84	51	23	51	+61
Against paying debts to loyalists	5	3	86– 32	54– 46	38–120	178–198	73	54	24	47	+49
Against admitting loyalists	8	4	137– 37	47– 66	30–115	214–218	79	42	21	51	+58
Favoring slaves, Negroes	15	5	154–228	131– 87	217–118	502–433	40	60	65	54	−25
For support of religion	7	3	63– 78	47– 53	79– 41	189–172	45	47	64	52	−19
For support of education	7	3	30– 96	56– 42	109– 25	195–163	24	57	81	54	−57
For support of theater	5	2	35– 83	28– 28	68– 41	131–152	31	50	62	46	−32

offices and few certificates, performed few services, built most of their own roads, hired their own ministers, paid for their own schools (if they had any), helped their own poor, provided most of their other needs, and asked only to be left alone. They resented paying taxes on land or other necessities; if other people wanted the government to spend money, they could tax themselves. As representatives of small property holders from relatively poor communities, always short of money, they naturally sought relief for debtors and an adequate supply of money at low interest rates. They voted against banks and the desires of businessmen and city folk. They resisted the return of well-to-do loyalists who would support the other side. They tended to be narrow-minded: their antiloyalist, anti-British prejudice formed part of this, as did their skepticism about state-supported colleges, their reluctance to obey the British treaty, and their unwillingness to grant power to Congress or to form a strong central government. They trusted no one but themselves (often with much reason), and this led to an emphasis upon simple democracy, in which they would regulate their own affairs without help from or interference by external, hostile, and probably corrupt outsiders.

To the commercial-cosmopolitans almost everything that governments did was beneficial as long as they themselves exercised power—as, in one way or another, they generally could. They approved of paying the debt, not simply because they received the interest and principal, but because they believed that governments should always maintain their credit, solvency, and reputation. They benefited from and saw the reason for paying good salaries to competent officials, establishing courts, improving transportation, aiding economic growth, providing a stable monetary system, and keeping order. They agreed to contribute money for these returns, but they wanted everyone else to share the expense and to pay their taxes promptly. They believed in collecting and paying private obligations as well. They approved of authority in government, supported Congress, and almost unanimously voted for the Constitution. As urbane men of broad views, they could easily forgive loyalists, support colleges, favor the economic and cultural growth of towns. The kind of democracy advocated by the other side they regarded as menacing, because it meant government by narrow men, who possessed little or no property, were unfit to rule, and really sought no government at all.

These two opposing attitudes and clusters of ideas appear not only in the voting but in other forms of expression. One of the best statements of the commercial-cosmopolitan side we owe to James Iredell and the town of Edenton, North Carolina.[10] Iredell, a lawyer, did not serve in the legislature but waged the battle outside it and encouraged his friends within it, while the town of Edenton naturally selected delegates from the urban elite. A series of resolutions from Edenton, which Iredell presumably wrote, called for maintaining public order, upholding the state's credit by paying the interest and principal of the debt, paying the officers and soldiers, and in general putting finances in good order. Liberal salaries for judges and the attorney-general would render them independent and attract good men. The townspeople opposed the return only of "open" loyalists (evidently not of others). They resolved against paper money and urged repeal of the state's stay law. They hoped to encourage the most useful manufactures and trade and to promote the settlement of merchants. To that end they recommended the removal of the tax on stock in trade. They applauded Washington's nationalistic circular letter, lamented the failure of the 5 percent impost, urged the necessity of union, and supported Congress in all its requests, including monetary ones.

On the other side, the Massachusetts farmers expressed agrarian-localist views in many lists of grievances during 1786. The Worcester County convention, for example, hoped to alter the location of the capital, print paper money, aid farmers and manufacturers rather than speculators and traders, abolish some courts, reduce salaries, stop using the money from the impost and excise for paying the state debt and apply it to the foreign debt instead, cut government costs, lessen the insolence and wealth of lawyers, deny the supplementary fund to Congress but instead pay holders of the old Continental money, delay the collection of the current tax, relieve those debtors owing money to loyalists, and amend the state constitution. To these kinds of people a newspaper writer, speaking for the commercial-cosmopolitans, recommended decorum, obedience, and reverence to their representatives, who had taken an oath to obey the laws and the constitution and therefore could not undertake any innovation. He assured everyone that the legislature would never emit paper, pass a tender act, scale down the state debt, or revise the constitution, because these measures were so obviously iniquitous. He closed by urging an enlargement of the

10. Griffith J. McRee, *Life and Correspondence of James Iredell* (New York, 1857–1858), II, 60–66.

powers of Congress, for "unless the spirit is laid asleep, which at-tributes all power, and subjects all property to the breath of a democratick assembly, we are a lost, undone people."[11]

An entertaining description of the Localist point of view was presented in what purported to be the soliloquy of a clam digger from the south side of Queens County on Long Island. He suggested that the legislature had given $500 to lawyers to rub up some old fusty books and that, everything considered, the state would be better off without the legislature or the lawyers. Every man should work for his living, declared the digger, who also vowed that, if given the power, he would pass a law making dried clams a tender for everything equal to gold.[12]

This article suggests that people of the time recognized the existence of characteristic political attitudes. The historian always welcomes such contemporary recognition, for without it he must question, if not the reality, then certainly the significance of his conclusions and wonder whether he has constructed a past that did not exist. He must inquire, in the present case, how the men of the Revolutionary era looked at the political alignments and whether they perceived the beginning of parties.

Men of the period preferred to describe rather than to analyze, and comparatively few commented on the theoretical implications of what they observed. Their newspapers and letters show them busy campaigning for election in a manner often new and calling for the choice of preferred candidates. "Crito" warned his Boston readers in 1785 that newspapers were deviating from the "good *old way*" by announcing men as eligible for representatives; the next step would be that men offered themselves as candidates, a "shameful" method.[13] Similarly a Connecticut correspondent bragged that, whereas in the middle and southern states "men meanly stoop to advertise for an office, or beg the votes of their countrymen," in Connecticut no election produced a dispute.[14] But that was ceasing to be true in both of these New England states. Within a few years candidates were "hawking" themselves, and newspapers carried tickets.[15] Elsewhere James Wilkinson bragged that he won by 240 votes after speaking for three and a

11. *Mass. Gaz.* (Boston), June 15, 19, 1787.
12. *New Haven Gaz.*, Apr. 20, 1786.
13. *American Herald* (Boston), Apr. 25, 1785.
14. *Columbian Herald* (Charleston), Dec. 4, 1786.
15. Thomas Dwight to Theodore Sedgwick, Springfield, Feb. 1, 1789, Sedgwick Papers, Box A, Mass. Hist. Soc.

half hours.[16] Philadelphia papers described the most energetic contests: "The ensuing election bids fair to produce a most violent
campaign. No exertions are spared on either side. All the arts of
electioneering are put in force. . . . Each party seems equally con-
fident of success."[17]

This politicking remained individual in most of the states, but
in Pennsylvania, New York, Rhode Island, and at the end, Massachusetts, groups of men campaigned together for recognized goals.
Meanwhile in all of the legislatures men had been combining into
sides, or factions, or blocs, or parties in the eighteenth-century
sense. This development aroused intense criticism in all sections of
the country, as a few examples will show. A South Carolinian set
it down as a maxim that "the strength and union of parties—the
ambition—the wealth—and even the popularity of individuals,
should be carefully watched and properly restrained in all repub-
lics,"[18] while Christopher Gadsden assured his readers that he was
"a professed disapprover of all political parties in our circumstances, and long to see *no* parties at all amongst us, but every
citizen *striving* to make each other as happy as he can."[19] A Maryland writer reported that the people's representatives were dis-
honest and ignorant because voters were influenced by "party and
faction," not reason and regard of fitness.[20] "The Impartial Exam-
iner" in New Jersey condemned parties as "the dangerous diseases
of civil freedom; they are only the first stage of anarchy, cloathed
in mild language."[21] "A Pennsylvanian" warned the voters to "distrust men of violent party spirit . . . [who] would wish to split
the state into factions"; instead they should choose men of property, education, integrity, and knowledge of foreign affairs.[22] From
London, William Bingham wrote that an inevitable result of popular assemblies occurred "when Individuals, possessed of popular
Talents, come forward, and put themselves at the Head of a Party,
and enlist in their Service a Set of inferiour Persons. . . . The
Sooner we can effectually destroy the Spirit of Party in Republican Governments, the more we shall promote the Happiness of

16. To James Hutchinson, Kentucky, Aug. 18, 1786, Society Collection, Hist.
Soc. Pa.

17. *Pa. Evening Herald* (Philadelphia), Oct. 5, 1785.

18. *The South-Carolina Gazette, and Public Advertiser* (Charleston), July 24,
1784.

19. *Gaz. of S.C.* (Charleston), Aug. 5, 1785.

20. *Md. Jour.* (Baltimore), Aug. 30, 1785.

21. *N.-J. Gaz.* (Trenton), Jan. 13, 1779.

22. *Pa. Jour.* (Philadelphia), Sept. 11, 1782.

Society."[23] In Dover, Delaware, an election oration exhorted the people to "be upon your guard against a party-spirit, or you will be misled,"[24] while beyond the Hudson, Richard Varick looked forward to a time "when all Party and Animosity will be absorbed in the general and Generous Sentiment of promoting the Common Good."[25] Still farther north a New Hampshire minister warned the legislature against forming combinations within the state in opposition to their own laws and government. They must guard against the spirit of faction, which would selfishly overturn the foundations of government. Instead they should support government and strengthen the hands of their rulers.[26]

Such hostility to parties raises the question of what interests they were presumed to threaten. Several of these comments indicate that the writers viewed them as dangerous to government. Thus a South Carolinian, noting that the state contained two "factions" or "sides," asserted that "one of these parties espouse the side of government" but the other did not. The people must "shun the insinuations of party as the wiles of a lewd woman," learn that the interest of the state was paramount to individuals, and acquiesce in its authority, he said.[27] Many writers decided that political divisions were inevitable: selfish men combined to seek their own ends and misled the people; others, through lack of understanding, also created divisions.[28] Moreover a republican government unhappily encouraged differences. "*Discord* and *faction* are evils to which popular governments are exposed. Where all the citizens claim a right of judging about the state of public affairs, it is to be expected that different opinions will prevail." The writer ended by remarking rather unhappily that everyone ought to pursue the public good.[29]

The reason for this unpopularity of parties appears in the contemporary analysis of their origin and composition (which quite

23. To ?, May 3, 1784, Gratz Coll., Old Congress, III, Hist. Soc. Pa.
24. *Pa. Packet* (Philadelphia), Oct. 15, 1776.
25. To Henry Glen, Poughkeepsie, Jan. 18, 1783, Glen Miscellaneous Manuscripts, N.-Y. Hist. Soc.
26. Samuel MacClintock, *A Sermon . . . June 3, 1784* (Portsmouth, 1784). A few other examples are "Philanthropos," *Conn. Gaz.* (New London), Apr. 4, 1783; *Pa. Jour.* (Philadelphia), Apr. 9, 1777; *The American Museum*, I (1787), 185–186.
27. *Gaz. of S.C.* (Charleston), Oct. 7, 1784.
28. For example, *Pa. Evening Herald* (Philadelphia), Aug. 24, Oct. 12, 1785.
29. *N.H. Mercury* (Portsmouth), Mar. 21, 1787. For the idea that parties arise inevitably in a free government, see also *Indep. Gazetteer* (Philadelphia), Sept. 24, 1787.

closely follows that outlined in the preceding chapter), for men of the Revolutionary generation readily identified conflicts between classes, interests, and cultures.

Differences in property existed in Revolutionary America, and although they ranked behind residence, occupation, and world view in political significance, they became important from time to time. Men of the period perceived them, often with regret, and introduced them into the political rhetoric in about the proper proportion—occasionally. A Pennsylvanian warned that "after a while the wealthy men of all parties will combine, for it is peculiar to wealth [that it creates] a uniformity of sentiment upon the subject of government."[30] So also a Marylander discussed the division between an aristocracy, or the power that property exercised, and a democracy, or the influence of the people as distinct from property. "Between these *two* powers, the aristocracy and democracy, that is the *rich* and *poor*, there is a constant warfare."[31] In South Carolina, Pennsylvania, and Massachusetts during Shays's Rebellion, men interpreted politics as involving a contest along class lines.[32] More often the terms they used, instead of rich versus poor, were aristocracy and democracy, which included economic differences in a larger whole. Thus Elbridge Gerry declared that in Massachusetts "there are two parties, one devoted to Democracy, . . . the other as violent in the opposite extreme," while Henry Livingston described New York's election as a contest "between Demo and Aristo."[33]

Conflicts among economic interest groups derived mainly from the obvious differences between farmers and traders. The dichotomy appeared in South Carolina, and from Virginia north the divergence became increasingly clear. A Virginian in 1787 hoped for an end to the idea that "seemed to prevail almost universally, that the Landed and Commercial Interests were opposed to each other."[34] Pennsylvanians condemned the jealousy of the country legislators toward the cities and people in trade.[35] Henry Living-

30. *Pa. Jour.* (Philadelphia), June 30, 1784.

31. "A Farmer," *Md. Gaz.* (Baltimore), Feb. 29, 1788.

32. E.g., William Hornby, in *Gaz. of S.C.* (Charleston), Aug. 19, 1784; William Whiting's account in Robert Treat Paine Papers, Mass. Hist. Soc.

33. Max Farrand, ed., *Records of the Federal Convention of 1787* (New Haven, 1911–1937), II, 647; Henry Livingston to Walter Livingston, Apr. 24, 1785, R. R. Livingston Papers, Box 14, N.-Y. Hist. Soc.

34. Alexander Donald to Jefferson, Richmond, Nov. 12, 1787, Boyd, ed., *Jefferson Papers*, XII, 346.

35. Samuel Vaughan to Richard Price, Mass. Hist. Soc., *Proc.*, 2d Ser., XVII (1903), 356.

ston, scion of a manor lord, complained that "our Damn Country Merchants ruin our Farmers,"[36] and the distrust between "the landed and the commercial interest" was lamented in New York's press.[37] In Massachusetts a Bostonian interpreted the division in the legislature as due to "a jealousy between the Country interest and that of the Sea Ports."[38] Economic interest received its ablest treatment from "A Citizen" of Rhode Island, who combined occupation with class. "The political creed of an individual may almost be ascertained with certainty from his connexions, or speculative prospects," he wrote.

Go to the counting-houses of the merchants, analize their political principles, and you will find their creed to be formed on the most minute calculation of private advantage. . . .

Indeed, the notions of private interest seem to decide the political principles of men of all stations in this State. Is he a man of opulence? Even wealth will not insure his patriotism. Pampered with the luxury of riches, he begins to covet ambition and power, and seeks honorary perferment. . . .

Scrutinize with attention the lower orders of life, and you will find the conduct of many decided by the illusive hope of benefiting by the countenance of those, whom in speculation they affect to despise.[39]

From the point of view of the commercial-cosmopolitan group, parties originated because farmers, men of small property, and those of little knowledge joined to oppose rule by the competent. The trouble in Massachusetts, according to "The Elector," resulted from licentiousness united with excessive democracy. Men in power should combine love of country, morality, spirit, firmness, independence, property, and knowledge of laws, history, and the constitution; to be truly independent a man "must, in some considerable degree, be autonomous of his constituents and of his place for support."[40] But instead such "men of sense and property" had lost influence. People no longer chose, as a matter of course, the best representatives, but "blustering ignorant men."[41] The legislature of

36. To Walter Livingston, Mar. 2, 1785, R. R. Livingston Papers, Box 14, N.-Y. Hist. Soc.

37. E.g., "A Citizen," *Indep. Jour.* (Philadelphia), Mar. 13, 1784; "A Merchant," *N.Y. Packet* (New York), Feb. 23, 1784.

38. Samuel Breck to Henry Knox, Boston, July 14, 1787, Knox Papers, XX, 131, Mass. Hist. Soc. See also "Real Farmer," *The Hampshire Chronicle* (Springfield), Oct. 22, 1788.

39. *Pa. Packet* (Philadelphia), Oct. 7, 1786.

40. *Mass. Gaz.* (Northampton), Mar. 30, 1787.

41. *Am. Herald* (Boston), Dec. 11, 1786.

the Bay State, wrote S. P. Savage, had fallen into the hands of men who, though perhaps honest,

> yet from the contractedness of their Education, and whose views never extended further than a small farm or a bond of 50 or 100 £ cannot, from long habit, be persuaded to view Matters on a large or national Scale—and are too apt to manage the great Affairs of Government as they do their own, who to determine whether John shall be paid 7/6 or 10/ will perhaps spend a Day at the Expense of 150 or 200 £ to their Constituents. . . . this is one of the great Evils of large Assembly, the Bulk of whom might for their real Service as well be asses as men. These sort of Men being unacquainted with the nature of Commerce view the Merchants as real positive Evils hence as well from Obstinancy as Ignorance, Trade, by which only a Nation can grow rich, is neglected.[42]

The same kind of men with the same faults—from this point of view—appeared in other states. "Eboracus" lamented that New York was governed by "men of low origin, no family, no property, and little education," instead of "independent gentlemen" with a good education, respect for religion, moral purity, and property.[43] In the same state "Americanus" agreed that no one could expect good government "when almost every office is in the hands of those who are not distinguished by property, family, education, manners or talents."[44] And from Carlisle, Pennsylvania, "Mentor" complained that "men without property, without connections, not born in your country, and only citizens of a day" had been elected to the legislature instead of men with education and a "considerable property."[45] The commercial-cosmopolitan group included, by general agreement, men of superior education, family, property, and ability. Hamilton observed that they were such as could think "continentally," while another writer stated that "men, by a more free intercourse with the world, enlarge their understanding, and acquire a more liberal way of thinking, besides more experience, have opportunities of comparing the customs, manners, and laws of one country with those of another."[46]

42. Samuel P. Savage to ?, Mar. 18, 1784, Apr. 19, 1784, Samuel P. Savage Papers, Box II, Mass. Hist. Soc.

43. *New Haven Gaz.*, Mar. 27, 1788.

44. *N.Y. Daily Advertiser*, Aug. 1, 1787. See also *An Address to the Free Electors of the State of New York* . . . (New York, 1786), calling upon electors to place the interest of the whole over that of the locality, for the latter was "a great cause of party faction and division, too prevalent in legislative bodies."

45. *Carlisle Gaz.* (Carlisle, Pa.), Sept. 27, 1786.

46. *N.-Y. Packet* (Fishkill), Sept. 12, 1782.

The agrarian-localists—Localists—sometimes chose such men to represent them, but they could not always be relied upon; as we have seen, a substantial number of country traders and professional men, presumably chosen to represent their districts, wound up on the other side. They were, as one writer pointed out, entertained and talked to, so that they "sooner or later fall under management."[47] As the rural miller Amos Singletary said in a well-known passage, "these lawyers, and men of learning, and moneyed men, that talk so finely, and gloss over matters so smoothly," expected to gain and hold power. In opposition the upstate New York radical Ephraim Paine stated the credo of the agrarian-localists: "I believe that the right of governing is inherent in the people: That they, to whom they delegate authority, ought to govern according to the will of the people: That whenever they, to whom authority is delegated, refuse to govern according to the known will of the people, the people in such case, have a right to re-assume that authority which they had delegated."[48]

Three perceptive descriptions of political alignments summarize contemporary opinion and point the way toward some general conclusions. The first, contributed by "The Free Republican," took a broad view of politics. Society, he observed, was divided into two parts: those who cultivated the earth, manufactured the produce of it, or in general depended upon their bodily labor; and those who subsisted on the first, including men of leisure who lived on inherited wealth, merchants, doctors, lawyers, and divines. The larger the latter's income, the harder the former must work. The result is conflict between the two, whether they are called rich and poor, high and low, patricians and plebeians, or by other words. He preferred "the few and the many." Literary men, he remarked parenthetically, joined the few out of dignity and pride and because they derived support from them. The common designations for the opposing groups in Massachusetts, he said, were "the gentlemen, and the common people." When the state drew up its constitution, he continued,

the distinctions I have described had long existed, and were strongly felt; for having been born and educated under a government, savouring highly of monarchical principles, the property of the citizens was very unequally accumulated, their employments exceedingly multiplied, and marked with different degrees of respectability and honour. A

47. "A Freeholder," *To the Inhabitants of Pennsylvania* . . . (Philadelphia, 1782).

48. *N.-Y. Packet* (Fishkill), Apr. 25, 1782.

democracy, for this people, would therefore have been despotic, and, in the course of a very few years, in all probability, have terminated in the tyranny of an individual. . . . A democratical government can never be free, unless there is an equality of rights and of property among the governed; because men are entitled to political power, in proportion to the rights they possess at entering into society.[49]

When "The Free Republican" wrote, in August 1784, he still expected to reconcile the two conflicting groups through the mechanism of a bicameral legislature. Three years later that attempt failed. After Shays's Rebellion, wrote "Atticus," it could be seen that thenceforth the state would contain two parties. "That one of these, that of the populace, would tend to general levelism, and democratic turbulence. That the other, that of the rich, and of men of austere political principles, would tend to an alteration of the constitution of our State, and the subjection of the people to a rigid aristocracy." The first, he continued, consisted of men with "small property, much embarrassed, and devoured by the interest of their debts. That of the latter, of men in large estates, especially those which consist in money." The most accurate designations he thought to be large estates and small estates, but "for convenience, we shall call them by names, invented long ago, the democratic and aristocratic factions." These parties, he argued, would always exist under free political institutions. Indeed—and here he struck a new note—parties were good, because Massachusetts could never become either a pure democracy or an aristocracy. The problem, he concluded, was to discover some third power to balance the two major protagonists.[50]

Far to the south, a Charlestonian reached a similar conclusion about the inevitability of parties. William Hornby, posing as "Democratic Gentle-Touch," pointed out that Carolinians were citizens of a "Democratic Republic" in which "*jealousy* and *opposition* must naturally exist, while there exists a difference in the minds, interests, and sentiments of mankind." If South Carolina became a despotism, "parties could not exist, as FEAR would then prevent them." Under a limited monarchy "parties always subsist; but the pivot on which they turn is *private*, not *public* interest." An aristocracy such as the wealthy Carolinians were trying to establish, usually lacked parties, "as the haughtiness of the RICH is the very soul of such a government." But, he insisted, "in a Democracy like ours, more springs are necessary, such as a *virtuous*

49. *Boston Magazine*, I (1784), 420–423.
50. *Indep. Chronicle* (Boston), Oct. 18, 1787.

jealousy of all who have united *arrogance* with their *power* of *influence*."[51] For Hornby's followers, as for the Massachusetts farmers, parties served as a vehicle for popular opposition to authority, inevitable in and essential to a democratic government.

This long investigation has succeeded in revealing the existence and origin of consistent political alignments during the Revolutionary era. We have found that, even in the absence of modern parties and pressure groups, the people's representatives formed distinct, continuous voting blocs. Chaotic, atomistic behavior did indeed appear, especially in some states during the war years, and perhaps on a third of the votes in assemblies where roll calls were numerous. Yet in two states (Massachusetts and South Carolina) virtually every vote produced the identical pattern that emerged from a thousand roll calls in ten states. The major characteristic of this pervasive pattern was the division of about three-fourths of the state representatives into two groups. The primary factors creating this pattern were: first, the sectional divergences within the states, most simply expressed as an opposition of the agrarian to the commercial areas; second, the conflict between men who farmed and those who did not; third, the contest between small and large property holders; and fourth, the differences between localists and cosmopolitans.

The same formative influences had long existed: why did they only now create parties within the legislatures? During the colonial period major questions of government were settled by and within local elites, consisting of the commercial-cosmopolitans—the merchants, professional men, great landowners, the social and cultural upper class—who occupied most of the elective or appointive offices and who usually curbed any dissent. The relaxation of authority after 1776, however, permitted the development of an opposition to challenge the old structure of power. Men could then debate the very form of government itself, economic policy, social issues, and other crucial questions. The Cosmopolitans favored an efficient government controlled by themselves and laws beneficial to their interest. The Localists, on the other hand, spoke for men who had previously lacked power and sought a political system founded on local self-government dominated by the majority. At first neither group had an organization, although the Cosmopolitans probably had always cooperated with one another. By the end of our period, however, both had begun to campaign actively

51. *Gaz. of S.C.* (Charleston), July 29, 1784.

and purposefully in several states. The division over the Federal Constitution coincided with party lines and intensified the dispute, encouraging interstate cooperation. Even those arch-localists, the Antifederalists, through the Federal Republican Committee in New York, began a correspondence that stretched from New Hampshire to South Carolina. Within a decade the process of nationalization of party was complete. The agrarian-localists formed the core of the Jeffersonian Republican party, and the commercial-cosmopolitans merged into Federalism.[52]

The relation between the American two-party system and the legislative blocs of the 1780s remains to be examined. Theoretically the two may prove identical, or we may find that the former developed quite separately from the latter. If the Cosmopolitan-Localist alignment continued into the 1790s and beyond, the most likely outcome seems to be a process by which the national parties adapted to and modified the state blocs. This appears the more probable, because the political alignments we have found grew logically out of the environment and strongly resembled the political divisions of the following decades. The process that created the Cosmopolitan and Localist blocs may be summarized as follows:

First, the comparatively democratic political institutions encouraged the rise of a legitimate opposition. In the absence of any central authority to enforce conformity, factions and blocs flourished.

Second, consistent divisions of opinion originated primarily from economic and political issues. Certain social and cultural questions, locally important, created different voting patterns, but economics and politics contributed the major impulse.

Third, the legislators polarized into two major groups that generally included a majority of representatives and senators.

Fourth, the factors determining political alignments comprehended the entire economic, social, political, and cultural environment, and together formed what might be called the political climate. No one single cause sufficed; instead representatives reacted to a set of factors. The most consistent bloc voters usually

52. The present research suggests the following political family tree:

   A. commercial-cosmopolitan dominant core = "High" Federalists
     1) commercial farmer wing = "Adams" Federalists
     2) artisan, etc., wing = first Federalists, then Republicans
   B. agrarian-localist dominant core = "Democratic" Republicans
     1) planter wing = "Old" Republicans

were those in whom all of the factors coincided, reinforcing one another, such as the wealthy, urban, cosmopolitan lawyer. Neutralism often occurred when the influences counteracted one another.

Fifth, the formative factors during the 1780s assumed roughly this order of importance: the legislator's residence or the nature of his constituency, whether he viewed the world as a cosmopolitan or localist, his occupation, and his economic status. Such influences as age, family background, political or military experience, and religion modified and contributed to the basic alignment, but they did not create one themselves.

Sixth, theorists adapted existing political ideology, so that it justified their objectives and their world view.

Seventh, the degree to which these voting blocs acquired some of the attributes of a modern party probably depended upon the existence of some decisive, crystallizing issue or local circumstance (e.g., the state constitution and the bank in Pennsylvania, Shays's Rebellion in Massachusetts, the money crisis in Rhode Island, the impost and state monetary policy in New York). Such particular circumstances gave political alignments their special form, as they did later during the Federalist era.

In the spring of 1787 "Plato" wrote that "the people of the United States are now divided, and have naturally thrown themselves into two great classes, or parties, and which are often distinguished by the names of the Mercantile and Landed Interests."[53] In this description the wise man proved to be both an acute political analyst and a prophet.

53. *U.S. Chronicle* (Providence), Apr. 19, 1787.

Appendix
The Party Leaders

The following capsule biographies describe the legislators who voted most consistently in the seven states treated in detail. Each legislative party is represented by about twenty men. The criteria vary from state to state depending upon circumstances. These legislators epitomize the character of their blocs, and the tables at the end of the section, which contrast the two groups, will repay careful examination.

If one or two principal books contain the biographical data, these are cited. Otherwise the facts come from miscellaneous sources, generally familiar to the specialist. For Massachusetts the 1771 tax lists supply valuable information about the parents and, with obvious reservations, about the sons. Such few New York tax lists as have survived supplement the essential wills published as part of the New-York Historical Society's *Collections*. The *New Jersey Archives* contain many volumes of probate records that, with the manuscript tax lists, furnish a mass of raw material. Basic for a study of Pennsylvania's politicians are the tax lists in the published *Archives*. The early issues of the *Pennsylvania Magazine of History and Biography* deserve special mention together with Eugene E. Doll's index to the first seventy volumes. Probate records in the state archival collections of Maryland, Virginia, and South Carolina help to fill in the gaps created by the shortage of local histories, and tax records exist for all three, those of Virginia being exceptionally complete.

MASSACHUSETTS

Cosmopolitans

BICKFORD, EBENEZER (9–0), of Salem (1737–1816), was a merchant. The son of Deacon John Bickford (1702–1788) a "shoreman" and yeoman, Ebenezer belonged to an old, reputable, but ordinary family.

Although he seems to have received no formal education, he sent a son to Harvard. Evidence in the 1771 tax list and Ebenezer's occupation suggests that he may have been well-to-do. He represented the town during 1786/1787 and 1787/1788. "Beckfork-Bickford Genealogy," *Essex Antiquarian*, VIII (1904), 60–64.

BOWDOIN, JAMES, JR. (9–0), of Dorchester, needs no sketch.

BRECK, SAMUEL (17–0), represented Boston during the years beginning 1784. His father, John (1705–1761), a merchant, left him £2,767. The family was prominent. Samuel (1747–1809) acquired a fortune as merchant and banker, assisted by foreign connections such as those gained by acting as fiscal agent for the French. He was an Episcopalian. Samuel Breck, *Genealogy of the Breck Family* . . . (Omaha, 1889), 18, 40.

BROOKS, JOHN (10–0), of Medford, a successful doctor, became a colonel in the Continental army and eventually a major general. A Calvinist who became a Unitarian, Brooks (1752–1825) remained politically consistent, supporting the Constitution and then the Federalist party. He received only a local education but joined the American Antiquarian Society. A member of the Society of the Cincinnati, he energetically opposed Shays's Rebellion. *DAB*, III, 79–80.

BROWN, BENJAMIN (14–2), of Lexington (1720–1801), descended from a respectable old family, his father, Joseph (1677–1764), serving as deacon, constable, clerk, selectman, and assessor. Benjamin, a fourth son, held the same office and attained that of justice of the peace. He also owned a small farm and can be called a farmer, though he may well have derived most of his income as a public official. He supported ratification. Charles Hudson, *History of the Town of Lexington, Middlesex County, Massachusetts* . . . (Boston, 1868), 27–28, of the genealogical register.

CARNES, JOHN (18–1), of Lynn (1723–1802), a Harvard graduate, began as a New Light minister. His father, John (1698–1760), a Boston pewterer, came from a good family (he was a captain in the British navy) and acquired a competence, leaving an inventory of £1,852 16s. 10d. The younger John earned a bare living as a minister, became a Boston innkeeper and a chaplain in the Continental army, and finally moved to Salem where he entered trade. His wife was well-to-do, and his sons prospered, but during the 1780s he was what probably should be called comfortably off rather than well-to-do. Carnes voted for ratification. Clifford K. Shipton, *Sibley's Harvard Graduates: Biographical Sketches of Those Who Attended Harvard College* . . . (Boston, 1873–1968), XI, 137–142; Oliver Ayer Roberts, *History of the Military Company of the Massachusetts, Now*

Called the Ancient and Honorable Artillery Company of Massachusetts (Boston, 1895–1901), I, 454–455.

CHOATE, JOHN (9–1), of Ipswich, was born and died in that town (1737–1791). The family was one of the town's most respectable, though his branch was not perhaps truly prominent. His father, Francis (1701–1777), earned his living successfully as blacksmith, shipbuilder, and shipowner. He also bought a farm and became an elder. John, the fourth surviving son, inherited the blacksmith shop, traded, and served as justice of the peace. He favored the Constitution. Ephraim Orcutt Jameson, *The Choates in America* (Boston, 1896), 37–38, 65–66.

CLARKE, THOMAS (17–3), of Roxbury, a "leatherdresser" and tanner, probably was born in Boston, where his father was a goldsmith of moderate property (Suffolk County Probate Records, LXXX, 194, 310). Clarke was chosen town clerk as well as representative for many years. Francis S. Drake, *The Town of Roxbury* (Roxbury, Mass., 1878), 380.

CUSHING, THEOPHILUS (13–2), of Hingham, belonged to a family that produced many prominent men, but his was a lesser branch. His father, Theophilus (1703–1779), was a miller and farmer, constable and selectman. Theophilus, Jr. (1740–1820), inherited the property and the office of selectman. He sat in the lower house eight terms, was a captain during the war, and ended as a state senator and brigadier general. In the eighties he was a prosperous miller. *History of the Town of Hingham, Massachusetts* (Cambridge, Mass., 1893), II, 161.

DAVIS, CALEB (20–0), of Boston, served in the legislature from 1776 to 1788. His father, Joshua (d. 1755), an innkeeper, left more liabilities than assets, and Caleb (1738–1797) was bound out as a housewright. His uncle however was a merchant, and Caleb himself married well, presently acquiring wealth as a sugar refiner and merchant. He became a deacon in the church and voted for ratification. His papers reveal the attitudes of a well-informed, upper-class Bostonian. Clarence Winthrop Bowen, *The History of Woodstock, Connecticut* (Norwood, Mass., 1926–1943), IV, 469–471; Suffolk Co. Prob. Recs., LI, 42, 81, LII, 100.

DAWES, THOMAS (19–0), of Boston, was the son of a perukemaker who died poor (Suffolk Co. Prob. Recs., XV, 880). Thomas (1731–1809) started as a mason, acquired property, and achieved status by marrying the granddaughter of merchant Edward Gray. He became a leading radical, helped to finance Samuel Adams, served as colonel in the militia, and ultimately acquired real wealth as a merchant and banker. He favored ratification. Henry W. Holland, *William Dawes, and his ride with Paul Revere* (Boston, 1878), 60–67.

GODDARD, JOHN (11–1), of Brookline, served continually from 1784 through 1792. The son of a farmer, John, Jr. (1730–1816), built up a considerable business as a teamster, furnishing three teams during the siege of Boston, and acted as commissary-general for the army in Massachusetts. He also owned a farm and produced sixteen children. Harriet F. Woods, *Historical Sketches of Brookline, Mass.* (Boston, 1874), 364–367.

HALE, JONATHAN (9–1), of Framingham, was born in Bradford to Jonathan (b. 1702), a farmer, who presently moved to Sutton. He eventually manufactured wool cards, erected a distillery, and served as selectman. Later he became trustee of an academy. He may have served as lieutenant colonel in the New Hampshire militia; the house records call him "Major." Josiah H. Temple, *History of Framingham, Massachusetts . . .* (Framingham, Mass., 1887), 574; Robert Safford Hale, *Genealogy of Descendants of Thomas Hale . . .* , ed. George R. Howell (Albany, N.Y., 1889), 119, 236–237.

HOLT, JOSHUA (10–1), of Andover, was the son of Nicholas Holt, who himself was a third-generation colonial but is otherwise unknown. Joshua (1730–1810) evidently was a farmer of moderate property but superior character. He sat in the legislature for twenty-one years, was chosen deacon, justice of the peace, member of various local committees, and captain of a company of minutemen. Sarah Loring Bailey, *Historical Sketches of Andover . . .* (Boston, 1880), 95, 294–295; Daniel S. Durrie, *A Genealogical History of the Holt Family in the United States . . .* (Albany, N.Y., 1864), 22–23.

JARVIS, LEONARD (8–1), of Boston, descended from a good Boston family. His great-great-grandfather, a sea captain, married a rich widow and settled in Boston as a prosperous merchant. His father, Leonard (1716–1760), was also a Boston merchant and married well, leaving a good, but not large, estate and six sons (Suffolk Co. Prob. Recs., LXIX, 149, 177). Leonard, Jr. (1742–1813), became first a doctor, then owner of a privateer during the war, and finally a merchant and treasurer of the state. He favored ratification. George A. Jarvis *et al.*, comps., *The Jarvis Family* (Hartford, 1879), 200–203.

JONES, JOHN COFFIN (10–0), of Boston, was a merchant, reputedly well-to-do, and a Harvard graduate of 1768. He evidently was born in Salem about 1750, engaged in trade there, and moved to Boston after the war. Jones was elected to the lower house in 1786, favored ratification, and became a Federalist.

MASON, JONATHAN (10-0), of Boston, was the son of a prominent, wealthy merchant, a Son of Liberty, deacon, and selectman. He graduated from the College of New Jersey (1774), studied law with John Adams and Josiah Quincy, and eventually acquired a good deal of Boston property as a banker. He became a strong Federalist. *DAB*, XXI, 370.

OTIS, SAMUEL ALLYNE (13-0), of Boston, sat almost constantly in the lower house. The youngest son of Col. James and brother of the more famous James, he married the daughter of the eminent Harrison Gray. He attended Harvard, became a well-to-do merchant before the war and prospered during it by supplying the Continental army, but went bankrupt afterwards. By 1786 he probably owned only moderate property, retaining, however, his office and prestige. He favored ratification and became a Federalist. Shipton, *Sibley's Harvard Graduates*, XV, 471–480.

TREADWELL, JOHN (8-1), of Ipswich, was born in Ipswich into a good family of prosperous farmers, his father leaving real estate worth £1,342. John (1735–1811) graduated from Harvard, became a minister for two decades at Lynn, but resigned and taught school for two years at Ipswich. At this time, when presumably a small property owner, he served in the house. He then moved to Salem, became a flour merchant, lawyer, judge, and zealous Federalist. Shipton, *Sibley's Harvard Graduates*, XV, 347–351; Thomas F. Waters, *Ipswich in the Massachusetts Bay Colony* (Ipswich, Mass., 1905–1917), II, 290–291.

WARD, RICHARD (14-0), of Salem, was the son of Joshua, a well-to-do tanner. He was born in Salem in 1741, married into a prominent family, and became a successful merchant. Little else is known. *Essex Institute Historical Collections*, XXXVI (1900), 249–251, LXXII (1936), 301; Sidney Perley, *The History of Salem, Massachusetts . . . 1626–1716* (Salem, Mass., 1924–1928), II, 102–104.

WINTER, FRANCIS (9-1), of Bath, was born in Boston, where he allied with Sam Adams and also graduated from Harvard. Talented and learned, he preached at Bath until 1787, starting as a Calvinist and ending as an Arminian. Later he farmed and practiced law informally. Parker McCobb Reed, *History of Bath and Environs . . .* (Portland, Me., 1894), 478–480.

Prominent men associated with the Cosmopolitans in Massachusetts included BENJAMIN AUSTIN (4-0), Boston ropemaker and Jeffersonian; JOHN BACON (6-1), Stockbridge minister, Antifederalist, and Republican; STEPHEN CROSS (7-1), Newburyport merchant and another Antifederalist-Republican; ELIJAH DWIGHT of Great Barrington (5-1), merchant, judge, and Federal leader; ELBRIDGE GERRY (6-0); JONATHAN

GLOVER (7–0), Continental colonel, merchant, and supporter of the Constitution; NATHANIEL GORHAM (4–0); LARKIN THORNDIKE (5–0), Beverly shipowner; and JOHN WILLIAMS (7–3), Federalist merchant and philanthropist from Deerfield.

The only neutrals of any importance were Gen. JOHN ASHLEY, JR., of Sheffield, wealthy lawyer and strong Federalist, and JOHN HILL of Berwick, a wealthy lawyer.

Localists

ADAMS, ISAAC (12–2), of Boxford, was born in Rowley. His father, Isaac, was presumably a farmer, but nothing is known of him. Isaac, Jr. (1713–1797), a Congregationalist, served briefly in the Continental army, attained the rank of captain, was chosen selectman, and represented Boxford regularly beginning in 1784. Evidently he farmed for a living. Sidney Perley, *The History of Boxford, Essex County, Massachusetts* . . . (Boxford, Mass., 1880), 391.

BODMAN, WILLIAM (13–2), of Williamsburg, also sat in the legislature regularly from 1784. He came from pioneer stock, his grandfather living in Hatfield before 1700. William (c. 1741–1825) moved to Williamsburg about 1770 and in time became one of the town's principal citizens and a justice of the peace. He was an Antifederalist. In the 1780s the town was emerging out of the frontier stage, but probably contained only farmers of small property. Phyllis Baker Deming, comp., *A History of Williamsburg in Massachusetts* (Northampton, Mass., 1946), 7, 24, 28.

BREWSTER, JONATHAN (9–1), of Worthington, served with Adams and Bodman. A fifth-generation New Englander, he was born in Preston, Connecticut, in 1759 and moved to Worthington (or his father of the same name moved) in 1777. Evidently a farmer, he held local offices but saw no military service. Either he or his father was a deacon. [James C. Rice], *Secular and Ecclesiastical History of the Town of Worthington* . . . (Albany, N.Y., 1853), 34–35.

BULLOCH, STEPHEN (13–2), of Rehoboth, descended from and continued a long line of small farmers. He served as a militia captain and in the legislature beginning in 1782. Richard LeBaron Bowen, *Early Rehoboth* (Rehoboth, Mass., 1945–1948), IV, 102.

CHAMBERLAIN, AARON (8–0), of Chelmsford, was perhaps the fourth son of Abraham (1653–1747), a Dedham housewright of above-average property. At any rate we find him—or one of the name—as a private in 1758, a member of the Chelmsford committee of correspondence, a deacon, selectman, and—again as a private—wounded at Concord in 1775. The tax list indicates that he was a small farmer. Wilson Waters, *History of Chelmsford, Massachusetts* (Lowell,

Mass., 1917), 171, 195, 214, 222, 309, 760; George Walter Chamberlain, *William Chamberlain of Billerica, Massachusetts* . . . (Portland, Me., 1911), 141.

CRANSON, ELISHA (11–1), of Ashfield, is not mentioned in the town history, although he served several years as representative. He was probably born in Marlborough about 1730, the son of Samuel, and arrived in Ashfield sometime before 1775 when he served a single term as selectman. He became captain of the militia in 1776 and died in 1804. He did not own a tavern, nor was he a professional man, so he almost certainly farmed for a living like his neighbors. Winfred Lovering Holman, "Cranson Bible Record," *New-England Historical and Genealogical Register*, XCVIII (1944), 282; N. B. Sylvester *et al.*, *History of the Connecticut Valley in Massachusetts* . . . (Philadelphia, 1879), I, 744.

DAVIS, ISRAEL, JR. (8–0), of Holden, cannot be certainly distinguished from his father (1717–1791). One was a town clerk, and one or both were often selectmen. Davis, Jr., served briefly as a private in the militia, attended the Congregational church, and—in the absence of contrary evidence—farmed. David Foster Estes, *The History of Holden, Massachusetts* (Worcester, Mass., 1894), 60, 255–256.

FORBES, DANIEL (9–1), of Brookfield, was born in Westborough to Daniel (1710–1780), locally prominent. Daniel, Jr. (1736–1808), the eldest son, moved to Brookfield about 1770, owned a chaise, farmed, and prospered. He voted against ratification. Frederick Clifton Pierce, *Forbes and Forbush Genealogy* (Chicago, 1892), 28–29, 45–46.

GLEASON, ISAAC (10–0), of Western, owned a shop of some kind in 1771 and a small amount of land. He was born in Sudbury in 1733 to Isaac (1705–1751) and died in 1820. He was chosen selectman, is referred to as captain, and presumably attended the town's only church, the Congregational. John Barber White, *Genealogy of the Descendants of Thomas Gleason of Watertown, Mass., 1607–1909* (Haverhill, Mass., 1909), 60, 289.

HAMILTON, ROBERT (9–1), of Conway, was born in Barre in 1732. His father had immigrated from Scotland. Robert became a lieutenant during the Revolution and owned a farm. Charles S. Pease, ed., *History of Conway (Massachusetts) 1767–1917* . . . (Springfield, Mass., 1917), 33, 205, 298.

MASON, CHRISTOPHER (12–0), of Swanzey, descended from a large landowner who immigrated in 1649. His father, Christopher (1702–1783), had four sons, of whom this Christopher (b. 1737) was the third. Probably the family land had been much subdivided; we have no indication of wealth, and he served as a private during the Revolution. He voted against ratification. *Representative Men and Old Families of Southeastern Massachusetts* . . . (Chicago, 1912), 1048.

MAYNARD, STEPHEN (14–0), of Westborough, a militia captain, was the town's wealthiest citizen—which meant in 1771 that he was a substantial farmer. At some point he acquired two slaves. A Congregationalist, he held various local offices, sat for several years in the legislature, and opposed ratification. Herman Packard De Forest and E. C. Bates, *The History of Westborough, Massachusetts* (Westborough, Mass., 1891), 190.

McFARLAND, WALTER (12–0), of Hopkinton, was the son of Ebenezer, evidently a local farmer. Walter (1749–1827) apparently was a farmer too though he also became a "civil engineer," which translated means surveyor. He was a militia captain and twice a selectman. Duane H. Hurd, ed., *History of Middlesex County, Massachusetts* (Philadelphia, 1890), III, 802.

METCALF, SAVEL (8–0), of Warwick, was the offspring of John (1704–1799), a coroner and tanner's son, who moved from Dedham to Bellingham. Savel probably was born there in the thirties. We know nothing else except that he served on the local committee of correspondence. Jonathan Blake, *History of the Town of Warwick, Massachusetts* . . . (Boston, 1873), 50; *N.-E. Hist. Gen. Reg.*, VI (1852), 175–176.

MOODY, SAMUEL (10–0), of Newbury, of an old family, became a colonel during the Revolution. He may have been a miller and a deacon (another Samuel confuses matters) and perhaps contributed to a grammar school in 1779. He belonged to the local committees. John J. Currier, *History of Newbury, Massachusetts, 1635–1902* (Boston, 1902), 406, 428, 584, 592.

NYE, DAVID (10–0), of Wareham, was born in that town in 1738. His father, David (1706–1796), moved to Douglas where he ran a tavern, but neither seems to have been an innkeeper in Wareham. David, Jr., held local offices, attended the Congregational church, became a captain in the militia, and died in 1816. George Hyatt Nye and Frank E. Best, comps., and David Fisher Nye, ed., *A Genealogy of the Nye Family* (Cleveland, 1907), 78, 122.

REED, BENJAMIN (9–0), of Mendon, left remarkably little mark for a man entitled "colonel." In 1771 he owned a very small farm. Probably he was only a captain during the war. He atypically led troops against the Shaysites, which perhaps accounts for his defeat for election in 1787.

SIBLEY, TIMOTHY (9–0), of Sutton, belonged to an old Sutton family; his father was a captain. None of the family was prominent. Timothy

(b. 1754) married the daughter of a Baptist minister and is called "colonel" though he is not listed among the Revolutionary officers. Arthur H. Radasch, *Barstow-Bestor Genealogy* (South Yarmouth, Mass.? 1964), 18.

SMEAD, DAVID (9-1), of Greenfield, came from a reputable old family. An ancestor was one of the town's first selectmen, and David (1732–1806) was its first justice of the peace. He was also a deacon, selectman, member of the Shaysite Hatfield Convention of 1786, and representative from 1780 until 1793. In 1771 the assessment list charged him with 2/3 mills, an ironworks, and a small farm, while by 1798 he and his children owned over $13,000 (about £2,000 in 1785 money) in real property. Halfway between the two dates he must have owned a substantial but not a large property. Francis M. Thompson, *History of Greenfield Massachusetts* (Greenfield, Mass., 1904–1931), II, 654, 718, 896.

STEBBINS, PHINEHAS (12-2), of Wilbraham, was born in Longmeadow in 1739. His father, Stephen (1711–1768), an early settler, taught school and farmed. Phinehas, a second son of four, also farmed, and became the town's first representative, captain in the militia, a Shaysite, an Antifederalist, and (in 1795) a Methodist. Ralph Stebbins Greenlee and Robert Lemuel Greenlee, *The Stebbins Genealogy* (Chicago, 1904), I, 172–173, 232.

THOMPSON, ISAAC (12-0), of Middleboro, like almost all Massachusetts legislators, came from an old Bay Colony family. His father was John (1727–1776), otherwise obscure. Isaac (1746–1819) held various local offices; he was known as a peacemaker and was pious. He seems to have been a farmer of moderate property. Charles Hutchinson Thompson, *A Genealogy of the Descendants of John Thomson of Plymouth, Mass.* (Lansing, Mich., 1890), 175.

WHITE, EBENEZER (9-1), of Rochester, descended from a long line of Plymouth County farmers. Ebenezer (1724–1804) presumably farmed too. He sat in the legislature during nineteen sessions and fought occasionally in the militia, attaining the rank of lieutenant colonel. Duane H. Hurd, ed., *History of Plymouth County, Massachusetts* (Philadelphia, 1884), 332.

Other representatives who voted on the same side included BENJAMIN BATES (6-0), of Mansfield, about whom almost nothing is known; NICHOLAS BAYLIES (7-1), Taunton iron manufacturer; EPHRAIM CARTER (7-0), of Lancaster, farmer and Antifederalist; WILLIAM CLARK (7-0), of Windsor, unknown; JOHN FESSENDER (7-0), of Rutland, farmer; JESSE JOHNSON (7-1), of Chester, farmer; EZEKIAH KNOWLTON (7-0), of Templeton, farmer; JOSEPH LOVELL (7-0), of Medway, farmer; PETER PENNEMAN (7-1), of Mendon, farmer;

OLIVER POND (7–0), of Wrentham, farmer; BENJAMIN SHELDON (7–1), of Northampton, Federalist, otherwise obscure; FRANCIS SHURTLIFF (7–1), of Plympton, Antifederal farmer; SETH SMITH (8–1), of Norton, farmer; DAVID SPEAR (7–1), of Palmer, farmer; ISAAC TOBEY (7–0), of Barre, carpenter; WILLIAM WARD (7–0), of Cummington, farmer; and DAVID WHITTIER (7–0), of Methuen, miller.

NEW YORK

Anti-Clintonians

BAYARD, NICHOLAS (23–0), of New York City, descended from one of the state's most prominent families, the members of which accumulated a fortune through commerce and in land and intermarried with other members of the elite. His father, a merchant, left a large estate consisting primarily of city lots. Nicholas (1733–1813) took no part in the Revolution (several of his relatives became loyalists) and probably lived off his inheritance. Indeed for a man of such a family he is singularly obscure. *Abstracts of Wills on File in the Surrogate's Office, City of New York, 1760–1766*, New-York Historical Society, *Collections*, VI (1897), 427–429.

BOYD, ROBERT (21–2), of New York City, sat earlier for Orange County. His father, Robert, immigrated from Ireland just as the war began, to inherit a large property left by his uncle Samuel, and probably died during the war. The property, which included an iron and scythe works, lay in the city, so Robert, Jr. (1734–1804), spent the war in Orange returning after the war to become, or resume, the occupation of a blacksmith (*N.Y. Packet*, Apr. 14, 1785). The war must have greatly diminished his inheritance for he paid only an average tax in 1786. William P. Boyd, *History of the Boyd Family and Descendants*, 2d ed. (Rochester, N.Y., 1912), 360–361.

BROOKS, DAVID (33–2), of New York City, took several forms. According to Ansel Wold, comp., *Biographical Directory of the American Congress*, rev. ed. (Washington, D.C., 1961), 741, he was born in Philadelphia in 1756, served as a lieutenant in the Pennsylvania line, was imprisoned from 1776 to 1780, studied law, and eventually became a Dutchess County judge, dying in 1838. The trouble with this account is that he served as a vestryman in Dutchess County in 1773, at the age of seventeen. A different David (b. 1736 in Wallingford, Connecticut) attended Yale, and some David died in New York City in 1795, thus preventing himself from attending Congress in 1797. A Maj. David Brooks was assistant clothier general for New York, 1780–1782, and owned modest property in the city in

1793. In this confusion the probabilities favor our man as being the major, lawyer, and later Federalist, other details being uncertain.

CORSEN, CORNELIUS (37–0), of Richmond, belonged to the sixth generation of a Dutch landowning family. His father, also Cornelius, was a justice of the peace who died in 1755 leaving bequests of £1,270, slaves, and more than a thousand acres. Born in 1731, Cornelius, Jr., inherited the "Manor of Castleton" containing over five hundred acres. He held three slaves in 1790. Ira K. Morris, *Morris's Memorial History of Staten Island, New York . . .* (New York, 1898–1900), II, 68–69; Charles William Leng and William T. Davis, *Staten Island and its People . . .* (New York, 1930), IV, 419.

DONGAN, JOHN C. (46–2), of Richmond, inherited an estate that his grandfather obtained as nephew of Governor Dongan. He owned six hundred acres on Long Island and considerable tracts in the city; his personal estate in Richmond was worth $10,000 in 1795. He became a New York City lawyer, a Federalist, regent of the state university, and eventually a drunkard. Morris, *Memorial History*, II, 107–111.

DOUGHTY, CHARLES (82–15), of Kings (c. 1728–1813), may in fact be two men of the same name, for one, son of Elias, lived in Flushing and married Margaret DeBovoise, while another was the son of John (d. 1757), married Mary Doughty, and moved from Jamaica to Brooklyn. The latter became a prominent attorney and probably is our man. Ethan Allen Doty, "The Doughty Family of Long Island," *New York Genealogical and Biographical Record*, XLIII (1912), 315–317.

GARDNER, NATHANIEL (23–0), of Suffolk, descended from one of Long Island's oldest and most notable families. His father, Col. Abraham (1721–1782), was a well-to-do landowner and traded with the West Indies. Nathaniel (1759–1804) graduated from King's College, studied medicine in Philadelphia, became a merchant in New York City, failed, and by 1786, when he served in the legislature, had reverted to medicine in East Hampton. Later he mortgaged his land, returned to the city, and evidently failed again. John Lion Gardiner, *Gardiners of Gardiner's Island* (East Hampton, N.Y., 1927), 170–173.

HAMILTON, ALEXANDER (26–1), of New York City, needs no introduction.

LIVINGSTON, PETER VAN BRUGH (37–1), of New York City, was the son of Philip, second lord of the manor. Peter (1710–1792) graduated from Yale, then married Councillor William Alexander's niece, and became a prosperous and—though an army contractor and privateer—honest merchant. He took the radical side in the Revolution. Although a Yale man he became trustee of the College of New Jersey, perhaps because he was both a Presbyterian and rich. After the war he retired except for a single year in the legislature. *DAB*, XI, 315–316.

LIVINGSTON, ROBERT C. (28–0), of New York City (1742–1790), son of the great landowner Robert of Clermont, graduated from Cambridge and thereafter bore "Cambridge" as a middle name. Poor health and (evidently) lack of talent kept him unimportant, while as the youngest son he inherited enough for comfort but not wealth. Florence Van Rensselaer, *The Livingston Family in America* . . . (New York, 1949), 93.

MERCEREAU, JOSHUA (47–4), of Richmond, descended from Joshua or John, an immigrant saddler, and Joshua who married a Corsen. Our Joshua (1728–1804) graduated from Columbia and became a lawyer, serving in the assembly regularly from 1777 to 1786. *N.Y. Gen. Biog. Rec.*, XXVII (1896), 195–197; Leng and Davis, *Staten Island*, IV, 511; Morris, *Memorial History*, II, 105.

RANDALL, THOMAS (33–1), of New York City, won fame as an English ship's captain and privateer. Thomas (c. 1723–1797) turned merchant and presently became a member of New York's Chamber of Commerce. Wealthy and an Episcopalian, he sided with the rebels and left the city during the war. Returning, he preserved or accumulated a large property. He favored ratification in 1788 but turned Republican later. John Austin Stevens, Jr., *Colonial Records of the New York Chamber of Commerce, 1768–1784, with Historical and Biographical Sketches* (New York, 1867), 157–158.

SANDS, COMFORT (36–3), of New York City, missed out on the family farm that went to his brother John. Comfort (1748–1834) received a good elementary education, entered trade at the age of twenty-one, and piled up a considerable fortune. He became prominent as a Revolutionary patriot, serving as auditor general. When the war ended, he returned to the city and again acquired wealth in trade and finance. *DAB*, XVI, 341–342.

SANDS, JOHN (30–2), of Queens, Comfort's older brother (see above), did inherit the farm, evidently a substantial but not a large property. John (1737–1811) remained a prosperous farmer. [Temple Prime] *Descent of Comfort Sands and of His Children* . . . (New York, 1886), 9, 21, 36–38.

THORNE, RICHARD (24–4), of Queens (b. 1743), inherited part of his father's large farm in Hempstead. He became a militia major, farmer, and shipowner, with eight slaves in 1790. *N.Y. Gen. Biog. Rec.*, XXII (1891), 174.

TROUP, ROBERT (17–1), of New York City (1757–1832), son of a ship's captain, graduated from King's College and studied law with John Jay. He rose to the rank of lieutenant colonel in the Continental army, practiced law, became a firm friend of Alexander Hamilton's and a Federalist. *DAB*, XVIII, 651–652.

VANDERBILT, JOHN (44–2), of Kings, was related only distantly to the more famous, later commodore. John (1739–1796), the son of a substantial farmer, entered trade, attended all the local congresses, served briefly as a major in the militia, helped found a local academy, rose to the position of senator, and accumulated a competent, though not a great, fortune. Thomas M. Strong, *The History of the Town of Flatbush, in Kings County, Long-Island* (New York, 1842), 100–101, 123.

VARICK, RICHARD (19–1), of New York City (1753–1831), belonged to an old but ordinary New Jersey family. He became Washington's efficient corresponding secretary, studied law, and ultimately achieved distinction as codifier of the state's laws, mayor of New York City, and founder of the American Bible Society. In 1786 he married Isaac Roosevelt's daughter. He was a Federalist. *DAB*, XIX, 226.

YATES, PETER WALDRON (21–1), of Albany, was Abraham Yates's nephew. His father was a blacksmith. Peter W. (1747–1826) practiced law and was chosen to the local committee of correspondence, but resigned and sat out the war. He became regent of the state university and member of the Continental Congress. Albany tax lists suggest that he owned a rather small property for a lawyer. *Biog. Dir. of Am. Cong.*, 1856; Jonathan Pearson, *Contributions for the Genealogies . . . of Albany* (Albany, N.Y., 1873), 184y.

Other principal legislators voting on the same side included the two wealthy BANCKER brothers of New York City, ADRIAN (22–4) and EVERT (43–10); WILLIAM DENNING (56–19), wealthy city merchant and future Republican; EGBERT BENSON (11–2), eminent lawyer and Federalist, then of Dutchess; WILLIAM DUER (8–0); DAVID GELSTON (30–8), Long Island merchant and later Republican; HENRY GLENN (36–12) and JAMES GORDON (39–17), both Albany traders and Federalists; Gen. JOHN LAMB (10–2), former radical; JOHN LAURENCE (22–4), city lawyer and Federalist; FRANCIS LEWIS, JR. (8–0), Queens County merchant and Federalist; JAMES (76–27) and JOHN (27–8) LIVINGSTON, both large landowners, the latter a later Republican; NICHOLAS LOW (10–3), city merchant and Federalist; WILLIAM MALCOLM (63–13), city merchant; HENRY REMSEN (23–4), city merchant; HENRY RUTGERS (18–2), now retired with great wealth; JOHN STAGG (27–8), city artisan and Republican; JOHN TAYLER (36–9), Albany merchant and much later lieutenant governor; HEZEKIAH VAN ORDEN

(12-1), Albany County farmer; and GULIAN VER PLANK (11-1), wealthy city merchant and Federalist.

Among major neutrals were WILLIAM GOFORTH, city shopkeeper; SAMUEL JONES, Queens lawyer who started as an Antifederalist, voted for ratification, and became a Federalist; JOHN LANSING, JR., also an Antifederal lawyer, but one who stayed Republican; CHRISTOPHER P. YATES, frontier Antifederal lawyer; and THOMAS YOUNGS of Suffolk, well-to-do landowner and Yale graduate. Gen. JOHN SMITH of Suffolk, who switched from Antifederalist to Federalist during the convention and ultimately became a Republican, tended to support the anti-Clintonians.

Clintonians

ADGATE, MATTHEW (60-3), of Albany, resided in New Canaan. Adgate (1737-1818) came from Connecticut, where his father, Matthew, was probably a farmer. He moved to New Canaan, a semifrontier town before 1767, farmed, and built a mill. Since he was lame he did not fight in the army but held a variety of local posts. He later became justice of the peace and opposed ratification. Mary E. Perkins, *Old Houses of . . . Norwich, 1600–1800 . . .* (Norwich, Conn., 1895), 172; Franklin Ellis, *History of Columbia County, New York* (Philadelphia, 1878), 320–322.

BAKER, ALBERT (69-5), of Washington, appeared from nowhere (one source says New York City) in 1768 as one of the first settlers at Sandy Hill. He constructed a sawmill and a "humble dwelling;" only much later was he able to expand his activities by adding a gristmill (1795) and a carding-and-fulling mill (1807). He opposed ratification. William Leete Stone, ed., *Washington County, New York . . .* (New York, 1901), 378; Crisfield Johnson, *History of Washington County, New York* (Philadelphia, 1878), 42.

BATCHELOR, ZEPHANIAH (28-1), of Montgomery, also materialized in a frontier area, in his case Caughnawaga. During the war he evidently was inactive and associated with the neutralist element. He possessed only a small farm, left no relatives, appeared for one year in the legislature and then vanished. *Public Papers of George Clinton . . .* (New York and Albany, 1899–1914), II, 621–622.

BECKER, ABRAHAM (51-7), of Albany, lived in Schoharie. Becker (1733-1818) came from a large Dutch family of farmers and was the sixth of seven sons. He served as a militia officer and presumably farmed. Another Abraham Becker, of German ancestry, came from New Jersey and served as a scout, and still a third, probably a relative, was considerably older. The identification is tentative. "Becker

Families," typescript, New York Genealogical and Biographical Society.

BRADNER, JOHN (24–3), of Orange, also appears out of the blue, no local history identifying his ancestry. Probably his father was Rev. John Bradner, a native of Scotland who served at Goshen's First Presbyterian Church, though a generation may have intervened. John owned a small property in Goshen and became the first supervisor of Minesink when it was created in 1788. E. M. Ruttenber and L. H. Clark, comps., *History of Orange County, New York* (Philadelphia, 1881), 664; Russel Headley, ed., *The History of Orange County, New York* (Middletown, N.Y., 1908), 231.

BURLING, EBENEZER S. (32–5), of Westchester, is equally obscure. Probably his father was Ebenezer who died in Eastchester in 1758 leaving land and mills. Ebenezer S. was a supervisor in that town, justice of the peace, and representative in 1785.

COOPER, GILBERT (91–10), of Orange, probably was born on Long Island to Abraham Cooper, whose £1,000 farm in Southampton was confiscated by the British, and who then fled to Saybrook, dying in 1784. He left £500 to his third son, Gilbert. Enough Long Islanders sought refuge in Orange County to make this connection possible, and no other Gilbert Cooper appears in the records. He owned two slaves in Haverstraw and sat in the legislature for a number of years.

DENNIS, JONATHAN (22–1), of Dutchess, cannot be traced at all, for the family name was apparently unique except in Rhode Island. He was an early resident of Beekmantown, which he served later as supervisor. He sat in the legislature for two terms.

DUBOYS, LEWIS (52–5), of Dutchess, was a somewhat atypical member of his party in that we know something about him. His father, Elias, was a captain who married the sister of Col. James Van Der Burgh. Lewis (1744–1824) started as a carpenter, presently ran an inn, bought some land, and traded. During the war he attained the rank of colonel in the Continental army and held the office of sheriff during the years 1781 to 1788. He paid a moderate tax in 1771 and lost his farm twenty years later. In between he probably owned substantial property. Duboys was an Antifederalist. *Dutchess County Historical Society Yearbook*, XX (1935), 71–82.

GRIFFIN, JACOB (51–5), of Dutchess (1749–1809), of unknown origin, ran a tavern, joined the local committee of safety, served as militia captain, and was a Presbyterian. He lived near Fishkill.

HOPKINS, DAVID (43–6), of Washington, was born in West Greenwich, Rhode Island, the son of a small farmer. He became a justice of the peace in that colony, but sold his property there and moved to

Hebron, New York, where he served as the town's first clerk, again held the office of justice, and sat in the legislature for many years beginning in 1778. In the senate (1786+) he supported the same side. He was a Presbyterian and Antifederalist. *The Salem Book* (Salem, N.Y., 1896), 51–53; Johnson, *Washington County*, 386.

HUSTED, EBENEZER (23–2), of Dutchess, belonged to a Connecticut family that settled in New York before 1700. None of the Husteds was prominent, and Husted evidently was a farmer of moderate property, living in the northwestern section of the county. He held local offices and attained the rank of captain in the militia.

LUDENTON, HENRY (52–1), of Dutchess, was born in Connecticut where his father was a farmer. Henry (1739–1817) enlisted in the militia, saw service as a private, married a Dutchess girl, and moved there about 1762, building the area's first sawmills and gristmills. He presently became locally prominent, holding the offices of justice of the peace, trustee of the Presbyterian church, and captain in the British army. He joined the local Revolutionary committees and became a colonel in the Dutchess County militia. These fairly high ranks seem to have earned him only a moderate property. He favored ratification in 1788. Ethel Mildred (Saltus) Ludington, *Ludington-Saltus Records*, ed. Louis Effingham de Forest (New Haven, 1925), 107, 152–153, 233.

McCRACKEN, JOSEPH (22–2), of Washington, immigrated from Worcester, Massachusetts, to Salem in 1767 where he bought a farm and built a brick house. A major in the Continental army, McCracken (1736–1825) lost an arm in the battle of Monmouth. By 1794 he held property above the average, but remained only a prosperous farmer. *Salem Book*, 73.

PAINE, BRINTON (88–3), of Dutchess, was born in 1737 in Windsor, where his father, Stephen, had a large farm. Brinton, the younger, joined his much better known relative, Ephraim, in Amenia, New York, about 1777. He served as a colonel and spent many months in prison. Later he moved to Elmira. He seems to have had no occupation other than farmer, and we do not know his economic status. H. D. Paine, ed., *Paine Family Records* . . . (Albany, N.Y., 1880–1883), II, 120.

PARKER, ICHABOD (54–3), of Washington, was living in Granville by 1782 and was still there in 1790, but is not listed as an early settler in the quite thorough county history. He served for two years in the legislature and opposed ratification. Since at least six of this party came from New England families and since this part of the state was settled from Massachusetts, Parker probably originated there, but he has not been traced.

SATTERLY, NATHANIEL (24–3), of Orange, was born in Setauket, Long Island, to a large and prosperous family. Probably the land was much divided. Nathaniel, the second of five sons, moved to Blooming Grove, Orange County, in 1760, where he built a gristmill, held local offices, and farmed. Charles J. Werner, *Genealogies of Long Island Families* . . . (New York, 1919), 80.

SNYDER, JOHANNIS (45–4), of Ulster, was born in Germany and served as militia colonel during the Revolution and as a justice of the peace. He had a son of the same name, a namesake lived in Albany County, and another Johannis Synder was building a mill near or in adjoining Orange County. Our Johannis (1720–1794) certainly lived in the Kingston area and belonged to the Dutch Reformed Church. The local histories make no effort to clarify matters. Nathaniel B. Sylvester, *History of Ulster County, New York* . . . (Philadelphia, 1880), 85; Probate Records, I, 185–186.

TAULMAN, PETER (28–3), of Orange, was born to an old family of Dutch farmers. He was a fourth son. According to the evidence in tax records, an older brother inherited most of the family property, but both paid a small tax. Taulman (1759–1826) became an adjutant in the Continental army and eventually moved west. Herbert S. Ackerman, "Talman-Tallman," mimeograph, N.Y. Gen. Biog. Soc.

THOMPSON, ISRAEL (27–1), of Albany (1741–1805), descended from a Welsh family. He was a prosperous farmer near Kingsbury, north of Albany, served in the militia during the French war, attained the rank of lieutenant colonel during the Revolution, and became an Antifederalist. *N.Y. Gen. Biog. Rec.*, XXXVI (1905), 276–278.

WISNER, HENRY III (23–2), of Orange, is not to be confused with his uncle Henry, Jr., a senator, congressman, Antifederalist, and more prominent man, who served in the lower house in 1788. Henry III (1742–1812) was the son of Capt. John Wisner (1722–1778), who owned a 280-acre farm. Henry III held no local offices unless some have wrongly been attributed to his uncle and seems to have derived his only importance from that relationship. G. Franklin Wisner, *The Wisners in America and their Kindred* . . . (Baltimore, 1918), 72, 82.

Other legislators voting consistently with the Clintonians included ISAAC BLOOM (10–1), Dutchess County shopkeeper; JACOB FORD (48–13), small farmer who moved from Connecticut to Columbia County; WILLIAM HARPER (100–22), small farmer and Antifederalist of the western frontier; THOMAS JANSEN (22–4), Ulster County farmer; ADAM MARTIN (22–4), Massachusetts-born miller and innkeeper of what was then the frontier in Washington County; MATTHEW PATTERSON (107–24), Dutchess County trader of substantial property who became an Antifederalist; EBENEZER PURDY (54–10), large farmer and future Republican of Westchester; EDWARD SAVAGE (75–19), small farmer, Antifederalist, Republican of Washington County, and JAMES TALMADGE (13–1), Dutchess County blacksmith and farmer.

NEW JERSEY

Cosmopolitans (West Jersey)

BOWEN, JONATHAN (90–14), of Bridgeton, Cumberland, came from a Baptist family that emigrated to Massachusetts in 1662. His father, Jonathan, died in 1782. The legislator owned a valuable farm along the Cohansey River, sat in the Convention of 1776, and voted for the Constitution in 1787. Thomas Cushing and C. E. Sheppard, *History of the Counties of Gloucester, Salem, and Cumberland, New Jersey* . . . (Philadelphia, 1883), 698–699.

BRICK, JOSHUA (20–1), of Maurice River, Cumberland, owned a substantial farm. His father John (d. 1757) had been an assemblyman and left an inventory of £2,270 in personal property, plus large amounts of land, but also left a number of children. Joshua seems not to have been well-to-do. He became justice of the peace before the war.

BURGEN, JOHN (49–9), of Hopewell, Cumberland, like Bowen descended from a Massachusetts family. His father left only a small property. John (1735–1793) became a prosperous farmer and moneylender, with £2,000 at interest in 1781. He probably owned about the same estate when he died. Cushing and Sheppard, *Gloucester, Salem, and Cumberland*, 699.

CLARK, THOMAS (55–5), of Greenwich, Gloucester, was the son of Jeffrey Clark, a Philadelphian who owned considerable real estate. Thomas (1737–1809) was a well-to-do Quaker farmer, leaving $12,435.22 in personal property and over eight hundred acres. He also surveyed and sat as a judge beginning in 1768. Frank H. Stewart, *Notes on Old Gloucester County, New Jersey* (Camden, N.J., 1917), 303.

DAVIS, DAVID (24–1), of Waterford, Gloucester, was the son of David (1694–1754), a large landowner, justice of the peace, and Quaker of Salem County. David, Jr. (1730–1806), inherited over a thousand acres and some slaves, which he freed. Salem County Historical Society, *Publications*, IV (1965), 37–40.

HALL, EDWARD (91–8), of Mannington, Salem, was the youngest son in a family of large landowners—his father, William, Jr., owned 2,000 acres. Edward himself owned only a modest farm of 240 acres.

Brought up a Quaker, he left his sect to become a militia colonel. Cushing and Sheppard, *Gloucester, Salem, and Cumberland*, 435–436.

JAMES, JAMES (21–0), of Piles Grove, Salem (d. 1807?), probably started as a cabinetmaker in Philadelphia and presently became a merchant and miller, owning seven hundred acres. He may have come from a Quaker family. He held no other offices and remains obscure.

LLOYD, EPHRAIM (39–8), of Lower Penn's Neck, Salem (d. 1795), cannot be traced. He held no office other than that of representative. He was a farmer and by the time of his death was well-to-do.

Low, JOSEPH (35–3), of Deptford, Gloucester (d. 1795), appears first in Philadelphia where he owned considerable property. He retained some or all of this and in addition owned a farm or farms in New Jersey totaling 478 acres in 1779, when he served a single term as representative.

MAYHEW, JOHN (52–9), of Pittsgrove, Salem, probably belonged to a family of large landowners who immigrated from Ulster early in the century. His father was also a John. John, Jr., became justice of the peace in 1763, judge in 1777, and eventually sat in the state senate. He was a Baptist and owned a farm of 157 acres, 3 horses, and 5 cattle in 1782. Probably the judgeship furnished his principal income.

MOTT, JAMES, JR. (35–4), of Middletown, Monmouth, was grandson of Gershom Mott, high sheriff and large landowner, and son of James Mott, who inherited part of the estate. In 1787 James, Sr., died leaving to his son, James, all of his land and to grandchildren £600 in bequests. Evidently he can be classified as well-to-do but barely so. He served very briefly as major and just as briefly in the assembly.

SHEPPARD, JOHN (57–0), of Greenwich, Cumberland, came from an old family. His father was probably John who left 385 acres and five sons. Sheppard (d. 1805) became a Quaker, entered trade, and eventually acquired a fortune. Cushing and Sheppard, *Gloucester, Salem, and Cumberland*, 687; Francis Bazley Lee, ed., *Genealogical and Memorial History of the State of New Jersey* (New York, 1910), I, 355.

SINNICKSON, THOMAS (66–12), of Salem town and Lower Penn's Neck, Salem, is one of the few well-known members of New Jersey's legislature. His father, Andrew, was a wealthy landowner, judge, and councillor. Thomas (1744–1817) became a merchant, justice of the peace, Episcopalian, and Federalist. He left a large property but probably was not wealthy at this earlier period. James Grant Wilson and John Fiske, eds., *Appletons' Cyclopædia of American Biography* (New York, 1887–1900), V, 542.

SMITH, JOSEPH (34–1), of Burlington town, Burlington, also came from a prominent family. His father, Samuel, was treasurer of West Jersey, a councillor, and a wealthy Quaker merchant, who left £6,000 in personal property. Joseph (b. 1742) married the daughter of Abel James, Philadelphia merchant, and also inherited £1,000 from an uncle. He seems to have lived off his real estate. R. Morris Smith, *The Burlington Smiths* (Philadelphia, 1877), is not a dependable source.

SMITH, RICHARD S. (43–0), of Burlington, Burlington County, was Joseph's brother (see above), and is not to be confused with his uncle, Richard Smith (1735–1803), who was a lawyer, diarist, neutralist, and member of the Continental Congress. Our Richard S. (1752–1796) was a merchant and Quaker like his father, and he voted for the Constitution. He left £10,000 in bequests in 1796. Lee, *Hy. of New Jersey*, 1400–1401, is unreliable.

THOMPSON, MARK (30–2), of Mansfield (now Warren), Sussex, was born across the Delaware in Montgomery County, Pennsylvania. His brother was a lawyer and business man of reputation. Mark (1739–1803) had settled in Sussex County by 1760, acquired a large tract of land, built a gristmill, and presently owned an iron forge, leaving $17,378.88½ (roughly £5,000) when he died. He attained the rank of colonel, went to the state senate, and eventually to Congress, where he was a Federalist. James P. Snell, comp., *History of Sussex and Warren Counties, New Jersey . . .* (Philadelphia, 1881), 713; *Biog. Dir. of Am. Cong.*, 1712.

TOWNSEND, ELIJAH (43–8), of Upper Cape May, belonged to an old family of the district that genealogists have not traced in detail. The founder, John, was a Quaker who immigrated first to Long Island and then to New Jersey. Elijah's father James (d. 1786) left two slaves and some land. The representative owned a mill in 1780, a tavern in 1785 (when he held office), and at other times about two hundred acres of land. Lewis Townsend Stevens, *The History of Cape May County, New Jersey . . .* (Cape May City, N.J., 1897), 37.

TOWNSEND, HENRY-YOUNG (28–5), of Upper Cape May, may have been a Quaker, but served as sheriff, militia captain, paymaster, and subsistence-master. Townsend (1744–1789) owned a tanyard, a gristmill, and 585 acres of which 100 was improved. His personal property was valued at £482 in 1790.

TOWNSEND, RICHARD (26–3), of Upper Cape May (d. 1802), served briefly as sheriff and two terms as representative. In the eighties he held 300 acres at most, though he added some land later on and left personal property worth $9,194.65.

TUCKER, SAMUEL (51-8), of Trenton, Hunterdon, probably came from Boston, where he had an aunt and cousin, though his wife was English, and genealogies do not clear up the matter. Tucker (d. 1789) was a Presbyterian and a trustee of the church in Trenton, but he had Anglican leanings and momentarily accepted an offer of British protection. Before the war he held important political posts and became a judge in 1776. He owned considerable landed property, and his personal estate was assessed at £5,977 15s. 1d. John Hall, *History of the Presbyterian Church in Trenton*, (New York, 1859), 200–203.

Affiliated with the foregoing were JOSEPH BIDDLE (73-16) of Burlington, wealthy farmer of prominent family; Gen. FRANKLIN DAVEN-PORT (18-4), Gloucester lawyer and Federalist; EPHRAIM HARRIS (21-6), Cumberland judge; BENJAMIN HOLME, well-to-do farmer of Salem; JOHN KILLÉ (12-0), wealthy Gloucester merchant and large landowner; CLAYTON NEWBOLD (12-1), large landowner of Burlington; JOSIAH SEELEY (15-3), well-to-do miller from Cumberland; WILLIAM SMITH (14-2), of Salem, small farmer; and NEZER SWAIN (23-6), Cape May shopkeeper.

Among the few assemblymen of some reputation were ABRAHAM CLARK, Republican lawyer and popular leader (East Jersey, 42-13); lawyer JONATHAN DAYTON, prominent Federalist and later Republican (neutral); Federalist FREDERICK FRELINGHUYSEN (neutral); trader and Federalist JOSIAH HORNBLOWER (East Jersey, 34-9); ROBERT MORRIS, wealthy lawyer, chief justice, and Federalist (East Jersey, 21-10); and JAMES and JOHN SCHUREMAN, merchant father and son, the latter a Federalist, both neutrals.

Localists (East Jersey)

ARNOLD, JACOB (41-3), of Morristown, Morris, was the son of Samuel Arnold, who came from Connecticut and built a tavern. Under Jacob (1749-1827) the tavern, which was commodious and reputable, with a 264-acre farm attached, became the center of the resistance movement. Arnold was a cavalry captain and sheriff. *New Jersey Archives*, IX, 22; Andrew M. Sherman, *Historic Morristown, New Jersey* (Morristown, N.J., 1905), 206–207.

BAKER, MATTHIAS (25-5), of Woodbridge, Middlesex, is obscure. Called a "farmer," he joined the town's committee of correspondence and served as justice of the peace. He belonged to the Elizabethtown Presbyterian Church.

BEARDSLEE, CHARLES (59-11), of Hardyston, Sussex, was born of pioneer stock. What we know of his earlier career is largely suppositious. Beardslee (1742–1803) may have served in the Revolutionary army. By 1780 he owned 520 acres and a sawmill. He attended the legislature continuously from 1784 to 1800, and left a substantial, though not a large, property. Alanson A. Haines, *Hardyston Memorial* (Newton, N.J., 1888), 29.

BLAIR, ROBERT (49–5), of Bedminster, Somerset, seems to have been an immigrant from Scotland. Blair (1748–1800) married a girl of good family and owned a two-hundred-acre farm. His son became a prominent merchant and his grandson a Presbyterian minister. He was a private during the war.

BLANCH, ISAAC (96–19), of Harrington, Bergen, another private, remains obscure. He married into a leading family of Orange County, New York, became a justice of the peace in 1776, and served on the local committee of observation. Tax lists indicate that he was a miller of small property.

CARMICHAEL, ALEXANDER (45–5), of Morristown, Morris (d. 1806), probably immigrated. He held a number of offices including that of sheriff and commissioner of forfeited estates. He also owned a small farm, but at the time of his legislative service (1779/1780) he may perhaps be considered an official. Later he prospered, contributing to a school and a library company. He was a Presbyterian.

COOK, ELLIS (126–26), of Hanover, Morris, descended from Ellis, a blacksmith, Ellis, a tavernkeeper, and possibly one or two more Ellises. Ours (1731?–1797) held a farm of moderate size, was probably a Presbyterian, and remains obscure.

COVENHOVEN, JOHN (41–4), of Freehold, Monmouth, belonged to a large family that arrived in 1630 and produced three or four Johns in the Revolutionary period. This John (d. 1803) was probably the colonel and justice of the peace who was a well-to-do (?) landowner and miller. He left an inventory of $18,656.49.

HENDERSON, THOMAS (77–8), of Freehold, Monmouth, was son of John (1697–1771), a farmer. Thomas (1743–1824) attended the College of New Jersey and practiced medicine for many years. A patriot, he was a colonel during the Revolution. Subsequent to his legislative career he sat in the Continental Congress and became surrogate. At this time (1782) he had a sizable farm and a mill. William S. Hornor, *This Old Monmouth of Ours* (Freehold, N.J., 1932), 151.

HENDRICKSON, DANIEL (21–2), of Holmdel, Monmouth (1728–1788), one of three of that name, was the son of Daniel, a prosperous, well-educated farmer. Also a farmer, he saw service as a captain (a cousin was a colonel) and was an elder in the Dutch Reformed Church. Hornor, *Old Monmouth*, 412.

KELLEY, DAVID (56–7), of Bernardston, Somerset (d. 1811), probably immigrated. He may have been a private. Local accounts scarcely mention him, yet he turns up as a justice of the peace in 1781 and judge in 1783/1784. Otherwise he had a small farm and left rather a small property.

LONGSTREET, CHRISTOPHER (49–5), of Newton, Sussex, like Kelley, is obscure. He probably moved from another part of the state, perhaps, for example, from New Brunswick where a blacksmith left property to his son by that name. He owned in 1774 a small farm, but did not make his mark as soldier or official until he served several years in the legislature.

MARSH, DANIEL (85–5), of Elizabethtown, Essex, descended from a family that arrived from New Haven in 1647 and multiplied. They were Presbyterians and farmers. His father was probably Daniel, a farmer (d. 1756). He did not serve in the Revolution, but held civil posts (e.g., commission of forfeited estates). He was a miller with a small amount of land. New Jersey Historical Society, *Proceedings*, LXIX (1951), 224–225.

NEILSON, JOHN (37–6), of New Brunswick, Middlesex, was the son of a doctor who immigrated from Ireland and settled as a merchant with his brother, established a large shipping business, and died just after John was born. John joined his uncle and succeeded him. He took a prominent part as a radical in the Revolution, rose to the rank of colonel, served as quartermaster, and then reentered trade. He voted for ratification in New Jersey's convention and remained a Federalist. W. Woodford Clayton, ed., *History of Union and Middlesex Counties New Jersey . . .* (Philadelphia, 1882), 468–470, 485, 490; *DAB*, XIII, 411–412.

SCHENCK, JACOB (18–2), of Windsor, Middlesex, a substantial farmer, inherited land from relations who were among the first settlers in the area. His father probably was Reoloff Schenck, Jr., of Freehold, Monmouth, a well-to-do brewer. Schenck is otherwise obscure.

SEBRING, REOLOFF (28–4), of Bridgewater, Somerset, descended from an early Dutch settler (Suebering) in Kings County, New York. His father (?) pioneered into New Jersey's hilly interior and left a large family. Reoloff presumably had a farm, served as captain and justice of the peace, and died leaving only £169 8s. 7d. in personal property.

SHREVE, ISRAEL (28–1), of Mansfield, Burlington, was the brother of Caleb and uncle of Isaac, both of whom sat in the legislature. His father was a well-to-do Quaker farmer and moneylender. Israel (1739–1799) became a colonel and justice of the peace and later moved to Pennsylvania where he remained a farmer.

SUYDAM, JACOB (51–6), of South Amboy, Middlesex, probably was the son of Cornelius (1768) who left farms to two sons but only £50 each to his youngest sons, including Jacob (d. 1805). Jacob was a private in the Revolution. When he died he owned a sizable farm in South Amboy and land in Somerset, so that he could leave £1,450 in bequests.

A few other important East Jerseymen were MELANCTHON FREEMAN (14–2), Middlesex doctor; JOAB HOUGHTON (49–9), Baptist farmer from Hunterdon; AARON KITCHELL (70–17) of Morris County, blacksmith who became a Republican; GARRETT LEYDECKER (17–2), Hackensack farmer; NATHANIEL SCUDDER (15–0), well-to-do Freehold doctor; THOMSON STELLE (30–7), small farmer of Middlesex; JOSEPH STILL-WELL (34–8), substantial farmer and judge from Monmouth; and HENRY VAN DYKE (35–8) of Somerset, substantial shopkeeper and colonel.

PENNSYLVANIA

Republicans

BULL, THOMAS (35–1), of East Nantmell, Chester, a well-to-do iron-master, was the son of William, an early settler. Thomas (1744–1837) received little schooling and started in life as a stonemason. He became manager of the Warwick furnace before the Revolution, in which he served as lieutenant colonel and was imprisoned. He was an Episcopalian, a Federalist, and reputedly wealthy, though tax records indicate that he was at most well-to-do during the eighties. William Henry Egle, "The Federal Constitution of 1787: Sketches of the Members of the Pennsylvania Convention," *Pennsylvania Magazine of History and Biography*, X (1886), 459–460.

CLYMER, GEORGE (56–3), of Philadelphia, a signer of the Declaration of Independence and the Constitution, was left fatherless when a child, but his uncle was a prosperous and well-educated merchant, whom Clymer (1739–1813) succeeded. An ardent "radical" before the war, he ended as a moderate Federalist. He was an Episcopalian, patron of the arts, bank president, and wealthy man. *DAB*, IV, 234–235.

DELANY, SHARP (41–4), of Philadelphia, was born in Ireland of a prominent family who also owned a large estate in New Jersey. Sharp (1739–1799) was in Philadelphia by 1759 where he married exceedingly well and became a druggist. He was politically active before the war, during which he fought as a captain and ultimately colonel in the Continental army. He subscribed £5,000 to the bank in 1780, yet the tax lists show him to be well-to-do rather than wealthy. Delany joined the Society of the Cincinnati and the American Philosophical Society. Like Clymer and Bull, he was an Episcopalian. John Spencer, *Genealogical Sketch . . .* (Chester, Pa., 1902), 69–98.

EVANS, SAMUEL (61–0), of Ashton, Chester, belonged to a Baptist family. His father, Col. Evans, attended the legislature for an even longer period, voting on the same side but not quite so consistently. Col. Evans and his three brothers received fifteen hundred acres from their father; thus the colonel was a substantial man. Samuel (1758–1805), however, held a rather small farm in 1785. He was a milita captain and became a judge later in life. Septimus E. Nivin, *Genealogy of Evans, Nivin and Allied Families* (Philadelphia, 1930), 29–30, 41.

FITZSIMONS, THOMAS (58–2), of Philadelphia, hardly requires a sketch. Fitzsimons (1741–1811), a signer of the Constitution, immigrated from Ireland as a poor boy and acquired wealth in trade and fame in politics. He was a Catholic. *DAB,* VI, 444.

GARDNER, PHILIP (81–3), of Hallam, York, voted on the same side but is virtually unknown. His name and its alternate spelling, Gartner, suggest a German ancestry. Peter Gartner was in Hallam by 1757. Tax lists reveal a substantial farmer with two stills and a slave.

HANNUM, JOHN (66–4), of East Bradford, Chester, a militia colonel during the war, was the son of a well-to-do Quaker farmer. By 1785 he paid the largest tax in his agricultural township, owning a mill and a sizable farm. Hannum (1742–1799) held many local offices and favored ratification. *Pa. Mag. Hist. Biog.,* XI (1887), 213–214.

HILTZHEIMER, JACOB (31–0), of Philadelphia, resided in and was chosen from the city, but derived his income from a sizable and exceptionally prosperous farm. Hiltzheimer (1729–1798) immigrated from Germany, served an apprenticeship to a goldsmith, leased land near the city, and presently raised some of the finest livestock in America. His diary is well known. He belonged to various scientific and benevolent societies, served as a vestryman in the German Reformed church and became a Federalist. Jacob Cox Parsons, ed., *Extracts from the Diary of Jacob Hiltzheimer, of Philadelphia* (Philadelphia, 1893), vii–viii.

HUBLY, ADAM (75–5), of Martick, Lancaster, descended from a German family, probably of farmers. Hubly (1747–1821) studied law with Edward Shippen and practiced. During the war he attained the rank of lieutenant colonel and a reputation for bravery. He held a variety of important civilian posts including those of justice of the peace and councillor. He favored ratification, became an Episcopalian, and helped support a college. The principal biographical sketch errs in calling him a Constitutionalist. *Pa. Mag. Hist. Biog.*, XXXIII (1914), 129–130.

LILLY, JOSEPH (93–4), of Heidelberg, New York, is obscure. Tax lists indicate that he was a substantial farmer, and he was a Federalist in 1800. He served four terms in the legislature.

MILLER, HENRY (74–0), of Yorktown, York, was born in Lancaster, the youngest son of a prominent landowner. Miller (1751–1824) studied law, married well, and moved to York in 1770. He served as lieutenant colonel in the Continental army and held various other offices, ending his career much later as a general. He led a brigade against the Whiskey Rebels, won an office under the Federalists, and lost it after Jefferson's election. See *Pa. Mag. Hist. Biog.*, XI (1887), 341–345, XII (1888), 425–431.

MORRIS, ROBERT (71–1), of Philadelphia (1734–1806), needs no sketch. See *DAB*, XIII, 219.

RALSTON, ROBERT (90–5), of Vincent, Chester, was probably the son of Robert who immigrated with his father from Ireland, though two other Roberts lived at the same time. This Ralston (1722–1814) was a small farmer. J. Smith Futhey and Gilbert Cope, *History of Chester County, Pennsylvania . . .* (Philadelphia, 1881), 703–704.

RITCHIE, MATTHEW (65–6), of Cecil, Washington, appeared as an agent of Virginia in 1777. His origins are unknown. Ritchie (d. 1798) was a Mason, sub-lieutenant, a justice of the peace, and a shopkeeper, picking up considerable land. In the nineties he represented George Washington in ejectment suits. Boyd Crumrine, *History of Washington County, Pennsylvania* (Philadelphia, 1882), 859.

ROBINSON, WILLIAM, JR. (56–4), of Northern Liberties, Philadelphia, is an obscure man despite his three years in the legislature. The records contain several men of the name who insisted on naming their sons William. Tax lists include one with a small estate, others with almost none. Speculation seems idle.

SALTER, JOHN (43–2), of Philadelphia County, may have been the lumber merchant who received £43 from the city committee of safety in 1776, or who was listed as a member of the firm "Salter Cooper and Redman" in 1786. Since he was chosen from the county, a more attractive guess is an Oxford substantial farmer, perhaps the same who served as a private in the Continental army. A Richard Salter in Burlington County, not far away, died in 1762 leaving a fairly large estate and three sons including a John.

TYSON, HENRY (60–5), of Windsor, York, is obscure. Clearly he was a substantial miller, with no military record and no other political offices. A genealogy of the family does not help; his background was certainly very plain.

WAYNE, ANTHONY (32–0), of Waynesboro, Chester (1745–1796), is the famous general. See *DAB*, XIX, 563.

WHELAN, TOWNSEND (44–2), of Uwchlan, Chester, descended from a respectable Quaker family. His father was a prosperous farmer and storekeeper. Townsend (d. 1790), the fourth son of five, served briefly in the militia as a private and practiced medicine though untrained. He remains obscure. John W. Jordan, ed., *Colonial and Revolutionary Families: Genealogical and Personal Memoirs* (New York, 1911), II, 663.

WILLING, RICHARD (86–8), of Haverford, Chester, was probably born in Philadelphia to Charles Willing (1710–1754) and the daughter of Joseph Shippen. Charles, the son of a prosperous Bristol merchant, acquired wealth in Philadelphia, served as mayor, and helped found the College of Philadelphia. The most prominent of his eleven children was Thomas, associate of Robert Morris. Richard (1745–1798) married well and settled quietly on a country estate. *Ibid.*, I, 128.

WORK, JOSEPH (74–4), of Donegal, Lancaster, probably was an immigrant from North Ireland. Work (d. 1796) married the daughter of Col. Jacob Cooke, another representative whose father came from Londonderry. Joseph became a captain and sheriff. Since he owned land but no farm animals he probably derived his income from his office. Lancaster County Historical Society, *Proceedings*, XII (1908), 305–306.

Among the many legislators associated with this party were SAMUEL ASHMEAD (31–5), Philadelphia merchant; SAMUEL J. ATLEE (26–2), Germantown lawyer; MARK BIRD (12–1), Berks ironmaster; HUGH H. BRACKENRIDGE (15–5), Pittsburgh lawyer and writer; GEORGE CAMPBELL (13–0), Philadelphia lawyer; DANIEL CLYMER (38–11), Berks miller; EVAN EVANS (80–12), Chester clothier-farmer; Gen. JAMES EWING (21–0) of York; the Quakers GEORGE (35–5) and ISAAC (57–19) GRAY of Blockley; HENRY HILL (63–7), Philadelphia merchant; GEORGE LOGAN (49–6), Philadelphia County farmer, Quaker, and Jeffersonian; WILLIAM MACLAY (19–4), frontier lawyer and Jeffersonian; and SAMUEL MEREDITH (29–0), Philadelphia merchant.

Principal neutrals included JACOB ARNDT, Northampton miller and official; JOHN CARSON, Dauphin storekeeper; WILLIAM COATS, Philadelphia brickmaker; JACOB ENGLE, Germantown cooper; PERCIFER FRAZER, Chester ironmaster; EMANUEL EYRE, Philadelphia shipmaker; ROBERT LOLLAR, Montgomery surveyor; NICHOLAS LUTZ, Reading miller; MOSES McLEAN, York surveyor-farmer; JOSEPH PARKE, Chester farmer; CHARLES PETTIT, Philadelphia merchant and Federalist; PETER RICHARDS,

Montgomery innkeeper; JOSEPH STRAWBRIDGE, Chester farmer (?); DAVID THOMAS, Chester tanner (?); and PETER TREXLER, Northampton farmer.

Constitutionalists

ALLISON, JAMES (29–2), of Cecil, Washington, arrived from Maryland just before the war and married into the locally prominent Bradford family. He served briefly in the Continental army and then acquired a substantial farm. A moral man, he belonged to the society for the abolition of slavery and was a Presbyterian elder. He opposed ratification. Crumrine, *Washington County*, 707.

ANTIS, FREDERICK (94–5), of Mahoning, Northumberland, was the son of a prosperous German Moravian farmer. Frederick (1730–1801) became an expert gunsmith who lost considerable property during the war, in which he served as colonel. He remained a substantial ironmaker but no more than that, was a justice of the peace and Antifederalist. S. Foster Damon, *One Line of the Pastorius Family of Germantown, Pennsylvania* . . . (Cambridge, Mass., 1926), 19–21.

BARR, JAMES (30–2), of Derry, Westmoreland (1749–1824), was born in Lancaster County of Scotch-Irish parentage and moved to the frontier as a young man. There he took the lead in the movement for independence, became a justice of the peace, a lieutenant (?), and small farmer. He opposed the Constitution. *Armstrong County Pennsylvania: Her People, Past and Present* . . . (Chicago, 1914), II, 752.

BEALE, THOMAS (33–2), of Milford, Cumberland, was the son of William Beale (1709–1800), an immigrant who accumulated a sizable property. Thomas (1737–1803), a Revolutionary soldier, moved west and obtained a large farm with a mill. He eventually sat as an associate judge. Mary (Beale) Hitchens, *The Beales of Chester County, Pa.* (Brooklyn, N.Y., 1957).

CLARK, ROBERT (91–7), of Dromore, Dauphin, came of pioneer stock. Brought up as a farmer, with a limited education, Clark (1740–1821) served as private and finally officer in the French wars. In 1776 he was chosen captain of the militia, rose to the rank of colonel, and also attained the dignity of a Presbyterian elder. He owned a small farm. William Henry Egle, *History of the Counties of Dauphin and Lebanon* . . . (Philadelphia, 1883), 474–475.

CULBERTSON, JOHN (33–0), of East Caln, Chester, the son of an immigrant, served as major in the state militia, owned a sawmill, a fulling mill, and a store, but he paid the tax of a substantial, not a well-to-do, property owner. He was probably a Presbyterian. Lewis R. Culbertson, *Genealogy of the Culbertson and Culberson Families*, rev. ed. (Zanesville, Ohio, 1923), 15–18.

DEAL (DALE), SAMUEL (81–5), of White Deer, Northumberland, appeared on the frontier by 1744, origin unknown. He pioneered, obtaining a small, not very valuable farm, served very briefly as a militia captain, and belonged to the Presbyterian church—none of which explains why he was elected three times to the legislature. Franklin Ellis and A. N. Hungerford, eds., *History of . . . the Susquehanna and Juniata Valleys . . .* (Philadelphia, 1886), 1299.

FINDLEY, WILLIAM (64–6), of Mount Pleasant, Westmoreland, a native of northern Ireland, immigrated at the age of twenty-two. Findley (1741–1821) tried his hand as weaver and teacher, married, and settled down as a farmer. A "radical," he was a militia captain during the war, after which he moved west and resumed farming. Although he received little schooling, he read widely and was elected to the American Philosophical Society. He served the Presbyterian church as an elder and his community as a legislator for many years, becoming a Constitutionalist, prominent Antifederalist, and Republican. *DAB*, VI, 385.

GILCHRIST, JOHN (31–1), of Franklin, Fayette, probably lived originally in Lancaster County where John Gilchrist, Sr., Esq. and John, Jr., both owned farms. The latter became first captain, then major in 1780, after which he disappears from the Lancaster records and turns up on the frontier with a 250-acre tract, five horses, and five cows. He was an Antifederalist. Franklin Ellis, *History of Fayette County, Pennsylvania . . .* (Philadelphia, 1882), 554, barely mentions him.

HOGE, JONATHAN (31–3), of East Pennsboro, Cumberland, was the son of a large farmer who moved against the tide into Pennsylvania from the Shenandoah Valley of Virginia. A brother, John, went to Princeton and became a Presbyterian minister. Jonathan (1725–1800) shared John's intellectual interests and was elected to the American Philosophical Society, but he remained a farmer. He held the office of justice of the peace and was chosen to the Supreme Executive Council as well as to local committees. He opposed ratification. William Henry Egle, *Pennsylvania Genealogies* (Harrisburg, Pa., 1886), 633–634.

KENNEDY, THOMAS (29–1), of West Pennsboro, Cumberland, cannot be traced; there were several of the name. One of these was a militia captain, Antifederalist, and Jeffersonian, and owned a small farm.

LATTIMER, ROBERT (47–2), of Allen, Northampton, was the eldest son of John Lattimer, a farmer. Robert owned a small farm. He was of

Scotch-Irish ancestry, a Presbyterian, and either he or a son served as a private in the Revolution. *The Scotch-Irish of Northampton County, Pennsylvania,* Northampton County Historical and Genealogical Society, *Publications,* I (1926), 33, 115, 118, 156.

McCLENE (McLENE), James (43–0), of Antrim, Cumberland, supposedly born in New London, received a good education from a Presbyterian minister and moved to Antrim in 1754. Here he developed a nice farm and distilling business. McClene (1730–1806) served in local conventions, the state constitutional convention, the Supreme Executive Council, and the Continental Congress. *Biog. Dir. of Am. Cong.,* 1285; *Pa. Mag. Hist. Biog.,* IV (1880), 93–94.

M'CALMONT, JAMES (90–8), of Letterkenny, Franklin, was probably the son of James, a Letterkenny small farmer. James, Jr. (1739–1809), was a famous Indian fighter, rising to the rank of major. After the war he settled down to farming on a 339-acre tract. He was a Presbyterian and an Antifederalist.

McDOWELL, JOHN (61–1), of Peters, Washington, a native of Ireland, immigrated when a young man and married the sister of David Bradford, radical politician. McDowell (1736–1809) pioneered, building a log cabin and presently a nice house. An Antifederalist, he served as a justice of the peace and an elder in the church and helped found an academy. Crumrine, *Washington County,* 869–870.

McFERRAN, WILLIAM (33–1), of Mount Bethel, Northampton, a Scotch-Irish Presbyterian, had arrived in that area by 1761, possibly as an immigrant. In 1779, just before his term in the legislature, he owned 294 acres, of which 80 was cleared and 20 sown, with three horses, four cows, and twelve sheep. Northampton Co. Hist. Gen. Soc., *Pub.,* I (1926), 519, 521, 579.

MERCER, JAMES (68–6), of Strasburg, Lancaster, moved from New York as a captain and twice married well. Mercer (d. 1804) presently attained the rank of colonel and owned a prosperous farm. Lancaster Co. Hist. Soc., *Proc.,* III (1899), 40.

MITCHELL, DAVID (31–1), of Peters of Rye, Cumberland, probably was a distiller, justice of the peace, Antifederalist, and Republican. Little else is known about him.

MONTGOMERY, WILLIAM (35–1), of Turbit and Mahoning, Northumberland, was born in Chester. Montgomery (1736–1816) attended the 1775 provincial congress, served as colonel in the militia, and in 1777 moved to Northumberland where he built a gristmill and a sawmill. He held other offices subsequently. Herbert C. Bell, ed., *History of Northumberland County, Pennsylvania . . .* (Chicago, 1891), 216.

PIPER, JOHN (58–2), of Colerain, Bedford, origin unknown, first appears in 1773 as a sheriff (a Virginia origin seems probable). Thereafter he continuously held important state offices and as colonel was exceptionally active in organizing the western militia. He owned three hundred acres, but undoubtedly made a living through his offices.

RHEA, JOHN (30–0), of Lurgan, Franklin, also probably made a career from officeholding. His father, a Scotch-Irish immigrant, pioneered. Rhea enlisted in the army at an early age, became a lieutenant colonel during the Revolution and a brigadier general later. After the war he became coroner. Much later he went to Congress as a Republican. Jordan, ed., *Col. and Rev. Families*, I, 639.

SMITH, ABRAHAM (84–3), of Antrim, Cumberland, and Franklin, was son of James, a small farmer. Abraham (d. 1813) also farmed, but made his reputation by becoming a militia colonel even before the Revolution. He was an Antifederalist. J. F. Richard, *History of Franklin County, Pennsylvania* (Chicago, 1887), 556.

WHITEHILL, ROBERT (88–8), of East Pennsboro, Cumberland, was an outstanding leader of the interior farmers. The son of a Scotch-Irish immigrant, Whitehill (1738–1813) received a good education and improved himself thereafter. He bought four hundred acres, built a stone house, and served his section politically in many capacities. He opposed ratification and became a Republican. He acquired more fame than property. *DAB*, XX, 131–132.

Other leading Constitutionalists included WILLIAM BROWN (49–7) of Lancaster, small farmer; JOHN CAROTHERS (49–9) of Cumberland, small farmer; JOHN CRAIG (69–8) of Lancaster, substantial propertyholder; JAMES EDGAR (22–2) of Washington, Antifederalist, Jeffersonian, and officeholder; JOHN HANNAM (27–3) of Washington, substantial landowner and Antifederalist; JOHN HARRIS (42–6) of Cumberland, immigrant, entrepreneur, and Antifederalist (not the founder of Harrisburg); GABRIEL HIESTER (28–3) of Berks, tanner-farmer of substantial property, Antifederalist, and Jeffersonian; JOHN LINDSEY (30–4) of Chester, farmer; ADAM ORTH (78–12) of Dauphin, substantial ironmaster and Antifederalist; THEOPHILUS PHILLIPS (29–2) of Fayette, substantial shopkeeper and Antifederalist; JAMES PORTER (41–6) of Lancaster, innkeeper; JOHN RALSTON (28–3) of Northampton, trader-farmer of substantial property; JOHN SMILIE (55–9) of Fayette, Irish immigrant, farmer, Antifederalist, Jeffersonian, and a principal spokesman; RICHARD WALLACE (24–2) of Westmoreland, substantial man of unknown occupation; and ALEXANDER WRIGHT (29–3) of Washington, frontier farmer, and Antifederalist.

MARYLAND

See my article "Political Parties in Revolutionary Maryland, 1780–1787," *Maryland Historical Magazine*, LXII (1967), 19–27, to which the following are added:

Cosmopolitans

CADWALADER, JOHN (24–4), of Kent, scion of a prominent Pennsylvania and Maryland family, and son of the eminent wealthy Dr. Thomas Cadwalader, attended the College of Philadelphia but did not graduate. Instead John (1742–1786) became a merchant with his brother Lambert. During the war he served as brigadier general in the Pennsylvania militia. He married a Lloyd and owned a rich Maryland estate including a hundred slaves. *DAB*, III, 398.

ELZEY, ARNOLD (25–3), of Somerset, came from an old Somerset family featuring a succession of Arnold Elzeys. They were all well-to-do landowners, reputable but not distinguished. Arnold was a doctor and large landowner assessed, in 1783, for £3,513 worth of taxable property. Clayton Torrence, *Old Somerset on the Eastern Shore of Maryland* (Richmond, 1935), 444.

FELL, WILLIAM (19–2), of Baltimore, inherited a large property created originally by merchant ancestors who invested in land and married extraordinarily well. William studied law and died very young. Annie Middleton (Leakin) Sioussat, *Old Baltimore* (New York, 1931), 72–74.

JOHNSON, EDWARD (19–3), of Calvert, an elusive figure, was most likely a doctor who owned 784 acres in the country and eventually moved to Baltimore, where he was admired and acquired a substantial property.

KEENE, WILLIAM (19–2), of Caroline, cannot be the son of Henry (d. 1749), a planter, because that William died in 1750. A possibility—but even two genealogies leave the issue doubtful—is the son of Newton Keene, from a Lancaster, Virginia family. Wills and inventories do not clarify the matter, and Keene himself was unimportant. He owned twenty-four slaves in 1790. An Eastern Shore family of Keenes was fairly prominent.

MANTZ, PETER (19–3), of Frederick, was probably a nephew of Peter Mantz, a shoemaker of Fredericktown and member of the Dutch Reformed Church, who in 1759 left a small property to his brother Casper and Casper's sons. Casper also lived in the town, probably also as an artisan, for his estate consisted of four lots and debts.

Peter dealt in real estate, surveying, buying and selling lots, and by the time of his term as delegate had obtained almost a thousand acres including "Mantzsylvania." His six slaves in 1790 suggest a substantial rather than a large property.

POLK, GILLIS (18–3), of Somerset, descended from an old Eastern Shore family of Presbyterians. He owned a small plantation with five slaves valued at £746 in 1783. A captain in 1781, he apparently died before 1790 but left no will.

TURNER, ZEPHANIAH (27–4), of Charles, was the eldest son of Samuel Turner, a planter who left £922 in real property and two plantations, which were probably small. Zephaniah owned fifteen slaves in 1790 and inherited one of the farms, but his office of auditor-general may have been more lucrative. He favored ratification.

Localists

BAKER, JEREMIAH (30–3), of Cecil, family unknown, rented a farm worth £1,000, which was confiscated during the Revolution. We find him petitioning for title, opposing the effort by Mark Alexander, a Cosmopolitan, to escheat the manor. Baker was a justice of the peace and judge of the orphan's court.

BEATTY, JOHN (25–3), of Frederick, is not identified in local histories or genealogies. He surely belonged in some way to the prominent family, but if so to a lesser branch, most likely that of John (1701–1749). He joined Israel Creek's Committee of Observation in 1775 and probably owned 166 acres. The census of 1790 does not include him. Mrs. R. S. Turk, *Beatty—Asfordby* ([New York], 1909), 101 *ff.*

BURGESS, EDWARD (80–5), of Montgomery, belonged to a prominent Virginia family of which the founder was the colonel and councillor, William Burgess. William's large estate remained almost intact through Capt. Edward, who had two sons, the younger of whom produced eight sons, our Edward being sixth in line. As a consequence the delegate inherited only several small farms worth all told £1,484. He became an Antifederalist. Joshua D. Warfield, *The Founders of Anne Arundel and Howard Counties, Maryland* (Baltimore, 1905), 49–50, 438–439.

HAMMOND, REZIN (18–2), of Baltimore County, was the son of Philip, an Annapolis merchant of a prominent, old, and wealthy family. Rezin (1745–1809) was a wealthy planter, radical, and colonel, who died a bachelor. Warfield, *Founders*, 178–184.

HOLMES, WILLIAM (24–2), of Montgomery, probably son of William, owned a small farm with eight slaves and another tract, totaling about £900. He opposed ratification.

McComas, James (20–2), of Harford, came from a large family of farmers. His father Daniel (1697–1765) owned about forty acres. James (1735–1791), a tobacco planter, added some land and was worth £1,400. He served on local committees and became a lieutenant colonel. Henry Clay McComas and Mary Winona McComas, "The McComas Saga," typescript, Library of Congress, 1950.

Wheeler, Ignatius (80–14), of Harford, a large landowner assessed for £2,837, was son of Luke Wheeler, a substantial farmer whose grandfather immigrated about 1658. Ignatius (d. 1793) served on local committees, became a colonel and justice of the peace, and bought a 535-acre property—probably his own rented land—for £120. Walter V. Ball, *The Butterworth Family of Maryland and Virginia* (Silver Spring, Md., 1960), 20–25; Walter W. Preston, *History of Harford County, Maryland* . . . (Baltimore, 1901), 224–225.

VIRGINIA

Northern Neck Bloc

Ball, James, Jr. (13–0), of Lancaster, was the eldest son of James, a colonel and sheriff who married a daughter of Richard Lee and whose father was a wealthy landowner. James, Jr. (1755–1825), also a colonel, served as justice of the peace and voted for ratification. His 1,745 acres and forty-nine slaves mark him as very well-to-do but not quite rich. Lyon Gardiner Tyler, ed., *Encyclopedia of Virginia Biography* (New York, 1915), I, 176–177.

Carrington, Paul (13–2), of Charlotte, voted with his brother Edward but, curiously, in opposition to his father, the very rich landowner George (1711–1785). Paul (1733–1818) did not attend college but studied law and practiced successfully. Previous to Independence he became king's attorney, major, justice of the peace, and a burgess. He played an important part in the Revolutionary movement and in the new government, eventually voting for ratification. His estate was no larger than James Ball's (above), but his legal practice probably entitles him to be called wealthy. *DAB*, III, 522.

Clapham, Josiah or Josias (11–0), of Loudon, probably is referred to in the will of Josias in 1749, who left 1,135 acres to his nephew Josias, if he would "come hear for it." This sounds as if Josiah had to immigrate to claim the property. He served as burgess and in the convention of 1774–1776, but otherwise remains unknown. Tyler, ed., *Encycl. Va. Biog.*, I, 212.

Corbin, Francis (25–2), of Middlesex, belonged to Virginia's elite. His father Richard left enough property so that even Francis (1759–

1821), the youngest of five sons, owned 4,394 acres. He studied at Cambridge, attended the Inner Temple, and became an able lawyer and Federalist. Francis Corbin, "The Corbin Family," *Virginia Magazine of History and Biography*, XXX (1922), 315–318.

EYRE, LITTLETON (14–1), of Northampton (c. 1760–1789), of an old but not really prominent (?) Eastern Shore family, attended William and Mary and voted for ratification. He had a large plantation with seventy-eight slaves.

FITZHUGH, DANIEL (14–2), of King George, is not the large landowner of Westmoreland but the son of Col. William of Marmion (d. 1791) and daughter of Col. William Beverley. Fitzhugh (b. 1758) certainly was a large landowner but may not have been wealthy. He voted for ratification but is not a conspicuous man. *Va. Mag. Hist. Biog.*, VIII (1900–1901), 93–94.

FITZHUGH, WILLIAM (12–0), of Stafford, is not the above Col. William but the son of Henry Fitzhugh (1706–1742) and a daughter of Robert Carter of Corotoman. One of Virginia's wealthiest men, he held many offices including that of representative to Congress.

LEE, RICHARD BLAND (17–1), of Loudon, a well-to-do planter, inherited his father Henry's Loudon estate—being one of five boys. Too young for military service, Richard (1761–1827) later went to Congress as an ardent Federalist.

LEE, RICHARD HENRY (10–0), of Westmoreland (1732–1789), needs no sketch. See *DAB*, XI, 117.

MADISON, JAMES (21–4), of Orange (1751–1836), needs no sketch. See *DAB*, XII, 184.

MARSHALL, JOHN (15–3), of Henrico (1755–1836), is the famous chief justice. See *DAB*, XII, 315. His father, Thomas, voted on the same side.

MASON, GEORGE (15–0), of Fairfax (1725–1792), is also familiar. See *DAB*, XII, 361.

NELSON, NATHANIEL (13–0), of York, was son of "President" William and Elizabeth, the only daughter of Nathaniel Burwell and the granddaughter of Robert "King" Carter. The second of five sons, Nelson (b. 1745) became a doctor and earned £5,000 sterling by marrying a daughter of John Page. Richard Channing Moore Page, *Genealogy of the Page Family in Virginia* (New York, 1883), 147.

NORVELL, WILLIAM (31–5), of James City, descended from a reputable family. A member of the 1776 convention and a consistent Federalist, Norvell (c. 1725–1802) freed his slaves when he died. He was a well-to-do planter. Tyler, ed., *Encycl. Va. Biog.*, I, 299; Lucile Gibson Pleasants, "Notes on the Norvell Family," *William and Mary Quarterly*, 2d Ser., XIV (1934), 147.

PAGE, MANN (16–1), of Spotsylvania, must be distinguished from his colleague, Mann Page of Gloucester (1766–1813), the extremely wealthy son of Gov. John Page, who voted on the same side (8–0). Mann of Spotsylvania (b. 1749) was son of Mann Page of Rosewell and Anne Corbin Taylor of Mt. Airy, and grandson of the Honorable Mann and Judith Carter. He had a huge estate including 143 slaves, but was not politically prominent.

STUART, DAVID (23–1), of Fairfax, a close friend of George Washington's, was the grandson of Rev. David and son of Rev. William Stuart. David (b. 1753) attended William and Mary, favored ratification, and owned a large (ninety-nine slaves) plantation.

THORNTON, WILLIAM (24–3), of King George, a wealthy planter, came from a good but not prominent family. He married a daughter of George Mason's, favored ratification, but never held important office.

TYLER, JOHN (10–1), of Charles City, was the son of John, a lawyer, and marshall of the Vice-Admiralty Court. Tyler (1747–1813) attended William and Mary, held the office of vice-admiralty judge for many years, and won the friendship of Jefferson and Henry. He became an Antifederalist, Republican, and defender of public education. *DAB*, XIX, 87.

Others associated with this group included HENRY BANKS (7–1), wealthy merchant chosen from Greenbrier; DANIEL BOONE (7–1), Kentucky frontiersman and entrepreneur; DANIEL C. BRENT (7–0), wealthy planter from Prince William; JAMES GORDON (9–0) of Lancaster, well-to-do planter; JAMES INNIS (6–1), Williamsburg lawyer, colonel, and Federalist; ZACHARIAH JOHNSON (27–7), Augusta merchant; LUDWELL LEE (7–1) of Prince William, wealthy lawyer; MANN PAGE (8–1) of Gloucester; LEVIN POWELL (8–0), Loudon entrepreneur and Federalist; CHARLES SIMMS (7–1), Fairfax lawyer and Federalist; ARCHIBALD STUART (26–6), lawyer from the Shenandoah Valley; HENRY TAZEWELL (14–3), wealthy Antifederal lawyer; and ALEXANDER WHITE (17–4), Frederick lawyer and Federalist.

A few principal delegates who followed a neutral course were EDWARD BLAND of Prince George; GEORGE BOOKER of Elizabeth City; CUTHBERT BULLITT of Prince William, the Antifederal lawyer; ISAAC COLES of Halifax; GEORGE JACKSON of Harrison; GEORGE and WILSON CARY NICHOLAS of Albemarle; JAMES PENDLETON of Culpeper; ROBERT SAYERS of Montgomery; BENJAMIN TEMPLE of King William; DANIEL TRIGG of Montgomery; WILLIAM WALKER of James City; WILLIAM WATKINS of Dinwiddie; and NATHANIEL WILKINSON of Henrico. The group includes five Antifederalists and four Federalists.

Southside Bloc

ANDERSON, GARLAND (18–3), of Hanover, son of Capt. Robert Anderson, a large landowner and vestryman, served as a burgess in 1771 and in the 1775 convention. He owned a large farm (seven hundred acres) and thirty-two slaves. Edward Lowell Anderson, *The Andersons of Gold Mine, Hanover County, Virginia* (Cincinnati, 1913).

BIBB, RICHARD (15–2), of Prince Edward, a shopkeeper, was the third son of John Bibb (1703–1769), a reputedly wealthy planter. When war began Richard (1752–1839) was studying for the Anglican ministry (he later became a Methodist), but he served in the army instead, rising to the rank of major. In 1783 he owned a large farm and thirty slaves, added six hundred acres during the next year or two, and took out a merchant license by 1788 at the latest. He was a trustee of Hampden-Sydney College. Later he moved to Kentucky, acquired wealth, and at his death freed fifty slaves. Charles William Bibb, comp., *The Bibb Family in America, 1640–1940* (Baltimore, 1941), 64–67.

CABELL, JOHN (11–2), of Buckingham, was the third son of the eminent Dr. William Cabell. John (1742–1815) inherited a large estate, served in a variety of local and state offices, and was a colonel. His brother, Samuel J., voted on the same side, served as a colonel in the Continental army and became first an Antifederalist, then a Republican. Alexander Brown, *The Cabells and Their Kin* (Boston, 1895), 153–157.

CHEATHAM, MATTHEW (9–1), of Chesterfield, appears without trace of a family background. He did not serve in the Revolution, though he is referred to much later as a colonel. He owned only six slaves in 1788. He was an Antifederalist and later a Republican.

COCKE, LEMUEL (10–1), of Surry, came from a fairly prominent family. His grandfather, Col. Thomas Cocke, storekeeper and large landowner, left a considerable property to three sons. Lemuel (d. 1756) had five sons. Lemuel, Jr., owned 1,854 acres and thirty-six slaves in 1787. He served on the local committee of safety and as a militia captain. He became an Antifederalist.

COLEMAN, JOHN (13–1), of Halifax, had been a shipbuilder in England, but after his arrival in Virginia about 1750, he turned planter, buying an estate worth over £3,000 in 1787. He became a vestryman and a justice of the peace. Wirt Johnson Carrington, *History of Halifax County* (Richmond, 1924), 149–150.

EDMUNDS, THOMAS (13–1), of Sussex, was the son of John Edmunds (d. 1770), a burgess of an old family. He served as captain, voted against ratification, and owned a large estate assessed for £3,804. Mary Stuart Green Edmunds, "Edmunds Family," *Tyler's Quarterly Historical and Genealogical Magazine*, XVII (1936), 60.

GATEWOOD, WILLIAM (19–1), of Essex, was the son of John (d. 1746) a well-to-do or wealthy landowner of good family who left sizable farms to five sons. William, a well-to-do planter, never became prominent. He voted against ratification in 1788. Zona (Gatewood) Canterbury, *A History of the Wyatt, New and Gatewood Lineage* (n.p., 1949), 44–50.

GOODALL, PARKE (24–1), of Hanover, probably inherited his tavern from his father Richard, a British immigrant. The tavern must have been extraordinary, for Goodall, a colonel in the war, had a sizable estate including thirty-two slaves. He was a justice of the peace and an Antifederalist. Rosewell Page, *Hanover County* (Richmond, 1926), 28; Tyler, ed., *Encycl. Va. Biog.*, II, 362–363; Hugh Blair Grigsby, *The History of the Virginia Federal Convention of 1788 . . .* , ed. R. A. Brock (Richmond, 1890–1891), II, 375.

HARRISON, CARTER H. (20–4), of Cumberland, of distinguished ancestry, was one of Virginia's richest planters. A graduate of William and Mary, Harrison (1726–1794) attended Middle Temple but never won fame. "Harrison of James River," *Va. Mag. Hist. Biog.*, XXXIV (1926), 183.

JONES, JOSEPH (24–3), of Dinwiddie, also one of the state's richest planters, served as a captain in the Revolution, was elected to the senate, and became, in turn, an Antifederalist and a Republican.

LANKFORD, BENJAMIN (33–5), of Pittsylvania (d. 1810), in contrast, owned a comparatively small (four hundred acres) farm. Lankford's background is unknown. By 1765 he had a farm and was a vestryman. Soon he became the county's first sheriff, presently justice of the peace, burgess, and militia captain. He opposed ratification and became a Republican. Tyler, ed., *Encycl. Va. Biog.*, I, 274; Maud Carter Clement, *The History of Pittsylvania County, Virginia* (Lynchburg, Va., 1929), 96 *n.*

LUCAS, JOHN (11–1), of Greensville, belonged to an old family that settled in Virginia before 1700. His father sat in the House of Burgesses. John was a captain in the Revolution and owned a sizable farm assessed at £500 in 1783. Silas Emmett Lucas, Jr., *The Powell Family . . .* (Sewanee, Tenn., 1961), 257–259.

NEW, ANTHONY (13–0), of Caroline, came from a good family of the lesser planter class. As the youngest of three sons, Anthony (1747–1833) was apprenticed to a chairmaker and apparently followed that trade. By the mid-eighties, however, he had served as justice of the peace and as captain in the Revolution, while acquiring a large farm with eighteen slaves. Eventually he moved to Kentucky and represented that state in Congress, voting with the Republicans. Canterbury, *Wyatt, New and Gatewood Lineage*, 35–42.

RENTFRO, JOHN (12–1), of Henry and Franklin, presumably came from an early Southside family. He had a small farm with four slaves, served as captain, and became justice of the peace in 1786. Marshall Wingfield, *An Old Virginia Court* (Memphis, 1948), 219–220.

RIDLEY, THOMAS (11–1), of Southampton, was the son of a farmer. Thomas (b. 1740), the youngest son, fought as a colonel in the Continental army and owned a 575-acre plantation with 30 slaves. G. T. Ridlon, *History of the Ancient Ryedales . . .* (Manchester, N.H., 1884), 482–485.

ROBERTSON, CHRISTOPHER (12–2), of Lunenburg, probably descended from an old Henrico County farm family. He served as justice of the peace and captain. In the eighties he owned a six-hundred acre farm with eleven slaves and left a personal estate of £1,834 11s. 8d. when he died. He voted against ratification and became a Republican. Landon C. Bell, *Cumberland Parish, Lunenburg County, Virginia. Vestry Book, 1746–1816* (Richmond, 1930), 282.

UPSHAW, JAMES (14–2), of Essex, was the son of Jeremiah, an Essex County farmer of old family. By 1767 Upshaw (1730–1806) was an Essex militia captain. He then moved to Caroline, where he became sheriff and lieutenant colonel (at a later date). His son, James, Jr., was a captain in the Virginia line. Upshaw owned farms in both Essex and Caroline, which combined made him a well-to-do large landowner. He was an Antifederalist and a Republican. *WMQ*, 2d Ser., XVIII (1936), 73.

WILSON, BENJAMIN (10–1), of Monongahela, was born in the Shenandoah Valley, where his father, an Irishman, had pioneered. Wilson became county clerk, colonel of the militia, slaveowner, and Federalist, but whether he should be called a farmer or an official is uncertain. Albert S. Bosworth, *A History of Randolph County, West Virginia . . .* (Elkins?, W.Va., 1916), 393–396.

Other delegates who voted on the same side included THOMAS BARBOUR (9–0), well-to-do planter and Antifederalist of Orange; DAVID BOOKER (7–0) of Amelia, Antifederalist and a farmer; ANTHONY BROWN (7–1) of Nansemond; RICHARD CARY, JR. (16–4) of Warwick, well-to-do lawyer; WILSON M. CARY of Warwick, wealthy planter; THOMAS COOPER (8–1) of Henry, Antifederalist with a thousand acres but of moderate wealth; JOHN GARLAND (7–0), substantial farmer of Henrico and Antifederalist; JOHN GUERRANT (7–1) of Goochland, small farmer,

Antifederalist, and Republican; BENJAMIN HARRISON (7-0) of Rock-
ingham (not of the famous family), farmer; CARTER H. HARRISON
(20-4) of Cumberland, wealthy planter; PATRICK HENRY (13-3);
JOHN PRIDE (7-1), well-to-do innkeeper and Antifederalist of Amelia;
SAMUEL RICHARDSON (18-4) of Fluvanna, well-to-do Antifederal
farmer; THOMAS SCOTT (8-1), wealthy Charlotte planter; CHARLES M.
TALBOT (9-0) of Campbell, small farmer; and JOHN TRIGG (12-5) of
Bedford, small farmer, Antifederalist, and Republican.

SOUTH CAROLINA

Cosmopolitans

CANNON, DANIEL (12-0), of Charleston, one of three artisans in this
group of men, is of uncertain origin, unless he was the son of John,
a small farmer, who died in 1763. He started as a carpenter and
seems to have regarded himself as one of them, for he was chosen
president of their society. He was also president of St. George Society, which implies an English birth. Even before the war he had
acquired at least two thousand acres of land, and he owned thirty-
one slaves in 1790. He voted for ratification.

DANIEL, ROBERT (16-1), of St. Thomas and Dennis, was the son of
Robert, a planter who died in 1739. Daniel (1730-1790) built up a
large plantation of some two thousand acres, primarily in rice, and
left £2,027 in personal property when he died. He favored ratification.

DARRELL, EDWARD (16-2), of Charleston, joined his father, Joseph, as
a merchant before the war. Darrell (1747-1797) was seized by the
British and returned to reestablish what has been called the largest
firm of native merchants. He married into the eminent Smith family,
favored ratification, and continued to be a Federalist. George C.
Rogers, Jr., *Evolution of a Federalist: William Loughton Smith of
Charleston (1758-1812)* (Columbia, S.C., 1962), 97-98, 401.

FLAGG, GEORGE (13-0), of Charleston, like Cannon began as an artisan
—a painter. He later entered trade in a small way and bought some
land but apparently never acquired wealth. His family background
remains unknown; probably he immigrated.

GRIMKÉ, JOHN FAUCHERAUD (13-1), of Charleston, might be considered
an artisan by upbringing though his father (John Paul), far from
being a typical artisan, was a silversmith who left a large estate
and sent his son to Cambridge. John F. (1752-1819) also attended
Inner Temple and returned to marry the daughter of Thomas Smith
of Broad Street, a wealthy merchant. He practiced law, joined the

Continental army as a captain, rose to the rank of lieutenant colonel, and was chosen judge in 1783. He favored ratification and became a Federalist. *DAB*, VII, 633.

HERIOT, ROBERT (13–0), of All Saints, appears without prior notice in 1766 when he bought 2,177 acres, presently adding 1,711 more. By 1790 he owned 128 slaves. Nothing else is known of him.

IZARD, RALPH (17–2), of St. James Goose Creek, belonged to one of the state's wealthiest families. Educated in England, Izard (1742–1804) was a cultured man, and his marriage to a New York, DeLancey girl perhaps contributed to his aristocratic inclinations. He served in Congress and became a steadfast Federalist. His son Walter voted on the same side. *DAB*, IX, 524.

JOHNSON, WILLIAM (16–2), of Charleston, is an obscure man. A blacksmith with little property, he favored ratification.

KARWON, THOMAS (11–1), of St. Thomas and Dennis, probably was the son of Crafton Karwon, who died in 1747. He was a wealthy planter who voted for the Constitution.

KINLOCH, FRANCIS (18–1), of Charleston, was the son of Francis, (1720–1767), a wealthy planter who left £32,000 in personal property when he died. Francis, Jr. (b. 1755), retained the wealth. He was a conservative during the Revolutionary era, voted for ratification, and remained a Federalist. H. D. Bull, comp., "Kinloch of South Carolina," *S.C. Mag. Hist. Biog.*, XLVI (1945), 63–66.

MANIGAULT, GABRIEL (13–1), of St. James Goose Creek, and JOSEPH (11–0), of Christ Church, were the sons of Peter Manigault, a very wealthy merchant and lawyer, who was the only son of the family's founder, Gabriel (1704–1781). Our Gabriel continued the family's trading tradition and in addition owned 210 slaves. Joseph was a wealthy planter. Both married into equally prominent families, favored ratification, and became Federalists. *DAB*, XII, 234.

MOTTE, ISAAC (13–0), of Charleston, was the son of Jacob Motte (1700–1770), a wealthy merchant. Isaac (1738–1795) married the daughter of Benjamin Smith (see William L. Smith, below) and maintained his position as one of the elite. Motte served as a colonel during the war, sat in Congress and in the state senate, and voted for ratification. A cultured man, he was president of the city's famous St. Cecelia Society. Emily Bellinger Reynolds and Joan Reynolds Faunt, comps., *Biographical Directory of the Senate of the State of South Carolina 1776–1964* (Columbia, S.C., 1964), 279.

PARKER, ISAAC (11–1), of St. Thomas and Dennis, was a wealthy planter who owned ninety-three slaves in 1790. He voted for ratification, but otherwise is obscure.

PARKER, JOHN, JR. (17–0), of St. James Goose Creek, belonged to a prominent old family. Parker (1735–1802) studied law at the Middle Temple and became a lawyer and well-to-do planter. He sat in the state senate and favored ratification. Reynolds and Faunt, comps. *Biog. Dir. S.C. Senate*, 286.

RAMSAY, DAVID (19–1), of Charleston, the famous doctor-historian, was born in Pennsylvania. His father was an immigrant of whom we know nothing except that he sent two sons to college. David (1749–1815) practiced medicine in South Carolina, where he acquired little property but a high reputation, except when he opposed slavery. Ramsay ardently supported the Constitution and the Federalist party. *DAB*, XV, 338.

READ, JACOB (13–1), of Charleston, was the oldest son of James Read, a rich merchant, planter, and member of Georgia's council. Jacob (1752–1816) studied law in England, saw service as a militia colonel, and then practiced law. He attended Congress, favored ratification, and remained a Federalist. *DAB*, XV, 425.

RUTLEDGE, EDWARD (15–1), of Charleston, does not require a sketch.

SMITH, PETER (11–1), of St. James Goose Creek, was the son of Thomas Smith of Broad Street, a wealthy merchant, cousin of William Smith (see below), husband of a Middleton, and related to the Motte, Elliott, Izard, Wragg, Moore, Rutledge, Bee, and Dry families. He was a wealthy planter and Federalist. Rogers, *Evolution*, 401–403.

SMITH, WILLIAM LOUGHTON (14–2), of St. James Goose Creek, cousin of the above, was a member of one of Carolina's most prominent families. Smith studied in England and Europe during the war, after which he returned to resume his rightful place as lawyer and great planter. He became one of the principal second-rank Federalists. *Ibid., passim.*

WASHINGTON, WILLIAM (13–1), of St. Paul's, oldest son of Baily Washington, a large planter of Stafford County, Virginia, was born there, and made his reputation as a cavalry colonel in the Continental army. Washington (1752–1810) then settled down on a 12,650-acre estate with 363 slaves, having married an Elliott and thus acquired much property. He voted for ratification and remained a Federalist. Henry A. M. Smith, "The Grave of Col. William Washington," *S.C. Hist. Gen. Mag.*, X (1909), 245–247.

WATIES, THOMAS (14–1), of Prince George Winyaw, was the son of Col. John Waties (d. 1760), a prominent planter, whose father William engaged in the Indian trade and acquired a huge landed estate. Waties (b. 1760) attended the College of Philadelphia, served as a captain during the war, and eventually became an eminent lawyer. He favored ratification.

Some other faithful adherents of this party were THOMAS BEE (11-0), eminent Federal lawyer; JOHN EDWARDS, JR. (9-1), Charleston merchant; THOMAS GADSDEN (10-0), well-to-do (at least) Charleston merchant; THOMAS HEYWARD, JR. (12-2) of Charleston, wealthy lawyer; WALTER IZARD (10-1); JAMES LADSON (11-0) of St. Andrew's, wealthy planter of prominent family; JOHN MATTHEWS (11-0) of Charleston, wealthy lawyer, governor, and future Republican; EPHRAIM MIKELL (10-1) of St. John's Colleton, wealthy planter of humble background; CHARLES C. PINCKNEY (13-2) of Charleston; and PLOWDEN WESTON (13-2) of Christ Church, merchant and ex-loyalist.

The principal neutrals included ROBERT BARNWELL of St. Helena, a wealthy landowner; ROBERT BAXTER of St. David's, a farmer; PATRICK CALHOUN of Ninety-six, well-to-do landowner and Antifederal leader; JOHN DICKEY of Prince Frederick, well-to-do planter; JOHN FENWICK of St. Peter's, also a well-to-do planter; HENRY PENDLETON of Saxe Gotha, a Virginian of humble origin who rose to a judgeship; Gen. ANDREW PICKENS of Ninety-six; BENJAMIN PORTER of Prince Frederick, wealthy planter; and WILLIAM A. WEGG of St. Helena, also a wealthy planter.

Localists

ANDERSON, WILLIAM (15-1), of Ninety-six, owns a name so common that his identity cannot be disentangled. He certainly possessed neither large property nor much importance.

BASKINS, ANDREW (15-2), of East of the Wateree, probably immigrated from Ireland to Virginia with his father, who died in 1750. Andrew (b. ca. 1730) settled in the Carolina backcountry, served as a private in the army, added some land, and became a justice of the peace. He opposed ratification. Raymond Martin Bell, *The Baskins-Baskin Family* (Washington, Pa., 1957), 29.

BLASINGAME, JOHN (13-0), of Upper or Spartan, had a small farm with no slaves. He later became a Federalist.

BRATTON, WILLIAM (15-2), of New Acquisition, immigrated from Ireland with his parents to Pennsylvania and then to the Carolina upcountry. Bratton (1742–1802) served as a colonel under Sumter and acquired a two-hundred-acre farm with five slaves. *Biog. Dir. S.C. Senate*, 185.

BUTLER, WILLIAM (15-0), of Ninety-six, moved to that area with his parents from Virginia just before the war. Butler (1759–1821) served as a captain in the Continental army and obtained 635 acres but bought no slaves. An Antifederalist, he later entered Congress as a Republican. *S.C. Hist. Gen. Mag.*, IV (1903), 296–300.

CRAIG, JAMES (16–0), of the district between the Broad and Catawba, started with a small farm and then purchased 2,290 acres in October 1787, but the land cost only £53. He owned seven slaves. Craig opposed ratification.

DRINNON, JOHN (17–1), of New Acquisition, seems to come from no family at all. He owned two hundred acres and no slaves.

FAIR, JAMES (12–0), of the district between the Savannah and Edisto, also appears from nowhere. One of that name owned 150 acres in 1775.

FERGUS, WILLIAM (17–1), of New Acquisition, owned one slave in 1790, a fact that completes our sketch.

FERGUSON, WILLIAM (13–1), of St. Bartholomew (d. 1789?), perhaps was born in 1753, the son of John Ferguson. In 1787 he owned 1,402 acres worth £365 10s. and thirty-two slaves. A 1789 inventory taken of his estate—if indeed the estate was his—totaled £2,953 15s. including forty barrels of rice and 750 head of cattle.

JONES, ADAM CRANE (16–1), of Ninety-six, remains obscure despite the first two names. He held a considerable amount of land and twenty-five slaves. Jones opposed ratification.

KNOX, JAMES (14–0), of the district between the Broad and Catawba, is entitled "Dr." in the records. Knox (d. 1794) bought 650 acres before the war, which he retained in 1794 as part of a £160 estate. Earlier, however, he owned twenty-nine slaves. He was an Antifederalist.

LOVE, ANDREW (17–0), of New Acquisition, was born in Pennsylvania and moved to Carolina with his father, who bought a 856-acre tract. Love (b. 1747) served as a colonel under Sumter and opposed ratification. *Biog. Dir. S.C. Senate*, 259–260.

LYLES, ARMANUS (16–2), of the district between the Broad and Catawba, first appears in 1753 when he married the daughter of a Bostonian. In 1773 he owned a 200-acre tract and by 1792 had a 525-acre farm and fourteen slaves.

McJUNKINS, SAMUEL (14–2), of the Upper or Spartan, owned a farm but no slaves. He held the rank of major but was reportedly too old to fight in the war. John Belton O'Neall Landrum, *Colonial and Revolutionary History of Upper South Carolina* . . . (Greenville, S.C., 1897), 111, 131.

MARTIN, JAMES (15–1), of New Acquisition, a doctor, served as a surgeon in the Continental army. Martin (d. 1797) owned seven slaves and an uncertain quantity of land (the name being not uncommon). He opposed ratification.

PALMER, JOSEPH (12–1), also of New Acquisition, seems to have been a farmer owning three slaves.

PATTEN, ROBERT (18–1), of the same district, owned ten slaves and was purchasing land while in the legislature, as were Palmer and Martin (above). Nothing else is known about him.

RAMSAY, JAMES (17–1), came from the same area, but had no slaves and bought only one hundred acres in 1784, though he probably held other property. The four men just noted may have had more property than the records reveal, but they certainly were neither important nor wealthy.

SIMKINS, ARTHUR (16–2), of Ninety-six, was born in Virginia in 1742 and moved to South Carolina in 1772. He promptly was chosen judge, member of the Provincial Congress, and a captain. Simkins opposed ratification and became a Republican. He owned seventeen slaves in 1790 and at some point joined the Baptist church. *Biog. Dir. S.C. Senate*, 307.

TURNER, JOHN (13–1), of the district between the Broad and Catawba, immigrated from Ireland before 1776 and became a farmer. By 1792 he had acquired 950 acres and ten slaves, paying thereon a moderate tax. He served as major and as a delegate to the Provincial Congress. *Ibid.*, 324.

WYLDS, JOHN (13–0), of the district between the Savannah and Edisto, a surveyor and farmer, accumulated nearly one thousand acres of land. He probably served as justice of the peace, senator, and captain, though the identification is uncertain. *Ibid.*, 339.

Other men who voted the same way were THOMAS BRANDON (11–0) of Upper or Spartan, substantial planter; LEVI CASEY (10–0) of Little River, small or substantial farmer, Continental officer, and Republican; BENJAMIN CUDWORTH (15–3) of the district east of the Wateree, moderate farmer who changed from Antifederalist to Federalist; JOHN GRAY (13–2) of the district between the Broad and Catawba, large farmer; JOHN LINDSAY (10–0) of the district between the Broad and Saluda; and Gen. THOMAS SUMTER (12–2) of the district east of the Wateree.

The well-known "radical" merchant ALEXANDER GILLON inclined toward the Localists, 9–4; RAWLINS LOWNDES, the conservative Antifederalist, preferred the Cosmopolitans, 7–3; and Dr. THOMAS TUDOR TUCKER, the eminent Republican, supported the Localists, 4–0.

Table A.1. Summary Table: Characteristics of Most Consistent Party Voters

	Localists		Neutrals		Cosmopolitans	
	No.	%	No.	%	No.	%
Residence						
Noncommercial farm	98	67	24	31	6	4
Commercial farm	43	29	42	55	82	58
Town	6	4	9	12	17	12
Major city	0	0	2	3	37	26
Uncertain			2			
Total	147	100	79	101	142	100
Occupation						
Farmer	86	59	23	29	18	13
Large landowner	15	10	19	24	25	18
Misc. nonfarmer	21	14	11	14	20	14
Professional	8	5	15	19	46	32
Trader	3	2	5	6	27	19
Unknown	14	10	6	8	6	4
Total	147	100	79	100	142	100
Economic status						
Moderate	79	54	25	31	18	13
Substantial	36	25	16	20	22	16
Well-to-do	17	12	20	25	40	28
Wealthy	7	5	12	15	54	38
Unknown	8	5	6	8	8	6
Total	147	101	79	99	142	101
Social origin						
Humble origin	52	35	23	29	25	18
Average family	64	44	30	38	50	35
Above-average family	8	5	9	11	16	11
Prominent family	4	3	9	11	37	26
Unknown	19	13	8	10	14	10
Total	147	100	79	99	142	100
Religion						
Episcopalian	9	14	7	29	37	50
Quaker	2	3	1	4	10	14
Congregational	13	20	6	25	12	16
Presbyterian	30	46	5	21	7	10
Dutch Reformed	5	8	2	8	4	5
Other	6	9	3	13	4	5
Total	65	100	24	100	74	100

Table A.1—Continued

	Localists		Neutrals		Cosmopolitans	
	No.	*%*	*No.*	*%*	*No.*	*%*
World view						
Localist	87	59	33	42	27	19
Cosmopolitan	10	7	15	19	60	42
Uncertain	50	34	31	39	55	39
Total	147	100	79	100	142	100
Vote on ratification						
Antifederalist	53	95	12	40	5	8
Federalist	3	5	18	60	55	92
Total	56	100	30	100	60	100
Age						
Under 40	19	27	14	37	40	42
40–49	31	44	15	39	30	31
50 and over	21	30	9	24	26	27
Total	71	101	38	100	96	100
Intellectual interest	8	5	11	14	47	33
Education	4	3	11	14	41	29
High civil or military office	39	27	25	32	51	36

NOTES: Episcopalians and Quakers voted more with the Cosmopolitans, and Presbyterians less, than their residence would predict.

Economic status operated independently of occupation and of residence; occupation operated independently of residence.

Men of prominent family voted more with the Cosmopolitans than their residence would predict, but that is not true of the other social ranks.

Age was a function of residence, not an independent variable.

National origin lacked significance.

Bibliographical Essay

The most important source for this book consisted of the state assembly journals. Most session laws and some compilations were published at that time and others since, and a number of records are available in microprint in the Early American Imprints series of the titles listed in Charles Evans's *American Bibliography*. However, the only complete collection of journals and laws forms part of the microfilm series listed in William Sumner Jenkins, comp., and Lillian Hamrick, ed., *A Guide to the Microfilm Collection of the Early State Records* (Washington, D.C., 1950; supplement, 1951). Every research library ought to contain the reels of both legislative journals and laws.

Supporting legislative records are seldom available except in the state archives. For this study petitions proved especially important. Together with resolutions and instructions of town meetings, gatherings of merchants, planters, townspeople, and other groups, they furnish valuable evidence about the ideas of ordinary voters.

Many of these expressions of opinions, as well as numerous formal and informal articles, appeared in the newspapers and magazines, which contain also quantities of other essential material. Several projects are duplicating on microfilm most of the papers, as listed in the most recent edition of *Newspapers on Microfilm*. Clarence S. Brigham's well-known *History and Bibliography of American Newspapers, 1690–1820*, 2 vols. (Worcester, Mass., 1947), locates newspapers that have not been reproduced. I used almost all of the newspapers and all of the magazines for this book.

Tax lists and inventories of estates help one to describe the social and economic attributes of localities and people. To the brief description of these in my *Social Structure of Revolutionary America* (Princeton, 1965), 290–295, I add a few footnotes: The probate records of

New Hampshire, of Suffolk and Hampshire counties in Massachusetts, and of Philadelphia are now available on microfilm. Those kept in Maryland's Hall of Records exceed in completeness the Virginia collection. The scattered Massachusetts tax lists, the extant Maryland tax lists for the 1780s, and the Delaware assessment lists are all on microfilm. The student will still find it necessary to visit the libraries, however, to use essential related records.

For this book I revisited the Massachusetts Historical Society, the New-York Historical Society, the New York Public Library, the Historical Society of Pennsylvania, and the Maryland Historical Society, as well as a few previously neglected, notably the Rutgers University Library and the library of the Pennsylvania Historical and Museum Commission. These provided new notes on the issues and on politics. Undoubtedly the numerous smaller private and public libraries contain much additional information. Much remains unknown concerning the history of every state.

Pamphlets, broadsides, and other publications of the period are available on microcard as indexed chronologically in Charles Evans's *American Bibliography*, together with its supplement by Roger P. Bristol (Charlottesville, Va., 1970), and topically by Clifford K. Shipton and James E. Mooney, *National Index of American Imprints through 1800: The Short-Title Evans*, 2 vols. (Barre, Mass., 1969). Of the more recent published works, genealogies and local histories furnished biographical data as discussed in chapter 2. The few good state histories rarely venture beyond political history and seldom analyze votes in detail. They suffer also from a concentration on national affairs, neglecting local issues. The best are Richard P. McCormick, *Experiment in Independence: New Jersey in the Critical Period, 1781–1789* (New Brunswick, N.J., 1950), Robert L. Brunhouse, *The Counter-Revolution in Pennsylvania, 1776–1790* (Harrisburg, Pa., 1942), E. Wilder Spaulding, *New York in the Critical Period, 1785–1789* (New York, 1932), Thomas C. Cochran, *New York in the Confederation: An Economic Study* (Philadelphia, 1932), Irwin H. Polishook, *Rhode Island in the Union, 1774–1795* (Evanston, Ill., 1969), and Philip A. Crowl, *Maryland during and after the Revolution* (Baltimore, 1943). The new study of Massachusetts by Van Beck Hall, *Politics Without Parties: Massachusetts, 1780–1791* (Pittsburgh, 1972), fully abreast of recent methodology, should stimulate similar studies elsewhere. I benefited from reading Jerome Nadelhaft's manuscript on South Carolina politics. For Georgia see Kenneth Coleman, *The American Revolution in Georgia, 1763–1789* (Athens, Ga., 1958). Jere Daniell's recent book on New Hampshire, *Experiment in Repub-*

licanism: New Hampshire Politics and the American Revolution, 1741–1794 (Cambridge, Mass., 1970), replaces all other works on that state. The footnotes indicate a few excellent articles. In general, despite the efforts of many scholars, we need much basic research on all phases of Revolutionary history, particularly the economic and social.

Index

AMERICAN HISTORY TITLES IN THE NORTON LIBRARY